OFFICIAL MILITARY HISTORICAL OFFICES AND SOURCES

OFFICIAL MILITARY HISTORICAL OFFICES AND SOURCES

Volume I: Europe, Africa, the Middle East, and India

Edited by Robin Higham

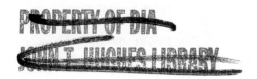

Greenwood Press
Westport, Connecticut • London

Library of Congress Cataloging-in-Publication Data

Official military historical offices and sources / edited by Robin Higham.
p. cm.
v. 1. Europe, Africa, the Middle East, and India—v. 2. The western hemisphere and the Pacific rim.
Includes bibliographical references and index.
ISBN 0–313–28684–1 (v. 1: alk. paper)—ISBN 0–313–30862–4 (v. 2: alk. paper)
1. Military history. 2. Military history—Archival resources. I. Higham, Robin D. S.
D25.5.O34 2000
355'.009—dc21 99–049148

British Library Cataloguing in Publication Data is available.

Library of Congress Catalog Card Number: 99–049148
ISBN: 0–313–28684–1

First published in 2000

Greenwood Press, 88 Post Road West, Westport, CT 06881
An imprint of Greenwood Publishing Group, Inc.
www.greenwood.com

Printed in the United States of America

The paper used in this book complies with the Permanent Paper Standard issued by the National Information Standards Organization (Z39.48–1984).

10 9 8 7 6 5 4 3 2 1

Copyright Acknowledgment

Every reasonable effort has been made to trace the owners of copyright materials in this book, but in some instances this has proven impossible. The editor and publisher will be glad to receive information leading to more complete acknowledgments in subsequent printings of the book and in the meantime extend their apologies for any omissions.

Contents

Preface

The essays and bibliographical lists contained in this and the companion book on the Western Hemisphere and the Pacific Rim supplement the information provided in my earlier book, *Official Histories*, published in 1970. Some entries cover historical offices, divisions, or sections not included in the 1970 publication. A few pieces cover offices no longer in existence, their interest lying in the historic time when they were written.

The approach used was to send letters to the various defense, naval, military, and air attachés listed in the U.S. State Department's *Diplomatic List*. For a variety of reasons there were delays at both ends of the process. In the end no answer was received from the various military historical offices in the following countries: Afghanistan, Albania, Algeria, Argentina, Bahrain, Bangladesh, Bolivia, Botswana, Bulgaria, Cameroon, Columbia, Côte d'Ivoire, Cuba, the Dominican Republic, Ecuador, Egypt, El Salvador, Ghana, Guatemala, Guinea, Haiti, Honduras, Iran, Jamaica, Kenya, Malaysia, Mexico, Morocco, Myanamar (Burma), Nigeria, Oman, Saudi Arabia, Senegal, Singapore, Sudan, Syria, Tanzania, Thailand, Tunisia, United Arab Emirates, Uruguay, Venezuela, Yemen, Yugoslavia, and Zaire. There are various reasons for the nonresponses:

1. The attachés either were not interested, did not understand the request, had no staff who did, or the like.
2. There is no historical office in that country, or as in number 1.

3. The English-language letter or the request for a response in English was a problem.
4. There was and remained confusion between a history of the activities of the armed forces and my request for an essay on the history of the historical office with a list or bibliography of the works published.
5. There was confusion as to what constitutes official military history.

To illustrate the difficulties, the original correspondence on Kansas State stationery follows, verbatim. In cases where no previous essay existed in the 1970 edition, Horst Boog's original contribution on the German Air Force was sent as an example.

Sir:

Please excuse the impersonality of this letter which is going to about 100 directors or chiefs.

As editor emeritus of MILITARY AFFAIRS and of AEROSPACE HISTORIAN, I have been asked to give the April 1990 presentation of the Military Classics seminar in Washington, D.C. This is a meeting attended by about 150 professionals, many of them manning official historical offices. I have been asked to talk about official histories on a world-wide basis.

I believe that you are aware of the work, OFFICIAL HISTORIES, which I edited about twenty years ago (information attached). That work was as complete as I was able to make it at that time. Since then, however, I have got to know many more of you, my colleagues, through the medium of the International Commission for Comparative Military History. That has been a stimulating and most enjoyable experience.

For some time it has been evident that the number of volumes which have been published since about 1968, when the work of preparing OFFICIAL HISTORIES (1970) publication began in earnest, has demanded that a supplement be produced. Moreover, there have been changes in the focus of the directorates of history, in the works being produced, and in attitudes towards such government publications. Thus, as the expression goes, it occurs to me that it would be a very good time to kill two birds with one stone, if material gathered for my April presentation could also be used for a supplement to OFFICIAL HISTORIES, a volume from which I have derived no monies.

Thus I am writing to ask you if it would be possible for you to do three things for this international effort?

1. Could you please send me a complete list of volumes published by your office and any predecessor organizations which are not already included in my first volume?
2. Can you supply me with an article of not more than 5,500 words on the history and development of the office and its series, either specially written or recently given or printed which I may have permission to reprint in English?

3. Can you please see that I receive nos. 1 and 2 both in the original language and in English by [revised] 1 May 1995?
4. If you know of any other official historical organizations in your country, would you please be kind enough to send me the name and address of the director and an indication, if it is not self-evident, of the directorate's connection to military history? Thank you.

Naturally, it should go without saying, that I will be most appreciative of any help which you can give me in publicizing the work of your office amongst our colleagues worldwide.

Hopefully we will get a chance to meet in Madrid next summer [1990]. Until then,

Good health!

Your sincerely,

Robin Higham, PhD

In some cases, after telephone conversations with the embassy staff in Washington, agreement was reached as to what was wanted, promises were made, yet the end result was still not usable. In one case the original version was returned for revision, but nothing further was ever received in spite of follow-up requests.

There have been delays in the work on my own part due to added responsibilities, commitments, and illness, and these lapses were used to try and get pieces through old and new contacts in the International Commission for Comparative Military History.

Delays have also been caused by the laws in one country that do not allow official communications to be in any language other than its own, while in another the author noted that he could do the translation but could not get anyone to type it. A further cause of delay was an original manuscript of 1,400 pages, a need to reduce this to workable size, and illness at the publisher as well.

In order to accommodate all of the entries, the original 1,400-page manuscript was split into three separate books—*The Writing of Official Military History*, which provides a background, and two books providing information on official historical offices and publications. The necessity of breaking the original work into three volumes was something of a challenge in organization. In the end, of course, any such division had to be somewhat arbitrary. Thus, Europe east to India and south to South Africa was deemed to be a suitable mix, while the newer concept of the Western Hemisphere and the Pacific Rim encompassed not only a large area, but one in which there has been a great deal of historical activity, even as the essays in the 1970 *Official Histories* demonstrated.

One of the very great drawbacks of a work with such a global span that has depended upon the good will of contributors around the world, especially when delays have been encountered, is that after one round of trying to get updated information, especially on publications since the original chapter was submitted was that busy offices could not spare the time or the interest. As a result, some of the chapters are not as up to date as was expected when the work began in 1988 and others, because of personal contacts and interests, are much more so.

In other cases, the concept of official histories was a convenient excuse to prevaricate. One delay lasted several years and was only resolved after a personal visit and a gift of two bottles of whiskey! In still another case, the article had to be rewritten by the editor to avoid paying a hefty fee for permission to reprint.

On the other hand, the contents of the work indicate how much international scholarly goodwill and tolerance of a slow publication schedule there is in the world military, naval, and air force historical community. It has been a pleasure dealing with my many contacts around the world.

Introduction

This Introduction and the Introduction in my 1970 book indicate a number of facets of official military history, from the general staff desire for usable operational lessons through the modern concern with scholarly standards and personal touches.

What is conceived of as official military history varies, from the Swiss view that they really do not have any to the Chilean view that while there is no such office, there are many works produced by officers which come close to having that *imprimatur*.

Official military historians have been and remain only as good as the evidence, training, energy, perspicacity, and time to do the job. Moreover, with each modern ministry creating as many as 2 million files in the 1939–1945 war, differing evidence is quite likely to turn up to suggest other interpretations of some points. In addition, moral positions and inculcated cultural norms apply to color the truth.

Most respondents were generous in providing their words in English. A few were not allowed or were not able to do so and so the editor or others had to provide a translation. In almost all cases where the titles of volumes or of positions were not self-evident, a translation has been provided. In a few cases, pieces from museums or military academies have been included because the whole of a service's historical activities are centered in one establishment.

One of the satisfying responses to the 1970 volume was that official historians around the world told me that at last they could know what each other had written. In these volumes I have not suggested what further research needs to be done, as I and my coeditors have in other bibliographical works, such as *A Guide to the Sources of U.S. Military History*. With those there was the further satisfaction of seeing the earlier suggestions taken up by the time later volumes appeared.

Official military historical services have originated at various times and places in a variety of guises, as illustrated by the chapters in this and the companion book, as well as in the 1970 book, *Official Histories*. In nearly all cases, the impetus came from the higher command wishing to capture the details and lessons of a recent campaign; to have a remembrancer. The approaches have also been very variable. In general, the armies have led, followed more reluctantly by the navies and, belatedly, by the new air forces.

Moreover, military history in both senses has gone in and out of military academies. Or, in the cases of neutral countries has become the military history department of the academy, with little or no research and public-action function. On the other hand, better established programs have secured themselves by branching out and producing neither campaign nor battlefield studies but respectable national history. Other times they have sortied into volumes on peacekeeping and other nonwar activities. Certainly, if enmities end, what will happen to the official historical offices?

Studies of the genesis of historical series suggest a rough rule of thumb that such series take at least twenty-five years to complete after a major war and sometimes up to half a century to appear. Moreover, there may be confidential versions which do not see the light of day until they go to the public archives thirty to fifty years after "publication."

Over the past century, official histories have become far more professional and respectable than they were at first. This is in part because history as a scholarly enterprise has changed. After the First World War, histories were judged to be too closely military and in some cases controversial, so the histories of the Second World War were started in a different atmosphere and with personnel generally trained in the evolving historical sciences. Moreover, some countries, such as Britain and Australia, initiated cabinet-level offices which oversaw from early in the war the gathering of a national record of total war on the 1914–1918 Australian model. Later, given the importance of intelligence, new works have now appeared on that delicate but fascinating subject.

Official volumes go through a period when they are the only tomes available that are written from government records, the archives being closed for thirty to fifty years. After the records are opened, there is inevitably a new view of their contents as scholars and the public are removed from events and perspectives change. Moreover, the government volumes inevitably neglected some topics, especially preparation for war and demobilization as well as technology in all its forms. These are occasionally covered in grand strategy books, but more often they are omitted. By the time authors wish to explore such neglected issues, the documents may have been destroyed, not to save reputations but because no one regarded them as valuable. Given the immense amount of documentation in the last century, as the historian Arnold Toynbee once declared, "The modern historian hopes for a good fire!" Perhaps so do official historians.

One of the issues in official military history has been who should command or head the historical office of each service. On the one hand, apart from being a sinecure for a retiring officer, the advantages of generals, admirals, or air marshals are that they have a entrées to the chief of staff and others, they themselves have had, hopefully, active service and command experience, and they have a network of those they have commanded that may stretch back some thirty years.

In theory, an officer of the armed forces should be familiar with documentation, but in fact they may not know more than regulations and orders closest to their own expertise. Because they are appointed late in life, senior officers are expensive and generally serve a limited term, though there are always exceptions. Civilian appointees may come up through the ranks or be selected from outside candidates. Their advantage usually lies in a superior educational/academic record, ability to write, and some administrative experience. Their weaknesses are lack of knowledge of military etiquette channels, discipline, and a monkish background. This is especially true when facing the day-to-day demands for quick answers to complex, precedent, and tradition-based questions.

In either case, the chief or director is usually supported by long-serving experts on the archives and publication processes. A civilian who does not offend or who does not face budget crunches may serve ten or more years. Some serve so long as to become a detriment to the field and the office.

The usefulness of a historical office to the General Staff it serves is determined by the attitude of the chief of staff or his deputies, tasks and access, significance of the historical subjects, the organization of the office or directorate and the demands upon its time, and the archival material available. While most historical offices either have their own libraries or museums, the essence of their research lies in perspicacious direction and archives that reflect the whole needs of the armed forces and are not solely concentrated on combat materials. Senior officers who are not familiar with the entire spread of military necessities do not know how to demand that archives acquire and not destroy the documentation of the invisible infrastructure. The same can apply to civilians. For their part, archivists tend to collect what historians wanted a decade and a half ago. And this is compounded by not asking units for the kind of materials that will be needed in the future. This is particularly important when long periods of peace lead to stagnation and then to crises in procurement, with time lags not being understood.

Service historical officers spend a considerable amount of time creating *esprit de corps,* validating acts of valor, and ensuring pension requirements are met, as well as writing combat history. This tends to be skewed, as it focuses on the frontline soldier to the detriment of the thirteen or more men and women behind the rifleman. As a matter of balance, very few histories have been written of the general staff itself, and this is the more surprising seeing as the foresight, doctrine, and efficiency of that body before war may be the key to wartime success or failure.

Among the reasons for there being secret as well as published official histories remains that drafts may, and usually are, circulated to principal participants for their comments. Generally, they may correct facts—whatever that word means—and they may protest to the point of demanding publication cease. However, those tactics are rarely successful. There may also be a much longer confidential version, as in the case of the history of British foreign policy in the Second World War, which eventually sees the light.

Notable in the years since the Second World War has been the professionalization and internationalization of the historical sections. Not only may they be headed by retired junior officers with doctorates instead of senior officers—though sometimes this is a political disadvantage—but their staffs have become officers in scholarly organizations. Moreover, increasingly the directorates of history have also convened their own conferences to encourage the interface between official historians and their colleagues in the profession. They have also initiated fellowships for graduate students and postdoctoral sojourns for scholars, often to the benefit of both sides in a world in which military history remains a major reader interest.

Moreover, as the pressure has mounted to reach the public, official volumes have been published by university presses and commercial houses, and the historical sections have authored, since the 1939–1945 war, paperbacks for the reading public and shorter serious studies for the professional officer corps. Sometimes these have been the products of staff colleges.

The U.S. government employed over 700 historians in the 1990s, more than 450 under the aegis of the Pentagon. Some are chroniclers, but most are engaged in historical research for in-house use, to benefit and enlighten the public, or both, as well as to justify budgets.

As long as the armed forces are engaged in warlike or peaceful activities, historical offices are likely to exist, unless a new generation of legislators and ministerial budget-cutters cannot comprehend the need for a national heritage and memory to prevent history repeating itself. Each generation rewrites history unless it chooses to forget it. In other cases, as now in France, history will have to be rewritten in a deeper and wider manner to set past actions in a new perspective not directly influenced by surviving participants. But the generation or two after those who were involved may still demand that history be written as they believe it happened.

Moreover, while evidence has always been doctored in the past through falsification of reports, loss of documents, weeding, and deaccessioning, as well as a narrowly conceived archival collections policy, new historians will face not merely the ravages of time and termites, but also audiovisual records and machine-readable computer materials which may be so manipulated that only slow, vast study and a very wide knowledge will allow the sifting of the truth and its encapsulation in what we still today call manuscript or book form. No matter how sophisticated the machines, the mind of man and woman must make the ultimate selections and decisions.

In this respect, it is interesting to note in reading these pieces which offices have taken a wider view of their work and which are still in the 1870 Prussian mold. It is also worth noting that in the Spanish-speaking countries, as well as in Brazil, history is done by officers associated with the Military History Commission, either before or after retirement, or they stimulated historical and cultural studies and books which became the source of the founding or the widening of the official service historical offices. These processes may have had the disadvantage that the works produced hew to the official line. On the other hand, they have had the advantage of being researched and written by officers who have intimately known the conditions under which activities and actions took place.

Surveying the essays and especially the attached bibliographies, it is worth noting that the approach to historical studies has changed much as it has in the profession as a whole. Thus, there is the shift from pure battle and campaign studies of special interest to the general staffs to a far wider view of military, naval, and air affairs, including the problems of the civilian support staff and their families. This is especially to be seen in the studies stemming from the Russo–Japanese War on the welfare of servicemen's families.

The historical offices of the armed services have frequently had relationships with museums. They have at various times been associated with museums under a common command, owned museums, or shared responsibilities with the establishments displaying the artifacts and honors of war. These relationships have been and remain related to cultural heritage as well as the country's military heritage. On the one hand the military has played a role in celebrations, such as a local march in conjunction with a fair, and on the other hand battle honors and their stories have been an integral part of inculcating pride in the service and *esprit de corps*. Both of these casas have been celebrated in battle paintings, portraits of leaders and family members in uniform, medals, and martial music. And closely related to the planning of parades and ceremonial occasions have been the protocol offices. For all these activities the archives, museums, and historical services have been utilized, and, indeed, they often have responsibilities over and beyond those to the general staff to provide past precedents for future planning.

Archives, museums, and historical offices also have to answer many questions, both from within and from outside the service. These may relate to pensions and campaign medal entitlements, or proposals to do thus and so which result from lack of institutional memory in the staff. Not infrequently, bad rules, regulations, and actions have been taken before the historians have been able to point to reinventing the wheel yet again. Not only do humans forget, but there are cycles of reform and change, some dictated by higher commanders' remembrance of conditions when they were young and newly commissioned.

Works from official military historical offices have changed greatly over the centuries. Strict campaign volumes have acquired joint authors to ensure fair and accurate treatment of the services involved, the breadth of coverage has expanded to recognize that it is the nation which goes to war, and changes in society have had to be included. This has resulted, as in the United Kingdom, in parallel civilian economic and medical series written by scholars and containing an immense amount of useful social information.

Starting in the 1930s Commissions of Military History arose, and under French leadership became the International Commission for Comparative Military History with annual meetings and publications. In most countries outside the Anglophone areas, these are supported by and housed in the appropriate ministry. The Portuguese Military History Commission is housed in the Ministry of Defense. It has as members the directors of the archives and museums of the three services, and produces the many volumes published. On top of this, funds may well be made available for tourism, allowing visitors to be invited officially and the expenses of their stay and sightseeing covered as a gesture of goodwill and hope for future military historical and touristic benefits.

Official military histories have a great deal of explicit and implicit information to offer. Like any historical work, they must be approached with skepticism and critiques must be consulted. However, they must also be placed in a balanced perspective, especially at the end of the twentieth century when there is a strong, vocal distrust of governments and leaders. It is also true that as archives are opened and researchers explore from different angles with varying strategies, there will need to be corrections and reassessments.

Reaching new conclusions may be hindered by the destruction of archives, either actively in war or pacifically in peace by archivists and others. This may well mean that imaginative new ways must be found to seek out additional or alternate copies in private archives, museums, and other official files to which, in the normal course, especially in the twentieth century, copies were routinely sent. Weapons makers, aircraft constructors, and shipbuilders may still have files. Medical materials especially are still likely to be found.

The essays and bibliographical lists presented here cover a wide variety of experiences of service historical offices, mostly since 1967. One of the rare guides to official histories and sources was compiled in 1926 by Waldo G. Leland and Newton D. Mereness for the Carnegie Endowment for International Peace. *Introduction to the American Official Sources for the Economic and Social History of the World War* ranges widely. Not only does it include information on the editorial process, but it also provides a breakdown—department by department and section by section—of government reports all the way to seed production in Kansas.

The British, having adhered pretty closely to the campaign model for the privately produced history of the Boer War, but with an official study of Japanese naval operations in the Russo–Japanese War as well as of the land side, produced only controversial campaign works for the 1914–1918 War, the naval and air force volumes being by civilian authors with a belated study of blockade by an economics scholar. However, due to the friction created and the bad press enjoyed by the naval and military volumes from "the last war," which were still trickling out after 1945, in 1939 the Cabinet Historical Office was created with the idea of describing the activities of a nation at war. Thus, there were campaign volumes authored by a triservice committee, civilian volumes by subject, and medical histories. Owing to the nature of doctors, quite a number of these clinical, surgical, and administrative tomes had been written in the past, and these are listed at the end of my 1999 book, *Writing Official Military History*. On the whole, the *United Kingdom History of the Second World War*, to give it its proper series title, proved to be pretty matter of fact and straightforward. Unlike the 1914–1918 volumes, here the controversy was limited to the four-volume *The Strategic Air Offensive against Germany* (London: Her Majesty's Stationers Office, 1961), authored by the noted historian of Europe, Sir Charles Webster, and Dr. Noble Frankland, who had done a tour as a navigator in Bomber Command. Evaluation of these raids was complicated by both the roars of wounded pride from the airmen and the reaction to the bombing of Dresden late in the war. This followed a cyclical pattern of emotions and assessments related to the Cold War and to the rise of a new generation without military experience.

The French have long had historical sections, but have only recently begun to produce volumes rather than articles on the military experience since the First World War, for which they have a large series. The difficulties have been compounded by attacks on survivors of the wartime Vichy government well into 1998. For the L'Armée de l'Air, the trauma of 1940 has just begun to be seen in a dispassionate manner.

Like the French, the Germans were defeated, but unlike the French they were also partitioned and so for political reasons had two military historical offices in succession to the older general staff office for the army, with the new offices handling all three service stories as well as special studies. Thus, Dr. Heider's essay (in Part 7) is of special interest, as it was written as the East German office was being closed after the reunification of Germany.

Of course, in the Soviet Union a grand historical establishment had been maintained largely behind closed doors. However, since the collapse of the Soviet Union, Russia is allowing outside scholars in, so the histories of the Great Patriotic War of 1941–1945 and perhaps also of earlier wars will most likely be revised.

In reading through or referring to these volumes, readers and researchers can have access to both sides of the story, and not just the English-language sources. English titles have been provided so that those with limited foreign languages can know what is available and what they may need to have translated, all of which is generally not available on a web site.

1

Austria

Austria: The Postwar Period

Erwin A. Schmidl, Vienna

No "official" military history as such was produced in Austria after 1945. This is partly due to this country's peculiar position at the end of World War II, being under Allied occupation for a decade, and partly a consequence of the Austrians' and Germans' rather reluctant attitude toward anything military after having experienced defeat in two world wars. The Austrian War Archives, the *Kriegsarchiv*, now fell under the authority of the Federal Chancellery, and understood itself as an archives only instead of the General Staff's research branch it had been earlier. It might be useful to add here that with the reorganization of the Austrian state archives in the 1980s, the post-1918 military files from the *Kriegsarchiv,* have been transferred to the new Archiv der Republik, both branches now being housed at the new archives building in Erdberg.

When the Austrian Federal Army was reestablished in 1955, a new research department (*Militärwissenschäftliche Abteilung*) was created, which in 1965 was incorporated into the Army Museum (*Heeresgeschichtliches Museum*), Austria's only federal museum to fall under the Ministry of Defense, rather than the Ministries of Education and Science. Although at first mainly concerned with analyzing recent or even contemporary conflicts (beside research on World War II, studies of the Middle East and Vietnam Wars were written), this became more and more an institution of serious historical research while the study of contemporary conflicts passed into the realm of the new defense academy. These activities are closely linked to the work of two historians: Johann Chr. Allmayer Beck, who served as director of the Army Museum 1965–1983, and Manfried Rauchensteiner, who was appointed to this position in 1992. It was mainly under the auspices of the Army Museum that a number of important studies were published from the 1960s on, with emphasis on twentieth-century military history. These are the nearest thing to "official" military historiography Austria has produced since 1945, and the most important of them are listed in the bibliography.

In order to emphasize the study of Austria's postwar military history and secure the relevant documents for research, a new branch, the Military Historical Service (*Militärhistorischer Dienst*) was created in 1989, under Manfried Rauchensteiner, within the ministry itself. Among the MIID's publications are a volume on the Austrian Armed Forces 1955–1970 and an interdisciplinary study on war memorials; in addition, a major project on Austrian participation in United Nations peacekeeping operations was initiated in 1990. Following Dr. Rauchensteiner's appointment as the new director of the Army Museum in mid-1992, a restructuring of Austrian military historical research facilities is likely to take place in the near future, although it is too early to give any details.

The common line in all these years has been to prove that military history is first and foremost a historical discipline. Therefore, close connection with other scholarly institutions, foreign and local, including civilian universities, has been maintained. The days when military history was considered the privileged pastime for general staff officers, studied principally with the potential application of any "lessons" in mind, are long over. At the same time, it is only with caution that one can speak about "official" military historiography any longer.

BIBLIOGRAPHY

This includes major publications only. For the sake of space, museum catalogues and the like are not listed here. However an illustrated catalogue to the museum's collections is available. *Heeresgeschichtliches Museum Wien*, was written by Liselotte Popelka and published by Styria (Graz) in German, English, French, and Italian editions.

Pre–World War II

Artl, Gerhard. *Die österreichisch-ungarische Sudtiroloffensive 1916*. Militärgeschichtliche Dissertationen österreichischer Universitaten 2. Wien: Bundesverlag, 1983. (A dissertation on Austria-Hungary's abortive 1916 offensive in the mountains of Southern Tyrol.)

Aus drei Jahrhunderten: Beitrage zue österreichischen Heeres-und Kriegsgeschichte von 1645–1938. Schriften des HGM 4. Wien: Bundesverlag, 1969. (A collection of essays ranging in topic from the Thirty Years War through the twentieth century.)

Der Dreißigjahrige Krieg: Beitrage zu seiner Geschichte. Schriften des HGM 7. Wien: Bundesverlag, 1976. (Essays on the Thirty Years War.)

Die k.k. Militärgrenze: Beitrage zu ihrer Geschichte. Schriften des HGM 6. Wien: Bundesverlag, 1973. (Essays on the military border.)

Forstner, Franz. *Premysl: Österreich-Ungarns bedcutendste Festung.* Militärgeschichtliche Dissertationen österreichischer Universitäten 7. Wien: Bundesverlag, 1987. (A study on the fortress of Premysl on the River San, now situated on the border between Poland and Russia, and its defense and fall in 1914–1915.)

Koch, Klaus. *Franz Graf Crenneville; Generaladjutant Kaiser Franz Josephs.* Militärgeschichtliche Dissertationen österreichischer Universitäten 3. Wien: Bundesverlag, 1984. (Biography of Francis Joseph's ADC.)

Koster, Maren. *Russische Truppen fur Prinz Eugen.* Militärgeschichtliche Dissertationen österreichischer Universitäten 6. Wien: Bundesverlag, 1986. (A dissertation about the first time Russian armed forces proceeded into Central Europe, during the 1730s War of the Polish Succession.)

Kurzmann, Gerhard. *Kaiser Maximilian I, und das Kriegswesen der österreichischen Länder und des Reiches.* Militärgeschichtliche Dissertationen österreichischer Universitäten 5. Wien: Bundesverlag, 1985. (A study on warfare and military organization under Emperor Maximilian I.)

Österreich zue See. Schriften des HGM 8. Wien: Bundesverlag, 1980. (Essays on Austria-Hungary's naval history.)

Ostler, Jurgen, II. *"Soldatenspielerei"? Vormilitärische Ausbildung bei Jugendlichen in der österreichischen Reichshälfte 1914–1918.* MHD–Sonderreihe. Wien: MIID, 1991. (A dissertation on premilitary training in Austria, 1914–1918.)

Military History, 1918–1938

Doppelbauer, Wolfgane. *Zum Elend noch die Schande.* Militärgeschichtliche Dissertationen österreichischer Universitäten 9. Wien: Bundesverlag, 1988. (A study on the social and economic situation of Austrian [ex-]officers after 1918.)

Hobelt, Lothar. *Die britische Appeasementpolitik.* Militärgeschichtliche Dissertationen österreichischer Universitäten 1. Wien: Bundesverlag, 1983. (A published dissertation on British appeasement policy.)

Kristan, Heribert. *Der Generalstabsdienst im Bundescheer der Ersten Republik.* Militärgeschichtliche Dissertationen österreichischer Universitäten 10. Wien: Bundesverlag, 1990. (In the Peace Treaty of 1919, the establishment of an Austrian general staff had been forbidden. This dissertation shows how the "clandestine" general staff worked in the interwar years.)

Schmidl, Erwin A. *Marz 38: Der deutsche Einmarsch in Österreich*. 2d. ed. Wien: Bundesverlag, 1988. (A study on the military aspects of Austria's 1938 annexation by the Third Reich.)

World War II

Rauchensteiner, Manfried. *1945: Entscheidung für Österreich*. Graz–Wien–Köln: Styria, 1975. (A photo volume to accompany the same author's *Krieg in Österreich*.)

Rauchensteiner, Manfried. *Der Krieg in Österreich 1945*. Schriften des HGM 5. 2d rev. ed. Wien: Bundesverlag, 1984. (The authoritative study on the closing days of World War II in Austria, the first edition was published in 1970.)

Austrian Military History, post-1945

Das Bundescheer der Zweiten Republik. Schriften des HGM 9. Wien: Bundesverlag, 1980. (Edition of documents about the Austrian Federal Army 1955–1980.)

Ein Heer für jede Jahreszeit. Wien: Bundesverlag, 1985. (Photo volume about Austria's Federal Army 1955–1985, an "army for all seasons," as implied by the title.)

Kernic, Franz. *Zwischen Worten und Täten: Die Wehrpolitik der Freiheitlichen 1949–1986*. Militärgeschichtliche Dissertationen österreichischer Universitäten 8. Wien: Bundesverlag, 1988. (A published dissertation on the Austrian Freedom Party's attitudes toward the military.)

Rauchensteiner, Manfried. *Spatherbst 1956: Die Neutralität auf dem prufstand*. Wien: Bundesverlag, 1981. (Austria's reaction, military and political, to the Soviet Union's intervention in Hungary in 1956.)

Rauchensteiner, Manfried, and Wolfgang Etschmann, eds. *Schild ohne Schwert; Das osterreichische Bundescheer 1955–1970*. Forschungen Zue Militärgeschichte 2. Graz–Wien–Koln: Styria, 1991. (Collection of essays on various aspects of Austrian military policy and organization in the 1950s and 1960s, the first of a series of volumes on the Austrian Federal Armed Forces post 1955.)

General Interest

Erwin, Pitsch. *Die Fliegerhorste des Bundesheeres in Krieg und Frieden*. Die Kasernen Österreichs 2. Wien: HGM, 1982. (A history of Austria's military airfields.)

Rauchensteiner, Manfried, and Erwin Pitsch. *Die Stiftskaserne in Krieg und Frieden*. Die Kasernen Österreichs 1. Wein: HGM, 1977. (A history of the Stiftskaserne, Austria's oldest military building continuously used for defense purposes.)

Rauchensteiner, Manfried, and Erwin A. Schmidl, eds. *Formen des Kriegs: Vom Mittelalter zum Low-Intensity-Conflict.* Forschungenzur Militargeschichte 1. Graz–Wien–Koln: Styria, 1991. (A collection of essays on warfare from the Middle Ages through the late twentieth century, including small wars and colonial warfare.)

Wo sind sie geblieben . . . ? Kriegerdenkmaler und militärischer Totenkult in Österreich. Schriften des HGM 12. Wien: Bundesverlag, 1992. (An illustrated study on war memorials in Austria, being the result of an interdisciplinary research project.)

Militärhistorische Schriftenreihe. (Sixty-five issues on topics ranging from Roman times through 1945 were published hitherto, each booklet dealing with a battle or campaign which took place within the present-day borders of Austria's Federal Republic).

2

Belgium

The Center for Historical Documentation

Based upon materials supplied by Professor Luc DeVos, Translated by Robin Higham

The Center for Historical Documentation (CDH) is the memory of the army, containing studies, reports of all sorts, campaign journals, reference works, theses, memoirs, and so on. Mementos are no longer without a home. In effect by the 1990s, the CDH had become the curator of all in its new home at Evere, alongside the other libraries and the general staff.[1]

HOME SWEET HOME

After leading a nomadic existence for some time, moving from place to place in la place Dailly at the Army Museum, then on Kortenberg Avenue in Brussels, over several months the Centre was moved in 1986 to be colocated with the other services at Evere prior to taking possession of its own block there even before the last stone was in place. There, Colonel (Brigade État Major [BEM]—member of the General Staff) Van Ruychevelt supervised the unpacking of 3,000 cases and the classifying and cataloguing of the documents.

A MEMOIR OF THE ELEPHANT WITHOUT HIS TRUNK

The mission of the CDH is in theory very simple. It is to collect, classify, repair, and conserve absolutely everything which in any way touches on the Belgian army since 1914. But in practice this task is as complicated as a Chinese fire drill. This collecting often means having to disassemble, classify, and restore, meaning also to annotate and compare. And conservation here sometimes means to restore.

The documents come from everywhere. Essentially, they come from the archives of the 1914–1918 war to the present and are placed at the CDH to the benefit of all.

The CDH now has the mandate of responding to all inquiries as best it can. It supplies copies of documents researchers request and it writes in response to all other queries punctually. Colonel Van Ruychevelt noted that the Centre receives about sixty visits and thirty written inquiries monthly.

In addition, the CDH has the following relationship with the Royal Army Museum. In effect the archives form an assemblage, and materials more than fifty years old are sent to the Museum. In principle all documents are open to researchers. There are, however, some limits relating to deontology [binding contracts or moral obligations] and military security, thus the penal code protects both public and private interests.

These small caveats having been made, let's enter the CDH.

SOUVENIRS

Since 1959, each unit or organism has had the duty to render an annual report, a complete daily diary of all the activities undertaken with a list of personnel and an account of the time they spent on annual exercises, ceremonies, and visits.

The Centre receives at least 343 reports a year, including those of reserve units recalled to duty during the year. These daily logs are examined by the CDH before being classified. This undertaking enables the files of each unit or organism to be updated. Since June 1985, the Centre has taken on the collection of reports of manuvers and exercises. Col. Van Ruychevelt personally holds all the files of the 1st (BE) Corps.

Perfection is not part of this world alone, for the Centre also holds numerous memorabilia and memoirs for the period from 1945 to the present. For this reason the Centre encourages those whom it helps to send in documents and photographs, either loaning or donating them to complete the pieces of the puzzle.

However, a short visit to the archives themselves reveals a very diverse set of materials on the shelves. In the profusion of campaign logs of the fusilier battalions, plans of fortifications, plans of abandoned barracks, unit photos, and photos of different types of material, there are some documents relating to the war in Korea, to events in the Congo, in Katanga and Shaka. There are the archives of the Ministry of Defense, as well, which also contain certain records of the exile government in London in World War II. And finally the archives hold numerous theses, memoirs, and reference works.

As part of its mission to aid the public the CDH has eight persons full time and a number of retired officers such as Colonel E. R. Vidick who, among other things, has the responsibility of putting historical reports sent in daily into their unit files.

And, again, General (e.r.) Gillet who, after a period of study became greatly interested in the road to peace in 1938, now is actually pursuing an immense study on the state of the Belgian Army on 28 May 1940, the movements coordinated after this date, and the life of those in the POW camps, work commandos, and disciplinary camps. Then there is M. Destrebecq, who punctually answers all the questions on the activities of air forces over Belgium, as well as those relating to the records of Belgians in the Royal Air Force in the Second World War.

Colonel Van Ruychevelt is concerned that without their volunteer help the CDH would not be what it is. Besides, who better than retired officers who have had the training, have served in the branch, and had the experience to be able to exploit with such understanding military documents?

When a visitor to the archives arrives at the CDH lecture hall he is greeted by the Chief of Staff Leroy, who regards it as a duty and a pleasure to fulfill his function of dispatcher (assessor). This is the starting place at the CDH and is an obligatory stop on the way to the records. Also librarian of the organization, he is responsible for the classification of documents. Among all the records, he is the finger and eye to the files arranged alphabetically by subject and author, by unit, by collection, and by theme. It is this graciousness at the start which the visitor finds when searching. M. Leroy never rests until the searcher has found the collection and his prey. If, by chance, the solution is not to be found at the CDH, the researcher will be given all possible help to locate it elsewhere.

The other personnel also provide guidance as far as they can as part of their "Public Function."

L'AVENIR DE CE PASSE (THE FUTURE OF THIS CHANNEL)

It is not possible to keep everything. We have said that documents over fifty years old become the concern of the Royal Army Museum. It is thus that sooner or later the quantity of documents and the information provided will undoubtedly create a loss of space. To mitigate this eventuality the Centre has microfilmed the most important documents, gaining time, space, and above all facility of manipulation.

One can always dream, but we live in an age of restrictions and operations which remain the priority.

HAUT SECRET (TOP SECRET)

Looking at the very confidential documents the CDH possesses, there is first a document taken off a German officer on 10 January 1940 who was in an aircraft forced to land at Méchelen-sur-Meuse. It is the plan for the invasion of Belgium, with a concentration particularly between the Sambre and the Meuse rivers. It is a document which was twice thought destroyed.

Second is the military plan of action for secret troops on the national territory in cooperation with the Allies. This plan of 31 March 1943 had been approved by M. Pieriot, Prime Minister of the Belgian government in exile in London. Amended many times, this is nevertheless the first such plan which places the Belgian Resistance Army in a time and space framework.

EN GUISE DE CONCLUSION (CONCLUSION)

"Man has need of functional roots," as Martin Gray has said. Regiments have a spirit, a character, and a soul like men, as a French general wrote. This is again true in the CDH archives, wherein the proof can be found. Seekers of today can find and retrieve there their roots drawn from the lessons of past actions.

Further inquiries should be addressed to

CDH
Quartier Reine Elisabeth
rue d'Evere
1140 Bruxelles
Belgium

NOTE

1. *Le centre de documentation historique: Mirror de notre histoire militaire* (The Center for Historical Documentation: Mirror of our military history). The original appeared in *Vox*, no. 10-86, 7–9.

A Short History of the History Department of the Belgian Royal Military Academy

Professor Luc DeVos, Translated by Robin Higham

As official military history was and still is done by the Staff of the Royal Military Academy, it is proper to provide this brief account.

At the time of its creation in 1834, the main aim of the Royal Military Academy was to train and form well-rounded [polyvalent] officers. And yet HRH Leopold I made it a point that the students in the academy were to receive a basically scientific training. This meant then that, during the first years of its existence, the course of Strategic Studies only had a tiny place in the curriculum.

Between 1834 and 1864 the course started with a short historical survey and came to include lectures on Fortifications, Organization and Recruitment, as well as Tactics and Strategy. In 1864 the course of Strategic Studies became a genuine course of Military History and represented 3 percent of the academic curriculum. In 1873 this course comprised the study of a series of battles ranging from the Ancient Greeks to the 1870–1871 conflict (for which information had started being gathered). As can be seen, the course of Military History was gaining momentum.

As early as 1887 a series of visits to Waterloo and Ligny were organized and atlases were being used. These would, however, only be completed by 1912. Students still had no handbooks and had to take notes during the lessons. The first handbooks only appeared in 1890. A little bit later (in 1912) both *History of Tactics* and *Introduction to the Royal Engineers* were published, where warcraft was examined in connection with this battalion. In 1906 there was a thorough study of the Russo–Japanese conflict and of the recruitment and organization of the French and German armies.

Between 1910 and 1914 the course of organization had to be updated taking into account the new Belgian laws on conscription. On the eve of World War I the course represented 6 percent of the academic curriculum of the RMA. After World War I the course of Strategic Studies gathered pace, but as the number of seminars could not increase, antiquity was superficially examined so as to spend most of the time studying the world conflict of 1914–1918. Staff Colonel Galet, commander of the RMA, reorganized the course of Strategic Studies and divided it into Military History, the 1914–1918 Belgian campaign, Organization, Strategy and General Tactics, Infantry Tactics, and Geography (which were seen as indispensable to understanding the course of history).

Between 1919 and 1927 the courses of Military History and Geography (from 1920 onward) were taught by Staff Captain-commander (soon-to-be Major) Van Overstraeten, also aide-de-camp to the Belgian king. As early as 1921 he published a book about military history entitled *The Principles of War Through the Ages*. He taught the events preceding the 1914–1918 war in a synthetic way and dwelt on the study of the Western Front at length. The course was enhanced by a visit to Waterloo, a detailed study of the use of tanks during the battle of Cambrai and a lecture on the use of aviation during World War I. The course on the 1914–1918 Belgian campaign aimed at a reappraisal of the aid given by our army to the Allies. The different colonial campaigns of our army were also studied.

At the end of World War II and after the reopening of the RMA on January 7, 1946, the Department of History at the RMA (called Royal since 1936) was led by Major (soon-to-be Professor) H. Bernard. The course comprised Military History, Organization and Tactics, as well as the history of Belgium, the study of defense problems, and Geography. In September 1967 Professor Jean-Léon Charles became the head of the department and did not change the courses fundamentally. But he understood the growing role of the media and helped to produce different TV series. Since 1988 the department has been led by Professor Luc Devos, who teaches the history of Belgium, of International Relations, of Wars, and of the world after 1945.

LISTE DES PUBLICATIONS DU CDH (Titles in French, Flemish, and Walloon)

Le combat de Bodange / Het gevecht van Bodange (The Battle of Bodange)

Le combat de Chabrehez / Het gevecht van Chabrehez (The Battle of Chabrehez)

Aan de 2000 doden van de 7, 17, 26 Linie Regimenten (The 7th, 17th, and 26th Infantry Regiments to the year 2000)
Historique du 14e Bataillon de Fusiliers (History of the 14th Fusiliers Battalion)
Historique du 13e Régiment de Ligne 1874–1914 (History of the 13th Regiment of the Line, 1874–1914)
Historique du 13e Régiment de Ligne 1918–1980 (History of the 13th Regiment of the Line, 1918–1980)
Historique du 12e Régiment de Ligne (History of the 12th Regiment of the Line). Tome I, 1830–1914; tome II, 1914–1918; tome III (A), 1919–1940; tome IV (B), 1944–1977.
Historiques des 8-16-38-58 Li 1939–40 / Historiek der 8-16-38-58 Li 1939–40 (The Story of the 8th, 16th, 38th, and 58th Line Regiments, 1939–1940)
Historique du 12e Bataillon de Fusiliers (History of the 12th Fusilier Battalion)
Historique de la cavalerie belge: son organisation de 1830 à 1970 (History of the Belgian Cavalry: Its organization from 1839–1970)
Geschiedenis van het Belgisch Leger: Deel 1 1830–1919 (The story of the Belgian Light Infantry, Part 1, 1830–1919)
Histoire de l'Armée Belge: Tome 2, 1920 à nos jours / Geschiedenis van het Belgisch Leger: Deel 2, 1920 tot heden (History of the Belgian Army, Vol. 2, from 1920 to our day)
De Infanterie: filiaties en tradities / L'Infanterie: filiations et traditions (The infantry: Lineage and traditions)
Filiations des unités de la Force Aérienne (The Lineage of Air Force Units)
La Prusse Orientale en 1944 et après (East Prussia in 1944 and after)
De l'Yser à Bruxelles / Van de Ijser tot Brussel (From the Yser River to Brussels)
Emblèmen en Eervolle Vermeldingen van de Eenheden / Emblèmes et Citations des Unités (Unit crests and citations)
Donnez-nous un champ de bataille / Geef ons een slagveld (Give us a field of battle)
Contribution à l'histoire du Congo Belge: Deuxième Guerre Mondiale (Contributions to the history of the Belgian Congo: Second World War)
L'Attaque aérienne des ponts du canal Albert (The air attack on the bridges over the Albert Canal)
Prix à enlever sur place (Prizes awarded)

Cartes du Lt Col Honoraire Bikar (The Maps of Hon. Colonel Bikar)

Armée Belge—Campagne de mai 40 (10 au 28 mai): Des fortifications permanentes—des positions occupées—des emplacements successifs des divisions et des itinéraires suivis (N° 34) / Belgisch Leger—Veldtocht mei 40 (10 tot 28 mei): Van de permanente versterkingen—van de bezette stellingen—van de opeenvolgende stellingen der divisies en de gevolgde marsroutes (N° 34) (Belgian Army in 1940 May [10–

28]. The Permanent Fortifications—positions occupied—the succession of positions occupied by various divisions and the itineraries followed)

Armée Belge—Mobilisation de 1939–1940 / Belgisch Leger—Mobilisatie van 1939–1940 (Belgian Army and the 1939–40 Mobilization)

Dispositif le 7 mai 40 à 12.30 Hr (préalerte) et mouvements jusqu'au 10 mai à 04.35 Hr (attaque allemande) (N° 40) / Opstelling op 7 mei 1940 te 12.30 (Vooralarm) en bewegingen tot 10 mei om 04.35 Hr. (Duitse aanval) (N° 40) ([The prealert] and the movements of 7 May 1940 to 0435 on 10 May when the Germans attacked)

The Campaign in Belgium, May 1940—Various Authors

Campagne de mai 1940 en Belgique (Spa) (N° 49)
Campagne de mai 1940 en Belgique (Stavelot) (N° 50)
Campagne de mai 1940 en Belgique (Durbuy) (N° 55)
Campagne de mai 1940 en Belgique (Vielsalm) (N° 56)
Campagne de mai 1940 en Belgique (Limerle) (N° 61)
Compagne de mai 1940 en Belgique (Neufchâteau) (N° 65)
Campagne de mai 1940 en Belgique (Arlon) (N° 68)
Campagne de mai 1940 en Belgique (Sterpenich) (N° 69)

RÉPERTOIRE DES MUSÉES D'HISTOIRE MILITAIRE, 1914–1918 ET 1940–1945

Courtesy of Colonel G. Lobet, Chef de Department, Centrum voor Historische Documentatie, Kwartier Koniquin Elisabeth, 1140 Brussels, Belgium

1. Centre de Documentation Historique des Forces Armées, Quartier Reine Elisabeth (Centre for the Historical Documentation of the Armed Forces), 1 Rue d'Evere, 1140 Bruxelles
2. Musée Royal de l'Armée et d'Histoire Militaire (Royal Army and Military History Museum), 3 Parc du Cinquantenaire, 1040 Bruxelles
3. Centre de Recherches et d'Etudes Historiques de la Seconde Guerre Mondiale (Centre for Research and Historical Studies of the Second World War), 4 Place de Louvain, 1000 Bruxelles
4. Musée de la Gendarmerie (The Police Museum), 2 Rue J. Wystman, 1050 Bruxelles
5. Musée des Chemins de Fer (The Railway Museum), Gare du Nord, Rue du Progès, 1000 Bruxelles
6. Musée de la Porte de Hal (The Hal Gate Museum), Avenue de la Porte de Hal, 1000 Bruxelles
7. Musée National de la Résistance (The National Museum of the Resistance), 14 Rue van Lint, 1030 Bruxelles

8. Fondation Auschwitz ASBL (The Auschwitz Foundation), 65 Rue des Tanneurs, 1000 Bruxelles
9. Musée de la Ligne KW 1940 (The 1940 KW Line Museum), Ancienne école de et à Longueville
10. Musée du 1 Bn PARA (The First Paratrooper Museum), Citadelle de Diest, 3290 Diest
11. Musée du Corps de Cavalerie Français 1940 (The French Cavalry, 1940, Museum), Ecole Communale, Chaussée de Wavre, 24, 5953 Jandrain
12. Musée Français des Combats de la lère Armée Française 1940 (The Museum of the Battles of the First French Army in 1940), Rue Tansoul, 5861 Cortil-Noirmont
13. Musée des Bérets Verts (The Green Berets Museum), Quartier SLt Thibaut, 5720 Flawinne
14. Citadelle de Dinant (The Castle of Dinant), 5500 Dinant
15. Quartier Général de Hitler 1940 (Hitler's headquarters, 1940), 6406 Bruyly de Pesche (Couvin)
16. Musée du Centenaire (The 100th Anniversary Museum), Jardin du Mayeur, 7000 Mons
17. Musée de la Tour Henri VIII (The Henry VIII Tower Museum), Rue des Remparts, 7500 Tournai
18. Historical Center, 6650 Bastogne
19. Musée de la Fraternelle du ler Bn d'Artillerie (The Fraternal Museum of the 1st Battalion of Artillery), Caserne SLt Heintz, 6650 Bastogne
20. Fort de Breendonck (Fort Breendonck), Brandstraat, 57, Route Nationale 1 Bis, Bruxelles-Anvers 2659 Breendonck
21. Musée du Camp de Bourg–Leopold (The Camp Bourg-Leopold Museum), Hôpital Militaire, Chaussée de Hechtel, 3970 Leopoldsburg

3

Czech Republic

The Historical Institute of the Army of the Czech Republic

Captain Petr Klučina, of the Institute

The Historical Institute of the Army of the Czech Republic is a successor of a number of the old Austro-Hungarian monarchial institutions which had various names in the past. In Spring 1919 a suggestion was put forward in the new Czechoslovak Parliament to create the basis for historiographical evaluation of the "great era of Czechoslovak history," meaning the history of the origins of the independent Czechoslovak state in 1914–1918, mainly including the history of the political and military anti-Austrian action. The attention, which the early institutions and organizations paid to the period of the Great War, was a general phenomenon: In most European states similar scholarly and documentary institutions were founded. They organized and published many works on the history of the Great War. In Czechoslovakia, the general interest in "responsibility for the war (*Krieschuldfrage*)" in questions of war aims, military operations, and so on was joined by an effort to show the historical reasons for the birth of the Czechoslovak state. At the beginning of the 1920s, three small institutions were founded:

1. *The Resistance Memorial (Památnik Odboje)*, which had the task to collect and preserve archive and museum material concerning the problems of political and military action aimed at the destruction of Austria-Hungary and emergence of an independent Czechoslovak state. Its activities comprised collecting, organizing, and preserving historical materials; it published a number of monographs, memoirs, and information and propaganda booklets.

2. *The National Liberation Archives (Archiv národního osvobození)*, a part of the Czech Land [Territorial] Archives, had a similar task, but while the Resistance Memorial concentrated on military actions, the National Liberation Archives focused on political actions. It built a library of historical and documentary literature concerning the Great War. The head of the institute, Jaroslav Werstadt, started to publish as editor a quarterly journal, *Naše revoluce* (Our revolution), which dealt with the histories of the anti-Austrian action and of the Great War in general.
3. *Military Archives and Museum of the Czechoslovak Republik (Vojenský archive a Museum Republiky Ceskoslovenské)* was an institute studying the "military past of Czechoslovakia"; e.g., Czechoslovak (in practice, Czech) military history since the ninth century.

On 28 October 1928, the tenth anniversary of the birth of the independent Czechoslovak state, all three institutions were amalgamated in the *Liberation Memorial (Památník osvobození)*, for which a new building in Prague-Zizkov was built. Thus a large institute was founded, well provided for in material and personnel, comprising branches for research, archives, and museum. It was incorporated into the Ministry of Defense and subordinated to the General Staff. According to its foundation charter its tasks were

1. To collect and preserve archival documents, museum items, and literature from the period of the Great War, from the period before 1914; e.g., the era of the Habsburg Monarchy and the period of the pre-Habsburg Czech state, all as far as military history of the territory of the Czechoslovak republic was concerned.
2. To publish and support publishing of sources concerning military history of Czechoslovakia, mainly for the period 1914–1918.
3. To collect material and to research the history of the army of the new Czechoslovak state.

The Liberation Memorial comprised, beside the director's office, four departments: The first was in charge of the so-called political archive of the first resistance and headed the library; the second was the so-called military archives of the resistance; the third comprised museum, photo archives, and the specialized library of old militaria (up to the nineteenth century); fourth was the research department, cooperating closely with other scholars interested in military history.

In the 1930s the Liberation Memorial organized many activities in the field of research, collections, museums, and exhibitions. The most significant research activities of the Liberation Memorial as well as those of its predecessor were connected with the historical quarterly *Naše revoluce.* It published in 1923–1938 a number of documents, scholarly studies, reviews, and information on publications at home and abroad concerning the history of the Great War in general and of the military and political history of Czechoslovakia in particular. Edited by Jaroslav Werstadt, who became the leading spirit of the research activities of the Liberation Memorial, the journal *Naše revoluce* became a respected historical periodical. The wide publication activities of the Liberation Memorial did not culminate however in a historical synthesis, although its staff helped with the great official publications, mainly those produced for the tenth and twentieth anniversaries of the Republic (*Deset let ceskoslovenské republiky*, Praha, 1928; *Ceskoslovenská armáda*, Praha, 1938).

After German occupation on 15 March 1939, the Liberation Memorial became an object of hatred and vengeance by the occupying power, as it was considered a bearer of Czechoslovak "Legionnaire ideology," which was regarded as anti-German. As a former part of the Defense Ministry, the whole Liberation Memorial (administration building, museum, archives) became the property of the Wehrmacht. Most of the leading personnel were arrested and imprisoned in concentration camps, while many others were active in the resistance movement. The archives survived thanks to the fact that the well-known Austrian military historian R. Kissling served there after being drafted into the Wehrmacht. Museum exhibits, on the other hand, were transported to Germany; luckily most of them were found after the war and returned. They were placed in the Schwarzenberg Palace at the Hradcany Castle in Prague, which thus became the Military Historical Museum.

After liberation in 1945 the Liberation Memorial was reconstituted and its departments closely followed the prewar tradition as far as ideas and organization were concerned. Their interest was broadened to include World War II, with an accent on the resistance at home and abroad. In February 1948, when the Communists gained power, they considered the tradition of the Czechoslovak Legions, especially in Russia, which was the basis of the research of the Liberation Memorial, as hostile to their ideology. The Liberation Memorial was disbanded and, in 1951, there was organized in its building an exhibition of "30 Years of the Communist Party of Czechoslovakia," which became the basis for forming the official Communist view of history. The original idea of using the buildings of the Liberation Memorial by the newly founded Institute of the Party History was not realized and a Military Historical Institute (Vojenský historický ústav) was placed there instead. Subordinated to the Main Political Directorate of the Ministry of National Defense, it was controlled in all aspects of its work by the Communist political/military organs. Its research work, developed on the basis of dogmatic Communist concepts characteristic of the 1950s, was organized by a Military Historical Department; all the archives became part of a Military Historical Archives, while all the museums were amalgamated into the Military Historical Museum, including the newly founded air museum in Prague-Kbely. The new institute also comprised a library, a documentation section, and a photo archive. It published a quarterly magazine called *Historie a vojenství*. A branch of the institute was opened in Bratislava.

In the 1950s the "scholarly" production of the institute was concentrated on the ideological fight with "Masarykism" and the "liberation legend," which contradicted the traditions and results of research of the former institute. Propaganda without any scholarly value dominated its work, though some results were achieved in collecting new material. After the XXth Congress of the Soviet Communist Party, and mainly from the beginning of the 1960s, a group of historians started to form in the Military Historical Institute to strive to overcome the dogmatic rigidity and to reawaken the prewar tradition of the Liberation Memorial. The institute gradually reassumed the character of a scholarly institution and published at the end of the 1960s a number of works pressing forward the progress of research. The climate of the "Prague Spring" in 1968 opened new perspectives for the research work of the institute.

After the Warsaw Pact invasion in August 1968 and the beginnings of the so-called normalization, the Military Historical Institute faced the third disaster in its short history. It was labelled a "nest of counterrevolution" and most of its research workers (above all the most able) were dismissed; the command of the institute was changed as a whole. The institute became once again an "ideological institution" of the party in the army. Its leadership was taken by unqualified newcomers, most of them without historical training, graduates of the "political" schools of the regime: the Military Political Academy and the Political University of the Communist Party. The journal *Historie a vojenství* lost the character of a scholarly review and became a propaganda magazine, commenting upon and rewriting the last resolutions of the party central committee or directives of the ministry. Some research continued only in the archives and museums.

After the fall of the Communist regime in 1989, the effort was resumed to once again give the discredited institute the character of a scholarly institution. Some of the staff released during the normalization returned, and new, younger historians graduating from the universities were added. To distinguish the new institute from the discredited old one it was renamed the Historical Institute of the Czechoslovak Army. It continues in the tradition of the prewar Liberation Memorial: It considers itself a specialized research institution for the history of the first and second resistances and military history, including military museums and archives.

After the dissolution of Czechoslovakia at the beginning of 1993, the structure of the institute was again changed. The Bratislava branch became an independent institution and the Czech institute was renamed the Historical Institute of the Army of the Czech Republic. It now consists of

1. *The Resistance Memorial*, the research branch, comprising three sections, specializing in military history, the First and Second World War resistance movements, and the contemporary history of the army.
2. *The Military Historical Archives*, with some fifteen kilometers of files of military origins from Austria-Hungary and the Czechoslovak Republic.
3. *The Military Historical Museum*, with three independent museums in Prague, in the Schwarzenberg Palace (exhibits to 1918), in the main office building (since 1914, with the stress on the history of resistance), and in Prague-Kbely (air and space museum and collection of heavy vehicles).
4. *The Military Historical Library*, charged also with publishing the journal *Historie a vojenství.*

BIBLIOGRAFIE K VOJENSKÝM DOJINÁM CESKOSLOVENSKA, 1914–1992 (BIBLIOGRAPHY TO MILITARY HISTORY OF CZECHOSLOVAKIA, 1914–1992)

Anger, J., and J. Dvoran. *Kvetnové povstání ceského lidu v roce 1945.* (May Uprising of the Czech People 1945). Praha, 1984.

Armáda—historie, tradice (Army, history, tradition). Praha, 1993.

Aron, L. a kol. *Ceskoslovenské opevnení 1935–1938* (Czechoslovak fortifications 1935–1938). Náchod, 1990.

Bárta, M., O. Felcman, J. Belda, V. Mencl, ved. aut. kol. *Ceskoslovensko roku 1968. Díl. II. Pocátky normalizace* (Czechoslovakia in 1968. Volume II. Beginnings of normalization). Praha, 1993.

Bencík, A., and J. Domanský. *21. arpen 1968* (21st August 1968). Praha, 1990.

Bílek, J. *Pomocné technické prapory 1950–1954. Vznik, Vývoj, organizace a cinnost* (Auxiliary technical battalions 1950–1954. Origins, Development, organization and activity). Praha, 1992.

Bittman, L. *Špionázní oprátky. Pohledy do zákulisí ceskoslovenské zpravodajské sluzby* (The deception game. Czechoslovak Intelligence Service viewed from behind the scene). Praha, 1992.

Bláha, S. *Co dal Masaryk armáde a brannosti národa* (What did Masaryk give the army and war preparedness of the nation). Praha, 1990.

Bosák, P. *Z bojových operácií na fronte SNP* (Combat operations at the front of the Slovak National Uprising). Bratislava, 1979.

Bouck, M. a kol. *Za národní osvobození, za novou republiku* (For national liberation, for a new republic). Praha, 1982.

Broft, M., and O. Mahler. *Praha V Kvetnu 1945* (Prague in May 1945). Praha, 1985.

Bursík, J. *Nelituj obeti* (No sorrow for sacrifices). Praha, 1992.

Cejka, E. *Zlomená krídla* (Broken wings). Praha, 1991.

Cejka, E. *Ceskoslovenský odboj na Západe* Sv. I–II (Czechoslovak Resistance in the West. Parts I–II). Praha, 1992.

Ceskoslovenské tankové vojsko v SSSR. Sborník studií a vzpomínek (Czechoslovak tank units in the Soviet Union. Miscellany studies and memoirs). Praha, 1978.

Ceskoslovensko a Izrael, 1945–1965. Dokumenty (Czechoslovakia and Israel, 1945–1965. Documents). Praha, 1993.

Ceský odboj a kvetnové povstání. Sborník dokumentu 1943–1945 (Czech Resistance and May Uprising. Miscellaneous documents 1943–1945). Praha, 1975.

Cílek, R. *Prokletí moci* (Curse of the power). Praha, 1991.

Cvancara, J. *Akce atentát* (Assassination attempt). Praha, 1991.

Dejiny Slovenského národného povstania. Sv. I–V (History of the Slovak National Uprising. Part I–V). Bratislava, 1984.

Destrukce cs.dustojnického sboru po únoru 1948 (Destruction of Czechoslovak Officers Corps after February 1948). Praha 1992.

Drska, P. *Ceskoslovenská armáda v národni a demokratické revoluci 1945–1948* (The Czechoslovak Army in the National Army Democratic Revolution 1945–1948). Praha, 1979.

Dufek, J. *Ceskoslovensko a Izrael. Studie* (Czechoslovakia and Israel. Studies). *Karel Kaplan, Vladimír Šlosar.* Praha, 1993.

Dvorský, J. *Naše vojško a ceskoslovenský ustojník v projevech T. G. Masaryka. Díl. I–II* (Our troops and the Czechoslovak officer in the speeches of T. G. Masaryk. Volume I–II). Praha, 1991.

Eyck, M. F. van. *Zemreli pro Anglii. Piloti 310., 312. a 313. ceskoslovenské perute, kterí bojovali a zemreli pro Anglii 1940–1945* (They died for England. Pilots of Nos. 310, 312 and 313 Czechoslovak Squadrons who fought and died for England 1940–1945). Praha, 1993.

Fajtl, F. *První doma* (The first at home). Praha, 1974.

Fajtl, F. *Létal jsem s Tristatrináctkou* (I flew with the No. 313). Praha, 1991.

Fajtl, F. *Podruhé doma* (Second return home). Praha, 1984.

Francev, V. *Ceskoslovenské tanky, obrnená auta, obrnené vlaky a drezíny 1918–1939. Jednotky obrnených vozidel cs, armády 1918–1939* (Czechoslovak tanks, armored cars, armored trains and trolleys 1918–1939. Armor units of Czechoslovak army 1918–1939). Praha, 1993.

Franek, O. *Zbrane pro celý svet* (Arms for the whole world). Brno, 1970.

Franek, O. *Dejiny koncernu brnenské Zbrojovky. Díl. I–II* (A history of the Zbrojovka Concern in Brno. Volume I–II). Brno, 1969–1970.

Frolík, J. *Špion vypovídá* (A spy's testimony). Praha, 1990.

Galandauer, J. a kol. *Slovník prvního ceskoslovenského odboje 1914–1920* (A dictionary of the First Czechoslovak Resistance 1914–1920). Praha, 1993.

Galandauer, J. a kol. *O samostatný ceskoslovenský stát 1914–1918* (For an independent Czechoslovak state 1914–1918). Praha, 1992.

Gebhart, J., A. Hájková, and J. Kuklík. *2245 dnu odporu. Podíl spoju a spojaru na národne osvobozeneckém zápase ceského lidu v letech 1939–1945* (2,245 days of resistance. The part of communications and signalmen in the struggle for national liberation of the Czech people in 1939–1945). Praha, 1980.

Gebhart, J., A. Hájková, and J. Kuklík. *Na frontách tajné války. Kapitoly z boju cs.zpravodajství proti nacismu v letech 1938–1945* (The Fronts of the Secret War. Chapters from the fight of Czechoslovak Intelligence against Nazism in 1938–1945). Praha, 1989.

Gebhart, J., and J. Šimovcek. *Partyzáni v Czskoslovensku 1941–1945* (Partisans in Czechoslovakia 1941–1945). Praha, 1984.

Gregorovic, M. *První ceskoslovenský odboj. Cs.legie 1914–1920* (The first Czechoslovak Resistance. Czechoslovak Legions 1914–1920). Praha, 1992.

Hejl, V. *Zpráva o organizovaném násilí* (A report on organized violence). Praha, 1990.

Historie vojska PVO ceskoslovenských pozemních vojsk (History of Czechoslovak Ground Forces AA units). Praha, 1970.

Holub, O. *Zrazené pevnosti* (Betrayed fortresses). Praha, 1982.

Holub, O. *Ceskoslovenské tanky a tankisté* (Czechoslovak tanks and tankers). Praha, 1980.

Holub, O. *Stüj. financní stráz!* (Stop [Who goes there?]. Financial guard!). Praha, 1987.

Honzík, M. *Za Heydrichem otazník* (A question mark behind Heydrich). Praha, 1989.

Honzík, M. *Legionári* (Legionnaires). Praha, 1990.

Hrabicovi, P. a Z. *Muz, ktorý velel muzum* (A man who commanded men). *K.Klapálek* Praha, 1988.

Ivanov. M. *Atentát na Reinharda Heydricha* (The killing of Reinhard Heydrich). Praha, 1987.

Jablonický, J. *Glosy o historiografii SNP. Zneuzivanie a falšovanie dejín SNP* (Comments on the historiography of the Slovak National Uprising. Misusing and falsifying its history). Bratislava, 1994.

Jablonický, J. *Povstanie bez legiend* (Uprising without legends). Bratislava, 1990.

Jelínek, Z. *Operace Silver A* (Operation Silver A). Praha, 1993.

Jelínek, Z. *Partyzánské organizátorské desanty v ceských zemích v letech 1944–1945* (Parachuted partisan organisers' groups in Czech lands 1944–1945). Roztoky u Prahy, 1984.

Jelínek, Z. *Západní paraskupiny a domácí odboj* (Western paragroups and resistance at home). Praha, 1992.

John, M. *Okupace cs.letišt v breznu 1939* (Occupation of Czechoslovak airfields in March 1939). Cheb, 1992.

Jozák, J. a kol. *Za obnovu státu Cechu a Slováku. Slovnéková prírucka* (For the renovation of the state of the Czechs and Slovaks. Dictionary handbook). Praha, 1993.

Kapetoly z vojenskej histórie Slovenska (Chapters from military history of Slovakia). Trencín, 1991.

Kaplan, K. *Tábory nucené práce v Ceskoslovensku v letech 1948–1954* (Forced labor camps in Czechoslovakia 1948–1954). Praha, 1992.

Karlický, V. *Ceskoslovenské delostrelecké zbrane* (Czechoslovak artillery weapons). Praha, 1975.

Klucina, P., A. Rgmanák, and K. Richter. *Clovek, zbran a zbroj v obraze doby. Díl. II* (Man, weapon and armor in the image of times. Part II). Praha, 1984.

Kokoška, J., S. Kokoška. *Spor o agenta A-54* (Dispute over Agent A-54). Praha, 1994.

Kolar, J. *Lidé z první rady* Praha, (People from the first row). 1985.

Koutek, J. *A národ se bránil* (And the nation fought on). Praha, 1987.

Koutek, J. *Tichá fronta* (Silent front). Praha, 1985.

Krajina, V. *Vysoká hra. Vzpomínky* (High game. Memoirs). Praha, 1994.

Kroupa, V. a kol. *Ceský antifašismus a odboj. Slovníková prírucka* (Czech antifascism and resistance. Dictionary handbook). Praha, 1988.

Krumbach, J. *Dvacet pet roku národního podniku LET Uherské Hradište a ctyrícet roku kunovické výroby letadel* (Twenty-five years of the national Company LET Uherské Hradište and forty years of aircraft production in Kunovice). Brno, 1976.

Kural, V., J. Moravec, F. Janácek, J. Navrátil, and A. Bencík. *Ceskoslovensko roku 1968. Díl. I. Obrodný proces* (Czechoslovakia in 1968. Volume I. Reforming process). Praha, 1993.

Kulka, E. *Zidé v Ceskoslovenské Svobodove Armáde* (Jews in the Czechoslovak Army of Svoboda). Praha, 1990.

Kulka, E. *Zidé v ceskoslovenském vojsku na Západe* (Jews in the Czechoslovak Army in the West). Praha, 1992.

Kural, V., J. Anger, and K. Müller. *Rok 1938. Mohli jsme se bránit?* (1938. Was our defence possible?). Praha, 1992.

Kyjev–Dukla–Praha. Sborník studií a vzpomínek (Kyjev–Kukla–Prague: Miscellany studies and memoirs). Praha, 1976.

Levora, V., and Z. Dvoráková. *Ze stalinských Gulagu do ceskoslovenského vojska* (From Stalin's Gulags into the Czechoslovak Army). Praha, 1993.

Loucký, F. *Mnozí nedoleteli* (Many did not complete the flight). Praha, 1989.

Lukešová, J. *Pravda o kvetnovém povstání v Praze* (The truth about the May Uprising in Prague). Praha, 1987.

Majer, P. *Vojenská akademie Hranice na Morave 1920–1990* (Military Academy in Hranice na Morave 1920–1990). Praha, 1991.

Minarík, P. Vznik a organizacní výstavba vojska PVO pozemního vojska v 60. letech (Origins and organizational development of the ground forces AA units in the 1960s). Praha, 1991.

Mlynárik, J. *Cesta ke hvezdám a svobode: M.R. Stefánik* (The journey to the stars and freedom). Praha, 1991.

Moravec, F. *Spión. jemiz neverili* (Master of spies). Praha, 1990.
Moudrý, P. *Bodáky v Ceskoslovensku* (Bayonets in Czechoslovakia). Praha, 1992.
Na všech frontách. Cechoslováci ve II. svetové válce (On all the fronts. Czechoslovaks in World War II). Praha, 1992.
Nemec, M. *Návraty ke svobode* (Returns to freedom). Praha, 1994.
Nemecek, V. *Ceskoslovenská letadla. Dil I. 1918–1945. Díl. II. 1945–1984* (Czechoslovak aircraft. Part I. 1918–1945. Part II. 1945–1984). Praha, 1983–1984.
Nesvadba, F. *Nez zahrmela dela* (Before the guns thundered). Praha, 1986.
Obraz vojenského prostredí v kinomatografii meziválecného Ceskoslovenska. Sborník (The image of the military in the movie industry of inter-war Czechoslovakia. Miscellaneous articles). Praha, 1992.
Pajer, M. *Krídla mírí na Memecko. 311. ceskoslovenská bombardovací perut v odbobí svého pusobení u Velitelství bombardovacího letectva RAF* (The wings head for Germany. 311th Czechoslovak Bomber Squadron during the period of service under RAF Bomber Command). Cheb, 1994.
Pajer, M. *Ve stínu slávy. Bojobý výcvik ceskoslovenských letcu, príslušníku bombardovacích a dopravních jednotek RAF ve Velké Británii v letech 1940 az 1945* (In the shadow of glory. Combat training of Czechoslovak airmen serving in RAF bomber and transport units in Great Britain 1940–1945). Cheb, 1992.
Pasák, T. *Generál Alois Eliáš odboj* (General Alois Eliás and the Resistance). Praha, 1990.
Pasák, T. *Kvetnové povstání ceského lidu v roce 1945* (The May Uprising of the Czech People 1945). Praha, 1980.
Pauliak, E. *Od povstania k oslobodeniu* (From uprising to liberation). Bratislava, 1985.
Pichlík, K. a kol. *Ceskoslovensko a jeho armáda, 1918–1989* (Czechoslovakia and its Army, 1918–1989). Praha, 1991.
Piskovský, P., M. Orság. *Zbrojovka Vsetín. padesát let závodu 1937–1987* (Zbrojovka Vsetín. Fifty years of the munitions factory 1937–1987). Vsetín, 1986.
Pivoluska, J. *Parabrigáda* (Parachute brigade). Praha, 1970.
Placák, B. *Partyzáni bez legend* (Partisans without legends). Praha, 1992.
Pokorná, A., P. Hofman, and E. Stehlík. *Ceskoslovenská armáda* (Czechoslovak Army). Praha, 1991.
Prehled dejin vojenské politiky KSC (A short history of military policy of the Communist Party of Czechoslovakia). Praha, 1988.
Prikryl, V. *Za Vlády tmy* (When darkness ruled). Praha, 1993.
Protifašistický národnoosvobozenecký boj na Slovensku v rokoch 1938–1945 (Antifascist national liberation struggle in Slovakia in 1938–1945). Bratislava, 1980.
Pucik, M. *Politické procesy v Ceskoslovensku v rokoch 1948–1954* (Political trials in Czechoslovakia 1948–1954). Bratislava, 1992.
Pulec, V. *Ceskoslovenská státní vyznamenání, státní castná uznání a ceny* (Czechoslovak state decorations, state citations and awards). Praha, 1980.

Rábon, M. a kol. *Ceskoslovenská zed. Tvrz Bouda. Ceskoslovenské opevnení z let 1935–1938* (Czechoslovak walls. Fortress Bouda. Czechoslovak fortifications from 1935 to 1938). Brno, 1993.

Radosta, P. *Protikomunistický odboj* (Anticommunist resistance). Praha, 1993.

Rajlich, J., and J. Sehnal. *Kocicí oci* (Cat's eyes). Praha, 1993.

Rajlich, J., and J. Sehnal. *Stíhaci nad Kanálem. Ceskoslovenský stíhací wing RAF 1942–1945* (Fighters over the Channel. The Czechoslovak Fighter Wing in the RAF 1942–1945). Praha, 1993.

Rajlich, J., and J. Sehnal. *Vzduch je naše more. Ceskoslovenské letectvo 1918–1939* (Air is our sea. Czechoslovak Air Force 1918–1939). Praha, 1993.

Rašla, A. *Neporazená armáda* (Undefeated army). Bratislava, 1969.

Richter, K. *Ceskoslovenský odboj na Východe* (Czechoslovak resistance in the East). Praha, 1992.

Richter, K. *Cesta K Sokolovu* (The road to Sokolovo). Praha, 1981.

Robejšek, P. *Obrana bez armády . . .* (Defense without an Army . . .). Praha, 1992.

Sacher, V. *Pod rozstríleným praporem* (Under a banner shot to pieces). Praha, 1991.

Sáda, M. *Ceskoslovenské rucní palné zbrane a kulomety* (Czechoslovak handguns and machine guns). Praha, 1971.

Sander, R. *Organizacní a dislokacní vývaj ceskoslovenské armády v letech 1918–1939* (Development of the organization and the dislocation of Czechoslovak Army 1918–1939). Praha, 1985.

Šára, F. *Tisk ve zbrani: Periodika cs. zahranicního odboje 1939–1945* (The press at arms: Periodics of Czechoslovak foreign resistance 1939–1945). Praha, 1988.

Sborník k 70. výocí zalození Vojenské akademie v Hranicích (Miscellaneous articles on the 70th anniversary of the Military Academy in Hranice). Hranice, 1990.

Sedm prazských dnu. 21.–27.srpen 1968 Dokumentace (Seven Prague days, 21st–27th August 1968. Documents). Praha, 1990.

Šín, Zb. *Historiografie obranné funkce cs.státu v právním rádu v letech 1918–1938* (Historiography of the defense function of the Czechoslovak state in the juridical order 1918–1938). Praha, 1973.

Sitenský, L, and Z. Hurt. *Stíhaci* (Fighters). Cheb, 1993.

Sitenský, L. *Z válecného deníku: Fotografie* (From a war diary: Photographs). Praha, 1991.

Sladek, O. *Pricházeli z nebe* (They came from the sky). Praha, 1993.

Slanina, J., and Z. Vališ. *Generál Karel Kutlvašr* (General Karel Kutlvašr). Praha, 1993.

Slovenské národní povstání a ceské zeme (The Slovak National Uprising and the Czech lands). Praha, 1974.

Slovenské národní povstání a náš odboj (The Slovak National Uprising and our resistance). Praha, 1975.

Slovenské národné povstanie. Nemci a Slovensko. Dokumenty ed. V. Precan (The Slovak National Uprising. Germans and Slovakia. Documents). Bratislava, 1971.

Šmoldas, Z. *Ceskoslovenští letci v boji proti fašismu* (Czechoslovakian airmen in the struggle against Fascism). Praha, 1987.
Sommr, J. *Od Tobrúku do Plzne* (From Tobruk to Plzen). Praha, 1992.
Svoboda, G. *Ti. kterí se nevrátili* (Those who did not return). Praha, 1992.
Svoboda, L. *Cestami zivota. I–II* (On the roads of life). Praha, 1971, 1992.
Svoboda, O. a kol. *Strucný slovník vojenství* (A concise dictionary of the military). Praha, 1984.
Svoboda, Zb. *Ceskoslovenská státní a vojenská symbolika* (Czechoslovak state and military symbolics). Praha, 1991.
Šolc, J. *Nikdo nás nezastaví Operace Anthropoid.* (No one can stop us). Praha, 1992.
Šolc, J. *Bylo málo muzu. Ceskoslovenští parašutisté na západní fronte za druhé svetové války* (There were few men. Czechoslovak paratroopers on the Western front during World War II). Praha, 1990.
Šolc, J. *Ve sluzbách prezidenta* (In the service of the President). *gen. Fr. Moravec.* Praha, 1994.
Šorel, V. a kol. *Češi a Slováce v oblacích* (Czechs and Slovaks in the skies). Plzen, 1993.
Špicák, M. *V armáde po Unoru* (In the army after February). Praha, 1968.
Štefanský, V. *Armáda v Slovenskom národnom povstaní* (The army in the Slovak National Uprising). Bratislava, 1983.
Titl, Z. *Organizace Ministerstva národní obrany a personálie v letech 1918–1939. Sv. I–II* (The organization and personal data of the Ministry of National Defense 1918–1939. Parts I–II). Praha, 1992.
Tomášek, D. *Konfidenti* (Confidential). Praha, 1991.
Trojan, E. *Betonová hranice* (Concrete frontier). Ústí n-Labem, 1994.
Váhala, R. *Smrt Generála* (The death of a general). *H.Píka* Praha, 1992.
Vališ Z, and J. Dvorák. *Generál Jaroslav Vedral-Sázavský* (General Jaroslav Vedral-Sázavský). Praha, 1994.
Vároš, M. *Poslední let generála Štefánika* (The last flight of General Štefánik). Bratislava, 1991.
Vávra, V. *KSC a armáda 1921–1938* (Communist Party of Czechoslovakia and the army 1921–1938). Praha, 1983.
Vávrovský, E. *Frýdek-Místek 14.brezna 1939 a za nacistické okupace* (Frýdek-Místek on 14 March 1939 and during Nazi occupation). Frýdek-Místek, 1984.
V boji za svobodu Ceskoslovenska. Kol. aut (In the struggle for the freedom of Czechoslovakia. Team authors). Praha, 1990.
Vojáci a "Prazské jaro" 1968 (Soldiers and the Prague Spring 1968). Praha, 1990.
Vojenská a další opatrení Ceskoslovenska v dobe povstání v Madarsku na podzim 1956. Sborník dokumentü (Military and other measures of Czechoslovakia during the Uprising in Hungary in Autumn 1956. Documents). Praha, 1993.
Vojenské dejiny Ceskoslovenska. Díl III. 1918–1939. Kol. aut (Military history of Czechoslovakia. Part III. 1918–1939). Praha, 1987.
Vojenské dejiny Ceskoslovenska. Díl IV. 1939–1945. Kol. aut (Military history of Czechoslovakia. Part IV. 1939–1945). Praha, 1988.

Vojenské dejiny Ceskoslovenska. Díl V. 1945–1955. Kol. aut (Military history of Czechoslovakia. Part V. 1945–1955). Praha, 1989.

Vojenské osoby, odsouzené státním soudem Praha, Brno, Bratislava v letech 1948–1952 (Military persons sentenced by the State Court in Prague, Brno, Bratislava 1948–1952). Praha, 1992.

Prísahali jsme republice. Pametní sborník k 50. výocí vzniku první ceskoslovenské vojenské jednotky v SSSR (We gave an oath to the Republic. Commemorative volume on the 50th anniversary of the first Czechoslovak military unit in the Soviet Union). Praha, 1992.

Zabudnutí velitelia (Forgotten Commanders). Bratislava, 1990.

Základní fakta o Ceskoslovenské armáde (Basic facts about Czechoslovak Army). Praha, 1991, 1992.

Zbrojní výroba. Konverze. Obranyschopnost (Armament production. Conversion. Striking power). Praha, 1993.

Zdrráhala, R. *Válcil jsem v poušti* (I fought in the desert). Praha, 1990.

Zdímal, M. *Memorandum: 1968–1990* Bratislava, 1992.

Zeny bojující v zahranicních jednotkách za druhé svetové války (Women fighting in units abroad during World War II). Praha, 1992.

4

Denmark

The Royal Danish Air Force Historical Collection

Bjorn Berg, Archivist

The first step taken to secure that important historical material was not lost was taken by chief of staff Royal Danish Air Force (RDAF), Major General Poul Zígler, 28 December 1966, when he issued a letter to all subordinate units requesting them to collect historical material connected to Danish military aviation and to send it to the headquarters. After a slow start, material and effects began to arrive and a few years later an office was established at the headquarters in Bedbaek. This office, together with collected historical materials, was moved on 1 December 1990 to Tactical Air Command, Karup (TACDEN).

The field of activity of the office now comprises

- Collection and registration of material relating to Danish military aviation history.
- Correspondence in relation to inquiries from authorities and from institutions and single persons re matters in connection with past military aviation history.
- Permanent or temporary loan of historical effects to museums and exhibitions.

At present the personnel of the RDAF Historical Collection comprises the officer in charge—a retired air force major—and one assistant (civilian) for the general work of the office.

DANISH OFFICIAL HISTORIES

These works contain bibliographies, references to records, illustrations, and so on.

Boeck, Johnstad-Moeller, and Hjalf Boeck. *Danmarks Haer* (Denmark's army). I–II. Copenhagen, 1934–1935.

General Staff. *Bidrag til Den store nordiske Krigs Historie* (Contribution to the history of the Great Nordic War). I–X. Copenhagen, 1929–1934.

General Staff. *Den dansk-tydske Krig i 1864* (The Danish–German War in 1864). I–III. Copenhagen, 1890–1892.

General Staff. *Frederik VI's Haer* (Frederik VI's army). Copenhagen, 1948.

The Museum of Arms and Uniform's book. *Treaarskrigen 1848–50* (The Three Year War 1848–50). I–II. Copenhagen, 1948.

Norup, P. *Haeren der ikke maatte kaempe* (The army that was not allowed to fight). Copenhagen, 1945.

Rockstroh, K. C. *Udviklingen af den nationale Haer* (The development of the National Army). I–III. Copenhagen, 1909–1926.

Stevens, Arne. *Vor Haer I Krig og Fred* (Our army in war and peace). I–II. Fredericia, 1943.

Vaupell, Ottol. *Den dansk-norske Haers Historie (The history of the Danish–Norwegian Army).* I–II. Copenhagen, 1872–1876.

5

Finland

Institute of Military Science, 1918–1989: A Brief History

Jarl Kronlund, War College
The Institute of Military Science
Office of Military History, Helsinki 1990

Toward the end of the Great War, from January to 4 May 1918, there was a Finnish civil war over what type of independent state the new nation would become. Immediately upon achieving independence from Communist Russia in December 1917, the defenseless country formed a historical section. The Liberation War History Committee, on the orders of its commander-in-chief, General C.G.E. Mannerheim, started at once, on 28 May 1918, to write up the recent war for independence.

THE BIRTH OF THE MILITARY ARCHIVES

On 25 May and 20 June, orders were issued to all units to send in materials so that they would be available to the Liberation War History Committee. Those who were being demobilized were asked to send their files to the new military archives established in the central military administration. As there was at that moment neither a military museum nor a library, the archives accepted donations of uniforms, maps, and books. The first set of regulations for the archives were in place on 31 July. The director of the central administration, an MA, took charge. The new archives were not, however, required to be the depository for the whole Defence Force.

The archives were divided into the history and administration departments, with an undefined division of labor. In early 1920 the mandate of the archives were broadened to have responsibility for the records of both peacetime and wartime formations of the Finnish Defence Forces. At the same time the archives became a single integrated unit. In May 1922 the Director, Guy Topelius, unsuccessfully proposed a Defence Force filing system. However, his efforts were not in vain, for after inquiries to the units as to what was desired, a forces-wide scheme was implemented. Temporary regulations for handling confidential and personal records were not in place until 1926, owing to clashes of personalities, the so-called Jaeger Rebellion, and confusion about work orders among the higher staff.

RESEARCH BECOMES SOLID

Office of Military History

The Liberation War History Committee was not very successful in producing a real history due to lack of continuity and absence of knowledge of the writing of military history. This led to a 1923 memorandum to the Minister of Defence in which it was suggested an office on military history should be established within the general staff (see Figure 5.1). Dr. Einar W. Juvelius had then stirred the waters with published articles, persuaded the chief of staff that it was not only an excellent idea but, equally important, that it was feasible and in the best interests of the armed forces. Thus, it came into being on 1 February 1925. Juvelius headed it on and off, as most of the officers appointed as director were too involved to take up their duties. And as the purpose of the military history unit was to work for the general staff, the Military Archives were transferred to its control on 17 April 1925, decreed in the 1970s to be the official birthday of the historical section.

According to the regulations, the duties of the Office of Military History were as follows:

1. To collect material concerning the Finnish wars and the defence forces and their history.
2. To publish those parts of this material that would benefit research.
3. To illustrate the Finnish war and defence forces' history through independent scientific studies.
4. To follow Finnish studies on war and defense forces' history.
5. To follow military history research in the rest of Europe, especially in the neighboring countries.
6. To carry out research on recent wars and the development of military forces in different countries, paying attention to the lessons which could be used by our own military establishment.
7. To maintain the Military Archives.

Figure 5.1
General Outline of Military–Historical Research in Spring 1925

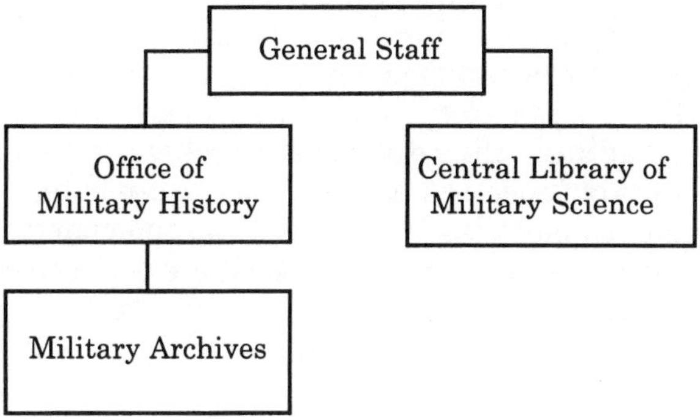

The Defence Forces had thus obtained unity in these efforts, including a separate Central Library of Military Science, and were all under one roof at Liisankatu 1, Helsinki. Furthermore, the General Staff College occupied the same building.

The Central Library of Military Science

At the same time, in March 1925, the acting chief of the general staff ordered that the various reference collections in unit libraries, which were of variable quality, should be shipped to the Central Library of Military Science. There the collections were weeded for works which would likely prove of use to the staff, service branch inspectors, and the corresponding military authorities. The library was used by students and faculty at the General Staff College, by officers of the Helsinki garrison, and as the lending service for those out in the garrisons. The library was not firmly reorganized and established until it moved to the former Uusimaa Barracks at Liisankatu 1 in 1927.

INSTITUTES OF MILITARY SCIENCE, 1927–1939

Military Archives

During the years up to 1926, the archives were organized and its duties clarified. In that year it was transferred from the general staff to the Ministry of Defence. Under temporary regulations promulgated on 1 January 1927, basic concepts were laid down which required that confidential be separated from unclassified documents and that units had the duty to send to the archives what was considered to be of historical value. The same regulation left the older Military Archives intact as the repository for items that had no other value than for historical purposes. From August 1927 the Military Archives began to grow as documents other than those relating to the War of Independence began to arrive (a move confirmed in 1934).

The Council of State thus divided the archives into an office and the departments of peacetime and wartime documents. In the meantime, the archives had also been serving as the central depository of the Ministry of Defence and its administrative branches, including the Civil Guard.

The director, Dr. Antti Kujala, significantly held the post from 1935 through the late 1960s.

The Founding of the Military Museum

The original collections in a military museum were those at the Hamina Military Academy started in 1861 and later transferred to Russia, of which Finland was a province in 1903. The Hämeenlinna Rifle Battalion's museum started in 1889, but was disbanded in 1903–1905. Most of the artifacts in these collections eventually wound up in the Vilpuri Museum and in the National Historical Museum of the Finnish state. However, the maps and photographs collected by the Liberation War History Committee were retained in the archives. At the same time, after the Great War artifacts were transferred to the Vilipuri Castle Museum and to that at Suomenlinna, from which they disappeared in the 1920s.

Not until Kaarle Soikkeli, MA, became archivist in 1926 did the Military Museum become active. His collecting encompassed not only what was on hand, but also the official transfer of war banners, guns, ammunition, and war medals. In the meantime, the Union of Finnish Officers had decided that there should be a proper military museum, but they did not have the political or fiscal wherewithal to bring it into being. Not until 1929 was the museum located in the basement at Liisankatu 1, where it opened on 18 October 1930.

The Military Museum only stayed a short time under the archivist, because in 1933 it had to be moved to Suomenlinna to provide more space for the incoming documents. Now governed by a three-member board, it remained under the Ministry of Defence. In the years before the Winter War of 1939–1940, the museum was divided into departments dealing with the Jaegers, the civil war, engineering, weapons, and naval affairs. Further departments were added to 1938 so that each branch of the services was represented.

The Central Library of the Defense Forces

When the Central Library of Military Science was moved to Liisankatu 1 in 1927, the collections of the General Staff, of the C-in-C, of the Helsinki Garrison officers, and the books from the Military Archives and the Railway Battalion were brought together, as well as an extensive collection of Russian literature left behind in 1917. However, the staff libraries of Naval Defence, the air force, and those of technical units were not affected. In 1939 the holdings stood at 40,000, of which about half were new works. Circulation had increased rapidly in the Central Library, with about 6,500 patrons annually using the facility.

In 1938 the new chief of the army staff decreed a reorganization in which the library was placed under the training department, but the librarian remained the same. A rival establishment was set up at Viipuri, together with twenty-two garrison reading rooms that got their volumes from the Central Library in Helsinki. Reference libraries were maintained in all staff establishments with sets of regulations and other important works. There were also thirty-six libraries for conscripts, of which four were for Swedish-language training.

The Office of Military History

Before the Winter War against the USSR the duties of the Office of Military History comprised a remarkable variety of tasks: the library, archives, museums, and Finnish military history.

The Office of Military History published seven volumes during its first fourteen years as a result of these studies. The first of these, *Suomen sotahistorian pääpiirteet* (The main features of Finnish war history), Volume 1, by Juvelius, dealing with the period up to 1617, and *Kuninkaallinen Savon jääkäririykmentti vuosina 1770–1910* (The Royal Savo Jaeger regiment in 1770–1910), by Aarne Huuskonen, were published in 1927. After the publication of a regimental history promulgation came to a ten-year halt. The next volume, by Werner Söderström Oy, was not published until 1938: The previous ones had appeared from Otava.

The 1920s volumes and the eight-part *Suomen vapaussota vuonna 1918* (The Finnish War of Independence in 1918), published by the Liberation War Committee, and the so-called participant's volume *Suomen vapaussota* (The Finnish Liberation War), competing with the aforementioned, marked the direction and the image for decades to come. The tradition was enhanced by *Hakkapeliittain Historia* (History of Finnish Cavalry in the Thirty Years' War in the 1600s), Volume 1, by Dr. Arvi Korhonen, successor to Dr. Juvelius, was published in 1938. At the end of the 1930s three other volumes were published: *Suomen itärajan syntyhistoria* (The origins of Finland's Eastern border) and *Suomen Jääkärien elämäkerrasto* (Biography of Finnish Jaegers) by Korhonen and Heimosodat 1918–1922, and *Taistelu Petsamosta* (Tribal wars in 1918–1922—The fight for Petsamo), by Eero Kuussari, the first part of a series, of which the others were not published.

In 1929 an experimental newspaper department was founded at the Office of Military History. Its duties were to follow the Finnish press and keep up a scrapbook collection. In addition, the department was to make the necessary corrections for newspaper articles and news items. It also provided both newspapers and magazines with articles describing the operations and duties of the army. As such, this was hardly military history work and in 1934 the department was transferred to general staff headquarters, where it eventually developed into the current information department.

INSTITUTES OF MILITARY SCIENCE, 1939–1945

The Winter War against the USSR, 1939–1940

In the immediate prewar maneuvers, three reserve officers joined the office staff, and all five members were transferred to the headquarters at Mikkeli upon the outbreak of hostilities. Colonel H. Nurmio, long associated with the office, kept the war headquarters diary while also attempting to keep track of the command and its plans for future historical work. How well-selected these materials were had yet to be evaluated in 1990.

During the Winter War the Military Museum at Suomenlinna was closed, the collections disbursed to safekeeping, and the facilities used for billeting soldiers. However its collections grew appreciably, as from March 1940 unit officers were ordered to confiscate items of historical interest, all of this under the direction of the archivist. Some of the 11,000 items were exhibited in Helsinki from January to June 1940 to boost the morale of the defenders, at the same time perpetuating the myth that the Finns were victorious.

The library at Viipuri was closed and once again the central establishment in Helsinki became the prime collection. The archives continued to exist in the basement of the General Staff College, but the staff was disbursed to other duties and the new documentation in the process of being created did not arrive until after the war ended. Then the archives became overfilled, but no decision on new space was made until the Continuation War began.

The Continuation War, 1941–1944, and the Lapland War, 1944–1945, against the USSR

Inspired by the German attack on Russia, the spirit of revenge, and the desire to recover lands lost in 1940, the Finns went on the offensive in mid-1941. As far as the Office of Military History, the archives, and the independent libraries were concerned, the arrangements for the Winter War were continued. The Military Archives had again been placed under the Office of Military History in the spring of 1941, following the precedent set in February for the museums.

During mobilization, the office staff was expanded to eight, five of whom were engaged in research. One result was that in 1942 Korhonen published the second part of *Hakkapeliitta,* (The history of the Finnish cavalry). The office was only evacuated from Helsinki to the countryside after the major bombing attacks began in early 1944, with the archives dispersed to Koskenkorva and Kokkola and the Central Library to Karkkila. The museum's holdings were evacuated in 1943–1944 to sixteen locations outside Helsinki. Other materials not yet accessioned were stored at depots, because the museum's storage facilities were cold and damp. In the meantime, thanks to an early Continuation War order, military officers were tasked with collecting for the museum, and this doubled the number of artifacts by 1945. The museum also put on exhibitions of the Soviets, as seen from the captured booty.

On 19 September 1944 the Finns and the Russians signed a truce, the terms of which required the Finnish army to be demobilized while the Lapland War continued against the Germans, the erstwhile allies. On 28 November 1944 the Institute of Military Science was ordered to revert to peacetime status.

THE INSTITUTE OF MILITARY HISTORY RESEARCH, 1945–1969

From the War to the 1950s

For just a couple of months after the war the Central Library and the Military Museums were placed again under the training organization. However, on 17 March 1945 they were returned to the Office of Military History, which had retained the Military Archives in any case (see Figure 5.2). Then the Military Museum suffered from the National Museum successfully claiming the bastion at Suomenlinna, leaving only a few square meters for the Naval Museum. In the meantime, all departments had been looking for

Figure 5.2
Organization as of March 1945

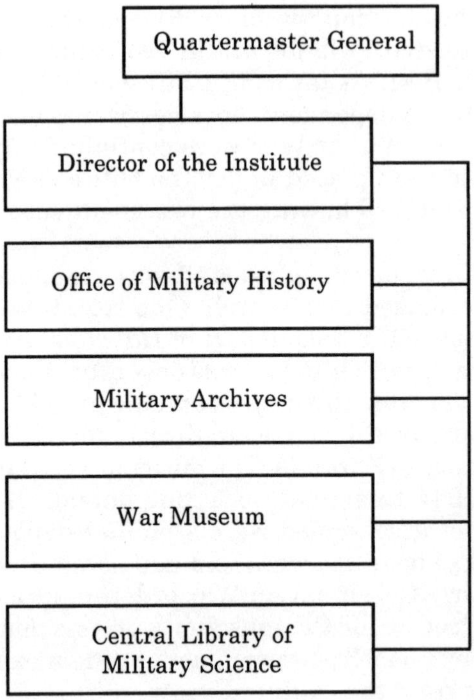

new and larger spaces. The museum people were helping to reopen or create the service branch depositories with the aid of officers' associations. The Military Archives found its present facilities at Siltavuorenranta 16. These facilities were adequate until the 1980s, when part of the collections had to be transferred to Hämeenlinna. Meanwhile, the Office of Military History was moved across the courtyard from the General Staff College to its present location at Maurinkatu 1. The administration of the Military Museum joined it there in 1949.

Changes in the 1950s

When the Defence Forces were reorganized in the early 1950s, the Institute of Military Sciences was expanded to include the Office of Military History, the Military Archives, the Military Museum, and once again the Central Library of Military Science. By the statute of 30 November 1952, the institute was placed in charge of the quartermaster-general. When a new director took over in December 1957, the duties of the chief of military history and director of the institute were split. He was succeeded by Colonel V. O. Terversmaki in 1969.

Under the statute of 1952 the duties of the institute were defined as the collection, organization, and storage of Defence Force documentation, literary, and artifactual material; the promotion of research and teaching of military history; to help other branches through the central and reference libraries; to preserve the traditions of the armed forces; to provide information and documentation as needed; and to publish.

Military History Research

From the end of the war against the Soviet Union, the story of that conflict had top priority. In December 1944 the new director started work on *Suomen sota 1941–1945* (Finland's war). The whole was coordinated by a committee appointed by the commander-in-chief and chaired by Major General A. J. Swenson and four others with a lieutenant as secretary. The series itself fully occupied the staff for many years in sorting and digesting all the materials available. Obviously the process of selection of documentation may have colored the narrative, but the four years spent editing it may have affected it even more. Thus, it was not until 1952 that the first volume appeared, and it was the second volume dealing with the July attack by the Karelian army.

In the meantime, there was a demand from both military and civilian readers for immediate accounts so that especially the political side of the war could be discussed while memories were fresh. This led then to the publication, in 1961, of Arvi Korhonen's *Barbarossa suunitelma* (The Barbarossa Plan and Finland). His volume led to considerable controversy, which in 1961 was named the driftwood theory, in that although it has been sunk several times, it keeps floating around. The theory itself related to the reasons for Finland's involvement in the Continuation War. The argument was also fed by the first volume of the official history, which finally saw the light of day in 1961.

The original ten-volume history of the 1941–1945 War series was expanded to eleven volumes when it was found that maintenance and supply had hardly been touched upon, and this concluding volume appeared in 1975 for the fiftieth anniversary of the founding of the Institute of Military Science together with a short history of the institute itself.

In the meantime, from 1948 to 1955 the Military Museum had published a six-part series, with summaries in English, on armaments, uniforms, equipment, fortifications, and other suitable topics. At the same time, a rejuvenated museum put on a series of historical exhibitions, with annual visitors numbering 3,000 except for that on the Winter War, which drew 8,000. The museum's artifact collection had grown to 40,000 items, with heavy equipment stored in various locations throughout the country, but in 1961 the continued lack of storage space caused the scrapping of quite a lot of material. That this could have been fatal was due to the late developments in the year of a reliable inventorying system. Concurrently, the museum was run by a board until 1953, when it was disbanded. In 1956 the Institute of Military History took charge.

Changing Trends in the 1960s and the Field of Military Research

Periodically in the 1920s and 1940s defence revision committees had been formed, but they lacked continuity. Thus it was not until the 1960s that long-term planning (PTS) became an essential part of the Defence Forces' activities (see Figure 5.3). In May 1967 a special committee was appointed to examine how the Institute of Military Sciences could be the base for new arrangements. Colonel Raunio's committee reported in spring 1968 and recommended that the guidelines for military historical research should focus primarily on meeting the war and fighting needs of the armed forces. Military Sciences were seen as real sciences which provide the groundwork for strategy, operational skills, tactics, organization, and equipment, as well as their development. The aim was to obtain a basic knowledge of the fields of strategy, operational art, and tactics from the study of military history and geography, economics, technology, psychology, and medicine as they related to war. The Raunio Report thus set the basis for the work of the institute in the 1970s. In 1969 a separate strategic research group was formed, and its task was to create a strategic assessment that would serve long-term planning.

Institute of Military Science, 1970–1980

In 1971 there was a generational review of the Defence Forces, under which the institute was reorganized again, and the Office of Strategic Studies given a permanent status, and the Institute of

Figure 5.3
Fields of Military Research

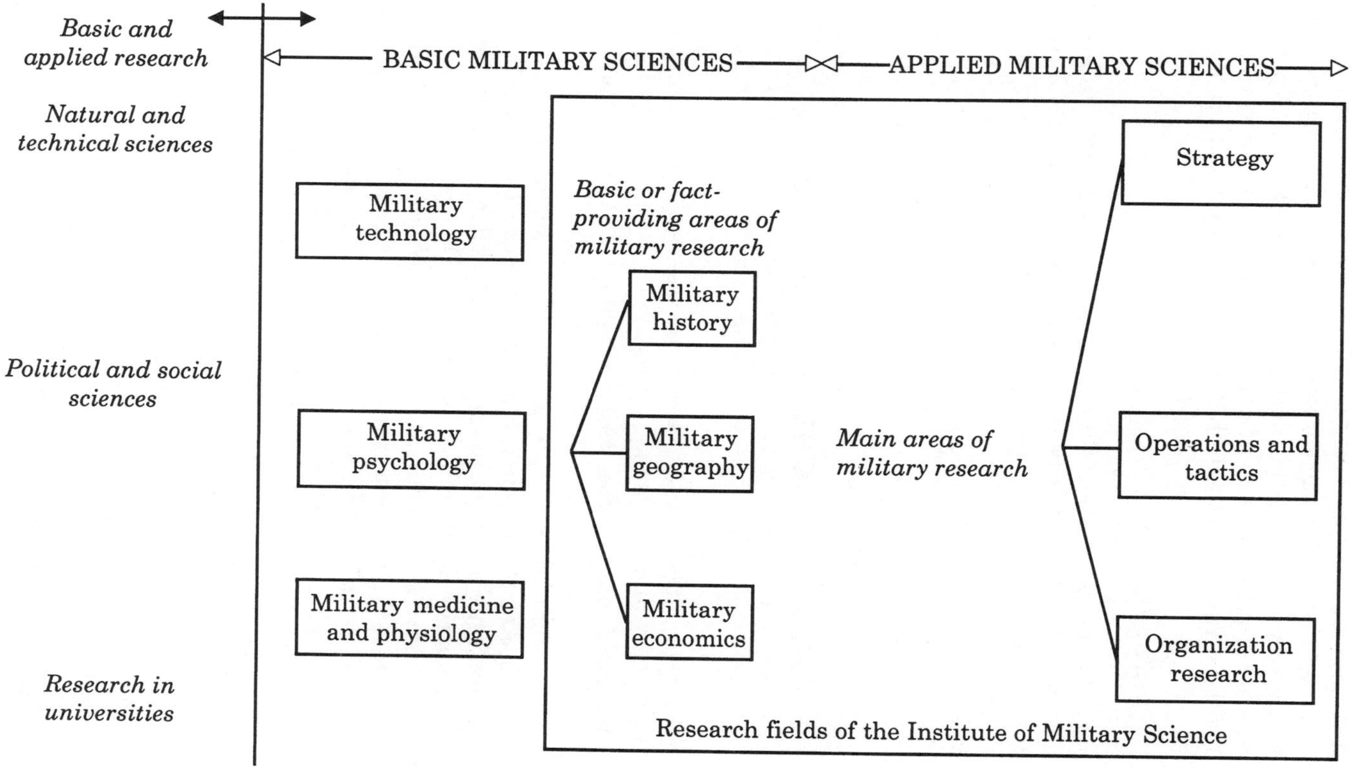

Military Research became the Institute of Military Science with a staff now numbering sixty people. The Office of Strategic Studies and the Office of Military History were almost exclusively research establishments. An administrative office took care of personnel, finances, maintenance, and communications. Its purpose was to allow the other divisions to be freed from day-to-day tasks.

Office of Military History

In the period 1958–1980 the office had had eight different directors and the staff shrank from eleven to three by 1965, which rendered the office impotent, so outsiders had to be hired to write military history. But the duties of the Office of Military History were gradually redefined and by 1975 they were as follows:

- To carry out military history research and publish research results according to the guidelines provided by the administration of the Defence Forces.
- To produce reviews, reports, statements, and statistics on issues concerning our country's military history and the development of the Defence Forces on the request by the general staff or by civil government offices.
- To follow, supervise, and assist the research and teaching of military history within the Defence Forces.
- To implement the tasks assigned to it by the General Staff.

Once the *Finland Wars in 1941–1945* series was published, the main resources were directed to writing the *Talvisota* (Winter War) volume. This involved research work, writing, and editing the material for the final published version. Document material had already been collected during the Winter War for future history books.

The most important manuscripts for the Winter War book were finished in 1975 and the series was published by WSOY (the government printing office) during 1975–1979. Apart from the Continuation War and Winter War history books, the office's own publishing activities were limited to one volume, *Suomen puolustusvoimat* (Finland's Defence Forces), which by the 1980s had had eight printings under various titles.

Six other books were published in the Institute of Military Science series. The most noteworthy were the two-part history of the Ministry of Defence, part 1 of the history of Finnish cavalry, and the biographies of the Finnish Jaegers.

The activities and staff of the Office of Strategic Studies were rather settled by 1975, but shorthanded. Therefore, part of the work had to be commissioned to outsiders, military and civilian experts for individual studies, as members of projects and as writers and collaborators for institute publications.

The duties of the Office of Strategic Studies had undergone a change during the first three years of operation. The main task, estimating the development of long-term military policy and strategy, remained unchanged. A new task was the attempt to define "the image of modern and future wars." In addition, the office endeavored to develop its own research methods.

As the Office of Military History did in its own sector, the Office of Strategic Studies also tried to develop links with Finnish and foreign researchers and research institutes. This was partly accomplished through its own four series:

- Studies on strategy.
- Documents on strategy and security policy.
- Facts on strategy.
- Research notes on strategy.

A total of twenty-five publications had appeared by 1981. One of their purposes was to increase the knowledge of security policy and the other was to satisfy the apparent need for information.

The Office of Strategic Studies staff with that of the Office of Military History took part in the teaching at the military schools and seminars.

The status of the Military Archives was strengthened when in 1972 the Ministry of Defense was also placed under its authority in matters dealing with filing documents. Thus, the Military Archives eventually became the central archives of the Defence Forces. Organizationally it was divided into the archives department and the office; the first was archival and the latter an assisting unit. The task of the archives department was to store, maintain and catalogue the documents received from the Ministry of Defence and the Defence Forces. In addition to the official documents, private collections were transferred to the Military Archives through the years. The archives gained a new dimension through exhibitions presenting the history of the different defense branches and services as seen in archival materials.

The Military Archives collections grew fast, thanks to the wars, in particular, and the material of the time of the Second World War actually covers half of the total (i.e., eighteen kilometers of shelves). All in all, there are thirty-two shelf kilometers of material. The Independence War archives are small compared with this, although they do have 200 shelf meters. There are 550 shelf meters of archival material on the army of the time of Finnish autonomy. The rest are peacetime archives produced by the Finnish Defence Forces.

It is natural that finding a document in this mass of material sources would be nearly impossible without the indexes created to help users. The search is further facilitated by the fact that the material is chronologically divided into four sections: the years 1812–1905, 1917–1939, and 1939–1944, and the archives after 1944. (From 1905 to 1917 Finnish records were sent to St. Petersburg.)

According to the statutes in force in Finland, in 1995 confidential archives were made available to the public up to the mid-1950s. The rest of the archives are also public in principle, but there are certain exceptions to this, mainly concerning private collections. A researcher has access to archives material by placing an order and having it delivered to the reading room.

The use of the Military Archives has steadily increased: Researcher visits increased from 1,800 in 1955 to nearly 3,000 by 1973. Currently more than 4,500 researchers annually visit the Military Archives, and of these a handful comes from abroad.

The Military Museum

The aftermath of the necessity of scrapping material in 1961 was the rise of eleven new branch museums with which the Military Museum made arrangements for dry storage space as a quid pro quo for helping them with their collections and exhibitions. At the end of the 1940s, as part of the peace agreement, the Finns raised the submarine *Vesikko* (Mink), which has been restored and was added to the museum in 1973.

At about this time the museum expanded not only its collecting to 79,000 objects by the 1980s and work with the branch museums, but began to undertake serious research into the provenance of its own materials, to which were added artifacts from Finnish participation in United Nations operations. It also acquired the picture collection of the Military Archives in 1977.

The Central Library of Military Science

The Central Library was severely handicapped in the years after 1944 by its location in the War Staff College building and the impression that that is all it was. Nor did it have the status of a university body. So, in the reorganization of 1972, it was designated a special public research library with the authority to acquire widely in the field of military studies and to make classified documents available to researchers as well as continuing to supervise the other

Defense Forces' libraries. Its collections thus began to grow at the rate of 2,000 to 3,000 items a year and had surpassed the 120,000-volume level by 1980.

The Development of the Institute of Military Science in the Latter 1970s

In spite of the reorganization, changes kept being made in the institute, at one moment consolidating and at another breaking it up into smaller units. Moreover, the institute began to participate in international projects and forums, starting with the joint Charles X Gustav project supervised by the Office of Military History at the Royal Swedish Militärhogskolan. The Military Museum joined the International Federation of Military History Museums under UNESCO. In 1978 the institute helped organize a colloquium in the International Commission for Comparative Military History at Hanasaari outside Helsinki. And the tempo has ever since increased.

THE CHANGE FROM AN INDEPENDENT RESEARCH INSTITUTE TO A DEPARTMENT OF THE WAR COLLEGE

Toward New Changes

In late 1979 the Ministry of Defence established a committee to consider a second framework for defense research, and this study was completed late in 1981 to govern the decade 1982–1991. This was a confidential matter, but Terversmäki knew that the Institute of Military Science had to sharpen its approach and to make its collections more useful. In addition, a sociological department was added in 1981, but by 1991 that had shrunk to but one researcher. The intended objectives had been leadership, organizational structure, intercommunications, and interbehavioral patterns. Military sociology became a more complex field than originally intended, and that delayed results.

In the 1980s the military historians began the task of reediting the history of Finland's wars of 1941–1945 and the writing of a history of the Defence Forces in peacetime, the latter a task directed by the author from 1984. At the same time, university professors were called in to guide various projects, including a cooperative one on Finland in the Second World War. As of 1982, a paid research director came aboard, both for the Institute and for the War College. At the same time, the organization stabilized with the establishment of specially tasked research groups for the purposes mentioned and in order to separate the administrative functions. Outsiders were brought in to write both books and articles. Some specialists were used as general consultants, owing to their military experience.

The Institute as Part of the War College

On 1 September 1985 the institute was integrated into the War College, and the director of the institute thus reported to the director of the War College as its scholarly research organ. But the office of scientific research into operational skills and tactics died.

Suomen puolustusvoimat, 1918–1939, a truly scholarly work, was published on the seventieth anniversary of the Defence Forces and presented to the president of Finland on 3 June 1988. The second volume of the peacetime history of the Finnish forces was finished and the publication of the reedited Continuation War History was completed in 1994.

EPILOGUE

On 1 January 1993 the War College, Battle School, and Cadet School were put under joint command, and the National Defence College saw the daylight. It meant changes also in the structure of the Institute of Military Science, which was divided into four parts, as shown in the National Defence College organization table. So the institute today consists of the Military and Military Archives at their former sites; the offices of Strategy and Military History were established as independent research and teaching units, in principle similar to those at the universities. Finally, the Library of Military Science became the Library of the National Defence College.

Though it has gained a lot with the renewal of the organization for the education of officers, a funny thing also happened because of this new legislation. The Institute of Military Science could not be suppressed, and so on this occasion it was decided that military science should include only archival and museum functions. Maybe oracles have spoken and shown the place of the future of military science.

DEPARTMENT OF WAR HISTORY OF NATIONAL DEFENCE COLLEGE

The National Defence College was founded in 1993. It united three formerly independent institutions, the Military Academy, the Battle School, and the War College (including the Institute of Military Science). All education of commissioned officers is now given at this one organization.

The college includes six departments, as well as the Military Museum, the Military Archives, and the National Defence College Library. One of the departments is the Department of War History. When the National Defence College was founded, almost all those who worked with military history were gathered to this new organization.

The Department of War History carries on the traditions of the Office of Military History of the Institute of Military Science, which had its traditions of reserching military history and making publications since 1918. Some other parts of the Institute of Military Science—the Office (now the Department) of Strategic Studies, the Military Museum, the Central Library of Military Sciences, and the Military Archives—became part of the National Defence College in 1993. Except for these four units, which are located in the central-city area of Helsinki, the National Defence College is located on the island of Santahamina in Helsinki.

The Department of War History is responsible for and coordinates instruction in war history and research in the Finnish Defence Forces. The main fields of tuition and research are the history of the theory of the art of war, the development of the art of war in the post–Second World War operations, and Finnish military history. All those fields are included in the curriculum of the Finnish officers. The objective is to support the instruction in war history, strategic studies, tactics, and leadership at the National Defence College.

Research work of the department focuses on the era after the Second World War. In recent years, special emphasis has been placed on theories of modern warfare, the Israeli and Soviet art of war, and terrorism. This research involves operation with departments of history at universities, foreign military schools, research institutes of war history at universities, foreign military schools, research institutes of war history, and relevant organizations in the field of military history.

The study of military history is included in the education of commissioned officers at all levels. All students of the first degree and the participants in the staff officer and general staff officer courses are also to do their research theses in the field of war history. Beginning in 1999 it is also possible to take a doctoral degree in military scences or military history at the National Defence College. Some of the best theses and other studies within our main research fields are printed in our publications.

After completing the first degree division, a student has a good knowledge of the main features of Finnish war history and of the central elements in the development of the art of war. At higher levels the objective is both to give the students a deeper knowledge of the development of the art of war and to deal with the development of the theories of war from antiquity to the present.

The department has seven employees: a chief of department, a professor, a senior research officer, a research officer, two researchers, and a project leader. They all have duties in research, teaching, and guiding. Four of them have doctoral degrees, and two are completing their doctoral studies. Three of the employees are officers, the rest are civilians.

Our contact information is as follows:

National Defence College
Department of War History
P.O. Box 7
00861 Helsinki
Fax +358–9–181 46535
http://www.sotahl.mol.fi

Those interested in Finnish military history may also want to consult or visit the Military Museum, the Military Archives, and the Library of the National Defence College. The have all existed in one form or another since the first years of Finnish independence. The Military Archives have about 40 shelf kilometers of documents, the Military Museum's collection includes over 200,000 items, and the Library of National Defence College has a collection of almost 180,000 volumes. Their contact information is as follows:

Military Museum
Maurinkatu 1
00171 Helsinki
Tel.: +358 9 181 26381
Fax: +359 9 181 26390

Military Archives
Työpajankatu 6
00580 Helsinki
Tel.: +358 9 181 55415
Fax: +358 9 181 55520

National Defence College Library
Maurinkatu 1
00170 Helsinki
Tel.: +358 9 181 26351
Fax: +358 9 181 26358

LITERATURE/RESOURCES

Det strategiska och säkerhetspolitiska forskningsarbetet vid Krigsvetenskapliga Institutet, esittelyasiakirja, numerotta. (Strategic and security policy research at the Institute of Military Science, introductory document.)

Guide to the Military Archives of Finland, a publication of the Military Archives. Helsinki, 1977.

Harinen, Olli. *Sotilassosiologian tutkimus,* maaliskuu 1990. (Research in military sociology.)

Kerkkonen, Karin, Kari Miskala, and Christian Perret. *Aikakauslehdet Sotatieteen keskuskirjastossa. Seppelöity miekka,* s. 155–183. Joensuu, 1987. (Periodicals in the Library of Military Science; *The Wreathed Sword,* pp. 155–183.)

Kirjastolehti 5/56, s. 96–97. (*The Library Journal* 5/56.)

Kirjastolehti 7/61, s. 170–171. (*The Library Journal* 7/61.)

Kronlund, Jarl. "A list of volumes published by the Office of Military History from 1968 to 1989." *Sota-historian toimisto* 24.1.1990.

Kronlund, Jarl. "Suomen puolustuslaitos 1918–1939: Puolustusvoimien rauhan ajan historia," *Sotatieteen laitoksen julkaisuja* XXIV, Porvoo, 1989. ("Finland's Defence Forces 1918–1939: The peacetime history of the Defence Forces"; *Publications of the Institute of Military Science* 24.)

Lappalainen, Matti. "Ken Härjillä kyntää." *Seppelöity miekka,* s. 7–14. Joensuu, 1985. ("He who plows with an ox"; *The Wreathed Sword,* pp. 7–14.)

Maunola, Kimmo. "Sotamuseon vaiheita viiden vuosikymmenen aikana." *Seppelöity miekka,* s. 211–234. Joensuu, 1985. ("The vicissitudes of the War Museum during five decades"; *The Wreathed Sword,* pp. 211–234.)

Puolustusministeriön esikuntakäskyt vuodelta 1925. Helsinki. (The staff orders of Ministry of Defence in 1925.)

"Seppelöity miekka—Sotatieteen Laitos 1925–1985." *Sotatieteen Laitoksen julkaisuja* XXII. Joensuu, 1985. ("Publications of the Institute of Military Science," *The Wreathed Sword* 1975.)

Sota-arkiston opas. Valtion arkiston julkaisuja 5. Helsinki, 1974. (*Guide to Military Archives in Finland.* Publication of the Finnish National Archives, no. 5.)

Sotahistorialliset erikoismuseot. Joensuu 1987. (The Military Historic Special Museums.)

Sotamuseotoimikunnan mietintö—Komiteamietintö 1983: 72. Helsinki, 1983. (Report of the Committee for Military Museums; 1983: 72.)

Sotamuseon tilastoja 1983–1989, Sotamuseo. Helsinki, 1989. (Statistics of Military Museum for 1983–1989.)

Sotamuseon toimintakertomus vuodelta 1945. Sotamuseo, Helsinki, Annual. (Annual report of Military Museum from 1945.)

Sotatieteellisen keskuskirjaston tilastotietoja 1962–1980. Sotatieteellinen keskuskirjasto. Helsinki, 1980. (Statistics of the Central Library of Military Science, 1962–1980.)

Sotatieteellisen tutkimustyön järjestäminen puolustusvoimissa. Toimikuntamietintö. Helsinki 27.3.1968. Sotatieteellinen keskuskirjasto. ("Rearrangement of scientific research within Finland's Defence Forces; Committee report of 1968." *The Library of Military Science.*)

Sotatieteen Laitos—toimintakertomus 1984. Helsinki, 1985. (Annual report of 1984 of the Institute of Military Science.)

Sotatieteen Laitos 1925–1975. Sotatieteen Laitoksen julkaisuja XV. Joensuu, 1975. ("The Institute of Military Science 1925–1975"; *Publications of the Institute of Military Science* 15.)

Syrjö, Sirkka. "Puolustusvoimien arkistotoimen järjestäminen—paperisotaa 1918–1928." *Seppelöity miekka,* s. 184–210. Joensuu, 1985. ("The organizing of the Archives of the Defence Forces in 1918–1928"; *The Wreathed Sword,* pp. 184–210.)

Viitasalo, Mikko. "Puolustusvoimien tutkimustoiminta ja sen kehittäminen 1980-luvulla." *Seppelöity miekka,* s. 22–34. Joensuu 1985. ("The research within Finland's Defence Forces and its development in the 1980s"; *The Wreathed Sword,* pp. 22–34.)

The War College. Helsinki, Archives.

Discussions and Interviews

Maunola, Kimmo. Foundation of Military Museums. Discussion in Helsinki, 14 March 1990.

Elfvengren, Eero. Foundation of Office of Military History and its first years in 1920s. Discussion in Helsinki, 19 March 1990.

Viitasalo, Mikko. The establishment of a post of a research director at the Institute of Military Science. Discussion in Helsinki, 3 April 1990.

6

France

Service Historique de l'Armée de l'Air (The French Air Force Historical Service)

Général Lucien Robineau, Chef,
Translated by Robin Higham

HISTORY

In December 1934 General Dénain, minister for air, wrote

> The Air Force does not actually have an historical service. The only work done for its benefit has been by the Army Historical Service. But now it is necessary to group the documents properly . . . so that the lessons of the 1914–1918 war can be studied. The present dispersion of these records throughout the Army Historical Service is a grave obstacle to this work.

This was the starting point for the first Air Force Historical Service (SHAA). Since 1930, in practice, there had been at the *Ecole militaire* (Military School) a modest aeronautical section under the Army Historical Service which did not allow the postwar reflexion on the air force needed.

The Historical and Geographical Service of the air force was thus created by decree of 20 December 1934 and in two years was forced to lead a quadruple life: the collection of archives, the editing of a *History of French Military Aviation,* the establishing of aerial maps for not only France itself but also for world air routes, and finally the organization and control of the Air Museum.

In 1935 the Army Historical Service turned over the records of the Headquarters (GQG) Aeronautical Directorate for the period of the First World War, while at the same time the air ministry began to turn over some of its documents. But in August 1936 it was dismembered and reduced to only an archives reattached to the Third Bureau. It was essentially "put to sleep" until 1939, when, considering "the preponderant part which historical studies played for the air force," Guy La Chambre, the air minister, created the Air Force Historical Service. This consisted again of all the sections of the older Historical and Geographical Service, with the exception of geographical studies, which disappeared, and the Air Museum, which became autonomous.

Caught in the maelstrom of 1940, from then on the SHAA knew numerous tribulations. A report of July 1941 showed it located at Négran near Amboise. After the Armistice it was transferred to Toulouse-Francazal and transformed into the French Air Force Archives and Museum Service. Its activities during the war were revived under orders from General Valin in January 1945: to research fighting patterns and to edit the general history of the war of 1939–1940, while also clandestinely working on the lessons of the 1939–1940 war, regulations for the air force, and photography. With very limited means, the editor recalled that he was the sole guardian of the air force archives, yet the central administration constantly called on him for information. Moreover, it was of the highest interest that the general staff of the air force have an organization able to reassemble and exploit the archives and use this body of materials for historical and technical work.

The Historical Archives section at Toulouse was dissolved on 15 March 1945 and the French Air Force Historical Service came into being in Paris. The instructions of May 1939 re the organization of the SHAA once again were in force. The collection of the archives as a whole and of the major commands in particular for the period 1940–1945, first of Vichy and then of the war in Indochina, was undertaken.

From 1948 to 1968 the SHAA was housed in the Denfert-Rochereau barracks at Versailles. In 1968 it was relocated to Vincennes, where together with the historical services of the army and navy it now forms the grand center of French military archives. Its present missions are the collection and conservation of the archives of the air force commands (see Figure 6.1). It has organized and developed both photographic and oral history sections. Its library is the documentary center. The research function has been enlarged and the corresponding work has resulted in a large number of articles and monographs, notably elaborated upon at national and international colloquia. The SHAA is also charged with the symbolism (heraldry) of the air force, both re insignia and pennants; it is the guardian of its service's traditions; and it establishes the lineage of units and presides over the award of component parts, both chartered and unchartered, of the patrimony, notably the colors.

Figure 6.1
Organizational Chart of the SHAA

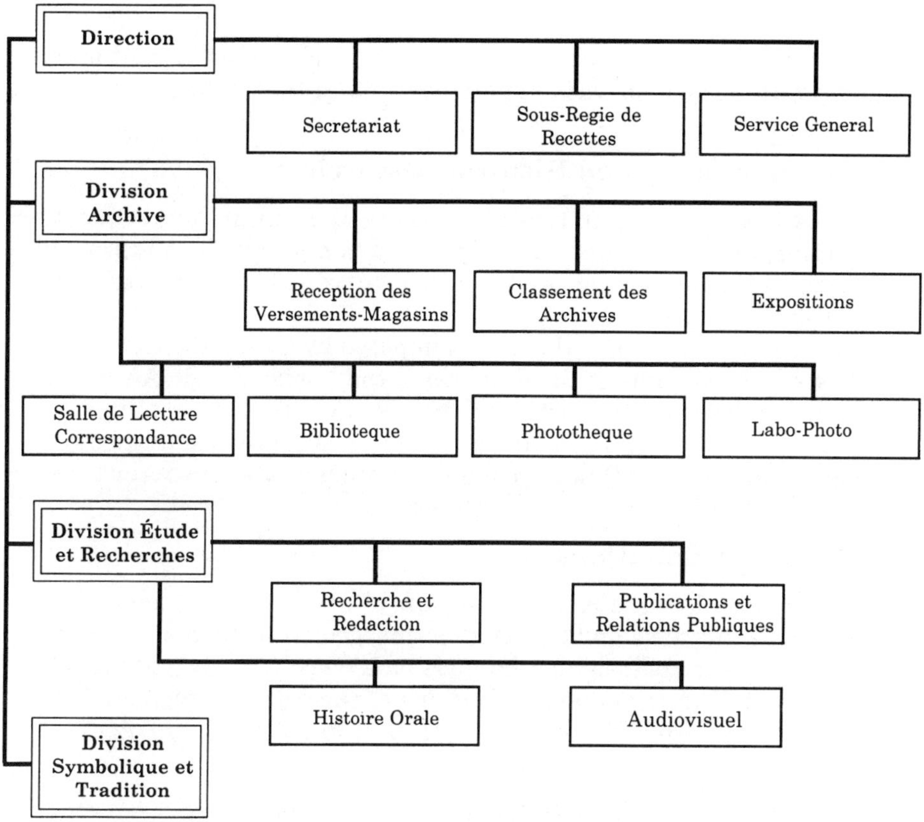

MISSIONS

Directly subordinate to the Chief of the Air Staff of the French Air Force, the SHAA is an organic unit of the air force. Its missions devolve from Ministerial Instruction No. 1502/DEF/EMAA/CAB of 27 May 1982 and can be described as follows:

The Archival Service

Exercising in the bosom of the air force the responsibilities conferred upon it by the legislature and to administer the archives, the SHAA assumes

1. The technical oversight of the Air Force Archives.

2. The conservation, the diagnosis, the classification, and the inventory of the archives as well as deaccessionings.
3. Archival communications.

On the other side, it also conserves, sorts, classifies, inventories, and publicizes the private papers donated to the SHAA.

Administrative and Historic Research

The SHAA uses the archives to respond to the numerous requests for information formulated by levels of command. In addition it examines the dossiers of veterans so as to provide evidence of their entitlements.

After the expiration of the delays imposed by law on the communication of the contents of the archives to the public, the SHAA works out their release for the history of the air force. To do this it employs the traditional means of writing and publication, without also neglecting the latest technological means, such as audiovisual works.

Keeper of Traditions

The SHAA is equally the guardian of air force traditions. The division "Traditions and Symbols" is charged with the management and conservation of insignias, banners, and flags. Already undertaken at the establishment of a unit, it is one of the organs which enables the service to show its total integration into L'Armée de L'Air.

THE ARCHIVES AND THEIR CLASSIFICATION SYSTEM

By the terms of Law No. 79-18 of 3 January 1979, which applies to all the French archival services, "The archives are to assemble the documents whatever their date, their form and their supporting material, products, or received from all bodies physical or intellectual, and by all organizations public or private, in the exercise of this activity." As a consequence, the archives of the SHAA can hold all forms of papers, photographs, slides, maps and plans, sound tapes, movies, video, and microfilm, as well as diskettes and supporting information.

The Air Force Historical Service has as its calling the collection, conservation, and control of all the records of the Air Force. It exercises this oversight through the intermediary of some "correspondents-archives" existing at nearly all levels of administration. At the same time it has a role in determining classifications, the conditions of storage and access, and, finally, in accord with legislation to make sure that nothing which is eliminated from the records is illegal.

The SHAA archives are composed of documents assembled from those of the general staff, the inspectorates, the departments, the major commands, the bases, and the air units in the course of their missions and functions: minutes, files of matters under discussion, logs of campaigns and operations (JMO), record books of orders and of aerial work (COTA), and accounts or reports of activities, including individuals' records and technical documentations related to air material. In parallel, the SHAA receives gifts and advance copies of particular items.

The oldest documents held by the SHAA are from 1909–1910. But the holdings for the period before the Second World War suffered in the debacle of 1940. The homogenous series only starts, therefore, after 1945.

The system of classification adopted for the documents is chronological or functional but some are closed: However, the war of 1914–1918, the interwar years, and wars overseas are all open; while general staff after 1945, high commands, air bases, flying units, and periodic support records of the different parts of the air force are guarded by declassification rules.

THE PHOTOGRAPHIC COLLECTIONS

Law No. 79-18 of 3 January 1979 provided that the quality of the archives must not be based solely upon documents. Plastic, photographs, negatives, and slides must have their proper place also in the activities of the SHAA.

Born in March 1976, the photo collection has as its prime mission to create the instruments for proper research in order to ease exploiting the photographic record produced by the Air Force together with the paper archives. The discovery of the richness of the documentation retained by the former members of the air force, and the evidence that this ran the peril of possible destruction, made it one of the set functions of this section, which has also devoted a large part of its time to their collection.

As to the documents produced by the air force, photographs accompany the operational record books; the files of archives of photographic laboratories of air bases are later added to the original holdings of personnel photographs; and both are deposited with or given to the SHAA.

Albums of contact prints allow the satisfaction of the varied demands of both researchers and the air force. The photographic laboratory works essentially for the benefit of the photo collection, for which it does the necessary copying to conserve documents lent to the SHAA by certain parties, preserves negatives thus created, and does the work of reproduction. At the same time, this section microfilms for security (that is to say those documents whose preservation by other means cannot be guaranteed) or for the completion of information (of documents of interest to the SHAA or given to it for reproduction).

The SHAA holds about 2,000,000 photographs, both public and private, in about 80,000 photo catalogues, and about 12,000 catalogues of maps, and a large number of posters relating to aviation.

THE LIBRARY

The role of keeper of the memory of the air force given to the SHAA extends equally to published documents (books, reviews, studies, and so on). These collections are held at the library, which has more than 11,000 volumes and 748 periodicals by title, of which 164 are current.

The library's principal concern is military aviation, both French and foreign, rather than civil (commercial or relating to space). At the same time, its holdings (*fonds*) also contain a large number of reference works on the twentieth century, allowing the history of aviation to be set into its historical, political, and economic milieu. In addition, it holds an important collection of both French and foreign works. It also gets a number of gifts and to this end keeps holdings closely related to aviation. Also a documentation service, the library makes available to lecturers and researchers biographical files, unit histories, and sound and audiovisual materials.

Open to everyone, the library is uniquely reserved as a consulting place. Sometimes the demand for works is such that they have to be borrowed on interlibrary loan.

ORAL HISTORY

Started in 1974, the Oral History Section's purpose is to collect the testimony of former military airmen and by the same token to broaden the sources offered to the historian, to enrich and deepen the understanding carried to the study of the archival materials.

By 1990, more than 600 veterans had already contributed their recollections of their various activities and particularly of the conditions under which they participated in the conflicts of the twentieth century (1914–1918, Morocco; 1939–1945, Indochina, Algeria, and Chad). These represent roughly two sessions a week. The choice is basically civil and military personalities who have held the highest responsible posts rather than those who simply carried out the orders: politicians, constructors, and engineers, as well as chiefs of the air staff, generals, senior officers, junior officers, and NCOs.

Until now (1990) the section has studied themes parallel to the great trends of history: Thus, the veterans of 1914–1918, the airmen of the Free French Forces, and the pilots sent to Suez in 1956 have been systematically interviewed for a well-determined period. Others have been led to recall the threads of their careers.

These interviews require a detailed preparation and a perfect knowledge of the subject's career. Recorded on magnetic tape, the interview, which is not straightforward, allows the interlocutor plenty of room for additional questions. At all times precise, the clarifications of these comments are the object of further questions. The length of each interview varies with the personality and the career of the person being taped.

The oral archival holdings thus represent and constitute important documentation put at the disposition of university professors. Strict conditions apply to the use of these tapes. The index of the first 145 interviews was published by the SHAA as Volume I. It contains for each a summary description of the interview to orient the researcher.

Through these innovative methods and the originality of its holdings, the Oral History Section offers historians a variety of often unedited information.

HISTORICAL RESEARCH

The SHAA had originally to live with researchers with diplomas in history who were employed to retrace the history of military aviation within the framework of the great political, economic, and technical phenomena of our century. They saw their articles appear in such various reviews as *La Revue historique des Armées* (The armed forces review), published jointly by the three French military services. In addition, they have participated in national and international colloquia in order to keep abreast of the latest research and to cooperate there. The researcher who is interested in the history of military aviation has numerous and varied resources available as noted earlier.

Reflecting the diversity of the sources, the history of French military aviation has a great richness and represents a vast field for investigation, properly concerning the combat history of the air force: the history of units, the history of the doctrine for their employment, and the story and analysis of campaigns. But the history of military aviation is not solely that of the military side; it also touches upon many other domains, such as politics, economics, diplomacy, and sociology, without overlooking intellectual history. It goes without saying that none of the studies are exclusive of the other. All of the evidence is connected.

THE AUDIOVISUAL SECTION

The unceasing and growing demand for images which characterizes our society led the SHAA to develop an audiovisual section. The section works to convey information on air force subjects. The sources for audiovisual compositions are to be found in the service itself: written archives, photographs, posters, illustrations, books, and so on.

The section possesses appropriate material which allows it to create presentations and is also endowed with a sound studio which makes it possible to put both images and sound on tape. In addition, the audiovisual section assumes the preservation of color photographs by duplicating them on slides.

For some time the SHAA has employed videotapes throughout the Air Force. On occasion of meetings organized by the EMAA (the État-major de L'Armée de L'Air; the air staff) or by units—exhibitions, open-house days, anniversaries—the audiovisual section creates slide shows to make the general public aware of the history of military aviation.

THE PUBLICATIONS SECTION

The SHAA publishes works by its authors based upon both its own archives and upon those of the sister services. Provided with the material ready for printing, publications sends it to the printer properly marked up for publication.

At the moment, the SHAA produces four kinds of publications:

1. The collection "Recueil d'articles et Etudes" (Miscellany of articles and studies), which principally regroups the contributions of the SHAA's historians to some studies, colloquia, and military historical reviews.
2. The collection "Travaux Universitaires" (University work) by which the SHAA wishes to be associated as much as possible with university professors and students, and has thus helped support publication in order to further the history of the Air Force.
3. The collection "Archives" publishes documents held by the SHAA archives, thus providing an inventory of the historical holdings.
4. The collection "Historique d'unités" publishes the histories of air force units.

These works are diffused widely throughout the air force and also to the many universities, archival services, libraries, history committees, and, in the same sectors, foreigners.

SYMBOLISM AND TRADITION

The SHAA has the honor to be "the keeper of traditions" of the air force through the division "Symbolism and Tradition," charged with assuring the maintenance of the heritage of current and disbanded units. The work of this division primarily benefits the air force alone, but it is also open to researchers and to private collectors.

The missions of the division are diverse:

1. To establish and put in order the affiliations of the air units (squadron and flights, groups, or wings) and to catalogue them by use (fighters, bombers, transports, helicopters, schools).
2. Similarly with names of traditions, insignia, and banners of units in the body of the regulations.
3. To confer, manufacture, or repair the flags placed in the care of units.
4. To guard and keep the flags of disbanded units.
5. To consult about the official traditions in the unity (research and historical constitution in light of the establishment of similar dossiers of insignia, banners, pennants, and traditional names, and to put in place the ceremony for the return of banners, pennants, and flags).
6. To respond to particular questions from the public.

The division has a nearly total collection of similar insignia for the air force and an incomplete collection of dissimilar ones. Gifts have enriched the collections, which have given value to the heart of the service. The insignia of current units are classed by special higher orders and territorially.

The similar insignia of disbanded units have been regrouped, as part of these were stationed in the former French departments of North Africa and in the former French colonies, the other set of the metropolitan insignias are arranged by the higher function or command to which they have belonged or to the base where they were stationed.

BIBLIOGRAPHY

Actes Colloque Air 1990. Colloque international: Précurseurs et prophètes de l'aviation militaire. Hommage à Clément Ader. Organisé sous l'égide du Comité national "Clément Ader" et sous le patronage de Monsieur le président de la République française, par le Service historique de l'armée de l'Air à Paris, les 8, 9 et 10 octobre 1990. Vincennes: Service historique de l'armée de l'Air, 1992. 354 p.; 24 cm. (Acta of the Colloquium Air 1990. International Colloquium: Precursors and prophets of military aviation in honour of Clément Ader).

Actes Colloque Air 1987. Colloque international: Histoire de la guerre aérienne, hommage au capitaine Georges Guynemer à l'occasion du

70è anniversaire de sa dispartion. Organisé par le Service historique de l'armeé de l'Air, avec l'Institute d'Histoire des Conflits contemporains, et le Centre d'histoire de l'Aéronautique et de l'Espace. Vincennes: Service historique de l'armée de l'Air, 1988. 395 p.; 24 cm. (Acta of the Air Colloquium 1987. International Colloquium: History of aerial warfare, in honor of Captain Georges Guynemer on the seventieth anniversary of his disappearance).

Les "as" de la guerre 1939–1945. Daniel Porret et Franck Thevenet; préf. du général Lucien Robineau. Vincennes: Service historique de l'armée de l'Air, 1991. 2 tomes, 292 et 322 p.; 11 planches (The "aces" of the 1939–1945 war).

Les "as" français de la Grande Guerre. Daniel Porret; préf. du général Charles Christienne. Vincennes: Service historique de l'armée de l'Air, 1983. 2 tomes, 342 + 376 p.; 24 cm. (French "aces" of the Great War 1914–1918).

L'aviation Militaire. Clément Ader. Réédition. Préf. du général Jean Fleury, chef d'état-major de l'armée de l'Air; avant-propos du général Lucien Robineau directeur de Service historique de l'armée de l'Air. Vincennes: SHAA, 1990. 379 p. Prix de vente: 100 F/120 F par correspondance (military aviation).

Du Ballon de Fleurus . . . au Mirage 2000. Les responsables de l'arme aérienne/S.H.A.A.; préf. du général d'armée aérienne Bernard Capillon, . . . ; introd. du général Charles Christienne, . . . Paris: Sirpa Air, 1984. 157 p.: photogr.; 38 cm. Prix de vente: 150 F/170 F par correspondance. (From the Balloon at Fleurus . . . to the mirage 2000. Those in charge of French military aviation).

Le general Pujo et la naissance de l'aviation française. Bernard Pujo; préf. du général d'armée aérienne Maurice Saint-Cricq. Vincennes: S.H.A.A., 1988. 235 p. Prix de vente: 60 F / 70 F par correspondance (General Pujo and the birth of French aviation).

Histoire orale. Inventaire des témoignagnes oraux. 1ére partie. Entretiens 1 à 145 / Véronique Debernardy-Lepère, Françoise de Ruffray; Emmanuel Breguet, Nicolas Kieffer, Pierre Ordonez. Vincennes: S.H.A.A., 1988. 412 p. Prix de vente: 60 F/70 F par correspondance (Index of oral history interviews).

Histoire du Groupe de Chassé 1/2 les Cigognes, 1914–1945. Texte adapté par Yves Brèche et Patrice Buffotot; préf. du général Charles Christienne. Vincennes: S.H.A.A., 1981. 293 p.: photogr.; 24 cm. (History of Fighter Group 1/2 les Cigones).

Historique de la 7ème Escadre de Chasse. Lieutenant-colonel Michel Caplet; adjudant-chef Guy Vaugeois. Vincennes: S.H.A.A., 1982. 2 tomes, 800 p.: ill. (History of the 7th Fighter Squadron).

Inventaire Sommaire des archives du Secretariat d'état à l'Aviation et du Secretariat General à la Defense Aerienne: 1940–1944. Patrick Facon, Françoise de Ruffray; sous la dir. de Madeline Astorkia. Vincennes: S.H.A.A., 1980. 213 p.; 24 cm. Index p. 201–213. (Summary inventory [finding aid] to the archives of the Secretary of State for Aviation and of the Secretariat-General for Air Defense, 1940–1944).

Un probleme de defense nationale: L'Aéronautique militaire au Parlement, 1928–1940. Dominique Boussard; av. pr. du général Charles Christienne. préf. de Jean-Baptiste Duroselle. Vincennes: S.H.A.A., 1983. 191 p.; 24 cm. (A national defence problem: Military aviation in parliament, 1928–1940).

Recueil d'articles et études: 1974–1975. Service historique de l'armée de l'Air. Vincennes: S.H.A.A., 1977. 302 p.: ill.; 24 cm. (Collection of articles and studies, 1974–1975).

Les Insignes de l'armée de l'Air, un élément de la symbolique militaire. P. Buffotot (Air Force insignia, an element of military symbolism).

Les Journaux de Marche et Opérations, garants de la tradition dans l'armée de l'Air. P. Buffotot (Operational record books, guarantors of Air Force traditions).

Morphologie de l'armée de l'Air 1924–1974: les officiers. D. Gaxie. (Morphology of the Air Force, 1924–1974: The officers).

L'image de l'aviateur française en 1914–1918. Une étude du milieu des aviateurs d'après la revue "la Guerre Aérienne." J.-P. Dournel (The image of the French aviator in 1914–1918. A study of the milieu of aviators as seen in the review *La Guerre Aerienne*).

L'industrie aéronautique française de septembre 1939 à juin 1940. Général C. Christienne (French air industry from September 1939 to June 1940).

Le Moral dans l'armée de l'Air française: de Septembre 1939 à juin 1940. P. Buffotot (Morale in the French Air Force from September 1939 to June 1940).

L'armée de l'Air pendant la bataille de France: du 10 mai à l'armistice. Essai de bilan numérique d'une bataille aérienne. P. Buffotot et J. Ogier (The Air Force during the Battle for France from 10 May to the Armistice. An attempt at a numerical balance of an aerial battle).

Les Ailes françaises dans le ciel au jour "J." Général C. Christienne (French wings in the sky on "J" Day).

L'Extraordinaire exploit d'un équipage du groupe Franche-Comté abattu le 19 août 1944 audessus de Toulon. P. Buffotot (The extraordinary exploit of a machine of the Group Franche-Comté brought down on 19 August 1944 near Toulon).

L'armée de l'Air en 1946. J.-P. Dournel (The French Air Force in 1946).

Recueil d'articles et études: 1976–1978. Service historique de l'armée de l'Air; préf. du général Charles Christienne. Vincennes: S.H.A.A., 1984. 228 p.; 24 cm. (Collection of articles and studies, 1976–1978).

L'Ecole Supérieure de Guerre et l'aviation dans l'entre-deux-guerres. Général C. Christienne (The Superior War College and aviation in the interwar years).

La politique aéronautique militaire des gouvernements française de 1919 à 1939. C. Deulin (Military aviation politics of French Governments from 1919 to 1939).

L'Armée de l'Air française et la crise du 7 mars 1936. Général C. Christienne et P. Buffotot (The French Air Force and the crisis of 7 March 1936).

La résistance au changement dans l'armée française entre les deux guerres. Un exemple: l'attitude de l'état-major de l'armée face aux problèmes posés par l'aviation militaire. Général C. Christienne (Resistance to change in the French Army between the wars, an example: The attitude of the general staff to problems posed by military aviation).

Aperçus sur la collaboration aéronautique franco-allemande (1940–1943). P. Facon et F. de Ruffray (Sketches of the [1940–1943] aeronautical collaboration: Franco–German).

Indochine 1945: le coup de force japonais et l'armée de l'Air. M. C. Mazaré (Indochina 1945: The Japanese blow and the French Air Force).

L'aviation et la guerre d'Espagne: la cinquième arme face aux exigences de la guerre moderne. M. Astorkia (Aviation and the war in Spain: The 5th arm faces the exigencies of modern war).

L'armée de l'Air française de mars 1936 à septembre 1939. Général C. Christienne (The French Air Force from March 1936 to September 1939).

L'aéronautique militaire française au Maroc (1911–1939). S. Lainé (The French Air Force in Morocco [1911–1939]).

Recueil d'articles et études: 1979–1981. Service historique de l'armée de l'Air; préf. du général Lucien Robineau. Vincennes: S.H.A.A., 1986. 290 p.: ill.; 24 cm. (Collection of articles and studies, 1979–1981).

Réarmement et reconstitution de l'armée de l'Air: 1942–1943. P. Facon (Rearmament and reconstitution of the French Air Force, 1942–1943).

Le plan VII: 1943–1944. P. Facon (Plan VII, 1943–1944).

Le plan V: 1938–1939. P. Facon (Plan V, 1938–1939).

L'armée de l'Air et les accords de Munich: étude de la presse parisienne de l'automne 1938. P. Papet (The French Air Force and Munich: A study of the Paris press in the autumn of 1938).

L'effort de guerre française dans le domaine aéronautique en 1914–1918. Général C. Christienne et S. Pesquiès-Courbier (The French war effort in aviation, 1914–1918).

Recrutement et formation des pilotes, 1917–1918. M. Hodeir (Recruitment and training of pilots, 1917–1918).

Le Haut commandement française face au progrès technique entre les deux guerres. Général C. Christienne (The French High Command and technical progress between the wars).

Danger aérien et architecture du IIIème Reich. M. Cluet (Aerial danger and architecture in the Third Reich).

Les bombardements aériens des usines sidérurgiques de l'Est en 1914–1918: l'enjeu économique, militaire et politique (The bombing of ironworks in the East, 1914–1918: The economic, military and political game).

Recueil d'articles et études: 1981–1983.
Service historique de l'armée de l'Air; préf. du général Lucien Robineau. Vincennes: S.H.A.A., 1987. 336 p.: ill.; 24 cm. (Collection of articles and studies, 1981–1983).

Alliances militaires et marchés d'avions pendant l'entre-deux-guerres: le cas français, 1936–1940. J. Ploquin (Military alliances and the sale of aircraft between the wars: The French case, 1936–1940).
L'armée de l'Air française à l'heure des pactes de Dunkerque et Bruxelles: 1947–1948. P. Facon (The French Air Force at the times of the Dunkirk and Brussels Pacts, 1947–1948).
Deux penseurs aéronautiques: Ader et Mitchell. Général C. Christienne (Two aeronautical thinkers: Ader and Mitchell).
Le Haut commandement aérien français et la crise de Munich: 1938. P. Facon (The French Air High Command and the Munich Crisis of 1938).
L'aviation populaire: entre les mythes et la rélité. P. Facon (Popular aviation: Between the myths and reality).
La visite du général Vuillemin en Allemagne: 16–21 août 1938. P. Facon (General Vuillemin's visit to Germany, 16–21 August 1938).
La coopération franco–alliée pendant la campagne de Tunisie: le problème aérien, 1942–1943. P. Facon (French–Allied cooperation during the Tunisian campaign: Air problems, 1942–1943).
L'armée de l'Air: sa place dans la défense nationale: 8 mai 1945–20 janvier 1946. P. Facon (The French Air Force and its place in National Defence, 8 May 1945–20 January 1946).
La R.A.F. dans la bataille de France au travers des rapports Vuillemin de Juillet 1940. Général C. Christienne (The RAF in the Battle of France as seen in the reports of General Vuillemin of July 1940).

Recueil d'articles et études: 1984–1985.
Service historique de l'armée de l'Air; préf. du général Lucien Robineau. Vincennes: S.H.A.A., 1991. 264 p.: ill.; 24 cm. (Collection of Articles and Studies, 1984–1985).

Overlord: la maîtrise de l'Air. Général C. Christienne (Air superiority at Overlord).
Un exemple de l'adaptation de l'arme aérienne aux conflits contemporains. P. Facon (An example of the Air Force to contemporary conflicts).
L'armée de l'Air et le problème du retour en France: 1943–1944. P. Facon (The French Air Force and the problem of the return to France, 1943–1944).
Puissance aérienne et puissance militaire française 1945–1948 (1ère partie). P. Facon (Air power and French military power, 1945–1948).
L'armée de l'Air et Dîen Bîen Phû. P. Facon (The Air Force at Dien Bien Phu).
Typologie et motivation des Forces aériennes françaises libres. Général C. Christienne (Typology and motivation of the Free French Air Forces).
Aperçus sur la doctrine d'emploi de l'aéronautique militaire française: 1914–18. P. Facon (Observations on the doctrine employed by French Military Aviation, 1914–18).

L'armée française et l'aviation: 1891–1914. P. Facon (The French Army and aviation, 1891–1914).
Le renouveau de l'armée de l'Air. P. Facon (The renovation of the French Air Force).
Les leçons de la campagne de Pologne vues par l'état-major aérien français: le rapport du colonel Bergeret aide-major général des forces aériennes (19 septembre 1939). P. Facon et A. Teyssier (The lessons of the campaign in Poland as seen by the French Air Force staff: The report of Colonel Bergeret, assistant chief of staff of the French Air Force [19 September 1939]).
L'école d'enseignement technique de l'armée de l'Air. P. Facon et A. Teyssier (The French Air Force School of Technical Maintenance).
L'armée de l'Air dans la bataille de France. Général L. Robineau (The Air Force in the Battle of France).
L'adaptation de l'armée de l'Air aux armes nouvelles. Général L. Robineau (The adaptation of the French Air Force to new weapons).
Les origines de la médecine aéronautique en France: l'expérience décisive de la grande guerre. A. Teyssier (The origins of aviation medicine in France: The decisive experience of the Great War).
L'Aéronautique de 1940 à 1943. A. Teyssier Aeronautics from 1940 to 1943).
Souvenirs du General Lauzin. Général Lauzin; préf. du général Charles Christienne. Vincennes: SHAA, 1979. 113 p.: photogr. 24 cm. (General Lauzin's Memoirs).

Service Historique de l'Armée de la Terre (The French Army Historical Service): Tradition and Evolution

Marcel Spivak, Director of Libraries,
Service Historique de l'Armée de la Terre,
Translated by Robin Higham

In contrast to the other historical services, whether French or foreign, the French Army Historical Service (Service historique de l'Armée de la Terre; SHAT) holds its own archives and assures their exploitation.

From the date of their creation by Louvois in 1688 to the present, it is plain that the missions of the Historical Service have changed, but its reason for being the memory of the nation in arms has remained essentially the same, and has been enlarged so that the SHAT receives and administers the archival records of all the organizations relevant to the Ministry of Defense.

Located in the Chateau de Vincennes, the SHAT holds some sixty linear kilometres of records, of which the oldest are of the seventeenth century. Use of the archives is governed by the Law of 1979, which allows access after thirty years with, however, certain restrictions, a function of the nature of the documents. These restrictions relate particularly to classified records, personnel records (a condition governed by type of service), medical records, those relating to military justice, and those which might compromise national security.

The public reading room at the archives is frequented by a widely varied public, but always with a hefty component of students and university faculty, whose research has to be preceded by or completed later by use of the holdings of the library, as much foreign as French. In this respect it should be noted that the library holds some 50,000 volumes in German out of a total of 600,000 volumes, as well as collections of periodicals and holdings in art, a research tool most precious in all regards.

But outside of its role as conservator which it considers, to be a very important aspect of the national patrimony, the SHAT also pursues a policy of publication of historical works going back to the 1890s.

Assuredly, Bonaparte wished to have prepared a report on his campaigns of 1798, but the renewal of the war did not allow the completion of this ambitious project. From this epoch came the War Memorial Depot, commenced in 1802, redone in 1925, above all for geography, even though some historical studies are to be found there.

It was between 1890 and 1914 that the Army Historical Section—ancestor of the present SHAT—carried to publication a considerable series of works based exclusively on military records. From this came the desire to study the history of those campaigns in which the French Army had participated, while avoiding very carefully all allusions to politicians and politics.

Between the two world wars, the historical section published a monumental work which marked the apogee of this historical method published up to 1914. This was *The French Armies in the Great War,* in 105 volumes and of which one of the collaborating authors was a name now well-known: De Gaulle. At the same time the service published the series *The French Armies Overseas* in twelve volumes, which appeared on the occasion of the Colonial Exposition of 1930 and remains a work much appreciated.

Since the end of the Second World War, the publications of the SHAT have focused upon the history of campaigns and operations in which the French Army participated, but, if these works have always been based upon the archives, their outlook has equally used foreign studies to obtain a more complete view of events.

Besides, several series of documentary publications on more recent conflicts have been sent to the press, such as on Indochina and Algeria, which are a notion of the work the archives does for the public.

In order to complete these series which pursue a nearly secular tradition, the SHAT also publishes works based upon the reminiscences (veterans have always been made use of to provide a many-sided view of events and to recreate as faithfully as possible great historical moments). A sign of the very close cooperation of the SHAT and the universities is that a number of military history theses appear in our publications.

Finally, *La Revue historique des Armées,* awarded a prize in 1954 by the French Academy and in 1981 by the Academy of Moral and Political Science, publishes articles which synthesize and illustrate the evolution of military history in the many areas which need to be covered. Its topical bibliography is a precise help to both students and researchers.

Not to be overlooked are the elaborate inventories of the records by the curators of the Service historique, because these specialized works enable researchers to find documents, and thus to enlarge the fields of research, and these reflect the new approaches in military history.

Also to be noted is the way in which the Service historique de l'Armée de Terre is not content simply to be the keeper of military archives—as important as that mission is—but also contributes to the diffusion of French military history, which is, in effect, the history of the nation itself in its many implications.

• • •

In the realm of ideas, the participation of both civil and military historians of the SHAT at international colloquia, the articles which they have published in diverse reviews, and the organization of expositions on the great themes of military history give testimony of this desire to deepen the understanding of historical problems and a pedagogical concern of the highest significance for the culture of what General de Gaulle called "a true idea of France."

WORKS PUBLISHED BY THE SHAT SINCE 1968, LISTED BY THEMES

Ancien Regime et Revolution

Lettres oubliées ou inédites de Turenne pour l'année 1652 par le capitaine A. de Menditte, éd. 1975 (Forgotten or unedited letters of Turenne for the year 1652 by Capt. A. de Mendittem).

Les relations franco-autrichiennes sous Louis XIV. Siége de Vienne (1683). éd. 1983 (Franco–Austrian relations under Louis XIV. Siege of Vienna, 1683).

Les commissaires des guerres et l'administration de l'Armée française, 1715–1730, par Claude Sturgill. éd. 1985 (The War Commissariat and the administration of the French Army, 1715–1730).

Les officers de l'armée royal combattants de la guerre d'Indépendance des Etats-Unis. De Yorktown à l'an II, par le capitaine Bodinier (thése). éd. 1983 (French officers of the Royal Army who fought in the United States during the War for Independence. From Yorktown to the Year II [1790]).

Dictionnaire des officiers de l'armée royale qui ont combattu aux Etats-Unis pendant la guerre d'Indépendance, par le capitaine Bodinier. éd. 1983 (Dictionary of the officers of the Royal Army who fought in the United States during the War for Independence).

Guibert ou le soldat philosophe (actes du colloque du centre d'études et de recherches sur les stratégies et les conflits de l'université Paris-Sorbonne), par J.-P. Charnay. éd. 1981 (Guibert or the philosophic soldier [proceedings of the colloquium held at the center for studies and research on strategies and conflicts of the University of Paris–Sorbonne]).

Les batailles aux frontières de Valma à Marengo (1792–1800), par les Cdts Bernède et Guelton. éd. 1989 (Battles on the frontiers from Valmy to Marengo [1792–1800]).

Parlement, gouvernement, commandement: l'armée de métier sous la troisième république (1871–1914) par Jean-Charles Jauffret (thèse de doctorat d'Etat). éd. 1987 (Parliament, government and command: L'armée de metier under the Third Republic [1871–1914]).

1919–1939

Les programmes d'armement de 1919 à 1939, par le contrôleur général HOFF. éd. 1982 (Armament programs of 1919 to 1939).

Les armées françaises en Orient après l'armistice de 1918, par le Général Bernachot (French armies in the East after the Armistice of 1918).

Tome I. *L'Armée française d'Orient—L'armée de Hongrie* (11 novembre 1918–10 Septembre 1919). éd. 1970 (The French Army in the East—The Army of Hungary [11 November 1918–10 September 1919]).

Tome II. *L'armée française d'Orient—L'armée du Danube* (28 octobre 1918–25 janvier 1920). éd. 1970 (The French Army in the East—The Army of the Danube [28 October 1918–25 January 1920]).

Tome III. *Le Corps d'occupation de Constantinople* (6 novembre 1920–2 octobre 1923). éd. 1972 (The Occupation Corps in Constantinople [6 November 1920–2 October 1923]).

L'Armée française de 1919 à 1939:

Tome I. *La reconversion* (1919), par le colonel Paoli. éd. 1969 (Demobilization [1919]).

Tome II. *La phase de fermeté* (1920–1924), par le colonel Paoli. éd. 1971 (The period of turmoil [1920–1924]).

Tome III. *Le temps des compromis* (1924–1930), par le colonel Paoli. éd. 1974 (The time of compromises [1924–1930]).
Tome IV. *La fin des illusions* (1930–1935), par le colonel Paoli. éd. 1976 (The end of illusions [1930–1935]).
Tome V. *Les problèmes de l'armée de terre* (1935–1939), par le Lt Col. Dutailly (thèse). éd. 1980 (The problems of the army [1935–1939]).

Deuxieme Guerre Mondiale

Les Grandes Unités française de la guerre, 1939–1945 (The large French units in the war of 1939–1940):
Tome I. *1939–1940 (Corps d'armée).* éd. 1967 (Army corps, 1939–1940).
Tome II. *1939–1940 (Divisions d'infanterie).* éd. 1967 (Infantry divisions, 1939–1940).
Tome III. *1939–1940 (Divisions d'infanterie coloniale et de cavalerie: secteurs fortifiés, groupements divers).* éd. 1967 (Colonial infantry divisions, cavalry, fortified sectors, and diverse groups, 1939–1940).
Tome IV. *1942–1944 (Campagne de Tunisie, de Corse, d'Italie et de l'île d'Elbe).* éd. 1970 (The campaign in France and Germany, 1944–1945).
Tome V. *1944–1945 (Campagne de France et d'Allemagne) 1ère partie: 3e D.I.A., 4e D.M.M., 9e D.I.C., 27e D.A.* éd. 1972 (The campaign in France and Germany, 1944–1945).
Tome V. *1944–1945 (Campagne de France et d'Allemagne) 2e partie: 1e D.M.I. (ex. 1e D.F.L.), 2e D.I.M., 10e D.I., 1e, 2e, et 5e D.B. éd.* 1975 (The campaign in France and Germany, 1944–1945, Part II).
Tome V. *1944–1945 (Campagne de France et d'Allemagne) 3e partie: les corps d'armée.* éd. 1975 (The campaign in France and Germany, Part III).
Tome V. *1944–1945 (Campagne de France et d'Allemagne) pochette de cartes, 9 planches.* éd. 1980 (The campaign in France and Germany, box of maps and nine plans).
Tome VI. *1944–1945 (la participation des F.F.I. aux opérations des fronts de l'Atlantique et des Alpes et à la réorganisation de l'Armée).* éd. 1980 (The participation of the F.F.I. in operations in the Atlantic and the Alps and the reorganization of the Army, 1944–1945).
Les Forces française dans la lutte contre l'Axe en Afrique, 1940–1943 (French forces in the struggle against the Axis in Africa, 1940–1943):
Tome I. *Les Forces française libres, 1940–1943,* par le chef de battalion Vincent. éd. 1983 (The Free French Forces, 1940–1943).
Tome II. *La Campagne de Tunisie, 1942–1943,* par Marcel Spivak et le colonel Léoni. éd. 1985 (The campaign in Tunisia, 1942–1943).
Le 3e groupe du 63e Régiment d'artillerie d'Afrique dans la campagne d'Italie, 1944, par le général François Valentin. éd. 1987 (The third battery of the 63rd Regiment of African Artillery in the campaign in Italy, 1944).
La participation française à la campaign d'Italie, par le colonel Le Goyet. éd. 1969 (French participation in the campaign in Italy).
Le Corps Expéditionnaire français en Italie (1943–1944), par le lieutenant-colonel Boulle (The French Expeditionary Corps in Italy, 1943–1944):
Tome I. *La Campagne d'hiver.* éd. 1971 (The winter campaign).

Tome II. *La campagne de printemps et d'été.* éd. 1973 (The spring and summer campaigns).

L'Union Soviétique en guerre, par le colonel A. Constantini (The Soviet Union in the war):

Tome I. *L'Invasion.* éd. 1968 (The German invasion).

Tome II. *Echec à la Wehrmacht.* éd. 1938 (The checking of the Wehrmacht [The German Army]).

Tome III. *De Kharkov à Berlin.* éd. 1969 (From Kharkov to Berlin).

Réarmement et réorganisation de l'armée de terre française (1943–1946), par le chef de bataillon J. Vernet. éd. 1980 (The rearmament and reorganization of the French Army [1943–1946]).

La Présence militaire française en Indochine (1940–1945), par le Lieutenant-Colonel Hesse d'Halzon (thèse). éd. 1985 (The French military presence in Indochina, 1940–1945).

Historiques des Unités combattantes de la Résistance (1940–1944), par le général de La Barre de Nanteuil (History of the fighting units of the Resistance, 1940–1945):

Série VIe région militaire (Series of the Sixth Military Region):

Dordogne, éd. 1974.

Charente, Charente-Maritime, éd. 1973.

Creuse, Corrèze, éd. 1974.

Gironde, éd. 1974.

Indre, éd. 1974.

Indre-et-Loire, éd. 1974.

Vienne, éd. 1974.

Haute-Vienne, éd. 1974.

Lot-et-Garonne, éd. 1974.

Deux-Sèvres et Vendée, éd. 1974.

Synthèse sur les treize départements, éd. 1974.

Série ex-VIIe région militaire (Series of the former Seventh Military Region):

Cher, éd., 1975.

Côte-d'Or, éd. 1976.

Saône-et-Loire, éd. 1976.

Nièvre, éd. 1976.

Haute-Saône et Territoire de Belfort, éd. 1977.

Yonne, éd. 1977.

Doubs, éd. 1977.

Jura, éd. 1977.

Synthèse sur les neuf départments de l'ex-VIIe région militaire, éd. 1977 (Overview of the nine departments of the former seventh military region):

Allier, éd. 1984.

Puy-de-Dôme, éd. 1985.

Haute-Loire, éd. 1986.

Cantal, éd. 1986.

Rapports d'activités du XXVe C.A. allemand en occupation en Bretagne (1940–1944), traduction et notes du Commandant Even, éd. 1978 (Reports of the activities of the 25th German C.A. in the Occupation of Brittany [1940–1944], a translation with notes).

Kriegstagebuch de l'état-major principal de liaison n 588 de Clermont-Ferrand (1er janv.–23 août 1944), du commandant Even, éd. 1975 (The war diary of the General Liaison Staff no. 588 in Clermont–Ferrand [1 January–23 August 1944]).

Haute lutte, par Maurice Passemard, 200 pages de croquis de combat, illustrations couleur, photos noir, cartes. (High struggle, 200 pages of combat sketches, illustrated in color, black and white photos, with maps).

Les Armées française au Levant (1919–1939), par le général Du Hays (The French Armies in the Levant, 1919–1939):

Tome I. *L'occupation française en Syrie et en Cilicie sous le commandement britannique* (nov. 1918–nov. 1919), éd. 1978 (The French occupation of Syria and Cilicie under British command [November 1918–November 1919]).

Tome II. *Le temps des combats* (1920–1921). éd. 1979 (The time of battles [1920–1921]).

La présence militaire française en Indochine (1940–1945), par le Lt Col. Hesse d'Halzon (thèse). éd. 1985 (The French military presence in Indochina [1940–1945]).

Le 27e B.T.A., Indochine, 1949–1954, par le général J. Le Chatelier. éd. 1987 (The 27th B.T.A., Indochina, 1949–1954).

La Libération du Laos, 1945–1946, par le général de Crèvecoeur. éd. 1985 (The liberation of Laos, 1945–1946).

La guerre d'Indochine 1945–1954, Textes et documents présentés par le Cdt Bodinier (The war in Indochina, 1945–1954, texts and documents):

Tome I. *Le retour de la France en Indochine,* 1945–1946, Préf. du général Delmas. éd. 1987 (The return of France to Indochina, 1945–1946).

Tome II. *Règlement politique ou solution militaire,* 1947, Préf du général Bassac. éd. 1989 (Political rule or military solution, 1947).

Insignes de l'Armée de Terre (Army Insignias)

Les insignes du Génie, par le major Dupire. éd. 1987 (Engineer insignia).

Les insignes du Train, par le colonel Huyon et le capitaine Mourot. éd. 1988 (Insignia of the supply corps).

Publications Diverses

Le fantassin de France, par le général Bertin. éd. 1988 (The French foot soldier).

Les origines militaires de l'éducation physique en France de 1774 à 1848, par Marcel Spivak. éd. 1972 (The military origins of physical education in France from 1774 to 1848).

Historique de l'ambulance vétérinaire 541 devenue 541ème groupe vétérinaire 1943–1977, par les généraux P. d'Autheville et E. Barrairon. éd. 1988 (History of the 541st Veterinary Ambulance, which became the 541st Veterinary Group, 1943–1977).

1688–1988. Mémoire de l'armée (catalogue de l'exposition du tricentenaire du SHAT). éd. 1988 (1688–1988. The Army in retrospect [catalogue of the TriCentenary exposition of the Service historique de l'Armée]).

Le Service historique de l'armée de terre et le Chateau de Vincennes. éd. 1988 (The Army historical service and the Chateau of Vincennes).

Guides Bibliographiques (Bibliographic Guides)

Guide bibliographique sommaire d'histoire militaire et coloniale française, par René Couret et Madeleine Lenoir. éd. 1969 (A summary bibliographic guide to military history and the French colonies).

Bibliographie de la campagne d'Indochine, par le commandant Désiré (Bibliography of the campaign in Indochina):

Tome I. *L'Indochine avant 1945.* éd. 1971 (Indochina before 1945).

Tome II. *Les données géographiques, économiques, humaines, politiques et diplomatiques.* éd. 1973 (The geographical, economic, humane, political, and diplomatic setting).

Tome III. *La campagne française d'Indochine*: (The French campaign in Indochina). 1ère partie: 1945–1950. éd. 1976 (First part, 1945–1950). 2ème partie: 1951–1954. éd. 1976 (Second part, 1951–1954).

Tome IV. *La campagne Vietminh. La fin de la campagne française et la relève américaine (1954–1956).* éd. 1977 (The Vietminh campaign. The end of the French campaign and the American takeover [1954–1956]).

Bibliographie des historiques des régiments depuis 1914, par le Commandant Rollot (Bibliographies of the histories of the regiments since 1944):

Tome I. *1ère partie: Ecoles, Infanterie de ligne.* éd. 1973 (First part: Schools, infantry of the line);*2ème partie: Infanterie territoriale, bataillons de chasseurs, troupes spécialisées: parachutistes, Corps francs, gendarmerie.* éd. 1974 (Second part: Territorial infantry, light infantry, special troops, parachutists, free corps, gendarmerie);*3ème partie: Infanterie d'Afrique du Nord, Infanterie de Marine, Légion étrangère.* éd. 1974 (Third part: North African infantry, marines, foreign legion).

Tome II. *Arme blindée et cavalerie, Train des équipages.* éd. 1974 (Armor and cavalry).

Tome III. *Artillerie, génie, transmissions, services.* éd. 1975 (Artillery, engineers, signals, supply services).

Inventaires des Archives Conservées au SHAT (Inventories of Archival Documents Preserved at the SHAT)

L*es contrôles des trouppes de l'Ancien Régime, par André Corvisier* (The muster rolls of troops in the Ancien Régime):

Tome I. *Une source d'histoire sociale, guide des recherches,* éd. 1968 (A source of social history, guide for research).

Tome II. *Inventaire des contrôles d'infanterie,* éd. 1970 (Inventory of the muster rolls of the infantry).

Tome III. *Inventaire des troupes à cheval, artillerie, milice, troupes suisses, gardes française, troupes des colonies et de la marine,* éd. 1970 (Inventory of horsed troops, artillery, militia, Swiss Guards, French Guards, colonial troops and marines).

Tome IV. *Supplément: Index des noms de régiments,* éd. 1970 (Supplement: Names of regiments).

Inventaire Sommaire des Archives de la Guerre (série N 1872–1919) (Brief Inventory of the Archives of War [series N, 1872–1919])

Introduction: Organization de l'armée française, guide des sources, bibliographie, par le colonel P. Guinard, J. C. Devos, J. Nicot, éd. 1975 (Introduction: Organization of the French Army, guide to the sources and bibliography).

Série 1 N à 14 N. *Cabinet du Ministre, Etat-major de l'Armée,* par J. C. Devos, J. Nicot, P. Schillinger et B. Waksman, conservateurs, éd. 1974 (Series 1N to 14N: Office of the minister, general staff of the army).

Série 15 N à 25 N. *Corps d'armées,* par J. Nicot, P. Schillinger et J. Ficat, éd. 1972 (Series 15N to 25N: Army corps).

Série 21 N à 25 N. *Corps d'armée, divisions, régiments,* par J. Nicot, éd. 1969 (Series 21 N to 25 N: Army corps, divisions, and regiments).

Série 26 N. *Répertoire numérique des journaux de marches et opérations (1914–1918),* par J. Nicot (Numerical list of the daily records of marches and operations).

Inventaire Sommaire des Archives de la Guerre (série N 1920–1940) (Summary Inventory of the War Archives [series N 1920–1940])

Tome II. *Etat-major de l'Armée, attachés militaires, directions et inspections,* par J. Nicot, B. Waksman, chef d'escadron de Menditte et capitaine Bodinier, éd. 1981 (The general staff of the army, military attachés, directions and inspections).

Tome III. *Grand quartier général, armées, corps d'armées, régions militaires, divisions, secteurs fortifiés, 1939–1940,* (sous-série 27 N à 33 N), par J. Nicot, éd. 1984 (Headquarters of the armies, corps, military regions, divisions, and fortified sectors, 1939–1940).

Tome IV. *Répertoire numérique des archives et journaux des marches et opérations des corps de troupes, 1919–1940,* (sous-série 34 N), par J. Nicot, éd. 1983 (Numerical list of the archives and daily reports of marches and operations of the troops, 1919–1940).

Etat des fonds privés du Service Historique de l'Armée de terre, par B. Waksman, Ph. Schillinger et M.A. Corvisier, conservateurs. 2 Tomes, 1981, 1988 (Register of the private holdings of the army historical service).

Répertoire des archives du Maroc, Série 3 H (1877–1960) fascicule I par le chef d'escadron A. de Menditte et Jean Nicot, conservateur, éd. 1982 (List of the archives of Morocco, Series 3 H [1877–1960]).

Inventaire des archives du Levant, Série 4 H (1919–1946) par Jean Nicot, conservateur, éd. 1984 (Inventory of the Levantine archives, Series 4 H [1919–1946]).

Inventaire des archives du Centre Militaire d'Information et de documentation sur l'Outre-Mer (CMIDOM). Sous-Série 15 H par Jean Nicot, conservateur, éd. 1987 (Inventory of the archives of the Center of Military Information and of the documentation overseas [CMIDOM, sub-series 15 H]).

Inventaire des archives de l'Indochine, Sous-Série 10 H (1867–1956) (Inventory of the Archives of Indochina, Subseries 10 H [1867–1956])

Tome I. par J.-C. Devos, J. Nicot, P. Schillinger, conservateurs, éd. 1989.
Tome II. par J.-C. Devos, J. Nicot, P. Schillinger, conservateurs, éd. 1987.
Inventaire des archives de Tunisie, Série 2 H (1881–1960), par Jean Nicot, éd. 1985 (Inventory of the Tunisian archives, Series 2 H [1881–1960]).
Inventaire analytique de l'article 5 des archives du Génie, "Communications de terre et d'eau, dessèchement" (1531–1877), par Nelly Lacrocq, éd. 1985 (Analytical inventory of Article 5 of the Engineer archives, "Communications relating to land and water, dryness," [1531–1877]).
Atlas des places fortes de France (1774–1788), par Nelly Lecrocq, éd. 1981 (Atlas of fortified places in France [1774–1788]).

Autres Publications d'Histoire Militaire (Other Publications in Military History)

1916: année de Verdun, par le Service Historique de l'Armée de terre; préf. de Alain Decaux, éd. 1988. Ouvrage couronné par l'Académie française (prix Maréchal Foch) (1916: The year of Verdun).
Les Insignes officiels de l'Armée de terre, par Jacques Mirlier, éd. IDM, 1987. 2 tomes (Official insignia of the Army).

Le Service Historique de la Marine (The French Navy Historical Service)

Rear Admiral Jean Kessler, Chief
Translated by Robin Higham

HISTORY

The Archives

It was at the end of 1660 that Colbert organized the naval archives, binding the correspondence in the magnificent registers bearing his coat of arms and installing them about 1680 at Saint-Germain-en-

Laye. In 1699 came the creation of a true naval and colonial archives depository at the Place des Victoires. In the meantime, in the ports the intendants pushed the creation of regional depositories.

For various reasons, in 1720 the Naval Council decided to create a depot for maps, plans, and ships' logs, until then mixed up with the other documents, a depot which constitutes the ancestor of the Naval Hydrographic and Oceanographic Service. In 1763 the archives were returned to Versailles, where they were housed in the same building with the Ministries of War and the Navy (actually the municipal library of Versailles), before in 1837 they were returned to the Rue Royale, Paris, close to the naval ministry.

The second empire had little interest in the naval archives. It was not until 1899 that the Navy Minister, Edouard Lockroy, decided that in order better to conserve the oldest material records dating from before the Revolution should be moved to the Archives nationales. From then until the present there has been no change in this practice. At last, in 1974, given the pressures on space at the Archives nationales, the naval archives were moved to the Queen's Pavillion at the Chateau de Vincennes on the east side of Paris.

The Libraries

The first historical and scientific (scholarly) library was at the Académie de Marine (a learned society) founded at Brest in 1752. Others were founded in the ports by decree of the Convention; thus, in the year VI, the libraries of the naval hospitals came into being. Finally, in 1820 the ministry's own library was created.

Historical Works

Under the Consulate there was an office for historical and legislative work, which after many adventures became the "historical section" of which Auguston Jal, author of the celebrated *Glossaire nautique,* became part from 1831 to 1852. The section was for a long time opposed by the archives, which it wished to annex. Dissolved in 1852, the historical section was not reestablished until 1918, when it was—by a proper turn of fate—reattached to the archives so as to sort and exploit all the documents which bore on the navy during the First World War.

The Naval Historical Service

It was in 1919 under Minister Georges Leygues, and benefitting from the determined direction of Capitaine de frégate Castex, who became the first chief, that the Service historique de la Marine was created, originally housed at Avenue Octave Gréard, and since 1974 at Vincennes. This latter decision had the advantage of uniting in one great location all of the service archives, libraries, and also the historical sections, and of doing away with the traditional hostilities between the archives and the historical services.

At the present time the service consists of four sections:

- the archives and libraries.
- the historical sections.
- *la Revue maritime,* for whose publication it is responsible.
- the Naval Museum (la musée de la Marine).

After the Second World War *la Revue maritime* and the museum were detached. In contrast, the Hydrographic Service deposited its very rich collections in the Pavillion de la Reine when this service was transferred to Brest—with the exception of its administration—and it was decided in 1970 to give to the E.N.A. (Ecole Nationale d'Administration) the prestigious property on the rue de l'Université. A part of its records is also deposited at the Archives nationales and the Bibliothéque nationale (the National Library).

Its Missions

Actually, the Naval Historical Service carries out three essential functions as well as its former ones. It is, first, a collection of naval archives that receive the outpourings of the central administration in the same way as with the naval units and branches, and for which responsibilities are defined by the archival law of 1979. It manages the specialized libraries in the historical, scholarly, and administrative spheres, both for the navy and for all interested citizens. It conducts, at least for the central administration, a certain number of studies and historical tasks, among which not the least is the elaboration of the course of maritime history used at the Higher War College (naval and interservice).

To these traditional missions others have been added: that of being the guardian of the symbolic patrimony (heritage) and the military traditions of the navy, in conjunction with the Naval Museum and in servicing the collections of the headquarters or general staff; and, finally, the mission to which the navy attaches great importance, participation in educational and cultural activities which have become more and more acceptable and have led the service to organize or to participate in a number of exhibitions, colloquia, and diverse national and international congresses.

Organization of the Service Historique de la Marine

This organization has two important characteristics. In the first place its independence, not only vis-à-vis the other historical services, but also equally of the Archives nationales, which has relations with the archives of all the other ministries, with the exception of those of defense and foreign affairs. The situation is very exceptional, since the majority of the great powers to the contrary have centralized their archives, not the least since they have been exploited on a historical plan.

Independence does not signify, however, lack of coordination. The archival problems at the level of the historical services are not fundamentally different from those of the general ordering of records which confronts the Archives nationales. Let us note that the keepers of the Ministry of Defense—now integrated in the Corps of Curators of the Patrimony—are the paleographic archivists, descended from the Map School like those of the Archives nationales. It is no less certain that the three military services have common responsibilities in many domains.

In order to respond to this need for coordination, they have created various commissions: the Committee on Defense archives, presided over by the secretary-general for administration of the Ministry of Defense, whose members include the director of the Archives of France and the director of the Diplomatic Archives, who mark well the similarity of their problems and needs; and the higher commission on the French archives, of which the competence extends together to the spheres of the archivists and to those of the heads of the historical services of the armed forces who are members, as they are also of the commission on diplomatic archives.

The second characteristic of the Naval Historical Service and one which is very correct for it is decentralization. The organization of the Naval Historical Service possesses in effect a regional aspect which is not present in the other military historical services, those of the army and the air force.

Dependent on the Naval Historical Service in the five ports (Cherbourg, Brest, L'Orient, Rochefort, and Toulon) are some local echelons of the archives and libraries which are the focal points for particularly rich and interesting collections on the local plane.

In the Queen's Pavillion at Vincennes is to be found the direction which rests in the chief of the Naval Historical Service, an admiral directly responsible to the chief of staff of the navy, and the keeper in chief, head of the naval archives and libraries, upon which depend equally at the scientific and the technical level the archives and libraries in the ports, beside those which are commonly called the central establishment. The central establishment contains a number of divisions:

- The archives and library service, already mentioned, is under the direction of the keeper in chief and is composed of

  the central archives, directed by a conservator.

  the central historical library, also directed by a conservator.

  the research section, which conducts historical and genealogical administrative research.
- The historical studies section, charged, to the benefit of the naval general staff, with doing studies and works of history. This is headed by a certified assistant professor, a doctor of letters, responsible for the course in maritime history at the Ecole supérieure de guerre navale.
- The oral history section, the responsibility of an instructor who is an assistant to the chief of the section of historical studies.
- A section concerned with the history of naval and tropical medicine, kindly run by a medical doctor with a university degree in history.
- The section on military symbolism, which is also charged with the military management of the navy's paintings.

In the ports the local organization precisely reflects that at the center, without the historical symbolic section, which exist only in Paris.

Also connected to the organic plan, and to satisfy certain specific fiscal requirements of the chief of naval history relevant to the local maritime authority of the military and administrative scheme, are found, again under the conservator of Patrimony, paleographic archivist:

- An archival depository which receives the records from the local command as well as the units affected and those reattached.
- A library.
- A research service.
- A modest set of workshops.

The important difference with Vincennes is to be found in the fact that at each port there is also an educational service which constitutes the navy's share of the responsibility for the proper teaching of naval history, in presenting to primary and secondary students a direct contact with preserved documents. They offer resources as rich as those in the departmental (provincial) archives and a privileged occasion to view the maritime heritage in the town or urban history—just as with the department—and not only with the navy locally.

The Background and the Collections

Under the force of the Law of 3 January 1979, the archives held in its depositories by the navy are not the property of the service, but are part of the national cultural patrimony. They constitute the memory of the nation. The exploitation of these archives is governed by strict rules. Thus, the records cannot be freely consulted until after a minimum delay of thirty years. But even to this rule there are a certain number of exceptions:

- There is a sixty-year rule for documents containing interesting information on the security of the state or of national defense, more generally for the records which touch upon intelligence.
- One hundred and twenty years in the case of personnel records, of which Vincennes holds some 300,000.
- One hundred years after the act was committed for records relating to cases taken before a court, including preliminary hearings (*parajudiciaire*).
- One hundred years for statistical inquiries related to dossiers on private persons.
- One hundred and fifty years for documents relating to the medical records of individuals.

A derogation to these rules can be granted by the minister on the special advice of the Historical Service.

The Historical Service, which not long ago worked solely for the benefit of the navy, has now become a public service, open to everyone, with the only restrictions on communications being those required by law. Until about fifty years ago the clientele was strictly composed of naval officers, either on active duty or retired. Today university types of all levels have become more and more numerous working at Vincennes.

The archives contain 42,000 ml (linear meters) of which 18,000 are in Paris; 4,000 in the repository of the Archives de France since the end of the last century are part of these numbers. Their accumulation has taken place at from 1,200 to 1,400 ml per annum. Qualitatively, the service retains at Vincennes the navy's records of the central administration and its directorates, plus those of some of the units stationed in Paris and its environs. Also preserved at Paris are unit operational records, just as with the administrative records, which it has been necessary to centralize for their effective use.

The echelons in the ports receive the records of those commands and of the units in the region, plus those of commands and units overseas. Thus, the archives at L'Orient contain those for the Indian Ocean, while the records from the Pacific, Dakar, and the West Indies–Guiana are at Brest, those concerned with the North are at Cherbourg, and at Toulon are those relating to the Mediterranean basin, North Africa, the Levant, and the Far East.

The sections at the ports also contain the most important older background materials, of which it is not possible to do more than cite a few examples:

- At L'Orient are the records of the East India Company.
- At Rochefort are those of emigration to the New World.
- At Toulon are the oldest records of French relations with the Levant.

The Naval Library holds some 300,000 volumes. The historical library at Vincennes contains some 170,000 volumes not counting maps, atlases, and the special charts of the Hydrographic Service, and is one of the foremost libraries in the world, specializing in questions of maritime history, explorations, and voyages. Along with this basic collection of printed materials, the library also boasts a very fine collection of manuscripts which continues to grow with new acquisitions (in the neighborhood of 1,000). As to the collections in the ports, even if their volume is not great, they are often nevertheless very rich, the most remarkable and the oldest being that at Brest, the records bequeathed by the Royal Naval Academy.

The Use of the Materials

Beside the use of the collections by researchers or historians, there are two types of official users: those from the research section and those from the historical section.

The Research Section

Three types of research have but narrow divides:

- administrative research.
- historical research.
- genealogical work.

The function of administrative research constitutes in effect an essential work of the Service historique de la Marine. It retrieves from its records those which permit the persons who have requested them to claim their rights under the administrative plan and to furnish the corresponding documents attesting to their needs in the most diverse of domains: battle maps, the validation of service records for pensions, and the corroboration of the right to a decoration.

The function of historical research is equally an important preoccupation: It responds to requests for information from both the general staff and from the units, be they only simple particulars. It permits the establishment and the furnishing of notices of the agreements, the researches, at the moment when a new unit is christened, such as intelligence on those who have previously carried the name. As to the questions posed by some particular persons, they can take the most diverse form: questions posed by ship lovers, by former sailors trying to retrace an activity or the ships upon which they were embarked, and by all those—and the list is numerous—who are doing nonuniversity research. Genealogical researchers, always the most numerous group, demand work that is often long and minute, for the most part of little interest to the service. Nevertheless, their work constitutes a mission of the service and is rendered as well as possible.

The Activities of the Historical Section

Recreated in 1916, the historical section has had a career encompassing diverse fortunes. Charged initially not only with the use of the contemporary operational archives, but also with their classification, with the publication of historical studies of use to the general staff, it was known until 1960–1965 as a section having at times a very important role to play.

It has counted among its effectives, and even as its head, known authors, some of them very prestigious: Paul Chack, A. Laurens, André Reussner, and Jacques Mordal wrote and published under the sign of the Service historique and under their own proper names works both numerous and brilliant.

Directed by Philippe Masson, assisted by an assistant professor and by a team of young historian national servicemen, the Historical Service produces research works and broad syntheses. It organizes colloquia and plays a role as a nearby guide to students and the universities. It also preserves relations with different historical institutes, both in France and abroad.

In the space of a generation, the field of action of the Historical Service has definitely continued to expand. It has become the guardian of the naval heritage and a center of research in the intellectual life of the country, and much more than at the end of the nineteenth century, its archives have not been limited to naval affairs, but now also include colonial affairs.

BIBLIOGRAPHY

Travaux de la Section Historique (Works of the Historical Section)

TSH1. Bayle (capitaine de frégate Luc-Marie), *Les corvettes FNFL de leur armement au 2 août, 1943.–1966 in-4°*, IV-227 p., cartes (The corvettes of the Free French Navy and their armament, 2 August 1943).

TSH2. Bayle (capitaine de frégate Luc-Marie), *Les opérations des sous-marins des FNFL.* 1967 in-4°, III-75 p. (Operations of Free French submarines).

TSH3. Bayle (capitaine de frégate Luc-Marie), *La 23° flottille de MTB FNFL 1942–1945 (Témoignagesdes officiers).* 1967 in-4°, XII-115 p. (The 23rd Free French Motor Torpedo Boat Flotilla [1942–1945] [Testimony of the officers]).

TSH4. Caroff (capitaine de frégate), *La campagne de Norvège, 1940.* (2° tirage, 1986), in-4°, XII-200 p., cartes (un fascicule complémentaire) (The campaign in Norway, 1940).

TSH5. Caroff (capitaine de frégate), *Les formations de la Marine aux armées, 1939–1945.* 1953 (2° tirage, 1984), in-4°, XIII-189 p. (Naval formations working with the armies, 1939–1945).

TSH6. Caroff (capitaine de vaisseau), *Les débarquements alliés en Afrique du Nord,* Novembre 1942. 1960 (2° tirage, 1987), in-4°, XVII-318 p., cartes (The Allied landings in North Africa, November 1942).

TSH7. Cras (Hervé), Mangin D'Ounce (capitaine de frégate Xavier), Masson (Philippe), *Les bâtiments de surface des FNFL,* 1975 in 4°, VI-170 p. (The surface ships of the Free French Navy, 1968).

TSH8. Masson (Philippe), *Les mutineries de la Marine française.* Tome II, 1919. 1975 in-4°, V-102 p. (The mutinies in the French Navy, 1919–1975).

TSH9. Masson (Philippe), *La crise de Suez, novembre 1956–avril 1957.* 1966, in-4°, V-273 p.m Avec encart, La crise de Suez et ses enseignements, 28 p., et cartes (The Suez crisis of November 1956–April 1957, with a supplement on the lessons of Suez).

TSH10. Michel (capitaine de vaisseau Jacques), *La Marine francaise en Indochine de 1939 à 1956.*

Tome I. Septembre 1939–Août 1945 *(The French Navy in Indochina, 1939 to 1956).*

TSH11. Tome II. *Août 1945–Décembre 1946* (August 1945–December 1946).

TSH12. Tome III. *Janvier 1947–Décembre 1949* (January 1947–December 1949).

TSH13. Tome IV. *Janvier 1950–Avril 1953* (January 1950–April 1953).

TSH14. Tome V. *Avril 1953–Mai 1956* (April 1953–May 1956).

TSH15. Muracciole (capitaine de frégate), *Historique de la Combattante, torpilleur des FNFL.* 1971, in-4°, III-91 p., cartes, photos (Story of the fighting destroyers of the Free French Navy).

TSH16. Reussner (André), *Les conversations franco-britanniques d'État-Major, 1935–1939.* 1969, in-4°, V-293 p. (The conversations between the French and British staffs, 1935–1939).

Collection Études Historiques

EH1. Aman (Jacques), *Une campagne navale méconnue á la veille de la guerre de Sept ans. L'escadre de Brest en 1755–1763.* 1973, in-8°, XXXI-203 p., cartes (The unknown campaign against Brest in the Seven Years' War 1755–1763).

EH2. Beauchesne (Geneviève), *Historique de la construction navale à Lorient de 1666 à 1770.* 1979, in-8°, XXXI-234 p. (The history of naval shipbuilding at Lorient from 1666 to 1770).

EH3. Caron (capitaine de frégate François), *La guerre incomprise ou les raisons d'un échec (capitulation de Louisbourg, 1758).* 1983, in-8°, XXX-475 p., planches et cartes hors-texte (The unappreciated war and the reasons for the defeat [the capitulation of Louisbourg, in 1758]).

EH4. Caron (capitaine de vaisseau François), *La guerre incomprise ou la victoire volée (bataille de la Chesapeake, 1781).* 1989, in-8°, VII-614 p., planches (The unappreciated war or the smashing victory at the Chesapeake, 1781).

EH5. Chaline (vice-amiral d'escadre), Santarelli (capitaine de vaisseau), *Historique des forces navales françaises Libres. Tome I (18-6-1940–3-8-1943).* 1989 (2° édition, 1990) in-4°, IX-462 p., cartes, photos (The history of the Free French Naval Forces, I. 18 June 1940–3 August 1943).

EH6. Delattre (capitaine de vaisseau G.), *Annales inédites de la flottille du fleuve Sénégal de 1819 à 1854. Tome I (seul paru), 1819–1835.* 1972, in-4°, XIV-432 p., cartes (The unedited annals of the Sénégal River Flotilla, 1819–1854, I. 1819–1835).

EH18. Guiglini (colnel Jean), *Les marques particulières des navires de guerre français de 1900 à 1950* (à paraître) (The particular classes of French warships pennant numbers from 1900 to 1950).

EH7. Lacroix (Jean-Bernárd), *Les Français au Sénégal au temps de la Compagnie des Indes de 1719 à 1758.* 1986, in-8°, IV-314 p. (The French in Sénégal at the time of the India Company from 1719 to 1758).

EH8. LePourhiet-Salat (Nicole), *La défense des iles bretonnes de l'Atlantique, des origines à 1860.* 1983, in-8°, XLV-376 p., planches hors-texte (un fascicule complémentaire) (The defense of the Atlantic islands of Brittany from the beginnings in 1869 to 1983).

EH9. Martel (Marie-Thérèse de), *Étude sur le recrutement des matelots et soldats des vaisseaux du roi dans le ressort de l'intendance du port de Rochefort, 1691–1697, Aspescts de la vie des gens de mer.* 1982, in-8°, XXXVI-406 p., carte (A study of the recruitment of sailors and soldiers on royal vessels at the start of the administration of the port of Rochefort, 1691–1697).

EH10. *Études d'officiers stagiaires à L'École de Guerre navale, rédigées entre 1949 et 1952 et relatives à la guerre de 1939–1945.* 1981, in-4°, 235 p., cartes (Study of the probatiaonary officers at the Naval War School, drafted between 1949 and 1952 and relative to the lessons of the war of 1939–1945).

EH17. Sabatier de Lachadenede (vice-amiral René), *La Marine française et la Guerre Civile d'Espagne, 1936–1939. (à paraître)* (The French Navy and the civil war in Spain, 1936–1939).

EH11. Salkin-Laparra (Geneviève), Marins et diplomates. *Les attachés navals, 1860–1914.* Essai de typologie. Dictionnaire biographique. 1990, in-8°, 500 p., index (Sailors and diplomats. The naval attachés, 1860–1914).

Colloques

EH12. *Guerres et paix, 1660–1815. Journées franco–anglaises d'historie de la marine, Corderie royale de Rochefort, 20–22 mars 1986.* 1987, in-8°, 329 p., planches (War and peace, 1660–1815. Anglo–French naval history conference at the Royal Ropeworks in Rochefort, 20–22 March 1986).

EH13. *Marine et technique au XIX° siècle.* Actes du colloque international, L'École militaire, 10–12 juin 1987 (Service historique de la Marine; Institut d'histoire des conflits contemporains). 1989, in-8°, X-650 p., figures, cartes (Navies and technology in the nineteeth century).

EH14. *Les Marines de guerre du dreadnought au nucléaire,* Actes du 2° colloque International, ex-École de Polytechnique 21–23 novembre 1988. 1991, in-8°, VI-570 p., figures, cartes (Navies from the *Dreadnought* to the nuclear age).

EH15. *Les Empires en Guerre et Paix, 1793–1860.* II° Journées franco–anglaises d'histoire de la marine, Portsmouth, 23–26 mars 1988. 1990, in-8°, 321 p., figures, cartes (Empires in war and peace, 1793–1860).

EH16. *Français et Anglais en Méditerranée, de la Révolution Française à L'Indépendence de la Grèce, 1789–1830.* III° Journées franco-britanniques d'histoire de la marine, Toulon, 14–16 novembre 1990 (à paraître) (The French and British in the Mediterranean, from the revolution to the independence of Greece, 1789–1830).

En Diffusion

D6. Masson Philippe, *La Marine Française et la mer Noire, 1918–1919.* Paris, Publications de la Sorbonne et Service historique de la Marine, 1982, in-8°, XI-669 p. (The French Navy in the Black Sea, 1918–1919).

D1. Masson (Philippe), Battesti (Michèle), *La Révolution maritime du XIX° siècle.* Paris, Lavauzelle, 1987, in-4°, 128 p., illustrations en noir et en couleurs (The naval revolution of the nineteenth century).

D2. Masson (Philippe), Battesti (Michèle), *Du dreadnought au nucléaire.* Paris, Lavauzelle, 1988, in-4°, 136 p., illustrations (From the *Dreadnought* to the nuclear age).

D3. Masson (Philippe), Battesti (Michèle), Favier (Jacques), *Marine et constructions navales, 1789–1989.* Paris, Lavauzelle, 1989, in-4°, 144 p., illustrations en noir et en couleurs (Navies and naval construction, 1789–1989).

D4. *Comité de documentation Historique de la Marine, Communications, 1986–1987 et 1987–1988.* 1989, in-8°, 208 p., planches, carte.

D5. *Comité de documentation Historique de la Marine, Communications, 1988–1989.* 1990, in-8°, 227 p., planches, cartes, photos.

D7. *Comité de documentation Historique de la Marine,Communications, 1989–1990.* 1992, in-8°, 159 p., figures, cartes, photos.

D8. *Comité de documentation Historique de la Marine,Communications, 1990–1991.* (à paraître).

7

Germany

East Germany

Paul Heider, Sometime Director,
Militärgeschichtliches Institut der DDR

PREFACE

The following article has itself become a document of contemporary history. The circumstances under which it has been written no longer exist. On October 3rd, 1990 the German Democratic Republic (GDR or Deutsche Demokratische Republik [DDR]) joined the Federal Republic of Germany (FRG or Bundesrepublik Deutschland [BRD]). The considerably reduced East German Army was taken over by the German Federal Armed Forces (*Bundeswehr*). The facilities of the former Institute of Military History (*Militärgeschichtliches Institut*/MGI) of the GDR are now the home of the Military History Research Institute (*Militärgeschichtliches Forschungsamt*/MGFA), which was transferred from Freiburg (in the south of Germany) to Potsdam in 1994. Thus, at the end of that year the dissolution of the MGI and its partial incorporation into the MGFA was completed.

This paper was written at the turn of the year 1989–1990. It was a time characterized by rapid political and social changes. The eventual outcome of the developments was by no means clear, in particular with regard to the relations between the two German states and their institutions. In accordance with the predominant political opinions in those days, my article was based on the assumption that the MGI would continue to exist within the framework of a reformed democratic GDR. Now free from political and ideological constraints, the author as well as other members of the institute explored a new conception of history, including a critical assessment of what had already been achieved. Taking into account the time when the article was written, the reader will realize that the considerations expressed therein could not avoid being fragmentary in nature and could scarcely go beyond the initial starting points.

Notwithstanding certain justified reservations, the presentation of the institute's achievements may show that there was a potential for a new conception of history among the historians at the institute. At least part of them had the will and the capacity for a new approach to history. My considerations expressed with regard to the perspectives of the MGI, however, were soon to become irrelevant. From March 1990—the date of the first free elections in the GDR—the transition of the GDR into the FRG developed with breathtaking speed. The accompanying changes of the elites affected the institutes of history and the respective chairs and with them the MGI accordingly. As early as September 1990, part of the staff was retired prematurely or had to look for an entirely different work. From the seventeen historians who had been employed on a provisional basis on October 3, 1990, only three younger colleagues eventually succeeded in getting permanent employment at the MGFA. The library of the MGI was incorporated into the collection of the MGFA and is open to the interested public. Some of the former staff of the MGI remain in contact with the MGFA and occasionally cooperate with it in an informal way.

• • •

This contribution is now (June 1992) only of historical interest. The Military History Institute no longer exists. The author wrote the contribution in the fall and winter of 1989–1990. It was a time of stormy change in the former German Democratic Republic, with still unclear perspectives of the wider development. When in late summer and fall of 1989 the protest movement discontent swelled more and more and assumed mass proportions, there was at first more freedom for the people in the DDR. Soon demands for social equalization with the Federal Republic appeared, and toward unification of both German states as well. In this situation the reformed government of the DDR hoped that the interests of the victorious powers of the Second World War, particularly the USSR, by which the existence of the two German states had been made possible, could prevent a complete dam break. But the government of the Federal Republic still did not believe the time was ripe for a reunification. They reckoned not only on strong opposition on the part of the Soviet Union, but also with resentments and reservations by their own allies. But in 1945 the German empire lay on the ground and the German partition was a result of tugs by the victorious powers on Germany. For forty-five years this appeared to be a firm part of the peace settlement of 1945. On this basis the government of the Federal Republic at first did not want to hand over relations to a liberalized DDR. But the DDR government submitted suitable proposals, and at a somewhat later moment there was even the idea that in a united German state and two German armies could exist next to each other for a certain time.

However, until the summer of 1990 all of these considerations were irrelevant. [I will not discuss here the foundations of carrying out] the process of the dissolution of the DDR and the annexation of its territory by the Federal Republic at a breathtaking speed. Those powers, which the democratically reforming DDR needed to continue, the existence of two German states with normalizing relations, lacked the backing of the people. Instead of volunteering for a new experiment, they sought protection in the scientifically powerful Federal Republic. That had far-reaching consequences for the planning of the political, social, and economic relations in the new federal lands of the territory of the former DDR in connection with which the consequences for the humanities are especially sweeping.

In congruence with the prevailing political opinion in the winter of 1989–1990, the author's contribution went on the continued existence of the Military Institute in a democratically renewed DDR. Counted among his considerations, it was soon arranged that objective research contacts with the Military History Research office of the Federal Republic could result and an enlargement and deepening of the existing international connections of the institute became possible. A fundamentally new view of the relations of science and politics came as a possibly sweeping change in the ideology of the field of military history, which the renewed use of science for politics excludes, appears to be an essential supposition. One must bear in mind the date of a contribution, indeed understand the then-current separate considerations which made for required unlimited necessary changes, and fragmentation had to remain and could scarcely be left out of a first draft.

Despite a necessary proviso to the considerations of the time of what we know today, the presented scientific results of the institute indeed show nevertheless that its researcher's intellectual powers were engaged in a new scientific understanding. Indeed, the subjective purpose of the realization of plurality in the consciousness from freedom of the science field was coming into being or was able to be at least not out of the question from the beginning. Investigating this angle and proving it was for the most part not allowed. The institute was dissolved. Valuable intellectual potential for the continued work on the military history of the DDR was lost. The researchers were prematurely retired or had to go to unfamiliar employment. With that, the fate of the military historians resembled the numerous other researchers of the former DDR. Besides ideologically and politically influenced decisions of the standard, established instances, the old Federal Republic of Germany contributed to this development as well by rashly throwing away the DDR identity of East German historiography from diverse foundations.

PUBLICATIONS OF THE *MILITÄRGESCHICHTLICHES INSTITUT DER DDR* (SELECTION)

German Abbreviations Retained in Translated Titles

BRD *Bundesrepublik Deutschland* (Federal Republic of Germany)

DDR *Deutsche Demokratische Republik* (German Democratic Republic)

KPD *Kommunistische Partei Deutschlands* (Communist Party of Germany)

NVA *Nationale Volksarmee* (National People's Army) (DDR)

SED *Sozialistische Einheitspartei Deutschlands* (Socialist Unity Party of Germany) (DDR)

Terms such as *Landsknecht, Landswehr, Reichswehr, Wehrmacht,* and *Bundeswehr* have specific chronological meaning within German history and remain untranslated.

General

1. Brühl, Reinhard, *Militärgeschichte und Kriegspolitik. Zur Militärgeschichtsschreibung des preußisch–deutschen General-stabes 1816–1945,* Berlin 1973, 431 S. (Military history and the politics of war. Illustrated by the historical military writings of the Prusso–German general staff, 1816–1945).
2. *Der deutsche Militarismus in Geschichte und Gegenwart. Studien, Probleme, Analysen.* Herausgeberkollektive unter Leitung von Karl Nuß, Berlin 1980, 301 S. (German militarism in history and the present. Studies, problems, analyses).
3. Förster, Gerhard; Otto, Helmut; Schnitter, Helmut, *Der preußisch–deutsche Generalstab 1870–1963. Zu Seiner politischen Rolle in der Geschichte,* Berlin 1964, 306 S.; erweiterte und überarb. Aufl., 1966, 575 S. (The Prusso–German general staff. Its political role in history).
4. Förster, Gerhard; Paulus, Nikolaus, *Abriß der Geschichte der Panzerwaffe,* Berlin 1977, 339 S.; 3. Aufl., 1982, 338 S. (Sketch of the history of Panzer force).
5. Förster, Gerhard; Hoch, Peter; Müller, Reinhold, *Uniformen europäischer Armeen,* Berlin 1978, 291 S. (Uniforms of European armies).

6. *Imperialistische Militärblockpolitik. Geschichte und Gegenwart.* Autorenkollektiv unter Leitung von Albrecht Charisius und O. A. Rsheschewski, Berlin 1980, 423 S. (Politics of imperialistic military alliances. Past and present).
7. *Klassenbrüder—Waffenbrüder. Gemeinsame revolutionäre militärische Traditionen der Nationalen Volksarmee der DDR und der Polnischen Armee.* Autorenkollektiv. Wissenschaftliche Gesamtredaktion Paul Heider und Eugeniusz Kozlowski, Berlin 1988, 373 S. (Class brothers—brothers in arms. Common revolutionary military traditions of the National People's Army of the DDR and the Polish Army).
8. *Kurzer Abriß der Militärgeschichte von den Anfängen der Geschichte des deutschen Volkes bis 1945.* Autorenkollektiv unter Leitung von Gerhard Förster, Berlin 1974, 471 S.; 2. Aufl., 1977, 422 S.; 3., erweiterte Aufl. unter dem Titel: Kurzer Abriß der deutschen Militärgeschichte, 1984, 437 S. (Short sketch of military history from the origins of the history of the German people to 1945).
9. Renn, Ludwig; Schnitter, Helmut, *Krieger, Landsknecht und Soldat,* Berlin 1973, 207 S. (Fighter, Landsknecht and soldier).
10. Schnitter, Helmut, *". . . also nötlich ist auch das Schwert." Streifzüge durch die deutsche Militärgeschichte,* Berlin 1984, 181 S. (". . . thus, the sword is also possible." Expeditions through German military history).
11. Schnitter, Helmut, *Von Salamis bis Dien Bien Phu. Schlachten aus drei Jahrtausenden,* Berlin 1987, 268 S. (From Salamis to Dien Bien Phu. Battles over three millennia).
12. *Wörterbuch zur deutschen Militärgeschichte.* Bd. 1, 2, Berlin 1985, 1119 S.; 2., durchgesehen Aufl., 1987, 1119 S. (Dictionary of German military history).
13. *Vom Bauernheer zur Volksarmee, Fortschrittliche Traditionen des deutschen Volkes.* Autorenkollektiv unter Leitung von Helmut Schnitter, Berlin 1979, 253 S. (From peasant to people's army. Progressive traditions of the German people).

Up to 1945

Series: Studies in Military History

14. Wunderlich, Werner, *Marine wider den Frieden. Zur Entwicklung der militärpolitischen, strategischen und operativen Konzeption des deutschen Militarismus im Ostseeraum,* Berlin 1961, 123 S. (Navy against peace. The development of grand strategic, strategic, and operational concepts of German militarism in the Baltic).
15. Herbell, Hajo, Saat des Verderbens. *Zur jüngsten Geschichte der Kriegsideologie des deutschen Militarismus, dargestellt an den "Schicksalsfragen der Gegenwart,"* Berlin 1961, 136 S. (Seed of ruin. The current history of war thought of German militarism presented within the context of the "destiny questions of the present").

16. Höhn, Hans, *Feuerkraft der Aggressoren. Zur Entwicklung der Artillerie in den Landstreitkräften des deutschen Militarismus von 1935 bis 1960,* Berlin 1961, 156 S. (Offensive firepower. The evolution of artillery in the ground forces of German militarism from 1935 to 1960).
17. Wünsche, Wolfgang, *Strategie der Niederlage. Zur imperialistischen deutschen Militärwissenschaft zwischen den beiden Weltkriegen,* Berlin 1961, 139 S. (Strategy of defeat. Imperialistic German military science between the world wars).
18. Oeckel, Heinz, *Volkswehr gegen Militarismus. Zur Milizfrage in der proletarischen Militärpolitik in Deutschland von der Mitte des 19. Jahrhunderts bis zum ersten Weltkrieg,* Berlin 1962, 145 S. (Volkswehr against militarism. The militia question in proletarian military politics in Germany from the mid-nineteenth century to the First World War).
19. Kolmsee, Peter, *Der Partisanenkampf in der Sowjetunion. Über Charakter, Inhalt und Formen des Partisanenkampfes in der USSR 1941–1944,* Berlin 1963, 132 S. (Partisan war in the Soviet Union. Concerning the character, contents, and forms of the partisan struggle in the USSR, 1941–1944).
20. Helmert, Heinz, *Militärsystem und Streitkräfte im Deutschen Bund am Vorabend des Preußisch–Österreichischen Krieges von 1866,* Berlin 1964, 263 S. (Military systems and military forces of the German Confederation on the eve of the Austro–Prussian war of 1866).
21. Otto, Helmut, *Schlieffen und der Generalstab. Der preußischdeutsche Generalstab unter der Leitung des Generals von Schlieffen 1891–1905,* Berlin 1966, 271 S. (Schlieffen and the general staff. The Prusso–German general staff under the direction of General von Schlieffen, 1891–1905).
22. Schnitter, Helmut, *Militärwesen und Militärpublizistik. Die militärische Zeitschriftenpublizistik in der Geschichte des bürgerlichen Militärwesens in Deutschland,* Berlin 1967, 273 S. (Military structure and military journalism. Military magazine journalism in the history of bourgeois military organization in Germany).
23. Förster, Gerhard, *Totaler Krieg und Blitzkrieg. Die Theorie des totalen Krieges und des Blitzkrieges in der Militärdoktrin des faschistischen Deutschlands am Vorabend des zweiten Weltkrieges,* Berlin 1967, 255 S. (Total war and blitzkrieg. The theory of total war and blitzkrieg in the military doctrine of Fascist Germany on the eve of the Second World War).
24. Oeckel, Heinz, *Die revolutionäre Volkswehr 1918/19. Die deutsche Arbeiterklasse im Kampf um die revolutionäre Volkswehr (November 1918 bis Mai 1919),* Berlin 1968, 326 S. (The revolutionary Volkswehr, 1918–19. The German working class in the revolutionary Volkswehr's struggle [November 1918 to May 1919]).
25. Ramme, Alwin, *Der Sicherheitsdienst der SS. Zu seiner Funktion im faschistischen Machtapparat und im Besatzungsregime des sogenannten Generalgouvernements Polen,* Berlin 1970, 324 S. (The security service of the SS. Its function in the Fascist power structure and in the occupation regime of the so-called general government of Poland).

26. Hübner, Werner, *Die Gesellschaft für Wehrkunde. Die Gesellschaft für Wehrkunde und ihre Rolle im System der Militarisierung Westdeutschlands (1952–1968),* Berlin 1970, 237 S. (The defense intelligence community. The defense intelligence community and its role in the plan to militarize West Germany [1952–1968]).
27. Helmert, Heinz, *Kriegspolitik und Strategie. Politische und militärische Ziele der Kriegführung des preußischen General-stabes vor der Reichsgründung (1859–1869),* Berlin 1970, 326 S. (War policy and strategy. Political and military aims of the war leadership of the Prussian general staff prior to the founding of the German Empire [1859–1869]).
28. Stenzel, Ernst, *Die Kriegführung des deutschen Imperialismus und das Völkerrecht. Zur Planung und Vorbereitung des deutschen Imperialismus auf die barbarische Kriegführung im ersten und zweiten Weltkrieg, dargestellt an den vorherrschenden Ansichten zu den Gesetzen und Gebräuchen des Landkrieges (1900–1945),* Berlin 1973, 232 S. (The warfare of German imperialism and international law. The planning and preparation of German imperialism by the barbaric war leadership of the First and Second World Wars in light of the prevailing views on the laws and usages of land warfare [1900–1945]).
29. Hoyer, Siegfried, *Das Militärwesen im deutschen Bauernkrieg 1524–1526,* Berlin 1975, 250 S. (Military organization in the German Peasants' War, 1524–1526).
30. Heider, Paul, *Antifaschistischer Kampf und revolutionäre Militärpolitik. Zur Militärpolitik der KPD von 1933 bis 1939 im Kampf gegen Faschismus und Kriegsvorbereitung, für Frieden, Demokratie und Sozialismus,* Berlin 1976, 311 S. (Antifascist struggle and revolutionary military policy. The military policy of the KPD from 1933 to 1939 in the struggle against fascism and war preparation, for peace, democracy, and socialism).
31. Schnitter, Helmut, *Volk und Landesdefension. Volksaufgebote, Defensionswerke, Landmilizen in den deutschen Territorien vom 15. bis zum 18. Jahrhundert,* Berlin 1977, 248 S. (People and provincial defense. Conscription, fortifications, and provincial militias in the German territories from the fifteenth to the eighteenth centuries).
32. Lakowski, Richard; Wunderlich, Werner, *Zwischen Flottenschlacht und Zufuhrkrieg. Die Entwicklung des seestrategischen Denkens im imperialistischen Deutschland in Vorbereitung des zaeiten Weltkrieges,* Berlin 1978, 242 S. (Between naval war and *Zufuhrkrieg.* The development of naval strategic thought in imperialistic Germany in preparation for the Second World War).
33. Kern, Wolfgang, *Die innere Funktion der Wehrmacht 1933–1939,* Berlin 1979, 266 S. (The inner workings of the Wehrmacht, 1933–1939).
34. Schmidt, Dorothea, *Die preußische Landwehr. Ein Beitrag zur Geschichte der allgemeinen Wehrpflicht in Preußen zwischen 1813 und 1830,* Berlin 1981, 251 S. (The Prussian *Landwehr.* A sketch of the history of general conscription in Prussia between 1813 and 1830).

35. Doehler, Edgar; Fischer, Egbert, *Revolutionäre Militärpolitik gegen faschistische Gefahr. Militärpolitische Probleme des antifaschistischen Kampfes der KPD von 1929 bis 1933,* Berlin 1982, 245 S. (Revolutionary military policy against the fascist menace. Military political problems of the KPD from 1929 to 1933).
36. Rahne, Hermann, *Mobilmachung. Militärische Mobilmachungsplanung und-technik in Preußen und im Deutschen Reich von Mitte des 19. Jahrhunderts bis zum zweiten Weltkrieg,* Berlin 1983, 308 S. (Mobilization. Military mobilization planning and implementation in Prussia and the German Reich from the mid-nineteenth century to the Second World War).
37. Geßner, Klaus, *Geheime Feldpolizei. Zur Funktion und Organisation des geheimpolizeilichen Exekutivorgans der faschistischen Wehrmacht,* Berlin 1986, 227 S. (Field security police. The function and organization of the field security police executive agency of the Fascist *Wehrmacht*).
38. Schnitter, Helmut; Schmidt, Thomas, *Absolutismus und Heer. Zur Entwicklung des Militärwesens im Spätfeudalismus,* Berlin 1987, 215 S. (Absolutism and the army. The development of military forces in the late Feudal Period).
39. Menger, Manfred, *Deutschland und Finnland im Zweiten Weltkrieg. Genesis und Scheitern einer Militärallianz,* Berlin 1988, 276 S. (Germany and Finland in the Second World War. Genesis and breakdown of a military alliance).

Series: Sketches in Military History

40. Förster, Gerhard, *Carl von Clausewitz. Lebensbild eines patriotischen Militärs und fortschrittlichen Militärtheoretikers,* Berlin 1983, 55 S. (Carl von Clausewitz. Biographical sketch of a military patriot and progressive military theoretician).
41. Lampe, Jürgen, *Rosa Luxemburg. Im Kampf gegen Militarismus, Kriegsvorbereitung und Krieg,* Berlin 1984, 63 S. (Rosa Luxemburg. In the fight against militarism, war preparation, and war).
42. Schnitter, Helmut, *Der Bauernkrieg in Thüringen,* Berlin 1984, 52 S. (The Pheasant's War in Thüringen).
43. Lakowski, Richard; Dorst, Klaus, *Berlin Frühjahr 1945,* Berlin 1985, 95 S. (Berlin, spring 1945).
44. Wolff, Willy, *Auf der richtigen Seite. Zum Wirken der Front-organisation des Nationalkomitees "Freies Deutschland,"* Berlin 1985, 55 S. (On the right side. The work of the front organization of the National Committee for a "Free Germany").
45. Schmiedel, Karl, *Johann Philipp Becker, General der Revolution,* Berlin 1986, 71 S. (Johann Philipp Becker, general of the revolution).
46. Gudzent, Christa, *Niedhardt von Gneisenau,* Berlin 1987, 63 S. (Niedhardt von Gneisenau).
47. Neffe, Dieter, *Kämpfe im Süden Afrikas (1652–1980),* Berlin 1987, 64 S. (Struggles in South Africa, 1652–1980).

48. Bauer, Frank, *Die Völkerschlacht bei Leipzig,* Berlin 1988, 63 S. (The people's battle near Leipzig).
49. Groehler, Olaf; Erfurth, Helmut, *Hugo Junkers. Ein politisches Essay,* Berlin 1989, 60 S. (Hugo Junkers. A political essay).
50. Usczeck, Hansjürgen, *Gerhard von Scharnhorst,* Berlin 1989, 55 S. (Gerhard von Scharnhorst).
51. Schnitter, Helmut, *Aber am Volk zweifle ich nicht. Thomas Müntzer—Theologe und Revolutionär,* Berlin 1989, 64 S. (But I do not doubt the people. Thomas Müntzer—theologian and revolutionary).

Monographs

52. *Auf antisowjetischem Kriegskurs. Studien zur militärischen Vorbereitung des deutschen Imperialismus auf die Aggression gegen die USSR (1933–1941).* Hrsg. unter Leitung von Hans Höhn, Berlin 1970, 477 S. (On the course of the anti-Soviet War. Studies of the military preparations of German imperialism for the aggression against the USSR [1933–1941]).
53. Clausewitz, Carl von, *Ausgewärische Schriften.* Herausgegeben von Gerhard Förster und Dorothea Schmidt unter Mitarbeit von Christa Gudzent, Berlin 1980, 546 S.; 2. Aufl., 1981, 546 S. (Select writings).
54. *Deutschland im zweiten Weltkrieg.* Autorenkollektiv unter Leitung von Wolfgang Schumann und Gerhart Hass. Bd. 1–6, Berlin 1974–1985, 644, 616, 670, 617, 702, 823 S. (Germany in the Second World War).
55. Dreetz, Dieter; Geßner, Klaus; Sperling, Heinz, *Bewaffnete Kämpfe in Deutschland 1918–1923,* Berlin 1988, 382 S. (Armed struggles in Germany, 1918–1923).
56. *Der erste Weltkrieg. Dokumente.* Ausgewählt und eingeleitet von Helmut Otto und Karl Schmiedel, Berlin 1977, 420 S. (The First World War. Documents).
57. *Fall Barbarossa. Dokumente zur Vorbereitung der faschistischen Wehrmacht auf die Aggression gegen die Sowjetunion (1940/41).* Ausgewählt und eingeleitet von Erhard Moritz, Berlin 1970, 437 S. (Operation Barbarossa. Documents concerning the preparation of Fascist *Wehrmacht* for the aggression against the Soviet Union, 1940–1941).
58. *Das Fiasko der antisowjetischen Aggression. Studien zur Kriegführung des deutschen Imperialismus gegen die USSR (1941–1945).* Hrsg. von Erhard Moritz, Berlin 1978, 361 S. (The fiasco of anti-Soviet aggression. Studies of the war leadership of German imperialism against the Soviet Union [1941–1945]).
59. Förster, Gerhard; Helmert, Heinz; Schnitter, Helmut, *Der zweite Weltkrieg. Militärhistorischer Abriß,* Berlin 1972, 587 S.; 5. Aufl., durchgesehen, bearb. und ergänzt von Paul Heider und Richard Lakowski, 1989, 394 S. (The Second World War. A military historical sketch).
60. *Geschichte der Militärpolitik der KPD (1918–1945).* Autorenkollektiv unter Leitung von Paul Heider, Berlin 1987, 450 S. (A history of the military policy of the KPD [1918–1945]).

61. Gneisenau, August Wilhelm Anton Neidhardt, *Ausgewählte militärsche Schriften.* Hrsg. von Gerhard Förster und Christa Gudzent, Berlin 1984, 475 S. (Selected military writings).
62. Hanisch, Wilfried, *Die Hundertschaften der Arbeiterwehr. Die Proletarischen Hundertschaften 1923 in Sachsen,* Berlin 1958, 105 S. (The hundred men of the workers' defense. The proletarian hundred in 1923 Saxony).
63. Helmert, Heinz, *Friedrich Engels. Die Anfänge der proletarischen Militärtheorie (1842–1852). Eine biografische Skizze,* Berlin 1970, 113 S. (Friedrich Engels. The origins of proletarian military theory, 1842–1852. A biographical sketch).
64. Hennicke, Otto, *Die Rote Ruhrarmee,* Berlin 1956, 117 S. (The red army of the Ruhr).
65. *Militarismus gegen Sowjetmacht 1917 bis 1919. Das Fiasko der ersten antisowjetischen Aggression des deutschen Militarismus.* Autorenkollektiv unter der Gesamtredaktion von Otto Hennichke, Berlin 1967, 303 S. (Militarism against Soviet power, 1917–1919. The fiasco of German militarism's first anti-Soviet aggression).
66. Müller, Norbert, *Wehrmacht und Okkupation 1941–1944. Zur Rolle der Wehrmacht und ihrer Führungsorgane im Okkupations-regime des faschistischen deutschen Imperialismus auf sowjetischem Territorium,* Berlin 1971, 356 S. (*Wehrmacht* and occupation, 1941–1944. The role of the *Wehrmacht* and its command agencies in occupation regimes of Fascist German imperialism on Soviet territory).
67. *1945. Das Jahr der endgültigen Niederlage der faschistischen Wehrmacht. Dokumente.* Ausgewählt und eingeleitet von Gerhard Förster und Richard Lakowski, Berlin 1975, 462 S.; 2. Aufl., 1985, 431 S. (The year of the final defeat of the Fascist *Wehrmacht.* Documents).
68. Nuß, Karl, *Militär und Wiederaufrüstung in der Weimarer Republik. Zur politischen Rolle und Entwicklung der Reichswehr,* Berlin 1977, 371 S. (The military and rearmament in the Weimar Republic. The political role and development of the *Reichswehr*).
69. *Okkupation–Raub–Vernichtung. Dokumente zur Besatzungs-politik der faschistischen Wehrmacht auf sowjetischem Territorium 1941–1944.* Hrsg. von Norbert Müller, Berlin 1980, 426 S. (Occupation–robbery–destruction. Documents on the occupation policy of the Fascist *Wehrmacht* on Soviet territory, 1941–1944).
70. Otto, Helmut; Schmiedel, Karl; Schnitter, Helmut, *Der erste Weltkrieg. Militärhistorischer Abriß,* Berlin 1964, 303 S.; 3., völlig überarb. und ergänzte Aufl., 1977, 420 S. (The First World War. A military historical sketch).
71. Scharnhorst, Gerhard, *Ausgewählte militärische Schriften.* Hrsg. von Hansjürgen Usczeck und Christa Gudzent, Berlin 1986, 440 S. (Selected military writings).
72. Schmiedel, Karl; Schnitter, Helmut, *Bürgerkrieg und Intervention 1918 bis 1922. Militärhistorischer Abriß des Bürgerkrieges und der ausländischen Intervention in Sowjetrußland,* Berlin 1970, 381 S. (Civil war and intervention, 1918 to 1922. Military historical sketch of the civil war and the foreign intervention in Soviet Russia).

73. Schützle, Jurt, *Reichswehr wider die Nation. Zur Rolle der Reichswehr bei der Vorbereitung und Errichtung der faschistischen Diktatur im Deutschland (1929–1933),* Berlin 1963, 249 S. (*Reichswehr* against the nation. The role of the *Reichswehr* in the preparation and establishment of the Fascist dictatorship in Germany [1929–1933]).
74. Wolff, Willy, *An der Seite der Roten Armee. Zum Wirken des Nationalkomitees "Freies Deutschland" an der sowjetisch–deutschen Front 1943 bis 1945,* Berlin 1973, 333 S.; 3., überarb. Aufl., 1982, 349 S. (On the side of the Red Army. The work of the "Free Germany" National Committee on the Soviet–German front, 1943 to 1945).
75. *Der zweite Weltkrieg. Dokumente.* Ausgewählt und eingeleitet von Gerhard Förster und Olaf Groehler, Berlin 1972, 587 S.; 3., überarb. und erweiterte Auf., 1989, 523 S. (The Second World War. Documents).

After 1945 (*Nationale Volksarmee*/Warsaw Pact)

76. *Armee für Frieden und Sozialismus. Geschichte der Nationalen Volksarmee der DDR.* Autorenkollektiv unter Leitung von Reinhard Brühl, Berlin 1985, 743 S.; 2., erweiterte Aufl., 1987, 807 S. (Army for peace and socialism. A history of the National People's Army of the DDR).
77. *Für den zuverlässigen Schutz der Deutschen Demokratischen Republik. Beiträge zur Entwicklung der Nationalen Volksarmee und des Systems der sozialistischen Landesverteidigung.* Redaktion unter Leitung von Günther Glasser, Berlin 1969, 355 S. (For the reliable protection of the German Democratic Republic. Contributions to the development of the National People's Army and the socialist provincial defense).
78. *Für ein sozialistisches Vaterland. Lebensbilder deutscher Kommunisten und Aktivisten der ersten Stunde.* Autorenkollektiv unter Leitung von Paul Heider, Berlin 1981, 292 S. (For a socialist Fatherland. Biographies of German communists and activists of the first rank).
79. Israel, Ulrich; Mehl, Hans; Schäfer, Knut, *Vom Küstenschutzboot zum Raketenschiff. Schiffe und Boote der Volksmarine,* Berlin 1986, 225 S.; 2., überarb. und erweiterte Aufl., 1989, 229 S. (From coastal gunboat to missile ship. Ships and boats of the People's Navy).
80. *Lebendige Tradition. Lebensbilder deutscher Kommunisten und Antifaschisten.* Herausgeberkollektiv unter Leitung von Paul Heider, Berlin 1974, 2 Halbbände zu je 321 bzw. 287 S. (Living tradition. Biographies of German communists and anti-Fascists).
81. *Militärpolitik für Sozialismus und Frieden. Grundfragen der Politik der SED zum militärischen Schutz der revolutionären Errungenschaften und des Friedens von der Gründung der DDR bis zur Gestaltung der entwickelten sozialistischen Gesellschaft.* Autorenkollektiv unter Leitung von Günther Glaser, Berlin 1976, 170 S. (Military policy for socialism and peace. Fundamental questions concerning the policy of the SED for the military protection of revolutionary achievements and peace from the founding of the DDR to the formation of the developing socialist society).

82. *Die Militär- und Sicherheitspolitik der SED 1945 bis 1988. Dokumente und Materialien.* Hrsg. und eingeleitet von einem Kollektiv unter Leitung von Klaus-Peter Meißner, Berlin 1989, 661 S. (The military and security policies of the SED, 1945 to 1988. Documents and materials).
83. *Die NVA in der sozialistischen Verteidigungskoalition. Auswahl von Dokumenten und Materialien 1955/1956 bis 1981.* Herausgeberkollektiv unter Leitung von Wilfried Hanisch, Berlin 1982, 490 S. (The NVA in the Socialist Defense Coalition. Selection from documents and materials, 1955–1956 to 1981).
84. *Zeittafel zur Militärgeschichte der Deutschen Demokratischen Republik 1949 bis 1984.* Autorenkollektiv unter Leitung von Toni Nelles, Berlin 1986, 569 S.; 2., erweiterte und durchgesehene Aufl., 1989, 658 S. (Chronology of the military history of the German Democratic Republic, 1949 to 1984).

After 1945 (*Bundeswehr*/NATO)

85. *Bundeswehr—antinational und aggressiv. Chronik, Fakten, Dokumente.* Ausgewählt und eingeleitet von Siegfried Zeimer, Berlin 1969,563 S. (Bundeswehr—Antinational and aggressive. Chronicle, facts, documents).
86. *Bundeswehr—Armee der Revanche. Probleme der Entwicklung der Bundeswehr.* Autorenkollektiv unter Leitung von Job von Witzleben, Berlin 1965, 516 S.; 2., völlig überarb. Aufl. unter dem Titel *Bundeswehr—Armee für den Krieg. Aufbau und Rolle der Bundeswehr als Aggressionsinstrument des west-deutchen Imperialismus,* Berlin 1968, 591 S. (*Bundeswehr*—Army of revenge. Problems of the development of the *Bundeswehr.* Completely revised edition under the title *Bundeswehr*—Army for war. The build up and role of the *Bundeswehr* as an instrument of aggression of West German imperialism).
87. Charisius, Albrecht; Mader, Julius, *Nicht länger geheim. Entwicklung, System und Arbeitsweise des imperialistischen deutschen Geheimdienstes,* Berlin 1969, 631 S.; 4., überarb. undergänzte Aufl., 1980, 783 S. (No longer secret. Development, doctrine, and method of operation of the imperialist German security service).
88. Charisius, Albrecht; Lambrecht, Rainer; Dorst, Klaus, *Weltgendarm USA. Der militärische Interventionismus der USA seit der Jahrundertwende.* Kurzgefaßter Überblick, Berlin 1983, 260 S.; 2., überarb. und erweiterte Aufl., 1984, 276 S.; 3., aktualisierte Aufl., 1985, 279 S. (The United States as world police. The military intervention of the USA since the turn of the century).
89. Dobias, Tibor; Charisius, Albrecht; Roschlau, Wolfgang, *Militärpolitik kontra europäische Sicherheit und Entspannung. Zur Reorganisation der Bundeswehr der BRD.* Ein dokumentarischer Abriß, Berlin 1975, 196 S. (Military policy against European security and détente. The reorganization of the *Bundeswehr* of the BRD).
90. Heimann, Bernhard, *Krieg in Vietnam 1946–1954. Die Aggression des französischen Imperialismus in Indochina,* Berlin 1987, 107 S. (War in Vietnam, 1946–1954. The aggression of French imperialism in Indochina).

91. Lambrecht, Rainer, *Der Krieg im Südatlantik,* Berlin 1986, 111 S.; 2., durchgesehene Aufl., 1989, 111 S. (The war in the South Atlantic).
92. *Militärgeschichte der BRD. Abriß. 1949 bis zur Gegenwart.* Autorenkollektiv unter Leitung von Tibor Dobias, Berlin 1989, 544 S. (Military history of the BRD. Sketch. 1949 to the present).
93. *Militarismus heute. Wesen und Erscheinungsformen des Militarismus der Gegenwart.* Autorenkollektivunter der Gesamtredaktion von Albrecht Charisius, Klaus Engelhardt und Horst Fiedler, Berlin 1979, 357 S.; 2. Aufl., 1981, 353 S. (Militarism today. The character and manifestations of present-day militarism).
94. *NATO–Chronik–Fakten–Dokumente. Zur aggressiven Militärpolitik des Nordatlantikpakts 1949–1982.* Autorenkollektiv unter Leitung von Tibor Dobias, Berlin 1983, 377 S. (NATO–Chronicle–Facts–Documents. On the military policy of the North Atlantic Alliance, 1949–1982).
95. *NATO—Staaten und militärische Konflikte. Militärhistorischer Abriß.* Autorenkollektiv unter der Redaktion von P. A. Shilin, Reinhard Brühl und Kazimierz Sobczak, Berlin 1988, 407 S. (NATO—states and military conflicts. A military historical sketch).
96. *NATO. Strategie und Streitkräfte. Die Rolle der Militärorganisatin des Nordatlantikpakts in der aggressiven Politik des Imperialismus 1949–1975.* Militärhistorischer Abriß. Autorenkollektiv unter Leitung von Albrecht Charisius und Wladyslaw Kozaczuk, Berlin 1976, 489 S.; 2., bearb. und erweiterte Aufl., 1980, 479 S. (NATO. Strategy and armed forces. The role of the military organization of the North Atlantic Alliance in the aggressive policies of imperialism, 1949–1975).

The Militärgeschichtliches Forschungsamt (Military History Research Institute) of the German Armed Forces

Wilhelm Deist and Roland Förster, of the Institute
Translated by William Voss

The MGFA was established in 1957, shortly after German forces, the *Bundeswehr,* were built up in 1955 as a result of the Cold War and as part of Western security. The MGFA has been a subdivision of the German Ministry of Defense, since a "Central Military Agency" (*Zentrale Militärische Dienststelle*) under the forces' deputy chief of staff (*Stellvertreter des General-inspekteurs der Bundeswehr*), to be exact, was established in 1957. It is led by the "*Amtschef*," a brigadier general (presently, in 1994, BGen Dr. Günter Roth).

One official task of the MGFA is the "research and publication of military history, seen as part of history in general, and conducted in accordance with the methods of academic historiography." This task is carried out by the research department (*Forschungsabteilung*) under the direction of the chief historian (presently Dir. and Prof. Dr. Wilhelm Deist).

In 1978 a new department for historical education (*Abteilung Historische Bildung*) was added to the MGFA. Basically, this department is responsible for the second official task of the MGFA, the "improvement of the historical education within the armed forces." The director of this department is the director of historical education and deputy chief of military history (presently Colonel [GS] Dr. Roland G. Foerster).

Looking at methods and approaches, military history has come a long way in the German forces. The Prussian and German general staff, as it existed from 1809 until the end of World War II, considered military history to be one of the most important and formative means of training the military mind. Using a strictly utilitarian approach, such a conception of military history avoided political, economic, and social implications and the interdependencies of military actions; therefore it was lacking to a considerable extent an analytical and critical scope.

When the MGFA was set up on 1 January 1957, it was clear from the very beginning that military history had to play its part in the new conception of the *Bundeswehr*. It had to be researched, published, and taught along the lines and standards of the scholarly approach of academic history. From then on, its major objective had to be the unabridged and unveiled examination of Germany's political and military past, in order to better understand the challenges of the present. This certainly did not exclude dealing with the history of strategies and operations, as long as analytical and critical methods were applied. Military history, therefore, as understood by the MGFA, has always meant the comprehensive analysis of the role of the military as an integral part of the overall political, economic, and social process within a national and international framework of reference.

Concerning the subjects and topics to be researched by the MGFA, they were determined by the very near past of German history (i.e., mostly the history of the twentieth century). It was clear that the causes, prerequisites and implications of World War II were given the highest degree of attention, concerning mainly German society and the *Wehrmacht* within the National Socialist (Nazi) regime from a German point of view. Another major field of research interest has been the results of World War II in Europe, particularly the integration of Germany's western zones of occupation into the Western world, the foundation of the Federal Republic, and the establishment of a military contribution for the defense of the West: in short, Germany's surprisingly quick rearmament and her inclusion in the Atlantic Alliance. Finally, the MGFA has started looking into the very complicated and diversified historical problem of the formation of NATO and the Western defense system, not from a German point of view this time, but from the perspective of the alliance itself.

In order to cover these three major research projects, the research department of the MGFA has set up several teams of historians under the responsibility of three project directors. The first project is a ten-volume series with the title *Das Deutsche Reich und der Zweite Weltkrieg.* This work was considered to be a particularly urgent assignment from the beginnings of the MGFA. After a vast number of documents, previously held by the former occupation forces, had been returned to German custody, and after extensive preparational work, it became possible to start research on a wide scale. The first volume was published in 1979, analyzing the political, economical, social, and ideological preconditions and causes for World War II in Germany. To date, six volumes have appeared (of Volume 5 only the first part of a double volume), and have met with broad and positive response. The MGFA is very proud that, following wide international interest, the complete work is being published by Oxford University Press in English. Volume 1 and 2 appeared in 1990 and 1991, respectively, and Volume 3 followed in 1993.

Since 1974 another group of scholars have researched and written a four-volume project in accordance with the aforementioned interest in postwar history, entitled *Anfänge westdeutscher Sicherheitspolitik 1945–1956* (Beginnings of West German security policy, 1945–1956). This work, like the previous one, is based on extensive research efforts, both at home and abroad. Its major research interest is directed at the question why, from virtually 1945 on, and within the scope of international power constellations, the three western zones of occupation formed a federal German state, later to become an integral part of the Western community and the Western defense system. Substantial armed forces were thus reestablished in Germany, merely ten years after the catastrophe of World War II and the Potsdam Conference. The first volume, covering a period from 1945 to 1950, was published in 1982; Volume 2 was presented to the public in 1990. Volume 3 was published in 1993 and Volume 4 was in the final stage of preparation in 1994.

The third major project, a history of NATO, has finished its conceptual phase. It requires a tremendous amount of research at various international archives, including the National Archives in Washington, D.C. and the archives in Ottawa, Canada, as well as access to NATO documents at Brussels, Belgium; the Public Record Office in London, Great Britain; and, as far as accessible, the Archive Nationale in Paris, France.

In addition, there are always a number of monographs which cannot be cited for want of space, but some of which must be mentioned. One of the first important publications of the MGFA was *Handbuch zur deutschen Militärgeschichte 1648–1939* (The guide to German military history, 1648–1939). It provides a survey and introduction to modern German military history for historians, especially teachers and students of the different academies and colleges of the *Bundeswehr*. Such a comprehensive work had not so far been available. To be mentioned also are two periodicals that are published by the MGFA. First there is the semiannual *Militärgeschichtliche Mitteilungen* (MGM), with its yearly bibliographical supplement *War and Society Newsletter,* that surveys more than 700 periodicals and collective works. It is directed rather at the academic military history community and enjoys popularity and a sound reputation among scholarly and military circles as well as the interested public around the world. From 1986 on, the MGFA has started to publish another historical journal, now called *Militärgeschichte. Neue Folge* (NF) (Military history: New consequences or conclusions).

Led by the director of historical education, the *Abteilung Historische Bildung* (AHB) (department of historical education) does not itself teach. But it is instrumental in developing general conceptions in this field for the entire armed forces, it is responsible for the training and permanent education of the instructors of military history in the *Bundeswehr,* and it prepares and publishes textbooks, teaching aids, and instructional material. In order to broaden historical consciousness within all members of the military community on a wide scale, it conducts national and international symposia on military history. It develops exhibitions on special problems of German military history, usually on those which are subject to controversial discussions by the public. And it prepares, conducts, and accompanies staff rides for German and allied units.

The publications of the department of historical education are serving the aforementioned purposes, for example, a three-volume series for all army units at brigade level and higher, called *Kriegsgeschichtliche Beispiele* (Case studies in the history of war). By preparing examples taken from the battlefields of World War II, the case studies of operational and—in a few cases—tactical leadership are intended to revive and develop operational thinking from an historical view.

A project under preparation is a general textbook on German military history for the period between the sixteenth century and the present time, called *Grundzüge der deutschen Militärgeschichte* (Outlines of German military history). It will help the instructors of military history guide their students—mostly officer cadets and junior officers—through the period of military history in an organized and systematic way. And it will serve the students as a text and reference book in their preparation for oral and written examinations. The book will also contain rich source material and a documentary supplement for "learning by research."

And finally, a project called "Studies in Strategic and Operational Thinking" will be a series of roughly ten to twelve slender volumes, each containing an in-depth analysis of the creation, conception, and implementation of one selected operational idea during World War II.

All these publications give a general view of the subjects worked on in the MGFA and prove at the same time the methodologically different forms of interpretation and presentation.

ANFÄNGE WESTDEUTSCHER SICHERHEITSPOLITIK 1945–1956 (THE BEGINNINGS OF WEST GERMAN SECURITY POLITICS)

Translated by Paul Hatley

1. Roland G. Foerster, Christian Greiner, Georg Meyer, Hans-Jürgen Rautenberg, Norbert Wiggershaus, *Von der Kapitulation bis zum Pleven-Plan*. 1982. 6 Karten, 4 Graphiken. XXV 940 S., 88,—DM (From the surrender to the Pleven Plan).
2. Lutz Köllner, Klaus A. Maier, Wilhelm Meier-Dörnberg, Hans-Erich Volkmann, *Die EVG-Phase*. 1989. 7 Karten, 5 Graphiken. XXVI, 915 S., 88,—DM (The EVG phase).
3. Hans Ehlert, Christian Greiner, Georg Meyer, Bruno Thoß, *Die NATO-Option*. 1993. 9 Karten, 12 Graphiken. XXI, 1220 S., 98,—DM (The NATO option).
4. *Wirtschaft und Rüstung, Sicherheit und Souveränität*. (Economy and armament, security and sovereignty).

Werner Abelshauser, *Wirtschaft und Rüstung in den fünfziger Jahren*. (Economy and armament in the fifties).

5. Walter Schwengler, *Der doppelte Anspruch: Souveränität und Sicherheit. Zur Entwicklung des völkerrechtlichen Status'der Bundesrepublik Deutschland (1949–1955)*. Ca. 900 S., 88,—DM (The double standard: Sovereignty and security. The development of the international legitimacy of West Germany).

Vom Kalten Krieg zur deutschen Einheit. Analysen und Zeitzeugenberichte zur deutschen Militärgeschichte 1945–1995. Im Auftrag des MGHFA hrsg. von Bruno Thoß. 1995. Ca. 800 S. mit rund 100 teilw. farb. Abb., 78,—DM (From the Cold War to German unity. Analyses and contemporary reports related to German military history 1945–1995).

In Preparation

Die Militär- und Sicherheitspolitik in der SOZ/DDR 1945–1990. Bibliographie. Im Auftr. des MGFA hrsg. von Hans Ehlert, bearb. von Hans-Joachim Beth (Military and security policies in the SOZ/DDR 1945–1990. Bibliography).

BEITRÄGE ZUR MILITÄRGESCHICHTE (LECTURES ON MILITARY HISTORY)

Die Bände 1–25 sind unter dem Reihentitel *Beiträge zur Militär- und Kriegsgeschichte* bei der Deutschen Verlags-Anstalt in Stuttgart erschienen. Sie sind seit 1989 beim Oldenbourg Verlag beziehbar (Volumes 1–25 appeared under the series title *Lectures on Military and Battle History* with the Deutschen Verlags-Anstalt in Stuttgart).

26. *Europa im Zeitalter Friedrichs des Großen.* Wirtschaft, Gesellschaft, Kriege. Im Auftrag des MGFA hrsg. von Bernhard R. Kroener, 1989. 316 S., 78,—DM Europe in the age of Frederick the Great).
27. Donald Abenheim, *Bundeswehr und Tradition. Die Suche nach dem gültigen Erbe des deutschen Soldaten.* 1989. XI, 260 S., 48,—DM (The West German army and tradition. The search for the valid inheritance of the German soldier).
28. Gerhard Schreiber, *Die italienischen Militärinternierten im deutschen Machtbereich 1943 bis 1945.* Verraten–verachet–vergessen. 1990. 642 S., 68,—DM. Ausgabe in italienischer Sprache: I militari italiani internati nei campi di concentramento del Terzo Reich 1943–1945. Traditi–Disprezzati–Dimenticati, Roma (Stato Maggiore dell' Esercito Ufficio Storico) 1992. 903 S., 45 000 Lira (Italian military internees in German areas of control 1943–1945. Betrayed–Despised–Forgotten.
29. Thomas Rohkrämer, *Der Militarismus der "kleinen Leute." Die Kriegervereine im Deutschen Kaiserreich 1871–1914.* 1990. 301 S., 78,—DM (Militarism of the "Little People." Military organizations in the German Empire 1871–1914).
30. Wolfgang Handrick, *Die Pragmatische Armee 1741 bis 1743. Eine alliierte Armee in Kalkül des österreichischen Erbfolgekrieges.* 1991. X, 350 S., 78,—DM (The practical army 1741 to 1743. An Allied army in the calculation of the War of the Austrian Succession).
31. Bernd Ebersold, *Machtverfall und Machtbewußtsein. Britische Friedens- und Konfliktlösungsstrategien 1918–1956.* 1992. XIV, 447 S., 88,—DM (Decline of power and consciousness of power. British strategies for peace and the resolution of conflict 1918–1956).
32. Michael Epkenhans, *Die wilhelminische Flottenrüstung 1908–1914. Weltmachtstreben, industrieller Fortschritt, soziale Integration.* 1991. XI, 488 S., 88,—DM. Ausgabe in englischer Sprache in Vorbereitung (Wilhelminian naval armament 1908–1914. Striving for world power

status, industrial advancement, social integration) (English edition in preparation).

33. *Generalfeldmarschall von Moltke. Bedeutung und Wirkung.* Im Auftrag des MGFA hrsg. von Roland G. Foerster. 1991. XXIII, 208 S. sowie 10 Abb., 78,—DM (General Field Marshal von Moltke. Significance and effect).
34. Wilhelm Deist, *Militär, Staat und Gesellschaft. Studien zur preußisch–deutschen Militärgeschichte.* 1991. XV, 432 S., geb. 78,—DM; brosch. 48,—DM (Military, state, and society. Studies in Prussian–German military history).
35. Ralf Schabel, *Die Illusion der Wuhnderwaffen. Die Rolle der Düsenflugzeuge und Flugabwehrraketen in der Rüstungspolitik des Dritten Reiches.* 1994. 316 S., 78,—DM (The illusion of the superweapons. The role of jet aircraft and air defense rockets in the armament policy of the Third Reich).
36. Manfred Zeidler, *Reichswehr und Rote Armee 1920–1933. Wege und Stationen einer ungewöhnlichen Zusammenarbeit,* 1993. 400 S., 78,—DM; Studienausgabe 1944, 48,—DM. Ausgabe in russischer Sprache in Vorbereitung (The German army and the Red army 1920–1933. Methods and phases of an unusual cooperation) (Russian edition in preparation).
37. *Das Nordatlantische Bündnis 1949–1956.* Im Auftrag des MGFA hrsg. von Norbert Wiggershaus und Klaus A. Maier. 1993. 324 S., 78,—DM (The North Atlantic Alliance 1949–1956).
38. Walter Manoschek. *"Serbien ist judenfrei." Militärische Besatzungspolitik und Judenvernichtung in Serbien 1941/42.* 1993. 210 S., 78,—DM; Studienausgabe 1995, 48,—DM ("Serbia is free of Jews." Military occupation policy and the extermination of Jews in Serbia 1941/42).
39. Johannes Hürter, *Wilhelm Groener. Reichswehrminister am Ende der Weimarer Republik (1928–1932).* 1993, XII, 401 S., 78,—DM (Wilhelm Groener. German army minister in the last days of the Weimar Republic [1928–1932]).
40. *"Unternehmen Barbarossa." Zum historischen Ort der deutsch-sowjetischen Beziehungen von 1933 bis Herbst 1941.* Im Auftrag des MGFA hrsg. von Roland G. Foerster. 1993. 188 S., 78,—DM ("Operation Barbarossa." The historical place of German–Soviet relations from 1933 to fall 1941).
41. Gerd von Gersdorff, *Adenauers Außenpolitik gegenüber den Siegermächten 1954. Westdeutsche Bewaffnung und internationale Politik.* 1994. 404 S., 88,—DM (Adenauer's foreign policy toward the victorious powers 1954. International politics and the arming of West Germany).
42. Holger Afflerbach, *Falkenhayn. Politisches Denken und Handeln im Kaiserreich.* 1994. XIII, 586 S., 88,—DM (Falkenhayn. Political thought and behavior in the empire).
43. *Die Wehrpflicht, Entstehung, Erscheinungsformen und politische-militärische Wirkung.* Im Auftrag des MGFA hrsg. von Roland G. Foerster. 1994. XVI, 262 S., 78,—DM (Compulsory military service. Origin, manifestations and political-military effect).

44. Roland Peter, *Rüstungspolitik in Baden. Kriegswirtschaft und Arbeitseinsatz in einer Grenzregion im Zweiten Weltkrieg.* 1995. XIV, 405 S., 88,—DM (Bild auf 4. Umschlagseite) (Armament policy in Baden. Military economics and labor deployment in a border region the Second World War).
45. Berthold Seewald, *Karl Wilhelm von Heideck. Ein bayerischer General im befreiten Griechenland (1826–1835).* 1994. XVI, 316 S. und 12 S. Abb., 78,—DM (Karl Wilhelm von Heideck. A Bavarian general in liberated Greece [1826–1835]).
47. Ralf Pröve, *Stehendes Heer und städtische Gesellschaft im 18. Jahrhundert. Göttingen und seine Militärbevölkerung 1713–1756.* 1995. XIV, 373 S., 88,—DM (Standing army and urban society in the eighteenth century. Göttingen and its military population 1713–1756).
49. Olaf Rose, *Carl von Clausewitz. Zur Wirkungsgeschichte seines Werkes in Rußland und der Sowjetunion 1836–1991.* 1995. VIII, 275 S., 88,—DM (Bild auf 4. Umschlagseite) (Carl von Clausewitz. The history of the effect of his work in Russia and the Soviet Union 1836–1991).
50. *Politischer Wandel, organisierte Gewalt und nationale Sicherheit. Beiträge zur neueren Geschichte Deutschlands und Frankreichs.* Im Auftr. des MGFA hrsg. von Ernst Willi Hansen, Gerhard Schreiber und Bernd Wegner. 1995. XII, 565 S., 78,—DM (Bild auf 4. Umschlagseite) (Political change, organized force and national security. Lectures on the recent history of Germany and France).
51. *Volksarmee schaffen—ohne Geschrei! Studien zu den Anfängen einer "verdeckten Aufrüstung" in der SBZ/DDR 1947–1952.* Im Auftrag des MGFA hrsg. von Bruno Thoß. 1994. 360 S., 78,—DM (Creating a people's army—without an outcry! Studies on the beginnings of "clandestine armament" in the SOZ/DDR 1947–1952).

In Preparation

Norwegen unter NS-Gewaltherrschaft (AT). Im Auftrag des MGFA und des Goethe-Instituts Oslo hrsg. von Arnim Lang und Ingeborg Probst (Norway under Nazi tyranny).

Arnim Lang, *Invasion und Gewaltherrschaft. Strukturen des Besatzungssystems in Norwegen 1940–1945* (AT) (Invasion and tyranny. Structures of the occupation system in Norway 1940–1945).

Jürgen Angelow, *Die Sicherheitspolitik des Deutschen Bundes im europäischen Gleichgewicht (1815–1866)* (The security policy of the German League in the European equilibrium [1815–1866]).

Martin Creutz, *Presselenkung im Kaiserreich. Strukturen und Strategien* (Direction of the press in the empire. Structures and strategies).

OPERATIONEN DES ZWEITEN WELTKRIEGS (OPERATIONS OF THE SECOND WORLD WAR)

1. Hans-Martin Ottmer, *"Weserübung." Der deutsche Angriff auf Dänemark und Norwegen im April 1940.* 1994. XVI, 217 S. mit 22 Abb.,

34, 80 DM ("Exercise *Weser*." The German attack on Denmark and Norway in April 1940).

2. Karl-Heinz Frieser, *Blitzkrieg-Legende. Der Westfeldzug 1940.* 1995. XXII, 474 S., 49, 80 DM (The Blitzkrieg legend. The Western campaign 1940).

In Preparation

Hans-Martin Ottmer, *Die Entwicklung des operativen Denkens seit Moltke d.Ä. bis zum Zweiten Weltkrieg* (The development of operational thought from Moltke the Elder to the Second World War).

Reinhard Stumpf, *Rommel in Afrika. Die deutsch–italienischen Operationen in Nordafrika (1941–1943).* Rommel in Africa. The German–Italian operations in North Africa [1941–1943]).

BEITRÄGE ZUR MILITÄR- UND KRIEGSGESCHICHTE (LECURES ON MILITARY AND BATTLE HISTORY)

Bände 1–25. Ab Band 26 erscheint die Reihe unter dem neuen Titel *Beiträge zur Militärgeschichte* beim R. Oldenbourg Verlag, München. Die vorhergehenden Bände sind dort beziehbar. (Volumes 1–25. After volume 26 the series appears under the new title *Lectures on Military History*).

9. Karl-Heinz Völker, *Dokumente und Dokumentarfotos zur Geschichte der deutschen Luftwaffe. Aus den Geheimakten des Reichswehrministeriums 1919–1933 und des Reichsluftfahrtministeriums 1933–1939.* 1968. 489 S. (vergriffen) (Documents and documentary photos on the history of the German Air Force. From the secret files of the German Army Ministry 1919–1933 and the German Air Ministry 1933–1939).
10. Klaus-Jürgen Müller, *Das Heer und Hitler. Armee und nationalsozialistisches Regime 1933–1940.* 1988. 726 S., 78,—DM (The army and Hitler. The armed forces and the National Socialist regime 1933–1940).
11. Ursula v. Gersdorff, *Frauen im Kriegsdienst 1914–1945.* 1969. 572 S. (vergriffen) (Women in military service 1914–1945).
12. Horst Rohde, *Das deutsche Wehrmachttransportwesen im Zweiten Weltkrieg. Entstehung—Organisation—Aufgaben.* 1971. 439 S. (vergriffen) (The transportation system of the German Army in the Second World War. Origin–Organization–Duties).
13. Klaus Reinhardt, *Die Wende vor Moskau. Das Scheitern der Strategie Hitlers im Winter 1941/42.* 1972. 355 S. (vergriffen) Ausgabe in englischer Sprache bei Berg Publishers, Oxford, erschienen. (The turn before Moscow. The failure of Hitler's strategy in the winter of 1941/42) (English edition available from Berg Publishers).
14. Klaus Olshausen, *Zwischenspiel, auf dem Balkan. Die deutsche Politik gegenüber Jugoslawien und Griechenland von März bis Juli 1941.* 1973. 375 S., 58,—DM (The Balkan interlude. German policy toward Yugoslavia and Greece from March to July 1941).

15. Manfred Kehrig, *Stalingrad. Analyse und Dokumentation einer Schlacht.* 1979. 680 S. (vergriffen) (Stalingrad. Analysis and documentation of a battle).
16. Generalfeldmarschall Wilhelm Ritter v. Leeb. *Tagebuchaufzeichnungen und Lagebeurteilungen aus zwei Weltkriegen.* Hrsg.: Georg Meyer. 1976. 500 S. (vergriffen) (Journal entries and situational assessments from two World Wars).
17. Wilhelm Deist, *Flottenpolitik und Flottenpropaganda. Das Nachrichtenbureau des Reichsmarineamtes 1897–1914.* 1976. 344 S., 48,—DM (Fleet policy and fleet propaganda. The bureau of information of the Imperial Navy Office 1897–1914).
18. Hans Umbreit, *Deutsche Militärverwaltungen 1938/39. Die militärische Besetzung der Tschechoslowakei und Polens.* 1977. 296 S., 48,—DM (German military administrations 1938/39. The military occupation of Czechoslovakia and Poland).
19. *Adjutant im preußischen Kriegsministerium Juni 1918–Oktober 1919. Aufzeichnungen des Hauptmanns Gustav Böhm.* Hrsg.: Heinz Hürten und Georg Meyer. 1977. 168 S., 28,—DM (Adjutant in the Prussian War Ministry June 1918–October 1919. Notes of Captain Gustav Böhm).
20. Gerhard Schreiber, *Revisionismus und Weltmachtstreben. Marineführung und deutsch-italienische Beziehungen 1919 bis 1944.* 1978. 428 S., 58,—DM (Revisionism and striving for world power status. Naval leadership and German–Italian relations 1919 to 1944).
21. Horst Boog, *Die deutsche Luftwaffenführung 1935–1945. Führungsprobleme–Spitzengliederung–Generalstabsausbildung.* 1982. 724 S., 78,—DM (The German air force leadership 1935–1945. Leadership problems–Leadership organization–General staff instruction).
22. Dieter Ose, *Entscheidung im Westen 1944. Der Oberbefehlshaber West und die Abwehr der alliierten Invasion.* 1986. 363 S. (vergriffen). Ausgabe in englicher Sprache bei Berg Publishers, Oxford, in Vorbereitung (Decision in the West 1944. The Supreme Commander of the West and the defense against the Allied invasion) (English edition in preparation with Berg Publishers).
23. Ernst-Heinrich Schmidt, *Heimatheer und Revolution 1918. Die militärischen Gewalten im Heimatgebiet zwischen Oktoberreform und Novemberrevolution.* 1981. 456 S., 58,—DM (Home army and revolution 1918. The military forces in the home area between October reform and November revolution).
24. Walter Schwengler, *Völkerrecht, Versailler Vertrag und Auslieferungsfrage. Die Strafverfolgung wegen Kriegsverbrechen als Problem des Friedensschlusses 1919/20.* 1982. 402 S., 58,—DM (International legitimacy, Versailles treaty and extradition question. The criminal prosecution of war crimes as a problem of the conclusion of peace 1919/20).
25. *Militärgeschichte. Probleme–Thesen–Wege.* Im Auftrag des MGFA aus Anlaß seines 25 jährigen Bestehens ausgewählt und zusammengestellt von Manfred Messerschmidt, Klaus A. Maier, Werner Rahn und Bruno Thoß. 1982. 500 S., 32,—DM (Military history. Problems–theses–methods).

Entscheidung 1870. Der Deutsch–Französische Krieg. Hrsg. vom MGFA durch Wolfgang v. Groote und Ursula v. Gersdorff. 1970. 403 S. (vergriffen) (Decision 1870. The Franco–Prussian War).

DAS DEUTSCHE REICH UND DER ZWEITE WELTKRIEG (THE GERMAN EMPIRE AND THE SECOND WORLD WAR)

1. Wilhelm Deist, Manfred Messerschmidt, Hans-Erich Volkmann, Wolfram Wette. *Ursachen und Voraussetzungen der deutschen Kriegspolitik.* 1979, Nachdr. 1991. 764 S. (Causes and prerequisites of German war policy).
2. Klaus A. Maier, Horst Rohde, Bernd Stegemann, Hans Umbreit. *Die Errichtung der Hegemonie auf dem europäischen Kontinent.* 1979, Nachdr. 1991. 439 S. (The creation of hegemony on the European continent).
3. Gerhard Schreiber, Bernd Stegemann, Detlef Vogel. *Der Mittelmerraum und Südosteuropa. Von der "non belligeranza" Italiens bis zum Kriegseintritt der Vereinigten Staaten.* 1984, Nachdr. 1994. XII, 735 S. (The Mediterranean and Southeast Europe: From the "non belligeranza" of Italy to the entry of the United States into the war).
4. Horst Boog, Jürgen Förster, Joachim Hoffmann, Ernst Klink, Rolf-Dieter Müller, Gerd R. Ueberschär. *Der Angriff auf die Sowjetunion.* 1987, Nachdr. 1993. XX, 1172 S. mit Beiheft (The attack on the Soviet Union).
5. Bernhard R. Kroener, Rolf-Dieter Müller, Hans Umbreit. *Organisation und Mobilisierung des deutschen Machtbereichs.* Teilband 1: *Kriegsverwaltung, Wirtschaft und personelle Ressourcen 1939–1941.* 1988, Nachdr. 1992. XVIII, 1062 S. (Organization and mobilization of the German sphere of control. Part 1: Wartime administration, economy and personnel resources, 1939–1941).
5. Bernhard R. Kroener, Rolf-Dieter Müller, Hans Umbreit *Organisation und Mobilisierung des deutschen Machtbereichs.* Teilband 2: *Kriegsverwaltung, Wirtschaft und personelle Ressourcen 1942–1945* (Organization and mobilization of the German sphere of control. Part 2: Wartime administration, economy and personnel resources, 1942–1945).
6. Horst Boog, Werner Rahn, Reinhard Stumpf, Bernd Wegner, *Der globale Krieg. Die Ausweitung zum Weltkrieg und der Wechsel der Initiative 1941–1943.* 1990, Nachdr. 1993. XX, 1184 S. (The Global War: The expansion to world war and the shift of the initiative, 1941–1943).

Gerhard L. Weinberg. *Eine Welt in Waffen. Die globale Geschichte des Zweiten Weltkrieges.* 1995. 1174 S., 98,—DM; ab 1.1.1996: 128,—DM (A World in arms. The global history of the Second World War).

Wilhelm Deist, Manfred Messerschmidt, Hans-Erich Volkmann, Wolfram Wette. *Uraschen und Voraussetzungen des Zweiten Weltkrieges.* 1989.954 S., 24,80,—DM (= Fischer tb 4432) (Causes and prerequisites of the Second World War).

Horst Boog, Jürgen Förster, Joachim Hoffmann, Ernst Klink, Rolf-Dieter Müller, Gerd R. Ueberschär. *Der Angriff auf die Sowjetunion.* 1991. 1377 S., 29,80,—DM (= Fischer tb 11008) (The attack on the Soviet Union).

Horst Boog, Werner Rahn, Reinhard Stumpf, Bernd Wegner. *Die Welt im Krieg 1941–1943.* Bd 1: *Von Pearl Harbor zum Bombenkrieg in Europa.* Bd 2: *Von El Alamein bis Stalingrad,* 1992. 655 S. und XII, 657–1354 S., 39, 90,—DM (= Fischer tb 11698 und 11699) (The world at war 1941–1943. Vol. 1: From Pearl Harbor to the Air War in Europe. Vol. 2: From El Alamein to Stalingrad).

Rolf-Dieter Müller. *Hitlers Ostkrieg und die deutsche Siedlungspolitik. Die Zusammenarbeit von Wehrmacht, Wirtschaft und SS.* In Verbindung mit dem MGFA. 1991. 238 S., 19, 80,—DM (= Fischer tb 10573) (Hitler's Eastern War and German settlement policy: The cooperation of the armed forces, economy and SS).

DER DEUTSCHE REICH UND DER ZWEITE WELTKRIEG (GERMANY AND THE SECOND WORLD WAR)

1. Wilhelm Deist, Manfred Messerschmidt, Hans-Erich Volkmann, Wolfram Wette. *The Build-up of German Aggression.* 1990. XXVIII, 799 S., 68£.
2. Klaus A. Maier, Horst Rohde, Bernd Stegemann, Hans Umbreit. *Germany's Initial Conquest in Europe.* 1991. XV, 444 S., 85£.
3. Gerhard Schreiber, Bernd Stegemann, Detlef Vogel. *The Mediterranean, South-East Europe, and North Africa, 1939–1941: From Italy's Declaration of Non-Belligerence to the Entry of the United States into the War.* 1995. Ca. 800 S., £135.

EINZELSCHRIFTEN ZUR MILITÄRGESCHICHTE (INDIVIDUAL WORKS IN MILITARY HISTORY)

1. Friedrich Forstmeier. *Odessa 1941. Der Kampf um Stadt und Hafen und die Räumung der Seffestung. 15. August bis 16. Oktober 1941.* 1967. 139 S. (vergriffen) (Odessa 1941. The battle for city and port and the evacuation of the naval fortress. 15 August to 16 October 1941).
2. Volkmar Regling. *Amiens 1940. Der deutsche Durchbruch südlich von Amiens. 5. bis 8. Juni 1940.* 1968. 130 S. (vergriffen) (Amiens 1940. The German breakthrough south of Amiens. 5 to 8 June 1940).
3. Hans-Otto Mühleisen. *Kreta 1941. Das Unternehmen "Merkur." 20. Mai bis. 1. Juni 1941.* 1977. 120 S. (vergriffen) (Crete 1941: Operation "Merkur"—20 May to 1 June 1941).
4. Gert Fricke. *"Fester Platz" Tarnopol 1944.* 1986. 161 S., 12,—DM ("Strong point" Tarnopol 1944).
5. Albert Merglen. *Geschichte und Zukunft der Luftlandetruppen.* Tit. d. Originalausg.: Histoire et avenir des troupes aéroportées. 1977. 175 S. (vergriffen) (History and future of airborne troops).

6. Hans Kissel. *Vom Dnjepr zum Dnjestr. Rückzugskämpfe des Grenadierregiments 683 (im Rahmen der 335. Infanteriedivision).* 9. März bis 12. April 1944. 1970. 113 S. (vergriffen) (From Dnieper to Dniester: Rearguard actions of Grenadier Regiment 683 [under the 335 Infantry Division]).
7. Herbert Schindler. *Mosty und Dirschau 1939. Zwei Handstreiche der Wehrmacht vor Beginn des Polenfeldzuges.* 2., veränderte Aufl. 1979. 167 S., 13,—DM (Mosty and Dirschau 1939: Two surprise coups of the armed forces prior to the beginning of the Polish Campaign).
8. Gert Fricke. *Kroatien 1941–1944. Der "Unabhängige Staat" in der Sicht des Deutschen Bevollmächtigten Generals in Agram, Glaise v. Horstenau.* 1972. 206 S. (vergriffen) (Croatia 1941–1944: The "Independent State" from the point of view of the German plenipotentiary general in Agram, Glaise von Horstenau).
9. Hubert Jeschke, *U-Boottaktik. Zur deutschen U-Boottaktik 1900–1945.* 1972. 120 S. (vergriffen) (U-Boat tactics. German U-boat tactics, 1900–1945).
11. Wilhelm Meier-Dörnberg. *Die Ölversorgung der Kriegsmarine 1935 bis 1945.* 1973. 111 S. (vergriffen) (The oil supply of the navy, 1935–1945).
12. Rudolf Steiger. *Panzertaktik im Spiegel deutscher Kriegstagebücher 1939 bis 1941.* 1977. 204 S. (vergriffen) (Ausgabe in englischer Sprache bei Berg Publishers, Oxford, erschienen (Armor tactics reflected in German war diaries, 1939–1941) (English edition available from Berg Publishers).
13. Heinrich Schuur, Rolf Martens, Wolfgang Koehler. *Führungsprobleme der Marine im Zweiten Weltkrieg. 1986.* 150 S., 12,—DM (Leadership problems of the navy in the Second World War).
14. Joachim Hoffmann. *Deutsche und Kalmyken 1942 bis 1945.* 1986. 214 S., 14,—DM (Germans and Kalmuks 1942 to 1945).
15. Rolf Elble. *Die Schlacht an der Bzura im September 1939 aus deutscher und polnischer Sicht.* 1975. 266 S. (vergriffen) (The battle on the Bzura in September 1939 from German and Polish perspectives).
16. Jürgen Förster. *Stalingrad. Risse im Bündnis 1942/43.* 1975. 172 S. (vergriffen) (Stalingrad. Cracks in the alliance 1942/43).
17. Klaus A. Maier. *Guernica 26.4.1937. Die deutsche Intervention in Spanien und der "Fall Guernica."* 1977. 164 S. (vergriffen) (Ausgabe in spanischer Sprache u.d.T.: Guernica 26.4.1937. La intervencion alemana en España y el "caso Guernica." Madrid: Ediciones Sedmay 1976. 214 S. (Guernica 26 April 1937. The German intervention in Spain and "Case Guernica").
18. Hans-Joachim Lorbeer. *Westmächte gegen die Sowjetunion 1939–1941.* 1975. 143 S., 10,—DM (Western powers against the Soviet Union, 1939–1941).
19. Joachim Hoffmann. *Die Ostlegionen 1941 bis 1943. Turkotataren, Kaukasier und Wolfgafinnen im deutschen Heer.* 1986. 197 S., 14,—DM (The Eastern Legions, 1941–1943: Turkotartars, Caucasians and Volga Finns in the German Army).

20. Heinz Magenheimer. *Abwehrschlacht an der Weichsel 1945. Vorbereitungen, Ablauf, Erfahrungen.* 1986. 163 S., 12,—DM (Defensive battle on the Vistula 1945: Preparations, order of events, experiences).
21. Adalbert v. Taysen. *Tobruk 1941. Der Kampf in Nordafrika.* 1976. 382 S. (vergriffen) (Tobruk 1941. The struggle in North Africa).
22. Hans Wegmüller. *Die Abwehr der Invasion. Die Konzeption des Oberbefehlshabers West 1940–1944.* 1986. 315 S., 17,—DM (The defense of the invasion: The conception of Supreme Commander West, 1940–1944).
23. Bertil Stjernfelt, Klaus-Richard Böhme. *Westerplatte 1939* (aus dem Schwedischen). 1979. 142 S. (vergriffen) (Westerplatte 1939 [from the Swedish]).
24. Bernd PhilippSchröder. *Irak 1941.* 1980. 138 S. (vergriffen) (Iraq 1941).
25. Hans-Otto Behrendt, *Rommels Kenntnis vom Feind im Afrikafeldzug. Ein Bericht über die Feindnachrichtenarbeit, insbesondere die Funkaufklärung.* 1980. 342 S. (vergriffen) (Rommel's knowledge of the enemy in the Africa Campaign: A report on intelligence work, especially radio interception). Published in English as: *Rommel's Intelligence in the Desert Campaign 1941–1943.* London: William Kimber, 1985.
26. Hans Meier-Welcker. *Aufzeichnungen eines Generalstabsoffiziers 1939–1942.* 1982. 240 S., 18,—DM (Notes of a general staff officer 1939–1942).
27. Joachim Hoffmann. *Die Geschichte der Wlassow-Armee.* 1995. 486, XVIII S., 32,—DM (Ausgabe in russischer Sprache u.d.T.: Istorija Vlasovskoj Armii. Perevod s nemeckogo, E. Gessen, Paris 1990. 379 S.,120 FF (= Issle dovanija Novejšej Russkoj Istorii. Pod obščej redakciej A. J. Solženicyna, 8) (The history of the Vlassov Army).
28. Volker Detlef Heydorn. *Nachrichtennahaufklärung (Ost) und sowjetrussisches Heerefunkwesen bis 1945.* 1985. 288 S. (vergriffen) (Short-range intelligence [East] and Soviet Russian Army radio to 1945).
29. Katriel Ben Arie. *Die Schlacht bei Monte Cassino 1944.* 1986. 418 S., 28,—DM. Gleichzeitig in der Schriftenreihe des Instituts für Deutsche Geschichte der Universität Tel-Aviv, Bd 8, erschienen (The Battle of Monte Cassino 1944).
30. Joachim Brückner. *Kriegsende in Bayern 1945. Der Wehrkreis VII und die Kämpfe zwischen Donau und Alpen.* 1995. 309 S., 26,—DM (War's end in Bavaria 1945: Defense Circle VII and the struggles between the Danube and the Alps).
31. Martin van Creveld. *Kampfkraft. Militärische Orgaanisation und militärische Leistung 1939–1945.* 1992. 232 S., 24,—DM (Fighting strength: Military organization and military achievement, 1939–1945).
32. Marlen von Xylander. *Die deutsche Besatzungsherrschaft auf Kreta 1941–1945.* 1995. 153 S., 28,—DM (The German occupation government in Crete, 1941–1945).
33. Uwe Brammer. *Spionageabwehr und "geheimer Meldedienst." Die Abwehrstelle im Wehrkreis X Hamburg 1935–1945.* 1989. 178 S., 24,—DM (Counterespionage and "Secret Message Service": The Office in Defense Circle X Hamburg, 1935–1945).
34. Rudibert Kunz, Rolf-Dieter Müller. *Giftgas gegen Abd el Krim. Deutsch-*

land, Spanien und der Gaskrieg in Spanisch-Marokko 1922–1927. 1990. 239 S., 32,—DM (Poison gas against Abd el Krim: Germany, Spain and the gas war in Spanish Morocco, 1922–1927).

35. Joachim Hoffmann. *Kaukasien 1942/43. Das deutsche Heer und die Orientvölker der Sowjetunion.* 1991. 534 S., 42,—DM (Caucasus 1942/43. The German Army and the oriental peoples of the Soviet Union).
36. Martin Raschke. *Der politisierende Generalstab. Die friderizianischen Kriege in der antlichen deutschen Militärgeschichtsschreibung 1890–1914.* 1993. 200 S., 32,—DM (The politicizing General Staff: The Frederician Wars in the writing of official German military history, 1890–1914).
37. Klaus Albrecht Lankheit. *Preußen und die Frage der europäischen Abrüstung 1867–1870.* 1993. 278 S., 42,—DM (Prussia and the question of European disarmament, 1867–1870).
38. Dieter Krüger. *Das Amt Blank. Die schwierige Gründung des Bundesministeriums für Verteidigung.* 1993. 257 S., 38,—DM (The Blank office: The difficult establishment of the Federal Ministry for Defense).
39. Joachim Ludewig. *Der deutsche Rückzug aus Frankreich 1944.* 1994. 368 S., 48,—DM (The German withdrawal from France 1944).
40. Sven Lange. *Hans Delbrück und der "Strategiestreit." Kriegführung und Kriegsgeschichte in der Kontroverse 1879–1914.* 1995. 159 S., 38,—DM (Bild auf 4. Umschlagseite) (Hans Delbrück and the "Strategy Dispute": War leadership and war history in the controversy, 1879–1914).

GRUNDZÜGE DER DEUTSCHEN MILITÄRGESCHICHTE (THE RUDIMENTS OF GERMAN MILITARY HISTORY)

Im Auftrag des Militärgeschichtlichen Forschungsamtes hrsg. von Karl-Volker Neugebauer

1. *Historischer Überblick.* Mit Beiträgen von Karl Diefenbach, Siegfried Fiedler, Bernhard R. Kroener, Karl-Volker Neugebauer, Heiger Ostertag, Hans-Martin Ottmer, Werner Rahn, Heinrich Walle und Manfred Zeidler. 1993. 484 S. (Historical overview).
2. *Arbeits- und Quellenbuch,* bearb. von Karl-Volker Neugebauer unter Mitwirkung vonm Heiger Ostertag. 1993. 464 S. Beide Bde zus. 88,—DM (Work and source book).

Napoleon I, und das Militärwesen seiner Zeit. Im Auftrag des Militärgeschichtlichen Forschungsamtes und der Rankegesellschaft—Vereinigung für Geschichte im öffentlichen Leben—hrsg. von Wolfgang v. Groote und Klaus-Jürgen Müller. 1968. 254 S. (vergriffen) (Napoleon I and the military of his time).

Napoleon I, und die Staatenwelt seiner Zeit. Im Auftrag der Ranke-Gesellschaft—Vereinigung für Geschichte im öffentlichen Leben—und des Militärgeschichtlichen Forschungsamtes hrsg. von Wolfgang v. Groote. 1969. 213 S. (vergriffen) (Napoleon I and the world in his time).

Wilhelm Zieger. *Das deutsche Heeresveterinärwesen im Zweiten Weltkrieg.* Hrsg. vom MGFA. 1973. XI, 708 S., 25,—DM (The German Army veterinary system in the Second World War).

Ines Reich. *Potsdam und der 20. Juli 1944. Auf den Spuren des Widerstandes gegen den Nationalsozialismus.* Begleitschrift zur Ausstellung des MGFA und des Potsdam-Museums. 1994. 104 S., 19,80 DM (Potsdam and 20 July 1944: On the trail of the resistance against National Socialism).

MILITÄRHISTORISCHE EXKURSIONSFÜHRER (MILITARY HISTORICAL EXCURSION GUIDES)

1. Richard Lakowski. *Seelow 1945. Die Entscheidungsschlacht an der Oder.* 1995. 260 S. (Seelow 1945: The decisive battle on the Oder).

Trag' diese Wehr zu Sachsen Ehr! Militärische Hiebund Stichwaffen Sachsens von 1700 bis 1918. Aus dem Bestand des Militärhistorischen Museums Dresden. 1994. 108 S. (Carry this weapon for the honor of Saxony! Military cutting and stabbing weapons of Saxony from 1700 to 1918).

VORTRÄGE ZUR MILITÄRGESCHICHTE (LECTURES ON MILITARY HISTORY)

1. *Einzelprobleme politischer und militärischer Führung.* Mit Beiträgen von Johann Christoph Allmayer-Beck, Horst Boog, Andreas Kraus, Manfred Messerschmidt, Eckardt Opitz, Kurt Peball. 1981. 133 S. (vergriffen) (Individual problems of political and military leadership).
2. *Menschenführung in der Marine.* Mit Beiträgen von Philippus M. Bosscher, Wilhelm Deist, Richard Plaschka, Olaf Preuschoft, Werner Rahn, Michael Salewski. 1981. 123 S. (vergriffen) (Leadership in the Navy).
3. *Menschenführung im Heer.* Mit Beiträgen von Johann Christoph Allmayer-Beck, Werner Gembruch, Gunter Holzweißig, Manfred Messerschmidt, Georg Meyer, Ernst Nittner, Manfried Rauchensteiner, Hans Senn, Bruno Thoß. 1982. 264 S. (vergriffen) (Leadership in the army).
4. *Entmilitarisierung und Aufrüstung in Mitteleuropa 1945–1956.* Mit Beiträgen von Alexander Fischer, Christian Greiner, Klaus A. Maier, Ulrich de Maizière, Wilhelm Meier-Dörnberg, Georg Meyer, Manfried Rauchensteiner, Jan Schulten, Hans-Erich Volkmann, Norbert Wiggershaus. 1983. 225 S. (vergriffen) (Demilitarization and arming in Middle Europe, 1945–1956).
5. *Der militärische Widerstand gegen Hitler und das NS-Regime 1933–1945.* Mit Beiträgen von Alexander Fischer, Othmar Hackl, Peter Hoffmann, Johann Adolf Graf v. Kielmansegg, Helmut Krausnick, Georg Meyer, Peter Sauerbruch, Gerd R. Ueberschär, Norbert Wiggershaus. 1984. 252 S. (vergriffen) (The military resistance against Hitler and the Nazi Regime, 1933–1945).
6. *Militärgeschichte in Deutschland und Österreich vom 18. Jahrhundert vis in die Gegenwart.* Mit Beiträgen von Johann Christoph Allmayer-Beck, Peter Broucek, Othmar Hackl, Gerhard Heyl, Friedrich Frhr.

Hiller v. Gaertringen, Friedhelm Klein, Manfried Rauchensteiner, Walter Rehm, Michael Salewsi. 1985. 212 S. (vergriffen) (Military history in Germany and Austria from the eighteenth century and into the future).

7. *Die Bedeutung der Logistik für die militärische Führung von der Antike bis in die neueste Zeit.* Mit Beiträgen von Horst Boog, Peter Broucek, Paul Heinsius, Diether Hülsemann, Walter Hummelberger, Wolfgang Petter, Horst Rohde, Jakob Seibert, Reinhard Stumpf. 1986. 285 S. (vergriffen) (The importance of logistics to military leadership from antiquity to most recent times).
8. *Friedrich der Große und das Militärwesen seiner Zeit.* Mit Beiträgen von Johann Christoph Allmayer-Beck, Hans Bleckwenn, Gustav-Adolf Caspar, Werner Gembruch, Dieter Hartwig, Bernhard R. Kroener, Ullrich Marwitz, Volker Schmidtchen. 1987. 192 S. (vergriffen) (Frederick the Great and the military of his time).
9. *Operatives Denken und Handeln in deutschen Streitkräften im 19. und 20. Jahrhundert.* Mit Beiträgen von Horst Boog, Lothar Burchardt, Karl-Heinz Frieser, Christian Greiner, Carl-Gero v. Ilsemann, Heinz Magenheimer, Wilhelm Meier-Dörnberg, Karl-Volker Neugebauer, Michael Salewski. 1988. 264 S. (vergriffen) (Operational thinking and practice in the German armed forces in the nineteenth and twentieth centuries).
10. *Die operative Idee und ihre Grundlagen.* Mit Beiträgen von Sampo Ahto, David M. Glantz, Christian Greiner, Werner Rahn, Horst Rohde, Günter Roth, Reinhard Stumpf, John E. Tashjean. 1989. 224 S., 29,80 DM (The operational idea and its bases).
11. *Sanitätswesen im Zweiten Weltkrieg.* Hrsg. von Ekkehart Guth. Mit Beiträgen von Wolfgang U. Eckart, Hubert Fischer, Heinz Goerke, Ekkehart Guth, Karl-Heinz Leven, Peter Riedesser, Hans Schadewaldt, Wolfgang Scholz, Rolf Valentin, Hana Vondra. 1989. 232 S. (vergriffen) (Medical services in the Second World War).
12. *Luftkriegführung im Zweiten Weltkrieg—ein internationaler Vergleich.* Im Auftraga des MGFA hrsg. von Horst Boog. Mit Beiträgen von W. A. Boelcke, H. Boog, L. Ceva, S. Cox, A. Curami, P. Facon, M. Forget, R. F. Futrell, A. Goldberg, O. Groehler, K. Gundelach, M. Handel, V. Hardesty, R. Higham, I. B. Holley, E. L. Homze, J. W. Huston, R. V. Jones, L. Kennett, G. Krebs, R. Kohn, M. Messerschmidt, J. H. Morrow, W. Murray, R. J. Overy, W. H. Parks, H. A. Probert, L. Robineau, M. Smith, R. Smith, J. Terraine, H. Trischler und W. Wark. 1993. 876 S., 49, 80,—DM. Ausgabe in englischer Sprache bei Berg Publishers, Oxford, erschienen (z.Z. vergriffen) (Air war leadership in the Second World War—An international comparison) (English edition from Berg Publishers).
13. *Die Zukunft des Reiches: Gegner, Verbündete und Neutrale (1943–1945).* Im Auftrag des MGFA hrsg. von Manfred Messerschmidt und Ekkehart Guth. Mit Beiträgen von Brian Bond, Josef Borus, Wilhelm Carlgren, Yves Durand, Warren F. Kimball, Paul Létourneau, Gernd Martin, Manfred Messerschmidt, Gerke Teitler und Olli Vehviläinen.

1990. 223 S. (vergriffen) (The future of the Reich: Opponents, allies and neutrals [1943–1945]).

14. *Militär und Technik. Wechselbeziehungen zu Staat, Gesellschaft und Industrie iim 19. und 20. Jahrhundert.* Im Auftrag des MGFA hrsg. von Roland G. Foerster und Heinrich Walle. Mit Beiträgen von Fritz H. Baer, Jobst Broelmann, Hartmut H. Knittel, Michael Salewski, Heinrich Walle, Rolf Wirtgen. 1992. 291 S., 34,80 DM (The military and technology. Interrelations of state, society and industry in the nineteenth and twentieth centuries).
15. *Gezitenwechsel im Zwieten Weltrieg? Die Schlachten von Char'kov and Kursk im Frühjahr und Sommer 1943 in operativer Anlage, Verlauf und politischer Bedeutung.* Im Auftrag des MGFA hrsg. von Roland G. Foerster. 1995. Ca. 210 S., ca. 34,80 DM (Turn of the tide in the Second World War? The battles of Kharkov and Kursk in the spring and summer of 1943 in operational conception, course of events and political significance).

Invasion 1944. Im Auftrag des MGFA hrsg. von Hans Umbreit.

Das Ende des Zweiten Weltkrieges in Europa. Die Kämpfe an der Oder, den Seelower Höhen und um Gerlin im Frühjahr 1945. Im Auftrag des MGFA hrsg. von Roland G. Foerster (The end of the Second World War in Europe. The battles on the Oder, the Seelow Heights and around Berlin in the spring of 1945).

ENTWICKLUNG DEUTSCHER MILITÄRISCHER TRADITION (DEVELOPMENT OF GERMAN MILITARY TRADITION)

1. Gustav Adolf Caspar, Ullrich Marwitz, Hans-Martin Ottmer. *Tradition in deutschen Streitkräften bis 1945.* 1986. 332 S. (vergriffen) (Tradition in German armed forces to 1945).
2. Hans-Joachim Harder, Norbert Wiggershaus. *Tradition und Reform in den Aufbaujahren der Bundeswehr.* 1985. 176 S. (vergriffen) (Tradition and reform in the building years of the West German Army).
3. Hans-Peter Stein. *Symbole und Zeremoniel in deutschen Streitkräften vom 18. bis zum 20. Jahrhundert.* Mit einem Beitrag von Hans-Martin Ottmer. 1986. 320 S. (vergriffen) (Symbols and the ceremonial in German armed forces from the eighteenth to the twentieth centuries).

KRIEGSTAGEBUCH DER SEEKRIEGSLEITUNG 1939–1945, TEIL A, 68 BÄNDE (WAR DIARY OF THE NAVAL WAR COMMAND 1939–1945, PART A, 68 VOLS.)

Sixty-eight volumes have been published in this series.

OPERATIVES DENKEN UND HANDEL IN DEUTSCHEN STREITKRÄFTEN (OPERATIONAL THINKING AND PRACTICE IN GERMAN ARMED FORCES)

1. *Operatives Denken bei Clausewitz, Moltke, Schlieffen und Manstein.* Hrsg. vom MGFA. 1989. 93 S. (vergriffen) (Operational thinking in

Clausewitz, Moltke, Schlieffen and Manstein). Ed. by MGFA. 1988. 83 S. (vergriffen).

2. *Entwicklung, Planung und Durchführung operativer Ideen im Ersten und Zweiten Weltkrieg.* Hrsg. vom MGFA. 1989. 143 S. (vergriffen) (Development, planning and realization of operational conceptions in World Wars I and II).
3. *Ideen und Strategien 1940. Ausgewählte Operationen und deren militärgeschichtliche Aufarbeitung.* Hrsg. vom MGFA. 1990. 209 S. (vergriffen) (Ideas and strategies 1940: Selected operations and their military historical reappraisal).
4. *Ausgewählte Operationen und ihre militärhistorischen Grundlagen.* Im Auftrag des MGFA hrsg. von Hans-Martin Ottmer und Heiger Osterrtag. 1993. 484 S. (vergriffen). Ausgabe in bulgarischer und russischer Sprache in Vorbereitung (Selected operations and their military historical bases) (Bulgarian and Russian editions in preparation).

Jakob A. Gilles. *Flugmotoren 1910 bis 1918.* Bearb. von Karl Köhler. Technisch überprüft und mit einem Nachwort versehen von Gustav Ewald. Hrsg. vom MGFA. 1971. XIII, 201, XXVII S. (vergriffen) (Aircraft engines, 1910–1918).

Deutsche Jüdische Soldaten 1914–1945. Im Auftrage des Bundesministeriums der Verteidigung hrsg. vom MGFA. 1987. 268 S., 9,80 DM (German Jewish soldiers, 1914–1945).

Die deutsche Flotte im Spannungsfeld der Politik 1848–1985. Vorträge und Diskussionen der 25. Historisch-Taktischen Tagung der Flotte 1985. Hrsg. vom Deutschen Marine Institut und vom MGFA. Mit Beitägen von G. Fromm, D. Mahncke, G. Moltmann, W. Rahn, J. Rohwer, M. Salewski, M. Stürmer und H. Vohs. 1985. 236 S. (vergriffen) (The German Fleet in the arena of political conflict, 1848–1985).

Seefahrt und Geschichte. Hrsg.: Deutsches Marine Institut, Militärgeschichtliches Forschungsamt. Red.: Heinrich Walle. 1986. 228 S. (vergriffen) (Seafaring and history).

Die französische Revolution und der Beginn des Zweiten Weltkrieges aus deutscher und französischer Sicht. Hrsg. vom MGFA. Mit Beiträgen von Robert Bassac, Gilbert Bodinier, Wilhelm Deist, Bernhard R. Kroener und Günter Roth. 1989. 103 S. (vergriffen) (The French Revolution and the origin of the Second World War from German and French perspectives).

Kreta. Kleiner kultur- und militärgeschichtlicher Wegweiser. Hrsg. vom MGFA. 2., überarb, u. erw. Aufl. 1989. 165 S. (vergriffen) (Crete: Tiny cultural and military-historical trailblazer).

Karl Bauer. *Gedächtnisprotokoll. Ein Prozeß in Minsk.* Mit Unterstitzung des MGFAa. 1990. 103 S. (vergriffen) (Memorial transcript. A trial in Minsk).

Von der Friedenssicherung zur Friedensgestaltung. Deutsche Streitkäfte im Wandel. Im Auftrag des MGFA hrsg. von Heinrich Walle. 1991. 400 S., zahlreiche Abb. (vergriffen) Ausgabe in russischer Sprache im Nauka Verlag der Wissenschaften, Moskau, erschienen; bulgarische Ausg. Sofia 1995; rumänische Ausg. in Vorbereitung (From peacekeeping measures to the form of peace: German armed forces in transition). (Russian edition from Nauka [also Bulgarian and Rumanian]).

Aufstand des Gewissens. Der militärische Widerstand gegen Hitler und das NS-Regime 1933–1945. Im Auftrag des MGFA hrsg. von Heinrich Walle. 4., überarb. und erw. Aufl. 1994. 18,—DM (Revolt of the conscience. The military resistance against Hitler and the Nazi regime, 1933–1945).

Siegfried Sorge. *Vom Kaiserreich zur Bundesrepublik. Aus den Schriften eines engagierten Offiziers und Staatsbürgers.* Im Auftrag des MGFA hrsg. von Werner Rahn. 1993. 144 S. (vergriffen) (From Empire to Federal Republic. From the writings of a committed officer and citizen).

Der Zweite Weltkrieg. Analysen, Grundzüge, Forschungsbilanz. Im Auftrag ades MGFA hrsg. von Wolfgang Michalka. 1990. XVI, 878 S., 34,80 DM (= Serie Piper, 811). Ausgabe in russischer Sprache im Progress Verlag, Moskau, in Vorbereitung (The Second World War: Analyses, essential features, balance of research) (Russian edition from Progress).

Zwei Wege nach Moskau. Vom Hitler-Stalin-Pakt zum "Unternehmen Barbarossa" 1939/41. Im Auftrag des MGFA hrsg. von Bernd Wegner, 1991. XIX, 664 S., 29,80 DM. (= Serie Piper, 1346). Ausgabe in englischer Sprache in Vorbereitung (Two routes to Moscow: From the Hitler–Stalin pact to "Operation Barbarossa" 1939/41) (English edition in preparation).

Stalingrad. Ereignis–Wirkung–Syumbol. Im Auftrag des MGFA hrsg. von Jürgen Förster. 1992. 501 S., 34,80 DM. (= Serie Piper, 1618). Ausgabe in russischer Sprache im Progress Verlag, Moskau, erschienen (Bild auf 4, Umschlagseite). Ausgabe in englischer Sprache in Vorbereitung (Stalingrad: Event–effect–symbol) (Russian edition from Progress; English edition in preparation).

Der Erste Weltkrieg. Wirkung, Wahrnehmung, Analyse. Im Auftrag des MGF A hrsg. von Wolfgang Michalka. 1994. XVI, 1062 S., 44,90 DM. (= Serie Piper, 1927) (The First World War: Effect, acceptance, analysis).

Ende des Dritten Reiches—Ende des Zweiten Weltkriegs. Eine perspektivische Rückschau. Im Auftrag des MGFA hrsg. von Hans-Erich Volkmann. 1994. XIV, 914 S., 39,90 DM. (= Serie Piper, 2056) (The end of the Third Reich—End of the Second World War: A perspectival reflection).

QUELLEN ZUR GESCHICHTE DES PARLAMENTARISMUS UND DER POLITISCHEN PARTEIEN (SOURCES FOR THE HISTORY OF PARLIAMENTARIANISM AND POLITICAL PARTIES)

Reihe 2: Militär und Politik (Series 2: The Military and Politics)

From the mission of the Commission for the History of Parliamentarianism and Political Parties and the Directorate of Military History, edited by Erich Matthias and Hans Meier-Welcker.

1. *Militär und Innenpolitik im Weltkrieg 1914 bis 1918,* bearbeitet von Wilhelm Deist. T. 1.2. 1970. 1:CLXXIII, 647 S., 2: S. 651–1530. 184,—DM (Military and domestic politics in the World War, 1914–1918).
2. *Zwischen Revolution und Kapp-Putsch. Militär und Innenpolitik 1918–*

1920, bearbeiter von Heinz Hürten. 1977. LXXVII, 378 S., 118,—DM (Between revolution and Kapp Putsch: Military and domestic politics, 1918–1920).

3. *Die Anfänge der Ära Seeckt. Militär und Innenpolitik 1920–1922,* bearbeitet von Heinz Hürten. 1979. LI, 314 S., 120,—DM (The early Seeckt period: Military and domestic politics, 1920–1922).
4. *Das Krisenjaahr 1923. Militär und Innenpolitik 1922–1924,* bearbeitet von Heinz Hürten. 1980. LXIII, 392 S., 148,—DM (The crisis year 1923: Military and domestic politics, 1922–1924).

Marine und Marinepolitik im kaiserlichen Deutschland 1871–1914. Hrsg. vom MGFA durch Herbert Schottelius und Wilhelm Deist. 2., mit einem ergänzenden Vorwort versehene Auflage 1981. 328 S., 36,—DM (The Navy and naval politics in imperial Germany, 1871–1914).

Wirtschaft und Rüstung am Vorabend des Zweiten Weltkrieges. Für das MGFA hrsg. von Friedrich Forstmeier und Hans-Erich Volkmann. 1981. 415 S., 32,—DM (Economics and armament on the eve of the Second World War).

Kriegswirtschaft und Rüstung 1939–1945. Für das MGFA hrsg. von Friedrich Forstmeier und Hans-Erich Volkmann. 1977., 420 S. (vergriffen) (Wartime economics and armament, 1939–1945).

Die deutsche Beraterschaft in China 1927–1938. Militär–Wirtschaft–Außenpolitik. Hrsg. in Verbindung mit dem MGFA von Bernd Martin. 1981. 504 S., 56,—DM (The German advisory group in China: Military, economic, and political issues in Sino–German relations, 1927–1938).

Manfred Messerschmidt. *Militärgeschichtliche Aspekte der Entwicklung des deutschen Nationalstaates.* 1988. 260 S. (vergriffen) (Military-historical aspects of the development of the German national state).

Wolfram Wette. *Gustav Noske. Eine politische Biographie.* 1988. 876 S. (vergriffen: Neuauflage in Vorbereitung) (Gustav Noske: A political biography).

Volker R. Berghahn, Wilhelm Deist. *Rüstung im Zeichen der wilhelminischen Weltpolitik. Grundlegende Dokumente 1890–1914.* Hrsg. vom MGFA. 1988. 426 S., 44,—DM (Armament under the sign of Wilhelminian world politics: Essential documents, 1890–1914).

Parlamentarische und öffentliche Kontrolle von Rüstung in Deutschland 1700–1970. Beiträge zur historischen Friedensforschung. Hrsg. vom MGFA und dem Arbeitskreis Historische Friedensforschung durch Jost Dülffer. 241 S., 28,—DM. (= Droste-Taschenbücher Geschichte, 917) (Parliamentary and public control of armament in Germany, 1700–1970. Lectures in the history of peace).

QUELLEN ZUR MILITÄRGESCHICHTE (SOURCES IN MILITARY HISTORY)

Serie A (Series A)

1. *Aus den Geburtsstunden der Weimarer Republik. Das Tagebuch des Obersten Ernst van den Bergh.* Hrsg. von Wolfram Wette. 1991. 263 S., 62,—DM (From the earliest hours of the Weimar Republic: The diary of Colonel Ernst van den Bergh).

In Preparation

Serie A (Series A)

Generalleutnant Johann Nicolaus von Luckner und seine Husaren im Siebenjährigen Kriege, hrsg. von Michael Hochedlinger (Lieutenant-General Johann Nicolaus von Luckner and his Hussars in the Seven Years' War).

Vizeadmiral Albert Hopman. Tagebücher, Briefe, Aufzeichnungen (1900–1941). Im Auftrag des MGFA bearb. und hrsg. von Michael Epkenhans (Vice-Admiral Albert Hopman: Diaries, letters, notes, 1900–1941).

Serie B (Series B)

Protokolle und Dokumente des Bundestagsausschusses für Verteidigung und seiner Vorläufer. Im Auftrag des MGFA hrsg. von Hans-Erich Volkmann unter Mitarbeit von Cynthia Flohr (Protocols and documents of the parliamentary commission for defense and its predecessors).

MILITÄRGESCHICHTLICHE STUDIEN (MILITARY-HISTORICAL STUDIES)

1. Joachim Ehlers. *Die Wehrverfassung der Stadt Hamburg im 17. und 18. Jahrhundert.* 1966. XIV, 273 S., 28,—DM (The state of defenses in the city of Hamburg in the seventeenth and eighteenth centuries).
2. Manfred Kehrig. *Die Wiedereinrichtung des deutschen militärischen Attachédienstes nach dem Ersten Weltkrieg (1919–1933).* 1966. IX, 254 S. (vergriffen) (The reestablishment of the German military attaché service after the First World War, 1919–1933).
3. Peter Fiala. *Die letzte Offensive Altösterreichs. Führungsprobleme und Führerverantwortlichkeit bei der österr.-ungar. Offensive in Venetien, Juni 1918.* 1967. XII, 157 S. (vergriffen) (The last offensive of old Austria: Command problems and commander responsibility in the Austro-Hungarian offensive in Venetia, June 1918).
4. Peter Bucher. *Der Reichswehrprozeß. Der Hochverrat der Ulmer Reichswehroffiziere. 1929/30.* 1967. VI, 524 S., 38,—DM (The German army trial: The high treason of the Ulm officers, 1929–1930).
5. Eckart Busch. *Der Oberbefehl. Seine rechtliche Struktur in Preußen und Deutschland seit 1848.* 1967. VI, 200 S., 28,—DM (The Supreme Command: Its legal structure in Prussia and Germany since 1848).
6. Lothar Burchardt. *Friedenswirtschaft und Kriegsvorsorge. Deutschlands wirtschaftliche Rüstungsbestrebungen vor 1914.* 1968. IX, 277 S., 30,—DM (Peacetime economics and provision for war: Germany's economic armament efforts before 1914).
7. Hans Umbreit. *Der Militärbefehlshaber in Frankreich 1940–1944.* 1968. XIII, 306 S. (vergriffen) (The military commander in France, 1940–1944).
8. Hagen Schulze. *Freikorps und Republik 1918–1920.* 1969. XI, 363 S. (vergriffen) (Free corps and republic, 1918–1920).

9. Johann Hellwege. *Die spanischen Provinzialmilizen im 18. Jahrhundert.* 1969. VIII, 471 S., 38,—DM (The Spanish provincial militias in the eighteenth century).
10. Eckardt Opitz. *Österreich und Brandenburg im Schwedisch-Polnischen Krieg 1655 bis 1660. Vorbereitung und Durchführung der Feldzüge nach Dänemark und Pommern.* 1969. X, 361 S., 38,—DM (Austria and Brandenburg in the First Northern War, 1655–1660: Preparation and execution of the campaigns in Denmark and Pomerania).
11. Rudolf Lenz. *Kosten und Finanzierung des Deutsch–Französischen Krieges 1870–1871. Dargestellt am Beispiel Württembergs, Badens und Bayerns.* 1970. X, 172 S., 24,—DM (Costs and financing of the Franco–Prussian War, 1870–1871: Portrayed in the examples of Württemberg, Baden and Bavaria).
12. Volkmar Bueb *Die "Junge Schule" der französischen Marine. Strategie und Politik 1875–1900.* 1971. IX, 185 S., 36,—DM (The "Young School" of the French Navy: Strategy and politics, 1875–1900).
13. Dieter Ernst Bangert. *Die russisch–österreichische militärische Zusammenarbeit im Siebenjährigen Kriege in den Jahren 1758 bis 1759.* 1971. XIV, 430 S., 48,—DM (Russian–Austrian military cooperation in the Seven Years' War in the years 1758 to 1759).
14. Wolf D. Gruner. *Das bayerische Heer 1825 bis 1864. Eine kritische Analyse der bewaffneten Macht Bayerns vom Regierungsantritt Ludwigs I. bis zum Vorabend des deutschen Krieges.* 1972. VIII, 439 S. (vergriffen) (The Bavarian Army 1825 to 1864: A critical analysis of the armed might of Bavaria from the beginning of the reign of Ludwig I to the eve of the German War).
15. Volker Wieland. *Zur Problematik der französischen Militärpolitik und Militärdoktrin in der Zeit zwischen den Weltkriegen.* 1973. VI, 290 S. (vergriffen) (Regarding the problematic nature of French military policy and military doctrine in the period between the World Wars).
16. Kurt Fischer. *Deutsche Truppen und Entente-Intervention in Südrußland 1918/19.* 1973. V, 160 S. (vergriffen) (German troops and entente intervention in southern Russia, 1918–1919).
17. Gotthard Breit. *Das Staats- und Gesellschaftsbild deutscher Generale beider Weltkriege im Spiegel ihrer Memoiren.* 1973. 245 S. (vergriffen) (German generals' views of state and society in both world wars, as reflected in their memoirs).
18. Wilfried Wagner. *Belgien in der deutschen Politik während des Zweiten Weltkrieges.* 1974. 324 S., 40,—DM (Belgium in German policy during the Second World War).
19. Justus-Andreas Grohmann. *Die deutsch–schwedische Auseinandersetzung um die Fahrstraßen des Öresunds im Ersten Weltkrieg.* 1974. IX, 283 S., 36,—DM (The German–Swedish dispute over the roads of Öresund during the First World War).
20. Antonio Schmidt-Brentano. *Die Armee in Österreich. Militär, Staat und Gesellschaft 1848–1867.* 1975. 553 S., 48,—DM (The army in Austria: Military, state and society, 1848–1867).
21. Klaus-Volker Gießler. *Die Institution des Marineattachés im Kaiserreich.* 1976. 332 S., 38,—DM (The naval attaché in Imperial Germany).

22. Jörg Calließ. *Militär in der Krise. Die bayerische Armee in der Revolution 1848/49.* 1976. VI, 232 S., 40,—DM (The military in crisis: The Bavarian army in the revolution of 1848–1849).
23. Gerhard W. Rakenius. *Wilhelm Groener als Erster Generalquartiermeister. Die Politik der obersten Heeresleitung 1918/19.* 1977. VII, 276 S., 38,—DM (Wilhelm Groener as the first quartermaster-general. The politics of the supreme command, 1918–1919).
24. Ernst W. Hansen. *Reichswehr und Industrie Rüstungswirtschaftliche Zusammenarbeit und wirtschaftliche Mobilmachungsvorbereitungen 1923–1932.* 1978. X, 272 S. (vergriffen) (The German Army and industry. Armament–economic coöperation and preparations for economic mobilization, 1923–1932).
25. Ulrich Marwedel. *Carl von Clausewitz. Persönlichkeit und Wirkungsgeschichte seines Werks bis 1918.* 1978. VIII, 304 S. (vergriffen) (Carl von Clausewitz: Personality and historical influence of his work to 1918).
26. Hans-Martin Ottmer. *Die Rubikon-Legende. Untersuchungen zu Caesars und Pompeius' Strategie vor und nach Ausbruch des Bürgerkrieges.* 1979. VII, 120 S., 28,—DM (The legend of the rubicon: Investigations into Caesar's and Pompey's strategies before and after the outbreak of the Civil War).
27. Karl-Volker Neugebauer. *Die deutsche Militärkontrolle im unbesetzten Frankreich und in Französisch Nordwestafrika 1940–1942. Zum Problem der Sicherung der Südwestflanke von Hitlers Kontinentalimperium.* 1980. VI, 192 S., 38,—DM (German military control in unoccupied France and in French Northwest Africa, 1940–1942: The problem of securing the southwest flank of Hitler's continental imperium).
28. Detlef Vogel. *Der Stellenwert des Militärischen in Bayern (1849–1875). Eine Analyse des militärzivilen Verhältnisses am Beispiel des Militäretats, der Heeresstärke und des Militärjustizwesens.* 1981. V, 217 S., 38,—DM (The status of the military in Bavaria, 1849–1875: An analysis of the military–civilian relationship in the examples of the military budget, the strength of the armed forces and the military justice system).
29. Reinhard Stumpf. *Die Wehrmacht-Elite. Rang- und Herkunftsstruktur der deutschen Generale und Admirale 1933–1945.* 1982. 399 S., 48,—DM (The German armed forces elite: Rank and background structure of the German generals and admirals, 1933–1945).
30. Gerhard Hecker. *Walther Rathenau und sein Verhältnis zu Militär und Krieg.* 1983. 542 S., 74,—DM (Walther Rathenau and his relationship to the military and war).
31. Ulrich Marwitz. *Staatsräson und Landesdefension. Untersuchungen zum Kriegswesen des Herzogtums Preußen (1640–1655).* 1983. 232 S., 48,—DM (Reason of state and state defense: Investigations into the nature of war in the duchy of Prussia, 1640–1655).
32. Rolf-Dieter Müller. *Das Tor zur Weltmacht. Die Bedeutung der Sowjetunion für die deutsche Wirtschafts- und Rüstungspolitik*

zwischen den Weltkriegen. 1984. 403 S., 54,—DM (The gateway to world power status: The significance of the Soviet Union for German economic and armament policies between the World Wars).

33. Günther Hebert. *Das Alpenkorps. Aufstellung, Organisation und Einsatz einer Gebrigstruppe im Ersten Weltkrieg.* 1988. 176 S., 40,—DM (The Alpine Corps. Establishment, organization and the action of a mountain division in the First World War).
34. Udo Ratenhof. *Die Chinapolitik des Deutschen Reiches 1871–1945. Wirtschaft–Rüstung–Militär.* 1987. X, 629 S., 96,—DM (The China policy of the German state, 1871–1945: Economics–armament–military).
35. Gerhard Horsmann. *Untersuchungen zur militärischen Ausbildung im republikanischen und kaiserzeitlichen Rom.* 1991. X, 260 S., 48,—DM (Investigations in military education in republican and imperial Rome).

MILITÄRGESCHICHTE SEIT 1945 (MILITARY HISTORY SINCE 1945)

1. *Aspekte der deutschen Wiederbewaffnung bis 1955.* Mit Beiträgen von Hans Buchheim, Kurt Fett, Peter Gosztony, Hans-Adolf Jacobsen, Paul Noack, Hans Tänzler, Gerhard Wettig. 1975. X, 228 S. (vergriffen) (Aspects of German rearmament to 1955).
2. Heinrich W. Nöbel. *Heer und Politik in Indonesien. Zielsetzung und Zielverwirklichung einer militärischen Organisation 1945–1967.* 1975. VII, 236 S., 32,—DM (Army and politics in Indonesia: Setting and realizing goals for a military organization, 1945–1967).
3. Oskar Weggel. *Milz, Wehrverfassung und Volkskriegsdenken in der Volksrepublik China.* 1977. VIII, 195 S., 36,—DM (Militia, state of defenses and belief in a people's war in the People's Republic of China).
4. Gunther Mai. *Westliche Sicherheitspolitik in Kalten Krieg. Der Korea-Krieg und die deutsche Wiederbewaffnung 1950.* 1977. VII, 207 S., 36,—DM (Western security policy in the Cold War: The Korean War and German rearmament, 1950).
5. Dietrich Wagner. *FDP und Wiederbewaffnung. Die wehrpolitische Orientierung der Liberalen in der Bundesrepublik Deutschland 1949–1955.* 1978. IX, 182 S., 36,—DM (FDP and rearmament: The defense policy orientation of liberals in the Federal Republic of Germany, 1949–1955).
6. Heinz-Ludger Borgert, Walter Stürm, Norbert Wiggershaus. *Dienstgruppen und westdeutscher Verteidigungsbeitrag. Vorüberlegungen zur Bewaffnung der Bundesrepublik Deutschland.* 1982. 230 S., 38,—DM (Service groups and West German defense contribution: Observations prior to the arming of the Federal Republic of Germany).
7. *Die Europäische Verteidigungsgemeinschaft. Stand und Probleme der Forschung.* Im Auftyrag des MGFA hrsg. von Hans-Erich Volkmann und Walter Schwengler. Mit Beiträgen von A. Breccia, A. Doering-Manteuffel, A. Fischer, P. Guillen, P. Jones, A. E. Kersten, W. Lipgens, K. A. Maier, W. Meier-Dörnberg, P. Noack, R. Poidevin, J. P. Rioux, H.-E. Volkmann, D. Cameron Watt, and W. Weidenfeld. 1985. 346 S.

(vergriffen) (The European Defense Community: The situation and problems in research).

8. *Die westliche Sicherheitsgemeinschaft 1948–1950. Gemeinsame Probleme und grundsätzliche Nationalinteressen in der Gründungsphase der Nordatlantischen Allianz.* Im Auftrag des MGFA hrsg. von Norbert Wiggershaus und Roland G. Foerster. Mit Beiträgen von D. Cameron Watt, L. De Vos, C. Greiner, P. Guillen, L. S. Kaplan, M. Knapp, W. Krieger, P. Létourneau, W. Loth, P. Melandri, N. Petersen, E. Pikart, R. H. Rainero, O. Riste, J. Schulten, K. Schwabe, G. Warner, N. Wiggershaus, und W. Woyke. 1988. 387 S., 65,—DM. Ausgabe in englischer Sprache bei Berg Publishers, Oxford, erschienen (The Western Security Community, 1948–1950: Collective problems and fundamental national interests in the foundational phase of the North Atlantic Alliance) (English edition published by Berg).
9. *Zwischen kalten Krieg und Entspannung. Sicherheits- und Deutschlandpolitik der Bundesrepublik im Mächtesystem der Jahre 1953–1956.* Im Auftrag des MGFA hrsg. von Bruno Thoß, und Hans-Erick Volkmann. Mit Beiträgen von E. Ambrose, D. Carlton, R. Fritsch-Bournazel, K. Gotto, C. Greiner, W. Loth, H.-J. Rupieper, D. Staritz, B. Thoß, und H.-E. Volkmann. 1988. VIII, 256 S., 45,—DM (Between Cold War and detente: Security policy and German policy of the Federal Republic in the system of the powers for the years 1953–1956).

MILITÄRGESCHICHTLICHE STUDIEN (STUDIES IN MILITARY HISTORY)

1. Rudolf Steiger. *Armor Tactics in the Second World War. Panzer Army Campaigns of 1939–41 in German War Diaries.* 1991. XIV, 288 S., £19.95.
2. *The Conduct of the Air War in the Second World War. An International Comparison.* Ed. by Horst Boog. 1992. XII, 775 S. (vergriffen).
3. Klaus Reinhardt. *Moscow—The Turning Point: The Failure of Hitler's Strategy in the Winter of 1941–42.* 1992. 480 S., £44.95.
4. *The Western Security Community 1948–1950. Common Problems and Conflicting National Interests during the Foundation Phase of the Atlantic Alliance.* Ed. Roland G. Foerster and Norbert Wiggershaus. 1994. 461 S., £44.95.

In Preparation

Dieter Ose, *The German Defence of Normandy.*

Das Rußlandbild im Dritten Reich, hrsg. von Hans-Erich Volkmann. Gedruckt mit Unterstützung des MGFA. 1994. VI, 466 S., 58,—DM (The image of Russia in the Third Reich).

Potsdam. Staat, Armee, Residenz in der preußisch–deutschen Militärgeschichte. Im Auftrag des MGFA hrsg. von Bernhard R. Kroener unter Mitarbeit von Heiger Ostertag. 1993. 637 S., 78,—DM (Potsdam: State, army, royal seat in Prussian–German military history).

Lernen aus dem Krieg? Deutsche Nachkriegszeiten 1918 und 1945. Beiträge zur historischen Friedensforschung, hrsg. vom Arbeitskreis Historische Friedensforschung mit Unterstützung des MGFA und der Arbeitsstelle Friedensforschung Bonn. Hrsg. von Gottfried Neidhart und Dieter Riesenberger. 1992. 448 S., 24,—DM. (= Beck'sche Reihe, 446) (Learning from war? German postwar periods 1918 and 1945. Lectures in the history of peace).

Hans-Joachim Harder. *Militärgeschichtliches Handbuch Baden-Württemberg.* 1987. 387 S. (vergriffen) (Military historical handbook of Baden-Württemberg).

Gerhard Söllner. *Für Badens Ehre. Die Geschichte der badischen Armee. Formation, Feldzüge, Waffen, Ausrüstung 1604 bis 1832.* Bd 1. 1995. 300 S., 98,—DM. (= Dokumente zur Landesgeschichte, Bd 23) (For the honor of Baden: The history of the Baden Army—formation, campaigns, weapons, armament 1604 to 1832).

Manfred Rauh. *Geschichte des Zweiten Welkriegs. Erster Teil: Die Voraussetzungen.* Hrsg. vom MGFA 1991. IV, 401 S., 68,—DM (History of the Second World War. Part I: The prerequisites).

Jörg Rüpke. *Domi militiae. Die religiöse Konstruktion des Krieges in Rom.* Hrsg. vom MGFA. 1990. 312 S., 68,—DM (*Domi militiae.* The religious construction of war in Rome).

30 Jahre Bundeswehr 1955–1985. Friedenssicherung im Bündnis. Im Auftrag des Bundesministeriums der Verteidigung zur Wanderausstellung herausgegeben vom MGFA. 1985. 406 S. (vergriffen) (Thirty years of the West German Army, 1955–1985: The securing of peace within the alliance).

Wolfram Wette. *Militarismus und Pazifismus. Auseinandersetzung mit den deutschen Kriegen.* 1991. XIII, 268 S., 29,80 DM (= Schriftenreihe Geschichte und Frieden, Bd 3) (Militarism and pacifism: Examination of the German wars).

Josef Anker. *Die Militärstrafgerichsordnung für das Deutsche Reich von 1898. Entwicklung, Einführung und Anwendung, dargest. an der Auseinandersetzung zwischen Bayern und Preußen.* 1995., 590 S., 138,—DM (The military criminal courts ordinance for the German Empire of 1898: Development, introduction and application, as portrayed in the dispute between Bavaria and Prussia).

BIBLIOTHECA RERUM MILITARIUM (LIBRARY OF MILITARY AFFAIRS)

Quellen und Darstellungen zur Militärwissenschaft und Militärgeschichte (Sources and Portrayals of Military Science and Military History)

1. Hannß Friedrich von Fleming. *Der vollkommene Deutsche Soldat.* Faks.-Dr. der Ausg. 1726. Mit einer Einl. v. W. Hummelberger. 1967. 16, 20, 808 S., 420,—DM (The complete German soldier).
2. Lorenz von Stein. *Die Lehre vom Heerwesen. Als Theil der Staatswißen-*

schaft. Mit einem Vorw. von E.-W. Böckenförde. Neudr. der Ausg. 1872. 1967. XVI, 274 S., 76,—DM (The teaching of things military: As a part of political science).

3. Flavii Arriani *Tactica* et Mauricii *Ars militaris.* Hrsg. von Joh. Scheffer. Faks.-Dr. der Ausg. 1664. Mit einer Einl. von W. Hahlweg. 1967. 14, 537 S., 110,—DM (Flavius Arrian's *Tactics* and Maurice's *The art of war*).
4. *Reglement vor die Königl. Preußische Infanterie von 1726.* Faks.-Dr. der Ausg. 1726. Mit einer Einl. von H. Bleckwenn. 1968. XLVIII, 642 S., 138,—DM (Regulations of the Royal Prussian Infantry from 1726).
5. *Corpus Iuris Militaris.* Hrsg.: Johann Christian Lünig. Faks.-Dr. der Ausg. 1723. Mit einem Vorw. von Lothar Paul. 2 Bde. 1968. 1: IX, 688 S. 2: S. 692–1464, 639 Sp., 640,—DM (The body of military jurisprudence).
6. Claudius Aelianus Tacticus. *The Art of Embattaling an Army or the Second Part of Aelians Tacticks.* Hrsg. und übers.: John Bingham. Facs. repr. of the ed. London 1631. With an introd. (in German) by Werner Hahlweg. 1968. XI, 159, 93 S., 248,—DM.
7. Max Jähns. *Militärgeschichtliche Aufsätze. Neudr. der Veröffentlichungen von 1816 (vielmehr richtig: 1867) bis 1903.* Mit einer Einführung von Ursula v. Gersdorff. 1970. XVIII, 329 S., 78,—DM (Military-historical essays: Reprinting of the publications from 1816 [more likely 1867] to 1903).
8. *La défense des états et la fortification à la fin du 19e siècle. Par Henry Alexis Brialmont.* Réimpr. de l'éd, 1895. Avec une introd. (en anglais) par Christopher Duffy. Nebst Atlas. 1967. Text: XLV, 349 S., Atlas: 17 Bl., 220,—DM (The defense of states and fortification to the end of the nineteenth century).
10. Wilhelm Rüstow. *Der deutsche Militärstaat vor und während der Revolution.* Photomechan. Nachdr. der Ausg. 1850. Mit einer Einl. von Gerhard Oestreich. 1971. XV, 209 S., 72,—DM (The German military state before and during the revolution).
11. Henri, duc de Rohan. *Le parfaict Capitaine. Autrement l'abrégé des guerres de Gaule des commentaires de César.* Neudr. der Ausg. von 1636. Mit einer Einführung von Werner Hahlweg. 1972. 15, 390 S., 98,—DM (The perfect captains: An abridgment of Caesar's commentaries on the Gallic Wars).
12. Johann Renner/Sebastian Heußler. *Kriegsmann New Kunstlich Fahnenbüchlein.* Faks.-Dr. der Ausg. 1615. Mit einer Einl. von Franz Gall. 1978. XXI. 31 Tafeln. 46,—DM (Soldier's new illustrated booklet of flags).
13. Vladimir Fedorov. *Evoljucija strelkovogo oruija (Entwicklung der Schußwaffen)* C. 1. 2. Fotomechan. perepe. izd. 1938–1939 g. Mit einer Einführung von W. Hahlweg. 1970. XX, 198, 314 S., 98,—DM (Development of firearms).
14. Th.A. le Roy de Grandmaison. *La petite Guerre.* Faks.-Dr. der Ausg. von 1756. Mit einer Einführung von Georg Ortenburg. 1972. XXXVIII, 417 S., 90,—DM (The little war).
15. *Stellenbesetzungen im Reichsheer vom 16. Mai 1920, 1. Oktober 1920 und 1. Oktober 1921.* Neudr. der Orig.-Ausg. 1920 bis 1921. Mit einer Einl.

von U. v. Gersdorff. 1968. X, 411 S., 78,—DM (Appointments in the German Army from 16 May 1920, 1 October 1920 and 1 October 1921).

16. Walter Elze. *Das deutsche Heer von 1914.* Neudr. der Ausg. 1928. *Der strategische Aufbau des Weltkrieges 1914–1918.* Neudr. der 2. Ausg. 1939. Mit einer Einl. von. U. v. Gersdorff. 1968. 77 S., 25,—DM (The German Army of 1914: The strategic construction of the World War, 1914–1918).
17. *Regulament und Ordnung des gesammten kaiserlichköniglichen Fuß-Volcks von 1749.* Faks.-Dr. der Orig.-Ausg. Mit einer Einl. von G. Ortenburg. 1.2, 1969. 1.: Textbd. XX, 302, 175 S., 2: Tafelbd. 117 Bl. Abb., 180,—DM (Regulation and ordering of the collective royal–imperial footsoldiery of 1749).
18. *Rang- und Quartierliste der Preußischen Armee von 1812.* Unveränderter Faks.-Dr. Mit einer Einl. von Werner Hahlweg. 1968. XXI, 239 S. (vergriffen) (Rank and quartering list of the Prussian army from 1812).
19. *Die Staatswehr. Wiseenschaftliche Untersuchung der öffentlichen Wehrangelegenheiten.* Von Gustav Ratzenhofer. Neudr. der Ausg. 1881. Mit einer Einführung von Hasso Kruggel-Emden. 1970. IX, XVI, 332 S., 78,—DM (Defense of the state: A scientific investigation of public defense matters).
20. Otto Morawietz. *Beiträge zur Geschichte und Technik der Handwaffen und Maschinengewehre. Zeitschriftenaufsätz 1940–1969.* 1973. 405 S., 240,—DM (Lectures in the history and technology of hand weapons and machine guns: Articles in periodicals, 1940–1969).
21. Charles Theophile Guichard. *Mémoires critiques et historiques sur plusieurs points d'antiquités militaires.* Faks.-Dr. der Ausg. 1774. Mit einer Einführung von Hans Zopf. 4 Bde. 1974. XXVII, 1631 S., 17 Falttaf. 440,—DM (Critical and historical memoirs about many issues of ancient military history).
22. Max Jähns. *Handbuch einer Geschichte des Kriegswesens von der Urzeit bis zur Renaissance.* Neudruck der Ausg. 1878–1880. Mit einer Einl. von Ursula v. Gersdorff. 1979. 2 Bde. Technischer Teil: Bewaffnung, Kampfweise, Befestigung, Belagerung und Seewesen. XLIV, 1288 S., Atlas: 100 Taf. in Fol., 420,—DM (Handbook of a history of the nature of war from earliest times to the Renaissance. 2 Volumes. Technical part: Armament, methods of battle, fortification, siege and sea warfare).
23. *Claudii Aeliani et Leonis Imperatoris Tactica sive De instruendis aciebus (graece et latine).* Neudr. der Ausg. Leiden 1613. Mit einer Einl. von Werner Hahlweg. 1981. XXVI, 18, 214, 6, 447, 7 S., 3 Tafeln. 240,—DM (Claudius Aelianus and the instructional tracts of Emperor Leo [in Greek and Latin]).
24. Bernard Poten. *Geschichte des Militär-, Erziehungs- und Bildungswesens in den Landen deutscher Zunge.* 5 Bde. 2215 S.; Registerband dem 5. Bd eingebunden. Neudr. der Ausg. Berlin 1889. 1982.600,—DM (History of the military, upbringing and educational systems in the German-speaking countries. 5 Vols.).
25. *Russisches Kriegsreglement von 1737. Kriegsreglement von der Pflicht und Schuldigkeit der General-Feld-Marschälle und der gantzen Generalitäat.* Faks.-Dr. der 2. Ausg. St. Petersburg 1737. Mit eine

Einl. von Dieter Bangert. 1976. LXXXVI, 878 S. (Russisch-deutsch). 175,—DM (Russian war regulation of 1737: War regulation on the duty of the general field marshals and of all generals).

26. Gerhard Johann David von Scharnhorst. *Über die Wirkung des Feuergewehrs. Für die Königl. Preußischen Kriegsschulen.* Neudr. der Ausg. von 1813. Mit einer Einl. von Werner Hahlweg. 1973. XXXIII, 112 S. mit 1 Plan. 42,—DM (On the effect of the gunpowder weapon: For the Royal Prussian Military Academies).

29. Georg Friedrich von Tempelhof. *Geschichte des Siebenjährigen Krieges in Deutschland.* Neudr. der Ausg. 1782–1801. Mit einer Einl. von Kurt Peball. 1977. 6 Bde. XXXXVIII, 2127 S., 35 Falttaf. (davon 4 koloriert). 1080,—DM (History of the Seven Years' War in Germany. 6 Vols.).

30. *Rangliste von 1808. Ranglist der Königliche Preußischen activen Truppen.* Faks.-Dr. der Ausg. Königsberg 1808. Mit einer Einl. von Werner Hahlweg. 1972. XVII, VI, 90, 27 S., 38,—DM (Rank list from 1808: Rank list of Royal Prussian active troops).

31. Gerhard Johann David von Scharnhorst. *Militärisches Taschenbuch zum Gebrauch in Felde.* Neudruck der 3. Aufl. 1794. Mit einer Einl. von Ulrich Marwedel. 1980. 27, 8, 480, 37 S. mit 8 Faltkarten. 146,—DM (Military pocketbook for use in the field).

32. Erzherzog Karl von Österreich. *Grundsätze der höheren Kriegskunst für die Generäle der österreichischen Armee.* Neudruck der Ausg. 1806. Mit einer Einl. von Walter Hummelberger. 1974. 22, IV, 92 S., 48,—DM (Principles of the higher art of war for the generals of the Austrian Army).

35. K. Hoburg. *Geschichte der Festungswerke Danzigs.* Text und Tafeln. Neudruck der Ausgabe Danzig 1852. Mit einer Einl. von Werner Hahlweg. 1986. VII, 185 S., XXI Tafeln. 88,—DM (History of the fortifications of Danzig).

36. Bredow/Wedel. *Historische Rang- und Stammliste des deutschen Heeres.* Neudruck der Ausg. 1905. Mit einer Einl. von Edgar Graf v. Matuschka. 1972. 2 Bde. XXI, 1444 S., 380,—DM (Historical rank and descent list of the German Army. Reprint of the 1905 edition).

37. *Denkwürdigkeiten der militärischen Gesellschaft zu Berlin.* 5 Bde. Neudruck der Ausgabe Berlin 1802–1805. Mit einer Einl. von Joachim Niemeyer. 1985. 2045 S. mit 25 Falttafeln. 520,—DM (Memorabilia of the Military Society of Berlin).

38.1: Georg Heinrich von Berenhorst. *Betrachtungen über die Kriegskunst, über ihre Fortschritte, ihre Widersprüche und ihre Zuverlässigkeit.* Nebst zwei Anhängen. Neudruck der 3. Aufl. 1827. Mit einer Einl. von Eckardt Opitz. XXVI, 562 S. (Observations on the art of war, its advance, its contradictions and its reliability).

38.2: *Aus dem Nachlasse von G. H. von Berenhorst.* Herausgegeben von Eduard von Bülow. 2. Abt Neudruck der Ausg. 1845 und 1847. 1978. XXVI, 227; VIII, 374 S., 280,—DM (From the personal papers of G. H. von Berenhorst).

39. *Rangliste der Kgl. Preuß Armee für das Jahr 1806, mit Nachrichten über das nachher. Verhältniß der darin aufgeführten Officiere und Militair-Beamten.* Neudruck der 2. Aufl. 1828, mit den seit dem

Erscheinen eingetretenen Veränderungen und ermittelten Berichtigungen. Dazu Namensregister mit Nachrichten über das nachher. Verhältniß der darin aufgeführten Officiere und Militair-Beamten, enthaltend die Seitenzahl eines Jeden in beiden Auflagen (Angefertigt im März 1835). Mit einer Einl. von Werner Hahlweg. 1976. XVI, X, 374, 102 S., 132,—DM (Rank listing of the Royal Prussian Army for the year 1806, with information thereafter: Relationship of the officers and military officials presented therein).

41. Feldmarschall Heinrich Freiherr von Hess. *Schriften aus dem militärwissenschaftlichen Nachlaß. Mit einer Einführung in sein Leben und das operative Denken seiner Zeit, herausgegeben von Manfried Rauchensteiner.* 1975. X, 475 S. mit 4 Portr. 110,—DM (Writings from the military–Scientific papers of Field Marshal Heinrich Freiherr von Hess: With an introduction to his life and the operational thinking of his time).
42. Hugo Grotius/John Selden. *Mare liberum und mare clausum.* Faks.-Dr. der Ausg. Lugd. Bat. 1618 und London 1635. Mit einer Einl. von Friedhelm Krüger-Sprengel. 1978. XLIV, 111; 26 unp., 304, 12 unp. S., 240,—DM (The open sea and the closed sea).
43. Henri Jomini. *Précis de l'art de la guerre, ou nouveau tableau analytique des principales combinaisons de la stratégie, de la grande tactique et de la politique militaire.* Neudruck der Ausg. 1855. Mit einer Einl. von H. R. Kurz. 1974. 2 Bde. XV, 415, 401 S., 240,—DM (Summary of the art of war, or new analytic tables of the principal contrivances of strategy, grand tactics, and military politics).
44. Gerhard Scharnhorst. *Aufsatzentwurf: Nutzen der militärischen Geschichte; Ursach ihres Mangels.* Faksmile der "Handschrift nach 1807" (Nachlaß Scharnhorst B Nr. 169). Umschrift und Einführung von Ursula v. Gersdorff. 1974. IV, XI, 27 B1., 10 S., 55,—DM (Essay outline: The use of military history; cause of its deficiency).
45. Carl von Clausewitz. *Verstreute kleine Schriften.* Zusammengestellt, bearbeitet und eingeleitet von Werner Hahlweg. 1979. XXV, 634 S (vergriffen) (Scattered short writings).
46. Johann Friedrich von der Decken. *Betrachtungen über das Verhältniß des Kriegsstandes zu dem Zwecke der Staaten.* Neudruck der Ausgabe Hannover 1800. Mit einer Einführung von Joachim Niemeyer. 1982. XXVI, 371 S., 98,—DM (Observations on the relationship of the level of war to the purposes of states).
47. Alexander von Zastrow. *Geschichte der beständigen Befestigung oder Handbuch der vorzüglichsten Systeme und Manieren der Befestigungskunst.* Neudruck der 3. Aufl. Leipzig 1854. Mit einer Einl. von Rudolf Schott. 1983. XI, 499 S., 20 Faltpläne. 160,—DM (History of the durable fortification, or handbook of the most advantageous systems and manners of the art of fortification).
48. *Rangliste der Königlich-bayerischen Armée für das Jahr 1811.* Neudr. der Ausg. von 1811. Mit einer Einl. von Othmar Hackl. 1982. LXXVI, 212, 40 ungezählte S., 82,—DM (Rank listing of the Royal Bavarian Army for the year 1811).
49. Gerhard von Scharnhorst. *Ausgewählte Schriften.* Zusammengestellt von Ursula von Gersdorff. 1983. XVIII, 520 S., 68,—DM (Selected writings).

50. *Ehrenrangliste des ehemaligen Deutschen Heeres. Auf Grund der Ranglisten von 1914 mit den inzwischen eingetretenen Veränderungen.* Hrsg. vom Deutschen Offizier-Bund. Neudruck der Ausgabe Berlin 1926. Mit einer Einführung von Friedrich-Christian Stahl. 1987. 2 Bde. XVII, 1310 S., 240,—DM (Honor rank listing of the former German Army: Based on the rank listings of 1914, including the changes since. Reprint of 1926 edition).
51. *Die Organisation der Landwehr in Preußen.* Nachdruck der in den Beiheften zum Militärwochenblatt 1845–1858 erschienenen Darstellungen zur Entwicklung der Landwehr und des Landsturms in den preußischen Provinzen. Mit einer Einleitung von Joachim Niemeyer (in Vorbereitung) (The organization of the Territorial Army in Prussia. Reprint of the portrayals of the development of the Territorial Army and the Home Guard in the Prussian provinces, appearing in the Supplements to the *Military Weekly*, 1845–1858).
52. Martin Richter. *Die Entwicklung und gegenwärtige Gestaltung der Militärseelsorge in Preußen. Historisch–kritische Denkschrift.* Neudruck der Ausgabe Berlin 1899. Mit einer Einf. von Arnold Vogt. 1991. XXIII, 203, IV, 114 S., 98,—DM (The development and present form of the military spiritual welfare service in Prussia: Historical–critical memorandum).
53. H.Dv. 487. *Führung und Gefecht der verbundenen Waffen (F.u.G.). Neudruck der Ausgabe 1921–1924 in 3 Teilen. Mit einer Einführung von Karl-Volker Neugebauer.* 1994. Getr. Zählung [767 S.], 125,—DM (Command and utilization of combined weapons [firearms and grenades]).

In Preparation

54. Jakob von Eggers. *Neues Kriegs-, Ingenieur-, Artillerie-, See- und Ritter-Lexikon,* 2 Bde, Dresden 1757 (New war, engineer, artillery, naval and knight's encyclopedia).
55. William Falconer. *An Universal Dictionary of the Marine.* London, 1780.

Handbuch zur deutschen Militärgeschichte 1648–1939, 6 vols. 1979–1981 (Handbook of German military history, 1648–1939).

Bibliographie zur Luftkriegsgeschichte (Teil 1: Literatur bis 1960), bearbeitet im MGFA von *Karl Köhler.* 1966. XII, 284 S. (= Schriften der Bibliothek für Zeitgeschichte, Weltkriegsbücherei, Stuttgart. N. F. der Bibliographien der Weltkriegsbücherei, H. 5) (vergriffen) (Bibliography of air war history [Part 1: Literature to 1960]).

Geschichte und Militärgeschichte. Wege der Forschung. Hrsg. von Ursula v. Gersdorff mit Unterstützung des MGFA. 1974. 381 S. (vergriffen) (History and military history: Methods of research).

Verteidigung im Bündnis. Planung, Aufbau und Bewährung der Bundeswehr 1950 bis 1972. Hrsg. vom MGFA. 1975. 502 S. (vergriffen) (Defense in the alliance: Planning, build-up and maintenance of the West German Army, 1950–1972).

German Air Force Monograph Project (of the Historical Research Division, Air University, Office of Air Force History, Headquarters USAF)

PUBLISHED MONOGRAPHS

Deichmann, General der Flieger a.D. Paul. *German Air Force Operations in Support of the Army*. 1962.
Drum, General der Flieger a.D. Karl. *Airpower and Russian Partisan Warfare*. 1962.
Morzik, Generalmajor a.D. Fritz. *German Air Force Airlift Operations*. 1961.
Nielsen, Generalleutnant Andreas. *The German Air Force General Staff*. 1959.
Plocher, Generalleutnant Hermann. *The German Air Force vs. Russia, 1941*. 1965.
Plocher, Generalleutnant Hermann. *The German Air Force vs. Russia, 1942*. 1966.
Plocher, Generalleutnant Hermann. *The German Air Force vs. Russia, 1943*. 1967.
Schwabedissen, Generalleutnant a.D. Walter. *The Russian Air Force in the Eyes of German Commanders*. 1960.
Suchenwirth, Prof. Richard. *Historical Turning Points in the German Air Force*. 1959.
Suchenwirth, Prof. Richard. *Development of the German Air Force, 1919–1939*. 1968.
Suchenwirth, Prof. Richard. *Command and Leadership in the German Air Force*. 1969.
Uebe, Generalleutnant a.D. Klaus. *Russian Reactions to German Air Power in World War II*. 1964.

UNPUBLISHED MONOGRAPHS

Deichmann, General der Flieger a.D. Paul. *The System of Target Selection Applied by the German Air Force in World War II*. 1956.
Deichmann, General der Flieger a.D. Paul and General a.D.E.A. Marquard. *Luftwaffe Methods in the Selection of Offensive Weapons*. 1954.
Drum, General der Flieger a.D. Karl. *The German Luftwaffe in the Spanish Civil War*. 1957.
Felmy, Generalleutnant a.D. Hellmuth. *The German Air Force versus the Allies in the Mediterranean*. 1955.

Gottschling, Oberst a.D. Kurt. *The Radio Intercept Service of the German Air Force.* 1955.

Grabmann, Generalmajor a.D. Walter. *German Air Force Air Defense Operations.* 1956.

Gundelach, Hptm. Karl. *The Effect of the Allied Air Attacks on the Ground Echelon of the Luftwaffe in Western Europe in 1944.* 1956.

Hertel, Generalingenieur a.D. Walter. *Procurement in the German Air Force.* 1955.

Hess, Obnerstleutnant a.D. Carl. *Air–Sea Rescue Service of the Luftwaffe in World War II.* 1955.

Jacob, Karl-Guenter. *The German Passive Air Defense Services.* 1957.

Kammhuber, General der Flieger a.D. Josef. *Problems in the Conduct of a Day and Night Defensive Air War.* 1953.

Kammhuber, General der Flieger a.D. Josef. *Problems of Long-Range All-Weather Intruder Aircraft.* 1954.

Kammhuber, General der Flieger a.D. Josef. *Fighter-Bomber Operations in Situations of Air Inferiority.* 1956.

Kesselring, Feldmarschall Albert. *Die Führung der Deutschen Luftwaffe im Kriege.* 1958.

Klee, Hauptman a.D. Karl. *Operation SEA LION and the Role of the Luftwaffe in the Planned Invasion of England.* 1955.

Kreipe, General der Flieger a.D. Werner, and Oberst a.D. Rudolf Koester. *Technical Training within the German Luftwaffe.* 1955

Maass, Generalleutnant a.D. Bruno. *The Organization of the German Air Force High Command and Higher Echelon Headquarters within the German Air Force.* 1955.

Mix, Oberst-Ingenieur a.D. *The Development of German Aircraft Armament to 1945.* 1957.

Neilsen, Generalleutnant a.D. Andreas L. *The Collection and Evaluation of Intelligence for the German Air Force High Command.* 1955.

Neilsen, Generalleutnant a.D. Andreas L. and Generalmajor a.D. Walter Grabmann. *Anglo-American Techniques of Strategic Warfare in the Air.* 1957.

Pickert, General der Flakartillerie a.D. Wolfgang. *Impact of Allied Air Attacks on German Divisions and other Army Forces in Zones of Combat.* 1958.

Pissin, Major a.D. Werner. *The Battle of Crete.* 1956

Riedmann, Oberst a.D. Johannes. *Die Technische Ausbildung in der Deutschen Luftwaffe.* 1956.

Schmid, Generalleutnant a.D. Josef "Beppo." *The German Air Force versus the Allies in the West, 1943–1945.* 1954.

Schroeder, Generaloberstabsarzt Prof. Dr. *Medical and Health Services in the German Air Force.* 1955.

Schwabedissen, Generalleutnant a.D. Walter. *Problems of Fighting a Three-Front Air War.* 1956.

Speidel, General der Flieger a.D. Wilhelm. *The German Air Force in the Polish Campaign of 1939.* 1956.

Speidel, General der Flieger a.D. Wilhelm. *The German Air Force in France and the Low Countries.* 1958.

Von Renze, General der Flakartillerie a.D. *The Development of German Antiaircraft Weapons and Equipment of All Types up to 1945.* 1958.

The Planning and Development of Bombs for the German Air Force, 1925–1945. 1955.

GERMAN DOCUMENT COLLECTION

The Document Collection consists of German military directives, situation reports, war diaries, strength reports, journals, maps, brief histories, charts, photographs, and summaries concerning the German Air Force from 1914 to 1945. The collection is arranged by topics. It is in the German language only.

Air-Sea Rescue
Intelligence
Miscellaneous German Records
Organization, Administration, and Procedures
Tactical Functions
Training
Book Collection
Photo Collection
Key Personnel Card File
German Monograph Project Index Cards
Microfilm

8

Greece

Hellenic Army General Staff, Army History Directorate, and the Greek Military Historical Archives

Hellenic Army Directorate of History

GENERAL

The Greek Ministry of Defense is in possession of a significant number of military archives. The archives are not kept at the same place and the same department. Thus, today there are the following military archives:

a. Hellenic Army General Staff (HAGS) Archives
   - Historical
   - General
   - Specific
   - Miscellaneous

b. Hellenic Navy General Staff Archives
   - Historical
   - General
   - Specific
   - Miscellaneous

c. Hellenic Air Force General Staff Archives
   - Historical
   - General
   - Specific
   - Miscellaneous

HISTORICAL ARCHIVES

When the term "military archives" is used, it applies to the records of the war periods of modern Greek history. The most significant and largest volume of those records pertains to the army, and the relevant material is kept at the Army History Directorate (AHD) of the HAGS.

The Army History Directorate is headed by a lieutenant general and is divided into six independent and self-contained offices having different areas of responsibility. These offices have as directors general officers, while in three of them philologists-historiographers serve as section chiefs.

The Army History Directorate keeps the following:

Historical records. The largest part of these are original and in manuscript form. They include event reports from company level to battalion level, large formation orders, orders from the general headquarters, orders of the day, calendars, and other material from the following periods:

- Greek–Turkish War, 1897
- Macedonian Struggle, 1904–1908
- Balkan Wars, 1912–1913
- First World War, Macedonian Front, 1914–1918
- Expedition to South Russia and Ukraine, 1919
- Expedition to Asia Minor, 1922–1923
- Second World War, 1940–1941
- Middle East Operations
- Korean War, 1950–1955
- Archives belonging to military personalities from several war periods
- The Northern Epirus Archives
- The National Resistance Archives
- Photographic Material Archives
- Cartographic Archives
- Historic Data Collection Archives
- Newspaper Archives
- Orders Archives

The part of the archival material that is not in manuscript form is typed and kept as an authentic copy of the original.

The library. The following can be found in the library:

- The historical publications of the Army History Directorate beginning with the Macedonian struggle up to the Expedition Corps of Greece in Korea as well as a large number of monographs.

- 10,000 volumes of international historical bibliography.
- All the army regulations and standing operating procedures, as well as organizational charts and circulars.

The AHD, as mentioned, is not the only agency being in possession of archives. Other such agencies are as follows:

The Military Archives Agency. This agency keeps those military archives of the modern Greek history which cover nonoperational, administrative matters. The information contained in these archives is accessible for an interested party after submitting a relevant application to the agency.

The War Museum. This museum has a wealth of photographic archival material and a collection of military uniforms.

Finally, every division of the HAGS, the HNGS (Hellenic Navy General Staff), and the HAFGS (Hellenic Air Force General Staff) is in possession of its own archival material.

Everything that has been mentioned is relevant to the Military Archives Services of the Greek Armed Forces concerning the last century. Older archival material is kept by the state general archives.

The historical archives of the AHD have been classified in a satisfactory manner. Catalogues make the access to the archives easy. From all the material, the part of it pertaining to the Macedonian Struggle, the Balkan Wars, and the First and Second World Wars is the best with regard to the way it has been recorded, catalogued, and maintained. In particular, the way this material has been catalogued has made its use efficient. The only problem is that cataloguing is a time-consuming process.

Currently a process is in progress, aiming at the computerization of all the archival material. The project targets facilitating the fast retrieval and photocopying of any relevant data. There are several benefits to be derived from this, the greatest of which is the reduction of use of the original material, hoping thus to better preserve it.

At this point it is worth mentioning that our archival material is accessible to researchers, historians, authors, other parts of the civil service, media correspondents, and students. Anyone interested only needs to submit to our directorate a specific application in which he or she should mention the reasons for wanting to do research using the archives. The application is then considered and approved, and afterward the interested party may begin his or her research with the help of the historiographer who is in charge of the office and his or her staff.

Of course, there are certain restrictions to the use of the archives, banning the (probably unwitting) ill-use of the documents as well as their removal from the agency. Also, users are not allowed to quote passages in full from the archives nor are they to photocopy a large number of pages, particularly if those make up a single and self-contained section of a file. Permission to photocopy is allowed for certain well-known documents which will be used by the researcher as special sections in his or her report, mentioning the source of the documents.

Evidently, access to uncatalogued archival material is rather difficult, while access to classified materials is, by law, impossible for thirty years.

The AHD is the keeper of all the archival material that has been rescued during all the war periods of the modern Greek history. This material is, as far as possible, a great aid for relevant research, and contributes, in effect, to the world truth. It also contains several pages in which struggles and liberating wars of superb beauty are narrated. Our country took part in those wars (within or outside its borders), sometimes as a Balkan ally and other times fighting for its national or the world freedom and justice. These are wars in which the moral strength of the Greeks made it possible to subject the matter to the spirit, fighting for world safety either as an immediate involved party or as a volunteer by the side of the allied forces or in the context of the U.N. decisions.

Photos in the Armed Forces Museum and some World War II 28/10/40 to 26/4/41 are in the Foreign Office section of the National Archives.

ADDRESSES OF THE GREEK MILITARY ARCHIVES AGENCIES

Army History Directorate (AHD), Thalou and Pittakoy 10, 10558 Athens, Greece. Tel.: 0030–1–3242961

Navy History Agency (NHA), Marconi 20, 10447 Botanikos, Greece. Tel.: 0030–1–3470610

Air Force History Agency, Delta Falirou, 17561 Pireus, Greece. Tel.: 0030–1–9223030

General Archives of State, Theatrou 6, 10552 Athens, Greece. Tel.: 0030–1–3218289

Greek Air Force History Service

Translated by Major General Konstantinos Kanakaris, MA (Ret.)

The Air Force History Service was formed on or about 1950 as a section of Branch A' of the air force general staff. This section was abolished in August 1956 and a new section of War Exhibitions was created under the Chief of Branch A', which in 1961 became a division. In 1962 the name of the War Exhibitions Division was changed to the Air Force History Division under the Branch Chief A', and later, from 1969, under the Branch Chief B' of the air force general staff (as BF). This division was renamed in 1983 the History Office under the assistant chief of the air force general staff.

The History Office was unified together with the Organization Office of the Air Force Museum and the Air Force Archives Office and a new independent unit of the air force general staff was constituted, titled "The Air Force History Service" under the director of public relations (A5).

The Air Force History Service is now housed in an air force building in Paleon, (Old) Falezon, where the Air Force Equipment Base (BAY) used to be. The service is now functioning with two basic offices: the History Office and the Archives Office. (The Museum Organization Office has been separated and constitutes a special unit at Tatoi Airfield.)

The mission of the service is to concentrate historical material, write air force history, and provide historical materials to officials and individuals, as well as concentrate the air force archives and microfilm them. The service also constitutes an advisory instrument of the air force general staff for historical matters and cooperates with the Hellenic Military History Committee and the International Commission for Military History in Paris.

The History Service is headed by an officer of the rank of wing commander and its personnel are both military and civilian.

The Air Force History Service has, so far, succeeded in the concentration, classification, and microfilming of the military archives (war reports, diaries, plans and operations orders, photographs, etc.). The work of an author that has been, so far, published, includes

- Volume A′ Air Force History 1908–1918
- Volume B′ Air Force History 1919–1929
- Volume C′ Air Force History 1929–1941
- Album and record of the airmen killed in action

This work narrates the events that have marked the evolution of the air force since its existence and, also, states the activities and contribution of the air force to Hellenic war history. For copies of the history individuals can write to the Hellenic Air Force Public Information Office.

Greek Army History

Major General Sotirios Ferendinos

HISTORICAL BACKGROUND

The service of Military Archives may be regarded as the core of the Army History Directorate. This service was established in 1910 in order to collect, keep, and make use of documents of a military nature.

In 1932 the service was given the name War Report Office and continued to collect and keep archive materials of military content. In a parallel manner this service started research activities and published a three-volume work on the "Wars in the Balkans 1912–1913." In 1954 it was named the Army History Directorate and from then on it undertook, now with a more intensified effort, research in the military history of modern Greece (from 1897 onward).

FIELD OF ACTIVITIES

In addition to the publishing activities resulting in twenty-seven volumes and six monographs, the Army History Directorate promotes research in modern Greek military history. The directorate also cooperates with universities, schools, colleges, various scientific associations, and the Hellenic Committee of Military History.

MAJOR COLLECTIONS

The archives of the Army History Directorate can be distinguished in operational commands, military units, war diaries, lists of dead and wounded persons in wartime, and so on. This material is arranged chronologically and by campaigns (e.g., the period of the 1897 Graeco–Turkish War, the Macedonian War of 1904–1908, the Balkan Wars 1912–1913, World War I 1914–1918, etc.) up to the Greek participation in the operation in Korea in 1950–1955.

Many of the documents of the archives of the Army History Directorate are originals signed by persons who in various periods played an important role in Greek History (King Constantine, P. M. El. Venizelos, General Dousmenis, General Plastiras, Field Marshal Papagos, etc.). The directorate also keeps a collection of laws and decrees of military content published in the "Newspaper of the Government" (from 1891 onward).

NONMANUSCRIPT MATERIAL

Within the Army History Directorate is a large library including old and new editions of Greek and foreign origin, arranged by sections: archaeology, Byzantine period, modern military history, dictionaries, and so on. The library is available for researchers. It is continuously enriched with new publications of military content.

FINDING AIDS

A large part of the archives of the directorate is easy to gain access to, thanks to existing catalogues.

PUBLICATIONS

A wide variety of books on the Greek Army and military history from the eighteenth century to 1955 has been published by the Directorate.

29. *The Medical Corps of the Greek Army during the Expedition to Asia Minor (1919–1922).* Publication of the Hellenic Army General Staff/History Dte. Athens 1968. Pp. 335.
30. *The Military Medical Service during the War in 1940–1941.* Publication of the Hellenic Army General Staff/History Dte. Athens 1982. Pp. 300.
31. *Preparation of the Greek Army towards War (1923–1940).* Publication of the Hellenic Army General Staff/History Dte. Athens 1969. Pp. 167.

32. *The Supplying of the Army with Weapons and Ammunition for the Artillery and Infantry in 1940–1941.* Publication of the Hellenic Army General Staff/History Dte. Athens 1982. Pp. 280.

Under a new program started in the mid-1990s, official Hellenic military history is being made available in English, starting with *The Abridged History of the Greek–Italian and Greek–German War of 1940–1941* (1998), with the following translations to follow:

1. *An Abridged History of the Balkan Wars, 1912–13*
2. *An Abridged History of the Participation of the Greek Army in the First World War, 1914–18*
3. *Index of the War Events of the Greek Nation*
4. *The Northern Epirus Fight, 1913–14*
5. *An Abridged History of the Greek Army, 1821–1997*

Historical Department of the Hellenic Navy

Commodore Costas Varfis

BACKGROUND

At first, there was a department the Hellenic Navy general staff (HNGS) called the "Naval Magazine." In February 1928 the name was changed to the Historical Department of the Hellenic Navy. The responsibilities of the Naval Magazine department were

1. To collect records, run the libraries, and be the historical staff of the Hellenic Navy in general.
2. To continue to edit the magazine *Naval Review.*

Until 1944, the Historical Department of the Hellenic Navy was a separate and independent department of the navy general staff. In 1945, the name was changed again, this time to "Historical Department of the Royal Navy." At the same time, it continued to belong to HNGS and had the following responsibilities:

1. The organization and management of records, libraries, and the Museum of the Royal Navy (R.N.).
2. The study of the *History of Wars* in which Royal Navy saw action.
3. The publication of naval magazines.
4. Enlightenment and cooperation with the Hellenic Maritime Union.
5. The management of the R.N.'s printing office.
6. The management of credits (finances) of the historical department of the R.N.

These responsibilities were divided on the following four divisions:

A′ Division: Records, Libraries, Museum

- Organization of records and libraries of the R.N., in general, in order to preserve and maintain all the serious papers and books and the like, and to make it easy to study them.
- Management of the central records and libraries of the R.N. and the supply and control of the libraries on each ship and in each naval division.
- Organization of the museum, which was a part of the Ethnological Committee of Greece, and which contained valuable historical finds.

B′ Division: Studies, Editions, Enlightenment

- Creation, according to the records of the R.N., of the Naval History of Wars on which the R.N. had taken part.
- Publication of the regular edition of the monthly magazine *Naval Review*, in which are included studies and information of concern to the R.N., both directly and indirectly.
- Publication of occasional articles on particular issues in both the Greek and foreign press concerned with Greek and foreign naval history.
- Cooperation with the Greek Maritime Union.
- Enlightenment of the crew of R.N.'s ships, in general, and of the people about the mission, action and history of the R.N.

C′ Division: R.N.'s Printing Office

- Management of the R.N.'s printing office, currently placed at the naval ministry's building and working under a special organization order.
- Handling of printing paper.

D′ Division: Accounting Office

- Estimation of the budget of the historical department and attendance of its realization as well as submitting of its annual accounts.
- Management of financial credits and incomes of the magazines the historical department publishes.

In 1952, according to a special order of HNGS, the historical department was moved to Votanicos. Although the department was camped there, it remained directly under the orders of the chief of HNGS.

TODAY'S SITUATION

Today, the department is known as the Historical Department of the Hellenic Navy. It is completely under the control of the Votanicos Command and continues to reside there.

The Historical Department of the Hellenic Navy has its own regulations of organization and Operation. A captain H.N. is the director and has the deriving responsibilities and obligations.

For the purpose of its existence, the Historical Department of the Navy has the following three divisions:

- A′ Division: Naval History, Naval Magazines
- B′ Division: Records of Warships and Naval Services, Micro-Photography of Records
- C′ Division: Printing and Bookbindery Office of the Hellenic Navy

Figure 8.1 shows the organization of the historical department. The most serious responsibilities of the department are the following:

Figure 8.1
Organization Chart of the Historical Department of the Hellenic Navy

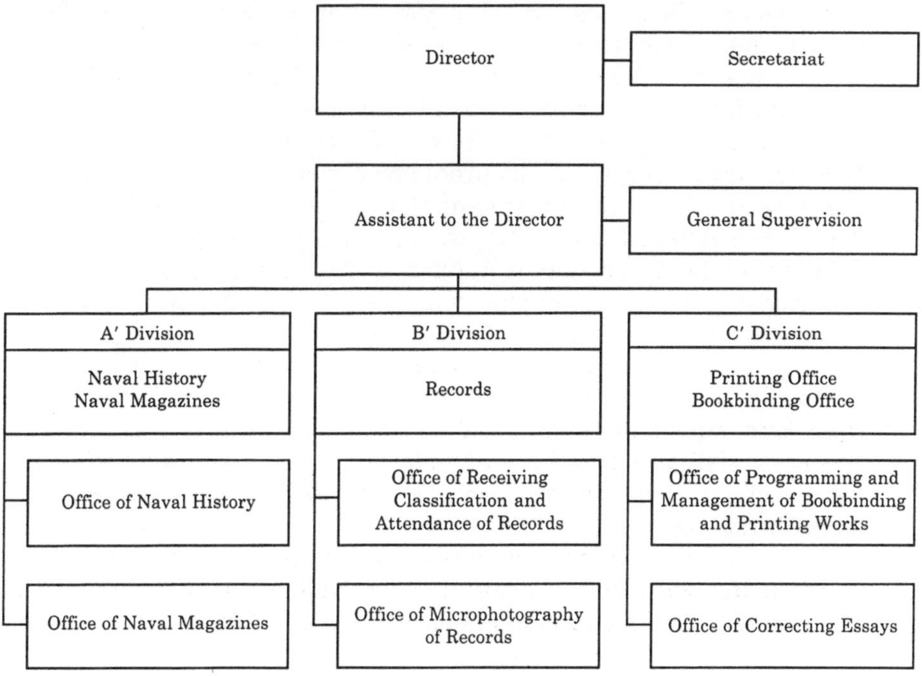

A′ Division

1. To select, preserve, classify, and inventory the existing historical records. To make them available for present and future use for the benefit of our services, as well as other interested parties not related to the Hellenic Navy (HN).
2. To offer information from these records for the writing of the naval history of the Hellenic Navy.
3. To publish, supervise, and manage naval magazines.

B′ Division

1. To preserve, microphotograph, classify, and inventory the records of naval services and warships of the Hellenic Navy.
2. To offer information on these records after an application by the interested services, individuals, or organizations.

C′ Division

1. To publish and bind every kind of paper and book which the Hellenic Navy needs.

NAVAL ISSUES

Among its other responsibilities through the years, the Historical Department has published some books, especially those of naval interest. These are noted in the following bibliography; this activity is also reflected in books published by other services of HN.

The magazine *Naval Review* has been published from 1917 till today, at first as a monthly magazine and later on every two months. Its mission is to contribute to the search for the science and the art of war at sea, the study of the problems of national defense, and for the information of the personnel of the Hellenic Navy about the Naval War Act and about the problems of national defense.

To complete its mission, it publishes chosen and sufficient studies, articles, critiques, information, special dedications, news, and dialogues from the columns of the magazine.

Up to 1987, along with the magazine *Naval Review*, the department also published a little magazine called *Spiritual Naval Culture*. This magazine contributed to the culture of the people, united the navy, giving texts of Greek and foreign literature, parts of some naval acts, and conjectural arts, as well as historical works with naval interests.

At the HN's printing office the monthly magazine *Maritime Greece* is published with the cooperation of the Hellenic Maritime Union.

All in all, the department has, since the 1920s, carried out a multitude of tasks, from preserving the records to seeing them printed, published, and distributed to the service and the Greek public.

BIBLIOGRAPHY

A/08 Torpedo. Description and Regulation, Navy Department, 1911.

Alexandris, Admiral C. A. *The Sea War in 1912–13.* Hellenic General Staff. n.d.

Alexandris, Admiral C. A. *The Naval Operations 1821–1829.* Hellenic Navy History Service, 1930.

Alexandris, Admiral C. A. *The Sea Force in the History of Byzantine Empire.* Hellenic Navy History Service, 1956.

Alexandris, Admiral C. A. *The Revival of Sea Force during Turkish Rule.* Hellenic Navy History Service, 1960.

Babouris, Epam. *The Greek Commercial Fleet during the Last War.* Naval Museum of Greece, 1986.

Bugler's Manual. Navy Department, 1937.

Cadet's Manual. Hellenic Naval Academy, 1976.

Canellopoulos, H. F. *Name List of Sailing Ships.* Aegean Naval Museum, 1987.

Catalogue and Description of the Greek Lighthouses and Lanterns. Navy Department, 1914.

Catevainis, G. M. *International Maritime Law Manual.* Hellenic Navy History Service, 1962.

Catsimpris, C. *Citizen's Training.* Hellenic Naval Academy, 1957.

Chrisanthis, A. *Lessons of Hydrography.* Vol. I, II, Hellenic Naval Academy, 1921–22.

Chrisanthis, A. *Hydrography.* Hydrographic Service, 1924.

Code of the Sea War. Navy Department, 1912.

Constantinidis, T. *Naval History and Tactics (Second Class of Combatants).* Hellenic Naval Academy, 1952.

Constantinidis, T. *Naval History and Tactics (C Class of Combatants).* Hellenic Naval Academy, 1952.

Constantinidis, T. *Naval History and Tactics (D Class of Combatants) (ASO Class & A Class of Mechanics)* Hellenic Naval Academy, 1954.

Constantinidis, T. *Ships, Captains and Companion Sailors.* Hellenic Navy History Service, 1954.

Constas, P. E. *1821's Naval Epic.* Hellenic General Staff, 1971.

Contogiannis, C. *Naval Geography.* Hellenic Naval Academy, 1928.

Damage Control Manual. Hellenic General Staff, 1959.

Destroyer's Discernments Call. Hellenic General Staff, 1951.

Dreadnoughts Type Kilkis-Limnos Lead's Direction Manual. Navy Department, 1918.

Efstathiou, G. *Hoveller. vol. D. North & East Coasts of the Aegean Sea.* Hydrographic Service, n.d.

Farmakopoulos, P. *Royal Navy's Economic Service Manual.* Hellenic Navy, 1957.

Farmakopoulos, P. G. *The War as Substance of the State.* Hellenic Navy History Service, 1940.

First Aid—Health Care. Hellenic General Staff, 1968.

Fokas, D. G. *The Royal Navy's Action in 1940–44.* Hellenic General Staff, 1968.

Fokas, D. G. *Greek Royal Navy's Annals in 1833–1873.* Hellenic General Staff, 1923.

Fokas, D. G. *Royal Navy's Action Report 1940–45.* Vol. I, II, Hellenic Navy History Service, 1953, 1954.

General Instructions for the Use of Modern Greek in Administration. Hellenic General Staff, 1982.

Georgios Caraiskakis Archives. Hellenic General Staff, 1924.

Giakoumakis, Commander D. M. *Manual of Administrative Concern (Care).* Hellenic General Staff, 1970.

Greek Seashores' Lighthouse Indicator. Hellenic Navy, 1977.

Hatzialexiou, D. *Nuclear Physics Lessons.* Hellenic Naval Academy, 1956.

Haziroglou, Th. *Russian and German Language Manual.* Naval Education Administration, n.d.

Hellenic General Staff. *Manual of Ships' Searching.* Navy Department, 1940.

Hydrography in Greece. Hydrographic Service, 1922.

Instructions for Convoy Escort. Hellenic General Staff, 1951.

Instructions for Convoy Formation. Hellenic General Staff, 1951.

Instructions for Lead Torpedo Direction. Hellenic General Staff, 1952.

Instructions for Search and Rescue of Submerged Submarine. Hellenic General Staff, 1960.

Internal Ballistics Study. Hellenic Naval Academy, 1924.

International Naval Law Orders During the War. Navy Department, 1915.

James, W. (dilligence from Captain Pagaras). *The British Navy During the Second World War.* Hellenic Navy History Service, 1948.

Katevainis, G. *Manual of the International Sea Law.* Hellenic Navy, 1962.

King, E. *The United States Navy during the War 1941–45.* Hellenic Navy History Service, 1949.

Likoudis, S. *Mediterranean.* vol. A., Navy Department, 1915.

Likoudis, S. *Greek Coast Lighthouse Indicator 1957.* Lighthouse Department, 1957.

Machines and Royal Ships Staff Duties Regulations. Navy Department, 1914.

Makris, M. *Instructions for Meteorological Observations.* Hydrographic Service, 1922.

Manual of Etiquette. Hellenic General Staff, 1976.

Manual of Maneuvers in Port and Under Way. Hellenic General Staff, 1951.

Manual of Operations and Anchorings. Hellenic Navy, 1914.

Manual of Psychological Operations (Propaganda). Hellenic General Staff, 1970.

Mezeviris, Gr. *Mediterranean and Its Strategic Importance.* Hellenic Navy History Service, 1957.

Mezeviris, Gr. *Strategy and Method for Using New Weapons.* Hellenic Navy History Service, 1959.

Mezeviris, Gr. *Conclusions of the Mediterranean Naval War.* Hellenic Navy History Service, 1961.
Mezeviris, Gr. *The Battle of Atlantic and the Submarine War 1914–18, 1939–45.* Hellenic Navy History Service, 1964.
Mezeviris, Gr. *The Pacific War in 1941–45.* Hellenic General Staff, 1967.
Michail, R. N. Th. *Lessons of Naval Machines* (1st Vol.). Hellenic Naval Academy, 1922–23.
Naval Cosmography. Hydrographic Service, 1928.
Naval Service's 1833–1937 Organic Regulations Manual. Navy Department, 1938.
Naval Stratology. Navy Department, 1922.
Operational Regulation for Naval School of War. Naval School of War, 1966.
Our Navy. Hellenic General Staff, 1950.
Paizis-Paradelis, C. *Hellenic Navy's Ships 1830–1979.* Hellenic General Staff, 1979.
Papavasiliou, Lieutenant Commander A. *Estimated Navigation and Sailing (Coasting).* Hellenic Naval Academy, 1937.
Papavasiliou, Lieutenant Commander A. *Types of Naval Calculations.* Hellenic Naval Academy, 1938.
Pharmakopoulos, P. *Hellenic Naval Academy's Economic Service Manual.* Hellenic Naval Academy, 1957.
Pharos, Th. *Description and Use of Navigations and Missions' Indicator.* Navy Department, 1914.
Principles and Elementary Description of the Gyro-Compass. Hellenic General Staff, 1914.
Radio Localization's Manual. Hellenic General Staff, 1951.
Raphtopoulos, C. *Steersman's Manual.* Navy Department, 1887.
Razis-Cotsicas, A. *Ship's Radial Manual.* Hydrographic Service, 1924.
Razis-Cotsicas, D. *Naval Cosmography.* Hellenic Naval Academy, 1928.
Royal Navy. *Royal Ships's Internal Service Manual.* Hellenic General Staff, 1938.
Royal Navy. *Restricted and Supervised Zones.* Hellenic General Staff, 1939.
Royal Navy's Prints Index. Hellenic Navy (n.d.).
Royal Navy's Uniforms Regulations. Hellenic Navy, 1939.
Royal Navy's Uniforms Regulations. Hellenic General Staff, 1956.
Simpsas, M. G. *The American Navy.* Hellenic Navy History Service, 1954.
Simpsas, M. G. *Navarino.* Hellenic General Staff, 1974.
Simpsas, M. G. *The Navy in the History of the Greeks.* Hellenic General Staff, 1982.
Stasinopoulos, E. *Old and Modern Turkey.* Hellenic Navy History Service, 1929.
Stathakis, N. A. *Dreadnought* Averof. *Chronicle of the Dreadnought of Victory.* Hellenic Navy, 1987.
Temporary Regulation of Best of Destroyers' Use. Hellenic General Staff, 1948.
Temporary Regulation of Landing. Hellenic General Staff, 1915.
Torpedo's A/08 Projects. Navy Department, 1911.
Turbine's Use Manual. Navy Department, 1931.

Von Hohenzollern, Prince F. J. *Emden* (translated by P. Segditsa). Hellenic General Staff, 1929.

Vourlakis, E. S. *Naval Meteorology* (1st part). Hellenic Naval Academy, 1949.

War Museum—Cartography of the Greek Area 15th–20th Century. Hellenic General Staff, 1986.

Wilson, H. W. *History of War Fleets.* Hellenic Navy History Service, 1937.

Zois-Moros, A. *Tide Elements for the Greek Ports.* Hydrographic Service, 1981.

9

Hungary

The Hungarian Military Archives and War-Historical Museum

Jozsef Kun, Director, Translated by William Voss

The following is an abridged version of articles by Jozsef Kun and by Janos Pongo, translated by William Voss, followed by that of László Veszprém.

In a number of countries, such as Australia, the military archives, the museum, and the historical section are either housed together or work in close conjunction, each at times producing publications. In the case of Hungary the establishment has been complicated by both the dominance of Vienna rather than Budapest and by the destructions of war, defeat, and occupation.

Both archives and museums promoted the military past to stimulate the present and were the handmaidens of military history.

Experiences show that the Hungarian Military Archives is not unknown in the circle of Austrian archivists, historians and researchers. Since its origins the archive has always stood in relation to Austrian organs, in first place with the State and War Archives, and also naturally with many archivists and historians who turned to us for explanations or have personally visited the archives. The circle of those interested has since changed, and from several quarters the wish has arisen—in as far as possible within the confines of an article—for the writing of a report about the past activity and continued existence of the Hungarian Military Archives. We approach this request with joy and hope that this small work can be a help for all those who wish to explore the holdings of our archives, or in another respect intend to take advantage of the archives.

The Hungarian Military Archives is a relatively young institution, whose origin is to be found in the unique past of the state. It was established barely four and one-half decades ago, in order to gather the written documents of Hungarian military history. The immediate reason for its founding was not subjects from past centuries, but rather from the First World War. The documents of the earlier military history of the Hungarian people were in the Hungarian State Archives, and the military writings from the later centuries and from the time of the Austro-Hungarian monarchy were, in contrast, kept at the Military Archives in Vienna. In this way, the latter archives became a treasure trove for the Hungarian researcher and historian.

Also at the time of the First World War, the K.u.K. (imperial and royal) order was in force, to wit that the K.u.K. army, as well as the units of the Honved (Hungarian) army, had to send their operational documents to the Vienna Military Archives. Only in 1915 did the War Minister decree that the Honved army and the units of the Hungarian royal home guard were to send their documents directly to the Hungarian State Defense Ministry. Here the documents were copied and the originals sent on to the Military Archives in Vienna. This work was carried out by Department 1/a of the Ministry for State Defense, and for this reason that department can be seen as a predecessor of the Hungarian Military Archives. Department 1/a consisted of several subdivisions, such as the archival and statistical subdivisions, as well as the subdivision created to handle the question of prisoners of war; the subdivision for military history joined these in 1918. In this form of organization the work succeeded until the fall of 1918.

The separation of Hungary from Austria brought with it the necessity for a satisfactory resolution of the question of the Military Archives, for the archival material of the army and especially the corps were threatened by losses. The founding of the Hungarian Archives and Museum as an independent institution lies in the period of the Hungarian Soviet Republic. The decree of the People's Commissariat for Military Affairs to this effect appeared on 8 April 1919.[1] This decree specified exactly the task of the institution: the gathering and preservation of files, which is still today the most basic task.

After the collapse of the Hungarian Soviet Republic (August 1919) the archive was subordinated to the command of Admiral Horthy, but later, however, again returned to the Ministry for State Defense. The peace treaty after the First World War specified the principal basis for further development. In fulfillment of Article 117 of the peace treaty of 1920, after several years of preparatory work in Baden by the representatives of the Austrian federal government and the Hungarian government, a final arrangement regarding the formerly joint archives and file collections was reached at Vienna on 26 May 1926. In this agreement Austria pledged to surrender to Hungary those files that could be seen as in spirit Hungarian. Regarding the joint material, it was determined that it would remain in Vienna. Regarding the processing of the joint materials, the Hungarian government could, with the approval of the Austrian federal government, send a certain number of representatives to Vienna. The delegates were to act as members of the Vienna Branch of the Hungarian Military Archives. This branch still remains today next to the Austrian Military Archives.

After its founding as an independent institution, the Hungarian Military Archives was housed in the building of the Hungarian State Archives, on its third and fourth floors. The military events that were played out here in the fall of 1944 had bad consequences for the materials stored in the archives. On 17 November 1944 a part of the officer corps transferred the archives to Balatonfuered and Suemeg; at a later time to Csepreg and Buek. The transfer involved much valuable material, of which only a small part returned to the archives after the war.

As a consequence of the military events, the wing of the building which had contained the depository of the archives was destroyed to its foundations. Of the sixty rooms, fully fifty-five were destroyed or were severely damaged.

After the Liberation in 1945 the question arose as to how the archives should function in the future. It was temporarily registered as a department of the Ministry for State Defense; the War-Historical Museum, primarily, took the valuable files secured from the ruins into custody. During this time processing and research projects had to be postponed, since the material was still not organized according to subjects. In spite of the difficult economic conditions of the state, the Ministry for State Defense took measures to find accommodations for the archives. In 1946 the current building of the archives was allocated (Budapest I. Kapisztran ter 2). During the war, however, this building had also been severely damaged. Only limited rooms were available for working space and depositories. Therefore, whole subjects had to continue to remain lying piled in the depository. The renovation and reconstruction of the building had already begun, however.

The activity of the archives in the period from 1946 to 1950 showed—for various reasons—only limited success. For example, there was a lack of archivists and the possibilities for accommodation were limited. The holdings of the archives went from one temporary location to another. The extraordinarily small number of personnel could never create order among the *Registraturen* (files that were raised by branches, institutes, or offices) that were transferred from the State Archives to the Military Archives. The complete reorganization of the collected materials had to be postponed to a later time.

The turning point in the development of our archives occurred in 1950–1951. From this time onward the institution received more and more support from the state in relation both to material and personnel questions. At that time, several university graduate students and young specialists were picked up. A special emphasis must also be placed on the large amount of state support that the archives received yearly after 1951. The greatest portion of this capital was used for the acquisition of modern iron shelving. Early in 1956, 4,167 metric lengths of these were installed. The institute received a photo lab, and a workplace for the restoration of paper was set up; appropriate work rooms, in adequate numbers, were made available for the employees of the archives.

The most important work of our archives has been the support of scientific (scholarly) research projects in order to best satisfy the demands of researchers. With this viewpoint in mind, a massive sifting-through of the material took place over the years. In this manner, the ordering of the most important possessions of the archives could again be achieved, which had been disrupted as a result of the Second World War.

The usefulness of an archive depends, naturally, not only on the ordering of its holdings. It also includes other aids which support the researcher and archivist in their work. The basic inventory (an archival aid which contains the most important data pertaining to the material. This includes space in the depository, year cycle, theme, name of the material, number, system of registration, research possibilities) in our archives was completed and every item received a fascicle designation (an archival aid which contains the most important data pertaining to the material: name of the archive, basic inventory-sentence number of the item, accommodation of the item, title of the item, and running number of the depository units in the item). As a result of the number of years elapsed, today all possessions of the archive are available for research projects. The most important task for the coming years will be the expansion and increase in number of the aids available to researchers, as well as the dissemination of researcher opportunities through detailed reports.

The most extensive connected holding is the archive of the General Command, which began its activity in 1740 and, worked without interruption until 1883.[2] In 1884 the IV Corps Command in Budapest took over the material and the modified function of the command; it operated under this name until 1914. To the files of the General Command were also added the material of the juridical department, the independent State-Military Court of Justice (1802–1871), as well as the Engineering and Fortification Administration (1803–1894). The total holding of the archives of the General Command consists of 11,466 fascicles.

This huge block of documents not only possesses military historical worth, but also provides an important source for economic, legal, and cultural historians concerned with this epoch. Those whose interest lies in the development of Hungarian society or have made the nationality problem the theme of their research also cannot afford to do without this material.

After the files of the General Command, the archive of the Royal Hungarian State Defense Ministry (1867–1945) contains the richest material, around 10,000 fascicles. The material of the State Defense Ministry of the Bourgeois-Democratic Revolution, and the People's Commissariat for Warfare of the Hungarian Soviet Republic, are not contained in this holding.

However, the documents of the War Ministry of the Hungarian Republic, which came into existence after the Bourgeois-Democratic Revolution (Documents of the Hungarian War Ministry 1 November 1918–21 March 1919, and the files of the People's Commissariat for Warfare of the Hungarian Soviet Republic 21 March 1919–3 August 1919) are handled specially.

The archives of the Royal Hungarian Honved High Command contain the most important military historical documents from the 1867 settlement to the end of the First World War (1867–1918). The Honved High Command was active without any great organizational alterations to the end of the First World War. The direction of Honved training, disciplinary supervision, and the accounting of military supplies fell under its sphere of activity. The State Defense Minister submitted his own decrees to the military authorities through the supreme commander of the Honved, and in the same way he also received their communications. The supreme commander of the Honved had the military authorities and corps at his disposal, but he had to report the most important orders to the State Defense Minister.

The archives of the so-called Red Army (USSR) Command took an important place in the list of the archives of the Supreme Commands. It is one of the most important sources for the struggles of the Red Army. The files encompass all areas of the activity of the Red Army. The division of the documents by content is as follows: documents of the operational, reconnaissance, and economic activity of the

Army Command; the documents of the consultant for aviation; Journal of the Supreme Command; collections of the army divisions.

Next to the archives of the State Defense Ministry—also including those of the Horthy era—the most meaningful documentary material is the archive of the general staff (VKF), which covers the period from summer 1919 to 1944. The material of the individual sections has been painstakingly sorted through, but it still provides an important source for the diplomatic, military–political, and army–organizational activity of the Horthy era.

The investigation of the history of the Second World War is severely hampered by the fact that the registries of the corps and higher units were either never sent to the archives or only sent in part. Because of this, the archives of the 2nd Royal Hungarian Army Command have taken on a still greater importance for investigations of the Second World War.

The archives of the Royal-Hungarian Szegedian Honved Law Chair (1870–1944) possesses the most extensive legal material. After this in size comes the archives of the Royal Hungarian Miskolcian Honved Law Chair (1915–1945). Both archives offer valuable documents from the First and Second World Wars regarding internal conditions, the moral and political situation of the army, the mood of the hinterland, and the left-oriented movements during the Second World War.

Less extensive, but highly valuable, are the court-martial files which we maintain from the Bach Epoch (1849–1860) and the Time of Absolutism (1860–1867). Here can be found the files of the K.u.K. Drumhead Courts-Martial and other military courts from the 1848–1849 Freedom War. This material consists of the following important foundations: documents of the Arad, Pest, Nagyvarad, Pecs, Kassa, and Pozsony courts; as well as the documents of the Gyoer, Gyoengyoes, Kecskemet, and Nagykanizsa summary courts.

In the material from the Bach Epoch the files of the so-called Military District Command (Pest, Pozsony, Sopron, Kassa, and Nagyvarad), as well as the Supreme Command of the 3rd Army, including therein the files of the Police Section (1850–1851), Justice Section (1848, 1849–1851), and Civil Section, are very interesting.

The records of the *Ungarische Leibgarde* (Hungarian Bodyguard), 1760–1850, and the *Koenigliche Leibgarde* (Royal Bodyguard), 1867–1918, are also kept here.

As to sheer mass of holdings, the material of the collection for the First World War is the richest, consisting of 4,152 fascicles. Unfortunately, the majority of the material is only available as copies.

Among the documents that came from the Austrian Military Archive are the operational reports of the different fronts; decrees of the higher command headquarters; daily reports of corps and formations; various instructions regarding organizational, material, and personal questions, and so on.

The Hungarian Military Archives and its Vienna branch declare themselves ready to be helpful to all researchers who desire to lay claim to detailed information in their work.

NOTES

1. Hadtöteneti Interesi Library, The Documents of the Hungarian Soviet Republic. 12th fasc. (Huenb. 638/lt.—1919).
2. For in-depth descriptions of the archive of the General Command, see K. Laszlo Jozsef, *Das im Jahre 1740 errichtete General-Commando* (Archivalische Mitteilungen, Jahrgang 1937); *Das Archiv des Ungarischen General-Commandos* (Der Bericht des Kriegshistorischen Instituts 1957/1).

The History of the Hungarian State War-Historical Museum: From Its Foundation until the End of the Second World War

Janos Pongo, Director, Translated by William Voss

SUMMARY

The idea of an institutional collection of war trophies and the erection of a Hungarian war museum first arose in 1867 at the time of the Dual Monarchy; but it would take still another half century before the Austro-Hungarian monarch would give his consent to its founding. The fundamental hindrance to this was to be found in the national–legal commitments, very disadvantageous to Hungary, which bound Hungary to Austria. The court in Vienna hindered all national attempts, especially those connected with the army. The issue of the museum was, unfortunately, also placed in this category.

The Hungarian ruling classes must also be held responsible for the delay. The provisional sources indicate that the responsible authorities wanted to resolve this issue within the bounds of loyalty; their efforts can be characterized by unnecessary caution, indeed fear and indecision, and therefore it meant little difficulty for the Vienna court to hinder, or at least delay, the issue.

Essays and studies in numerous—especially military—periodicals fostered the idea of a war museum. In addition, occasional petitionary cases brought the issue of a war museum to the fore, and this idea was also presumably nurtured in various forms in public opinion. In the *Katonai Lapok* (military papers) from 16 January 1886 we read of the need to reaffirm the martial spirit in young people, so that their military education will not fall behind those of other nations. And that can happen most effectively through an institution in which the great deeds of forefathers provide an example, where exhibits and trophies are bound together with the Hungarian Army and its bravery.

The successful war-history exhibition during the millennial celebrations of 1896 inspired the public. The rich war-historical material collected could have provided a sound basis for the establishment of a war museum. However, in spite of the many discussions and agreements, the project still failed to go forward at this time.

The Hungarian Hussar exhibition at the Paris World's Fair in 1900 provided another opportunity, which once again failed to be used. The worthwhile collection was deposited in the Ludovika War Academy, where it perished or was lost during the First World War. In 1908 Jeno Pilch wrote an article about the establishment of the museum, but this effort also went without success.

In the years prior to the First World War, the problem arose of moving the Hungarian art treasures, among which were also the war trophies, to Hungary from Vienna. In connection with these endeavors, the idea of the creation of a war museum arose once again. The issue came before the parliament, but did not bring the desired results.

Public opinion—at the fore of which was the war-history committee of the Hungarian Academy of Sciences—demanded in the first year of the war, with renewed strength, the creation of the Hungarian War Museum. This demand remained continually on the order of the day and developed, at the end of the war—all bureaucratic obstacles having been overcome—into a finished plan, which now only needed the blessing of the Almighty.

Regarding the basic obstacle to the founding of the museum, here is the fate of a petition put together at the beginning of the war: Immediately after the outbreak of the First World War, the secretary of the Balaton Museum Union, Dr. Arpad Csak, directed a petition to the Hungarian State Defense Minister, wherein he proposed that through the outbreak of the war the opportunity for collecting war trophies, and therewith also establishing a war museum, had arisen. He suggested the recruiting zones of the troops going into war as the location for the collection.

This petition was also directed at the joint Austro-Hungarian Minister of War. The answer indicates clearly the inclination of the Vienna ruling circle: The War Minister did not agree to the collection of objects in recruiting zones, because this was already exactly prescribed in the regulations. The most important problem—the founding of the Hungarian War Museum—was simply left without an answer, probably because no paragraph pertained to that.

The war trophies and war booty, to which the joint War Minister made claim, streamed to Vienna until the Army Museum there could not hold them all. After 1916 the Vienna government planned a new building of the Army Museum, which would be well able to hold the horde in its wide, special rooms. This secret plan came, however, to the attention of the Hungarian government, and because of this event the Hungarian State Defense Minister took the issue of the war museum again in hand. The first known draft from July 1917 of "Promemoria Regarding the Founding of the Hungarian War Museum" said that it would be desirable to establish in Budapest a war museum accessible to anyone, in which the memorial items and war trophies won in heroic battles by troops supplied by Hungary should announce to posterity the glory of past times. The period of the collection was limited, as a precaution, to only the First World War, and it was emphasized that if objects from earlier epochs or from the year 1848 should surface, when the nation stood in conflict with the ruler, this might arouse the envy and mistrust of certain groups; in order now to avoid all unpleasantries, it should be stipulated at the museum's founding that it would collect particularly only the objects of the World War.

It emerged from the plan that the head of the Vienna Army Museum and Military Archives showed himself ready to give over the specified material. According to the plan, the archives were also to be absorbed into the organization of the museum, which would be expanded because of this addition: subdivision of the Section 1/a in the State Defense Ministry.

On 9 September 1917 a new plan under the title "Project for a Popular War Museum" was announced by the joint Ministers of War. It is our opinion that, because they could no longer afford to ignore this problem, the purpose of the project was to skew the matter in those directions which Vienna felt desirable. The essential part of the project was that the Hungarian museum might concern itself exclusively with the role of the hinterlands and gather objects relevant to them, because everything that happened at the fronts and stood in immediate relationship to military operations was left to the Army Museum in Vienna.

This plan was so insulting to a de jure independent state that even the Hungarian State Defense Ministry, which certainly could not be seen as hostile to the court, naturally declined.

The issue of the war museum was addressed publicly for the first time in March 1918 with the discussion of the new construction of the Army Museum, as the joint Ministers of War demanded that the Hungarian State Defense Minister read the plan for the Hungarian War Museum.

After this discussion the Hungarian side demanded that a symposium be convened, where the head of Department 1/a of the State Defense Ministry was commissioned to work out a corresponding petition. This project appeared on 27 July 1918 as a draft of the Hungarian State Defense Minister, who was directed to make the presentation to the emperor and obtain the ultimate resolution. This rough draft was based on the "Promemoria" (it was a detailed, concrete variant of it); according to this, the museum would consist of three units: (1) the Hungarian Pantheon, (2) the actual museum, (3) the Hungarian War Archives. Twenty-five million kroner were to be budgeted for the initial displays. The museum building was planned to be on the Gellertberg, where the capital offered the property free of charge.

But with only the emperor's approval of the final plan lacking, it was not to be, because of the revolutionary events of the fall of 1918. The collapse of the monarchy and the independence of Hungary made this very highest acceptance superfluous, and two weeks after the victory of the middle-class democratic revolution, in spite of the difficult internal political conditions, this old demand became reality.

At the time that the governments held their discussions, without regard for the resistance of Vienna, the foundations were quietly laid, and as in November 1918 the greatest obstacle was done away with, a new scientific and cultural institution under the name "War Historical Archives and Museum" materialized.

A founding document was probably not drawn up. The announcement of the founding went on without ceremony in November 1918. The organizational basis was Department 1/a of the State Defense Ministry; within this the archives subdivision, established in November 1915, was installed and then expanded into the archives and museum. The first written document from which can be concluded the founding of the museum is a decree from 20 November 1918, in which Lieutenant-Colonel Janos Gabanyi, the head of the previous archives subdivision, called upon all military units and organs to gather war-historical material and save it for posterity. The first concrete references which report the museum's founding as a fact stem from a letter draft of 14 January 1919. The head of the archives and museum, Lieutenant-Colonel Janos Gabanyi, sought contact with the head of the Committee for the Surrender of Hungarian Treasures and Files Present in Vienna. In this letter Gabanyi reported that he was entrusted in November 1918 with the leadership of the War-Historical Archives and Museum, and in this capacity desired to contact the committee and seek support.

The archives subdivision had the assignment of making copies of operations reports that the War Archive in Vienna would surrender. From the beginning, the subdivision gathered military objects, among other things, photographs, paintings, soldiers' songs, flags, commemorative medals, insignia, prisoner-of-war banknotes, and later also weapons and so forth.

The new institution was housed in the Buda Fortress—in the building of the National Archives—its personnel consisted in December 1918 of thirteen officers, sixty-three clerks, illustrators, and typists, and nine orderlies, of whom eighteen belonged to the museum.

Although financial difficulties persisted right up to the Hungarian Soviet Republic of 1919, the war commissioner's department provided within the resulting limits for the activities of the museum. The first details regarding these activities actually stem from the time of the Hungarian Soviet Republic, when the collection consisted of 1,200 larger museum pieces, 24,000 photographs, a greater number of badges, coins, and insignia, and the library of approximately 1,000 volumes.

There remains intact a decree of the war commissioner's department ordering every Military-District Command to gather material pertinent to the revolutions of 1918 and 1919.

The new institution was certainly organizationally a subdivision of the State Defense Ministry, but it led a seemingly independent life after its founding, especially because of the isolated accommodations and special responsibilities. At the end of 1919 the formal dependency also ended, and the Hungarian War Archives and Museum began its own life.

The most important function of the new museum was naturally collecting, for which the immediate postwar period appeared especially suited. After the peace treaty of 1920, which established the present state and organization of the army, several units were dissolved, others reorganized, and a considerable amount of military material remained abandoned. Since the museum enthusiastically gathered this material, the available space in the State Archives soon became too small, since the archival holdings also grew rapidly. Therefore, a part of the new institution was housed in the Maria Theresa Barracks. By this transfer, however, only the problem of the archives, which needed to use the museum space, could be resolved; the museum, on the other hand, had to limit a reduced collecting activity and minimal restoration of holdings to the barracks, which were neither architecturally nor dimensionally suitable.

In April 1922 the museum was temporarily subordinated to the Ministry of the Interior. Since the museum and archives had undergone a development which contributed to the independence of both institutions, the division into two was officially completed on 15 November 1922, and both institutions were subordinated to the Ministry of Culture and Education. Healthier conditions for further development were thereby created, but the fundamental material problems still awaited a solution.

The most important of these was the question of accommodation. The available part of the Maria Theresa Barracks was storagewise no longer adequate for the housing of the material. A portion of the artillery and train material went first into a pavilion far from the barracks, and after 1926 also in the northern and western part of the Promenade of the Buda Fortress before the Nandor Barracks. In such circumstances there could be no discussion of an exhibition.

The inadequacy of the number of personnel signified the next difficulty. The number was raised in 1923 first to twenty, and then in the same year reduced to ten; the material, however, had tripled in size by 1927. Under such circumstances skill and education of any consequence among museum workers could not even be considered; this would come to cause the museum many difficulties later on.

Beside these difficulties, financial concerns were constantly on the agenda. The purchase of materials broke off almost completely, and acquisition occurred through gathering of antiquated or newly released objects of the army.

The selection of pertinent materials, which the Vienna Army Museum delivered to Hungary, also fell under the area of the museum's concerns. In this way, nearly 2,000 valuable pieces came into the possession of the Hungarian War-Historical Museum. The staff also took part in the assessment of war-historical matters and the gathering of the uniforms and pieces of equipment of the Honved (Hungarian) Army, where they represented heraldic and traditional historical viewpoints. The staff contributed to the propagation of the matter of the museum with special articles in the press and on the radio. Contributors and volunteer staff were sought, and contacts with other institutions and staffs were created. Some personnel from the museum helped with exhibitions at other museums. In order to improve the material situation of the museum, the Hungarian War Museum Union was established, whose newspaper, *Hadimuzeumi Lapok* (War Museum Papers), represented the interests and problems of the museum, and above all campaigns were organized that contributed to the solution of financial questions. Since there were no exhibitions, on certain days of the week the collection of the museum was made accessible to the members of the union.

At the end of the 1920s, a definite improvement occurred, which was related to the political and economic consolidation of the state.

At the end of 1926 the western part of the Nandor Barracks was renovated, and with the move in 1929 the war-historical collection received its final residence. Meanwhile, in 1927 the museum had been expanded through an independent economic department with three people, and the temporary staff was raised to eight, so that it reached the level of 1923. However, the needs of the museum were much greater—almost four times as much—and they remained unmet. The final number fluctuated around thirty.

In 1928 the museum was once again subordinated to the War Ministry. With the resolution of the basic problems, the question of exhibitions could be put on the agenda. At the end of 1929 the State Defense Minister demanded a basic, detailed description of the collections and of the capabilities of the museum. In order to ensure expertise and impartiality, outstanding specialists were selected for this task: the general director of the National Museum, Prof. Dr. Balint Homan, and the well known military historian and war-historical expert of the National Museum, Prof. Dr. Zoltan Toth. Their special report was—in spite of its in many ways tendentious attitude—an important document for the history of the museum. The most important conclusions were that the collections of the museum were heterogeneous, the cause of which was to be found in the circumstances of its founding; qualitatively and quantitatively seen, the material of the more recent epochs was more suited for exhibitions, and therefore the 1848–1849 Freedom War—eventually changed to 1715—was suggested as a beginning period; one-third of the collections had to be disposed of; a scientific procedure for preservation was lacking; and the committee was critical of the fact that no experts headed the military-scientific institutions, which brought forth the disdain of outstanding specialists and negatively influenced the development of the institution. In this respect, however, the War-Historical Museum was mentioned as an exception, because its leader, Colonel Kamil Agghazy, won the recognition of the two men.

The problem of incorporation into the state's museum structure was also mentioned, and supported with concrete suggestions. To further perspective development, the bringing together of the military objects of the National and War-Historical Museums was suggested, through which a collection impressive by European standards might come into being. This question had already come up at the founding of the museum, but until 1929 had never satisfactorily been settled.

How the museum and State Defense Ministry received this special report can only be reconstructed through scattered references. A variant relative to bringing together the collections remained on the agenda until the middle of the 1930s; namely, that the National Museum would retain seven rooms in the building of the War Museum, where its own objects and those of the War-Historical Museum would be exhibited, and to which the further exhibitions of the museums would be added. As an epochal limit, and at the same time a collection limit, the year 1715, the date of the creation of the standing Hungarian army, was stipulated, and was accepted by the State Defense Ministry. For the materials outside of this epoch an exchange was worked out.

The question of exhibitions arose—for unknown reasons—again in 1935, because the State Defense Minister desired a written report about the exhibition plan. In this draft the surrender of the seven rooms at the National Museum are no longer mentioned, and 1715 was planned as the starting point. On 28 October 1935 the heads of both museums signed an agreement in which the epochal limit of collection activity was established in writing. The War-Historical Museum was promised a part of the exhibit of the Rakoczi Freedom War (1682–1699), as well as of the cannon collection, which could be nicely accommodated on the promenade in front of the museum building. The exchange of a few objects was also established, and the idea that the ultimate goal would be to unite the two collections was emphasized.

The conditions for the exhibitions were first met in 1936, when the renovation of the building was almost done and the bare minimum preparation of materials had been completed. The opening of the museum was also pushed forward by the minister in order to strengthen martial spirit and minimize the destructive influences of the army.

The museum celebrated its opening on 29 May 1937, and on 30 May the first exhibition was opened to the public. This event was an important turning point in the history of the museum. Through this its position was established, and through the opening of the exhibitions it was drawn into the bloodstream of the museum system of the state. From this time onward, exhibitions became the focus of work. The exhibition area was expanded to thirty-six rooms and covered military history from 1715 to the present.

The directive regulating the activity of the museum during the 1939–1945 War stipulated, among other things, the arrangement of exhibitions of the most current military themes so that the museum would reflect most recent events. Therefore, at the beginning of 1942 the occupation actions of 1938 and the first events on the Soviet front were shown, which was supposed to serve the spirit of anti-Soviet propaganda. The number of visitors rose from 26,220 in 1937 to 55,000 in 1943.

The last year in which the museum was still active at full intensity was 1943. At the beginning of 1944, before the systematic Russian bombardment of Budapest, the commandant of the museum ordered that the materials and most valuable pieces of the exhibitions be packaged and removed, and that from the less valuable or duplicate objects a reduced exhibition planned in only seven rooms be arranged.

In this condition, in October 1944 the museum received the order from the State Minister of Defense to evacuate. The materials were housed in November in the Castle Somlovar in Transdanubia. In March 1945, an order was received to send the materials to Germany. In this difficult situation the staff fled, and the collection remained without supervision.

During the Battles for Liberation, because of their central location, most of the buildings of the Buda Fortress were destroyed, including the War Museum. The southernmost part was leveled to the foundations, the main walls were badly damaged, the dividing walls were destroyed, and the remaining objects of the collection disappeared under the rubble.

With this dreadful picture ends the first part of the study that traces the development of the museum from the founding up to 1945. The Liberation brought, not only to the life of the people but also to the history of the museum, a stage certainly not free of obstacles, yet an unbroken one, which should provide the theme of a second study.

Hadtörténelmi Intézet és Múzeum (Institute and Museum of War History)

László Veszprém, Director

During the period of the Austro-Hungarian monarchy the documents on the Hungarian war history were stored in Vienna, first in the Heeresmuseum and in the Kriegsarchiv. In the last days of the monarchy, on 27 July 1918, it was decided to establish an independent Hungarian museum, but it was not organized and opened until after the collapse of the monarchy.

The collections of the new museum increased proportionately as groups were surrendered from the Heeresmuseum and at the Kriegsarchiv in Vienna in accordance with an agreement made at Baden bei Wien on 28 May 1926 by the Hungarian National Museum re objects of the post-1715 period (that is, during the setting up of the standing army). The museum was opened to the public in its present building in the castle of Buda on 29 May 1937. During World War II the collections suffered heavy damage: some 70 percent of the holdings were destroyed. The museum only opened again to visitors in 1949. Its main collections are weaponry, war technical material and equipment, uniforms, flags, objects of fine arts, decorations, books, and leaflets. Its open-air exhibition of military technical materials—armored cars, airplanes, and so on—is under reconstruction. Today (1995) it has a collection of more than 500,000 items.

Beside the museum, the most important department of the Institute and Museum of War History is the War History Archives (*Hadtörténelmi Levéltár*) founded at the same time as the museum. It keeps the documents of the national military authorities, the Ministry of Defense, the regional authorities, institutions in the fields of sanitation, law, military academies, secondary schools, and so on. Today it has a collection of 6,500 linear meters of documents. It has had a permanent office at the Kiegsarchiv in Vienna since 1920.

The Library of Military Sciences (*Hadtudományi Köyvtár*) originally belonged to the archives, but since 1923 it has been an independent department of 180,000 volumes of books and journals. The Collection of Maps (*Hadtörténelmi Térképtár*) has the same story—separated from the archives in 1954 and for now the biggest map collection in the country with its 300,000 items. In the first decades the center of historical researches was the archives, but by 1953 the Institute of War History (*Hadtörténeti Intézet*) had been established with a scholarly (scientific) personnel of some ten to twenty historians. Since 1961 even the name of the institution has been changed to the present Institute and Museum of War History.

Today this institution publishes the scientific quarterly founded originally in 1888, the *Journal of Military History* (*Hadtörténelmi Közlemények*), and the museum the irregular *Bulletin of the Museum of War History* (*Országos Hadtörténeti Múzeum Értesítôje*) and the *Booklets of the Museum* series (*Múzeumi füzetek*). The Library for Military Sciences publishes two bibliographical series: The annual *Bibliography of Publications on War History in Hungary* (*Magyarországon megjelent hadtörténelmi irodalom bibliográfiája*), and the *Abstract of Foreign Journals of Military History* (*Külföldi hadtörténelmi folyóiratok repertóriuma*).

BIBLIOGRAPHY OF PUBLICATIONS EDITED BY THE INSTITUTE AND MUSEUM OF WAR HISTORY

A basic problem is that the most important monographs written by the researchers of the institution have been published by others, after 1951 by the national military publishing house Zrínyi. Nevertheless, here is a comprehensive survey of these publications:

Hadtörténelmi szemelvények a világháborúbó (Selected documents on World War I). Budapest, War History Archives, 1926. p. 425., with one map.

A magyar Királyi honvédség története 1868–1918 (History of the Hungarian Royal Honvéd Army 1868–1918). Ed. István Berkó. Budapest, War History Archives, 1928. p. 601., with 12 plates.

A világháború 1914–1918. Különös tekintettel Magyarországra és a magyar csapatok szereplésére (World War I 1914–1918. With special respect to Hungary and for the activity of Hungarian troops). Vols. 1–10. Budapest, Stádium, 1928–1942. With 9 boxes of maps.

A Zrínyi Katonai Kiadó kiadványai 1951–1980 (Bibliography of the publications of the Military Publishing House Zrínyi 1951–1980). Ed. Library of Military Sciences. Budapest, Zrínyi, 1980. p. 506.

Mutató a Hadtörténelmi Közlemények évfolyamaihoz 1888–1978 (Of the *Journal of Military History*). Vols. 1–2. Ed. Library of Military Sciences. Budapest, 1956–1979. pp. 309, 175.

Gyalókay, Jenô, et al. *Hadifogoly magyarok története* (History of Hungarian prisoners of war). Vols. 1–2. Budapest, Atheneum, 1930. pp. 590, 588.

Godó, Ågnes. *Magyar–lengyel kapcsolatok a második világháborúban* (Polish–Hungarian relations during World War II). Budapest, Zríyi-Kossuth, 1976. p. 447.

Dombrády, Lóránd. *Hadsereg és politika Magyarországon, 1938–1944.* (The army and politics in Hungary, 1938–1944). Budapest, Akadémiai, 1986. p. 400.

———. *A magyar gazdaság és hadfelszerelés 1938–1944* (Hungarian economy and war industry). Budapest, Akadémiai, 1981. p. 291.

Zachar, József. *Idegen hadakban* (Hungarian soldiers in foreign armies). Budapest, Magvetô, 1984. p. 496.

Magyarország hadtörténete (War history of Hungary). Vols. 1–2. Budapest, Zrínyi, 1985. pp. 671, 657.

Horthy-Magyarország részvétele Jugoszlávia megtámadásában és megszállásában, 1941–1945 (Hungary's participation in the attack and occupation of Yugoslavia/Belgrade). Zrínyi, Budapest, Vojnoist Inst., 1986. p. 566.

Bencze, László. *Bosznia és Hercegovina okkupációja 1878-ban* (Occupation of Bosnia and Hezegovina in 1878). Budapest, Akadémiai, 1987. p. 243.

Dombrády, Lóránd-Tóth. *Sándor: A magyar Királyi honvédség 1919–1945* (The Hungarian Royal Honvéd Army, 1919–1945). Budapest, Zrínyi, 1987. p. 461.

Szakály, Sándor. *A magyar katonai elit 1938–1945* (The Hungarian military élite). Budapest, Magvetô, 1987. p. 272.

Zachar, József. *Franciaország magyar marshallja, Bercsényi László* (Hungarian marshal of France, László Bercsényi). Budapest, Zrínyi, 1987. p. 308.

Bona, Gábor. *Kossuth Lajos Kapitányai* (Captains of the War of Independence of 1848–49). Budapest, Zrínyi, 1988. p. 781.

———. *Tábornokok, törzstisztek a szabadságharcban* (Generals and field officers in the war of independence of 1848–49). 2nd ed. Budapest, Zrínyi, 1987. p. 426.

Szakály, Sándor. *A magyar tábori csendôrség* (The Hungarian military police). Budapest, Zrínyi, 1990. p. 154.

Makai, Ågnes-Héri, Vera. *Kitüntetések* (Decorations). Budapest, Zrínyi, 1990. p. 236.

CATALOGUES

A magyar királyi Hadtörténelmi Levéltár iratanyagának áttekintése (Survey of the holdings of the Royal War History Archives). Budapest, 1930. p. 308. With supplements of 1934, p. 112, of 1937, p. 107, of 1941, p. 104.

A Hadtörténelmi Levéltár fondjainak jegyzéke. Feudális és kapitalista kor (Fonds of the War History Archives. Periods of feudalism and capitalism). Budapest. 1980. p. 222.

COLLECTION OF MAPS OF WAR HISTORY

Csendes, László. *A Habsburg birodalom és az Osztrák-magyar monarchia térképeinek katalógusa* (Catalogue of maps of the Habsburg Empire and the Austro-Hungarian monarchy). Budapest, 1981. p. 200.

Jankó, Annamária. *Ipoly, Márta: Katonai vonatkozású térképek a Habsburg birodalom és az Osztrák-magyar monarchia korából, 1700–1919* (Maps of military interests from the period of the Habsburg Empire and the Austro-Hungarian monarchy, 1700–1919). Budapest, 1982. p. 77.

Ipoly, Márta. *Malmok, ipari és gazdasági létesítmények az elsô katonai felmérés térképszelvényein 1782–1785* (Mills, industrial and farming enterprises on the maps of the first military land surveying in Hungary, 1782–1785). Budapest, 1982. p. 220.

MUSEUM OF WAR HISTORY

Series *Magyar Királyi hadtörténelmi múzeum kiadványai* (Publications of the Hungarian Royal Museum of War History). One of the more important is Béla, Bevilaqua-Borsody. *Dürer Albert Erôdítési tervei és a XV–XVI századi török probléma* (A. Dürer fortification plans and the Turkish problem of the fifteenth and sixteenth centuries). No. 2, 1928, p. 15.

Dezsényi, Miklós. *Tengeri és folyami hajóhadaink kimagasló fegyvertényei 1052–1942* (Feats of arms of the Hungarian Navy 1052–1942). No. 13, p. 203.

Barcsay-Amant, Zoltán-Erdéyi. *Gyula: A magyar lovassport története, 1526–1849* (History of Hungarian horsemanship, 1526–1849). No. 14, p. 56.

Series *A Honvéd Levéltár és Múzeum hadtörténeti kiadványsorozata* (Publications of war history of the Archives and Museum of War History). Vajda, Pál. *Oroszok a magyar szabadságharoról* (Russians in the Hungarian War of Independence, 1848–1849). No. 1, 1949, p. 82, with 7 plates.

Artemev, N. *Magarország felszabadítása. A Szovjetunió és a Szovjet Hadsereg segísége Magyarországnak* (Liberation of Hungary. The help of the Soviet Union and that of the Red Army to Hungary). No. 2, 1950, p. 101.

Series *A Honvéd Levéltár és Múzeum múzeumi kiadványsorozata* (Publications in the field of the museum of the Archives and Museum of War History). Barczy, Zoltán. *A szabadságharc katonái. Az 1848–1849. évi magyar hadsereg egyenruhái* (Soldiers of the war of independence. Uniforms of the Hungarian Army of 1848–1849). No. 1, 1950, p. 143.

Szentneményi, Béla. *Budavár hadiépítészete* (Military architecture of the Castle of Buda). No. 2, 1950, p. 146.

Lugosi, József. *Szélpuskák* (Arquebuses à vent). No. 2, 1981, p. 22, with 8 plates.

———. *Szuronyok Magyarországon a 18. századtól napjainkig* (Bayonets in Hungary from the eighteenth century till today). No. 3, 1981, p. 48.

Bezzeg, Mária. *A múzeumi elméleti kutatások szükségességérôl* (The necessity for theoretical researches in the field of museology). No. 4, 1988, p. 27.

PERIODICALS

Hadtörténelem (War history). January 1921–1922.
Hadimúzeumi Lapok (Pages from the Museum of War History). December 1925–December 1927, and later as a supplement of the review *Historia* (History). March 1928–December 1932.

10

India

The Indian Historical Division

G. B. Singh, Director

The name of the historical section, Ministry of Defense has changed to History Division. It has published the following as part of the history of the Indian Armed Forces of the Indian Union, post-partition series:

1. *Operation Polo—The Police Action against Hyderabad 1948* (1972).
2. *Operation Vijay* (Victory)—*The Liberation of Goa and Other Portuguese colonies in India, 1961* (1974).
3. *The Congo Operation, 1960–63* (1976).
4. *CFI or Indian Troops in Korea, 1953–54* (1976).
5. *History of the Operations in Jammu and Kashmir, 1947–48* (1987).
6. *Operation Shanti* (Peace)—*The Indian Army on the Peace Mission in Egypt, 1956–67* (1990).
7. *Military Costumes of India* (also as *Sharatiya Sainik Vesha—Bhusa* [Hindi]) (1991).
8. *Stories/Tales of Bravery/Heroism* (also as *Veerta Ki Kahaniyan* [Hindi]) (1995).

The address of the History Division is c/o the Ministry of Defense, West Block No. VIII, R. K. Puran, *New Delhi-110066,* India. The first eight volumes listed may be obtained from the Controller of Publications, Government of India, Civil Lines, *New Delhi-110006,* India. The last two volumes have been published privately by Allied Publishers in New Delhi.

11

Israel

The History of the I.D.F. Military History Department

I.D.F. Information Office

The Military History Department was established in 1952 as a section directly subject to the Chief of Operations. Its major activity was to process and to publish the *Independence War Book.* The section had a big budget and many personnel with which it established the Independence War archives. After that much research, work was accomplished by the head of the section and by other military historians.

Debriefing Before Creating an Image

If a historian wants to know exactly what happened in a certain battle, he must debrief the warriors immediately after the battle, when they are still shocked and tired. Then their testimonies are reliable. To do that the historian must accompany the warriors.

During the Independence War it couldn't be done. Therefore, the historians had to trust the reports and the letters which were written after the battle and which were less reliable. To solve that problem they used photographs to refresh the memory of the warriors and interviews to recover necessary information of the war.

The Course of Time of the Independence War

A controversial question is how long the War of Independence lasted. The war started a day after the United Nations decision of November 29, 1947. But when did the war end? Did it end when

Jordan and Syria signed the Armistice Agreement, or did it end when the forces returned to their borders? Research must be organized by periods or limits in time.

The War Phases

Another question is how to determine a war's phases. It is acceptable to determine these according to who initiated them. The Independence War began when Arabs attacked a Jewish bus. The first stage, therefore, was initiated by the Arabs who lived in Palestine. The first stage ended in March 1948. By that time the Jewish population had spread all over the country. Then the second stage began. Operation "Nachshon" saw the initiative move to the Hagana. The aim was to create a contiguity of all the places assigned to the Jewish state and to create corridors to those which were supposed to be in an Arab zone. The Arab invasion of Palestine began the third stage. The fourth stage was a combined initiative: The Jews opened operation "Brosh" while Syria planned to break through the bridgehead of Mishmar Hayarden to the road between Rosh-Pina and Metula. Finally, the Jews started several operations in the North and the South: "Yoav," "Horev," and others.

The Essence of the Independence War History

A troublesome question is this: What is the history of the Independence War?

- Is it a history of battles?
- Is it a tactical operational history?
- Is it a history of conflicts on the battlefield?
- Is it necessary to describe all the factors which led to the war?

War Financing and Diplomatic Activity

How much did the war cost? How will the issue of human life appear in this balance? Where will the expenses in cash appear? But those questions weren't investigated. It is known that the Jews of the Diaspora helped to finance the War of Independence, but there is more than that to research.

There was also the diplomatic and political activity. Jews had to achieve recognition as the State of Israel. Therefore, there was a strong connection between their military activity and their political chances. As the latter and political support sometimes enabled certain operations to take place while denying others, it was vital to answer these questions.

The Independence War—War or Campaign

Was the War of Independence a war or a campaign? Both Arab and Jewish historians have tried to cope with this question. The Arab historians claim that they never lost in the war, but only in a campaign. The answers depend on how one defines these conceptions. If the war aim is to break the enemy's willingness to fight, then the Jews never won the war, the Independence War was a campaign, and the fight is still going on in 1992.

Conflict between Two Rights

There is a deep conflict between two rights: The right of the state to keep its documents in secret and the right of the public to know. Historians and researchers need documents and papers for their work, but the state did not have to give them access to its archives. Therefore, historians did not have all the information they needed and their researches were not complete.

The Sources Problem

The written sources of the Independence War are limited. The State of Israel and the I.D.F. (Israeli Defense Forces) were formed in 1948 from the underground. The first rule in an underground is to keep silence. The less you know and write the better. The people who had been in the underground continued keeping silent. They kept documents or they destroyed them. That's how important information was lost, especially during the first years.

In 1955, the new branch was ruled by the Head of the Training Department. Since the chief was not a military officer, he concentrated on the Independence War research, and the head of the Lessons Production Section was directly under the orders of the head of the Combat Doctrine Department (which was then called the Department of Research and Development). In August 1956 an officer was again appointed head of the Military History Branch, and because of that the Lessons Production Section was restored to the Military History Branch.

The branch organization at the end of 1957 was as follows:

Regular

1. Head of the branch—Lieutenant Colonel.
2. Two senior officers—Majors.
3. One staff officer assistant—First Lieutenant (compulsory service).
4. One N.C.O.— First Sergeant (compulsory service).
5. Two clerks— Corporals (compulsory service).

Reserves

1. Three Majors.
2. One First Lieutenant.
3. Two Sergeants.
4. One Corporal.
5. One Private.

The Branch Structure and Missions

In the late 1950s there were two sections:

The Lessons Production Section

The section dealt with

1. Research of the special operations (reprisals, etc.).
2. The "Kadesh" War research.
3. Publishing a collection of lessons from theaters of operations for the senior commanders.
4. General military history training.

The section dealt with the training subject only superficially.

The Independence War Section

The section dealt with

1. Contracting with researchers for work on the Independence War.
2. Storing and organizing the Section Independence War Archive.
3. Training the I.D.F. on the Independence War.

Officers that Joined the Branch

In addition to the two sections, there were other officers who joined the branch:

1. A Lieutenant Colonel who researched the subject of Jerusalem during the Independence War.
2. A Major who dealt with the research on the Foreign Military History.

There was also an academic sergeant (in regular service) who was responsible to the Section Archive.

Except for directing the heads of the sections, the head of the Military History Branch dealt with the following subjects:

1. The I.D.F. archive.
2. The I.D.F. spokesman.
3. The I.D.F. museum project.
4. Editorial boards.
5. The chief educational officer (for publications and perfections).
6. The Tel Aviv University (Military History Cathedra).
7. War games.

The Training and Doctrine Commander's Instructions

On April 23, 1958, the head of the training department set new instructions concerning the branch tasks. His initial point was that the branch carries a heavy debt of summarizing the War of Independence and the "Kadesh" War (1956), the work of the branch must be reflected in the I.D.F.'s work or there would not be lessons to apply. Therefore, Major General Zorea ordered that

1. The main aim of the branch is to translate operational lessons (as quickly as possible) into war theories, training plans, and guidance courses. This information must be shared with other branches, such as the training branch.
2. The branch's lesser aims are summarizing the War of Independence of 1948 and summarizing the "Kadesh" War of 1956.
3. The main aim must be completed even if the lesser ones were not.

Then the general ordered maximum use of the budget and to prepare files in order to cover different subjects and not to print an official history.

THE MILITARY HISTORY BRANCH AND ITS ASSIGNMENTS ACCORDING TO I.D.F. SUPREME COMMAND INSTRUCTIONS

The Supreme Command instructions from March 1, 1961, assigned the Military History Branch the following functions:

1. The responsibility for writing the military history of the I.D.F. and other armies, so that doctrines and military procedures could be assessed and adopted.
2. The task of concentration, registration, and accumulation of material which concerned I.D.F. organization, occurrences, considerations, decisions, and operations through all the I.D.F.'s units and elements.
3. Writing the military history of the Independence War and of "Kadesh" and publishing it as an official history.

4. Researching and deriving lessons from special operations.
5. Guiding the I.D.F. archive in its defined duties when they concerned military history branch tasks.
6. Staff responsibility for the I.D.F. museum in subjects relating to the general staff.
7. Creating and maintaining contacts with scholars and civil educational institutions (both at home and abroad).

In the early 1960s the chief of Military History abolished, according to the general instructions, the Independence War section, leaving the two senior officers in the branch to deal with all the subjects they were ordered to cover without having a clearly defined role. Work on Jerusalem during the War of Independence was continued by a civilian. The Military History Branch made the War of Independence a staff work in order to be able to finish the task. Since preparing the original staff research, nothing had been done. The branch had published no chronology of the Independence War except little booklets about certain operations (see book list).

From the end of 1963 until 1965, there was only one senior officer in the branch. Furthermore, from August 1964 until February 1965 a major was the only senior officer, and he acted as the chief of Military History. One April 21, 1965, a lieutenant colonel was appointed to the job of the chief of Military History, and until the beginning of the Six Day War of 1967 the section staff was five officers and three clerks. But that was too few personnel to cover a war when it began. A document telling about this situation was presented to the head of the training department in March 1965. In a meeting which was held December 18, 1966, it was settled that in wartime there would be established teams of three to four men who would cover historic events in the Supreme Command, in the corps, and in the Territorial Commands. The proposition remained on paper only, until the Six Day War. Therefore it was decided during the alert period to reinforce the branch with two staff officers and six students from the Command and General Staff College—two Majors and four Lieutenant Colonels.

The alert period and the Six Day War were covered as follows:

1. The Supreme Command post was covered by the head of the Military History Branch.
2. The general staff departments and the different Territorial Commands were covered by the branch teams which were in the field.

At the end of the war the teams had to deliver their material to the branch. After the war, when the head of the training department returned to his regular duty, it was decided that

Stage A: Collecting the material was the general staff's responsibility.

Stage B: Processing the material was the training department's responsibility.

Stage C: Writing the war history and publishing a book was a training department responsibility.

The head of the training department decided to reconstruct the battles of the war. Therefore, the branch prepared a list of battles which should be reconstructed. The branch collected information up to November 1967. To be able to continue working, the branch increased its staff with six regular officers and four clerks in compulsory service. Still, the branch lacked personnel, vehicles, recording tapes, equipment, and so on, in order to succeed in covering all the units. Yet a procedure had been fixed. According to this plan the first stage was to concentrate on the unit and formation levels. The second stage was to cover the Supreme Command, divisions, and commands.

The archives was organized according to this procedure. When the first stage ended, the branch presented, in June 1968, an offer to the chief of the general staff which concluded a work plan to the Six Day War book. On June 22, in a meeting which was held in the office of the chief of the general staff, the offer was confirmed, and it was decided that two versions of the book would be written: one classified and one open. By early 1968 the second stage of the work had begun.

On September 1, 1969 the intermediate report of the Six Day War was presented with the assistance of the I.D.F.'s archives. Two years later, in 1972, the branch distributed the full research of the Six Day War for comments, but the process was stopped with the beginning of the Yom Kippur War in October 1973.

Another big project which the branch had begun was publishing annual summaries of routine security measures. The project started in 1964 and still continues. The aim of this project was to concentrate on the main events of routine security in order to be able to follow the security of Israel during peacetime.

In 1968, while researching the Six Day War, the Military History Branch became a department because the branch facilities was unable to handle the burgeoning Six Day War research. Therefore, the department holdings were increased and the Chief of Military History became a colonel.

After the Six Day War, the department organization was adjusted to the research. There were

- The Supreme Command Post Research Branch under a lieutenant colonel.
- The command's Research Branch under a lieutenant colonel.
- The Enemy Branch headed by a lieutenant colonel.

- The Routine Security Section. The head of the section was a major. (In 1971–1972 the section became a branch and the major became a lieutenant colonel.)
- The administration officer was a major.

In the beginning of 1971 a major came to the department as the head of the research on the past section to produce the work about the Arab–Israeli conflict from the end of the Independence War till 1963. (Later on a civilian who worked for the I.D.F. wrote the continuation of the work from 1964 to 1974.)

In 1972 (after finishing the Six Day War research) the Military History Department was asked to assist in establishing the Ministry of Defense History Unit. In September 1972 a new lieutenant colonel came to the department as the head of the Routine Security Branch, and soon became the officer in charge of the Ministry of Defense History Unit. He, one officer, and three shorthand clerks gathered material on such different subjects as procurement of arms from the Six Day War, arms development, security manufacture, and more. The unit was subject to the Minister of Defense's assistant, Zvi Sur, and used for special operations. In the summer of 1973 the chief of the general staff decided to separate this unit and the Military History Department. The unit became independent and the staff returned to the department.

When the Six Day War research ended, most of the senior officers left the department and were replaced. (In 1971–1972 there was also a publishing section whose head was a lieutenant colonel and later a major).

Just before the 1973 Yom Kippur War the department organization was

- Colonel—the chief of the Military History Department.
- Lieutenant colonel—the head of the War Research Branch.
- Lieutenant colonel—the head of the Routine Security Branch.
- Lieutenant colonel—a researcher.

In 1973, just when the chief of Military History wanted to publish an unclassified work on the Six Day War, the Yom Kippur War started.

THE DEPARTMENT DURING THE 1973 WAR

The chief of Military History functioned as the historian for the deputy chief of the general staff. He was in charge of the survey of the Supreme Command. A lieutenant colonel and a major were in the Northern Command. A lieutenant colonel, the head of the Combat Doctrine Branch, and another lieutenant colonel, the head of the Manoeuvres Branch, were in the Southern Command. In the different divisions were a reservist and a major.

All of them gathered information in order to write after the war. In September 1974 the chief of Military History was replaced. At that time there were

- The Supreme Command Research Branch—a lieutenant colonel and a captain. (The section had ceased to exist after the Six Day War, but was reestablished after the Yom Kippur War.)
- The Northern Command Research Branch—a lieutenant colonel and a major.
- The Southern Command Research Branch—a lieutenant colonel.
- The Enemy Research Branch—a lieutenant colonel.

RESEARCH ON THE YOM KIPPUR WAR

In the beginning of September 1975 the chief of Military History was ordered to start research on the Yom Kippur War. So as to describe the operational activity of the I.D.F. during the war and not the political background, he was ordered to "give the senior officers of the I.D.F. a readable book which will educate them about the history of the last war." The chief of Military History hoped that he would be able to complete the research in a short time, based on five general reviews which were made in the department and in the services (different teams dealt with the following subjects) about the Supreme Command, the Northern and Southern Theaters, the air force, and the navy. He wanted to summarize these general reviews and not to engage in new research.

The chief wanted to write the story from the I.D.F.'s point of view. But while doing this more information came in about the air force, the navy, routine security measures during the cease-fire, and so on. Each chapter draft was distributed to the heads of the different teams, their remarks were received, and then a discussion was held with the chief of Military History. The final version was completed in the editorial board and was passed to the field security department which classified it secret. So, instead of writing a short general overview, the department started to write a full, researched work which described and analyzed each day of the war. The department also used open sources such as newspapers, books, brigades' memorial books, and so on.

The editorial board of the Yom Kippur War book was the historical writer, a lieutenant colonel (in reserve service), the Supreme

Command Team, the War Team's secretary, and all the others were of the same rank: the Enemy and the International Relations Team, the Southern Command Team, and the Northern Command Team.

After the war the department succeeded in establishing a reserve cadre. Until then the department had to search for reservists whenever it needed them.

In September 1975 the chief of Military History was replaced again, first, until December 1975, by a lieutenant colonel. In December 1975 a colonel replaced the latter. During the next eight years the department continued the research and publication on the Yom Kippur War (see the publications list). As a result of a general reduction in the I.D.F. organization, there were in 1981 only three branches in the department: the Training and Routine Security Branch, the Supreme Command Branch, and the Administration Branch, all headed by lieutenant colonels.

"PEACE FOR GALILEE" WAR, 1983

When the war began, the department sent its officers and reservists to the Northern Command and the various divisions in order to cover the war and to collect information for later research. An officer sat also in the Supreme Command post.

After the war, the Administration Branch became a section, there were only two branches (as noted), and the department continued to gather information.

In September 1983 the chief of Military History was replaced. In the next four-year period the department dealt with the Yom Kippur War research, and also started the plan for research on the later war.

In October 1987 the former chief of the Military History Department was replaced, and the title changed to the chief of Military History.

Today the Military History Department is writing up the "Peace for Galilee" War. There are two branches in the department which deal with this:

1. The Strategic Level Research Branch—one lieutenant colonel and one major—are researching the strategic point of view of the war.
2. The Battles Research Branch—a lieutenant colonel and two majors—are working on the main battles and theaters during the war.

The administration section of the department assists the research by transcribing lots of recorded cassettes into stanograms which are used as information sources. And, in order to complete the work as quickly as possible, the department has also hired civilian researchers.

In addition to the war research, the department is also summarizing the subject of routine security (including the Intifada Affair). The department is also completing the research on the "Kadesh" and Atririon Wars that were neglected over the years. The department continues to teach the subject of military history to the I.D.F. officers course and at the Command and General Staff College.

CIVIL CONNECTIONS

The military history department also has professional connections with the Military and Diplomatic History Trends and the Strategic Research Institute at Tel Aviv University, with the Herzel Institute for Zionizsm Research at the Haifa University, and with the Davis and Truman Institutes at the Hebrew University in Jerusalem. The chief of the Military History Department is a member of the Israeli Commission of Military History. He is also the I.D.F. representative on the International Commission of Military History, and he supervises the Military History final papers which are written each year by high school students. The department also has periodical meetings with military correspondents in which it helps to produce different programs for television or the newspapers. Beside all that, the department is connected with Maarachot, the editorial house of the I.D.F., which it assists in writing military works and essays.

CHIEFS OF THE MILITARY HISTORY DEPARTMENT

1. Lieutenant Colonel Netanel Lorech: 1952–1955.
2. Lieutenant Colonel Mordechay Bar-On: 1955–1956.
3. Lieutenant Colonel Gabriel Luria: 1956–1963.
4. Lieutenant Colonel Avraham Ayalon: 1965–1974.
5. Colonel Bezalel Amir: 1974–1975.
6. Colonel Uri Algom: 1975–1983.
7. Colonel Ehud Ramot: 1983–1987.
8. Colonel Beny Michalson: 1987 forward.

Israeli Defense Publications

The original list contained classified titles. These have been deleted. Hence the gaps in the numbering.

PUBLICATIONS BY THE MILITARY HISTORY DEPARTMENT

War of Independence

.1 אינדקס מפת קרבות מלחמת העצמאות (רשימת הקרבות לפי חתך גאוגרפי), אפריל 1955.

1. *Index of War of Independence Battle Maps* (List of battles arranged according to a geographic cross-section), April 1955.

.2 מבצע "ברוש" - 18–9 ביולי 1948, מדריך סיור, 1956.

2. *Operation "Brosh"—July 9th–18th 1948, A Reconnaissance Guide,* 1956.

.3 מלחמת העצמאות - ראשי פרקים להסברה, מאי 1957.

3. *War of Independence—Outline for Clarification,* May 1957.

.4 מלחמת העצמאות - ראשי פרקים להסברה, עזרי אימון (מפות וטבלות לשמושו של המפקד המסביר), מאי 1957.

4. *War of Independence—Outline for Recounting, Training Aids* (Maps and charts for the use of the explaining commander), 1957.

.5 "יואב", שלב א׳ - 20–15 באוקטובר 1948, 1957.

5. *Operation "Yoav"—Stage I—15th–20th October 1948* (The breakthrough to the Negev in the War of Independence), 1957.

.6 מבצע "חורב", 1958.

6. *Operations "Horev"* (The final routing of the Egyptian Army from Israel), 1958.

.7 מבצע "חורב" ומעורבות המעצמות (דצמבר 1948 - ינואר 1949), נובמבר 1982.

7. *Operation "Horev" and the Superpowers Interfering* (December 1948–January 1949), November 1982.

.8 תולדות מלחמת הקוממיות, פברואר 1959.

8. *History of the War of Independence,* February 1959.

.9 מבצעי חטיבה 7 (מ"בן נון" עד "דקל", 25 במאי 1948 - 17 ביולי 1948).

9. *The 7th Brigade Operations* (From "Bin-Nun" to "Dekel," 25 May 1948–17 May 1948).

FROM THE WAR OF INDEPENDENCE TILL OPERATION "KADESH"

.11 מבצע "אלקיים" (קרב משטרת חאן-יונס ומוצב 132 במבואות עבסאן, 31-30 באוגוסט 1955), 1956, מסווג.

11. *Operation "Elkayam"* (The battle of the Han-Yones police and Post 132 at the entrance to Abasan, August 30th–31st, 1955).

BETWEEN "KADESH" AND THE SIX DAY WAR

33. חטיבה 45 במלחמת ששת הימים - צפון השומרון, יוני 5-7 1967, ינואר 1988.

33. *45 Brigade in the Six Day War—Northern Samaria, June 5th–7th 1967,* January 1988.

BETWEEN THE SIX DAY WAR AND THE YOM KIPPUR WAR

41. רא"ל בר-לב, דברים 1968-1971, נספח ד', לוח ארועים משולב, מסווג.

41. *Lieutenant General Bar-Lev, Speeches 1968–1971,* Appendix IV: Combined Tables of Incidents, n.d.

YOM KIPPUR WAR

71. נהול המלחמה - חלק ב', מתקפת הנגד בשטחנו (8 באוקטובר 1973), ספטמבר 1983, מסווג.

71. *The Conduct of War.* Vol. II: *The Counterattack in Israeli Territory (October 8th 1973)*, September 1983.

117. מקראה משלימה להסטוריה צבאית, ספטמבר 1988.

117. *Completed Anthology to Military History and Meditation,* September 1988.

FROM YOM KIPPUR TILL 1989

99. ספר המדינה (3 כרכים), מסווג.

99. *The State Book*—Three Volumes.

GENERAL

100. קרבות מופת (ארבל, קנה, לויטן), 1956.

100. *Classic Battles (Arabela, Cannae, Leuthen),* 1956.

101. פרשיות קרב (קרבות קאסרין - קרב דיאן ביאן פו), 1958.

101. *Battle Accounts (Battles of Kasrin, Battle of Dien-Bien-Fu),* 1958.

102. פרשיות קרב - קרב ההגנה בכיתור ("כיס דמיאנסקי"), 1959.

102. *Battle Accounts—Defense Battle in Encirclement* ("Demianski Pocket"), 1959.

107. קרב היתקלות בין עוצבות שריון (פרשת קרב פורוחובקה במלחה"ע השניה בחזית בריה"מ), 1965.

107. *An Encounter Engagement between Armored Formations* (Porhavka battle episode in World War II on the Soviet front), 1965.

108. סיני כמרחב ספר באספקלריה היסטורית, 1969, מסווג.

108. *Sinai as a Border Zone in Historic Perspective,* 1969.

109. פרוגרמה למוזאון צה"ל - 1947-1973, מצע לדיון, מרס 1979, מסווג.

109. *Program for the I.D.F. Museum—1947–1973, Proposal for Discussion,* 1979.

110. מערכות קשר, מאי 1979, מסווג.

110. *Maarachot Kesher* (the Signal Corp Newspaper), May 1979.

112. פנקס כיס לקצין ההסטוריה, אוגוסט 1980. חסווג.

112. *The History Officer Pocket Notebook,* August 1980.

122. תולדות צה"ל בראי מלחמותיו, פרקי הסטוריה צבאית עד מלחמת יוה"כ, אפריל 1988.

122. *The I.D.F.'s Chronology through Israel's Wars,* (Military history chapters to Yom-Kippur War), April 1989.

129. המלחמה נגד המחבלים ברודזיה בין השנים 76-77 (מבצע "אלנד" ומבצע "מניאטלה"), אוגוסט 1988.

129. *The Fight against Terrorists in the Rhodesian War between the Years 76–77* (Operations "Eland" and "Maniatela"), August 1988.

131. רוז'ה טרינקייה, לוחמה נגד מהפכנות, 1989.

131. Rog'ee Trinkye, *Warfare: A French View of Counter-Revolutionary Warfare,* 1989.

132. בעיני אויב - 3 פרסומים ערביים על מלחמת העצמאות, 1954.

132. *In the Eyes of the Enemy, Three Arab Publications on the Independence War,* 1954.

133. מעבר למסך - ועדת חקירה פרלמנטרית עירקית על מלחמת העצמאות, 1955.

133. *Beyond the Curtain—An Iraqi Parliamentary Commission on the War in Israel,* 1954.

134. קרבות תש"ח - 23 פרשיות קרב במלחמת העצמאות, 1955.

134. *The Battle of 1948—23 Battle Accounts during the War of Independence,* 1955.

BOOKS AND ARTICLES BY HISTORY DEPARTMENT RESEARCHERS

Books

1. א. אילון, חטיבת גבעתי במלחמת העצמאות, 1959.

1. A. Ayalon, *The Givati Brigade in the War of Independence,* 1959.

2. שם, חטיבת גבעתי נגד הפולש המצרי, 1963.

2. A. Ayalon, *The Givati Brigade against the Egyptian Invader* (The Egyptian invasion of Israel in the War of Independence), 1963.

3. א. אורן, בדרך אל העיר - מבצע "דני", 1976.

3. E. Oren, *On the Road to the City—Operation "Danny"* (The freeing of Lod and Ramla in the War of Independence), 1976.

4. י. קורדובה, מדיניות ארה"ב במלחמת יוה"כ, 1987.

4. Y. Cordoba, *U.S. Policy in the Yom Kippur War,* 1987.

5. ש. גולן, מרות ומאבק בימי מרי, 1945-1946, 1988.

5. S. Golan, *Allegiance in the Struggle, 1945–1946* (The struggle against British policy and occupation of Palestine by the Hebrew underground organizations), 1988.

Articles

The list is arranged according to wars and periods, within each period according to periodicals in chronological order. Articles discussing more than one period are marked with an asterisk.

War of Independence

Maarachot

6. נ. לורך, הבעיות ההסטוריוגרפיות של מלחמת העצמאות, כרך 45.

6. N. Lorch, *On Problems of Military Historiography of the War of Independence,* 75.

7. ג. לוריא, התכניות למבצע "חירם", 145.

7. G. Luria, *The Planning of Operation "Hiram,"* 145 (The freeing of the Galilee in the War of Independence).

8. שם, מבצע "חירם", 149.

8. G. Luria, *Operation "Hiram,"* 149.

9. * א. אילון, מחקר השוואה - מלחמת העצמאות, מבצע "קדש" ומלחמת ששת הימים, 191-192.

9. *A. Ayalon, *A Comparative Study—the War of Independence, Operation "Kadesh," the Six Day War*, 191–192.

10. * א. אורן, המאבק לעצמאות, 1945-1947, 230.

10. *E. Oren, *The Struggle for Independence, 1945–1947,* 230.

11. א. אילון, הרקע להקמתה של מדינת ישראל, 241.

11. A. Ayalon, *The Background of the Establishment of the State of Israel,* 241.

12. א. אורן, הקרב בפרברי ירושלים, אפריל 1948, 234-244.

12. E. Oren, *The Battle in the Outskirts of Jerusalem, April 1948,* 234–244.

13. א. אילון, המעורבות העירקית במלחמת העצמאות, 246.

13. A. Ayalon, *The Iraqi Involvement in the War of Indcpendence,* 246.

14. א. אורן, הקרב בפרברי חיפה, אפריל 1948, 251-252.

14. E. Oren, *The Battle in the Outskirts of Haifa, April 1948,* 251–252.

15. * נ. לורך, קץ המלחמות וסיום המאבקים, 257.

15. *N. Lorch, *The End of Wars and the Termination of Conflicts,* 257.

16. 1948 - אוסף תעודות, 263-264 (מתייחס למלחמת העצמאות).

16. *1948—Collection of Documents,* 263–264 (Relating to the Israeli War of Independence).

17. א. אורן, ימשימות הסדר ויעדים ובטחון, 270-271.

17. *E. Oren, *The Settlement's Missions and Goals—and Security,* 270–271.

18. שם, מטרות ותוצאות במלחמת העצמאות, חלק I, 279-280.

18. E. Oren, *Aims and Results in the War of Independence I,* 279–280.

19. שם, שם, חלק II, 281.

19. E. Oren, *Aims and Results in the War of Independence II*, 281.

20. י. בנדמן, הלגיון הערבי במלחמת העצמאות, 295-299.

20. Y. Bandman, *The Arab Legion—in the* [Israeli] *War of Independence,* 229–295.

21. נ. לורך, האולטימטום הבריטי במבצע "חורב", 294-295.

21. N. Lorch, *The "British Ultimatum" during "Horev,"* 294–295 (With the response of M. Gazit in Vol. 297).

22. א. אלגום, קרבות חירבת מאחז, 294-295.

22. E. Oren, *The Repulse of the "Army of Deliverance" from Mishmar-Haemek,* 294–295 (A Kibbutz repulsing of an attack by Arab semi-regular forces in the Israeli War of Independence).

23. א. אורן, הדיפת חיל המשלוחממשמר העמק, 294–295.

23. U. Algom, *The Battles of Hirbet-Mahaz,* 294–295 (Prior to the I.D.F. breakthrough to the Negev).

24. א. אורן, המשבר בפקוד העליון - ועדת החמישה, 298.

24. E. Oren, *The Crisis in the Supreme Command—Commission of the Five Ministers,* 298 (The search for a Commander-in-Chief in the Israeli War of Independence).

25. נ. לורך, האולטימטום הבריטי - עובדה או מיתוס? , 298.

25. N. Lorch, *The British Ultimatum, Myth or Fact,* 298 (Response to M. Gazit).

26. א. אורן, לא היה אולטימטום אבל איום כן, 298.

26. E. Oren, *There Was No Ultimatum, But There Was a Real Threat,* 298–303 (Response to N. Lorch).

27. שם, "מחתרות", "צבא סדיר", "ההגנה" (ארגוני ההגנה היהודיים), ו"צבא הגנה לישראל", 308.

27. E. Oren, *"Underground," "Regular Army," the "Haganah" (Jewish self-defense organization) and the I.D.F.,* 308.

28. צ. לבקוביץ, ציוד ואספקה, חיל האספקה, 310.

28. Z. Levkovitch, *Equipment and Supplies, Supplying Service and Supply and Transportation Corps,* 310.

29. א. אורן, עסקת דה–פקטו? מבצעים ומדיניות במרכז הארץ, סתיו 1948, 311.

29. E. Oren, *"De-Facto Deal?" Policy and Operations in the Center of the Country, Autumn 1948,* 311.

Maarachot Shiryon (Armor)

30. ש. גפני, גדוד 89 תופס את בית גוברין,-מערכות שריון 7–8.

30. S. Gafni, *The 89th Battalion Captures Bet-Guvrin,* 7–8.

31. שם, גדוד 89 תופס את משטרת עירק–סואידן.

31. S. Gafni, *The 89th Battalion Takes the Fortress,* 7–8 (The capturing of the famous Iraq–Sueidan police station).

32. י. ציזקינד, פעילות שריון בעירק אל מנשיה, 21.

32. Y. Ziskind, *Armour Activity in the Iraq El-Manshia,* 21 (I.D.F. armor in one of the I.D.F.'s first armored operations).

Maarachot Kesher V'Electronica (Signal and Electronics)

33. ג. שריג, תקשורת במבצע "אהוד", 73, 90.

33. G. Sarig, *Communications during Operation "Ehud,"* 73, 90.

34. שם, שרותי הדואר הצבאיים במלחמת העצמאות, 74.

34. G. Sarig, *Military Postal Service in the War of Independence,* 74.

35. שם, תקשורת במבצע "נחשון", 77.

35. G. Sarig, *Communications during Operation "Nahshon,"* 77.

36. שם, תקשורת במבצע "הראל", 79.

36. G. Sarig, *Communications during Operation "Harel,"* 79 (The capturing of the road to the encircled Jerusalem).

37. שם, תקשורת במבצע "בלק", 80.

37. G. Sarig, *Communications during Operation "Balak,"* 80 (The aerial train to Israel).

38. שם, צעדים ראשונים במלחמת העצמאות, 85.
38. G. Sarig, *First Steps in the War of Independence,* 85.

39. שם, התכנית הפלשתינאית, 91.
39. G. Sarig, *The Palestine Scheme,* 91.

40. שם, חיל הקשר בסוף מלחמת העצמאות, 94.
40. G. Sarig, *The Signal and Electronics Corps at the End of the War of Independence,* 94.

41. * שם, מלחמת ישראל כפי שהיא מצטיירת על פי טלגרמות, 1948–1973, 100.
41. *G. Sarig, *Israel's War Seen through Telegrams, 1948–1973,* 100.

42. שם, קשר בחטיבה 8 במלחמת העצמאות, 102.
42. G. Sarig, *Communications in the 8th Brigade in the War of Independence,* 102.

43. שם, תקשורת במבצע "דני", 105.
43. G. Sarig, *Communications during Operation "Danny,"* 105.

44. שם, קשר בחטיבה 7 במבצע "חירם", 107.
44. G. Sarig, *Communications in the 7th Brigade During Operation "Hiram,"* 107.

45. שם, תקשורת במבצע "חורב", 108.
45. G. Sarig, *Communications during Operation "Horev,"* 108 (The final routing of the Egyptian enemy from Israeli territory).

Skira Hodshit (Monthly Review)

46. נ. לורך, צמתים בקבלת החלטות במלחמת העצמאות, 77/11.
46. N. Lorch, *Crossroads of Decisionmaking in the War of Independence,* 77/11.

47. א. אורן, הסדרים - מבנה לעצמאות, 3-4/82.
47. E. Oren, *Settlement—an Infrastructure for Independence,* 82/3–4.

48. א. אילון, הבטחון הלאומי הישראלי, 2-3/83.
48. A. Ayalon, *Israel's National Security,* 83/2–3.

49. א. אורן, מרסון עצמי לטוהר הנשק, 2-3/84.
49. E. Oren, *From "Self-Restraint" to "Parity of Arms,"* 84/2–3.

50. שם, יגאל ידין במלחמת העצמאות, 6/84.
50. E. Oren, *Y. Yadin in the War of Independence,* 84/6.

51. שם, דויד בן גוריון במלחמת העצמאות, 1/86.
51. E. Oren, *David Ben-Gurion in the War of Independence,* 86/1.

Geographic Collections

52. א. אורן, הנגב בתקופת המרי, מאבק והמלחמה לעצמאות, ארץ הנגב, 1979.
52. E. Oren, *The Negev in Resistance, Struggle, and the War of Independence* (The Negev—the southern half of Israel in the struggle for independence), in *The Negev Land*, 1979.

53. שם, באר שבע בקרבות הנגב, 1939–1949, ספר באר שבע, 1979.
53. E. Oren, *Beer-Sheva in the Negev Battles, 1939–1949,* in *The Beer-Sheva Book,* 1979.

From the End of the War of Independence until Operation "Kadesh" (The Sinai Campaign, 1956)

Maarachot

54. ש. גפני, תפיסת רפיח, חלק I, 107–108.

54. S. Gafni, *The Capture of Rafiah* I, 107–108.

55. שם, שם, חלק II, 109.

55. S. Gafni, *The Capture of Rafiah* II, 109.

56. שם, תפיסת צומת רפיח, 112.

56. S. Gafni, *The Capture of the Rafiah Crossroads,* 112.

57. שם, מצומת רפיח לתעלת סואץ, 115.

57. S. Gafni, *From the Rafiah Crossroads to the Suez Canal,* 115.

58. שם, קרב המיתלה, 144.

58. S. Gafni, *The Mitla Battle,* 144 (In the Sinai Campaign, the first airborne operation).

59. מ. אילן, שמוש בגורם ההפתעה במבצע "קדש", 178–179.

59. M. Ilan, *Utilization of the Surprise Factor in Operation "Kadesh,"* 178–179.

60. נ. בר און, רוח הלחימה במבצע "קדש". 140.

60. N. Bar-on, *The Fighting Spirit in Operation "Kadesh,"* 140.

61. ש. גפני, חץ שחור לעזה, 254.

61. S. Gafni, *A Black Arrow to Gaza,* 254 (A retaliation operation against the Egyptians, 1955).

62. מ. בר און, עסקת מצריים–צ'כוסלובקיה, שאלה של זמן, 306–307.

62. M. Bar-on, *The Egyptian–Czechoslovakian Deal—A Question of Dating,* 306–307 (The arms deal between Egypt and Czechoslovakia, 1955).

Maarachot Kesher V'Electronica (Signals and Electronics)

63. ג. שריג, תקשורת במבצע "כנרת", 101.

63. G. Sarig, *Communications during Operation "Kinneret,"* 101 (A retaliation operation against the Syrians, 1955).

64. שם, מסקנות קציני קשר לגבי מבצע "קדש", 97–98.

64. G. Sarig, *A Signal Officer's Conclusions at the End of Operation "Kadesh,"* 97–98.

Skira Hodshit (Monthly Review)

65. א. זוהר, מבצע סיני כנקודת מפנה, 81/10.

65. A. Zohar, *The Sinai Campaign as a Turning Point,* 81/10.

66. מ. בר און, מערכת סיני – גורמים והשגים, 86/10–11.

66. M. Bar-on, *The Sinai Campaign—Causes and Achievements,* 86/10–11.

67. נ. לורך, בן גוריון והמעצמות במבצע "קדש", 86/10–11.

67. N. Lorch, *Ben-Gurion and the Superpowers during "Kadesh,"* 86/10–11.

68. ש. גפני, החדירה בהגנת רפיח במבצע "קדש", 11-10/86.
68. S. Gafni, *Penetration of the Rafiah Defences in "Kadesh,"* 86/10–11 (M. Pails response—87/1).

Geographic Collections

69. ש. גולן, הקרב על מי הירדן, ארץ הגליל, 1983.
69. S. Golan, *The Battle over the Waters of the Jordan,* in *The Galilee Lands,* 1983 (The series of incidents and retaliation operations caused by the Arab attempts to stop Israel from using the Jordan waters).
70. י. בנדמן, חצי האי סיני בתפיסת האסטרטגיה המצרית, ספר סיני, 1987.
70. Y. Bandman, *The Sinai Peninsula in Egypt's Strategic Perception, 1949–1967,* in *The Sinai Book,* 1987.

From the End of Operation "Kadesh" until the Six Day War

Maarachot

71. א. אילון, צעדי מלחמה, 187-186.
71. A. Ayalon, *War Moves,* 186–187 (In the Six Day War).
72. ש. גפני. נשק אנטי טנקי. 187-186.
72. S. Gafni, *Recoilless Guns against Tanks,* 186–187 (Israeli recoilless guns in the Sinai in the Six Day War).
73. מ. שריג, חדירת המוצבים ברמה"ג, 187-186.
73. M. Sarig, *Penetration of Posts in the Golan Heights,* 186–187 (In the Six Day War).
74. י. בנדמן, איך הערבים רואים את הרקע למלחמת ששת הימים,102-191.
74. Y. Bandman, *How the Arabs See the Background of the Six Day War,* 102–191.
75. א. אילון, פעולת "סמוע", 262-261.
75. A. Ayalon, *Operation "Grinder" ("Samoa"),* 261–262 (A retaliation operation against the Jordanians, 1966).

Skira Hodshit (Monthly Review)

76. א. אילון, התהליך שהביא את מלחמת ששת הימים, 5/86.
76. A. Ayalon, *The Process that Brought About the Six Day War,* 86/5.

From the End of the Six Day War until the Yom Kippur War

Maarachot

77. י. בנדמן, מדיניות המאבק של נאצר. 223.
77. Y. Bandman, *Gamal and El-Nasser's Struggle Policy,* 223.
78. שם, הדרכה מורלית בצבא המצרי בשנים שקדמו למלחמת יוה"כ, 237.
78. Y. Bandman, *Moral Guidance in the Egyptian Army in the Years Preceding the Yom Kippur War,* 237.

79. א. זוהר, על מלחמת ההתשה, 257.

79. A. Zohar, *About the War of Attrition,* 257 (The four-year war of attrition fought after the Six Day War).

80. ב. מיכלסון, מבצע "תופת", 292–293.

80. B. Michelson, *Operation "Inferno" (Karame),* 292–293 (Response to the article, 297).

81. א. זוהר, מבצעי "אסקורט" ו"רביב", 297.

81. A. Zohar, *"Eskort" and "Raviv,"* 297 (Two Israeli raids behind Egyptian lines in the war of attrition in which a Russian-made radar installation was captured and brought to Israel).

Skira Hodshit (Monthly Review)

82. בטחון שוטף נגד פעילות חבלנית עוינת יוני 1967–יוני1969, 6/69.

82. A. Ayalon, *Current Security Against Hostile Activity, June 1967–June 1969,* 69/6.

83. צ. לבקוביץ, סכום פעילות חודשי - ספטמבר, 8/69–9.

83. Z. Levkovitch, *The Summits of the Month of September,* 69/8–9 (Two Arab summits on the Arab–Israeli conflict).

84. א. זוהר, אפיון מבצע "קדש", 9/86.

84. A. Zohar, *Characterization of the War of Attrition,* 86/9.

The Yom Kippur War

Maarachot

85. א. אורן, גדוד טנקים בקרבות הגולן, סופר ע"י בני- קצין בגדוד, 234–235.

85. E. Oren, *A Tank Battalion in the Golan Campaigns—Told by Benny, an Officer in the Battalion,* 234–235.

86. י. בנדמן, מלחמת יום כיפור בספרות העולמית, 238–239.

86. Y. Bandman, *The Yom Kippur War in World Literature,* 238–239.

87. חוקרי מחלקת היסטוריה (לא מוזכרים שמות). כרך 240.

87. History Department Researchers (no names mentioned), 240.

88. י. בנדמן, כיצד ראו המצרים את מלחמת יוה"כ, 245.

88. Y. Bandman, *How the Egyptians Saw the Yom Kippur War,* 245.

89. צ. איתן, הקרב על האגם המר. 247–248.

89. Z. Eytan, *The Battle by the Bitter Lakes,* 247–248.

90. י. בנדמן, מצרים במלחמת יוה"כ: מטרות המלחמה ותוכניות ההתקפה, 250.

90. Y. Bandman, *Egypt Towards the Yom Kippur War: War Aims and Offensive Plans,* 250.

91. D. Inbar, *The Battle for the Capture of the "Ohra" Locality,* 253.

92. Y. Cordoba, *The Political Background of the American Airlift,* 256.

93. R. Rojansky, *The "Mezach" Stronghold in the Yom Kippur War,* 258–259.

94. Y. Bandman, *The Iraqi Expeditionary Force,* 258–259.

95. A. Ayalon, *October 14th 1973—Why It Was Erased from History* (A heavy Egyptian armor attack on October 14, 1973, which the I.D.F. repulsed).

96. D. Inbar, *The Jordanian Army in the Yom Kippur War,* 266.

97. Y. Cordoba and Y. Bandman, *The Soviet Nuclear Threat at the End of the Yom Kippur War,* 266.
98. Z. Eytan, *October 8th—the Entire War Machine Did Not Run Smoothly,* 268 (On October 8 the I.D.F. tried prematurely, and failed, to wipe out the Egyptian invading forces in the Sinai and across the Suez Canal to Egypt).
99. A. Zohar, *The Yom Kipper War Strategic Decisions,* 276–277.
100. Y. Cordoba, *The U.S. Policy on the "Preemptive Strike,"* 276–277 (On the part of Israel).
101. Z. Eytan, *"Dove-Cote"—Planning and Execution Tested under Fire,* 276–277 ("Dove-Cote" was the code name of the I.D.F. defensive plan in the Sinai before the Yom Kippur War).
102. S. Golan, *War Aims,* 289–290.
103. Y. Cordoba and Y. Bandman, *The Egyptian 3rd Army crosses the Suez Canal,* 296.

Hirhurim V'Irurim (Thoughts and Criticism)

104. א. לביא, גבעה אחת ושני קרבות (תל שמס), 1.
104. A. Lavi, *One Hill—Two Battles (Tel Shams),* Pamphlet #1. (Efforts to capture Tel Shams in the Golan Heights in the Yom Kippur War).
105. צ. איתן, שנויים במבנה הכוחות ומשימותיהם לפני כניסתם לקרב, 3.
105. Z. Eytan, *Changes in the Composition of the Armoured Forces and Their Missions before Engaging in Battle,* 3.

Skira Hodshit (Monthly Review)

106. א. אילון, המוכנות הלאומית ערב מלחמת יוה"כ, 8/83.
106. A. Ayalon, *National Readiness (In the Wake of the Yom Kippur War),* 83/8.

Geographic Collections

107. א. אורן, מהגנה להתקפה במלחמת יוה"כ, ספר סיני, 1987.
107. E. Oren, *From Holding-Defence to Counter-Crossing in the Yom Kippur War,* in *The Sinai Book,* 1987 (The counter-crossing of the Suez Canal by the I.D.F.).

I.D.F. MILITARY HISTORY DIVISION PUBLICATIONS

1. אל"מ בני מיכלסון, ההסטוריה של צה"ל בארבע תקופות, עיתון צה"ל, קיץ 1988.
1. I.D.F. Journal, Summer 1988, Col. Benny Michelson, *A History of the I.D.F. through Four Decades.*
2. סא"ל בן ציון טחן, מערכת סיני, 1960.
2. Lt. Col. Ben-Zion Tahan, *The Sinai Campaign,* 1960.
3. סא"ל אברהם אילון, מלחמת ששת הימים, 1968.
3. Lt. Col. A. Ayalon, *The Six Day War,* 1968.
4. תאור מבצעים משולבים במלחמת ששת הימים מפי מפקדים, גזרת סיני, 1967.
4. *The Six Day War Description of Combats by Commanders, Sinai Front,* 1967.

5. ענף הסטוריה צבאית של חיל האויר, חיל האויר במלחמת יוה"כ, 1975.

5. Historical Branch Israeli Air Force, *The Air Force in the "Yom Kippur War,"* 1975.

6. מלחמת יוה"כ, אוקטובר 1973, 1981 (הרצאה).

6. *The "Yom Kippur War," October 1973,* 1981 (Lecture).

7. תקרית הליברטי, 8 ביוני 1967, 1982.

7. *The "Liberty" Incident, 8 June 1967,* 1982.

8. אל"מ בני מיכלסון, מבצע "תופת" - לחימה בגדה המזרחית של הירדן, מרץ 1968, 1984.

8. Col. Benny Michelsohn, *Operation "Tofet" ("Inferno") Fighting East of the Jordan River* (March 1968), 1984.

9. אל"מ אורי אלגום וסא"ל יעקב אידל, מלחמת "שלום הגליל", (הרצאה), 1984.

9. Col. Uri Algom and Lt. Col. Ya'Acov Idel, *"Peace for Galilee" War,* 1984 (Lecture).

OTHER OFFICIAL PUBLICATIONS

10. מרכז ההסברה הישראלי, הסכסוך הערבי ישראלי לפני מלחמת ששת הימים ומאז, ירושלים 1973.

10. Israel Information Center, *The Arab Israeli Conflict before 1967 and Since,* Jerusalem, 1973.

11. סדרת הסברה ישראלית, הארועים שהובילו למלחמת ששת הימים והלקחים, ירושלים 1972.

11. Israel Information Series, *Menace, the Events That Led up to the Six Day War and Their Lessons,* Jerusalem, 1972.

12. סדרת הסברה של המזרח התיכון, מסמכים ותעודות ממלחמת יוה"כ, ירושלים 1973.

12. Middle East Information Series, *Statements and Documents on the October 1973 War,* Jerusalem, 1973.

13. קצין חינוך ראשי, מלחמת ששת הימים, ת"א, 1967.

13. I.D.F. Chief Education Officer, *The Six Day War,* Tel Aviv, 1967.

14. דובר צה"ל, מלחמות ישראל-ערב, 1975.

14. I.D.F. Spokesman's Office, *The Israeli–Arab Wars,* 1975 (a collection).

OTHER NONOFFICIAL RECOMMENDED PUBLICATIONS

15. אריה חשביה, סקירה של הסטוריה צבאית בינ"ל, ת"א, 1979.

15. Arie C. Hshavia (ed.), *Revue International d'Histoire Militaire,* Tel Aviv, 1979.

16. לואיס וויליאמס, אספקטים בסכסוך הישראלי-ערבי, ת"א, 1975.

16. Louis Williams (ed.), *Military Aspects of the Israeli–Arab Conflict,* Tel Aviv, 1975.

17. ג'ון ודויד קמחי, משני עברי הגבעה, לונדון 1970.

17. Jon Kimche and David Kimche, *Both Sides of the Hill,* London, 1960.

18. חוסיין - מלך ירדן, מלחמתי עם ישראל, ניו יורק, 1969.

18. Hussein of Jordan, *My "War" with Israel,* New York, 1969.

19. יעקב בר סימן טוב, מלחמת ההתשה הישראלית-מצרית, 1969-1970, ניו יורק 1980.

19. Yaacov Bar-Siman-Tov, *The Israeli–Egyptian War of Attrition, 1969–1970,* New York, 1980.

20. שי פלדמן, הפשיטה על אוזירו, ת"א, 1981.
20. Shay Feldman, *The Raid on Osiraq,* Tel Aviv, 1981.
21. דויד בן גוריון, ישראל, הסטוריה אישית, לונדון, 1972.
21. David Ben-Gurion, *Israel, a Personal History,* London, 1972.
22. מיכאל בר זוהר, ביאוגרפיה על דויד בן גוריון, לונדון 1971.
22. Michael Bar-Zohar, *The Armed Prophet: A Biography of Ben Gurion,* London, 1966.

23. יגאל אלון, הקמת צה"ל, לונדון 1971.
23. Maj. General Yogal Allon, *The Making of Israeli's Army,* London, 1971.
24. חנוך ברטוב, דדו, 48 שנים ו20 יום, ת"א, 1981.
24. Hanoch Bartov, *Dado, 48 Years and 20 Days,* Tel Aviv, 1981.
25. אברהם אדן, על שתי גדות הסואץ, סאן רפאל, 1980.
25. Avraham (Bren) Adan, *On the Banks of the Suez,* San Rafael, Calif., 1980.

26. מרדכי גור, הקרב על ירושליים, ניו יורק, 1978.
26. Mordechai Gur, *The Battle for Jerusalem,* New York, 1978.
27. קהלני אביגדור, עז 77, ווסטפורט, 1984.
27. Avigdor Kahalani, *The Heights of Courage,* Westport, 1984.
28. סעד אל שאזאלי, חציית התעלה, סאן פרנסיסקו, 1980.
28. Shazaly Saad El. *The Crossing of the Suez,* San Francisco, 1980.
29. יגאל אלון, מגן דויד.
29. Yigal Allon, *Shield of David.* 1966.

30. משה דיין, יומן סיני, ניו יורק, 1966.
30. Moshe Dayan, *Diary of the Sinai Campaign,* New York, 1966.
31. דיין משה, ספור חיי, ניו יורק 1976.
31. Moshe Dayan, *The Story of My Life,* New York, 1976.
32. שבתאי טבת, טנקי תמוז, ניו יורק 1968.
32. Shabtai Teveth, *The Tanks of Tamuz,* New York, 1968.
33. עוזי נרקיס, שחרור ירושליים: קרב 1967, לונדון 1973.
33. Uzi Narkiss, *The Liberation of Jerusalem: The Battle of 1967,* London, 1973.

12

Italy

The Italian Air Force Historical Office

Colonel Giovanni de Lorenzo, Chief

The Italian Air Force Historical Office was formed on 25 January 1926 as the Historical Section of the Royal Italian Air Force's Staff Office with the duty of "firstly collecting and reorganizing as much archival material of historical importance as possible and to classify it; in order to be able in the future to use it to compile an official account of the new Service's development and use, in peace and at war." Currently the office, which reports to the 5th Department of the Air Force Staff, comprises four sections: library, historical materials, publications, and historical research.

The section's first chief was Lt. Col. Ercole Morelli, who gathered much documentary material in the navy and army archives and eventually in 1927–1929 compiled the *Cronistoria dell'Aeronautica Militare Italiana* (chronicle of Italian military aviation) (seven volumes, completed with an eighth in 1968) and the monographs on units employed during the Great War (the series comprises currently twelve boxes of papers, including in part some later materials). The World War I papers available run to some 250 boxes, to which should be added another 300 relating to personnel and are stored at Bagni di Tivoli.

On 14 May 1927 the Historical Section became the Historical Office and on 1 June Lt. Col. Morelli was confirmed as its chief. His first tasks were the compilation of lists of deceased personnel (which, continuously updated, now runs to fourteen boxes), twenty-four panels with photos of Gold Medal holders and the motivations for the decoration (also updated over the years with new awards), the two volumes of the *Albo d'Oro* (Golden Roll of Honor), and the abstract of all war bulletins regarding the air service.

In the 1930s the Historical Office participated in the organization of several exhibitions and the establishing of an Air Force Museum within the Air Force Academy. The service's activity in these years is documented by the various units' *Memorie storiche* (Historical memoranda) (thirty-two boxes), *Raid e crociere* (Flights and cruises) (six), *Airship Wing* (thirty-five), *Airfields* (sixteen), *1st Department–Operations Division 1936–1940, and Service Division 1937–1941*. Other collections cover operations in East Africa (376 boxes for the 1935–1938 period) and OMS, the Italian code name for the involvement in the Spanish Civil War (102 boxes). Other papers from the Air Force Staff 1st Department cover years 1932–1950 and compensate in part for the loss of the Air Minister's cabinet papers prior to 1937 (post 1937 cabinet papers are held, also in Rome, by the Archivio Centrale dello Stato).

On 3 June 1940 operational units started keeping a daily *Diario Storico* (Operational Record Book), of which the office holds 395 bound volumes for 1940, 427 for 1941, 275 for 1942, 95 for 1943, 40 for 1944, and 28 for 1945. To these should be added the other World War II documentary collections: *Seconda guerra mondiale* (divided in thirty subsections), *SAS* (the air transport service, eighty-nine boxes plus eighty covering personnel), *Divisione difesa* (thirty-three), *SIOS* (205, also including technical aircraft material which adds to an extensive handbook [manual] collection), plus several different types of periodical *Aircraft* situations.

The Historical Office survived the disbanding of the Air Force Staff decreed on 16 September 1943 by Gen. Aldo Urbani, who following the armistice with the Allies had become Air Force Commissioner. This foresight enabled Capt. Angelo Lodi, who served with the office, to compile already by 1946 the book *L'Aeronautica italiana nella guerra di liberazione* (The Italian Air Force in the War of Liberation). This difficult period is also covered by the twenty-two boxes of the *Aeronautica Nazionale Repubblicana* collection.

The return of peace brought about the return to the *Memorie Storiche*, initially compiled quarterly and later made annual. Obviously, access to recent documentation, which includes a collection on *Operazione Locusta* (the code name for Italy's involvement in the Gulf War), is regulated by security considerations. The office holds no personnel files, which are kept by the General Directorate of Military Personnel, but the archives do contain some 1,200 A and B forms up to 1962, listing personnel on strength with units, as well as some 650 *Libretti personali* (personal diaries). There are also some 250 flight logs and a *Relazione varie* collection (thirteen boxes). Although the office does not have its own photo archive (which, however, also exists within the 5th Department), its collections include a number of photo albums and incomplete material on badges and insignia.

The Library Section operates the Air Force Central Library and the Periodicals Collection, totalling some 45,000 volumes. Computer cataloguing is underway. The section also oversees the operation of about eighty unit libraries in the field.

The Publications Section is tasked with the production of books published by the office: About ten books are released annually. Among the most recent are the *Direttive tecnico operative di Superaereo* (Technical Operating Directives of the High Command) (4 volumes), the two volumes on air force architecture, and the first volume of the collected works of Giulio Douhet, all compiled or written by external authors. Books are sold by mail (payment can be made by postal order on giro account 597005 in the name of Comando RESCAM-Servizio Amministrativo) or over the counter at the main air events.

The Historical Materials Section was formed to oversee the Air Force Museum at Vigna di Valle and to coordinate the recovery, cataloguing, restoration, and exhibition of aircraft and related items, as well as their distribution to units, museums, or other interested parties. A very productive relationship is entertained with the Gruppo Amici Velivoli Storici, the society for the preservation of historic Italian aircraft.

The Historical Office is open to the public during normal working hours. Documentation can be studied within existing security and confidentiality regulations and, for small quantities of papers, xeroxing facilities are available. Some queries can be answered by post, although researchers with large projects are advised to undertake them personally.

The office is located in the former Telecomdife building, within the air staff complex, within walking distance from Rome's central railroad station and thus linked to every part of the city. Access can be gained from the Passes Office on Viale dell'Università 4.

Mailing Address

Stato Maggiore Aeronautica, 5 Reparto, Ufficio Storico, Viale dell' Università 4, 00185 Roma, Italy. Telephone: +39.6.4986.5214

Ufficio Storico

Translated by Robin Higham

CATALOGO DELLE PUBBLICAZIONI, MAGGIO 1995

A.T.A. *Il convegno degli Aviatori Transoceanici 60 anni dopo* (60th anniversary meeting of the Transoceanic airmen).

Alegi, G., Catalanotto, B. *Coccarde Tricolori* (The tricoloured roundel).

Arena, N. *La Regia Aeronautica 1939–43. Vol. 1* (The Italian air force, 1939–1943, Vol. 1).

Arena, N. *La Regia Aeronautica 1939–43. Vol. 2* (The Italian air force, 1939–1943, Vol. 2).

Arena, N. *La Regia Aeronautica 1939–43. Vol. 3* (The Italian air force, 1939–1943, Vol. 3).

Arena, N. *La Regia Aeronautica 1939–43. Vol. 4* (The Italian air force, 1939–1943, Vol. 4).

Arena, N. *La Regia Aeronautica. Dall'Armistizio alla cobelligeranza. Vol. 1* (The Italian air force from the Armistice to Cobelligerency, Vol. 1).

Arena, N. *La Regia Aeronautica. Dall'Armistizio alla cobelligeranza. Vol. 2* (The Italian air force from the Armistice to Cobeelligerency, Vol. 2).

Botti, F., Cermelli, M. *La teoria della Guerra Aerea* (The theory of aerial warfare).

Casini, G. *Il Gruppo Buscaglia alla vigilia e dopo l'armistizio* (Group Buscaglia to the watch and after the Armistice).

Catalanotto, B., Pratt, H. *In un cielo lontano: 70 anni di Aeronautica Militare* (In a distant sky—70 years of military aviation).

Circi, M., Guglielmetti, *A. Gli attuali reparti A.M. dell'aviazione per la marina* (The present division of air army from naval air).

Curami, A., Rochat, G. *Giulio Douhet. Scritti 1901–1915* (The writings of Giulio Douhet, 1901–1915).

Dalla Tomba, G. *Tomaso dal Molin* (Thomas de Moline).

De Marchi, I. *Gli Aeroplani Italiani 1945–1991* (Italian aircraft, 1945–1991).

Farina, P. *Professione Trasporto. La 46ª Brogata Aerea* (Professional air transport. The 46th aerial brigade).

Ferandini, C. A., Zavattini. *Tradizioni aeronautiche della città di Mantova* (The aeronautical traditions of the city of Mantua).

Ferrone, E. *Tra cielo e mare. Idrovolanti e anfibi nell' aviazione mondiale* (Between sky and sea: Seaplanes and amphibians of world aviation).

Garello, G. *Regia Aeronautica e armée de l'air* (The regia aeronautica [Royal air force] and the air army).
Giorleo, A. *Palestra azzurra. L'A.M. e il paracadutismo. Cronistoria* (The Azure gym: The air army and the parachutists. chronology).
Giuffrida, O. *Buscaglia e gli Aerosiluranti* (Buscaglia and the aerial torpedo).
Gori, C. *10° Stormo* (The 10th flight).
Gori, C. *SM.79. Produzione–Evoluzione–Versioni* (SM.79: Production, evolution, and marks).
Greenfield, R. *Decisioni di comando* (Command decisions).
Guidi, G. *C.M.A.S.A.*
Lattanzi. *L'opera scientifica di Alessandro Guidoni ingegnere militare* (The scientific work of Alessandro Guidini, military engineer).
Lioy, V. *1918–1958. 40° anniversario di Vittorio Veneto* (1918–1958. 40th anniversary of the battle of Vittorio Veneto).
Magnani, G. *Cronistoria della 46ª aerobrigata* (Chronicle of the 46th air brigade).
Marcon, T. *Quarant'anni due idroscali* (Forty years of seaplane stations).
Masini, G. *Il commissariato militare aeronautico nel suo profilo storico. Vol. 1* (The military aeronautical commission and its technical story. Vol. 1).
Masini, G. *Il commissariato militare aeronautico nel suo profilo storico. Vol. 2* (The military aeronautical commission and its technical story. Vol. 2).
Mattesini, F., Cermelli, M. *Direttive tecnico-operative di Superaereo Vol. 1 (tomo I e II)* (Technical and operational directions of the high command of the air force. Vol. 1, parts 1 and 2).
Mattesini, F., Cermelli, M. *Direttive tecnico-operative di Superaereo Vol. 2 (tomo I e II)* (Technical and operational directions of the high command of the air force. Vol. 2, parts 1 and 2).
Mayer, G. *Economia Militare. Storia e teoria* (Military economy: History and theory).
Mayer, G. *L'evoluzione del Bilancio della Difesa dal 1975 ai primi anni '90* (The evolution of the balanced defence from 1975 to the beginning of the 1990s).
Mencarelli, I. *Personaggi aeronautici rilevanti* (Remarkable aeronautical personalities).
Mencarelli, I. *Amedeo di Savoia Aosta-Ancillotto-Balbo-Baracca.*
Mencarelli, I. *Baudoin-Bernasconi-Biseo-Bonmartini-Brack Papa.*
Mencarelli, I. *Caproni-Castoldi-Crocco-Da Schio-De Bernardi.*
Mencarelli, I. *De Pinedo-Donati-Ferrarin-Forlanini-Freri.*
Mencarelli, I. *Guidoni-Keller-Locatelli-Maddalena-Mecozzi.*
Mencarelli, I. *Moizo-Nobile-Padri dell'ala rotante-Palli-Piccio.*
Mencarelli, I. *Pionieri del volo bellico-Ruffo Fulvo di Calabria.*
Mencarelli, I. *Salomone-Scaroni-Stoppani-Usuelli-Valle-Zappata.*
Pedriali. *Guerra di Spagna e Aviazione Italiana* (The war in Spain and Italian aviation).
Pelliccia, A. *La Regia Aeronautica. Dalle origini alla 2 G.M.* (The Italian air force from its origins to the Second World War).

Pelliccia, A. *La lotta nello spazio* (The struggle in space).
Pesce, G. *Maurizio Mario Moris.*
Pesce, G. *Storia della radio in aviazione* (The history of aviation radio).
Pesce, G. *Vigna di Valle* (The vineyard in the valley).
Piola Caselli, C. *C. Lucangeli nel bicentenario del suo volo a Roma* (The bicentennial of C. Lucangeli's flight at Rome).
Porro, A. *Natale Palli.*
Ranisi, M. *L'architettura dell'Aeronautica Militare* (Military aeronautical architecture).
Ranisi, M. *L'architettura della Regia Aeronautica* (Architecture of the Regia Aeronautica).
Rea, A. *Accademia aeronautica* (Air academies).
Rebora, E. *I precedenti del volo su Vienna* (The precedents for the flight to Vienna).
Ricci, C. *Il C.A.I. sul fronte della Manica* (The Italian air corps on the English Channel front).
Scaroni, S. *Missione militare aeronautica in Cina* (The military air mission in China).
Scarpa, C., Sezanne, P. *Le decorazioni al valore della Repubblica Italiana* (Decorations for valor of the Italian Republic).
Setti, M. *L'aliante militare* (The military glider).
Sezanne, P. *Le decorazioni del Regno di Sardegna e del Regno d'Italia. Vol. 2* (Decorations of the Kingdom of Sardinia and of the Kingdom of Italy. Vol. 2).
SMA. *Columbus '92 (libro + video Vhs)* (Columbus '92—book and video).
Strada I. *2° Stormo* (2nd flight).
Straulino, L. *Bibliografia aeronautica italiana dal 1937 al 1981* (Bibliography of Italian aviation from 1937 to 1981).
Straulino, L. *Il servizio tecnico caccia nella Guerra di Liberazione* (The armaments service during the war for liberation).
Tappero Mrelo, G. *W. Mitchell e la dotrina militare USA tra le due G.M.* (Billy Mitchell and American military doctrine during the Second World War).
Trotta, A. *Medaglie d'Oro al Valore Aeronautico* (Gold medals for valor in the air).
Ufficio Storico A.M. *Cronistoria dell'A.M. (1884–1915), 8 Volumi* (History of Italian military aviation from 1884 to 1915).
Ufficio Storico A.M. *Medaglie al Valor Aeronautico* (Medals for valor in the air).
Ufficio Storico A.M. *Medaglie d'Oro al Valor Militare* (Gold medals for military valor).
Ufficio Storico A.M. *Ordine Militare d'Italia 1911–1964* (The military orders of Italy, 1911–1964).
Ufficio Storico A.M. *I reparti decorati dell'A.M.* (The decoration divisions of military aviation).
Ufficio Storico A.M. *Stemma dell'A.M.* (The coats of arms of the air arm).
Zizzi, G. *Storia ed evoluzione della propulsione aerea* (The story of the evolution of aerial propulsion or the history of aircraft engines).

LIBRI IN CORSO DI STAMPA (BOOKS IN PRESS, 1995)

Arena, N. *La Regia Aeronautica 1939–43 Vol. 2.*

Cosci, S. *Colorazioni ed insegne dei velivoli e degli elicotteri dell'A.M. dal '45 ai giorni nostri* (Colors and insignia of aircraft and of helicopters of the air arm from 1945 to the present day).

Licheri, S. *Storia del volo e delle operazioni aeree da lcaro ai giorni nostri* (The story of flight and of air operations from Icarus to the present day).

Mattesini, F. *L'attività aerea italo-tedesca nel Mediterraneo* (Italo–German air operations in the Mediterranean).

Palaca A. *Reparto alta velocità* (The high-speed divisions).

Pedriali F. *L'Aeronautica italiana nelle guerre coloniali La Guerra d'Etiopia 1935–36* (Italian air force during a colonial war: The war in Ethiopia, 1935–1936).

Ranisi, M. *Aeroporti italiani* (Italian airports).

Zamparelli, F. *Diritto internazionale e attività militare nello spazio extra-atmosferico* (International rights and military activity in Space).

Stato Maggiore dell'Esercito Italia

General Pier Luigi Bertinaria, Chief

ORIGINS AND DEVELOPMENT

The Military Office of the Kingdom of Sardinia Royal Army Staff Corps, from which the present Army Staff Historical Office stems, was created by the Royal Corps General Commandant on 16 July 1853, as laid down in the Order no. 712, which was drawn up in Turin on 1 July 1856 and, despite 130 years having passed and changes of any kinds having occurred, it is still perfectly up to date.

The first of the ten Articles of the "Instructions" ordered the Historical Office "to gather and arrange all those documents and news useful to give an exact and thorough knowledge of the Army and of the Kingdom's Military Organizations" and "to draw up, on the basis of authentic documents gathered in the Royal Corps' Files or elsewhere, the full history of Italian military campaigns and events, as well as of all the most memorable happenings concerning recent wars."

This particular task was the responsibility of the Military History Section, which was the second of the three sections into which the office was divided. Documentary material began with those of the 1848–1849 campaigns and the Eastern War (Crimea), by the reports drawn up by commandants, by a certain number of monographs written by officers charged to study the various Italian regions, and finally by all those magazines to which the Royal Staff Corps was a subscriber.

As we can see, this office was absolutely modern at its beginning. If, in one respect, the intention to gather evidence of our best patriotic traditions was somewhat romantic, the new requirement to prepare texts founded, as much as possible, on philosophical positivist thought was not. The intent was not only to define the truth and, if possible, to restore it, but also to draw lessons from past events. But the enthusiasms of the office in the climate of the First War of Independence, which showed that Italian unity was not an unattainable dream, had to be accompanied by a severe realism in political, military, diplomatic, ideological, and conspiratorial spheres.

The Historical Office, dealing with such important material, fostered technical and historical studies, yet remained the same for just four years: in fact, on 25 March 1860 five great Departmental Commands were established, having their seats in Turin, Alessandria, Brescia, Parma, and Bologna. Special record offices, independent from the Main Military Office, were created in each. What had been gathered so far remained at the Royal Staff Corps Military Record Office of Turin. The correspondence regarding the 1859 campaign was added to it, but all the documents concerning our 1860–1861 military history were lacking: reports, relations, agendas, and all the correspondence of the Tuscan Army and the Central Italy League Army. In 1861 the VI Great Command was created in Naples, in 1862 the VII Great Command was created in Palermo, and the Southern Army's documents were kept in the respective record Offices.

The office in Rome could centralize all the documents in a rational way, but the nine moves from 1872–1962 were not yet over. The handwritten, iconographic, printed documents were enriched with many historical memiors and journals, drawn up by the different army divisions—having the first ones yearly and the second ones on a two-months schedule—both in peacetime and in wartime, and thanks to much financial support. A Record Office was created, which is valuable and unique in its aims, and imposing in its dimensions.

But in this Record Office there are several gaps due to the fact that, during the Second World War, the big units couldn't always send their historical journals to the office, and because of the numerous ups and downs that occurred in the 1943–1945 period. In fact, in 1943, as a result of the development of the war and of the government intention to proclaim Rome an "open city," the precaution was taken of evacuating several military bodies, including the Historical Office, which was moved from Rome to Orvieto in the month of May, with its staff at full strength and with all its archives—a load of about 120 tons. The setting up of the Historical Office at Orvieto was not easy. The Record Office was housed in the Cathedral Museum, while its internal library was housed part in the Faina Palace, part at the Momicchioli Club, and part in other premises. The huge load of material coming from Rome was followed by other monthly shipments of war documents. This was the situation when the armistice was signed on 8 September 1943. So, before going under cover, the office staff hid historical materials for safety and from the Germans. They quickly selected particularly confidential and delicate documents (like those concerning Northern African and Russian campaigns), which were sent back to Rome and concealed in the Vittoriano for the whole period of German occupation. This operation was made possible thanks to the sensibility, courage, and patriotism of Professors Alberto Maria Ghisalberti and Emilia Morelli. Other material, considered of a specific interest for our enemy, was packaged in cases and walled up in the cathedral's basement, where it was recovered, intact, after Liberation.

In November 1943 a representative of the Republic of Salo Army constituted a new historical office which was endowed with all material available at Orvieto. In the month of January 1944 this office moved from Orvieto to Trescore (Bergamo) by rail and mail, but most of the documents arrived damaged or in a great confusion, due to illegal openings or cases breaking.

Many events followed which caused a new transfer of a great many documents from Trescore to Villa Novara-Ardizzano (Novara) in November 1944. This move was very important as far as the amount and relevance of the documents in question was concerned, since they dealt with the war in progress and were addressed to the Supreme Command. Unfortunately, these documents were damaged by a fire and by the firemen. It's not easy to determine which damage was the most serious: The fact remains that several collections of appendices to the Supreme Command war diary were lost, too. Moreover, part of the material fell into German hands.

At the same time, in the South of Italy (Lecce), another Historical Office had been constituted at the army staff and, notwithstanding its reduced dimensions as for cadres and possibilities, it was important enough to assure a certain continuity in the historical services and later to allow a rather satisfactory gathering of documents concerning the regular Armed Forces and the "Corpo Italiano di Liberazione."

On 4 July 1944, Rome was freed by the Allied Forces and members of the former staff of the Historical Office returned to its original seat. Of course, it was not possible to carry on much activity: Staff was lacking, there were no premises, administrative and procedural problems arose, but the office was still there and it could reestablish its own organization.

The situation improved considerably in the month of July 1944, when army staff moved from Lecce to Rome and the two historical sections were reunited, thus giving the office back most of its former physiognomy and its normal activity.

In 1967, after filming and photocopying it, the U.S. government restored all the Italian material which, at first, had been requisitioned by the German forces and subsequently seized, in 1945, by the U.S. forces in Germany. That's the reason why none of the publications issued by this office mention the collection of Italian Army Records microfilms, which were kept in the National Archives in Washington. All the restored publications have in fact the same record number as the material that has never left the office. But it is necessary to point out that the Historical Office Archives are not the only depositories of the documents relative to the Ministry of War, but only those pertaining to the army units in peace and in wartime. So political, administrative, and registration documents are not there. However, a certain number of the documents relative to military attachés prior to 1925 are. The consultation of the existing documents is dependent on the regulations provided by current laws (L. No. 1863, 17.2.1962, D.P.R. No. 1409, 30.9.1963). Request for authorization to consult the documents must be forwarded to the Historical Office and must contain the exact indication of the material to be consulted and the reason.

PRESENT STRUCTURE AND TASKS

The main office tasks are as follows:

- Processing of reports and historical studies together with other external cultural organizations.
- Gathering of all the documents that can have a historical interest for other army bodies.
- Processing of studies concerning heraldic flags, crosspieces, arms, and mottos, as well as preparation of grant ordinances.

All these tasks involve manifold activities. First of all, it is necessary to keep all the documentary material up to date, as its importance and confidential nature are never sufficiently stressed. Equally important for its programmatic and creative aspects is the preparation of historical works, which are always preceded by scrupulous and even comparative researches.

The Historical Office establishes connections and also assists individuals, as authors, university teachers, and scholars concerned with the drawing up of articles and history books, in their bibliographic reference work.

The office, which is a lifelong member of the Istituto per la Storia del Risorgimento Italiano and the Società Geografica Italiana and a member of the Istituto Nazionale per la Storia del Movimento di Liberazione in Italy, is always ready for fruitful cooperation with other organizations having an honest interest in military history and a sincere faith in truth. The Historical Office also takes part in congresses and meetings on historical sciences in Italy and abroad and sometimes it also undertakes their organization.

It is also useful to stress office participation in some Research Boards recently established by MOD (Ministry of Defense), such as: "Research Board for a historical digression on Giuseppe Garibaldi and his military deeds" (Ministerial Decree, 20 July 1981) and "Research Board for a historical survey of Armed Forces and the War of Liberation" (Ministerial Decree, 5 May 1983). The last had the task of investigating the historical and sociopolitical elements which had determined the reestablishment of the armed forces and their participation in the Liberation during the 1943–1945 campaign and had its official seat in the office itself. Both committees enhanced and organized very interesting study congresses. Unfortunately, not every contribution has been printed, only those which have some bearing on topics dealt with by International Congresses: "Giuseppe Garibaldi, General of Freedom" (Rome, 28–31 September 1982) and "Eighth September 1943. The Italian Armistice after 40 years" (Milano, 7–8 September 1983).

As far as international relations are concerned, the Historical Office has solid dealings with other similar European and American offices, as well as with the Commission Internationale d'Histoire Militaire (ICCMH), on behalf of which it has also edited the *Revue Internationale d'Histoire Militaire* (No. 10 in 1951 and No. 39 in 1978). Moreover, since 1975 it has been attending yearly programs organized by the ICCMH.

The Historical Office also fields inquires from ex-servicemen, in order to grant them all the allowances provided for by the current laws.

Consequently, the Historical Office consists of three sections: The first deals with planning and publishing and with the organization of meetings and congresses; the second handles research and documentation and includes the archives; the third checks on war allowances.

There are also two very specialized and well-furnished libraries. The Central Military Library, of about 200,000 volumes, was founded by the Decree of General Pelloux, Minister of the War, on 27 September 1891. Actually, the library has a much longer history going back to 1814, when the King of Sardinia founded in Turin the Biblioteca del Corpo Reale dello Stato Maggiore e della Topografia. In 1854 General Alfonso La Marmora decided to unify the Biblioteca dello Stato Maggiore and the Biblioteche dei Regi Corpi di Artiglieria e Genio, so the new institution became the Biblioteca delle Armi Speciali, and, in 1859, the Biblioteca Militare. The 1891 Pelloux Decree really just unified the Military Library, the Ministry of the War Library, and the Rome Recruiting Area Library as the Central Military Library, the name which it still has. Later, by the 31 January 1893 Decree, the Biblioteca dell'Ispettorato di Sanità Militare was added.

The library is also rich in magazines: more than 1,000 titles amounting to 25,000 volumes.

The Historical Office's second library is the Artillery and Engineers Library, which stems from the Artillery and Fortifications Library, created in Turin in 1729, and cooperating with the Artillery and Fortifications Technical Schools, instituted by Carlo Emanuele III. This library subdivides all 60,000 volumes into twenty-nine sections. Both libraries, which are furnished with author and subject catalogues, can be frequented by civil scholars.

Other military libraries, which do not organically belong to the Historical Office, are open to civil and military scholars: the Garrison Libraries of Novara, Milano, Verona, Padova, Bologna, Napoli, Palermo, and Cagliari, and also the Military Geographic Institute Libraries of Florence, the Technical School of Turin, the Military Academy of Modena, and the War School of Civitavecchia. They keep up on military sciences, as well as being rich in manuscripts and ancient works, widely exceeding one million volumes and becoming every year greater and greater thanks to major new contributions.

Stato Maggiore dell'Esercito: Ufficio Storico

CATALOGO BIBLIOGRAFICO, FINO AL 1990 (BIBLIOGRAPHICAL CATALOGUE, UP THROUGH 1990)

Sigle e Abbreviazioni (Signs and Abbreviations)

BUS Bollettino dell'Ufficio Storico (Bulletin of the Historical Office)

MSM Memorie Storiche Militari (Military Historical Memories)

SSM Studi Storico Militari (Military Historical Studies)

pp. numero delle pagine del volume o dell'articolo (number of pages in the volume or article)

pag. numero della pagina del volume o del periodico (page number in the volume or periodical)

fasc. fascicolo (issue)

f.t. fuori testo (outside of the text)

b/n bianc e nero (black and white)

carta in genere carta topografica (in generic topographical map)

STUDI MONOGRAFICI

Garibaldi, Giuseppe, Jr. *La battaglia del Volturno* (The battle of Volturno). 1981.

Scala, Edoardo. *La guerra del 1866 ed altri scritti* (The war of 1866 and other writings). 1981.

Isastia, Anna Maria. *ll volontariato militare nel risorgimento—La partecipazione alla guerra del 1859* (Military volunteers of the Risorgimento—the participation in the war of 1859). 1990.

STUDI BIOGRAFICI

Mondini, Luigi. *Un'immagine insolita del Risorgimento* (An unusual image of the Risorgimento). 1977.

Autori vari. *Il Generale Giuseppe Garibaldi* (General Giuseppe Garibaldi). 1982.

Tamborra, Algelo. *Garibaldi e l'Europa* (Garibaldi and Europe). 1983.
Alessandro Mola, Aldo. *Garibaldi Generale della Libertà, Atti del Convegno Internazionale* (Garibaldi, general of liberty, Acta of the International Conference). 1984.
Bogliari, Francesco, and Carlo Traversi. *Manfredo Fanti* (Manfred Fanti). 1980.

ARTICOLI E CURIOSITA

Gallinari, Vincenzo. *Le riforme militari di Cesare Ricotti* (The military reforms of Caesar Ricotti).
Loi, Salvatore. *Gli ideali del Risorgimento italiano nell'indipendenza latino-americana* (The ideal of the Risorgimento in the independence of Latin America). 1978.
Trotta, Leonetti Caterina. *Eroine del Risorgimento* (Heroines of the Risorgimento). 1979.
Loi, Salvatore. *L'irredentismo all'inizio del secolo in atti di Archivi ufficiali e privati* (The nineteenth century irredentist movement as seen in public and private archives). 1979.
Corso, Anna Letizia. *Callimaco Zambianchi e la spedizione nello Stato romano* (Callimaco Zambianchi and the expedition to Rome). 1980.
Del Negro, Piero. *Guerra partigiana e guerra di popolo nel Risorgimento* (Partisan warfare and People's War in the Risorgimento). 1981.
Oreste, Bovio. *Il congedamento dell'Esercito meridionale garibaldino* (The demobilization of the southern Garibaldian army). 1982.
Mrcheggiano, Arturo. *Venezia nella rivoluzione del 1848–1849* (Venice in the revolution of 1848–1849). 1983.
Polo Friz, Luigi, and Viviani, Ambrogio. *Le istruzioni di Giuseppe Garibaldi per la campagna di Francia nel 1870* (The instructions given Guisseppe Garibaldi for the French Campaign of 1870). 1983.
Isastia, Anna Maria. *Il volontariato militare nella seconda guerra d'indipendenza* (Military volunteers in the Second War of Independence). 1984.
Tuccari, Luigi. *Memora sui principali aspetti tecnico-operativi della lotta al brigantaggio dopo l'unità (1861–1870)* (Memories of the principal aspects of technical operations during the struggle against Brigandage after unification [1861–1870]). 1984.
Calabresi, Ennio. *La medaglia commemorativa dei Mille* (The medal commemorating the 1,000). 1984.
Tuccari, Luigi. *L'impresa di Massaua (1885): cento anni dopo* (The impact of Massua [1885]: 100 years later). 1987.

STUDI BIOGRAFICI

Bianchini, Alessandro. *Tancredi Saletta a Massaua (memoria, relazione, documenti).* (Tancredi Saletta at Massowa [memorials, accounts, documents]). 1987.

ARTICOLI E CURIOSITA

Biagini, Antonello. *Italia e Turchia (1904–1911): gli ufficiali italiani e la riorganizzazione della gendarmeria macedone* (Italy and Turkey [1904–1911]. Italian officials and the reorganization of the Macedonian Constabulary). 1977.

Dell'Uomo, Franco. *La Divisione d'Africa* (The partition of Africa). 1977.

Loi, Salvatore. *Dal "Fondo Umberto Salatores": un ciclo operativo coloniale* (About "Fondo Umberto Salatores": A cycle in colonial operations). 1978.

Biagini, Antonello. *La questione d'Oriente del 1875–1878 nei documenti dell'U.S. dello SME* (The Eastern question of 1875–1878 in the documents of the foreign office). 1978.

Cecchini, Ezio. *Organizzazione, preparazione e supporto logistico della campagna 1935–1936 in Africa Orientale* (Organization, preparation, and logistical support for the campaign in Ethiopia, 1935–1936). 1979.

Montanari, Mario. *Il progetto Africa Orientale e i suoi sviluppi* (The East African plan and its development). 1987.

Petrilli, Piero. *La guerra d'Etiopia e le prime esperienze italiane di corazzaati* (The war in Ethiopia and the first Italian experience with armor). 1988.

Longo, Luigi Emilio. *Gli Alpini in Africa* (The Alpini in Africa). 1988.

DOCUMENTAZIONE UFFICIALE

Ufficio Storico. *Vol. IV—Tomo 3° bis—Le operazioni del 1917 (ottobre–dicembre)—documenti* (Operations of October–December 1917—documents). 1967.

Ufficio Storico. *Vol. IV— Tomo 3° ter— Le operazioni del 1917 (ottobre–dicembre)—carte* (Operations of October–December 1917—maps). 1967.

Ufficio Storico. *Vol. V— Tomo 1°—Le operazioni del 1918—Le operazioni del 1918 (Gli avvenimenti dal gennaio al giugno). Narrazione* (The operations of 1918 [The events of January to June]. Narrative). 1980.

Ufficio Storico. *Vol. V—Tomo 1° bis—Le operaziono del 1918—Le operaziono del 1918 (gennaio–giugno). Documenti* (The operations of 1918 [January to June]. Documents). 1980.

Ufficio Storico. *Vol. V—Tomo 1° ter—Le operaziono del 1918—Le operaziono del 1918 (gennaio–giugno). Carte e schizzi* (The operations of January to June 1918. Maps and sketches). 1980.

Ufficio Storico. *Vol. V—Tomo 2°—Le operazioni dl 1918 (La conclusione del conflitto). Narrazione* (The operations of 1918 [The end of the war]. Narrative). 1988.

Ufficio Storico. *Vol. V—Tomo 2°—Le operazioni dl 1918 (La conclusione del conflitto). Documenti* (The operations of 1918 [The end of the war]. Narrative). 1988.

Ufficio Storico. *Vol. V—Tomo 2°—Le operazioni dl 1918 (La conclusione del conflitto). Carte* (The operations of 1918 [The end of the war]. Maps). 1988.

Ufficio Storico. *Vol. VI—Tomo 1°—Le istruzioni tattiche del Capo di Stato Maggiore dell'Esercito anni 1914–1915–1916* (The tactical instructions given by the chief of staff of the army in 1914, 1915, and 1916). 1932.

Ufficio Storico. *Vol. VI—Tomo 2°—Le istruzioni tattiche del Capo di Stato Maggiore dell'Esercito anni 1917–1918* (The tactical instructions of the chief of staff of the army, 1917–1918). 1980.

Ufficio Storico. *Vol. VII—Tomo 1°—Le operazioni fuori del territorio nazionale—Il Corpo di Spedizione Italiano in Estremo Oriente* (Operations outside of the national territory—the Italian expeditionary force in the Far East). 1934.

Ufficio Storico. *Vol. VII—Tomo 2°—Le Operazioni fuori del territorio nazionale—Soldati d'Italia in terra di Francia—narrazione* (Operations outside the national territory—Italian soldiers in France—narrative). 1951.

Ufficio Storico. *Vol. VII—Tomo 2° bis—Le Operazioni fuori del territorio nazionale—Soldati d'Italia in terra di Francia—documenti* (Operations outside the national territory—Italian soldiers in France—documents). 1951.

Ufficio Storico. *Vol. VII—Tomo 2° ter—Le Operazioni fuori del territorio nazionale—Soldati d'Italia in terra di Francia—carte e schizzi* (Operations outside the national territory—Italian soldiers in France—maps and sketches). 1951.

Ufficio Storico. *Vol. VII—Tomo 3°—Le operazioni fuori del territorio nazionale—Albania, Macedonia, Medio Oriente—narrazione* (Operations outside the national territories—Albania, Macedonia, Middle East—narrative). 1983.

Ufficio Storico. *Vol. VII—Tomo 3° bis—Le operazioni fuori del territorio nazionale—Albania, Macedonia, Medio Oriente—documenti* (Operations outside of the national territories—Albania, Macedonia, the Middle East—documents). 1981.

Ufficio Storico. *Vol. VII—Tomo 3° ter—Le operazioni fuori del territorio nazionale—Albania, Macedonia, Medio Oriente—Carte.* (Operations outside of the national territories—Albania, Macedonia, the Middle East—maps). 1981.

STUDI MONOGRAFICI

I Paesi dell'Intesa

Biagini, Antonello. *In Russia tra guerra e rivoluzione La missione militare italiana 1915–1918* (In Russia through war and revolution—the Italian military mission, 1915–1918). 1983.

Altri Studi

Montanari, Mario. *Le truppe italiana in Albania (Anni 1914–29 e 1939)* (Italian troops in Albania, 1914–1929 and 1939). 1978.

Mazzetti, Massimo. *L'industria italiana nellande guerra.* (Italian industry during the war). 1979.

Gallinari, Vincenzo. *L'Esercito italiano nel primo dopoguerra 1918–1920* (The Italian army during the postwar period, 1918–1920). 1980.

Pieri, Piero, and Rochat, Giorgio. *La prima guerra mondiale 1914–1918—Problemi di Storia militare* (The First World War, 1914–1918—problems in military history). 1986.

Cadioli, Beniamino, and Cecchi, Aldo. *La Posta Militare italiana nella prima guerra mondiale* (The Italian military postal service in the First World War). 1978.

ARTICOLI E CURIOSITA

Brugioni, Antonio. *Piani strategici italiani alla vigilia dell'intervento nel primo conflitto mondiale* (Secret Italian flights to observe the intervention in the First World War).

Garibaldi, Anita Italia. *Dal Piave alla Mosa* (From the Piave to Mosa). 1982.

GLI ANTECENDENT

von Plehwe, Friedrich Karl. *Il Patto d'Acciaio* (The Ajaccio Pact). 1970.

von Plehwe, Friedrich Karl. *Da Mussolini a Badoglio—Una testimonianza tedesca* (From Mussolini to Badoglio—German witness). 1976.

Montanari, Mario. *L'Esercito italiano alla vigilia della 2ª Guerra Mondiale* (The Italian army of the eve of the Second World War). 1954.

DOCUMENTAZIONE

Gallinari, Vincenzo. *Le operazioni del giungo 1940 sulle Alpi Occidentali* (The operations of June 1940 in the Western Alps). 1981.

Rainero, Romain H. *Mussolini e Petain—Storia dei rapporti tra l'Italia e la Francia de Vichy (10 giugno 1940–8 settembre 1943)* (Mussolini and Pétain—the history of the relations of Italy and Vichy France [10 June 1940–8 September 1943]). 1990.

Fronte dei Balcani (The Balkan Front)

Montanari, Mario. *La Campagna di Grecia. Tomo 1°—testo; Tomo 2°—documenti; Tomo 3°—schizzi e fotografie; Tomo 4°—indici* (The campaign in Greece—text, documents, sketches and photographs, index). 1980.

Loi, Salvatore. *Le operazioni delle Unità italiane in Jugoslavia (1941–1943)* (The operations of Italian units in Yugoslavia [1941–1943]). 1978.

Fronte dell'Africa Orientale (Operations in East Africa)

Rovighi, Alberto. *Le Operazioni in Africa Orientale (glugno 1940–novembre 1941). Volume I—Narrazione; Volume II—Documenti* (Operations in East Africa [June 1940–November 1941]). 1988.

Fronte dell'Africa Settentrionale (The North African Front)

Montanari, Mario. *Le operazioni in A.S.—Vol. I—Sidi el Barrani* (The operations in the Western Desert—Sidi Barrani]). 1985.

Montanari, Mario. *Le operazioni in A.S.—Vol. II—Tobruk* (The operations in the Western Desert—Tobruk). 1985.

Montanari, Mario. *Le operazioni in A.S.—Vol. III—El Alamein* (The operations in the Western Desert—El Alamein). 1989.

Fronte Russo (The Russian Front)

De Franceschi, Constantino, and de Vecchi, Giorgio. *Le operazioni delle Unità italiane al fronte russo (1941–1943)* (Operations of Italian forces on the Russian front [1941–1943]). 1977.

De Franceschi, Constantino, and de Vecchi, Giorgio. *I servizi logistici delle Unità italiane al fronte russo (1941–1943)* (The Italian supply services on the Russian front [1941–1943]). 1975.

Teatro Italiano (The Italian Theater)

Santoni, Alberto. *Le operazioni in Sicilia e in Calabria (luglio–settembre 1943)* (Operations in Sicily and Calabria [July–September 1943]). Stilgrafica, Roma, 1983. Graficart, Formia, 1989.

RELAZIONI SULLE OPERAZIONI, 1943–1945 (OPERATIONS, 1943–1945)

Conti, Giuseppe. *Il Primo Raggruppamento Motorizzato* (The first motorized division). 1984.

DOCUMENTAZIONE VARIA (VARIOUS DOCUMENTATION)

Lanfaloni Antonio. *L'azione dello Stato Maggiore Generale per lo sviluppo del movimento di liberazione* (The actions of the general staff in the development of the liberation movement). 1975.

Mazzaccara, Carlo, and Biagini, Antonello. *Verbali delle riunioni tenute dal Capo di SM Generale. Vol. I—26 gennaio 1939–29 dicenbre 1940* (Records of the meetings held by the chief of the general staff [26 January 1939–29 December 1940]). 1982.

Biagini, Antonello, and Frattolillo, Fernando. *Verbali delle riunioni tenute dal Capo di SM Generale. Vol. II—1 gennaio 1941–31 dicenbre 1941* (Records of the meetings held by the chief of the general staff [1 January 1941–31 December 1941]). 1984.

Biagini, Antonello, and Frattolillo, Fernando. *Verbali delle riunioni tenute dal Capo di SM Generale. Vol. III—1 gennaio 1942–31 dicenbre 1942* (Records of the meetings held by the chief of the general staff [1 January 1942–31 December 1942]). 1985.

Biagini, Antonello, and Frattolillo, Fernando. *Verbali delle riunioni tenute dal Capo di SM Generale. Vol. IV—1 gennaio 1943–7 settembre 1943* (Records of the meetings held by the chief of the general staff [1 January 1943–7 September 1943]). 1987.

Biagini, Antonello, and Frattolillo, Fernando. *I Documenti della II G.M.—Diari storici del Comando Supremo. Vol. I—11 glugno 1940–30 Agosto 1940. Tomo I—Diario.* 1986; *Tomo II—Allegati.* 1986. (Documents of the Second World War—the diary of the supreme command. Vol. I. 11 June 1940–30 August 1940. I. diary; II. enclosures).

Biagini, Antonello, and Frattolillo, Fernando. *I Documenti della II G.M.—Diari storici del Comando Supremo. Vol. II—1 settembre 1940–31 dicenbre 1940. Tomo I—Diario.* 1988; *Tomo II—Allegati.* 1988 (Documents of the Second World War—historical diary of the supreme command. Vol. II. 1 September 1940–31 December 1940. I. diary; II. enclosures).

Biagini, Antonello, and Frattolillo, Fernando. *I Documenti della II G.M.—Diari storici del Comando Supremo. Vol. III—1 gennaio 1941–30 aprile 1941. Tomo I—Diario.* 1989; *Tomo II—Allegati.* 1989 (Documents of the Second World War—historical diary of the supreme command). Vol. III. 1 January 1941–30 April 1941. I. diary; II. enclosures).

Salvatore, Loi. *La Brigata d'assalto "Italia" (1943–1945)* (The assault brigade "Italia" [1943–1945]).

STUDI MONOGRAFICI (MONOGRAPHIC STUDIES)

Sul Periodo 1940–1943 (fino alla data dell'armistizio) (For the Period 1940–1943 [to the date of the Armistice])

Fronte dell'Africa Settentrionale (The North African Front)

Mancinelli, Giuseppe. *La prima controffensiva italo-tedesca in Africa Settentrionale (15 febbraio–18 novembre 1941)* (The first Italo–German counteroffensive in the Western Desert [15 February–18 November 1941]). 1974.

Fronte Russo (The Russian Front)

Inaudi, Giuseppe. *La notte più lunga. La battaglia del Solstizio d'inverno sul Don* (The longest night. The battle of the Solstizio Cauldron on the Don). 1979.

Fabio, Mantovani (Trad.). *L'Italia nella Relazione ufficiale sovietica sulla Seconda Guerra Mondiale* (Italian–Soviet official relations during the Second World War). 1978.

Sul Periodo 1943–1945 (For the Period 1943–1945)

Torsiello, Mario. *Le operazioni delle Unità italiane nel settembre–ottobre 1943* (The operations of Italian units from September to October 1943). 1975.

Lollio, Luciano. *Le unità ausiliarie dell'Esercito italiano nella guerra di Liberazione—Narrazione—Documenti* (The auxiliary units of the Italian army during the war for liberation—narratives and documents). 1977.

Scala, Edoardo. *La riscossa dell'Esercito* (The recovery of the army). 1948.

Vari, Autori. *La guerra di liberazione—Scritti nel trentennale* (The war of liberation—writings of the past thirty years). 1976.

Vari, Autori. *La guerra di liberazione—Scritti nel trentennale (2^ edizione)* (The war of liberation—writings over thirty years [Second Edition]). 1979.

Salvatore, Loi. *I rapporti fra Italiani e Alleati nella Cobelligeranza* (The report on Italian and Allied cobelligerency). 1986.

SAGGI BIBLIOGRAFICI, CRONOLOGIE E STUDI BIOGRAFICI (VARIOUS BIBLIOGRAPHICAL, CHRONOLOGICAL, AND BIOGRAPHICAL STUDIES)

Ufficio Storico. *Bollettini di guerra del Comando Supremo 1940–1943.* (War bulletins of the supreme command, 1940–1943). 1970, 1973.

Ufficio Storico. *Saggio bibliografico sulla Seconda Guerra Mondiale. III Volume 1966–1968* (Bibliography of the Second World War. Volume III, 1966–1968). 1969.

Ufficio Storico. *Saggio bibliografico sulla Seconda Guerra Mondiale. IV Volume 1969–1970.* (Bibliography of the Second World War. Volume IV, 1969–1970). 1971.

Ufficio Storico. *Saggio bibliografico sulla Seconda Guerra Mondiale e conflitti successivi. V Volume* (Bibliography of the Second World War and successor conflicts. Volume V). 1972.

Ufficio Storico. *Saggio bibliografico sulla Seconda Guerra Mondiale e conflitti successivi. VI Volume* (Bibliography of the Second World War and successor conflicts. Volume VI). 1974.

Ufficio Storico. *Saggio bibliografico sulla Seconda Guerra Mondiale e conflitti successivi. VII Volume* (Bibliography of the Second World War and successor conflicts. Volume VII). 1976.

Fasanotti, Enzo. *Bibliografia della Seconda Guerra Mondiale* (Bibliography of the Second World War). 1980.

Marziano, Brignoli. *Raffaele Cadorna 1889–1973* (General Raffaele Cadorna, 1889–1973). 1982.

Longo, Luigi Emilio. *Francesco Saverio Grazioli* (Francesco Saverio Grazioli). 1989.

ARTICOLI, CURIOSITÁ, TESTIMONIANZE, DIARI (ARTICLES, CURIOSITIES, TESTIMONIALS, DIARIES)

Cruccu, Rinaldo. *L'Italia e la Corsica nella seconda Guerra Mondiale* (Italy and Corsica in the Second World War). 1977.

Branca, Ugo. *Ricordi d'Albania* (The record of Albania). 1977.

Mazzetti, Massimo. *L'armistizio con l'Italia in base alle relazioni ufficiali anglo-americane* (The Italian armistice as the basis for official relations with the Anglo-Americans). 1978.

Cruccu, Rinaldo. *Il contributo delle Forze Armate italiane alla resistenza all'estero* (The contribution of the Italian armed forces to the resistance abroad). 1979.

Sierpowski, Stanislaw. *Il contributo dei polacchi alla liberazione dell'Italia* (The contribution of the Poles to the liberation of Italy). 1979.

Minniti, Fortunato. *Gli aiuti militari italiani alla Finlandia durante la guerra d'inverno* (Italian military aid to Finland during the winter war). 1980.

Zurlo, Teodoroo. *Emergenza "E" (tesi di laurea)* (Emergency "E" [Graduate Thesis]). 1979.

Montanari, Mario. *L'impegno italiano nella guerra di Spagna* (The Italian impact on the war in Spain). 1980.

Santoni, Alberto. *Il duello tra le risorse informative italo-tedesche e l'Ultra Secret britannico durante la guerra nel Mediterraneo* (The duel in Italo–German information resources and the British ULTRA secret during the war in the Mediterranean). 1981.

Calderini, Giorgio. *Relazione sulle azioni svolte dal II/27° rgt. f. in A.S. dal al 23.11.1941* (Stories of the actions of the II/27th regiment fighting in North Africa from to 23 November 1941). 1981.

Fiore, Lanfranco. *L'Esercito italiano di fronte alla guerra di Liberazione* (The Italian army facing the war of liberation). 1982.

Gallinari, Vincenzo. *L'Esercito italiano nella campagna di Tunisia* (The Italian army in the campaign in Tunisia). 1983.

La Bua, Giuseppe. *Aspetti militari dell'occupazione italiana di Rodi (tesi di laurea).* (Military aspects of the Italian occupation of Rhodes). 1983.

Giambartolomei, Aldo. *Campagna di Russia 1942–1943: la guerra del 6° Reggimento Bersaglieri* (The campaign in Russia, 1942–1943: The 6th Bersaglieri regiment's war). 1983.

Ferrari, Dorello. *Il plano segreto di Balbo* (Balbo's secret flight). 1984.

Adami, Giuseppe. *Relazione sul ripiegamento del 5° reggimento alpini della linea del Don (15–31 gennaio 1943) (testimonianza)* (The story of the retreat of the 5th Alpini regiment along the line of the Don [15–31 January 1943]). 1984.

Weiss, Luigi. *La 2ª batteria del CL gruppo da 149/13 alla caduta di Tobruk (testimonianza)* (The 2nd battery of light artillery of the 149th/13th at the fall of Tobruk). 1984.

Saccarelli, Silvio. *Note e considerazioni della battaglia di El Alamein* (Notes and considerations on the battle of El Alamein). 1985.

Graziani, Angelo. *Il ritorno dal Montenegro: il rimpatrio* (The return to Montenegro—the Repatriation). 1985.

Basso, Alessandro. *L'armistizi dell'8 settembre 1943 in Sardegna* (The armistice of 8 September 1943 in Sardinia). 1985.

Gabriele, Mariano. *La forza di spedizione brasiliana (F.E.B.) nella Campagna d'Italia (settembre 1944–aprile 1945)* (The Brazilian expeditionary force (FEB) in the campaign in Italy [September 1944–April 1945]). 1986.

Capizzi, Manlio. *La Divisione "Ravenna" in Russia (testimonianza)* (The "Ravenna" division in Russia). 1985.

Zavattaro Ardizzi, Piero. *Diario dall'8.9.1943 al 18.3.1945 (testimonianza)* (Diary for 18 September 1943 to 18 March 1945). 1986.

Braca, Giovanni. *Il 1° "Gruppo bande di confine" (testimonianza)* (The first interned band). 1986.

Fatutta, Francesco. *Difesa costiera e guerriglia sul litorale croato-dalmato* (Coast defense and guerrillas on the Croatian–Dalmation Littoral). 1986.

Postiglioni, Umberto. *Il X reggimento arditi* (The brave 10th regiment). 1986.

Ferrari, Dorello. *La difesa della costa italiana nella 2ª G.M.* (Italian coastal defenses in the Second World War).

Amati, Giuseppe. *Grecia 1943–44. Dal presidio di Tembi della "Pinerolo" alla banda dei diciotto (testimonianza)* (Greece, 1943–1944. From the garrison at Tembi of the "Pinerolo" to the band of Eighteen). 1987.

Viglione, Francesco. *Tentativo di ricostruzione di un mattiono di guerra del 132° reggimento carri "Ariete"* (The attempt at a reconstruction of a morning of war of the 132nd armored regiment "Ariete"). 1987.

Longo, Luigi Emillio. *L'incursione britannica sull'acquedotto pugliese (febbraio 1941)* (The British attack on the Boxer aqueduct [February 1941]). 1988.

Vannucchi, Francesco. *Aspetti e problemi della spesa militare in Italia nel secondo dopoguerra* (Aspects and problems of Italian military expenditures during the Second World War). 1988.

Schierano, Mario. *Situazione delle truppe italiane nell'isola di Creta dopo l'8 settembre 1943* (The situation of Italian troops isolated on Crete after 8 September 1943). 1988.

Migliavacca, Renato. *Gli artiglieri della "Figore" nel combattimento di NAQB RALA (Alamein) 24 ottobre 1942* (The "Figore" artillery in the battle of El Alamein). 1979.

OPERE STORICO-MILITARI VARIE (VARIOUS MILITARY-HISTORICAL WORKS)

Storia Antica (Ancient History)

Moscardelii, Giuseppe. *Cesare duce—Una lettura del Bellum Gallicum* (The leadership of Caesar—a reading of *The Gallic Wars*). 1973.

Liddell Hart, B. H. *Scipione Africano* (Scipio Africans) 1975.

Angelini, Antonio. *L'arte militare di Flavio Renato Vegezio* (The military art of Flavius Renato Vegetius). 1984.

Storia Moderna e Contemporanea (Modern and Contemporary History)

L'eta'Della Rinascenza (The Renaissance)

Barone, Enrico. *I grandi capitani dell'età moderna* (Great captains of the modern era). 1982.
Tomassini, Luciano. *Raimondo Montecuccoli capitano e scrittore* (Raimondo Montecuccoli, captain and author). 1978.
Raimondo, Luraghi. *Le opere di Raimondo Montecuccoli—Edizione critica. Volume I: Trattato della guèrra; Volume II: Delle battaglie. I—Tavole militari—Discorso della guerra contro il Turco—Della guerra col Turco in Ungheria—Dell'Arte militare—Delle battaglie. II.* (The works of Raimondo Montecuccoli—critical edition. I. Treatises on War; II. On Battle. [I] Military tables, discourses on the war against the Turks—of the war against the Turks in Hungary, on the art of war—on battle [II]).

L'Eta' Risorgimentale e Contemporanea (The Age of the Risorgimento and the Present)

STUDI DOCUMENTALI (DOCUMENTARY STUDIES)

Scarpa, Costantino, and Sezanne, Paolo. *Le Decorazioni Al Valore dei Regni Di Sardegna e d'Italia (1793–1946).* (Decorations for valour of the Kingdom of Sardinia [1793–1946]). 1976.
Scarpa, Costantino, and Sezanne, Paolo. *Le Decorazioni al Valore del Regno di Sardegna e d'Italia—Le decorazioni commemorative—Volume I* (The decorations of the kingdom of Sardinia and of the kingdom of Italy commemorative decorations). 1982.
Scarpa, Costantino, and Sezanne, Paolo. *Le Decorazioni al Valore del Regno di Sardegna e d'Italia—Le decorazioni commemorative—Volume II* (The decorations of the kingdom of Sardinia and of the kingdom of Italy commemorative decorations). 1985.
Scarpa, Costantino, and Sezanne, Paolo. *Le Decorazioni al Valore del Regno di Sardegna e d'Italia—Le decorazioni al Merito—Volume I* (Decorations for Merit). 1987.
Scarpa, Costantino, and Sezanne, Paolo. *Le Decorazioni Al Valore Delia Repubblica Italiana* (Decorations for valour of the Italian Republic). 1981.
Roselli, Floro. *Tribunale Speciale per la Defesa dello Stato Decisioni emesse nel 1927* (Special tribunal for the defence of the state, decisions issued in 1927). 1980.
Roselli, Floro. *Tribunale Speciale per la Defesa dello Stato Decisioni emese nel 1928* (Special tribunal for the defence of the state, decisions issued in 1928). 1983.
Roselli, Floro. *Tribunale Speciale per la Defesa dello Stato Decisioni emesse nel 1929* (Special tribunal for the defence of the state, decisions issued in 1929). 1983.

Roselli, Floro. *Tribunale Speciale per la Defesa dello Stato Decisioni emesse nel 1930* (Special tribunal for the defence of the state, decisions issued in 1930). 1984.

Roselli, Floro. *Tribunale Speciale per la Defesa dello Stato Decisioni emesse nel 1931* (Special tribunal for the defence of the state, decisions issued in 1931). 1985.

Roselli, Floro. *Tribunale Speciale per la Difesa dello Stato Decisioni emesse nel 1932* (Special tribunal for the defence of the state, decisions issued in 1932). 1986.

Roselli, Floro. *Tribunale Speciale per la Difesa dello Stato Decisioni emesse nel 1933* (Special tribunal for the defence of the state, decisions issued in 1933). 1987.

Roselli, Floro. *Tribunale Speciale per la Difesa dello Stato Decisioni emesse nel 1934* (Special tribunal for the defence of the state, decisions issued in 1934). 1989.

Roselli, Floro. *Tribunale Speciale per la Difesa dello Stato Decisioni emesse nel 1935* (Special tribunal for the defence of the state, decisions issued in 1935). 1990.

Studi Monografici (Monographic Studies)

Panetta, Rinaldo. *L'Esercito per il Paese 1861–1975.* (The army in the country, 1861–1975). n.d.

Biagini, Antonello. *Note e relazioni de viaggio nei Balcani* (Notes and account of a journey in the Balkans). 1979.

Biagini, Antonello. *Documenti italiani sulla guerra russo-glapponese (1904–1905)* (Italian documents on the Russo–Japanese War [1904–1905]). 1977.

Autori vari. *L'Esercito italiano dall'Unità alla grande guerra (1861–1918)* (The Italian army from unification through the Great War [1861–1918]). 1980.

Talpo, Oddone. *Dalmazia—Una cronaca per la storia 1940–1941* (Dalmatia—a chronicle of the history, 1940–1941). 1985.

Talpo, Oddone. *Dalmazia—Una cronaca per la storia 1942* (Dalmatia—a chronicle for the history, 1942). 1990.

Rovighi, Alberto. *Un secolo di relazioni militari tra Italia e Svizzera 1861–1961* (A century of Italian–Swiss military relations, 1861–1961). 1987.

Il Pensiero Militare e L'Arte Della Guerra (Military Thought and the Art of War)

Maravigna, Pietro. *Storia dell'arte militare moderna. Tomo I—Rinascenza—Epoca delle monarchie assolute* (Renaissance—epoch of absolute monarchies). 1982.

Maravigna, Pietro. *Tomo II—La Rivoluzione francese e L'Impero.* (The French Revolution and Empire). 1982.

Maravigna, Pietro. *Tomo III—Dalla restaurazione alla Prima Guerra Mondiale* (From the Restoration to the First World War). 1982.

Marselli, Nicola. *La Guerra e la sua storia* (War and its history). 1986.
Marselli, Nicola. *La vita del Reggimento—Osservazioni e ricordi* (The life of the regiment—observations and records). 1989.
Fuller, J.F.C., and Trad. Giampaolo, Giannetti. *Le battaglie decisive del mondo occidentale e la loro influenza sulla storia. Volume I: Dalle origini alla battaglia de Lepanto* (The military history of the Western World. Vol. I. From the origins to the Battle of Lepanto). 1988.
Fuller, J.F.C., and Trad. Noviello, Raffaele. *Volume II: Dalla sconfitta dell'Armada Spagnola alla battaglia de Waterloo* (Vol. II. From the defeat of the Armada to Waterloo). 1988.
Fuller, J.F.C., and Trad. Noviello, Raffaele. *Volume III: Dalla guerra civile americana alla fine della II guerra mondiale* (Vol. III. From the American Civil War to the end of Second World War). 1988.
Di Lauro, Ferdinando. *Saggi di storia etico-militare* (Essays in the history of military ethics). 1925.
Botti, Ferruccio, and Ilari, Virgilio. *Il pensiero militare dal primo al secondo dopoguerra (1919–1949)* (Military thought of the First and Second World Wars, 1919–1949). 1985.
Muscarà, Francesco. *Storia dell'Osservazione aerea dell'Esercito* (History of aerial observations in the army). 1974.
Stefani, Filippo. *La storia della dottrina e degli ordinamenti dell'Esercito italiano. Volume I. Dall'Esercito piemontese al'Esercito di Vittorio Veneto* (The history of doctrine and of the ordinances of the Italian army. Vol. I. From the Piedmontese army to the army of Vittorio Veneto). 1984.
Stefani, Filippo. *Volume II. Tomo I—Da Vittorio Veneto alla 2ª Guerra Mondiale* (From Vittorio Veneto to the Second World War). 1985.
Stefani, Filippo. *Volume II. Tomo II—La 2ª Guerra Mondiale* (The Second World War). 1986.
Stefani, Filippo. *Volume III. Tomo I—Dalla guerra de liberazione all'arma atomica tattica* (From the liberation war to atomic tactics). 1987.
Stefani, Filippo. *Volume III. Tomo II—Dagli anni cinquanta alla ristrutturazione* (From the fifth year to the Restoration). 1989.
Ceva, Lucio, and Curami, Andrea. *La meccanizzazione dell'Esercito fino al 1943. Volume I. Narrazione. 1989; Volume II. Documentazione. 1989* (The mechanization of the army to the end of 1943. Vol. I. narrative; Vol. II. documentation).
Cecchini, Ezio. *Le istituzioni militari* (Military institutions). 1986.

OPERE ILLUSTRATE (ILLUSTRATED WORKS)

Miscellanea (Miscellany)

Bovio, Oreste. *Le bandiere dell'Esercito* (The army band). 1985.
Bovio, Oreste. *Le bandiere dell'Esercito* (The army band, second edition). 1991.
Di Lauro, Ferdinando. *L'Esercito italiano—Dal 1° centenario* (The Italian army, the first century). 1962.

Puletti, Rodolfo. *L'Esercito e i suoi corpi—Sintesi storica. Volume I* (The army and its units—a short history). 1971.
Puletti, Rodolfo, and Dell'Uomo, Franco. *L'Esercito e i suoi corpi—Sintesi storica. Volume II. Tomo I e II* (The army and its units—a short history. Vol. II). 1973.
Pirrone, Giorgio. *L'Esercito e i suoi corpi—Sintesi storica. Volume III. Tomo I* (The army and its units—a short history. Vol. III). 1979.
Floris, Giovanni. *L'Esercito italiano nell'arte* (The army in art). 1977.
Ufficio Storico. *L'Esercito italano* (The Italian army). 1982.
della Volpe, Nicola. *Fotografie militari* (Military photography). 1980.
della Volpe, Nicola. *Cartoline militari* (Military map catalogue). 1983.
Bovio, Oreste, and della Volpe, Nicola. *L'Esercito Italiano nella 1ª Guerra Mondiale—Immagini* (The Italian army in the First World War—images). 1978.
Viotti, Andrea. *L'uniforme grigioi-verde (1909–1918)* (The grey–green uniform of 1909–1918). 1984.
Ufficio Storico. *Esercito anno XVII* (Army year 17). 1989.
Bovio, Oreste, Brialdi, Camillo, Cruccu, Rinaldo, and della Volpe, Nicola. *L'Esercito Italiano nella 2ª Guerra Mondiale—Immagini* (The Italian army in the Second World War—images). 1978.
Fara, Amelio. *La metropoli difesa* (Metropolitan defense). 1985.
Fara, Amelio. *La carta de Ignazio Porro* (Ignazio Porro's maps). 1986.
Bovio, Oreste. *L'araldica del'Esercito* (Army heraldry). 1985.
della Volpe, Nicola. *Esercito e Propaganda nella Grande Guerra* (The army and propaganda in the Great War). 1989.
Viotti, Andrea. *Uniformi e distintivi dell'Esercito Italiano nella seconda Guerra mondiale 1940–1945* (Uniforms and badges of the Italian army during the Second World War). 1988.
Ales, Stefano. *Le Regie truppe sarde (1773–1814)* (The Royal Sardinian army [1773–1814]). 1989.
Ales, Stefano. *L'Armata Sarda della Restaurazione (1814–1831)* (The Sardinian armed forces of the Restoration [1814–1831]). 1987.
Ales, Stefano. *L'Armata Sarda e le riforme Albertine (1831–1842)* (The Sardinian army and the Albertine reforms [1831–1842]). 1987.
Ales, Stefano. *Dall'Armata Sarda all'Esercito italiano (1843–1861)* (From the Sardinian army to the Italian army [1843–1861]). 1990.

Saggistica Varia (Various Essays)

Autori vari. *Atti del Primo Convegno Nazionale di Storia Militare* (Acts of the first national conference of military history). 1969.
Autori vari. *Revue Internatinale d'Histoire Militaire n. 39* (The international review of military history, No. 39). 1978.
Autori vari. *Il problema dell'Alto Coimmando dell'E.I. dal Risorgimento al Patto Atlantico—Atti del Convegno* (The problems of the high command of the Italian army from the Risorgimento to the Atlantic treaty—acts of the conference). 1985.

Autori vari. *L'8 settembere 1943—L'armistizio italiano quaranta anni dopo. Atti del Congresso di Milano (7–9 settembre 1983)* (Eighth September 1943—the Italian armistice forty years afterward. Acts of the congress of Milan [7–9 September 1983]). 1985.

Autori vari. *La Cobelligeranza italiana nella lotta de liberazione dell'Europa. Atti del Congresso di Milano (17–19 maggio 1984)* (Italian cobelligerency during the struggle to liberate Europe. Acts of the congress of Milan [17–19 May 1984]). 1986.

Di Gangi, Antonino, Baldo, Antonella, and Ravetto, Giuseppe. *Musei, Sacrari e Monumenti militari* (Museums, shrines, and military monuments). 1989.

Bovio, Oreste. *L'Ufficio Storico dell'Esercito. Un secolo di storiografia militare* (The historical office of the army. A century of military historiography). 1987.

Terrone, Alfredo. *Le cinquecentine della Biblioteca Militare Centrale* (The 150 years of the Central Military Library). 1990.

Autori vari. *L'immagine delle Forze Armate nella Scuola italiana. Atti del Convegno (Firenze, 8–9 dicembre 1984)* (The image of the armed forces by the Italian school. Acts of the conference [Florence, 8–9 December 1984]).

Autori vari. *Le Forze Armate dalla Liberazione all'adesione dell'Italia alla NATO. Atti del Convegno (Torino 8–10 novembre 1985)* (The Italian armed forces from the liberation to Italy's adhesion to NATO. Acts of the conference at Turin [8–10 November 1985]). 1986.

Boeri, Giancarlo, and Crociani, Piero. *L'esercito borbnonico dal 1789 al 1815* (The Bourbon army from 1789 to 1815). 1989.

Russo, Flavio. *La difesa costiera del regno di Napoli dal XVI al XIX Secolo* (The coastal defence of Naples from the sixteenth through the nineteenth centuries). 1989.

Brugioni, Antonio, and Saporitii, Maurizio. *Manuale delle ricerche nell'Ufficio Storico dello Stato Maggiore dell'Esercito* (The army historical office's manual for research on the general staff of the army). 1989.

Terrone, Alfredo. *Catalogo bibliografico delle opera edite dall'Ufficio Storico (Dalle origini al 1985)* (Bibliographical catalogue of the works of the army historical office [from the beginning to 1985]). 1985.

Ministero della Guerra. *Volontari dell'Esercito nella guerra di Spagna* (Army volunteers during the war in Spain). 1996.

Marcheggiano, Arturo. *Diritto umanitario e sua introduzione nella regolamentazione dell'Esercito italiano (Leggi ed usi di guerra)* (Humanitarian rights and their introduction into the regulations of the Italian army). 1990.

Biagini, Antonello. *L'Italia e le guerre balcaniche* (Italy and the Balkan wars. 1990.

Ufficio Storico della Marina Militare

Translated by Robin Higham

SERIE I: LA MARINA ITALIANA NELLA SECONDA GUERRA MONDIALE (THE ITALIAN NAVY IN THE SECOND WORLD WAR)

Fioravanzo, G. Vol. I. *Dati Statistici.* 2ª ed. 1972 (Statistics).

Ufficio Storico. Vol. II. *Navi Militari Perdute.* 5ª ed. 1975 (Warships lost).

Nortarangelo, R. rev. G. P. Pagano. Vol. III. *Navi Mercantili Perdute.* 3ª ed. 1986 (Merchantmen lost).

Fioravanzo, G. Vol. IV. *Le Azioni Navali in Mediterraneo—Dal 10 giugno 1940 al 31 marzo 1941.* 3ª ed. 1976 (Naval actions in the Mediterranean from 10 June 1940 to 31 March 1941).

Fioravanzo, G. Vol. V. *Le Azioni Navali in Mediterraneo—Dal 1 aprile 1941 all'8 settembre 1943.* 2ª ed. 1970 (Naval actions in the Mediterranean from 1 April 1941 to 8 September 1943).

Cocchia, A. Vol. VI. *La Difesa Del Traffico Con L'Africa Settentrionale—Dal 10 giugno 1940 al 30 settembre 1942.* 2ª ed. 1977 (The defense of the traffic to North Africa from 10 June 1940 to 30 September 1942).

Cocchia, A. Vol. VII. *La Difesa Del Traffico Con L'Africa Settentrionale—Dal 1 ottobre 1942 Alla Cadula Della Tunisia.* reissued 1992 (The defense of the traffic to North Africa from 1 October 1942 to the loss of Tunisia).

Lupinacci, P. F. Vol. X. *Le Operazioni in Africa Orientale.* 2ª ed. 1976 (Operations in East Africa).

Lupinacci, P. F. Vol. XI. *Attivita in Mar Nero E Lago Ladoga.* 3ª ed. 1972 (Activities in the Black Sea and Lake Ladoga).

Ubaldini, U. Mori. Vol. XII. *I Sommergibili Negli Oceani.* 2ª ed. 1976 (Submarines in the ocean).

Bertini, Bertini. Vol. XIII. *I Sommergibiliin Mediterraneo* (Submarines in the Mediterranean) Tomo I—1972; Tomo II—1992 reprint.

De Risio, C., rev. G. P. Pagano. Vol. XIV. *Mezzi D'Assalto.* 4ª ed. 1992 (Landing operations).

Fioravanzo, G. Vol. XV. *La Marina Dall' 8 settembre 1943 Alla Fine Del Conflitto.* 2ª ed. 1971 (The navy from 8 September 1943 to the end of the War).

Levi, A. Vol. XVI. *Avvenimenti In Egeo Dopo L'Armistizio.* 2ª ed. 1972 (Events in the Aegean after the armistice).

De Risio, C. Vol. XVII. *I Violatorido Blocco.* 2ª ed. 1972 (Violations of the blockade).

Lupinacci, P. F. Vol. XVIII. *La Guerra Di Mine.* 2ª ed. 1988 (Mine warfare).

Franti, M. Vol. XIX. *Il Dragaggio*. 1969 (Dredging).
Fioravanzo, G. Vol. XXI. *L'Organizzazione Della Marina Durante Il Conflitto* (The organization of the navy during the war). Tomo I—1972; Tomo II—1975; Tomo III—1978.
Rauber, V. Vol. XXII. *La Lotta Antisommergibile*. 1978 (The antisubmarine battle).

SERIE II: LE NAVI D'ITALIA (THE ITALIAN NAVY)

1. *Le Navi Di Linea Italiane (1861–1990)*. 4ª ed. 1995 (Italian warships [1861–1990]).
2. *I Sommergibiliitaliani (1898–1990)*. 4ª ed. 1996 (Italian submarines [1898–1990]).
3. Pollina, P. M. *Le Torpediniere Italiane (1881–1990)*. 2ª ed. 1974 (Italian torpedoboats [1881–1990]).
4. Giorgerini, G., and A. Nani. *Gli Incrociatori Italiani (1861–1975)*. 4ª ed. 1976 (Italian cruisers [1861–1975]).
5. Fioravanzo, G., P. M. Pollina, G. Riccardi, and F. Gnifetti. *Cacciatorpediniere Italliani (1900–1971)*. 3ª ed. 1971 (Italian torpedoboat destroyers [1900–1971]).
6. *I Mas, Le Motosiluranti e Gli Aliscafi Italiani (1906–1992)*. 1993 (Italian motortorpedoboats, human torpedos, and hydrofoils [1906–1992]).
7. Bargoni, F. *Esploratori, Fregate, Corvette Ed Avvisi Italiani (1861–1974)*. 3ª ed. 1974 (Italian scouts, frigates, corvettes, and dispatch boats [1861–1974]).
8. *Almanacco Storico Delle Navi Militari D'Italia (1861–1991)*. 2ª ed. 1996 (Historical almanac of the Italian navy [1861–1991]).
9. Bargoni, Gay. *Gliesplorator Italiani*. 1996. (Italian naval scouts).

SERIE III: POLITICA NAVALE (NAVAL POLITICS)

1. Gabriele, M. and G. Friz. *La Flotta Come Strumento Di Politica Nei Primi Decenni Dello Stato Unitario Italiano*. 1973 (The fleet as an instrument of policy in the first decade of united Italy).
2. Bernardi, G. *Il Disramo Navale Fra Le Due Guerre Mondiali (1919–1939)*. 1975 (Naval disarmament in the interwar years).
3. Bernardi, G. *La Marina, Gli Armistizi e Il Trattato Di Pace (settembre 1943–dicembre 1951)*. 1979 (The navy from the armistice to the peace treaty, September 1943–December 1951).
4. Gabriele, M. and G. Friz. *La Politica Navale Italiana dal 1885 al 1915*. 1982 (Italian naval politics from 1885–1915).
5. Santoni, A. *Storia e Politica Navale Dell'Eta Contemporanea*. 1993 (The history of Italian naval policy in the contemporary era).
6. Santoni, A. *Storia e Politica Navale Dell'Ultimo Cinquantennio*. 1996 (The history of Italian naval policy in the last 50 years).
7. Giorgerini, G., and R. Nassigh. *Il Potere Marittimo—Il Pensiero Navale Italiano Dal Dopoguerra Ad Oggi*. 1996 (Sea power—Italian naval thought from the end of the war to the present).

SERIE IV: OPERE VARIE (VARIOUS WORKS)

1. Gabriele, M. *Operazione C.3: Malta.* 2ª ed. 1990 (Operation C.3 against Malta).
2. Leva. F. *Storia Delle Campagne Oceaniche Della Marina* (The history of the oceanic campaigns at sea). Vol. I (1861–1882)—1992; Vol. II (1881–1900)—1992; Vol. III (1901–1923)—1992; Vol. IV (1923–1959)—1993.
3. Fioravanzo, G. *Storia Del Pensiero Tattico Navale.* 1973 (The history of tactical naval thought).
4. Di Paola, L. *L'Istituto Idrografico Della Marina (1872–1972).* 1973 (The naval hydrographical institute).
5. Galuppini, G. *La Bandiera Tricolore Nella Marina Sarda.* 2ª ed. 1987 (The tricolor flag of the Sardinian navy).
6. Galuppini, G. *Divise Per Secondi Capi, Sottocapi e Comuni Anno 1890.* 2ª ed. 1986 (Uniforms of the lower officers, underofficers and other ranks in 1890).
7. Radogna, L. *Cronistoria Delle Unita Da Guerra Delle Marine Preunitarie.* 1981 (Chronicle of the Preunification navy of the war of unification).
8. Galuppini, G. *Lo Schnorchel Italiano.* 1986 (Italian schnorkel submarines).
9. Galuppini, G. *La Preghiera Del Marinaio.* 1987 (The sailor's prayer).
10. Ferrante, E. *La Grande Guerra in Adriatico Nel LXX Anniversario Della Vittoria.* 1987 (The Great War in the Adriatic on the 70th anniversary of victory).
11. Fulvi, L., T. Marcon, O. Miozzi, rev. G. Manzari. *Le Fanterie Di Marina Italiane.* 2ª ed. 1995 (Thc Italian marines).
12. Bargoni, F. *Tutte Le Navi Militari D'Italia (1861–1995).* 1996 (All Italian warships, 1861–1995).
13. Mattesini, F. *La Battaglia Di Punta Stilo.* 1990 (The battle over the writing pointer).
14. Bargoni, F. *L'Impegno Navale Italiano Durante La Guerra Civile Spagnola (1936–1939).* 1992 (The Italian commitment during the Spanish Civil War).
15. Gabriele, M. *Sicilia 1860: Da Marsala Allo Stretto.* 1991 (Sicily 1860: From Marsala to Stretto).
16. Mattesini, F. *Betasom: La Guerra Negli Oceani (1940–1943).* 1993 (Betasom: The Oceanic War, 1940–1943).
17. *Le Memorie Dell'Ammiraglio De Courten (1943–1946).* 1993 (Memoirs of Admiral de Courten).
18. *Claudus—Pittore Del Mare.* 1993 (Claudus—pictures of the sea).
19. Romano, Roberto Vittorio. *Eduardo De Martino.* 1994.
20. *La Battaglia Dei Convogle.* 1994 (The battle of the convoys).
21. *L'Aviazione Di Marina.* 1996 (Naval aviation [provisional title]).

SERIE V: EDIZIONI ESERCITO–MARINA–AERONAUTICA (EDITIONS ARMY–NAVY–AIR)

1. Scarpa, C., and P. Sézanne. *Le Decorazioni Al Valore Dei Regni Di Sarsdegna e D'Italia (1793–1946).* 1976 (Decorations for valor of the kingdoms of Sardinia and of Italy [1793–1946]).

2. Scarpa, C., and P. Sézanne. *Le Decorazioni Al Valore Delia Repubblica Italiana.* 1981 (Decorations for valour of the Italian Republic).
3. Scarpa, C., and P. Sézanne. *Le Decorazioni Del Regno Di Sardegna e Del Regno D'Italia: Le decorazioni commemorative.* Vol. I. 1982 (The decorations of the Kingdom of Sardinia and of the Kingdom of Italy commemorative decorations).
4. Scarpa, C., and P. Sézanne. *Le Decorazioni Del Regno Di Sardegna e Del Regno D'Italia: Le decorazioni commemorative.* Vol. II. 1985 (The decorations of the Kingdom of Sardinia and of the Kingdom of Italy commemorative decorations).
5. Scarpa, C., and P. Sézanne. *Le Decorazioni Del Regno Di Sardegna e Del Regno D'Italia: Le decorazioni al Merito.* Vol. I. 1987 (Decorations for merit).
6. Scarpa, C., and P. Sézanne. *Le Decorazioni Del Regno Di Sardegna e Del Regno D'Italia: Le decorazioni al Merito.* Vol. II. 1992 (Decorations for merit).

SERIE VI: TRADUZIONI (TRANSLATIONS)

1. Mahan, Alfred T. *L'Influenza Del Potere Marittimo Sulla Storia 1660–1783.* 1994 (The influence of sea power upon history, 1660–1783).

SERIE VII: I DECORATI AL VALORE DELLA MARINA (NAVAL DECORATIONS FOR VALOR)

Miozzi, O. Vol. I—*Ordine Militare Di Savoia—Ordine Militare D'Italia.* 1991 (The military order of Savoy—the military order of Italy).

Miozzi, O. Vol. II—*Medaglie D'Oro al Valoe Mililtare.* 1992 (The gold medal for military valor).

Miozzi, O. Vol. III—*Medaglie D'Argento al Valore Militare.* 1996 (The silver medal for military valor).

Miozzi, O. Vol. IV—*Medaglie Di Bronz al Valore Military.* In process (The bronze medal for military valor).

Miozzi, O. Vol. V—*Medaglie al Valore Di Marina.* In process (The naval medal of valor).

SERIE IX: COMMISSIONE ITALIANA DI STORIA MILITARE (THE ITALIAN COMMISSION OF MILITARY HISTORY)

1. *L'Italia in Guerra: Il Primo Anno, 1940.* 1991 (Italy in the war: The first year, 1940).
2. L'*Italia in Guerra: Il Secondo Anno, 1941.* 1992 (Italy in the war: The second year, 1941).
3. *L'Italia in Guerra: Il Terzo Anno, 1942.* 1993 (Italy in the war: The third year, 1942).
4. *L'Italia in Guerra: Il Quarto Anno, 1943.* 1994 (Italy in the war: The fourth year, 1943).
5. *L'Italia in Guerra: Il Quinto Anno, 1944.* 1995 (Italy in the war: The fifth year, 1944).

13

Jordan

Brigadier S. A. El-Edroos (ret., Pakistani Army). *The Hashemite Arab Army, 1908–1979.* Amman, Jordan: Publishing Committee, 1980.

14

Lebanese Republic

Lebanese Republic, Ministry of Defense, Army Command, Directorate of Orientation

Directorate of Orientation

The Lebanese Army Command Historical Committee has the following duties:

1. The Historical Committee, in charge of writing the history of the Lebanese Army, is part of the Military National Heritage—Historical Department—attached to the Directorate of Orientation in the Army Command. The committee's mission is the following: to register, classify, and record every parchment, document, and photograph linked with the history of the army.
2. Grouping, updating, and classifying the record of historical events in the different departments.
3. Preparing and writing Lebanese military history.
4. During wartime (1976–1990), the committee had to stop its work, and some documents linked with the army and its history disappeared or were burned.
5. The Army Command appointed a temporary committee made up of officers specialized in the field of military history, which issued several publications in order to rewrite the military history of the Lebanese Army from its creation in 1945 until now. At the same time, and once this committee has finished its work, the Directorate of Orientation pursues the task by collecting the recording documents it might need.

There are currently some publications on the history of the Lebanese Army approved of by the Army Command; they are the following:

Staff General Samy Rihana. *The Current History of the Lebanese Army*, Volumes I and II.
Staff General George Faghali. *The Levant Army in Lebanon: Organization and Military Operations.*
Lieutenant Col. Ahmad Ellow. *History of Lebanese Military Institutions: Creation and Development 1916–1958.*

The following booklets were issued by the Directorate of Orientation from January 8, 1992, to the present:

The Military Establishment: Three Years of Building and Sacrifice.
The Army and Independence.
Independence: Hands to Build and an Army to Protect.
From Security Stability to National Stability.
The First of August 1994: Unlimited Sacrifices.
The Army Golden Jubilee 1945–1995, 50 Years Preserving the National Heritage and Being Faithful to the Oath.

15

The Netherlands

The Historical Section of the Royal Netherlands Navy, the Institute for Maritime History of the Naval Staff of the Royal Netherlands Navy, The Hague

Dr. P. C. van Royen, Director

The Historical Section of the Royal Netherlands Navy (RNN) was established 1 September 1946. The task of this office was to assemble data for the historiography of the operations of the Royal Netherlands Navy during the Second World War and in the Dutch East Indies during the postwar period. Head of the section was retired Vice-Admiral G. W. Stöve. From the start, the work of the section consisted solely of assembling data and documents on the subject mentioned. Obviously, collecting this kind of material meant an immense effort.

In the following years a beginning was also made with compiling chronologies of the war and excerpts of the countless documents. In 1950 Stöve was succeeded by Captain J. C. d'Engelbronner. During the 1950s the work of the Historical Section was not changed fundamentally. The collecting of data, summarizing documents, and the construction of a chronological framework took most of the time of the people involved. After the death of d'Engelbronner in 1961, Commodore J. F. van Dulm took over. By that time the work of the section was considerably extended. Naval and maritime history as a whole was going to be the main work of the section. According to the order issued, "It may no longer be a department which only concerns itself with World War II, it must become a department which stands on an academic level, which in the first place studies Netherlands maritime history and as much as possible puts this on record. It has to be a department that can answer all questions in this sphere, can give lessons and lectures and form a valuable section of the Naval Staff."

It then was stipulated that from then on each academic assistant had to be someone with a proven great interest in maritime history and at the same time one who had studied history at a university for at least three years. Under the guidance of van Dulm, the Historical Section developed into the kind of department the aforementioned order demanded. In 1972, after van Dulm retired, F. C. van Oosten took over his position. During his "reign" the quantity of work done by the Section increased every year and the last military personnel were replaced by civilians. In 1978 the office became the Department of Maritime History of the Naval Staff. However, through the years the number of staff members remained at just about the same level: nine.

When in 1972 van Oosten became head of the Historical Department, the department employed a growing number of professional historians. More and more the department developed a less exclusive naval character. After twelve years of service van Oosten left in 1984 and was followed by G.J.A. Raven, a full-time maritime and naval historian, educated at Leyden University. During the 1970s as well as during the 1980s the various archives and the library of the department increased impressively. The library in particular was increased by taking over the heritage of the former naval library. Most of the archives consist of personal documentation and collections donated by former naval personnel. In the meantime the photographic archives of the department has increased exponentially.

During Raven's administration the first steps were taken in the realm of the computerized world. This "digital revolution" in many respects meant a diminishing of the daily routine, the possibility of automation of the research in naval and maritime history, and, of course, the introduction of a different way of keeping libraries, archives, and other data collections. As for the external world, more frequent relations were kept with the University of Leyden, and the various societies and museums interested in Dutch maritime and naval history. Moreover, the department managed to issue a new and commercial series on Dutch naval and maritime history (*Bijdragen tot de Nederlands marinegeschiedenis*). It was to Raven's merit that he managed to issue a new series on Dutch naval historical subjects. At the end of 1990 he left the department and was followed by P. C. van Royen.

From 1991 on the tasks of the department remained basically the same. The accent of the management, however, was put on the integration of the work of all members of the staff with all possible means. Next to that, the introduction and growing use of the computer bore fruit. For instance, the library was connected to a national network of university libraries. Service to the naval staff and to the public gained priority over specialized research into naval and maritime history. Or, to put it differently, the demand dictated the supply. The groups paid extra attention to are the naval staff and the Royal Netherlands Navy, the media, the (professional) students of maritime and naval history, and the public interested in maritime and naval history. Relations with universities became more frequent. Within the naval organization the position of the department changed as it was connected closer to the two naval museums. Within this maritime historical setting the Institute for Maritime History acts as a *trait d'union* between the naval staff and the naval museums in Den Helder and Rotterdam. The change of accent toward a more public-relations attitude so far effected an ever-growing stream of questions and information concerning the various aspects of the maritime and naval history of the Netherlands. The same can be said of the number of researchers visiting the library of the institute.

The staff nowadays consists of two full-time historians, one editor of the yearbook of the RNN, a full-time photographer and archivist (the photo and film archives of the department count more than a quarter of a million items), and two librarians and archivists and one assistant (the library of the department counts 20,000 books alone, some of them dating from the seventeenth century; the collection of journals comprises more than 500 various periodicals) to take care of the maritime historical library. Next to that the archives of the department shelter just about 600 meters of various personal collections and archival materials. Most of these collections have had to be reorganized. Since 1993, with the aid of a library computer system, nearly half of the 20,000 volumes have been entered in an integrated data system. The stream of incoming and outgoing information is handled smoothly by the secretary of the institute, while responsibility for the management and administration is the director's. This short story would not be complete without mentioning the fact that the institute relies greatly upon the assistance and expertise of many volunteers. By the end of 1994 more than ten volunteers were involved in working for the institute.

BIBLIOGRAPHY

Contributions to the History of Maritime Affairs

J.M.G.A. Dronkers, *De admiraals van het Koninkrijk Holland (1806–1810): een bijdrage tot de studie van de maritieme geschiedenis van Nederland* (The admirals of the kingdom of Holland [1806–1810]: A contribution to the study of the maritime history of the Netherlands) ('s-Gravenhage, 1967 & 1973).

F. L. Diekerhoff, *Journael gehouden op 's Landts Schip d'Eendracht door de Heer Aert van Nes, Lt. admrl van Holland ende van Westvriesland inden jare 1667* (Journal kept on board the Ship of the Nation d'Eendracht by Mr. Aert van Nes, lt. admrl. of Holland and West Friesland in the year 1667) ('s-Gravenhage, 1967).

K. Twigt, *De opleiding in de Koninklijke Marine in het begin van deze eeuw* (The Royal Netherlands Navy training in the beginning of this century); R. F. Scheltema de Heere, *Enige scheepstypen uit de 19e en 20e eeuw* (Some types of ships from the nineteenth and twentieth century); Ph. M. Bosscher, *Journaal van luitenant-admiraal M. A. de Ruyter aan boord van 's lands schip De Zeven Provinciën, die betrekking op de Vierdaagse Zeeslag* (Journal by Lieutenant-Admiral M. A. de Ruyter on board the ship of the nation De Zeven Provinciën, relating to the four-days' sea-battle) ('s-Gravenhage, 1968).

F. L. Diekerhoff, *Het marine-uniform tot 1809* (The naval uniform until 1809) ('s-Gravenhage, 1969).

K. Twigt, *De Koninklijke Marine in het begin van de 20e eeu* (The Royal Netherlands navy in the beginning of the twentieth century); A. G. Vromans, *De scheepsmacht in de wateren van Bengkalis in het jaar 1924* (The shipping power in the waters of Bengkalis in the year 1924) ('s-Gravenhage, 1969).

R. F. Scheltema de Heere, *Dreadnoughts in de Middellandse zee, tot 1918* (Dreadnoughts in the Mediterranean until 1918) ('s-Gravenhage, 1970).

A. F. Lancker, *Zr.Ms. Borneo in Borneo (Borneo in Borneo);* K. Twigt, *De Koninklijke Marine in het begin van de 20e eeuw* (The Royal Netherlands navy in the beginning of the twentiethth century) ('s-Gravenhage, 1972).

G. M. de Vries, *Pompen, paapen en kiellichten. De geschiedenis van het loodswezen op de Eems* (Pumping, buoying and keel lifting: The history of pilotage on the Eems) ('s-Gravenhage, 1977).

H.A.G.J.P. van Hanswijck de Jonge, *Vijf jaar troepen varen (1946–1950)* (Five years of sailing troops [1946–1950]) ('s-Gravenhage, 1979).

N. Geldhof, *Verkennen en bewaken. Dornier Do 24K vliegbotten van de Marine luchtvaartidienst* (Making reconnaissance flights and guarding. Dornier Do 24K flying-boats of the naval fleet air arm) ('s-Gravenhage, 1979).

G.K.R. de Roos, *De marinierskant van het verhaal, november 1960–november 1962* (The marines' side of the story, November 1960–November 1962) ('s-Gravenhage, 1979).

F. C. Backer Dirks, *Schetsen van de Gouvernementsmarine I* (Sketches of the governmental navy I) ('s-Gravenhage, 1980).
M.J.C. Klaassen, *Adelborstenopleiding te Hellevoetsluis-Feijenoord-Enkhuizen 1803–1812* (Naval cadet training in Hellevoetsluis-Feijenoord-Enkhuizen 1803–1812) ('s-Gravenhage, 1986).
G. M. Veenman, *Van gaffelzeil tot spinnaker. 40 jaar zeilend opleidingsschip der Koninklijke Marine Hr.Ms. Urania* (From trysail to spinnaker. Fourty years of the Royal Netherlands navy sailing training ship Hr.Ms. *Urania*) ('s-Gravenhage, 1981).
J.P.M. Wanders, *Emblemen van de Koninklijke Marine* (Badges of the Royal Netherlands navy) ('s-Gravenhage, 1982).
O. G. Ward, P. C. Boer en G. J. Casius, *The Royal Netherlands Military Flying School 1942–1944* ('s-Gravenhage, 1985).

Contributions to Dutch Naval History

F. M. van Elderen, *Erfprins. Van Fort Lasalle tot marinekazerne* (Erfprins. From Fort Lasalle to naval barracks) (Amsterdam, 1985).
L. Brouwer (e.a.), *Tussen vloot en politiek. Een eeuw Marinestaf 1886–1986* (Between fleet and politics. A century of naval staff 1886–1986) (Amsterdam, 1986).
A. N. de Vos van Steenwijk, *Het marinebeleid in de Tweede Wereldoorlog* (Naval policy in the Second World War) (Amsterdam, 1986).
A. van Dijk, *Voor Pampus. De ontwikkeling van de scheepsbouw bij de Koninklijke Marine omstreeks 1860* (Off Pampus. The development of shipbuilding in the Royal Netherlands Navy around 1860) (Amsterdam, 1987).
G.J.A. Raven (ed.), *De Kroon op het anker. 175 Jaar Koninklijke Marine* (The crown on the anchor. 175 years of the Royal Netherlands navy) (Amsterdam, 1988).
R. H. van Holst Pellekaan, I. C. de Regt en J. F. Bastiaans, *Patrouilleren voor de Papoea's. De Koninklijke Marine in Nederlands Nieuw-Guinea 1945–1960* (Patrolling for the Papuas. The Royal Netherlands Navy in Dutch New Guinea 1945–1960) (Amsterdam, 1989).
R. H. van Holst Pellekaan, I. C. de Regt en J. F. Bastiaans, *Patrouilleren voor de Papoea's. De Koninklijke Marine in Nederlands Nieuw-Guinea 1960–1962* (Patrolling the Papuas. The Royal Netherlands Navy in Dutch New Guinea 1960–1962) (Amsterdam, 1990).
L.L.M. Eekhout, *Het Admiralenboek. De vlagofficieren van de Nederlandse marine 1382–1991* (The book of admirals. Flag officers of the Royal Netherlands Navy 1382–1991) (Amsterdam, 1992).

Other Publications

M.J.C. Klaassen, *Adelborstenopleiding Delft-Medemblik-Breda 1816–1857* (Naval cadet training Delft-Medemblik-Breda 1816–1857) (Den Helder, 1979).
M.J.C. Klaassen, *Adelborstenopleiding Willemsoord 1854–1979* (Naval cadet training Willemsoord 1854–1979) (Den Helder, 1979).

D.C.L. Schoonoord, *De Mariniersbrigade 1943–1949. Wording en inzet in Indonesië* (The Marine Brigade 1943–1949. Origin and employment in Indonesia) ('s-Gravenhage, 1988).

L.L.M. Eekhout (e.a.) (red.), *500 Jaar Marine* (500 years of the Dutch Navy) (Amsterdam, 1988).

G. Jungslager, *Recht zo die gaat. De maritiem–strategische doelstellingen terzake van de verdediging van Nederlands-Indië in de jaren twintig* (Straight it goes. The maritime–strategical aims concerning the defense of the Dutch Indies in the twenties) ('s-Gravenhage, 1991).

L.L.M. Eekhout, *Emblemen van de Koninklijke Marine* (Badges of the Royal Netherlands navy) (Leeuwarden, 1991).

A.M.C. van Dissel, W.H.C. van Straten en J. M. Oudendorp, *50 jaar MARVO, een halve eeuw Marinevoorlichting.* (50 years MARVO, half a century of the naval information service) ('s-Gravenhage, 1993).

Contributions to Dutch Naval History (Small Series)

A.M.C. van Dissel en J. R. Bruijn, *Bij de MARVA. Vrouwelijke militairen in dienst van de Koninklijke Marine 1944–1982* (With the MARVA. Female soldiers serving in the Royal Netherlands Navy 1944–1982) (Amsterdam, 1994).

Yearbook of the Royal Netherlands Navy

F. C. van Oosten, *Jaarboek van de Koninklijke Marine 1982* (Yearbook of the Royal Netherlands Navy 1982) ('s-Gravenhage, 1986).

M. K. Zaagman, *Jaarboek van de Koninklijke Marine 1983* (Yearbook of the Royal Netherlands Navy 1983) ('s-Gravenhage, 1986).

M. K. Zaagman, *Jaarboek van de Koninklijke Marine 1984* (Yearbook of the Royal Netherlands Navy 1984) ('s-Gravenhage, 1989).

M.C.F. van Drunen, *Jaarboek van de Koninklijke Marine 1985* (Yearbook of the Royal Netherlands Navy 1985) ('s-Gravenhage, 1991).

M.C.F. van Drunen, *Jaarboek van de Koninklijke Marine 1986* (Yearbook of the Royal Netherlands Navy 1986) ('s-Gravenhage/Bergen, 1992).

M.C.F. van Drunen, *Jaarboek van de Koninklijke Marine 1987* (Yearbook of the Royal Netherlands Navy 1987) ('s-Gravenhage, 1988).

M.C.F. van Drunen, *Jaarboek van de Koninklijke Marine 1988* (Yearbook of the Royal Netherlands Navy 1988) ('s-Gravenhage, 1989).

M.C.F. van Drunen, *Jaarboek van de Koninklijke Marine 1989/1990* (Yearbook of the Royal Netherlands Navy 1989/1990) ('s-Gravenhage/Amsterdam, 1990).

M.C.F. van Drunen, *Jaarboek van de Koninklijke Marine 1990* (Yearbook of the Royal Netherlands Navy 1990) ('s-Gravenhage/Bergen, 1991).

M.C.F. van Drunen, *Jaarboek van de Koninklijke Marine 1991* (Yearbook of the Royal Netherlands Navy 1991) ('s-Gravenhage/Bergen, 1992).

M.C.F. van Drunen, *Jaarboek van de Koninklijke Marine 1992* (Yearbook of the Royal Netherlands Navy 1992) ('s-Gravenhage/Bergen, 1993).

M.C.F. van Drunen, *Jaarboek van de Koninklijke Marine 1993* (Yearbook of the Royal Netherlands Navy 1993) ('s-Gravenhage/Bergen, 1994).

The Historical Section of the Royal Netherlands Army since 1967

Piet Kamphuis, Director

In 1968 the Military Historical Section underwent an extensive reorganization. The three history bureaus were merged into one Writing and Research Bureau. In addition, a Documentation and Information Bureau was established in 1972. To coordinate the activities of the two bureaus a general staff was created. The Bureau of Ceremonies, which had been added to the Military Historical Section in 1962, was transferred back to the staff of the commander in chief in 1969. The entire organization remains largely the same to this day.

With the appointment of Dr. C. M. Schulten as head of the Military Historical Section in 1974, the directorship was assumed for the first time by a civilian rather than by a military official. Dr. Schulten's appointment heralded the beginning of a more professional approach to the study of military history. Academically educated historians came to replace the military officers, who, competent and knowledgeable though they were, had lacked the benefit of academic training. This transformation was completed in 1983. Today, the section's researchers, whether civilian or military, all have an academic degree. Most have completed a doctoral dissertation or are in the process of doing so. The staff of the Documentation and Information Bureau, who are in charge of the various collections, are also highly qualified and able to work with computers. The outcome of all this is that today the Military Historical Section consists mainly of civilian personnel. The military personnel who work at the section are usually doing compulsory service.

The tasks and activities of the Military Historical Section can be summarized as follows:

1. To trace and examine sources and material for the recording of national military history, including the military contribution to the official recording of the history of the Netherlands.

2. To examine the archives of the army, the former Netherlands East Indies' Army, and other military files included in government, provincial, and municipal archives at home and abroad.
3. To collect, maintain, and preserve military historical documentation from the earliest period up to the present time.
4. To provide services to the armed forces, in particular the Royal Netherlands Army and its arms and branches, by providing information and advice on (military) historical matters, and by issuing publications and giving lectures.
5. To provide services to individuals and organizations outside the armed forces, in particular to answer written and telephone inquiries from journalists, historians, and others and to assist visitors who wish to view the collections or use the library.
6. To arrange scientific publications and lectures. To maintain relations with the history departments of Dutch universities and with sister organizations at home and abroad.

Internally, the tasks are divided as follows. The general staff handles the administration. The Documentation and Information Bureau administers the collections—the library, the documentation center, and the photograph and film archive. Anything pertaining to the field of military history and related sciences may be included in the collections. Approximately 250 visitors are received annually. In addition, the Documentation and Information Bureau handles about 1,000 written inquiries each year.

The task of the Military Historical Section is to engage in scientific research and publish its results. The historians who work at the bureau all have their own specializations. Not only Dutch military history is studied, but much work is still being done on the Netherlands East Indies as well. The section publishes the following periodicals:

- *Mededelingen van de Sectie Militaire Geschiedenis Landmachtstaf* (Journal of the Military History Section of the Netherlands army staff), which was established in 1979 and appears once or twice a year. It is the leading periodical of its kind in the Netherlands.
- *Bijdragen van de Sectie Militaire Geschiedenis* (Contributions of the Military History Section), a series of monographs, bibliographies, and source material, started in 1977.
- A series of brochures describing the current working and living conditions of army personnel, started in 1986.

In addition, the historians of the Writing and Research Bureau regularly contribute to scientific magazines and more popular publications.

In 1987 the Military Historical Section started up a new activity, taking upon itself the organization of the exhibition *The Sweetest*

Spring, which highlighted the Canadian contribution to the liberation of the Netherlands in 1944–1945 and the postwar relations between the two countries. The exhibition was opened on 10 May 1988 in Ottawa by Her Majesty Queen Beatrix and attracted a great deal of attention, especially from Canadian veterans. In 1989 the Military Historical Section produced an audiovisual documentary, *Je Maintiendrai*, dealing with the history of the Royal Netherlands Army.

BIBLIOGRAPHY

Amersfoort, H., *Drukken voor Defensie. IUB en CDP 1948–1988,* 's-Gravenhage, 1989 (Printing for the Department of Defense).

Amersfoort, H., *Koning en Kanton. De Nederlandse staat en het einde van de Zwitserse krijgsdienst hier tye lande 1814–1829,* 's-Gravenhage, 1988 (King and Canton. The Dutch state and the end of Swiss military service in the Netherlands).

Amersfoort, H., and L. L. Doedens, *Spot op de Landmacht. Honderd jaar politieke prenten over het Nederlandse leger,* 's-Gravenhage, 1991 (Political cartoons on the Dutch army).

Amersfoort, H., and P. H. Kamphuis (eds.), *Je maintiendrai. A concise history of the Dutch Army 1568–1940,* The Hague, 1985.

Amersfoort, H., and P. H. Kamphuis (red.), *Mei 1940. De strijd op Nederlands grondgebied,* 's-Gravenhage, 1990 (May 1940. The struggle on Dutch territory).

Amersfoort, H., and P. H. Kamphuis (eds.), *Revue internationale d'histoire militaire. No. 58. Edition néerlandaise,* La Haye, 1984.

de Bruin, T. D., *Orgaan der Nederlandsch-Indische Officiersvereeniging 1915–1942/1949–1951,* 's-Gravenhage, 1990. (A selective and annotated bibliography).

de Moore, J. A., *Indisch Militair Tijdschrift (1870–1942). A selective and annotated bibliography,* 's-Gravenhage, 1983 (The Indian military magazine).

Groen, P.M.H., *Marsroutes en dwaalsporen. Het Nederlands militair-strategisch beleid in Indonesië 1945–1950,* 's-Gravenhage, 1991 (Dutch military strategic policy in Indonesia).

Groen, P.M.H., J.A.M.M. Janssen, and C. M. Schulten, *Stoottroepen 1944–1984,* Dieren, 1984 (Storm troops 1944–1984).

Groen, P.M.H., and G. Teitler (eds.), *De Politionele Acties,* Amsterdam, 1987 (The political activities).

Heshusius, C. A., *KNIL-Cavalerie; Geschiedenis van de Cavalerie en Pantsertroepen van het Koninklijk Nederlands-Indisch Leger (1814–1950),* Emmen, 1978 (KNIL-cavalry; History of the cavalry and armored forces of the Royal Netherlands East Indian Army [1814–1950]).

Heshusius, C. A., and H. L. Sqitzer, *Het Koninklijk Nederlands-Indisch Leger 1830–1950,* 's-Gravenhage, 1977 (The Royal Netherlands East Indian army 1830–1950).

Hoffenaar, J., and F. M. Kert, *The sweetest spring/Heureux printemps/ De mooiste lente,* Ottawa, 1988.

Hoenen, J.C.G.W., and P. H. Kamphuis, *De bevrijding van Goirle (27 october 1944),* 's-Gravenhage, 1983 (The liberation of Goirle).

Hoffenaar, J., C. M. Schulten, and H. L. Zwitzer, *1 Divisie "7 december,"* Amsterdam, 1986 (First division "7 December").

Hoog, A.B.C.M. 'op't, and Th. M. van Koppen, *De Prinses Julianakazerne,* 's-Gravenhage, 1988 (The Princes Juliana Barracks).

Janssen, J.A.M.M., *Cantinezorg in het Nederlandse leger vóór de Tweede Wereldoorlog. Enkele fragmenten uit de voorgeschiedenis van de CADI,* 's-Gravenhage, 1982 (Canteens in the Dutch army before World War II).

Janssen, J.A.M.M., *Commissie van Proefneming 1866–15 December 1981,* 's-Gravenhage, 1981 (Commission of Testing 1866–15 December 1981).

Janssen, J.A.M.M., *Curatorium KMA 1961–1986: een kwart eeuw toezicht op de opleiding tot beroepsofficier KL en KLu aan de Koninklijke Militaire Academie te Breda,* 's-Gravenhage, 1986 (Curatorium Royal Military Academy 1961–1986).

Janssen, J.A.M.M., *De Legerraad 1945–1982,* 's-Gravenhage, 1982 (The army council 1945–1982).

Janssen, J.A.M.M., *Op weg naar Breda. De opleiding van officieren voor het Nederlandse leger tot aan de oprichting van de Koninklijke Militaire Academie in 1828,* 's-Gravenhage, 1989 (On the road to Breda. The education of officers for the Dutch army up to the foundation of the Royal Military Academy in 1828).

Janssen, J.A.M.M., B. Schoenmaker, and C. M. Schulten, *Nederland en Nassau-Dietz,* 's-Gravenhage, 1988 (The Netherlands and Nassau-Dietz).

Kamphuis, P. H., *Het Algemeene Nederlandsche Vredebond* (1871–1901), 's-Gravenhage, 1982 (The General Dutch Union for Peace [1871–1901]).

Kamphuis, P. H., *Het drama bij de Wassenaarse Slag,* Amsterdam\Dieren, 1985 (The drama at the "Wassenaarse Slag").

Kamphuis, P. H., and C. M. Schulten, *Van Staats tot Koninklijk. Gids ter begeleiding van de historische expositie in het Armamentarium te Delft,* Delft, 1986 (From state to royal army).

Kamphuis, P. H., B. van Opzeeland, and A. Tjepkema, *Blauwe baretten tussen twee vuren in Libanon,* Amsterdam, 1981 (Blue Berets between two fires in Lebanon).

Klinkert, W., *Het Vaderland verdedigd. Plannen en opvattingen over de verdediging van Nederland 1874–1914,* 's-Gravenhage, 1992 (Plans and viewpoints concerning the defense of the Netherlands).

Klinkert, W., and J.W.M. Schulten, *Mobilisatie in Nederland en België 1870–1914–1939,* Amsterdam, 1991 (Mobilization in Holland and Belgium).

Maalderink, P.G.H., *De Militaire Willems-Orde sinds 1940,* 's-Gravenhage, 1982 (The military order of William I since 1940).

Maalderink, P.G.H., B. J. Kasperink-Taekema, and C. M. Schulten, *Koeps Commandotroepen 1942–1982,* Roosendaal, 1982. (The Dutch commando forces 1942–1982).

Molenaar, F. J., *De strijd op Nederlands grondgebied tijdens de Tweede Wereldoorlog. Deel III-7. De luchtverdediging mei 1940.* 's-Gravenhage, 1970 (The battle on Netherlands territory during World War II. Part III-7. Air defense May 1940).

Nortier, J. J., *Acties in de Archipel. De intelligence operaties van NEFIS III in de Pacific-Oorlog,* Franeker, 1985 (Action in the Archipelago. The intelligence operations of NEFIS III in the Pacific war).

Nortier, J. J., *De Japanese aanval op Nederlands-Indië,* Rotterdam, 1988 (The Japanese attack on the Dutch East Indies).

Ommen, A. F., *Voor trouwe dienst. De trouwe-dienst medaille voor militairen beneden de rang van officier ingesteld in 1825,* 's-Gravenhage, 1986 (For loyal service. The loyal service medal for N.C.O.'s instituted in 1825).

Ringoir, H., *Afstamminge en voortzettingen der Artillerie,* 's-Gravenhage, 1979 (Origins and continuation of the artillery).

Ringoir, H., *Afstammingen en voortzettingen der Genie en Trein,* 's-Gravenhage, 1979. (Origins and continuation of the engineering corps and the train).

Ringoir, H., *Afstamminge en voortzettingen der Infanterie,* 's-Gravenhage, 1977 (Origins and continuation of the infantry).

Ringoir, H., *Hoofdofficieren der Infanterie van 1568 tot 1813,* 's-Gravenhage, 1981 (Field officers of the infantry from 1568 to 1813).

Ringoir, H., *Nederlandse generals van 1568 tot 1940,* 's-Gravenhage, 1981 (Dutch generals from 1568 to 1940).

Ringoir, H., *Vredesgarnizoenen van 1715 tot 1795 en 1815 tot 1940,* 's-Gravenhage, 1980 (Peace garrisons from 1715 to 1795 and from 1815 to 1940).

Schulten, C. M., *Frank van Bijnen 1910–1944,* 's-Gravenhage, 1985. (Frank van Bijnen 1910–1944).

Schulten, C. M., *Jonkheer P. J. Six. Amsterdammer en verzetsstrijder,* Nijmegen, 1987 (P. J. Six, esq. Amsterdammer and resistance fighter).

Schulten, C. M., *Toen, nu en straks Milva 1944–1979,* 's-Gravenhage, 1980 (The women's military department 1944–1979).

Schulten, C. M., and F.J.H. Th. Smits (eds.), *Grenadiers en Jagers in Nederland,* 's-Gravenhage, 1981 (Grenadiers and riflemen in the Netherlands).

Teitler, G., *De Indische defensie en de bezuinigingen,* 's-Gravenhage, 1985 (East Indian defense and the budget cuts).

Teitler, G., *De kolonels en generals van het KNIL,* 's-Gravenhage, 1982 (The colonels and generals of the Royal Netherlands East Indian army).

Teitler, G., and J. Hoffenaar (red.), *De Politionele Acties: Afwikkeling en Verwerking,* Amsterdam, 1990 (The Politional Actions. Completion and digestion).

Ten Raa, F.J.G., *De Uniformen van de Nederlandse Zee- en Landmacht,* 2dln, 's-Gravenhage, 1980. (facsimile van de uitgave van 1900) (The uniforms of the Dutch sea and land forces).

van den Doel, H. W., *H. J. Mulder en de strijd buj MILL. Een episode uit de Nederlandse artilleriegeschiedenis,* 's-Gravenhage, 1990 (H. J. Mulder and the battle of Mill).

van Hoof, J.P.C.M., *Langs wal en bastion. Hoogtepunten uit de Nederlandse vestingbouw,* Utrecht, 1991. (Highlights of Dutch fortification).

van Hoof, J.P.C.M., *Utrecht als militaire stad,* 's-Gravenhage, 1989 (Utrecht as military city).

van Hoof, J.P.C.M., *Willem Lodewijk van Nassau. Noorderling en Nederlander,* 's-Gravenhage, 1990 (Willem Lodewijk van Nassau. Northerner and Dutchman).

van Ojen, G. J., *De strijd op Nederlands grondgebied tijdens de Tweede Wereldoorlog. Deel IV–1 en 2. De Binnenlandse Strijdkrachten.* 's-Gravenhage, 1972 (The battle on Netherlands territory during World War II. Part IV–1 and 2. The forces of the interior).

van Ojen, H. J., *Leven en werken van Henri Koot (1883–1959),* 's-Gravenhage, 1978 (Life and work of Henri Koot [1883–1959]).

van Peelen, Th., and A.L.J. van Vliet, *"Zwevend naar de dood,"* Arnhem 1944, Velp, 1976. ("Gliding to death," Arnhem 1944).

van Popta, E. W., and H. Ringoir, *De Koninklijke Landmacht in ansichtkaarten,* Zaltbommel, 1975 (The Royal Netherlands army in postcards).

van Popta, E. W., and C. M. Schulten, *Nederlandse militaire voertuigen,* Bussum, 1978 (Dutch military vehicles).

Verhoeff, L., *Soldatenfolklore,* 's-Gravenhage, 1977 (Soldiers' folklore).

Zwitzer, H. L., *Documenten betreffende de Eerste Politionele Actie (20 juli 1947–4 augustus 1947),* 's-Gravenhage, 1983 (Documents on the first politional action).

Air Force History Section of the Royal Netherlands Air Force (RN1AF)

Rik Schreurs, NCO of the RN1AF

The Air Force History Section formed part of the Military History Section of the general staff until 1961. It then became an independent section of the air staff, which it still is today. With some slight changes in the name such as Section Military Aviation History in 1981, the name was definitively changed to Air Force History Section (Sectie Luchtmacht Historie; SLH) in 1989. Being part of the air staff and linked to the cabinet of the commander in chief of the RN1AF, its initial tasks were fourfold:

- To document the history of military aviation in the Netherlands (with the exception of the Naval Air Arm) and the publication of that history.
- To document the history of military aviation in the former Netherlands East Indies and publication of that history.
- To record information about military aviation history; i.e., photos and diaries of the squadrons.
- To coordinate the management of relevant archives in cooperation with the Central Archive Facilities of the Ministry of Defense.

In the early years the section produced a number of publications. From the beginning of the 1970s, however, the section's prospects started to look less bright. The reason for a decline in its activities can be found in the fact that the section became understaffed. After an expansion in number of persons employed in the second half of the 1960s, the section dwindled from over twenty collaborators to a mere five. In fact, this was the same number as in 1961. Conscripts have always been an important component of the section's cooperators. Right now the Section employs seven civilians and one conscript officer. This number is increased by volunteers and apprentices from the universities.

Also, the unfortunate linkage to the Military Aviation Museum at Soesterberg air base, from 1978 onward, made the activities of the section less distinct. As a result of this link, the head of the Historical Section of the air staff was at the same time Director of the Military Aviation Museum. Because of his being entangled in the daily routine of the museum, the original activities of the section almost came to a standstill.

To put an end to this unsatisfactory situation, the Air Force Council decided to disconnect the Air Force History Section from the Military Aviation Museum in 1989 and transfer it to The Hague in 1991.

Today, the Air Force History Section is the official historian of the RN1AF. Therefore, it has become the main point for historical consultation within our air force. It serves as a collective air force memory, indispensable to prove our identity as the youngest branch of the forces. The tasks set out in 1961 have been maintained, and it should be pointed out that by publishing books and brochures and providing information, the Air Force History Section contributes considerably to the image of the RN1AF.

In view of the latter task, providing information, it is important to mention the vast collection of written and audiovisual material concerning the history of the RN1AF. The roughly 1,000 diaries of the separate units and squadrons of the RN1AF are part of this collection, as well as the approximately 30,000 photos related to miliary aviation. Our archive and photo/video collection are in principle open to the public for consultation.

However, with the regeneration of the section in 1989 a new mandate expanded the tasks already given. The Defense White Paper of 1990 stressed the government's intention to pay more attention to the Dutch war veterans and their respective organizations. Its concern here is those who served in the navy, the army, and the air force during the Second World War or in the Netherlands East Indies over the period 1945–1950. Also those who served in Netherlands New Guinea until its transfer to Indonesia in 1962 are also included. This is a completely new angle of Dutch defense policy, since the Netherlands, despite its war experiences and unlike other countries, failed to develop a veterans' policy. It is the section's task to update the addresses of the veterans of the RN1AF for reunions.

Beside activities in the field of education, we are in the process of setting up a data bank of crashed aircraft. The unique position of our country in the Second World War as a corridor for aircraft between the United Kingdom and Germany makes it useful to set up a data bank of the around 7,000 aircraft that crashed on Dutch territory between 1940 and 1945. It marks the popularity of our section and the history of military aviation in general that this work is mainly done by volunteers.

Head of the Air Force History Section: Dr. J.A.M.M. Janseen
Head of the Documentation and Information Office: Mr. H. Th. M. Kauffman
Address: Air Force History Section, Postbox 20703, 2500 ES The Hague
Telephone: 070 318 8630

Since the reorganization of the Air Force History Section in 1989, the following brochures and books have been published:

BROCHURES

Scoenmaker, B., *Voor langdurige eervolle dienst. Het ontstaan en de geschiedenis van het officierskruis,* Brochure no. 1, Soesterberg 1990.

Jongh, Th. J. de, *Van Rudelsheimstichting tot Van Helsdingenkazerne. Biografie van J. P. van Helsdingen (1907–1942),* Brochure no. 2, The Hague 1991.

Starink, D., *Gevechtsvliegtuigen voor de Klu......... De geschedenis van de keuzebepaling en de aanschaf,* Brochure no. 3, The Hague 1991.

Ommen, A. F. van, *Voor trouwe dienst,* Brochure no. 4, The Hague 1992.

Lutgert, W. H., and R. de Winter, *"Voor hen die vielen."* Jackson 1992. *Verslag van de Nederlandse herdenking in de Verenigde Staten,* Brochure no. 5, The Hague 1992.

BOOKS

Winter, R. de, *Hendrik Walaardt Sacré 1873–1949. Leven voor de Luchtvaart,* The Hague 1992.
Lutgert, W. H., and B. Sorgedrager, *322 Squadron. Sporen van zijn verleden, lijnen in zijngeschiedenis,* The Hague 1993.
Lutgert, W. H., *"Ab Origine Flexibilis," Luchtmacht Stafschool 1949–1991,* The Hague. *Supplement,* The Hague 1993.
Doreleijers, E.H.J.C.M., and R. de Winter, *Luchtmacht-structuren in beweging. 80 Jaar luchtmachtorganisatie,* The Hague 1994.

16

Poland

The Military Historical Institute, Warsaw, Poland (1967–1995)

Colonel Tadeusz Panecki, Director

At the end of the 1960s three main centers in the field of military history were formed in Poland: the Military Historical Institute (MHI), the Military Political Academy (dissolved in 1990), and the Academy of the General Staff (from 1990 known as the Academy of National Defense). The best specialist scientific (scholarly) cadre was concentrated in these three, where research was conducted on Polish and international military history. The historians from those institutions have published some most important works.

In addition, military history in the Polish armed forces was studied at the war colleges, at the headquarters of the various armed forces (for example, in the headquarters of air force and the navy), and also at both the Museum of the Polish Armed Forces and at the Central Military Library.

Two departments were created at universities: the Department of Military History of the History Institute at Adam Mickiewicz University in Poznań and the Department of Military History of History and Archives at Mikolaj Kopernik University in Toruń. However, the Military Historical Institute, Warsaw, continues to be the most important institution in the field of military history. From the mid-1960s the Military Historical Institute conducted research chiefly on the following: the history of war and Polish military science, the history of Polish military traditions, the Polish armed effort during World War II, and the history of the Polish People's armed forces. At that time the MHI published a lot of valuable works from a scientific viewpoint, but there were also works of propaganda and even unscholarly pieces. This was a result of the political and ideological "corset" which crimped the activities of the Military Historical Institute until 1989. The institute as a cell of the "ideological front" also had the tasks forced on it by the Main Political Board of the Polish Army, an organ of the Communist Party in the armed forces.

The Military Historical Institute has also conducted educational activities: In 1972 the institute received the competence to grant scientific degrees: i.e., doctorates and from 1986 the scientific degree of assistant professor. Ten persons have regularly attended the doctors' postgraduate seminars at the MHI. Every year several postgraduate studies have been finished and examinations taken to qualify as assistant professor.

Great political changes took place after 1989, when the communist system was overthrown, leading to a restoration of full independence and Polish sovereignty, and these have not been without influence on the image and activity of the Military Historical Institute. It has regained, in the full sense of the word, scientific character. Now it can conduct studies in an unrestricted way on all aspects of Polish and international military history.

In July 1990 the director of the Military Historical Institute, civilian professor Andrzej Zahorski, was acclaimed one of the best Polish military historians. After his death in December 1992, professor Andrzej Ajnenkiel has taken up his duties.

Besides scientific tasks and educating researchers for the purposes of the armed forces of the Republic of Poland, the Military Historical Institute after 1989 has acted as the historical service of the Polish Army.

An important task of the institute is conducting research on Polish and international military history and publishing the results. As of now the MHI can investigate, without any limits and suppressions, those aspects of our history which were forbidden during the communist period: for example, Polish–Russian and Polish–Soviet relations.

The scientific staff of the institute consists of forty persons, including six professors and six Ph.D.'s. Scientific researchers work in three sections. The institute has its own search base: i.e., the scientific library of over 60,000 volumes and 1,000 titles of scientific journals and periodicals, the documentation center (with 3,000 archival units, 3,500,000 microfilm frames, and 27,000 maps as well as photographs), and a bibliographic center. The Scientific Council of the Military Historical Institute includes most distinguished representatives of the military-historical sciences in Poland.

The results of that search by the Military Historical Institute's staff are published as scholarly books and articles. The institute edits two periodicals *Wojskowy Przeglad Historyczny* (Military historical review) and the yearbook *Studia i materialy do Historii Wojskowo ci* (Studies and materials on the history of military affairs).

The Military Historical Institute has permanent scientific contacts with all important Polish scholarly centers, such as the Polish Academy of Sciences, universities, and officers' academies. There is cooperation as well with foreign historical services and institutes of military history of the armies of neighboring countries and other European countries, as well as with those in the United States and Canada.

From 1965, the Polish Commission of Military History, which is based on the Military Historical Institute, has been a member of the International Commission on Military History (CIHM). To express the international activity of Polish military historians, Col. Prof. Tadeusz Panecki, deputy director of the Military Historical Institute, was elected to the Bureau of the CIHM in 1990 at Madrid and again in 1995 at Quebec.

In August 1994 the MHI and the Polish Commission in Warsaw organized the International Colloquium of the CIHM under the title "National Insurgencies after 1794." This was a great scientific achievement for the Military Historical Institute, as can be seen in the proceedings published in 1996.

Bibliography 1967–1995: The Military Historical Institute

Urszula Olech, Polish Military Historical Institute

1. Wybór, I. Oprac, and Czeslaw Grzelak. *Agresja sowiecka na Plosk w świetle dokumentów 17 września 1939. T. i: Geneza i skutki agresji* (Soviet aggression on Poland in the light of documents, September 17, 1939. Vol. I: Origins and results of aggression). Warszawa: 1994.
2. Kozlowski, Eugeniusz, and Jan Wimmer. *L'Armee aux epoques des grandes transformations sociales* (The army in the great epoch of social transformation). Varsovie: 1980.

3. Komorowski, Krzysztof. *Armia Krajowa: dramatyczny epilog* (Home army: Dramatic epilogue). Warszawa: 1994.
4. Stawecki, Piotr. *Armia Polska we Francji, 1917–1919* (Polish army in France, 1917–1919). Warszawa: 1983.
5. Bauer, Krzysztof. *Wojsko koronne powstania kościuszkowskiego.* (The Polish army in the Kościuszko uprising). Warszawa: 1981.
6. Biegański, Witold. *Regularne jednostki Wojska Polskiego na Zachodzie. Formowanie, dzialania bojowe, organaizacja, metryki dywizji i brygad* (Regular units of the Polish armed forces in the West. Formation. Combat actions, organization; certificates of divisions and brigades). Warszawa: 1961.
7. Biegański, Witold. *Wojsko Polskie we Francji 1939–1940* (Polish armed forces in France, 1939–1940). Warszawa: 1967.
8. Biegański, Witold. *Zaczeloe sie w Coëtquidan: z dziejów polskich jednostek regularnych we Francji* (It happened in Coëtquidan: From the history of the Polish regular units in France). Warszawa: 1977.
9. Biskup, Marian. *Trzynastoletnia wojna z Zakonem Krzyzackim, 1454–1466* (Thirteen years war with the Teutonic Order, 1454–1466). Warszawa: 1967.
10. Ciechanowski, Konrad. *Armia "Pomorze" 1939* ("Pomorze" Army, 1939). Warszawa: 1983.
11. Ciechanowski, Konrad. *Ruch oporu na Pomorzu Gdańskim 1939–1945* (Resistance movement in Gdańsk Pomerania 1939–1945). Warszawa: 1972.
12. Derejczyk, Stanislaw and Olech Urszula. *Polacy w I wojnie światowej: problematyke wojskowa: bibliografia* (Poles in World War I: Military problems: Bibliography). Warszawa: n.d..
13. Dyskant, Józef W. *Cuszima 1905* (Tsushima 1905). Warszawa: 1989.
14. Dyskant, Józef W. *Flotylle rzeczne w planach i dzialaniach wojennych II Rzeczypospolitej* (River Flotillas in combat actions during the Second Republic). Warszawa: 1991.
15. Dyskant, Józef W. *Zatoka Swieźa, 1463: przebieg dziaalań wojny trzynastoletniej na morzu i wodach śródladowych na tle rozwoju źeglugi w polowie XV wieku* (Swieźa Bay, 1463: Progress of actions of Thirteen Years War on the sea and inland waters on the background of development of navigation in the mid-fifteenth century). Warszawa: 1987.
16. Feret, Stanislaw. *Polska aztuka wojenna 1918–1939* (Polish art of war, 1918–1939). Warszawa: 1972.
17. Gać, Stanislaw. *7 dywizia piechoty, Historia 7 luźychkiej dywizji piechoty* (History of the 7th Lusatian infantry division). Warszawa: 1971.
18. Godlewski, Jerzy Romuald. *Bitwa nad Bzura: historyczne studium operacyjne* (The battle of Bzura: Historical operational study). Warszawa: 1973.
19. Góra Stanislaw. *Partyzantka na Podlasiu 1863–1864* (Partisan movements on Podlasie, 1863–1864). Warszawa: 1976.
20. Harz, Maria. *Bibliografia zbrodni katyńskiej: materialy z lat 1943–1993.* Przedm. Janusz K. Zawodny (Bibliography of the Katyń crime: Materials from 1943–1993. Intro. by Janusz K. Zawodny). Warszawa: 1993.

21. *Histoire militaire de la Pologne. Problèmes choisis. Dissertations, études, esquisses.* Ed. W. Biegański et al. (Military history of Poland. Select problems, dissertations, sketches). Varsovie: 1970.
22. *Historia wojskowoś ci polskiej: wybrane zagadnienia.* Ed. Witold Biegański, Piotr Stawecki, Janusz Wojtasik (Polish military history: Selected problems). Warszawa: 1972.
23. Iwanowski, Wincenty. *Operacje okra żajace II wojny światowej na europejskim TDW: studium wojskowo-historyczne* (Encircling operations in the European theatre of war actions: Military-historical study). Warszawa: 1973.
24. Jaczyński, Stanislaw. *Zygmunt Berling: mi dzly slawa a potepieniem* (Zygmunt Berling: Between fame and condemnation). Warszawa: 1993.
25. Jaśtak, Zbigniew. *Szlakiem wojsk chemicznych 1943–1945* (The story of the chemical units, 1943–1945). Warszawa: 1966.
26. Kaczmarek, Kazimierz. *Polacy na polach Lużyc* (Poles on Lusatian fields). Warszawa: 1980.
27. Kieniewicz, Stefan, Andrezej Zahorski, and Wladyslaw Zajewski. *Trzy powstania narodowe: Kościuszkowski, listpadowe, atyczniowe* (Three national uprisings: Kościuszko, November, January). Warszawa: 1992.
28. Klimecki, Michal, and Wladyslawv Klimczak. *Legiony Polskie* (Polish legions). Warszawa: 1990.
29. Kozlowski, Eugeniusz. *Wojsko Polskie w latach 1936–1939: próby modernizacji i rozbudowy* (Polish armed forces, 1936–1939: Attempts at modernization and development). Warszawa: 1974.
30. Krassowski, Boguslaw. *Polska kartografia wojskowa w latach 1918–1945* (Polish military cartography, 1918–1945). Warszawa: 1974.
31. Krawczyk, Edward. *Demobilizacja i pokojowa organizacja Wojska Polskiego w latach 1920–1921* (Demobilization and peace organization of the Polish armed forces in 1920–1921). Warszawa: 1971.
32. Krzemiński, Czeslaw. *Wojna powietrazna w Europie 1939–1945* (Aerial war over Europe, 1939–1945). Warszawa: 1989.
33. Majewski, Ryszard. *Cecora, rok 1620* (Cecora, 1620). Warszawa: 1970.
34. Markowski, Wladyslaw. *Zaopatrzenie medyczno-sanitarne Warszawy i Modlina w wojnie obronnej 1939* (Medical and sanitary aid in Warsaw and Modlin during the September 1929 campaign). Warszawa: 1985.
35. *Military Technique, Policy and Strategy in History* Ed. Witold Biegański et al. Warszawa: 1976.
36. *Na oczach Kremia: tragedia walacz cej Warszawy w świetie dokumentów rosyjskich.* Przedm. Andrzej Ajnenkiel (Under Kremlin's eyes: A tragedy of fighting Warsaw in the light of Russian documents. Collated by Andrzej Chmielarz). Warszawa: 1994.
37. Ajnenkiel, Andrzej, et al. *Naczelni wodzowie i wyźsi dowódcy Polskich Sil Zbrojnych na Zachodzie* (Commanders in Chief and Higher Commanders of Polish Armed Forces in the West). Warszawa: 1995.
38. Nalepa, Edward J. *Oficerowie Armii Radzieckiej w Wojsku Polskim 1943–1968* (Officers of Soviet armed forces in the Polish armed forces, 1943–1968). Warszawa: 1995.

39. Nalepa, Edward J. *Wojsko Polskie w grudniu 1070* (Polish armed forces in December 1070). Warszawa: 1990.
40. Nowak, Tadeusz M. *Rozwój techniki rakietowej w świetle europejskich traktatów XIII–XVII wieku* (Development of rocket techniques in the light of European treaties from the thirteenth to seventeenth centuries). Warszawa: 1995.
41. *Obrona Warszawy w 1939 r. Wybór dokumentów wojskowych* (Defense of Warsaw in 1939: Selected documents). Warszawa: 1968.
42. Pachoński, Jan. *Legiony Polskie: prawda i legenda, 1794–1807. 4 t* (Polish legions: The truth and legend, 1794–1807. 4 Vols.). Warszawa: 1969–1979.
43. Plewczyński, Marek. *Armia Koronna, 1506–1567: zagadnienia struktury narodowoś ciowej* (The army of the Kingdom of Poland, 1506–1576: Problems of nationality structure). Warszawa: 1991.
44. *The Policy and Strategy of Poland in the Second World War 1939–1945: Materials Prepared for the 14th International Congress of Historical Sciences in San Francisco.* Ed. Boand W. Biegański et al. Warszawa: n.d.
45. Biegański, Witold, et al. *Polish Resistance Movement in Poland and Abroad 1939–1945.* Warszawa: 1987.
46. *Polska technika wojskowa do 1500 roku* (Polish military technique to 1500). Scientific ed. Andrzej Nadolski. Warszawa: 1994.
47. *Polskie tradycje wojskowe* t. 1, 3 (Polish military traditions. Vols. 1 and 3). Ed. Janusz Sikorski. Warszawa: 1990–1995.
48. *Powstanie Kościuszkowskie 1794: dzieje militarne* (Kościuszko uprising 1794: The military history). Scientific ed. Tadeusz Rawski. Warszawa: 1994.
49. Rawski, Tadeusz. *Wojna na Balkanach 1941: agresja hitlerowska na Jugoslawi i Grecj* (War in the Balkans, 1941: Nazi aggression against Yugoslavia and Greece). Warszawa: 1981.
50. Rzepniewski, Andrzej. *Wojna powietrzna w Polsce—1939 na tie rozwoju lotnictwa Polski i Niemiec* (Aerial war over Poland—1939, the background of the development of the Polish and German air forces). Warszawa: 1970.
51. Rzepski, Stanislaw. *38 pulk artyierii lekkiej* (38th Light Artillery Regiment). Warszawa: 1971.
52. Ryźewski, Waclaw. *Trzecie powstanie ślaskie, 1921: geneza i przebieg dzialań bojowych* (Third Silesian uprising, 1921: Origins and progress of combat actions). Warszawa: 1977.
53. Sawicki, Tadeusz. *Front wschodni a powstanie warszawskie* (The Eastern Front and the Warsaw uprising). Warszawa: 1986.
54. Sikorski, Janusz. *Zarys historii wojskowo ści powazechnej do końca wieku XIX* (International military history to the end of the nineteenth century: An outline). Warszawa: 1972.
55. Skibiński, Franciszek. *Rozwa źania o sztuce wojennej* (Considerations of the art of war). Warszawa: 1972.
56. Stawecki, Piotr. *Nast pcy komendanta, Wojsko a polityka wewnetrzna Drugiej Rzeczypospolitej w latach 1935–1939* (Successors of the

commendant, the army and the internal policy of the Second Republic in 1935–1939). Warszawa: 1969.
57. Stawecki, Piotr. *Polityka wojskowa Polski 1921–1926* (Military policy of Poland, 1921–1926). Warszawa: 1981.
58. Sulek, Zdzislaw. *Sprzysieżenie Jakuba Jasińskiego* (The Jakub Jasiński conspiracy). Warszawa: 1982.
59. Tarczyński, Marek. *Generalicja powstania listopadowego.* Wyd. 2 (The generals of November uprising. 2 ed.). Warszawa: 1988.
60. *Uźródel niepodleglości, 1914–1918: z dziejów polskiego czynu zbrojnego* (The origins of independence, 1914–1918: From the history of Polish armed actions). Scientific ed. Piotr Stawecki. Warszawa: 1983.
61. Wimmer, Jan. *Historia piechoty polskiej do roku 1864* (History of Polish infantry to 1864). Warszawa: 1978.
62. Wimmer, Jan. *Wiedeń 1683: dzieje kampanii i bitwy* (Vienna 1683: History of the campaign and of the battle). Warszawa: 1983.
63. *Wojna obronna Polski 1939. Wybór źródel* (The defensive war, 1939. Selection of sources). Worked by Mieczyslaw Cieplewicz et al. Warszawa: 1968.
64. *Wojna polsko-szwedzka 1655–1660* (Polish–Swedish War, 1655–1660). Ed. Jan Wimmer. Warszawa: 1944.
65. Wojtasik, Janusz. *Idea walki zbrojnej o niepodleglość Polski, 1864–1907: koncepcje i próby ich realizacji* (The idea of armed fighting for the independence of Poland, 1864–1907: Conceptions and attempts at their realization). Warszawa: 1987.
66. Wróblewski, Jan. *Armia "Prusy" 1939* ("Prusy" Army, 1939). Warszawa: 1986.
67. Wróblewski, Jan. *Samodzielna Grupa Operacyjna "Polesie" 1939* (The independent "Polesie" operational group, 1939). Scientific ed. Mieczyslaw Cieplewicz. Warszawa: 1989.
68. Wróblewski, Wieslaw. *Moskwa 1941* (Moscow 1941). Warszawa: 1987.
69. Wrosek, Mieczyslaw. *Wojny o granice Polski Odrodzonej, 1918–1921* (Wars for the reestablishment of Poland's frontiers, 1918–1921). Warszawa: 1992.
70. Cieplewicz, Mieczyslaw, et al. *Zarys dziejów wojskowoś ci polskiej w latach 1864–1939* (An outline of Polish military history, 1864–1939). Warszawa: 1990.

17

Portugal

Portuguese Military History

General Manuel Freire Themudo Barata, President, Portuguese Commission of Military History

Although the entire history of Portugal from its foundation to the present day constitutes a repository of military history, the fact is that it was never considered as such outside the scope of the military structures themselves, and even there its study and dissemination has only been institutionalized in a fragmentary fashion. Both the army and the navy have their own historical archives and have fostered many works of dissemination and research. It was only after the realization of the XVIII International Meeting, however (which took place in Greece in 1988 under the aegis of the International Military History Commission, Portugal being represented by an observer), that the Ministry of National Defense promoted the constitution of a commission comprising representatives of the armed forces and of the Departments of Education and Culture. The aim of the commission is to institutionalize the research, study, and dissemination of military history.

Thus, in 1989, the Portuguese Military History Commission (PMHC) was formed, directly answerable to the Minister for National Defense. Its functions include

- Promoting the research and study of military history within military colleges and the universities.
- Cooperating and participating in the activities of the International Military History Commission.
- Promoting and encouraging the publication of historical and military works.

The Portuguese Commission of Military History comprises

- The presidency.
- An advisory committee.
- A secretary general.

The presidency is comprised of one representative from each of the three arms of the armed forces and one from the Portuguese Academy of History. The advisory committee is comprised of twelve members, six military and six civilian academics, all with renowned competence in the field of military history.

The Portuguese Commission has taken part in the annual meetings of the IMHC and developed major activity, such as

- An annual national meeting with the presence of an eminent personality from the IMHC.
- Active cooperation with the universities, organizing conferences, postgraduate courses, and "Military History Day."
- The organization, annually, of two national prizes: one aimed at authors of works on military history published each year, or hitherto unpublished—the National Defense Prize (*Prémio Defesa Nacional*); the other for young people, with presentation in various forms (music, painting, dance, theatre, etc.), in which the contents must be original—the Youth and Defense Prize (*Prémio Juventude e Defesa*).
- The participation in the Sympoisum "Tordesilhas—V Century," organized by the Brasilian Institute of Geography and Military History, at Rio de Janeiro, with a representative delegation.

Since its formation the Portuguese Commission of Military History edited (or coedited) the following publications:

Actas do I Colóquio de História Militar. "Para uma visão global da História Militar," 1992 (For a global vision of military history).

Actas do II Colóquio de História Militar. "Panorama e perspectivas actuais da História Militar," 1993 (Panorama and current perspectives of military history).

Actas do III Colóquio de História Militar. "Portugal e a Europa—Sec. XVII a XX," 1994 (Portugal and Europe—from the seventeenth to the twentieth centuries).

Actas do IV Colóquio de História Militar. "A História Militar de Portugal no Séc. XIX," 1994 (Portugal's military history on the nineteenth century).

Actas do V Colóquio de História Militar. "Do Infante e Tordesilhas," 1955 (The Infante and Tordesilhas).

Participações Portuguesas em Colóquios Internacionais, 1993 (Portuguese participations in international congresses).

Barroca, M. J. *Do Castelo da Reconquista ao Castelo Românico (Secs. IX a XII),* 1994 (From the reconquest castle to the Romanic castle [ninth to twelfth century]).
Raueber, C. A. *Les Renseignements, la Reconnaissance et les Transmissions Militaires du Temps du Napoleon—l'exemple de la Troisième Invasion du Portugal, 1810,* 1993 (The intelligence, the reconnaissance, and the military transmissions in Napoleon's period—the example of the third invasion of Portugal, 1810).
O Conde Lippe e Portugal, 1991 (The Count Lippe and Portugal).
No Centenário do General Barros Rodrigues, 1991 (On General Barros Rodrigues' centennial commemoration).
Bessa, Carlos. *Relações entre Portugal e a Polónia e Cinquentenário da Invasão de Varsóvia,* 1995 (Relationships between Portugal and Poland and the Fiftieth Anniversary of the Warsaw Invasion).

It could be said that Portuguese Military History began with the scribes and chroniclers of the sixteenth century who have given us detailed reports of our military actions and travels. Although written in the style peculiar to that time, they contain references to almost all the activities which took place during the fifteenth and sixteenth centuries.

At the beginning of the nineteenth century the navy made a first attempt at publishing the Annals of the Portuguese Navy but got no further than the year 1640. At the end of that century and on the threshold of the twentieth century many different studies about the past of our navy were published. But it was only in 1969 that the Naval History Study Center was formed (the forerunner of the Navy Academy set up in 1978), which centralizes and broadcast all the historical activities of our navy. Naval History has been taught at the Naval College since 1864. A close connection with the universities has been fruitful, with the curriculum including several courses on our naval history.

After the era of scribes and chroniclers, many historical works were published about the army, mostly on individual initiative. However, the Military Academy functions as a center for the study and dissemination of the history of the Portuguese Army.

It was only after the creation of the Military History Commission (to which the director of the Military History Archives belonged) at staff headquarters in 1923 that an attempt was made to structure the historical and cultural activities of the army. In 1959 this commission, directly answerable to the chief of staff, became the Military History Department, under the vice chief of staff in 1976. On that date the Army Library merged with the Military History Department.

The History Archives Bulletin has been published continuously since 1934. It is a very rich repository of Portuguese military history. Special mention must also be made of the valuable work carried out by the Army Historical Department in the area of military archaeology, namely with the recovery and preservation of castles and other military monuments together with places of historical and military interest.

It was only in 1952 that the air force became independent within the armed forces, with the fusion of the 5th Aeronautical Arm of the army with naval aviation. All its historical data up to that date is scattered throughout the archives and libraries of the army and navy. Even after its emancipation in 1952, only certain works and individual initiatives have emerged on the scene of national aeronautical history, such as the publication of the description of the major air raids carried out by our military and naval aviators, and also numerous articles in *Revista do Ar* of the Aero Club de Portugal, and in *Mais Alto*. The exceptions are

- "História da Forca Aérea Portuguesa" by Colonel Edgar Cardoso, three volumes published with Air Force support.
- "História das Tropas Para-quedistas" by members of a panel appointed for the purpose, five volumes published by the Paratroop Command, part of the air force.
- "Os Aviões da Cruz de Cristo—75 Anos de Aviacão Militar em Portugal" by Engineer Mário Canongia Lopes, published with air force support.
- "Spitfires and Hurricanes" by Engineer Mário Canongia Lopes.

With the appearance of the Portuguese Military History Commission in 1989, a growing need was felt to create within the air force an organ which would provide a response to the requests of that commission and at the same time support its representatives. This led to the creation of the Office of Aeronautical History Studies, which quite soon after merged with the Air Force History Commission with the basic aim of activating a historical archive and promoting the collection of all air force history, scattered throughout all the units and other organs and even in private hands.

The creation of the Portuguese Military History Commission is proof of the interest the Ministry of Defense has in historical and military activities. Consequently, relevant legislation was published during 1993 and 1994 which integrated the historic and cultural bodies of the three arms of the armed forces in their organic structure under new, well-defined forms.

Thus, the navy has the following cultural bodies:

- Navy Academy
- Maritime Museum
- Central Library

- Vasco da Gama Aquarium
- Calouste Gulbenkian Planetarium

The Navy Academy has succeeded the Maritime History Study Center and as such acts as the organizer of all these navy activities. All these organs are directly answerable to the navy chief of staff, who is assisted by a cultural committee through which all these activities are coordinated.

The army has a Division of Documentation and Military History (integrated in the functional area of Personnel Command) responsible for supervising documentation treatment and archives and the use of the libraries, together with research, conservation, and dissemination of the army's historical and military heritage. This Division of Documentation and Military History comprises executive bodies responsible for activities which include the military museums, monuments, and places of historic and military interest, and also the Heraldry Office.

The air force has also formed a Historical and Cultural Commission, directly answerable to the chief of staff, which coordinates the activities of collection, conservation, study, and dissemination of the air force historical and cultural heritage. The commission coordinates the activities of the history archives, the Air Museum, and the magazine *Mais Alto*.

BIBLIOGRAPHY

Subsidios para o Esforco Militar Português na Década de 50 (Assistance for the Portuguese military effort on the 50s), Ernesto A. L. Ferreira de Macedo, DSHM, 1988, Vol. I, 340 pp., Vol. II, 339 pp.

Le Genie Français au Portugal sous l'Empire (French engineers in Portugal under the Empire), António Pedro Vicente, DSHM, 1984, 288 pp.

Alcácer-Quibir—A vertente táctica (Alcacer-Quibir—the tactical aspect), F. Alcide de Oliveira, DSHM, 1988, 45 pp.

Aljubarrota Dissecada (Aljubarrota examined point by point), F. Alcide de Oliveira, DSHM, 1988, 130 pp.

Dicionário Temático de Arquitectura Militar e a Arte de Fortificar (Thematic dictionary of military architecture and the art of fortification), António L. Pires Nunes, EME-DSHM, 1991, 249 pp.

A Defesa dos Acores durante a II Guerra Mundial (1939–1945) (The Azores defense in World War II [1939–1945]), Manuel de Sousa Meneze, DSHM, 1988, 133 pp.

Resenha Histórica das Campanhas de Africa (1961–74) (Historical review of the African campaigns [1961–74]), Comissâo para o Estudo das Campanhas de Africa, CECA.

- *Enquadramento* (General bracket), 1988 (2nd ed.), 532 pp.
- *Angola,* 1989, 363 pp.
- *Guiné (Guinea),* 1989, 219 pp.
- *Mocambique (Mozambique),* 1989, 325 pp.
- *Condecoracoes (Medals and Badges of honour)*
  Tomo I—Torre Espada, Valor Militar, 1990, 358 pp.
  Tomos II/III—Cruz de Guerra, 1991/1992, 546 pp., 468 pp.

Subsidios para a Doutrina aplicada nas Campanhas de Africa (Assistance for the application of doctrine in the African campaigns), CECA, 1990, 327 pp.

Publications of the Navy Academy

Translated by Robin Higham and William S. Reeder, Jr.

Cte. Teixeira da Mota. *A Viagem de António de Saldanha em 1503 e a Rota de Vasco da Gama no Atlǘntico Sul* (The voyage of Antonio de Saldanha in 1503 and the route of Vasco da Gama in the South Atlantic). 1971.

Prof. Dr. Virgínia Rau. *Achegas p/o Estudo da Construção Naval Durante os Séculos XVII e XVIII Na Ribeira do Ouro-Porto* (Advances in the study of naval construction during the seventeenth and eighteenth centuries on the Ribeira do Oun-Oporto). 1971.

Eńg. J. M. dos Santos Simões. *Saveiros da Baía* (Of the bay). 1977.

Prof. Dr. Armando Cortesão. *Descobrimento e Cartografia das Ilhas de S. Tomé e Príncipe* (The discovery and maps of the islands of Sao Tomé and Principe). 1971.

Alberto Iria. *Caíques do Algarve no Sul de Angola* (Coasting Vessels from the Algarve in the South of Angola). 1971.

E. H. Serra Brandão. *Novos Conceitos de Agressão e Legitima Defesa em Direito Internacional* (New conceptions of aggression and legitimate defense in international affairs). 1973.

Damião Peres. *Fernão de Magalhães e o Problema da Communicação do Atlántico com o Pacífico* (Ferdinand Magellan and the problem of passing from the Atlantic to the Pacific). 1973.

J. H. Gago de Medeiros. *O Encoberto mos Jerónimos* (The secrets of the hieronomy). 1973.

J. Soeiro de Brito. *Evolução Recente dos Métodos de Navegação* (The recent evolution of methods of navigation). 1972.
Silva Gameiro. *A Viagem Aérea Lisboa–Funchal em 1921* (The flight from Lisbon to Funchal in 1921). 1973.
Alberto Cutileiro. *A Vida Faustosa das Galeotas Reais Subsídios Para a História das* (The luxurious life of the Royal Galiots). 1973.
Maurício de Oliveira. *O Almirante Pereira da Silva—Exemplo de Devoção* (Admiral Pereira da Silva—an example of devotion). 1973.
Hernáni Cidade. *O Mar na Formação e Robustecimento na Defesa e Ilustração de Portugal* (The sea in the formation and strengthening of the defense and illustration of Portugal). 1973.
Arquiduque Otão de Habsburgo. *Os mares e a Política Mundial* (The seas and world politics). 1973.
Luís Filipe Thomaz. *Notas Sobre a Vida Marítima em Timor* (Notes about maritime life at Timor). 1977.
Sarmento Rodrigues. *Celestino Soares—Marinheiro, Patriota, Humanista, Escritor* (Celestino Soares—seaman, patriot, humanist, writer). 1973.
Sarmento Rodrigues. *Algumas Informações Sobre o Rio Douro, Seu Curso em Portugal e Sua Navegção* (Some information about the Douro River, its course in Portugal and its navigation). 1972.
Ramos Pereira. *Fontoura da Costa* (Fontoura da Costa). 1973.
Braga Paixão. *Uma Comissão de Serviço de Fontoura da Costa no Ministério do Reino* (Fontoura da Costa's commission as minister of the kingdom). 1973.
Sarmento Rodrigues. *Fontoura da Costa—Governador em Cabo Verde* (Fontoura da Costa—governor of Cape Verde). 1973.
Leandro Tocantis. *O Capitão-Mor Pedro Teixeira, Precursor da Transamazónica* (Captain-General Pedro Teixeira, precursor of Transamazonia). 1973.
Fernando Vasco da Costa. *O Futuro dos Portos* (On the future of harbors). 1973.
Mexia Salema. *Marrocos Pitoresco (breves imagens)* (Picturesque Morocco [a few pictures]). 1973.
Alberto Iria. *Ex-votos de Mareantes e Pescadores do Algarve (região e náutica)* (Votive offerings of sailors and fishermen of the Algarve). 1973.
Guilhermino de Magalhães. *A Evolução da Arte da Guerra Naval* (On the evolution of the art of naval warfare). 1973.
Rodrigues Santos. *Uma Vitória do Espírito no Céu Virgem do Atlántico Sul* (A spiritual victory in the virgin sky of the South Atlantic). 1973.
Gago de Medeiros. *Os Lusíadas e o Pacto do Atlántico* (The Portugese and the Atlantic Treaty). 1973.
Hernáni Cidade. *Luís de Camões: Honesto Estudo Misturado a . . .* (Luis de Camoëns: Honest balanced study of . . .). 1973.
Virgínia Rau. *Portugal e o Mediterráneo no Século XV* (Portugal and the Mediterranean in the fifteenth century). 1973.
Pimentel Barata. *Introdução á Arqueologia Naval: A Crítica da Documentação Plástica* (Introduction to naval archeology: A critique of plastic documentation [falsified documents]). 1973.

A. Teixeira da Mota. *O Comandante Abel Fontoura da Costa, Historiador da Marinha dos Descobrimentos* (The Commandant Abel Fontoura da Costa: Naval historian of discoveries). 1973.

Elaine Sanceau. *A Vida a Bordo duma Náu da Índia de Quinhentos* (The life on board a large Indiaman of the sixteenth century). 1974.

Dr. Alberto Iria Júnior. *Oficiais e Náus da Carreira da Índia no Século XVII (novos documentos do Arquivo Histórico Ultramarino)* (Officers and ships on the route to India in the seventeenth century [new documents from the naval historical archives]). 1974.

C/Alm. Ramos Pereira. *Henrique Lopes de Mendonça. Investigador e Historiógrafo de Alto Nivel Intelectual Que Muito Honrou o País e significou a Armada* (Henriques Lopes de Mendonça: Researcher and historian of an intelluctual high level that honored his country and dignified the navy very much). 1974.

Eng. Arantes e Oliveira. *A Engenharia de Estruturas, Especialidade Irmã da Arquitectura Naval* (Structural engineering, especially closely related with naval architecture). 1977.

Dr. Cortêz Pinto. *O Feitiço das Astronáuticas e as Três Divisas de D. Manuel* (The witchcraft of the astronautics and the three devices of D. Manuel). 1974.

Prof. Dr. Virgínia Rau. *Um Florentino ao Serviço da Expansão Ultramarina Portuguesa—Francisco Corbinelli* (A Florentine in the overseas expansion service of the Portuguese—Francisco Corbinelli). 1974.

Dr. José Pedro Machado. *Fim dos Medos Antigos no Atlântico* (The end of the ancient fears of the Atlantic). 1974.

Luís de Albuquerque. *O Códice de Bastião Lopes* (The codex of Bastiao Lopes). 1974.

José de Oiveira Boléo. *A Actividade Marítima no Índico e no Pacífico em Tempos Pregâmicos* (East Indian and Pacific maritime activity in the pre-gamic times). 1975.

Dr. Hernâni Cidade. *Fernando Oliveira, "Uomo Universale," Era Também Filósofo* (Fernando Oliveira "Universal Man," philosopher). 1976.

Alberto Cutileiro. *O Combate do Caça-Minas "Augusto de Castilho" Com o Submarino Alemão "U.139" Visto Através do Relatório do 1° Oficial* (The fight of the minesweeper *Augusto de Castilho* with the German submarine *U-139* as seen in the first officer's report). 1976.

Guilhermino de Magalhães. *A "Rota do Cabo" na Estratégia e na Economia do Ocidente* (The "Cape Route" in the strategy and economics of the West). 1976.

Octávio Lixa Filgueiras. *Comentários Técnicos da Tese do Moçarabismo Náutico* (Technical comments on the thesis of the Nautical Mozarabism). 1975.

Dr. Filipe F. Reis Thomaz. *Nina Chatu e o Comércio Português em Malaca* (Nina Chatu and Portuguese trade in Malacca). 1976.

Viriato Tadeu. *Aspectos da Crise do Petróleo* (Aspects of the fuel crisis). 1976.

Luís de Albuquerque. *Gil Eanes, o Cabo Bojador* (Gil Eanes and Cape Bojador). 1984.

Viriato de Sousa Campos. *Damião Gois—Humanista, Cronista e Mártir* (Damiao Gois—humanist, chronicler, and martyr). 1976.

João Farrajota Rocheta. *Os Navios de Carga e a Sua Evolução Futura* (Cargo ships and their future evolution). 1977.

A. Teixeira da Mota. *Acerca de Algumas Recentes Reuniões Internacionais de Interesse Para a História Marítima* (Concerning the several recent international reunions of interest to maritime historians). 1977.

Joaquim B. V. Soeiro de Brito. *Características Métricas de Alguns Sistemas Coordenados no Plano* (The metric characteristics of some coordinate systems in the plan). 1977.

Octávio Lixa Filgueiras. *A Jangada de S. Torpes—Um Problema de Arqueologia Naval* (The raft of St. Torpes—a problem of naval archeology). 1977.

Luís de Albuquerque. *Dois Documentos Sobre a Carreira do Trato de Moçambique* (Two documents about the trade route to Mozambique). 1977.

Braga Paixão. *Sá da Bandeira, Na Pasta da Marinha* (Sá da Bandeira, at the navy portfolio). 1974.

Octávio Lixa Filgueiras. *Museus de Marinha e de Arqueologia Naval* (Navy and naval archeology museums). 1978.

Eng. José Rodrigues dos Santos. *Marinha Mercante 1967–1968—Impacto da Revolução Tecnológica nos Armamentos Convencionais* (The merchant marine, 1967–1968—the impact of the technological revolution upon conventional armaments). 1978.

Viriato Tadeu. *Diaporama de Malta* (Diapositives [slides] of Malta). 1977.

Norberto Lopes. *A Magnífica Aventura de Gago Coutinho e Sacadura Cabral* (The magnificent adventure of Gago Coutinho and Sacadura Cabral). 1978.

Octávio Lixa Filgueiras. *A Propósito da Protecção Mágica dos Barcos* (About the magical protection of the ships). 1978.

António Cardoso. *Missão a Mombaça* (Mission to Mombassa). 1978.

A. Teixeira da Mota. *Cartas Portuguesas Antigas n Colecção de Groote Schuur* (Antique Portuguese maps collected by Groote Schuur). 1978.

Viriato Tadeu. *Evocação de Wenceslau de Moraes (diaporama do japão)* (The evocation [speech] of Wenceslau de Moraes [diapositives of Japan]). 1978.

Alberto Cutileiro. *Alguns Subsídios Para a História da Banda da Armada* (A few contributions toward the history of the navy band). 1981.

Barahona Fernandes. *Moderna Cartografia Náutica Portuguesa* (Modern Portuguese nautical cartography). 1978.

Dr. Luís Filipe Reis Thomaz. *Aspectos do Comércio Marítimo Português na Ásia do Sueste no Século XVI* (Aspects of Portuguese maritime trade with Southwest Asia in the sixteenth century). 1978.

Octávio Lixa Filgueiras. *Os Barcos da Nazaré no Panorama da Nossa Arqueologia Naval* (Ships of Nazaré in the panorama of our naval archeology). 1978.

Dr. Alexandre Marques Lobato. *Sobre a Intervenção Comercial Portuguesa no Oriente no Século XVI—Organizaçao, Formas e Métodos* (On Portuguese commercial intervention in the Orient in the sixteenth century—organization, forms, and methods). 1978

C/Alm. Emmanuel Ricou. *Os Barcos Vikingues de Roskilde e Sobre a Recuperação do Navio Wasa* (Viking ships from Roskilde and the recovery of the Wassan navy). 1978.

Gago de Medeiros. *Os Açores—Descobrimento, Geoestratégia, Guarnição, Geopolitica: Perspectivas Económicas* (The Azores—discovery, geostrategy, governance, geopolitics: Economic perspectives). 1981.

Dr. Hamo Sassoon. *Trabalhos de Arqueologia Submarina no Navio Portugês Afundado no Porto de Mombaça* (The work of the undersea archaeologists of the Portuguese ship sunk in the port of Mombassa). 1983.

António Tengarrinha Pires. *Caravelas dos Descobrimentos* (The caravelles of discovery). 1978/1990.

Romano Caldeira. *Correio Marítimo Português* (Portuguese maritime mail). 1981.

Emmanuel Ricou e António Cardoso. *A Participação do Museu de Marinha na 3ª. Conferência do Internacional Congress of Maritime Museums, realizada em Mystic Seaport* (Communications of the third conference of maritime museums held at Mystic Seaport [Conn., USA]). 1979/1980.

Braga Paixão. *O "Adamastor" Em Lourenço Marques em 1899* (The *Adamastor* in Lourenco Marques in 1899). 1981.

Academia de Marinha. *Sarmento Rodrigues In Memorian* (Memorial to Sarmento Rodriques). 1983.

Fernando Castelo Branco. *Subsídios Para a História do Bugio* (Contributions to a history of the "Bugio"). 1979/1980.

José da Cruz Moura da Fonseca. *A TSF na Armada—O seu Septuagésimo Aniversário e Algumas Páginas da Sua História* (The TSF of the Navy—on the 70th anniversary and some pages of his history). 1979/1980.

E. H. Serra Brandão. *A Nova Ordem Dos Oceânos* (The new order of the oceans). 1979/1980.

Eng. Viriato Tadeu. *Um Bosquejo Histórico da Cultura da Marinha e a Fundação da Casa Pia* (A historical outline of naval culture and the foundation of the Casa Pia). 1981.

Luís Valente de Oliveira. *A Elaboração de uma Carta de Princípios Para o Ordenamento do Litoral da Europa* (Elaboration of a chart of principal ports for the coast of Europe). 1979/1980.

Margarida Garcez Ventura. *Uma Época de Indefinição do Direito Marítimo—A Embaixada de João da Silveira em França (1512–1530)* (An epoch of uncertainty in maritime right—the embassy of Joao da Silveira in France [1512–1530]). 1981.

Ilídio do Amaral. *A Redescoberta do Mundo na Segunda Metade do Século XX—Missão Landsat* (The rediscovery of the world in the second half of the twentieth century—the Landsat mission). 1979/1980.

Dr. Luís de Albuquerque. *Uma Tradução Portuguesa de Navegação Especulativa de António Naiera* (A Portuguese translation of speculative navigation of Antonio Naiera). 1981.

Coronel Laguarda Trias. *Discordância Dimensional Entre El Atlântico Y El Mediterrâneo em Las Cartas Portulanas* (Conflicting measurements between the Atlantic and the Mediterranean on the Portulana maps). 1981.

Octávio Lixa Filgueiras. *Uma Presumível Herança Germânica na Construção Naval Tradicional Portuguesa* (A presumed German legacy in traditional Portuguese naval construction). 1979/1980.

Octávio Lixa Filgueiras. *Os Painéis Introdutórios da exposição de Oslo—critérios e conceitos* (Introductory pictures of the Oslo exposition—standards and concepts). 1981.

C/Alm. Manuel E. Leal Vilarinho. *Alguns Aspectos da Paremiologia: A Influência da Expansão Marítima nos Provérbios Portugueses.* (Some aspects of myology: The influence of maritime expansion on Portuguese proverbs). 1981.

Eng. Viriato Tadeu. *Evocação de Sacadura Cabral* (Evocation of Sacadura Cabral). 1982.

Francisco Alberto Cutileiro. *Bocage Guarda-Marinha—A Sua Vida e A Sua Época* (Naval Cadet Bocage—his life and his epoch). 1982.

Francisco Alberto Cutileiro. *Posto de Capitão-de-Mar-e-Guerra da Armada Real e o seu Primeiro Regimento* (The rank of flag captain of the Royal Fleet and its first rule). 1982.

Nuno Valdez dos Santos. *Setecentos Anos de Estudos Navais em Portugal* (Seven hundred years of naval studies in Portugal). 1985.

Herculano Vilela. *Atuns de Portugal Continental* (Tunnies of continental Portugal). 1982.

Academia de Marinha. *Teixeira da Mota (1920–1982). In Memorian* (Memorial to Teixeira da Mota [1920–1982]). 1982.

José Nogueira Rodrigues Branco. *O Grande Estaleiro Naval do Estuário do Tejo* (The great naval dockyard in the Tagus Estuary). 1982.

Alberto Cutileiro. *A Origem do Glorioso Corpo de Fuzileiros da Armada* (On the origins of the glorious corps of fleet fusiliers [shipboard marines]). 1982.

Henrique Alexandre da Fonseca. *A Propósito do Bicentenário da Criação da Companhia de Guard-Marinhas e da Sua Academia* (About the bicentennial of the raising of the naval-cadet company and its academy). 1982.

Octávio Lixa Filgueiras. *Introdução ao Caderno de Todos os Barcos do Tejo Tanto de Carga e Transporte Como de Pesca, por João de Sousa, Lente d'Arquitectura Naval* (Introduction to the notebook of all vessels on the Tagus both cargo and transport as well as fishing vessels by Joao de Sousa, professor of naval architecture). 1985.

E. H. Serra Brandão. *As Relações Internacionais Antes de Hugo Grotius* (International relationships before Hugo Grotius). 1983.

Joaquim B. V. Soeiro de Brito. *Características Métricas de Alguns Sistemas Coordenados na Esfera* (Metric characteristics of some coordinate systems in the sphere). 1983.

V/Alm. Pedro Fragoso de Matos. *As Origens da Baía do Lobito* (On the sources of Lobito Bay). 1983.

António Tengarrinha Pires. *A Caravela dos Descobrimentos II (A—Mareação de Bolina)* (The Caravelles of Discovery II [A. Hauling the wind sailing]). 1983.

Eng. José Carlos Gonçalves Viana. *O Mar Nas Origens e No Futuro de Portugal (numa perspectiva tecnológica)* (The sea in the past and future of Portugal from a technological perspective). 1984.

Henrique Alexandre da Fonseca. *A Colónia de Sacramento* (The Sacramento settlement). 1984.

Nuno Valdez dos Santos. *A Hierarquia Naval* (The naval hierarchy). 1984.

Prof. Dr. Luís de Albuquerque. *Gil Eanes e o Cabo Bojador* (Gil Eanes and Cape Bojador). 1984.

Guimarães Lobato, Lixa Filgueiras, Manuel Carrelhas, Rodrigues Branco, Santos Viegas, and M. Leitão. *1º. Painel das Caravelas* (The first panel on caravelas). 1984.

José V. Carneiro e Menezes. *Medidas Sanitárias ao Tempo de D. Afonso V e de D. João II* (Sanitary measures at the time of King Alfonso V and of King John II). 1985.

Maria Emília Madeira Santos. *Capelo e Ivens, Um Fecho Europeu Para Uma Tradição Nacional* (Copelo and Ivens: A European close to a national tradition). 1985.

Dr. Brian R. Stuckenberg. *Recent Studies of Historic Portuguese Shipwrecks in South Africa.* 1985.

V/Alm. António Tengarrinha Pires. *Caravela dos Descobrimentos II (B—Uso da Bolina)* (Caravels of discovery II [B. The use of the bowline]). 1985.

Nuno Valdez dos Santos. *A Artilharia Naval e os Canhões do Galeão "Santiago"* (Naval gunnery and the cannons of the galleon *Santiago*). 1985.

J. N. Rodrigues Branco. *Utilização da Fotografia na Obtenção de Formas de Casco de Uma Embarcação* (Use of photography to obtain the shape of the hull of a vessel). 1985.

Gabriel Lobo Fialho. *Atuns das Ilhas Adjacentes—Auxílio na Sua Captura por Métodos de Detecção Remota* (Tunnies of the adjacent islands—aid for fishing for them by methods of remote detection). 1986.

Dr. Francisco C. Domingues. *Problemas e Perspectivas da Arqueologia Naval Portuguesa dos Séculos XV–XVII; Obra Historiográfica de João da Gama Pimentel Barata* (Problems and perspectives of Portuguese naval archeology of the fifteenth to seventeenth centuries: The historical work of Joao da Gama Pimentel Barata). 1986.

Academia de Marinha; Eng. F. Rocheta. *Evocação da Memória de Cap. M.G. EMQ José Rodrigues dos Santos* (An evocation of the memory of Flag Captain Jose Rodrigues dos Santos). 1986.

Cte. António Estãcio dos Reis. *O Dique da Ribeira das Naus* (The dam of "Ribeira das Naus"). 1988.

José V. Carneiro e Menezes. *Almirante—O Termo e o Seu Significado* (Admiral—the term and its significance). 1988.

Eng. Carlos R. Lourenço. *Notas Sobre a Navegação ao Tempo das Descobertas* (Some notes on navigation at the time of the discoveries). 1986.

Cor. Nuno Valdez dos Santos. *Pedras Que Falam do Mar* (Stones that speak of the sea). 1986.

Prof. Arq. Lixa Filgueiras. *Na Descoberta de Portugal* (Discovering Portugal). 1987.

Cte. Henrique da Fonseca. *O Arsenal da Ribeira do Ouro* (The arsenal of the Ribeira de Ouro). 1987.

Coronel Laguarda Trias. *Pilotos Portugueses En El Rio de La Plata Durante El Siglo XVI* (Portuguese pilots in the Rio de la Plata in the sixteenth century). 1992.

José V. Carneiro e Menezes. *Apoio Sanitário nas Armadas de Outrora* (The medical support of our former navy). 1987.

V/Alm. António Tengarrinha Pires. *Caravela dos Descobrimentos II (C—Bolina na Costa Portuguesa)* (Caravels of the discoveries II. [C—bowline on the Portuguese coast]). 1987.

Cte. Saturnino Monteiro. *A Propósito da Batalha do Golfo de Oman; Sugestão de Corrigenda às Legendas de Dois Desenhos de Uma das Estampas da "Portugali Monumenta Cartografica"* (About the Battle of the Gulf of Oman: Suggestions for correcting one of the Plates of the "Portuguese Monument Cartographic"). 1988.

Dr. Maria Emília Madeira Santos, Dr. Francisco Contente Domingues, Cte. Gabriel Lobo Fialho. *X Aniversário do Instituto Nacional de Portos. "Notas Para a História dos Pilotos em Portugal" "Pilotagem, uma Arte ou Uma Ciência?"* (Tenth anniversary of the National Institute for Harbors: Notes for a history of Pilotage in Portugal. Pilotage: An art or a science?). 1988.

Eng. Carlos Lourenço. *A 5ª. Volta do Largo—As Navegações Atlticas a Rodear Ventos Ponteiros* (The fifth turn out to sea—the Atlantic navigations skirting the contrary winds). 1988.

Cor. Valdez dos Santos. *A Marinha na Época da Restauração* (The navy of the period of the restoration). 1988.

Prof. Fukuo Shibata, Eng. Viriato Tadeu. *Propulsão Electromagnética de Navios. Sonho ou Realidade em Marcha* (Electromagnetic propulsion of ships: Dream or reality?). 1988.

Cte. Estãcio dos Reis. *Concerto Para Dois Globos* (Agreement between two globes). 1988.

Dr. Maria Emília Madeira Santos. *João Pereira Dantas, um Homen da Expansão Europeia. A Experiência na Carreira da Índia. The notícia na Corte de Paris* (Joao Pereira Dantas: A man of the European expansion. The experiences of the career of India, news in the court of Paris). 1988.

Cte. Henrique Alexandre da Fonseca. *A Propósito da Passagem do 4º. Centenãrio da Derrotta da Invencível Armada* (About the fourth centenary of the defeat of the Invincible Armada). 1988.

Cor. Valdez dos Santos. *Um Desconhecido Tratado de Marinharia do Século XVIII* (An unknown naval treaty of the eighteenth century). 1989.

Cte. Eduardo Henrique Serra Brandão. *A Equidade na Delimitação dos Espaços Marítimos* (Toward equity in the demarcation of maritime spaces). 1989.

V/Alm. Henrique Afonso da Silva Horta. *Poluição Marítima* (Maritime pollution). 1989.

Cte. António Pereira Cardoso. *Os Descobrimentos Marítimos, as Plantas e os Animais* (Maritime discoveries—plants and animals). 1989.

Cte. Henrique Alexandre da Fonseca. *Os Estaleiros da Ribeira das Naus* (The shipyards of the *Ribeira das Naus*). 1989.

V/Alm. António Tengarrinha Pires. *Caravela dos Descobrimentos II—A Caravela de Meados do Século XV* (The caravel of discoveries II—a caravel of the middle of the fifteenth century). 1990.

Coronel Nuno Valdez dos Santos. *A Representação das Armas Nacionais nas Peças de Artilharia* (The representation of the national arms in artillery guns). 1991.
V/Alm. Afonso da Silva Horta. *A Marinha, Ramo das Forças Armadas e Serviço Público* (The navy: Branch of the armed forces and public service). 1990.
Cap. Ten. Maestro Manuel Baltazar. *A Música na Vida do Homem do Mar* (Music in the life of sailors). 1990.
Cte. António Cardoso. *A Viagem de Bartolomeu Dias em 1487/8 Vista Por Um Marinheiro* (The voyage of Bartolomeu Dias in 1487/8 seen by a sailor). 1990.
Dr. Francisco J. S. Alves. *A Arqueologia Subaquática em Portugal. Uma Questão Inadíavel* (Underseas archeology in Portugal: An urgent search). 1990.
Cte. António Luciano Estácio dos Reis. *Uma Oficina de Instrumentos Náuticos na Fábrica da Cordoaria* (Nautical workshop instruments at the Cordoaria factory). n.d.
Cte. Armando Saturnino Monteiro. *O Poder Naval Português, Esse Desconhecido* (Portuguese naval power, that unknown). 1992.
Dr. Rebbeca Catz. *Cristóvão Colombo nos Açores* (Christopher Columbus at the Azores). 1991.
Cte. António Sérgio Pereira Cardoso. *A Epopeia dos Descobrimentos Maritimos Continua-se nas Bandeiras no Brasil* (The epic of the maritime discoveries continued in the "Bandeiras" of Brazil). 1991.
Cte. António Luciano Estãcio dos Reis. *O Primeiro Navio Português que Atravessou o Canal de Suez* (The first Portuguese naval vessel to traverse the Suez Canal). 1991.
Eng. José Carlos Gonçalves Viana. *Uma Estratégia Para a Marinha Mercante Portuguesa* (A strategy for the Portuguese merchant marine). 1991.
Prof. Manuel Cadafaz de Matos. *No Segundo Centenário da Viagem filosófica de Alexandre Rodrigues Ferreira, Por Terras do Brasil* (In the second century of the philosophical travel of Alexandre Rodriques Ferreira, through the lands of Brazil). 1991.
Prof. Dr. Per M. Bruun. *Sea Level Rise and Its Consequences for Coastal Areas.* 1991.
Alm. Rogério de Oliveira, C/Alm. António Malheiro do Vale, Cte. António J. da Silva Soares. *Sessão Comemorativa do 70°. Aniversãrio da 1ª. Travessia Aérea no Atlântico Sul por Sacadura Cabral e Gago Coutinho em 1922* (The commemorative session of the seventieth anniversary of the first aerial crossing of the South Atlantic by Sacadura Cabral and Gago Coutinho in 1922). 1992.
Cor. Nuno Valdez dos Santos. *Os Regimentos Navais do Marquês de Pombal* (The naval regiments of the Marquis de Pombal). 1992.
Dr. Jean-Ives Blot, Dr. Maria Luisa Blot. *O Interface História-Arqueologia: O Naufrágio do "San Pedro de Alcântara" Peniche 1786* (The interface between history and archaeology: The wreck of the *San Pedro de Alcantara* in Peniche 1786). 1992.

Eng. Carlos Eugénio R. Lourenço. *Desde Quando se Mediram Alturas dos Astros no Mar?* (When was the altitude of the stars first measured at sea?). 1992.

Prof. Dr. Carlos Almaça. *Viagem Filosófica de Alexandre Rodrigues Ferreira no Contexto Histórico-Natural da Sua Época* (The philosophical voyage of Alexandre Rodrigues Ferreira in the historic natural context of his epoch). 1992.

Dr. Ângela Domingues. *Um Novo Conceito de Ciência ao Serviço da Razão de Estado: A Viagem de Alexandre Rodrigues Ferreira ao Norte Brasileiro* (A new idea of science in the service of reasons of state: The travel of Alexandre Rodrigues Ferreira to Northern Brazil). 1992.

Dr. Miguel Faria. *A Escola de Desenhadores de História Natural da Ajuda e a Viagem Filosófica de Alexandre Rodrigues Ferreira* (The directors school of natural history of the Ajuda and the philosophical voyage of Alexandre Rodrigues Ferreira). 1992.

Dr. Fernando Lourenço Fernandes. *A Armada de 1500 e as Singularidades de Arribada na Escala do Atlântico-Sul* (The fleet of 1500 and the singularities of arrival at the South Atlantic latitudes). 1993.

Prof. Dr. Humberto Baquero Moreno. *A Navegação Entre Douro e Minho na Idade Média* (The navigation between the Douro and the Minho rivers in the Middle Ages). 1993.

Dr. Rainer Daehnhardt. *Origens Desconhecidas da Construção Naval em Portugal* (The unknown origins of naval construction in Portugal). 1993.

Dr. Maria Benedita Almeida Araújo. *Enfermidades e Medicamentos nas Naus Portuguesas (Séc. XVI a XVIII)* (Illnesses and medications in Portuguese vessels from the sixteenth through the eighteenth centuries). 1993.

Cte. Saturnino Monteiro. *A Evolução do Pensamento Naval Português* (The evolution of Portuguese naval thought). 1993.

Eng. José Caro Proença. *Encobrimentos nos Descobrimentos* (Conquerors of the discoveries). 1993.

Eng. José de Almeida Santos. *As Berlengas e os Piratas* (The Berlengas and the pirates). 1994.

Cte. António Cardoso. *A Provável Viagem de Cristovão de Mendonça à Australia em 1522* (The probable route of Cristovao de Mendonca to Australia in 1522). 1994.

Manuel Fernandes. *Livro das Traças de Carpintaria* (The book of carpentry plans). 1989.

Fernando de Oliveira. *Livro da Fábrica das Naus* (The book of Shipbuilding). 1991.

José de Vasconcellos e Menezes. *Armadas Portuguesas—Os Marinheiros e o Almirantado* (Portuguese fleets—sailors and the admiralty). 1989.

José de Vasconcellos e Menezes. *Armadas Portuguesas—Apoio Sanitário* (Portuguese fleets—medical support). 1987.

José de Vasconcellos e Menezes. *Armadas Portuguesas—Hospitais no Além Mar na Época dos Descobrimentos* (Portuguese fleets—overseas hospitals in the age of discoveries). 1993.

António Estácio dos Reis. *O Dique da Ribeira das Naus* (The dam of the shipbuilding river).

Fernando Pedrosa. *Cristovão Colombo—Corsário em Portugal 1469–1485* (Christopher Columbus: Corsair in Portugal, 1469–1485). 1989.

Dr. J. Alberto Iria. *As Caravelas do Infante e os Caíques do Algarve* (The prince's caravels and the Algarvian caiques). 1991.

Edições Conjuntas da Academia de Marinha e Instituto de Investigação Cientifica e Tropical. *Vice-Almirante A. Teixeira da Mota In Memorian* (In memory of Vice-Admiral A. Teixeira da Mota). 1982.

Cte. António Marques Esparteiro. *O General dos Galeões do Estado da Índia—António de Figueiredo e Utra (1678–1751)* (The general condition of India galleons—Antonio de Figueiredo e Utra [1678–1751]). 1982.

Cte. António Marques Esparteiro. *Catálogo dos Navios Brigantinos (1640–1910)* (Catalogue of brigantine vessels [1640–1910]). 1976.

M. M. Sarmento Rodrigues. *Relatório da Viagem Aérea Lisboa—Rio de Janeiro por Sacadura Cabral e Gago Coutinho* (Report of the flight from Lisbon to Rio de Janiero by Sacadura Cabral and Gago Coutinho). 1922.

Cte. Sousa Machado. *Centenário de Hermenegildo Capelo e Roberto Ivens* (The centennial of Hermenegildo Capelo and Roberto Ivens).

Cor. Nuno Valdez dos Santos. *Apontamentos para a História da Marinha Portuguesa* (Notes for the history of the Portuguese navy). 1991.

António Marques Esparteiro. *Dicionário de Marinha (Português–Inglês)* (Portuguese–English naval dictionary). 1975.

António Marques Esparteiro. *Dictionary of Naval Terms (English–Portuguese).* 1974.

António Marques Esparteiro. *Três Datas Que Importam à Independência do Brasil* (Three dates important to the independence of Brazil). 1972.

Humberto Leitão. *O Régulo Timorense D. Aleixo Corte-Real* (D. Alexio, the little king of East Timor). 1970.

V. Rau, V. Campos, A. Júnior, J. Barata. *Elementos da História da Ilha de S. Tomé* (Elements of the history of the island of São Tomé). 1971.

A. J. da Silva Soares. *Macau à Margem dos Arranha-Céus—Album de Aguarelas* (From Macao to Margem on the *Arranha-Céus*—album of watercolors). 1993.

Vários. *I Simpósio de História Marítima—As Navegações Portuguesas no Atlântico e o Descobrimento da América* (First Symposium on Naval History—Portuguese navigation on the Atlantic and the discovery of America). 1994.

Inácio Guerreiro. *A Carta Náutica de Jorge de Aguiar de 1492* (The 1492 nautical chart of Jorge de Aguiar). 1992.

Vários. *Memórias da Academia de Marinha,* Volume I (1971), II (1972), III (1973), IV (1974), V (1975), VI (1976), VII (1978), VIII (1978), IX (1979/80), X (1981), XI (1982), XII (1983), XIII (1984), XIV (1985), XV (1986), XVI (1987), XVII (1988), XVIII (1989), XIX (1990), XX (1991) (Memories of the Naval Academy).

18

South Africa

South African State and State-Sponsored Military Historical Research, 1924–1995

Colonel Dr. Jan Ploeger, Former Chief
Translated by Major I. J. van der Waag, M.M.M.

In its simplest form, history is the expressed memories of the past resulting from a human need to know the origin of a matter or an issue. These expressed memories are carried over either orally or in writing. Already in the fifth century before Christ, the Greek historian Thucydides (c.471 B.C.–c.400 B.C.), consciously strove to obtain the closest possible verisimilitude to the actual events which took place during the Peloponesian wars (431 B.C.–404 B.C.). In this respect, this early historian already jostled such factors as objectivity and subjectivity.

Those historians who, through the centuries, were honest with themselves, with the available sources, and with their future readers came to the increasing realization that absolute objectivity was impossible. With this conviction, the historian must nevertheless continually strive for the highest degree of objectivity and attempt to reach the truth.[1] Not all historians have always been willing or able to follow this golden rule; and today numerous examples in this regard can be encountered.

Over centuries of historical practice, the field of study for researchers and writers increased considerably and split into the various subdivisions, as, for example, political history and cultural history. Both military history and research have always been particularly popular. J. Huizinga declared that military history, as a division of cultural or technical history, maintains an independent and important place within the general concept of history.[2] Examples are

Sir Edward Creasy's *The Fifteen Decisive Battles of the World: From Marathon to Waterloo* (London, 1887) and Lt. Alfred von Müller's *Der Krieg in Süd-Afrika 1899/1900 und seine Vorgeschichte* (Berlin, 1900).

Sir Edward Creasy's then-authoritative study first appeared in 1851 and by 1887 had seen thirty-two reprints. He concentrated only on battles and in his introduction emphasized: "how the chain of circumstances is to be linked together, that the smallest skirmish, or the slightest occurrence of any kind, that ever occurred, may be said to have been essential, in its actual termination to the whole order of subsequent events."[3]

Lt. von Müller, in turn, began with a concise political history of the Boer republics and with statistics on the opposing forces, before devoting himself fully to military events.[4]

In our own century, the practice of descriptive military history has gone its course, while at the same time attention has been given to military history and research. The following example clearly shows the differences between the various fields of the practitioners of the mentioned schools.

In the foreword to *Je Maintiendrai; A Concise History of the Dutch Army* (The Hague, 1985), the editors of this study declared

> Although the authors of this survey of Dutch military history certainly do not ignore campaigns and battles, they make it clear that the description of an army in peacetime cannot only be just as fascinating as what has been described as drum-and-trumpet history, but certainly as instructive for the purpose of gaining an understanding of the course of historical events.
>
> After all, once it is decided to continue a political struggle by military means, and the writers of battle histories proceed to sharpen their pencils, it will still take some considerable time before any army can be raised from scratch.[5]

The editors went on to add, "The outcome of military confrontations usually depends more on the organization, training, discipline and other facets of any army in peacetime than on the ingenious tactical instinct of a commander during the fighting itself."[6]

When these expositions are accepted, it follows that military history and military-historical research embraces campaign history, unit and regimental history, and so on.

The publications of Dr. H. H. Curson, one of South Africa's pioneers with regard to certain aspects of military history, fall within this framework. Curson was a prolific writer and produced inter alia *Colours and Honours in South Africa, 1783–1948* (1948); *Regimental Devices in South Africa, 1783–1954* (1954); *The S.A. Field Artillery in German East Africa and Palestine, 1915–19* (1958, with Brigadier F. B. Adler and Major A. E. Lorch); and *The History of the Kimberley Regiment* (1963).[7]

Of importance too, are the views expressed by Peter Warwick and Professor S. B. Spies in their introduction to *The South African War—The Anglo–Boer War, 1899–1902* (London, 1980). They concentrated attention on the following aspects:

> The book is organized in three parts: the advent of war, the war itself, and its aftermath. Each part is opened by a short narrative account of the period under review. The chapters that follow deal with both the *military* and *political history* of the war, and above all, with its *social history*, an element that has often been neglected in the past.[8]

AIMS OF EARLY WRITERS: PROBLEMS

In light of these observations, it is enlightening to concentrate on the aims of early writers on the Anglo–Boer War (1899–1902) and also to spend a little time studying the problems they encountered.

The Transvaal official war historian, N. Hofmeyr (1880–1932), who before the war taught history at the Pretoria State Gymnasium, started during the first months of the war with the writing of *Zes maanden bij de Commando's* (Six months with the commandos) and completed the work in April 1901 in Oudtshoorn.[9]

What goals did this first official war historian of the South African Republic set for himself? His work was, as he himself stated, not meant to defend or refute one or other favorite tenet with regard to the war. He also avoided giving criticism and avoided the field of politics. He wanted to tell what he saw, experienced, thought, and felt while he participated in the war. He stood on the side of the republics and made no claim to "*schoon-klinkende, maar voor de meeste menschen onmogelijke onpartijdigheid*" (nice sounding, but for most people impossible impartiality). And to this meaning Hofmeyr added that it did not prevent him from seeing the good and noble in the opposing party.

His driving force in this regard was that the gulf between the two White races was already so large and reconciliation and cooperation between them was so necessary for the material, intellectual, moral, and religious well-being of South Africa that it was the duty of every patriot to assist with the closing of the gulf and the promotion of desirable harmony.[10]

While Hofmeyr frankly stated his point of view, the Dutch writer W. F. Andriessen in the foreword to his *Gedenkboek van den oorlog in Zuid-Afrika* (Amsterdam–Cape Town, 1904) posed a number of questions to his readers: Had the time already arrived to place the war in an impartial, historical light? Is it within human reach, after everything that had been said and written during the struggle, to obtain the truth?[11] But Andriessen's all-important question was whether there was anybody in the world who had sufficient, authentic documents to make a just opinion. Such an opinion, according to Andriessen, could not be troubled by biased glorification or vituperation.

While he thus saw these questions and hurdles, Andriessen came to the conclusion that he could collect the facts and arrange them chronologically. These facts could then be presented—without partial views and prejudiced opinions—to the reader. In this way, the recollection of important events could be preserved and planted in the memory of the next generation. It would also apply to collected examples of patriotism, courage and contempt of death, faithfulness, and the performance of duty.

Andriessen was convinced that combatants on both sides believed that they had entered the war for a noble purpose: The Boer wanted to free himself from British interference, while his opponent was brought up with the proud belief that each attack on the authority of the monarchy was intolerable. This writer saluted all the fallen soldiers.[12]

Already before Andriessen presented these thoughts to his readers, Captain Dr. W. Vallentin's two-part work entitled *Der Burenkrieg* appeared in Leipzig.[13] This writer, who had spent some time in the South African Republic before the war, clearly stated that his work did not have a military-scientific nature. It was also not his intention to produce romantically colored war experiences. He intended to present to the German people a detailed, understandable, and unvarnished description of the great freedom struggle. The tragic end to this struggle brought embitterment to the heart of every thinking person. Captain Dr. Valletin further expressed the wish that his work would be a monument to the great heroic struggle that his Germanic kinsmen in South Africa had made for freedom and justice.[14]

Even earlier, in 1902, the first volume of the standard reference work *The Times History of the War in South Africa, 1899–1900*, had appeared in London under the editorship of L. S. Amery.[15] In his introduction, Amery stressed the desirability first to sketch prewar political developments. This was done from a historical perspective, Amery added, "though at so short an interval of time from the events themselves it is impossible altogether, on some occasions, to avoid a controversial tone. Absolute impartiality in dealing with so momentous and so recent a conflict of political principles and political ambitions is perhaps hardly attainable."[16]

Furthermore, Amery frankly declared that the first volume was written by himself from this point of view; and to this he connected the thought "that the essential right and justice of the controversy have been with his own country, and that the policy which has been pursued by the British Government has been both politically and morally, justifiable."[17]

The second volume of the series appeared on 11 April 1902 and Amery explained that he first had to describe the historical development, the organization, and the most notable characteristics of the two strong, disparate military systems before he could commence with the story of the armed struggle.

Amery emphasized that he, in contrast to Dr. Conan Doyle, always worked critically and did not escape by using a picturesque, imaginative style. According to himself, he strove to present his readers with the story as it really happened. To Amery, his story was critical, but at the same time impartial and unprejudiced. He also emphasized that he wrote his work after he had thoroughly consulted and evaluated all of the available sources.

If Amery had already received information from all quarters, he was aware of the inclusion of incorrect facts and faulty conclusions. He exploded these errors, presenting his criticism in full.[18]

These examples of writers who concentrated on the Second Anglo–Boer War (1899–1902) during or shortly after the sweeping event is only a limited sample. This is also the case of the various goals they set themselves and also with regard to the questions which vexed them.

The first part of *Die Kämpfe der deutschen Truppen in Südwestafrika* (Berlin, 1906), a publication produced by Military History Section Number 1 of the German general staff, appeared in 1906.[19] The building materials for this official publication were of official origin. Before these details appeared in book form, they were published as articles in the quarterly journal *Viertelheften für Truppenführung und Heereskunde*. The purpose of the publicity, which was officially given to the German campaign against the Heroro's, was to give the German people a view of the hardships of the German troops in the field and their courageous action in combat. These achievements deserved the gratitude of the country and the general staff saw it as their duty to release a picture of the campaign. For this reason, the book was published before all of the pertinent sources were available.

SOUTH AFRICAN OFFICIAL MILITARY-HISTORICAL WRITING RESULTING FROM THE UNION'S PARTICIPATION IN THE FIRST WORLD WAR (1914–1918)

Two years after the formation of the Union of South Africa (1910), the young state, by Act No. 13 of 1912 (the *Defence Act*), had a defense organization with provision for a Permanent Force, a Coast Garrison Force, an Active Citizen Force, various reserves and a cadet organization.[20]

The First World War broke out in 1914 and on 4 August Britain, together with the entire British Empire, including the Union of South Africa, entered the struggle. Six days later the Union cabinet, under Prime Minister General Louis Botha (1862–1919), declared its willingness to invade German South West Africa. The House of Assembly approved this decision by a large majority (92–12). There was resistance among the Afrikaners who, under the leadership of men like General C. R. de Wet (1854–1922), Brigadier General C. F. Beyers (1869–1914), and others, started the "armed protest" or "rebellion."

By February 1915 this event belonged to the past and the government, after having despatched troops to Port Nolloth and Lüderitz Bay, gave its full attention to military operations against German South West Africa.[21]

After the end of the campaign, Union troops were sent to the Western Front (France) and German East Africa, where they were still in the field at the cessation of hostilities in November 1918.

In total, some 140,000 White troops, 200 nurses, 1,900 Coloured soldiers, and approximately 15,000 members of the native labor contingents served on the various fronts. Some 120,000 uniformed members of the Union Defence Force served on the home front.[22]

During the term of office of Colonel Hendrik Mentz, DTD, as Minister of Defense, the official publication *The Union of South Africa and The Great War 1914–1918* appeared in 1924. The order for the printing of the book was given to the government printer on 17 October 1923.[23] One thousand copies were printed. The printer and distributer of this valuable work of 230 pages, which was compiled by the general staff in Pretoria, was the South African government printer and the price per copy was fixed at fifteen shillings and six pence.

As far as can be ascertained, the writer of this official war history was Captain (later Major) J.G.W. Leipoldt, a brother of the famous poet–writer–doctor Christian Frederik Louis Leipoldt (1880–1947). Regarding this officer, it is known that he was on the staff of the South African Military School in Bloemfontein in 1913 and that he served with Captain Nobbs in the Intelligence Service during the German Southwest Africa Campaign.[24] The foreword of the official history declared, "The main purpose kept in view has been to record the effort and achievement of South Africa as a whole, bearing in mind the old adage 'too may trees and one fails to see the wood.'"[25] As result of this policy, the description of the achievements of the various units and regiments was left to the historians who would write these detailed histories.

According to the writer, South Africa's participation in the First World War did not come about without problems. One of these was the fact that the war efforts of the other dominions were centralized and of the same nature. South African activities, on the other hand, as a result of circumstances, did not bear much relation to each other.[26]

There were the operations in connection with the capture of certain objectives in German South West Africa. As a result of the rebellion in the Union, these operations had to be stopped briefly. Attention was temporarily given to the quelling of the rebellion and thereafter the campaign was continued. There was talk of two, even three related enterprises which in other respects differed greatly.

While the rebellion was sketched to show the connection with the military activities in German South West Africa, the actual war in this area started and finished in 1915.

Thereafter, a successful attempt was made in the Union to raise an infantry brigade under Brigadier General Henry Timson (Tim) Lukin (1860–1925) to represent South Africa on the Western Front (France). These troops arrived in England for training in November 1915, and a month later were sent to Egypt where they helped defeat the Senussi. Thereafter the brigade left for service in France, where they entered the line on the Somme.

Ample place was given in the *Official History* for the description of the battles for Deville Wood (Bois d'Elville), Warlencourt, Arras (Atrecht), the third battle for Ieper, and the German offensive (November 1917–March 1918), as well as battles of the final year of the war (1918). Sufficient attention is given to that part of the campaign in German East Africa which led to the assumption of the Allied command by Lieutenant General J. C. Smuts (1870–1950), in February 1916. As is known, General von Lettow Vorbeck and his troops surrendered on 25 November 1918 at Abercorn.

Some 182 pages of the *Official History* are dedicated to South African participation on the various fronts. The text is illustrated with photographs and maps and the whole forms a reliable, understandable, reasonably superficial guide for laymen and academics who desire more knowledge on and insight into the subject in question.

The book closes with valuable data on the role of the South African heavy artillery, the South African Signal Company, the South African Medical Corps, the railway and other specialized companies, including the Cape Coloured transport companies, the administration, a list of South Africans who were awarded the Victoria Cross, and a list of casualties.[27]

With the publication of the *Official History*, a particularly readable source of military-historical value was sent into the world. It was and still is a monument of lasting value with regard to the South Africans who participated in the titanic struggle, in which more than 12,000 individuals brought the greatest offering—their lives (8,551 Whites, 709 Coloureds, 3,192 Blacks).

Years before this official publication saw the light, Lieutenant General J. C. Smuts had emphasized that many of the less important theaters of the First World War would demand the attention of historians and military students as the campaigns launched in these regions took place under unusual circumstances. General Louis Botha's campaign in German South West Africa, according to Smuts, would always serve as a model desert campaign. In his opinion, the enemy made the mistake of believing that supply and transport problems (of inter alia water) would be insurmountable for the attacker. A brilliant and daring strategy showed the contrary. The 1916 campaign in German East Africa is a striking example of a successful military operation in a tropical theater. Despite a determined enemy, natural obstacles, and climatological problems, a large area was occupied within ten months.[28]

BRIGADIER GENERAL J. J. COLLYER'S IMPORTANT PUBLICATIONS OF 1937 AND 1939

In 1936 Brigadier General J. J. Collyer, CB, CMG, DSO, the former chief of the general staff of the Union Defence Force (UDF), during the campaigns in German South West and German East Africa, rounded off the introduction to an important military-historical study, which appeared as an official publication under the title, *The Campaign in German South West Africa 1914–1915* (Pretoria, 1937).

In his introduction, the writer emphasized the following valuable statement: "We learn wisdom from failure much more than from success. We often discover what will do by finding out what will not do; and probably he who never made a mistake never made a discovery."[29] It was as a result of this statement that Brig. Gen. Collyer strove, in his study, to emphasis previous mistakes. In so doing he wished to prevent the same errors from reoccurring under similar circumstances in the future.

One of the mistakes of 1914, according to him, was that with the exception of a small cadre of professional soldiers, use was made of members of the Active Citizen Force (ACF). The ACF was numerically too small and an unforeseen and thus unplanned expansion had to take place. Such a situation should be prevented in the future by immediately expanding the Permanent Force.[30]

In Chapter 14, the writer made a number of disparate suggestions as a means, in the case of future war, to prevent the mistakes of the past. In 1914 there was inter alia a shortage of trained staff officers and in the future commanders and troops, who would have to participate in mobile warfare, would have to receive better training than was the case in the past.[31]

These remarks are but a few of those mentioned and discussed in Collyer's publication. This book, in essence a training manual, could also claim more comprehensivity than the part in the *Official History* of 1924 dealing with the same subject.

A large number of excellent maps were added to the text and by this means a distinguished academic study of the first campaign was produced independently by the Union of South Africa.[32] This publication carries the characteristics of a military history with a didactic and moralizing approach. In 1939, a translated version of the 1937 study appeared under the title, *Die veldtog in Duits Suidwes-Afrika 1914–1915*.[33] In May of the same year, Brig. Gen. Collyer published his next study, *The South Africans with General Smuts in German East Afrika 1916* (Pretoria, 1939), and the translation, *Die Suid-Afrikaners met Generaal Smuts in Duits Oos-Afrika 1916* (Pretoria, 1939). Both publications were official and, like their predecessors, were published by the government printer in Pretoria.[34]

As in his previous study, the writer also emphasized the value of military experience and the study thereof in this publication. From such a study, in his opinion, they could only benefit. On the grounds of this conviction, he included the following quote from De Peucker in his introduction: "In peace time history becomes the true means of learning war and of determining the fixed principles of the art of war."[35]

In his introduction the writer further emphasized, inter alia, that the Union troops in 1916 acquired extremely valuable experience of warfare in an exceptionally difficult terrain—namely, East Africa. Collyer was furthermore of the opinion that each future war in Africa, south of the equator, would become more important, as this would be the arena for the application of South African troops in a war for the defense of the Union. In this connection, the writer referred to a declaration by the Union's Minister of Defense on 13 October 1937 that the military policy was based on the supposition that the Union would remain a member of the British Commonwealth. He further surmised that the Union Defence Force would see combat on the African continent and that the theater of war would lie between the Cape of Good Hope and the equator.[36]

A foreword by General J. C. Smuts preceded this introduction. He, too, emphasized the didactic aspects of the writer's work and recommended the book to those students interested in tropical warfare. He believed that Brig. Gen. Collyer's work was more a military-technical overview of the war. It was, in his opinion, the splendid story of an enormous human achievement, in which the Belgian and South African troops, the actual heroes of the campaign, were praised.

To this Smuts added the following thoughts:

> They have received scant recognition. After all, was East Africa not one of the little side-shows of the Great War? The honours have gone to those of their comrades who went to the Western Front. Deville Wood, Marrières Wood and other battle centres in France are the high lights in the South African War record.
>
> Let us not grudge the heroes of the Western Front the glory that is theirs, and that is South Africa's. But equally, let us not forget that there was no less heroism in East Africa, no less endurance to the utmost limit of human nature, no less a contribution to the heroic record of South Africa.
>
> Thousands of them lie there, in the furthest north of our African Trek.[37]

Brig. Gen. Collyer devoted fourteen chapters to the background to and the unfolding of the campaign in 1916. He devotes attention to those lessons which, according to himself, are based on his own personal experience in the campaign.[38] These lessons include the necessity to prepare for a war or campaign, the use of mounted infantry in the tropical bushveld, the administrative lessons (transport, supplies, medical services, lines of communication), and the tactical lessons.

Collyer's study appeared two years before Part 1 of Lt. Col. Charles Hordern's official *Military Operations East Africa* (London, 1941), of the series *History of the Great War*. This series was compiled under the supervision of the Historical Section of the Committee of Imperial Defence and rested upon research into official documents. This volume of this series contains the story of the military operations in German East Africa during the period from August 1914 through to September 1916.[39] Both *The Union of South*

Africa and the Great War and Collyer's study on the campaign in German East Africa appear in the bibliography.[40]

THE OFFICIAL PUBLICATIONS OF THE UNION WAR HISTORIES SECTION

To the best knowledge of the writer, no scientifically responsible description of the section is in existence.

Before the outbreak of the Second World War, Major Leipoldt and later Brig. Gen. Collyer were responsible for the writing of the official war histories. A fully fledged section known as the Union War Histories Section was established at the end of 1940 or the beginning of 1941. This was housed initially under the Department of Defense and, later, in the Office of the Prime Minister. J.A.I. Agar-Hamilton (later Col., Prof. Dr.), a senior lecturer in the History Department at the University of Pretoria, acted as head of this section. He initially enjoyed war leave, but left the service of the university in 1946 and headed the section until 1961.[41]

Under his able leadership and with the help of a number of excellent coworkers, Colonel Agar-Hamilton consulted an impressive collection of official and unofficial documents and published a trilogy which would give new direction to South African military history. In these publications, the new policy was clearly visible. In many respects the content is of a quality far superior to the already mentioned studies on South African participation in the First World War.

It is known that, at an unknown time, a committee under Prof. Dr. H. B. Thom, then professor of history at the University of Stellenbosch, was appointed to assist Col. Agar-Hamilton. On 7 November 1943, the Prime Minister (Gen. J. C. Smuts) decided to add an advisory committee.[42]

In 1952 this advisory committee consisted of Prof. Dr. H. B. Thom (chairman), Lt. Col. G. Graham Botha, Mr. D. de Waal Meyer, Prof. I. S. Fourie, Mr. G.W.R. de Mare, Prof. A. F. Hattersley, and Dr. C. Beyers.[43] After Dr. Beyers's retirement as Chief Archivist of the Union, his place was filled by, Dr. A. Kieser.[44]

Colonel Agar-Hamilton, editor in chief, was assisted by assistant editors Dr. Eric Axelson, Maj. L.C.F. Turner (military), and Capt. J. E. Betzler. Commander H. R. Gordon-Cumming, OBE, RN, accepted responsibility for a part of the content of *War in the Southern Oceans 1939–1945* (Cape Town–London–New York, 1961). At one time Capt. J. E. Betzler was employed as archivist–translator, while he held the post of assistant editor in 1961. Cartographer P. Alton did valuable work and this group was assisted by a number of assistant researchers, typists, and so on.[45]

In the then Union the editor in chief had unlimited access to official war documentation and already in 1942 had commenced a study of the fall of Tobruk. With regard to his first work, *Crisis in the Desert May–July 1942* (Oxford: Oxford University Press, 1952), help was received from members of the permanent force who had knowledge of the subject. In England, help was received from the head of the Historical Section of the British Cabinet as well as from a large number of British officers. Similar assistance was received from New Zealand, the United States, Italy, Pakistan, and Germany. These unpublished sources were gratefully used, together with the large number of publications which appear immediately after the war. In this respect, the bibliography is revealing (pp. 345–346).

These and other undisclosed sources were used by the editor in chief and Assistant Editor Turner to compile *Crisis in the Desert May–July 1942.* The research work on the fall of Tobruk was followed by work on the German offensives on the Gazala Line, Field Marshal Erwin Rommel's offensive against Egypt, his victory at Mersa Matruh, and the end of his advance at El Alamein.[46]

This was only a small part of an area of research which, through the passage of time, was studied by the authors and their coworkers. And, as a result of all these different aspects, the mentioned publication is divided into three parts: The Gazala Line, Tobruk, and Alamein.

With this background, it should be clear that with the publications of the section military historiography in this country entered a new era.

With regard to the publication of *The Sidi Rezeg Battles 1941*, in 1957, Agar-Hamilton and Turner studied the actions of 1 SA Infantry Division, with the great desert offensive of November 1941 as background, and working through all the available data presented twenty chapters (pp. 1–467) and added a conclusion. As with its predecessor, this authorative study was accompanied by ample photographic material, maps, useful appendices, a valuable source list, and an index.

Inter alia, official documents of the 8th Army as well as the *Panzergruppe Afrika* were consulted. The writers did everything within their capability to solve burning questions with regard to the Crusader battles.[47]

The introduction to *War in the Southern Oceans 1939–45* mentions that the first overview of the activities of the South African Navy was compiled by Cdr. H. R. Gordon-Cumming, OBE, RN. Thereafter, Maj. Turner made an extensive strategic study of naval activity at the Cape of Good Hope and the southern oceans. Furthermore, data on the SAAF, generated by Dr. Eric Axelson, was fruitfully used. Captain Betzler and Cdr. Gordon-Cumming undertook research at the British Admiralty and, in 1954, Capt. Betzler also went to Germany.

The writers commenced their story with the cruise of the *Admiral Graf Spee* and the sinking of the *Watussi* (1939) and followed with the series of German raids in the Atlantic and Indian Oceans, both important shipping lanes. Enemy submarine activity followed until, in 1944, the tide turned against the Axis. Included in this extremely important work are appendices on the German submarines as well as the South African vessels and crews seconded to the Royal Navy.[48]

A review of the activities of the Union War Histories Section, even after considering the gaps in our knowledge, highlights the following facts. In addition to the authorative publications, a large number of manuscripts were compiled. By 1961, only a small part of these valuable data had been published. There were also valuable photographic material, periodicals, military-historical brochures, newspaper cuttings, photostats, official and unofficial publications, and operational maps.

A fourth unnamed publication had almost been completed when the section was closed in 1961. The activities of the advisory committee had stopped on 31 July 1959.

After the disbandment of the Union War Histories Section, the military archives in its custody were transferred to the Military-Historical Section of the South African Defence Force. The other archives were initially transferred to the Central Archives Depot, Pretoria and later transferred to the Military-Historical Section.[49]

Military historians and ex-servicemen lamented the closure of the Union War Histories Section. They wanted to see a full, written record of South Africa's participation in the Second World War. This they saw as necessary so that the entire world would remember what the South Africans had done. Already in 1941, Carl Birkby had expressed another thought in the introduction to his unofficial *Springbok Victory*: "I hope you will like this book, for it tells the extraordinary story of an extraordinary war, the like of which may never be known again in the world's history, because the methods of warfare have changed so greatly."[50]

And, in 1965, another renowned writer on South African participation in the Second World War, Lt. Col. Harry Klein, testified in *Springboks in Armour: The South African Armoured Corps in World War II* (Cape Town, Johannesburg), "A story of high endeavour and great military achievement lies behind the short-lived history of the South African Tank Corps. Born of humble beginnings early in 1940, the infant Corps wrote a brilliant chapter in South Africa's annals of war before being absorbed by the South African Armoured Corps in 1943." The following accolade of praise for the same unit, came from Lt. Gen. George E. Brink, CB, CBE, DSO: "As one who had part in the birth, organization and training of the South African Tank Corps and subsequently had several of the Units in my command in East Africa, Abyssinia and North Africa I shall always look back with pride and affection on the achievements of that grand body of men who made up the personnel of that splendid Corps."[51]

Could all the unpublished stories of the actions of these and other South African soldiers on land, at sea, and in the air be allowed to rest in the archives? And could those who had given the highest sacrifice be forgotten? One South African who argued along these lines was Lt. Gen. George E. Brink.

THE ACHIEVEMENTS OF LT. GEN. GEORGE EDWIN BRINK (1889–1971)

In his foreword to Cmdt. (later Col.) Neil Orpen's *East African and Abyssinian Campaigns* (Cape Town, Johannesburg, 1968), Mr. C. G. Kerr, chairman of the War History Advisory Committee, detailed the circumstances under which the Union War Histories Section closed its doors in June 1961 after the Advisory Committee had been disbanded in July 1959.

Lt. Gen. Brink, in his capacity as chairman of the Council of Corps, Regimental and Kindred Associations, requested a review of the decision of 1961. He was informed that the archives of the former section had been transferred to the Central Archives Depot and were accessible to researchers. The former editor in chief of the former section planned a further four volumes detailing the history of the South African Air Force (SAAF), the campaign in Abyssinia, the campaign in Italy, and the gaps in the military operations in North Africa. In 1961, Gen. Brink emphasized the fact that unless sufficient funds were collected at an early date these works would never appear.

A call was made to all ex-servicemen's organizations and R10,000 was collected. Thereafter, at the request of Gen. Brink, Col. D. Ollemans resurrected the War Histories Advisory Committee and, before his death, further financial support was obtained from three newspaper groups. As a result, the committee appointed Cmdt. (later Col.) N.N.D. Orpen, Order of the Star of South Africa (Civilian) Class 4 (Officer), JCD, to research and draw up a manuscript on the history of the East African campaign. Cmdt. Neil Orpen, M.A. (Cantab) was a former journalist who was to become one of

South Africa's leading military historians. During the Second World War he served with 2 Light Anti-Aircraft Regiment in Egypt and Cyrenaica and was captured at Tobruk. After the war he continued his journalistic career and his military activities as commanding officer of the Cape Field Artillery. In the future he would achieve fame as a first-rate military historian.

At the same time, Mr. James Ambrose Brown was appointed to record the history of the South African Air Force during the Second World War.

At this stage, the Advisory Committee realized that the funds would not be sufficient and a call was made upon trade and industry. This call was wholeheartedly supported and encouraged by the influential Sir Keith Acutt.

When the Union War Histories Section closed in 1961, the prime minister, Dr. H. F. Verwoerd, suggested that Gen. Brink approach the then Department of Education, Arts and Science for a subsidy. This request was allowed and Prof. Dr. D. W. Kruger was the first representative of the National Council for Social Research (Pretoria) to sit on the Advisory Committee. General R. C. Hiemstra, Commandant General of the South African Defence Force (SADF) encouraged this enterprise and appointed Cmdt. (later Col.) Ploeger and Capt. E. Jonker to represent the SADF on the Advisory Committee. Until his retirement in 1973, Col. Ploeger was responsible for verifying the manuscripts in terms of the archives held in the custody of the Military Historical and Archival Service (MHAS) of the SADF.[52]

In 1968 the Advisory Committee consisted of Mr. C. G. Kerr (chairman); Lt. Gen. G. E. Brink, CB, CBE, DSO; Brig. J. T. Durrant, CB, DFC; Col. W.P.F. McLaren, OBE; Col. J. Williams, DSO, DFC; Lt. Col. K. T. Gilson, DSO; Cmdt. G. R. Duxbury; Maj. R. D. Meeser, MC; Maj. R. J. Southey, ED; Messr L. H. Walton and L.E.A. Slater; Capt. K. Hunter; Cmdt. (later Col.) Dr. Jan Ploeger and Capt. E. Jonker (for the MHAS, SADF); Prof. Dr. D. W. Kruger (for the National Council for Social Research); and Maj. E. B. Edmeades (honorary secretary).[53]

In the second part of the series, which appeared in 1970, chairman C. G. Kerr wrote, "Behind all this lies the formidable energy and sagacity of General George Brink, now in his 81st year, whose drive and enthusiasm remain undimmed."[54] Everybody who at some time had the privilege of working under Lt. Gen. Brink will confirm this quotation without underestimating the work of all the others who contributed to the realization of a large objective.

George Edwin Brink (1889–1971) was a born Free Stater. [Gen. Brink's military career began in 1913 and he rose steadily up the ladder as a staff officer in the First World War, campaigning with General Smuts in South West Africa. After a course at Camberley, U.K., he served at Roberts Heights for many years as, among other duties, commandant of the S.A. Military College, then to Cape Command from whence he was sent on a tour of Britain, Germany, France, Italy, and Denmark to study organization and physical training. Upon his return he became Deputy Chief of the General Staff. He trained the South African Army until October 1940, when he took the First S.A. Division to campaign in East Africa and then in the Western Desert until invalided in early 1942 back to South Africa, where as in 1918 he prepared the army for demobilization. He retired in 1948 and became active in many military-historical activities—editor. Lt. Gen. G. E. Brink passed away before the publication of Cmdt. N.N.D. Orpen's *War in the Desert.* Chairman C. G. Kerr's remark in the foreword to this work was characteristic: "General Brink died before publication of this book, but he guided the author throughout."[55]

The *South African Forces World War II* series is testimony to General Brink's stamina and undescribable love and respect for the South African defense organization, which was trained to defend and in war to offer the highest sacrifice.

DETAILS REGARDING THE *SOUTH AFRICAN FORCES WORLD WAR II* SERIES

By way of introduction, mention was already made of the initiative of Lt. Gen. G. E. Brink, the origin and objectives of the Advisory Committee, and the choice of two writers for this series. The committee wished to make use of Cmdt. Orpen for the writing of the history of the land war, while Mr. James Ambrose Brown would cover the South African Air Force. Orpen had already achieved fame through his study, *Prince Alfred's Guard 1856–1966* (Cape Town, 1967).[56]

Today Orpen is regarding as one of the leading military historians in South Africa.[57] Mr. James Ambrose Brown had achieved fame as a writer of prose. His novel, *The Return*, appeared in 1971. This was a dramatized fictional story written against the background of events in South West Africa between 1904 and 1922. It won a prize of R2,000 in the English section of the literary contest during the republic festival.[58]

Brown was responsible for volume 2 of the series (i.e., *A Gathering of Eagles*, 1970) and Volume 4 (i.e., *Eagles Strike*). These two volumes sketch the role of the SAAF in the military operations in East Africa (1940–1941), Egypt, Cyrenaica, Libya, Tunisia, Tripolitania, and Madagascar (1941–1943).

With regard to the role of the SAAF in Europe, the Advisory Committee was fortunate to obtain the cooperation of Lt. Gen. H. J. Martin, BA, SM, CBE, DFC, Belgian *Croix Militaire (I)*. Lt. Gen. Martin was, until his retirement in 1968, Chief of Defence Staff, SA, and had, during the North African campaign, commanded 12 Squadron SAAF and later 3 Wing SAAF. After the war, he served as quartermaster general and chief of the air force. He had a good knowledge of the documentation in the custody of the Military Archives, having spent his prewar career as a journalist.

While Cmdt. Orpen wrote Volume 5 of the series (i.e., *Victory in Italy*), he and Lt. Gen. Martin worked together on Volume 6 (*Eagles Victorious*, 1977) and Volume 7 (*South Africa at War*, 1979). Thereafter these two writers produced the two parts of Volume 8 (*Salute the Sappers*, 1981, 1982). These two parts were published by the Sappers Association (Johannesburg).

Thus, between 1968 and 1982, the following volumes of the *South African Forces World War II* appeared:

1968—Volume 1

Cmdt. Neil Orpen, *East African and Abyssinian Campaigns* (Cape Town, Johannesburg), pp 390 (with photographs, maps, etc). This work is the authorative account of the South African contribution to the victory over the Italians in East Africa (1941) and the military operations of the East African Force in cooperation with the Sudanese troops in Eritrea.

1970—Volume 2

James A. Brown, *A Gathering of Eagles. The campaigns of the South African Air Force in Italian East Africa June 1940–November 1941 with an introduction 1912–1939* (Cape Town, Johannesburg, London), pp 342. This work contains a fully documented account of the air war in Kenya, Somaliland, Abyssinia, Sudan, and Eritrea.

1971—Volume 3

Cmdt. Neil Orpen, *War in the Desert* (Cape Town, Johannesburg), pp 538. Contains those parts of the operations in North Africa not covered by Agar-Hamilton. Particular attention is given to the roles played by 1 and 2 South African divisions.

1974—Volume 4

James Ambrose Brown, *Eagles Strike. The Campaigns of the South African Air Force in Egypt, Cyrenaica, Libya, Tunisia, Tripolitania and Madagascar 1941–1943* (Cape Town, Johannesburg, London), pp 448. The obvious title gives thorough insight into the content of the work, which is rich in photographs and maps.

With the following volumes, Lt. Gen. Martin replaced Ambrose Brown as the writer of the air war.

1975—Volume 5

Cmdt. Neil Orpen, *Victory in Italy* (Cape Town, Johannesburg), pp 340. This is the captivating story of 6 South African Armoured Division from the battle of Cassino to the collapse of the German forces in Italy. Attention is also given to South African units from the landing in Sicily.

1977—Volume 6

Lt. Gen. H. J. Martin and Col. Neil Orpen, *Eagles Victorious. The Operation of the South African Air Forces over the Mediterranean and Europe, in Italy, the Balkans and the Aegean, and from Gibraltar and West Africa* (Cape Town, Johannesburg, London), pp 494. This work gives the reader a clear picture of the role played by South Africans—in comparison to their American, British, and other allies—in the battle for air superiority.

1979—Volume 7

Lt. Gen. H. J. Martin and Col. Neil Orpen, *South Africa at War. Military and Industrial Organization and Operations in Connection with the Conduct of the War, 1939–1945* (Cape Town, Johannesburg, London), pp 405. Although an earlier attempt was made to describe this facet of the war, this work was pioneering. In this valuable study, attention is given to war production and war expenses, the battle against the submarines, the relationship between Gen. Sir Pierre van Ryneveld and Field Marshall Smuts, and the postwar era.

In his foreword to this volume, C. G. Kerr mentioned that this volume would end the series, but that the Advisory Committee had been approached to see to the writing and publication of the history of the Sappers—the South African Engineer Corps. This request was approved and Col. Neil Orpen and Lt. Gen. H. J. Martin set to work. The result was the following:

1981—Volume 8/1

Neil Orpen and Lt. Gen. H. J. Martin, *Salute the Sappers. The Formation of the South African Engineer Corps and Its Operations in East Africa to the Battle of Alamein* (Cape Town), pp 507.

A year later, the second part of this volume appeared under the following title:

1982—Volume 8/2

Neil Orpen and Lt. Gen. H. J. Martin, *Salute the Sappers. The Operations of the South African Engineer Corps in the North African and Italian Theatres of War from the Battle of El Alamein to the End of World War II, with a Brief Description of Subsequent Developments* (Cape Town), pp 424.

A monumental series was closed with the appearance of these works, which enabled academic and lay historians, both locally and abroad, to consult an authorative series on the honorable role played by South Africans during the Second World War.

OFFICIAL PUBLICATIONS OF THE DOCUMENTATION SERVICE DIRECTORATE, NATIONAL DEFENCE FORCES (NDF), AND ITS PREDECESSORS (1968–1995)

Mention was made in the preceding paragraphs of the very real support given by the South African Defence Force with regard to the *South African Forces World War II* series. This support included, inter alia, the access to the archives of the South African Defence Force, including the unpublished manuscripts of the Union War Histories Section. Furthermore, personnel of the Military Historical and Archival Service acted in a quality-control capacity.

It can be shortly mentioned here that the establishment of a fully-fledged military archives was achieved on 14 June 1950, with the appointment of a Staff Officer Archives. The Archives Depot began to function with effect from January 1953 and this position became *de jure* on 16 August 1967, following official approval from the Minister of Defense. On the same day the Military Historical Section was renamed SADF Archives.[59]

Until 29 June 1968, the SADF Archives controlled the military-historical and archival activities of the former Military-Historical Section. On this day, the SADF Archives together with the other functions of the former Military Historical Section were brought under the umbrella of the Military-Historical and Archival Service.

In October 1972, the organization was renamed the Central Documentation Service and became a full-fledged directorate on 1 February 1975.

In 1969, the MHAS had started a military-history journal called *Militaria*, which is still in existence today.[60] In addition to *Militaria*, another series was also started:

1. Cmdt. J. Ploeger, *The Fortification of Pretoria; Yesterday and Today* (Publication no. 1, 1968). pp 95, illus., maps. Also published in Afrikaans.[61]
2. W. Otto, *Die Spesiale Diensbataljon, 1933–1973* (Publication no. 2, 1973). pp 149, index, illus. With contributions by Brig. J. N. Blatt, Col. J. Ploeger, and Maj. F. J. Jacobs.
3. Cmdt. C. M. Bakkes, *Die Britse Deaurbraak aan die Benede-Tugela op Majubadag 1900* (Publication no. 3, 1973). pp 106, index, illus., maps.
4. Maj. F. J. Jacobs, Lt. R. J. Bouch, S. du Preez, R. Cornwell, *South African Corps of Signals* (Publication no. 4, 1975). pp 107, illus.
5. Capt. R. J. Bouch (ed.), *Infantry in South Africa, 1652–1976* (Publication no. 5, 1977). pp 276, illus., maps.
6. Maj. J. E. Rabie, *Generaal C. R. de Wet se krygsleiding by Sannaspos en Groenkop* (Publication no. 6, 1980). pp 67, index, illus., maps.
7. Maj. A. E. van Jaarsveldt et al., *Militêre Geneeskunde in Suid-Afrika, 1913–1983* (Publication no. 7, 1983). pp 119, index, illus.
8. Cmdt. C. J. Nöthling (ed), *Ultima Ratio Regum (The last argument of kings); Artillery History of South Africa* (Publication no. 8, 1987). pp 432, illus.
9. Capt. I. J. van der Waag, *A History of the South African Defence Force Institute (SADFI), 1914–1990* (Publication no. 9, 1991). pp 165, index, illus., maps.

All of these publications were furnished with illustrations, maps, and useful indexes. While these works were compiled by personnel of the Documentation Service Directorate and its predecessors, assistance was also given with regard to other official, departmental publications. In this connection, the following may be mentioned: Kenneth A. Maxwell, John M. Smith, *Per aspera ad astra 1920–1970. SA Air Force Golden Jubilee Souvenir Book / SA Lugmag Goue Jubileumgedenkboek* (Johannesburg, 1970); Commodore J. C. Goosen, SM, *South Africa's Navy; The First Fifty Years* (Cape Town, 1973), and Wilhlem Gruther's translation, *Ons Vloot; Die eerste vyftig jaar* (Kaapstad, 1973);[62] L. Jooste, *The Art of War; An Introduction to Military Art in South Africa* (Pretoria, n.d.); and Commander J.M.M. Imrie, *The Military Band in South Africa* (Pretoria, 1976).

MILITARY-HISTORICAL PUBLICATIONS OF THE INSTITUTE FOR HISTORICAL RESEARCH OF THE HUMAN SCIENCES RESEARCH COUNCIL, 1972–1986

The Human Sciences Research Council (HSRC) has already been mentioned with regard to the provision of financial assistance to the Union War Histories Advisory Committee.[63] It must, however, be emphasized that the HSRC also undertook military-historical research. For this purpose, the Institute for Historical Research was established.

Under the leadership of Cmdt. (Dr.) C. M. Bakkes, a number of source publications with a military-historical orientation were prepared and annotated by the personnel of the institute. From 1972 until 1986, the following source publications appeared:

1. A. G. Oberholster (ed.), *Dagboek van H. C. Bredell 1900–1904*, 1972.
2. J. P. Brits (ed.), *Diary of a National Scout; P. J. du Toit 1900–1902*, 1974.
3. O.J.O. Ferreira (ed.), *Geschiedenis, werken en streven van S.P.E. Trichardt; Luitenant Kolonel der vroegere Staatsartillerie Z.A.R. door hemzelve beschreven*, 1975.
4. C. E. Eloff (ed.), *Oorlogsdagboekie van H. S. Oosterhagen Januarie–Junie 1902*, 1976.
5. Thariza van Rensburg (ed.), *Oorlogsjoernaal van S. J. Burger 1899–1902*, 1977.
6. O.J.O. Ferreira (ed.), *Krygsgevangenschap van L. C. Ruijssenaers 1899–1902*, 1977.
7. A. G. Oberholster (ed.), *Oorlogsdagboek van Jan F. E. Celliers 1899–1902*, 1978.
8. Thariza van Rensburg (ed.), *Camp Diary of Henrietta E. A. Armstrong; Experiences of a Boer nurse in the Irene Concentration Camp, 6 April–11 October 1901*, 1980.
9. O.J.O. Ferreira (ed.), *Memoirs of General Ben Bouwer as written by P. J. le Riche*, 1980.
10. A. P. Smit and L. Mare (eds.), *Die beleg van Mafeking*, 1985.
11. A. Wessels (ed.), *Anglo–Boer War Diary of Herbert Gwynne Howell*, 1986.

It will be seen from the titles that these publications deal, either partly or entirely, with the Second Anglo-Boer War. General Ben Bouwer's memoirs run through to 1914. The reminiscences of (later Col.) H. C. Bredell deal chiefly with President S.J.P. Kruger's sojourn in Europe. The camps were a product of the war, and the diary of Jan F. E. Celliers reflects a high degree of sensitivity. His diary was his place of escape, enabling him to maintain psychological stability.[64] Petrus Jacobus du Toit cried out, "Oh, God of Gods, hast thou let us over to ourselves, hast thou forsaken thy children, is there no help, no remedy, no peace? If our case is a hopeless one, what can I do to stop it? All is a mystery, I shall act soon, yes this very day or tomorrow."[65] Thus, some of these diaries were interpreted as the inner, psychological battles within a people at war.

THE ARCHIVES YEAR BOOK SERIES (1938)

Some years before the appearance of the first volume of the official *Archives Year Book for South African History* in 1938, the well-known historian Prof. Dr. J.L.M. Franken, of the University of Stellenbosch, pleaded the desirability of such a series.[66] The government made money available and the then chief archivist of the Union, Mr. (later Dr.) C. Graham Botha saw to the realization of this dream. Botha was assisted by an editorial committee consisting of Assistant Chief Archivist Dr. Coenraad Beyers, Prof. Dr. H. B. Thom, and Mr. P. J. Venter, MA (archivist, secretary).

In his introduction to the first volume of the series, the chief archivist stressed that the year book would be used to draw public attention to archival issues and the fruits of scientific, historical research.

The passage of time has proved that the *Archives Year Book* series, which appears to this day, meets an important need of the academic and lay communities. Divergent facets of historical research are still brought to public attention.

Military-historical themes are not neglected. The following military-historical studies are mentioned in the index, which is updated with each volume and is alphabetically arranged according to the surname of the writer:

Bakkes, C. M., *Die Militêre Situasie aan die Benede-Tugela op die Vooraand van die Britse Deurbraak by Pietershoogte (26 Februarie 1900).* (1967, part 1).

Barnard, B. J., *'n Lewensbeskrywing van Majoor Henry Douglas Warden.* (1948, part 1).

Barnard, C. J., *Robert Jacob Gordon se Loopbaan aan die Kaap.* (1950, part 1).

Campbell, Dr. W. B., *The South African Frontier, 1865–1885; A Study in Expansion.* (1959, part 1).

Cilliers, J. H., *Die Slag van Spioenkop (24 Jan 1900).* (1960, part 2).

Coetzee, C. G., *Die Kompanjie se besetting van Delagoabaai.* (1948, part 2).

Davey, A. M., *The Siege of Pretoria, 1880–1881.* (1956, part 1).

De Villiers, C. J., *Die Britse Vloot aan die Kaap, 1781–1806.* (1969, part 1).

De Villiers, J., *Hottentotregimente aan die Kaap, 1781–1806.* (1970, part 2).

De Villiers, J., *Die Cape Regiment, 1806–1817; 'n Koloniale Regiment in Britse Diens.* (1989, part 1).

Grimsehl, H. W., *Onluste in Modjadjiland, 1890–1894.* (1955, part 2).

Hattingh, J. L., *Die Irenekonsentrasiekamp.* (1967, part 1).

Kotze, J. S., *Die Kaapse Staande Mag, 1872–1882.* (1993).

Mouton, Dr. J. A., *Genl Piet Joubert in die Geskiedenis van Transvaal.* (1957, part 1).

Nel, H. F., *Die Britse Verowering van die Kaap in 1795.* (1972, part 2).

Smith, K. W., *The Campaigns against the Bapedi of Sekhukhune 1877–1879.* (1967, part 2).
Snyman, J. H., *Rebelle-Verhoor in Kaapland gedurende die Tweede Vryheidsoorlog met Spesiale Verwysing na die Militêre Howe (1899–1902).* (1962).
Snyman, Dr. J. H., *Die Afrikaner in Kaapland, 1899–1902.* (1979, part 2).
Van Heerden, Dr. J. J., *Die Kommandant-generaal in die Geskiedenis van die Suid-Afrikaanse Republiek.* (1964, part 2).
Van Jaarsveld, F. A., *Die Veldkornet en sy aandeel in die opbou van die Suid-Afrikaanse Republiek tot 1870.* (1950, part 2).
Van Niekerk, M., *Adlof Schiel en die Duitse Komando.* (1951, part 2).
Van Wyk, A. J., *Dinizulu en die Usoto-opstand van 1888.* (1979, part 1).
Van Zyl, Dr. M. C., *Die uitbreiding van die britse gesag oor die Natalse Noordgrensgebiede 1879–1897.* (1966, part 1).
Wales, J. M., *The Relationship between the Orange Free State and the Rolong of Thaba'Nchu during the Presidency of J. H. Brand, 1864–1888.* (1986, part 1).[67]

The editorship of the *Archives Year Book* rests with the Director of Archives and the Archives Commission.

STATE HISTORIANS AND THEIR ACTIVITIES, 1959–1994

In 1959 the then Union government decided to create the post of state historian and Dr. Johann Hendrik Breytenbach was appointed in this capacity. Dr. Breytenbach had served since 1939 in various archival depots and, since 1940, had devoted himself to an in-depth and uninterrupted study of the sources dealing with the Second Anglo–Boer War. Before his appointment as state historian, he had worked during his free time on this topic. After his appointment in 1959, he devoted himself to his topic in a full-time capacity. His task was to record the military history of the Second Anglo–Boer War with a view to the publication of his findings.[68]

Various reasons, according to Dr. Breytenbach, led to the government's decision to record this history. In the first place, this war was the largest and most glorious of wars fought in South Africa. It touched the citizens of both republics as well as the inhabitants of the Cape and Natal colonies. It produced men like generals C. R. de Wet, L. Botha, and J. H. de la Rey, who, as a result of the roles they played, achieved world fame. This war, like no other event, focused the attention of the whole civilized world on South Africa.

Despite this, a history of the whole war had not been scientifically recorded. Dr. Breytenbach attributed this to the vast amount of archival material pertaining to the war, which made it impossible for any individual who did not make it his life work to complete it.[69]

Second, those works which did deal with the war had several serious hiatuses. In this connection, Dr. Breytenbach declared

In die geval van die grootste massa daarvan is waarheid en verdigsel so met elkaar vermeng as gevolg van die sentimente van die skrywers dat hulle nie 'n getroue beeld gee van wat werklik gebeur het nie. Die paar uitsonderinge word weer daardeur gekenmerk dat hulle almal op onvolledige en oorhaastige navorsing berus.[70] (The overwhelming majority of them did not present a true picture, in view of the sentiments of the writers and the resulting mix of truth and fabrication. The few exceptions were, however, characterized by incomplete and hasty research.)

In this case, it was correctly stated that only a few writers were aware of the enormous amount of material in the South African archival depots, and their works were never published. It was further argued that these works were not academically grounded and many were already out of print. In view thereof, the government came to the following conclusion:

Daar bestaan dus 'n ernstige behoefte aan 'n omvattende werk waarin die verloop van die oorlog aan die hand van alle beskikbare bronne binne in en buite Suid-Afrika beskryf word, en waarin alle feite wat genoem word behoorlik in voetnote verantwoord word.[71] (A serious need exists for a comprehensive account of the war, based on all available sources, both in South Africa and abroad, and in which all facts are properly footnoted.)

Dr. Breytenbach worked under the supervision of a committee initially appointed by the government for this purpose. The first committee consisted of Prof. Dr. A. N. Pelzer, Prof. Dr. F. J. du T. Spies, and Dr. T. S. van Rooyen, all of the Department of History at the University of Pretoria.[72]

Over the years, the following volumes of the series *Die geskiedenis van die Tweede Vryheidsoorlog in Suid-Afrika 1899–1902* (The History of the Second War of Independence in South Africa 1899–1902) appeared:

1969—Volume 1

Die Boere-offensief October–November 1899 (The Boer offensive October–November 1899), pp 508, with illustrations, maps, index. This publication, together with those which were to follow, appeared by order of the Minister of National Education and under the supervision of the Department of History, University of Pretoria.

1971—Volume 2

Die Eerste Britse offensief November–Desember 1899 (The first British offensive November–December 1899), pp 513, as above.

1973—Volume 3

Die stryd in Natal Januarie–Februarie 1900 (The war in Natal January–February 1900), pp 594, as above.

1977—Volume 4

Die Boereterugtog uit Kaapland (The Boer retreat from the Cape), pp 513, as above.

1983—Volume 5

Die Britse opmars tot in Pretoria (The British advance to Pretoria), pp 587, as above.

State Historian Dr. J. H. Breytenbach reached retirement age on 31 October 1972, but decided to continue with his official activities after his retirement.

Breytenbach's successor as State Historian, Dr. J. A. Mouton, also had a long connection with the State Archives. His official task was to record the origin and development of the concentration camp system. Dr. Mouton passed away a year later.

Dr. Mouton was succeeded in 1973 by Col. (Dr.) J. Ploeger, after the latter's retirement as Senior Staff Officer Archives and Research, South African Defence Force. After approximately seven years of further research, a number of chapters on the civilian aspects of the war were produced. Furthermore, histories of each separate concentration camp for Whites was compiled, with an overview of the camps for Blacks. In so doing, a total of 100 chapters were produced. Col. (Dr.) Ploeger retired in 1983, but undertook to complete the project. His service ended in February 1987. The chapters cover the way of life, experiences, morale, and dilemma of people in captivity. No further developments have taken place since Dr. Ploeger's death in 1994.

CONCLUSION

In this contribution, the writer—within the boundaries of his ability and the extent of his knowledge—gives an overview of South African state and state-sponsored military-historical research since 1924. This contribution is undoubtedly, but not purposefully, incomplete. Notwithstanding these shortcomings, the reader will have an impression of the advances made over the years. These advances are recognized with gratitude.

NOTES

This paper is reprinted with permission from *Militaria; Military History Journal of the South African National Defence Force* 19, 4 (1989): 15–36. It has been revised and updated.

1. F. A. van Jaarsveld and J. I. Rademeyer, *Teorie en metodiek vir geskiedenisonderrig* (Johannesburg, 1960), pp. 15–65.

2. J. Huizinga, *De wetenschap der geschiedenis* (Haarlem, 1937), pp. 119–121.

3. E. Creasy, *The Fifteen Decisive Battles of the World: From Marathon to Waterloo in Order Categorical* (London, 1887), p. x.

4. Alfred von Müller, *Der Krieg in Süd-Afrika 1889/1900 und seine Vorgeschichte* (Berlin, 1900), pp. 1–46.

5. H. Amersfoort and P. H. Kamphuis (ed.), *Je Maintiendrai: A Concise History of the Dutch Army* (The Hague, 1985), p. 7.

6. Ibid.

7. An overview of Dr Carson's books and articles (1943–1963) has been taken up in the front of the last mentioned publication. Page numbers are not given.

8. P. Warwick, S. B. Spies, *The South African War: The Anglo–Boer War 1899–1902* (London, 1980), p. 6 (emphasis added).

9. N. Hofmeyr, *Zes maanden bij de Commando's* ('s-Gravenhage, 1903). He was appointed as Historian of the War by the Executive Council of the South African Republic.

10. Ibid., p. 5.

11. W. F. Andriessen, *Gedenkboek van den Oorlog in Zuid-Afrika* (Amsterdam and Cape Town, 1904), pp. ix–x.

12. Ibid., p. x.

13. W. Valletin, *Der Burenkrieg* (Wald-Solingen, Leipzig, 1902), p. v.

14. Ibid., p. vi.

15. L. S. Amery, *The Times History of The War in South Africa 1899–1900* (London, 1900), pp. iii et seq.

16. Ibid., pp. v–vi.

17. Ibid., p. vi.

18. Ibid., Volume 2 (1902), pp. v et seq.

19. *Die Kämpfe der deutschen Truppen in Südwestafrika* (Berlin, 1906), Erstes Heft, Vorwork.

20. *Official Year Book of the Union of South Africa and of Basutoland, Bechuanaland Protectorate, and Swaziland* (Pretoria, 1921), pp. 408 et seq.

21. C.F.J. Muller (ed.), *Vyfhonderd Jaar Suid-Afrikaanse Geskiedenis* (Pretoria and Cape Town, 1968), pp. 352 et seq.

22. *Official Year Book*, no. 4 (Pretoria, 1921), p. 411.

23. *The Union of South Africa and the Great War, 1914–1918* (Pretoria, 1924). Mentioned on the back of the title page.

24. Piet van der Byl, *From playgrounds to battlefields* (Cape Town, 1971), pp. 145–146. During his term of service in the SADF, the writer could ascertain that Major L. was the author.

25. *The Union of South Africa,* p. 4.

26. Ibid., p. 3.

27. The Official History is divided as follows: the campaign in GSWA and the rebellion, pp. 10–60; the campaign in GEA, pp. 63–93; the S.A. Infantry Brigade in France, pp. 100–182; the S.A. Heavy Artillery, pp. 185–189; the S.A. Signal Company, pp. 189–200; the S.A. Medical Service, pp. 200–205; the railway companies and so on, pp. 207–208; the administration, pp. 211–224. Victoria Crosses earned by South Africans, pp. 225–228. South African casualties, pp. 229–230.

28. J.H.V. Crowe, *General Smuts' Campaign in East Africa* (London, 1918), pp. v–vi.

29. J. J. Collyer, *The Campaign in German South West Africa 1914–1915* (Pretoria, 1937), preface.

30. Ibid.

31. Ibid., pp. 165–173.

32. Ibid., p.173.

33. The 1937 edition encompassed 180 pages, while the 1939 edition encompassed 196 pages. Both were printed by the government printer, Pretoria, as official publications.

34. English edition: red cover, 299 pages of text and index, twenty-one multicolored operational maps. Afrikaans edition: green cover, 308 pages of text and index, twenty-one multicolored operational maps.

35. J. J. Collyer, *Die Suid-Afrikaners met Generaal Smuts in Duits Oos-Afrika 1916* (Pretoria, 1939), p. xi.

36. Ibid., p. xv.

37. Ibid., pp. ix–x.

38. Ibid., pp. 268–298 (Afrikaans edition); pp. 260–289 (English edition).

39. London, 1941, pp. 603 (text and index), 67 maps (See *Official Histories* I [1970]).

40. Ibid., p. xix.

41. *Ad Destinatum Gedenkboek van die Universiteit van Pretoria* (Johannesburg, 1960), pp. 112. Details regarding J.A.I. Agar-Hamilton.

42. J.A.I. Agar-Hamilton, L.C.F. Turner, *The Sidi Rezeg Battles 1941* (Cape Town, London, New York, 1957), p. vi. Neil Orpen, *East African and Abyssinian Campaigns* (Cape Town, Johannesburg, 1968), p. iii. The Union War Histories Advisory Committee was established in 1943. In 1945 the designation was changed to the War History Advisory Committee. This committee was disbanded on 31 May 1979. See "'n Kort geskiedenis van die Militêre Informasieburo," Archives News July 1983, 41.

43. J.A.I. Agar-Hamilton, L.C.F. Turner, *Crisis in the Desert May–July 1942* (Cape Town, London, New York, 1952), p. x.

44. Ibid.: *The Sidi Rezeg Battles 1941,* p. 6. With regard to the life and work of Chief Archivist Dr. Coenraad Beyers, see W. B. van der Vyver, "Dr Coenraad Beyers," *SA Archives Journal* 1976, pp. 33–37.

45. See the foreword of each of the publications.

46. *Crisis in the Desert,* p. vii et seq. Print of 4,000, pp. 368.

47. *The Sidi Rezeg Battles*, p. 505.
48. L.C.F. Turner, H. R. Gordon-Cumming, J. E. Betzler, *War in the Southern Oceans 1939–1945* (Oxford: Oxford University Press, 1961), p. 288.
49. E. J. Smith, "Die Unie-Oorlogsgeskiedenis," *Archives News*, October 1961, p. 20; and idem, July 1963, pp. 38–46.
50. C. Birkby, Springbok Victory (Johannesburg, 1941), author's note, Cape Town, 1 September 1941. The writer was SAPA's first war correspondent with the troops in East Africa.
51. Harry Klein, *Springboks in Armour* (Cape Town, Johannesburg, n.d.), pp. vi–vii.
52. *East African and Abyssinian Campaigns* (Oxford: Oxford University Press, 1968), p. iii; James Ambrose Brown, *A Gathering of Eagles* (Oxford: Oxford University Press, 1970), p. vi.
53. *East African and Abyssinian Campaigns,* pp. iii–iv. The amended composition of the committee is mentioned in the following volumes of the series.
54. *A Gathering of Eagles,* p. v.
55. *War in the Desert,* p. v.
56. With maps and sketches, p. 346. The Department of Education, Art and Science sponsored part of the research.
57. See Neil Orpen, *The Cape Town Highlanders* (Cape Town, 1970), p. 396.
58. James Ambrose Brown, *The Return* (Cape Town, Johannesburg, 1971), p. 191.
59. *Archives News*, July 1983, p. 38 et seq.
60. *Militaria* and other similar journals have not been studied for the purposes of this article.
61. This publication owed its existence to the official decision to restore forts Klapperkop and Schanskop. Impression: 2,500 copies (Afrikaans), 2,500 copies (English).
62. The book was subsidized by the South African Marine Corporation and was compiled by the South African Navy under the editorship of Commodore J. C. Goosen, SM.
63. The terminal date (1986) is based upon information provided by Mrs. A. van Zyl, HSRC publications.
64. A. G. Oberholster, MA (ed.), *Oorlogsdagboek van Jan F. E. Celliers 1899–1902* (Pretoria, 1978), p. 7.
65. J. P. Brits, MA (ed.), *Diary of a National Scout; P. J. du Toit 1900–1902* (Pretoria, 1974), p. 33.
66. *Archives Year Book for South African History* (Cape Town, 1938), Volume 1, Part 1, Preface.
67. Ibid., Volume 43, Part 1 (Pretoria, 1980), pp. 377–384.
68. *Archives News,* December 1982, p. 21; ibid., October 1978, p. 10; and J. H. Breytenbach, *Die Geskiedenis van die Tweede Vryheidsoorlog in Suid-Afrika 1899–1902* (Pretoria, 1969), Volume 1, p. ix.
69. J. H. Breytenbach, *Die Geskiedenis van die Tweede Vryheidsoorlog in Suid-Afrika 1899–1902* (Pretoria, 1969), Volume 1, p. ix.
70. Ibid.
71. Ibid.
72. Ibid.

19

Spain

Museo Naval de Madrid (Naval Museum of Madrid)

Office of the Director

The Naval Museum, a cultural entity and state property reporting to the secretary of the navy, is governed by a patronage consisting of diverse military and civil personnel. Its mission is to exalt naval glories, to centralize as many elements as possible so as to contribute to the study and knowledge of past sea life and nautical art, and to create in the present generations a genuine affinity and affection for the sea.

It was created in 1843: Since that date it has been quartered in various official buildings. At present it occupies space in the present navy headquarters, Montalban Street No. 2, Madrid. It is commissioned under prescribed procedures as approved by ministerial order dated 19 July 1949, which has suffered some modifications with respect to the corporation and in other ways.

The majority of the objects on display have been gathered and collected since the very foundation of the museum: many of them came from the Philippine Islands, from Spanish maritime establishments in Central and South America before their independence, and from donations by naval personnel. There are more than 2,000 models, pictures, flags, passports, and other diverse objects, some on display and some in storage.

FUNCTION

The Patronage

The museum depends entirely on a patronage, at present consisting of a president, twelve elected officials, and ten appointees.

Included in the group of elected officials are the captain generals of the two Maritime Zones, the commander generals of the fleet, and the admiral in chief of the Central Naval Jurisdiction. Included in the second group are university personnel, teachers, and other patrons. The patronage has sufficient legal status to acquire and accept donations, to exchange effects and property of the museum, and to invest the funds and the donations that it receives.

In order for any object to leave—for example, pictures, engravings, sculpture, books, and maps—the express authorization in full of the patronage is required, or authorization from its permanent commission (the objects when loaned have to be guaranteed by an insurance at a value specified by the patronage). The loaning of objects must be handled by a trust worthy person selected by the museum, and the objects, from the time they leave the museum until their return, must be guarded by museum personnel, who are to be charged with all the packing and delivery expenditures, the round trip of the personnel, and residence at the exposition site.

The patronage studies each petition with utmost interest and agrees that nothing will leave the museum unless the display or exposition in question has a positive artistic or national importance. The transfer of museum pieces is moderately restricted, if possible, in order to avoid the loaning of pictures and models, which deteriorate with frequent removals.

The entire patronage must meet from time to time, as well as those in the Permanent Commission. The entire committee must meet two times a year, the permanent commission when the necessities of service demand it.

Personnel

With the approval of the patronage, an admiral or chief appointed by the secretary of navy will direct the museum: At present the director is an admiral of the armada, Don Jose Ignacio Gonzalez-Aller Hierro; second in command are three chiefs of the distinguished corps of the armada, as well as one civil person, who are in charge of the four areas which the Museum is organized in. These areas are auxiliary department of the direction; area of conservation, investigation and exhibition, Area of general services and Area of administration of peripheral organs. In order to take care of the foreign personnel, there is a public relations woman who speaks French and English, acting as interpreter, a very necessary function due to the increase of foreign investigators. The personnel also includes various craftsmen (model restorers) and those in charge of the card files.

The library functions under the direction of a librarian who is in charge of the topographic, onomastic, and author and title card files. The number of volumes, and keep in mind that this is a specialized library, has exceeded the 10,000 mark.

For the service of investigators, publicists, magazines, and newspapers, the museum has a photographic card file, which at present contains more than 16,000 references, and a specially designated room so that the investigators can work comfortably without being disturbed by visitors.

Visits

The museum is open every day of the year, except for Mondays when it is closed for cleaning, and the entire month of August. Visiting hours are in the morning. Admission is free for everybody.

Exposition

The installations of the Naval Museum have been renovated in order to give it the decorum befitting the valuable pieces on display; a museum which, in ship models, historical and cartographical background, portraits of naval admirals, and various antique pieces, has international prestige.

Naval Historical Institute

This center, in charge of studying all things regarding the Spanish Navy, was created by decree on June 1942. Included in its investigations are activities of the past, voyages, discoveries, maritime letters, and documents. The institute is a part of the Superior Council of Scientific Investigations, supreme directive and origin of the Spanish Culture.

From its foundations until the present time, it has published numerous books which are listed in the attached bibliography. It has as its core the Naval Museum, since its manuscript funds and specialized library serve authors as a means of consultation and investigation.

As can be observed in the list of publications, all the books deal more or less entirely with naval themes. There are many and varied authors, both naval and civilian. The museum works with the Superior Council of Scientific Investigations, through which all the editions, once published, pass to the Scientific Library of the council, where the books are sold.

Museo Naval de Madrid: Publications

Office of the Director

Campo Muñoz, Juan del. *Breve historia del Palacio del Viso del Margués.* Madrid: Museo Naval, 1988 (Short history of the Palace of Glass of the Marquis).

Cerezo Martinez, Ricardo. *Años cruciales en la historia del Mediterráneo, 1570–1574.* Madrid: Junta Ejecutiva del IV Centenario del la Batalla de Lepanto, 1971. 320 p. (The crucial years in the history of the Mediterranean, 1570–1574).

Cerezo Martinez, Ricardo. *La expedición Malaspina 1789–1794. I Circunstancia Histórica del viaje.* Ministerio de Defensa. Museo Naval (The Malaspina expedition, 1789–1794: The circumstances of the journey).

Conmemoración del IV Centenario de la Batalla de Lepanto 1571–1971. Madrid: Ministerio de Información y Turismo, 1971 (Commemoration of the fourth centenary of the Battle of Lepanto, 1571–1971).

Cortes Albacar, Martin. *Breve compendio de la esfera y el arte de navegar.* Madrid: Museo Naval (A short compendium of the compass and the art of navigation).

Chaves, Alonso de. *Quatri Partitu en cosmografía practica y por otro nombre Espejo de Navegantes.* Transcripción, estudio y notas por Paulino Castañeda, Mariano Cuesta y Pilar hernández. Madrid: Instituto de Historia y Cultura Naval, 1983. 422 p. (The fourth division in cosmographics and for another number of seafaring mirrors).

Chocano Higueras, Guadalupe. *Naves del Descubrimiento "La Santa María, La Pinta y la Niña."* Madrid: Museo Naval, 1985 (The ships of discovery: The *Santa Maria,* the *Pinta* and the *Nina*).

Escalante de Mendoza, Juan de. *Itinerario de navegación de los mares y tierras occidentales. 1575.* Estudios y comentarios por Roberto Barreiro-Meiro. Madrid: Museo Naval, 1985 (Itinerary of the navigation of the Western seas and lands).

Fernandez Duro, Cesáreo. *Armada española desde los reinos de Castilla y Aragón.* 9 vol. 1985–1903. Madrid: Museo Naval, 1972 (The Spanish fleet since the reigns of Castilla and Aragon).

Fernandez Gaytan, José. *Banderas de la Marina de España* (1785–1985). Madrid: Museo Naval, 1985 (Flags of the Spanish navy, 1785–1985).

Guillen Tato, Julio. *Los tenientes de navío Jorge Juan y Santacilla y Antonio de Ulloa y la Torre Guiral y la medición del meridiano.* Madrid, 1973. 274 p. (The ship's lieutenants of Jorge Juan and Santacilla and Antonio de Ulloa and of La Torre Guiral and the measurement of the meridians).

Higueras Rodriguez, María Dolores. *Costa NW de América. Album Iconográfico de la Expedición Malaspina.* Museo Naval (The coast of NW America. Paintings from the Malaspina expedition).

La forma de la Tierra. Medición del Meridiano. (1736–1744). Catálogo. Ministerio de Defensa. Ministerio de Educación y Ciencia. Ministerio de Cultura. En colaboració con la Comisión Quinto Centenario. Madrid: Museo Naval, 1987 (The shape of the earth: Measuring the meridians, 1736–1744).

Martin-Meras, Luisa y Ribera, Belén. *Catálogo de Cartografía Histórica de España del Museo Naval.* Museo Naval, 1990 (Catalogue of historic Spanish maps in the Naval Museum).

Martinez Montero, Homero. *El apostadero de Montevideo.* Prólogo de Julio Guillén Tato. Madrid: Instituto Historico de Marina, 1968. 272 p. (The departure from Montevideo).

Nuñez Iglesias, Indalecio y Fernandez Nuñez, Pedro. *El coloquio de Brion.* Madrid. Museo Naval, 1977. 247 p. (The colloquium at Brion).

Olesa Muñido, Francisco Felipe. *La galera en la navegación y el combate.* Madrid, IV Centenario de la Batalla de Lepanto, 1971. 2 vol. Tomo I: el buque suelto y Tomo II: Formaciones y dispositivos (The galley under sail and in combat).

Ordenanzas del Buen Govierno de la Armada del Mar Océano de 24 de enero de 1633. Barcelona, 1678. Edición facsimil. Madrid: Instituto Histórico de Marina, 1974 (Ordinances to better govern the Ocean War Fleet of 24 January 1633).

O'Scalan, Timoteo. *Diccionario marítimo español.* Madrid: Imprenta Real, 1831. Edición facsímil. Madrid: Museo Naval, 1974 (Spanish maritime dictionary).

San Oui Aladrén, Pilar y Zamarron Moreno, Carmen. *Colección de documentos de Vargas Ponce que posee el Museo Naval.* 2 vol. Madrid: Museo Naval, 1979 (Collection of the documents of Vargas Ponce in the possession of the Naval Museum).

Vellerino de Villalobos, Baltasar. *Luz de Navegantes.* Edición facsímil. Estudio y comentarios de María Luisa Martin-Merás. Madrid: Museo Naval, 1984 (Knowledge of navigation).

Vigon Sanchez, Ana María. *Catálogo de los documentos referentes a la independencia de Colombia, existentes en el Museo Naval y Archivo de Marina "Bazán."* Madrid: Instituto Histórico de Marina, 1969 (Catalogue of documents relating to the independence of Columbia, existing in the Naval Museum and in the Naval Archives "Bazan").

Vigon Sanchez, Ana María. *Guía del Archivo General de Marina "Don Alvaro de Bazán."* Madrid: Instituto Histórico de Marina, 1985 (Guide to the naval archives-general "Don Alvaro de Bazan").

Vigon Sanchez, Ana María. *Colección Antonio de Mazarredo.* Madrid: Museo Naval, 1987. 270 p. (The Antonio de Mazarredo Collection).

Malaspina, Alejandro. *La expedición Malaspina 1789–1794. Diario General del viaje.* Estudio introductorio Ricardo Cerezo. Tomo II. 2 vol. Ministerio de Defensa. Museo Naval (The Malaspina Expedition, 1789–1794: General log of the voyage).

The Military Historical Service of Spain

Office of the Chief,
Translated by Duane C. Young and Robin Higham

ORIGINS

The origin of the Military Historical Service goes back to the so-called Depot of War, a dependent organization of the Staff Corps, begun in 1810 and organized then into Historical and Geographical Sections with the mission to "gather the documents that could facilitate the control of their studies and decisions." Subsequently, the Historical Section constituted the War of Independence (1809–1814) Archive. By 1841 it had become the Historical and Statistical Section with a new mission, that of organizing the archive of the Carlist War (1834–1839). Later the archive of the War of Independence increased with the "Friar's Document Collection," compiled by the missionary Brother Joaquin of Seville, which, from 1924 to 1942, had been deposited in the Romantic Museum and which dealt with, among other themes, the war against the Napoleonic Invasion.

Coordinated with the section mentioned, the Historic Commission of the Campaigns in Morocco was created in 1927, a department whose holdings were added to those with that of another section formed the previous year, both with the objective of studying and publishing on the Spanish operations in Morocco.

With the advent of the Republic in 1931, the Depot of War was dissolved, leaving the Historic Commission of Morocco to continue its work until interrupted in July 1936, the date of the National Uprising.

The National Military Libraries, later integrated into the Military Historical Service, originated within the Museums of Artillery and Engineers, of notable importance in their time, because their history is intimately joined to that of the museums.

The Royal Military Museum was created in 1756, becoming effective in 1803, the date at which it undertook the responsibility for the artillery weapons that defrayed the cost of its formation. Under artillery responsibility, and including other branches of the military art, especially those of artillery and engineers, the museum settled in the Palace of the Counts of Monteleón, a building already occupied by the Artillery Park. The holdings of the Royal Museum came from the existing fonds in the central arsenal, those that provided the collections of artillery and engineers and the models of Montalembert (on the subject of artillery and fortification). It was dismantled during the French invasion of 1808, and with the material remaining in the hands of the French until their evacuation, the Military Museum was restored and enlarged. By Royal Order of 8 March 1816 the museum was moved to the Palace of Buenavista (today the general headquarters of the army), where it remained in a precarious situation. In 1827 it was ordered to catalogue the materials concerning the artillery and engineers, giving space to two museums, one for each arm, within the same building. The enlargement of the other offices of the Ministry of War forced the removal of the Museum of Engineers, though the Artillery Museum remained there. The library of the latter was made independent in 1848, constituting the Archive of the Faculty of Artillery.

The Museum of Engineers was established in the Palace of San Juan and in 1843 its library became autonomous, uniting with those of the academy, the Corps Archive, and the Topographical Depot. In 1905 both outbuildings passed to the Warehouses of the Engineers, located in a wing of an enormous caserón (barracks) in the street of Martyrs of Alcalá (currently the headquarters of the Historical Service). In 1910 the library published its catalog, noting 16,935 records, a number which had risen by the time of the publication of the supplement in 1927. From 1911, museum and library (that had incorporated the segregated Museum of Artillery), constituted one administrative unit. In 1932, the archives of the Museum of Engineers added an important document and map collection from the Section of Engineers of the Depot of the War, remaining so until 1936. Subsequently, the museums were fused into the current Museum of the Army, and the libraries were combined into the current Central Military Library (with the same headquarters as the Historical Service).

Upon creating the Military Historic Service on 8 November 1939, all the historic holdings of the old Depot of the War, the Historic Commission from Morocco, as well as the Libraries of Artillery, Engineers, and others were brought into a single organization for all the missions.

The Historical Service was given the general mission of gathering military experiences, in order to adjust the organization and employment of the armed forces, as well as the diffusion of military culture. To this end the Historical Service was organized in two sections: Historical and Bibliographical.

The Historical Section received the assignment of adding to its holdings with the Archive of the War of Liberation, thus gathering all the documents of both sides in one place. Also, it was given the function of inspecting the rest of the military archives. The secondary missions were established as

- Editing the history of the Spanish Army and other military institutions.
- Studying the War of Liberation, the campaigns in Morocco and overseas, as well as modern wars of special interest.

The Bibliographical Section was constituted in the Central Military Library as well as in other dependent regional ones. The purpose was to compile the holdings of bibliographic and cartographic documents of the museums and libraries of artillery and engineers.

CURRENT ORGANIZATION

The Military Historical Service is an organ of the general headquarters of the Spanish Army that, under the direction of a General of Division, developed from 1988, in a General-Secretary, Section of Administration, and two subdirections: the Military History, Archives, and Libraries, and the Museum of the Army.

With a staff of 150 people, 25-percent civil personnel, in the several centers, it has assignments to

1. File, inventory, edit, and publish documents and related historic topics with the military institution and the profession of arms.
2. Organize, classify, and display, in worthy and adequate manner, weapons, flags, and objects that perpetuate the actions of the army and are of military-historical interest.
3. Welcome and encourage the individual authors who deal with military thought along with the greater history and military personalities.
4. Diffusion of the military historical culture in the army.
5. Military-historical research.
6. Propose distinctions for and naming of units.
7. Pursuit of the histories of the corps and units.
8. Maintain relations with the Royal Academy of History and other civil organizations dedicated to the specialty.

The Subdirection of Military History, Archives, and Libraries is organized into a General and Technical Secretary, Administration, Military History Magazine, Archives, Libraries and Historical Studies, and Publications.

The Section of Historical Studies is composed of six divisions: the War of Independence, Overseas, Campaign in Africa, War of Liberation, Heraldry, and Histories of the Spanish Army. In parallel it develops courses on heraldry, uniforms, and military music.

The divisions cited base their research in the following documentary archives:

1. Antique Documents. With dates of 1724 to 1894, they consist of 7,291 records divided in two large groups: *Originals,* on general topics European, Asian, African, and Oceanic, and *Transcripts,* taken of the archives of the Crown of Aragón and of the Indies.
2. Collection of Count Clonard. It contains forty-six files of documents and manuscript copies referring to the history of the corps and several other matters, with dates from 1442 to 1870.
3. Aparici Collection. It consists of fifty-eight volumes and a total of 6,346 transcript documents of diverse archives, the oldest being of 1560 and the most recent of 1800.
4. Archives of the Wars in Italy. Original documents of 1742 to 1795, contents in eighteen files that refer to the behavior of Spanish troops in Italy.
5. Archives of the War of Independence. It consists of seventy-four files, with documents of 1807 to 1824. One must add the Document Collection of the Friar, which contains, among others, periodic publications and documents of the Napoleonic invasion, some 1,010 volumes dating between 1738 and 1824.
6. Archives of Africa. With documents dated between 1720 and the end of the War with Morocco. It contains documents in 1,208 files.
7. Archives of the Civil War. Divided into three groups, containing more than 16,000 documents, assembled in 3,061 files. The groups refer to documents of the general headquarters of the Generalismo, of the Nationalist Zone, and of the Republican Zone. The correspondence here are very numerous due to the large collection of newspapers. Among the documents of the general headquarters are aerial photographs contained in fifty-five portfolios.
8. Maps and Plans. Comprising a collection of 8,348 plans, that total more than 30,000 sheets (since several of them constitute a single plan [leaf]), divided into General, European, Asian, African, American, and Oceanic Sections. The cartographic collection on South America fortifications of the eighteenth century has great value, comparable to any other in the world.

A collection of 7,274 classified references complete the documentary holdings, in connection with the historic cartography, and they refer to "descriptions" and military "reconnaissances" and records of "fortifications" of the seventeenth, eighteenth, and nineteenth centuries.

The publications carried out up to the present time are varied. Among others, we will mention six volumes of *Overseas Cartography* (the seventh awaiting editing); the *History of the Spanish Army* (two volumes); *Military History Magazine,* published (biannually) and in whose edition in the month of June reproduced a study of General Franco, Chief of the State, of the Battle of San Quintin (in number 71); the *Army of the Bourbons* (two volumes); the *Civil War* (eighteen monographs and others waiting for editing); the *War of the Independence* (five volumes); and others of historical interest.

The Bibliographic Section of the Historical Service, part of the Central Military Library from its creation in 1939, picked up the bibliographic holdings of the Library of Engineers, of the Archives of the Royal Corps of Artillery (Faculty of Artillery Archive), and other lesser materials. Deserving preferential mention is that part dedicated to the Museum of Military Literature, which combines the works of military topics and those of military authors, whatever their themes. Counting some bibliographic holdings, all told there are over 400,000 volumes, mainly on topics in military arts and sciences, historical geographical, technical and engineering, and in minor number those that are related to mathematics, physics, and chemistry, as well as other very notable hand-written and biographical works.

The holdings of iconográfia consist of collections and albums of French, English, Prussian, North American, Swiss, and other Europeans and Americans. All are of great artistic value and were published in the first half of the nineteenth century. The total of these holdings exceeds some 700 sheets of Spanish uniforms and 800 of the foreigners.

THE MILITARY ARCHIVES OF SEGOVIA

The General Military Archives was created by Royal Ordinance of Queen Regent Maria Cristina of 22 June 1898, and integrated in the Military Historical Service, where the subarchives of the Ministry of War that existed in Alcalá de Heneres, Aranjuez, Guadalajara, and Segovia would be reassembled. The archive occupies twenty-five rooms within the fortress, all high ceilinged with different panelling. There are thirteen rooms above and twelve below.

The documentation preserved in the General Military Archives are the following:

1. The personal records from all sources.
2. Military Administrative material of artillery, engineers, sanitary corps, offices, and corps, whatever their source.

3. The procural matters of the Ministry of the War, General Addresses of Carabineros and the Civil Guard, Commandant General of the Disabled, and Halbadiers and Depot of the War.
4. The business of the paymaster and ordnance-general of war, quartermaster-general, commissariart.
5. The papers of the Supreme War and Navy Council, Advisory War Council, and Military vicar-general.
6. The records received from captains, generals, exempt general commands, subinspections, governors, and military commands.
7. The corresponding documentation from the corps.
8. The proceedings of the overseas general box, and depots of flags and embarkations.
9. The causes, summaries, and governmental dossiers, administrative and informational in folio, of all proceedings.

One of the sections most attractive to researchers is the overseas, whose documentation covers the territories that were formerly ours: Cuba, Puerto Rico, Santo Domingo, Mexico, Guatemala, Honduras, El Salvador, Louisiana, Florida, Panama, Colombia, Venezuela, Ecuador, Peru, Chile, Bolivia, Argentina, the Philippines, and Cochinchina. There is also that of Brazil, although it was not Spanish. Today this section is being reorganized in the headquarters of the service in Madrid.

The Army Museum was made part of the Military Historical Service in 1988 and installed in the northern part of the old Royal Palace of the Pensioners (Palaeio Reol del Buen Retiro), which by the wishes of the Count Duke de Olivares was built in the Baroque style by the Spanish architect Alonso Carebonell (1632), its form was lowered under the direction of General Urrutia in 1803, and then actively reorganized for General Bermidez de Castro in 1940. It now is an important reflection of the military history of Spain.

On the principal facade facing Mendez Nunej, the famous Mariner Street hero of the campaign in the Pacific in 1866, there is inside one holding of more than 31,000 items in many rooms from the less to the more important.

The Queen's Room records the exploits of the Spanish Infantry, especially in the nineteenth and twentieth centuries. It contains the last two flags flown at Guantanamo (Cuba) and Mindanao (Philippines), as well as glass cases devoted to Cervantes and numerous illustrious generals.

The Monarch's Room (the former royal throne room) was designed for Velázquez and painted in part for the same, representing all the coats of arms and each of the kingdoms which are components of the Spanish Monarchy. In addition are the four paintings of the famous battle, such as the "Surrender of Breda" by the same painter. There are also centennials of objects of major interest, flags of honor, the bust of the Great Captain, and so on.

The Hall of Arms possesses an unsurpassable collection of portable arms and complete set for some countries and others only of a time period, before the twentieth century. The "Tizona" of El Cid, whose leaf was of the ninth century, exhibits the sword, sabres, pistols, culverins, and flintlocks. Outstanding are the hand cannons used by Hernan Cortés.

The Room of Armor contains the gift of the Ducal House of Medinaceli. There is an equestrian armor and 38 meter galley among whose artifacts are three of Gonzolo Fernández de Córdova, the Grand Commander, the sword of Suero de Qurñones, presented to Juan II of Castille (1406–1454) by the Ducal House, and the reverse of the flag carried by Pizzaro during the conquest of Peru.

The Arab Room is decorated in the style of the Alhambra in Granada. It contains the tunic and two swords of great worth of the last Grenadine (Moorish) king, Boabdil, and an autographed letter of the Order of the Catholic Epiphany of those who went to Africa.

The Colonial Room is a showcase with fifty-four flags and standards of overseas units, and reproductions of the flags of the regiments Navarra, España, and Princesa, who fought for their independence against the British on the side of the North Americans.

The Room of Independence and the War of 1860 in Africa commemorates the heroes of the War of Independence, including Castaños, Wellington, and Palafox, and the peace of Tetuan in 1860 (in Africa).

The Room of Charles I includes the campaign tent used by the Emperor in Tunis, the Imperial Banner of 1535, and so on, and a letter autographed by Lord Nelson as governor of Tenerife.

Other rooms are the Room of the Heroines, the room of the Civil War (1936–1939), the room of the Cavalry, the room of Africa in the twentiethth century, and the room of Miniatures. In the section of the Army Museum in the Alcazar of Toledo there are important holdings and collections of modern arms.

THE HISTORICAL MAPROOM OF THE ARMY GEOGRAPHIC SERVICE

The Geographic Section of the Depot of War had a parallel development to that of the historical service. In 1939, at the end of the Civil War, it was established independently as the Army Geographic Service, maintained under the jurisdiction of the Geodetic and Topographical School.

The Geographic Service possesses in its historical geographical archives a group of 329 atlases classified by century. The sixteen of the sixteenth century stand out as a collection of great value: handwritten parchments, letters in (portulano) style, three translations of the Geography of Ptolemy by Tonsino (1507), Villanovo (1535), and Miguel Servet (1541), the seven editions of the *Theatrum Orbis Terrarum* of Ortelio, as well as the *Civitatis Orbis Terrarum* of Braun. The thirty-four atlases of the seventeenth century were published by Dutch cartographers with several Mercator and other editions, including the ten volumes of the *Blavin Geography*. The 124 atlases of the eighteenth century refers to the French, German, and Italian geographers who competed then with the Spanish geographers Tomas Lopez and his son, Juan, together with Tofiño, Jorge Juan, and Antonio of Ulloa. The 128 atlases of the nineteenth century and the forty-two of the twentieth century are compound works of the principal cartographers of several nationalities, the Germans being the more outstanding.

The map library of the service contains 30,000 maps and guides, some of those parchments of the sixteenth century, the majority of the eighteenth and nineteenth centuries, relating to Spain and America.

The modern map library is universal and contains 25,000 specimens of various countries, in editions of the nineteenth and twentieth centuries. Completing their archives, they hold some 7 million plates from military cartography in current use, or in process of being published.

Both organizations, the Military Historical Service (SHM) and the Geographical Service of the Army (SGE), are integrated in the Direction of Technical Services of the General Headquarters of the Army.

BIBLIOGRAPHY

Museo del Ejercito (The Army Museum)

"El Museo del Ejercito Español" Director de la obra: Manuel de Heredia y Lozano, Colabora Luis López Anglada (Cor. de Infantería) (The Spanish Army Museum).

Edición bilingüe español–ingles (Bilingual edition in Spanish and English).

"Guiá del Museo del Ejercito" (Realización del Museo). Editor: José Mª Fiestas. 1984 (Guide to the Army Museum).

"Museo del Ejército, Guia del visitante." 2ª edición. 1951 The Army Museum Visitors' guide).

Revista de Historia Militar (Military History Review)

Revista de Historia Militar. 1982 (Military history review).

La Guerra de la Independencia. 1983 (The war for independence): Toma I: Antecedentes y Preliminares. (1966) (Vol. I: Antecedents and preliminaries); Toma II: La primera campaña de 1808. (1989) (Vol. II: The first campaign of 1808); Tome III: La segunda campaña de 1808.

(1974) (Vol. III: The second campaign of 1808); Tome IV: Campaña de 1809. (1977) (Vol. IV: The campaign of 1809); Tomo V: Campaña de 1810. (1981) (Vol. V: The Campaign of 1810).

Historia (Histories)

Coronel Juan Guillermo de Mraguiegui: Un personaje americano al servicio de España (1777–1840). 1982 (Colonel Juan Guillermo de Mraguiegui: An American in the Spanish service).

La guerra del Caribe: Reedición en 1990. Aportación del Servicio Histórico Militar a la conmemoración del V Centenario. (The war in the Caribbean: Reissued in 1990 as part of the Military Historical Service's 500th anniversary celebration).

Fortalezas (Fortresses)

El Real Felipe del Callao. Primer Castillo de la Mar del Sur. 1983 (The royal ship *Philip of Castille).*

Las fortalezas de Puerto Cabello. 1988 (The fortresses of Porto Cabello).

Estudios sobre la Guerra de España (1936–1939) (Studies of the Spanish Civil War [1936–1939]).

La guerra de minas en España. 1948 (The War of the Mines in Spain).

Partes Oficiales de guerra (1936–1939). 1978 (The official factions of war [1936–1939]).

Monografías (Monographs)

La marcha sobre Madrid. 1982 (The campaign against Madrid).

La lucha en torno a Madrid. 1984 (The struggle about Madrid).

Regimiento Mixto de Artillería núm. 2. 1965 (Composite Regiment of Artillery No. 2).

Regimiento de Zapadores núm. 1 para Cuerpo de Ejército. 1965 (The Zapadores regiment: The first parachute corps in the Army).

Erjército de los Borbones. Tomo I. Reinados de Felipe V y Luis I (1700–1746). 1990 (The army of the Bourbons: Vol. I. Reigns of Philip V and Louis I [1700–1746]).

El Ejército de los Borbones. Tomo II. Reinados de Fernando VI y Carlos III (1746–1788). 1991 (The army of the Bourbons: Vol. II. Reigns of Ferdinand VI and Carlos III [1746–1788]).

Historial del Regimiento Lanceros del Rey. 1989 (History of the Royal Lancers Regiment).

Organización de la Artillería española en el siglo XVIII. 1982 (Organization of the Spanish artillery in the eighteenth century).

Las Campañas de la Caballería española en el siglo XIX. Tomos I y II. 1985 (The Spanish cavalry's campaigns in the nineteenth century).

Bases documentales del carlismo y guerras carlistas de los siglos XIX y XX. Tomos I y II. 1985 (The documentary basis for Carlismo and the Carlist Wars of the nineteenth and twentieth centuries).

Evolución de las Divisasen las Armas del Ejército español. 1982 (The evolution of the insignia of the divisions of the Spanish Army).
Historia de tres Laureadas: El Rigimiento de Artilleria no. 46. 1984 (The history of three Laureates: The 46th Artillery Regiment).

Heráldica (Heraldry)

Tomo I: *Tratado de Heráldica Militar* (I. Treaty [Handbook on military heraldry]).
Tomo II: *Tratado de Heráldica Militar.* 1984 (II. Treaty [Handbook on military heraldry]).
Cerramientos y Trazas de Montea (Closing and recording the plans of bases).

Carpetas de Láminas (Files of Illustrations)

Ejército Austro-húngaro (The Austro-Hungarian Army).
Caballería europea (European cavalry).
Milicia Nacional local voluntaria de Madrid (Local volunteers of the National Militia of Madrid).
Ejército alemán, siglo XIX (The German Army in the nineteenth century).
Carlos III. Tropas de Casa Real (Carlos III's Royal Household Troops).
Ejército Francés (Siglos XVIII y XIX) (The French Army in the eighteenth and nineteenth centuries).
Carlos III. Estados Militares de España (Charles III. The condition of the Spanish Army).
Primer Regimiento de la Guardia Real de Infantería (The First Royal Infantry Guards Regiment).
Tropas de Ultramar (Troops overseas).

Observaciones (Observations)

Todas estas obras pueden adquirirse en la "Sección de distribución de obras" de este Servicio Histórico Militar (calle Mártires de Alcalá, núm. 9.28025 Madrid). También se remite por correo certificado contra reembolso, con el incremento correspondiente (All inquiries should be addressed to the Distribution Section, Military Historical Section at the address above).

Ortros Organismos de Interes Historico-Militar (Other Organizations with an Interest in Military History)

Real Armerí, organizado en 1983 en su situación actual, puede decirse que fuéiniciado por Felipe II (The Royal Arsenal, organized in 1983 in the same place where Philip II was buried).

Instituto de História y Cultura Naval, Museo Naval de Madrid (The Institute of Naval and Historical Culture, The Naval Museum of Madrid)

Servicio História y Cultura del Ejército del Aire: Instituto de História y Cultura, Museo de Aeronàutica y Astronáutica (The Historical and Cultural Service of the Air Force: Institute of History and Culture, the Air and Space Museum).

Direcciones (Addresses in Madrid)

Servicio Histórico–Militar, Mártires de Alcalá, 9.
Tfno: (91) 5.47.03.00; Fax: (91) 5.59.43.71

Muse del Ejército (The Military/Army Museum), Mendez Nuñez, 1.
Tfno: (91) 5.21.12.85; Fax: (91) 5.31.46.24

Servicio Geográfico (Geographical Service), Dario Gazapo, 8. Tfno: (91) 7.11.49.49; Fax: (91) 7.11.50.32

Dirección de Servicios Tecnicos (The Directorate of Technical Services), Alcala, 51. Tfno: (91) 5.21.29.60; Fax: (91) 5.32.27.71

The Historical and Cultural Service of the Spanish Air Force

Office of the Chief,
Translated by William S. Reeder, Jr.
and Robin Higham

ORIGINS

The predecessors of the Air Force Historical and Cultural Service came into being with the official creation of the Commission of Military History under the presidency of the director of CRESDEN (Centro Superior de Estudios de la Defensa National) and was formed to provide a single voice for the three service military history offices. At that time there was no historical section of the air staff. This led to the conclusion that it was vital to have such an establishment on solid grounds and to start with a small, capable organization.

The manner of birth of the Seminar of Historical Aeronautical Studies (Seminario de Estudios Historicos Aeronatuticos) (SHEA) was created by Order 3/81 of 9 January 1981, initiating, among other tasks, the publication of the book *Great Flights of Spanish Aviation* (Grande Vuelos de la Aviacon Española). Those who participated in this work did so voluntarily and independently of their official duties.

Other things important to the successful propelling of the seminar to a place in the existing organization consisted of the celebration in a dignified manner of the fiftieth anniversary of the flight from Sevilla to Cuba by Capt. Barbaran and Lt. Collar, which was completed in June 1983, and there was no doubt that the goal was entirely achieved with the activities in Seville and Madrid.

At the conclusion of this phase of the seminar, it was thought that the process had matured enough to allow it to be transformed into a concrete organization with assigned personnel and appropriate purposes. So from this period of gestation came the idea of the Historical and Cultural Institute, which would be an expansion of the Historical and Cultural Service of the air staff, which in its turn would be the equal of the historical services of the army and the navy.

CREATION

The new air staff branch was created by Royal Decree No. 1632/1983 of 1 June, which partially modified the decree 1108/1978 of 3 May that year, which had established the original structure of the air staff. The modification consisted of substituting between the organization constituting the headquarters of the air force (AFHQ) and the Museum of Aeronautics and Astronautics for the Historical and Cultural Service and of codifying the ultimate missions and organization. The method was justified by the need to create an organ similar to that which existed in the Ministry of the Army and War with the initiative to undertake and facilitate historical investigations imperative for staff papers and for the study and dissemination of the special air history and culture.

PRESENT ORGANIZATION

Purpose

The SHYCEA (Historical and Cultural Service of the Air Force) is directly subordinate to the chief of the air staff, who directs what historical aeronautical investigations are to be undertaken, especially as relates to the divulging and dissemination of knowledge and understanding of aeronautics and astronautics in Spanish aviation history and its principal feats. Also to this end is the collection, restoration, custody, and display of these items relating to the patrimony (heritage) of the air force, the assignment historically of credit for valor, and those pieces worthy of being conserved in the general (holdings) and illustrations of the past history of the air force.

The Patron of the SHYCEA

The patron, directly under the chief of the air staff, is the superior organ which gives the directions the SHYCEA needs and for whom it works. The entire *patronato* consists of

The president, who is the chief of the air staff
The vice-president, who is the director-general of the SHYCEA
The general head of the Logistical Transport and Support Command
The vice-chief of the air staff of the Spanish Air Force
The head of the Personnel Command
The director-general of Technical Services
The director-general of the Higher Air War College
The head of the Association (Cartek General) of the Air Force
The director-general of economic affairs
The general-director of the Institute of Aeronautical History and Culture
The director-general of the Air Museum
The secretary, who is also the secretary of SHYCEA

The council (*Pedran*), a fully incorporated body, handles subject matters as well as advice, and also the authority of the state administration (the government) and, in addition, the relations of the air force with companies and industry who (adscription) subscribe to (peuda) an interest in the functions (property) of the SHYCEA.

The whole council (*patronato*) meets at least once a year, usually in the first quarter, in order to keep current with the reports of the SHYCEA relating to its activities and accomplishments as a result of the directions given by the council in the previous year. Likewise (*senalara*), new directions are given to follow up on those projects marked for continuation in the following year.

The Organizational Structure of the SHYCEA

The Management of the SHYCEA

The direction of the Historical and Cultural Service of the air force is under the orders of a senior officer of the air staff, who in any situation carries out his assigned primary functions:

1. Establishment, starting with the fixed directives, for the Council, to carry out the tasks assigned to the different offices, directing and coordinating activities so as to bring them to a successful conclusion.
2. To maintain relations with the DRISDEN (Directorship of Cultural Action and Historical Patrimony) and both with the Army Historical Service and the Historical and Cultural Institution of the navy and, in general, with the public and private users of the end products of the SHYCEA.
3. To edit and publish *The Review of Aeronautics and Astronautics.*

In order to carry out these functions, the directorate is divided into the following sections:

- Secretariat General
- Historical and Cultural Aeronautical Institute
- The Air Museum

Secretariat General

This is the organ charged with carrying out the administrative functions necessary to make the SHYCEA run efficiently. The office is commanded by a senior official from the air staff at all times.

The Aeronautical Historical and Cultural Instituto (IHCA)

This is the fundamental organ of the SHYCEA, responsible for historical investigations and especially the promulgation and distribution of aeronautical findings, particularly as they relate to the air force.

Always under the direction of a senior official of the air force staff, the office carries out the following primary functions:

1. The stimulation, facilitation, and encouragement of historical investigations, especially in history of Spanish aviation.
2. To make known the aeronautical and astronautical heritage of Spanish aviation.
3. To exalt the aeronautical accomplishments of Spanish aviation and to spread the word about them.
4. To garner by purchase, gift, or acquisition through collaboration documentation or works of historical aeronautical value, such as writings, photographs, and audiovisual items.
5. To compile, classify, archive, take care of, maintain, reconstruct, and exhibit, with the administrative aim of the investigation and study of their significance.

The IHCA is itself divided into the following:

CENTER FOR DOCUMENTATION

This is the establishment in charge of receiving, classifying, preserving, restoring, and maintaining written documents, maps, photographs, and audiovisual materials which pertain to the productions of the ICHA, which in the end will be utilized by whoever is interested in researching the history of Spanish aviation.

The Central Library of the air staff is still connected to the center because of the similarity of activities of both organizations. The center is also commanded by a senior air force officer at all times.

THE GENERAL ARCHIVES OF AIR FORCE HISTORY

This body is charged with collecting, classifying (cataloguing), archiving, caring for, restoring (in each case along administrative lines), and the investigation and study of air force documentation entrusted to it. It too is always commanded by a senior air force officer.

Publications

Grandes Vuelos de la Aviacion Española (1983). Varios autores (Great flights of Spanish aviation).

Aviones Militares Españoles (1986). Autores: Jesús Salas Larrazábal, José Warleta Carrillo y Carlos Pérez San Emeterio (Spanish military aviation, or the Spanish Air Force).

La Medicina Aeronautica (1987). Autor: Pedro Gómez Cabeza (Aeronautical medicine).

El Dominio del Aire (1987). Versión en castellano del libro de Guilio Douhet (A Spanish version of Douhet's *The Command of the Air).*

Entre el Añil y el Cobalto (1ª Edición 1987, 2ª Edición 1991). Autor: Emilio Herrera Alonso (Between the ring and the cobalt bomb).

Historia de la Aviacion Española (1988). Varios autores (History of Spanish aviation).

El Poder Aereo: Clave de la Supervivencia (1988). Versión en castellano del libro de Alexander P. Severky (Spanish version of *Victory through Air Power*).

El Archivo General e Historico del Aire, Castillo de Villaviciosa de Odon (1989). Autor: Fernando Fernández-Monzón Altolaguirre (The general and historical air archives at the notorious Villa de Odon).

Sabre: Comienzo de Una Epoca (1989). Autores G. Avila Cruz y J. L. González Serrano (The F-86 Sabre—the beginning of an era).

El Infante Don Alfonso de Orleans (1991). Autor: José R. Sánchez Carmona (Prince Don Alfonso de Orleans).

Aeroplano (Revista de Historia, publicada anualmente desde 1983) (*The Aeroplane*, a review published annually since 1983).

The Air Museum

The Air Museum was authorized in 1966 by Decree 1.437 of 16 June. It belongs to the Air Ministry and is located on the outskirts of Madrid. It opened on 21 May 1981, when the public was admitted. In 1983 it inaugurated the Historical and Cultural Service of the Spanish Air Force (SHYCA), including in the latter the functions of the parent organization.

The SHYCA was established under O.M. 32/84 with the duties, as with the museum, to acquire, to take care of, and to conserve the best heritage of the Spanish Air Force and to make known and exalted the best relevant feats of Spanish aviation.

The installations of the museum are divided between the headquarters of the air force, under the direction of a staff officer, and the 10,500 square-meter facility at Carretera N-V Madrid Extremadura, where on the outskirts the artifacts are repaired, stored, and exhibited. The public is admitted daily except on Mondays, from 1,000 to 1,400 hours. The price of admission is 50 pesetas. Under some circumstances the fee is waived.

Under the supervision of a general staff officer of the AFHQ, the museum has the following functions:

1. The collection, rehabilitation, custody, conservation, and exhibition of those aircraft which have been significant in the history of the Spanish Air Force and to which particular significance is attached.
2. The acquisition of new materials or items (*fonds*) which support its mission.
3. To expose and diffuse the history of Spanish aviation and to mediate the exposition in conjunction with others.
4. Technical relations with organizations at the same level, especially those on both the military and civil sides dedicated to aviation.

The Air Museum is organized as follows:

- The secretary-general is authorized to carry out the administrative functions in order to make the museum efficient.
- The Historical-Technical Section is the organization charged with maintaining the library and archives of technical documentation, cataloguing the holdings relating to the heritage, and seeking out and locating new materials of interest to the museum.
- It is under the charge of an official of the superior general staff of the Spanish Air Force.
- The Section on Permanent Traveling Exhibits is charged with those functions and is likewise under the charge of an official in AFHQ.

The principal collections consist of some sixty-five aircraft, from the first aircraft in Spain (the monoplane Vilanova-Acedo of 1911) to one of the prototypes of the recent CASA C-101. There is a fine collection of engines used by the Spanish Air Force. There are also about 100 models in one-tenth scale for single-engined and one-fifteenth scale for multiengined aircraft. In addition, the collections contain armaments, propellers, navigation instruments, and the like.

Museum Publications

As part of its functions, the museum has issued the following publications:
Guía del Museo del Aire (Guide to the Air Museum).
Aeronaves del Museo (Aircraft of the Air Museum).
Guerra Aérea sobre el Marruecos Español (The air war over Spanish Morocco).
Maquetes del Museo (Scale models in the Air Museum).
Boletin del Museo (The bulletin of the Air Museum).
Un joven Museo (A beautiful new museum).
Posters, recordings, and other publications for the young.

In the publishing program are the following:

Maquetas del Museo, 2ª serie (Models in the museum, second series).
En busca de la aventura aérea (The search for aerial adventure).
Uniformidad en la Aeronáutica Militar Española (Spanish Air Force uniforms).
La Aerostación Militar Española (Spanish military airfields).
Motores de la Aviación Española (Spanish aero engines).
Nuestros Pioneros (Our pioneers).
Boletín del Museo, periodicidad trimestral (The quarterly Bulletin of the Air Museum).

20

Sweden

Sweden

Eric Norberg, Director General, Riksarkivet

There are no "official histories" in Sweden. The historians of the Military Historical Department of the Royal Military Staff College publish their works as private individuals and there is no more or less official version of their work. This also applies to the works published by the Royal Military Archives—with the exception of printed guidebooks—and the Defense Museums.

After consultations with the department, above all Klaus-Richard Böhme, I have found it reasonable to mention only what has been published as joint efforts of the department during later years, and in this category I can find only the one-volume work *Sveriges militära beredskap 1939–1945* (The Military preparedness of Sweden 1939–1945), Köping, 1982. This is a general summary of a project resulting in about twenty dissertations treating Sweden and the Second World War. The project started as a pure military project but was transformed in the 1960s into a cooperation between the Military Staff College and the University of Stockholm.

21

Switzerland

Switzerland

Jürg Stüssi-Lauteburg, Berne

There is a historical service located at Berne. It does not, however, publish official histories. What has happened is that retired general officers have from time to time written with some official support of activities, usually in their own time. These manuscripts have been vetted for security matters and then published privately. The following is a list of those volumes.

Schweizer Kriegsgeschichte (Swiss military history), by order of the Chief of the General Staff, Oberkriegs-kommissariat Theophil Sprecher von Bernegg; compiled by Swiss historians under the direction of Colonel M. Feldmann and Captain H. G. Wirtz with contributions from . . . etc. etc. 12 vols. Bern: 1915–1935.

Von der 7. Armeedivision zur Felddivision 7 (From the Seventh Army Division to Field Division Seven) published by the headquarters of Field Division 7, Herisau: 1988.

50 Jahre Felddivision 8 1938–1988 (Fifty years of Field Division Eight 1938–1988) published by the headquarters of Field Division 8, Kriens: 1988.

100 Jahre Eidgenössische Waffenfabrik Bern 1871–1971 (100 years of the confederate weapons factory at Bern 1871–1971). Bern: 1971.

125 Jahre Eidgenössische Munitionsfabrik Thun 1863–1988 (125 years of the confederate munitions factory at Thun 1863–1988). Thun: 1988.

125 Jahre Eidgenössische Konstruktionswerkstätte Thun (125 years of the confederate construction workshop at Thun). Thun: 1988.

50 Jahre Armee-Motorfahrzeugpark Thun (50 years of the army motor vehicle depot at Thun). Thun: 1973.

22

Turkey

The History of the Turkish Military

LTG Alâatin Güven, Turkish Army (Ret.)

The starting point of Turkish history is the Huns, so Turkish military history began around the end of third century B.C., some twenty-two centuries ago.

Geographically—one of the fundamentals of history—Turkish military history extends from the Pacific Ocean and the Great Wall of China in Asia to the Hungarian lowlands in Europe, again from the Siberian and Russian steppes in Asia to the Indian Ocean in the south, as well as including the Mediterranean to the northern coast of Africa.

Since the horseman was an essential part of the Turkish army, horses were widely used in the military operations, thus resulting in very high mobility. Instead of settling down, the Turks chose to march to new lands every time. In this respect, keeping their own records of military operations and events was totally ignored. On the other hand, some indigenous nations with whom the Turks had relations or against whom they fought have very important records which shed light on the history of the Turkish military. For instance, the Chinese chronicles constitute very valuable sources for Turkish history. Because of their continuous relations with the Turks in Asia, the Arab and Persian records provide helpful highlights as well. Also, through their combat with the Turks, Roman, Slav, Byzantine, Hungarian, Venetian, and Austrian records contain useful materials.

During their migration from Asia to western lands the Turks had fought the nations they met on their way. After they had arrived at the Caspian Sea region, they divided mainly into two branches. The first branch moved to the northwest through the Crimea to the Hungarian lowlands and even as far as modern Finland. The other and larger branch moved south of the Caspian Sea through Persia and Iraq to Anatolia and settled there, where they established the Seljuk Empire and then the Anatolian Principalities. After the confrontation with Byzantium in 1453, they established the Ottoman Empire, one of the greater empires of the world at that age. The military power played a major role in this progress.

Due to the training, management, and discipline provided and devotion to the sultan, the Ottoman army was the most efficient and effective of its day, achieving many great conquests. The government was able to expand its borders and won many victories, the army playing the key role in creating an empire. But as the law of nature suggests, the Ottoman Empire passed through the phases of birth, growth, and death and disappeared from sight in 1921.

While its enemies were constantly developing their internal structures and institutions during the Industrial Revolution, being on the decline, the Ottoman Empire was unable to keep up with progress. Also, the army lost the qualities that had been acquired. The increasing number of defeats was a quiet warning of the need for a reform of the military (i.e., to modernize the army according to Western standards). As a result of this, in the nineteenth century the statesmen and especially the sultans shifted their attention to the West.

Selim III (1789–1807) initiated reforms in the military institutions which aimed to achieve Western standards. The next sultan, Mahmut II, was more cautious. Being aware of the lessons of the past he took coercive measures and abolished the by-then-undisciplined Janissary organization in 1826, at a time when the army was at peace. As a result of this, attempts to establish a Western military organization were facilitated. Military educational activities were Europeanized with the addition of foreign specialists.

THE EDUCATION OF THE TURKISH MILITARY PRIOR TO THE ESTABLISHMENT OF HISTORICAL SCIENCE

As is already well known, international historical science became evident at the end of eighteenth century. It is accepted that the starting point of this era is the French Revolution in 1789. The trend of nationalism spread out to many countries after this event. The Ottoman Empire was a multinational state like many others of the day. Having been provoked by this trend, the minorities caused many problems. The invasions by Napoleon Bonaparte's army in Europe and in the Middle East after the French Revolution stimulated minorities in many countries. This nationalist trend also affected the Ottoman Empire. Earlier in the eighteenth century—during Peter the Great's reign—Russia's hostile attitude toward the Ottoman Empire had caused a series of Ottoman–Russian Wars.

In fact, the Ottoman Empire had already established an educational structure in the manner of European military schools. The Naval College (Mühendishane-i Bahri-î Humayûn) and the Artillery College (Mühendishane-i Berri-i Humayûn), which were founded in the second half of eighteenth century, are the two examples of this.

Thus, European military methods and educational organizations were replacing those of the Ottoman Empire. At the beginning, military educational commissions were imported from France. Though initiated during the reign of the reformist Sultan Selim III, these did not last for long, because Selim III was killed during a rebellion.

After the 1870–1871 Franco–Prussian War, German commissions replaced the French and took the leading role in improving the Turkish Army and military organizations.

After this brief review of the military reorganization, we now may pass on to the education in military history.

THE EDUCATION IN MILITARY HISTORY AND COMPLETE ORIENTATION TOWARD THE WEST

It is accepted that the teaching of military history in Turkish military institutions progressed parallel to the reorganization of the Turkish army in a European fashion. Military history was scheduled as a course at the third year of Artillery College, which was established during the reign of Selim III in 1795.

The attempts to establish a school in the Western manner were initiated in March 1845 and the Military or War College (Mekteb-i Harbiye) was established in Istanbul in 1846. The Staff College was introduced shortly afterwards (in 1847–1848) as an extension of the War College and in order to train staff officers as well.

Military history courses were included in the curricula of the Military and Staff Colleges in 1865. The Military History of the Ottoman Empire and war history courses were also introduced to the Staff College's curricula during 1868–1880. In addition to these, war history courses and important war case studies (during von der Goltz's period), art of war and the military history of the Ottoman Empire courses were scheduled during 1881–1883, 1884–1895, and 1895–1901, respectively. Important war case studies and art of war courses were also included during 1901–1908.

THE FOUNDATIONS OF THE HISTORY OF TURKISH MILITARY AND MILITARY RECORD KEEPING

Establishing an organization to record Turkish military history began quite late. Because military courses were included in the curricula of the military colleges, the first books on this subject were written by enterprising instructors and officers.

But since the Ottoman Empire was a multinational society, history books written at that time consisted only of the dynastic chronology. As a result of this, historical methodology was totally disregarded while keeping records of wars, although publications were punctual.

The chroniclers (*vak'a nüvis*), who were a part of the governmental structure, kept annual records. However, these records contained no comment nor were they connected to each other. It is clear that the chroniclers were not as neutral as their official titles would suggest. The historical records, or more realistically the war chronologies, were kept by civilians and officers after the establishment of military colleges in the Western manner.

The introduction of systematic studies of military history coincided with the German–Turkish cooperation during the First World War. Having concluded an alliance, Germany and the Ottoman Empire collaborated in all military aspects.

As a result of regarding history theoretically, an organization was established on March 23, 1916, called *Karargâho-i Umumi*, the 16th section of general staff in Istanbul. It was responsible for military history.

From then on military history acquired an official status which was executed formally by individual officers and civilians. There were also efforts to establish archives during this period. After that, military history studies were put on a firm basis by the "regulations for war diaries and documentary files" which were enacted in 1917.

This first section of the military history division then became the 8th section of the general staff on November 10, 1919, and classification of military documents was initiated. The main topics of this classification were

1. Wars prior to the Balkan Wars of 1912–1913
2. The Balkan Wars
3. The First World War

4. Military medical history
5. Military veterinarian history
6. The archives

The General Staff Military History Section was renamed the Military History Registration Committee on July 3, 1920, and continued to study military history.

Because of the reorganization throughout the whole country during 1921 to 1926, this section's name changed many times. It became the Military History Committee in 1921. Then its name was changed twice in 1922, from General Staff Council to History of Warfare Section. It was at last called the History of Warfare Department in 1926. It was under the chief of the general staff and renamed the History of Warfare and Geographic Council in 1944. From then on it moved to its current building in Ankara, and in 1951 took the name History of Warfare Department. It became one of the joint departments of the general staff as the History of Warfare Directorate in 1967. Finally, in 1978 it took its current name as the General Staff Military History and Strategical Research Directorate and continued to support the Turkish Armed Forces with both national and military history.

The department's main interests are military history, strategical research, archives, studies on international military history, and military culture sites (Military Museum and the Mehteran Division). The department's activities concerning military history are as follows:

- The Ottoman Empire period (1299–1920)
- The Balkan Wars (1912–1913)
- The First World War (1914–1918)
- The Turkish War of Independence (1919–1922)
- The Period of the Grand National Assembly of Turkey (1920–1923)
- The Turkish Republic (1923–)

The Military History Commission of Turkey continues its research within its own body as well as cooperating with legal organizations (universities and the Society of Turkish History). Through the history seminars, which have been given every two years since 1983, civilian researchers and official historians have gathered together to highlight aspects of military history. The Turkish Military History Commission has been a member of the International Commission of Comparative Military History (ICCMH) since 1974. In this respect it is possible for it to cooperate with military historians of different nations. In order to extend the areas of collaboration, a most successful international colloquium was held in Istanbul in 1993.

Through the military seminars and colloquia we make use of data supplied by the Atatürk Kültür Dil ve Tarih Yüksek Kurume (Atatürk Culture and Language Assembly), Türk Tarih Kurume (History Assembly of Turkey), and instructors from history departments of the universities. The names and the addresses as of 1993 of these departments concerning official military history are

Atatürk Kültür Dil ve Tarih Yüsek Kurum Başkanligi 06680 Ankara

Atatürk Ara tirma Merkezi Başkanligi 06680 Ankara

Türk Tarih Kurumu Başkanligi 06050 Ankara

The address of the Directorate of History and of the Turkish Commission of Military History is Atatürk Kültör Dil, Tarih Yüsek Kurum, Baskan—Ligi, 06680 Ankara, Turkey.

Bibliography

MILITARY HISTORY PUBLICATIONS (BEFORE 1930)

Ahmet (Süvari Yüzbaşı); *Türk Istiklâl Harbi'nin Başında Milli Mücadele,* Büyük Erkän-ı Harbiye Reisliği 10 ncu Şubesi, Ankara, 1928, 126 Sayfa, 29x19, Fihrist, Giriş, 9 Fotoğraf, 10 Kroki, 1 Harita, Çizelge (Istiklâl:17) (National defense at the beginning of the Turkish War of Independence).

Ahmet Cemal (Erkân-ı Harbiye Kolağası); *Plevne Müdafa-sı.* Kütüphane-i İslam, İstanbul, 1316 (1900), 160 Sayfa, 14x20, Fihrist, Önsöz, Giriş, Bibliyografya (93 Seferi:36) (The defense of Plevne).

Ahmet Cevat (Paşa); *Tarih-i Askeri-i Osmani,* İstanbul, Kırkanbar Matbaası, 1883, 287 Sayfa, 27x19 (Tarih:917) (The military history of the Ottoman Empire).

Ahmet Muhtar (Ferik, Topçu Erkân-ı Harbiyesi'nden Mütekait); *1244–1245 Türkiye Rusya Seferi ve Edirne Muahedesi Yahut Vakitsiz Seferin İbret ve İntibah Dersle-ri.* 2 Cilt, Büyük Erkân-ı Harbiye Onuncu Şubesi, Ankara, 1928, 234 Sayfa, 25x18, Fihrist, 17 Adet Cetvel, Bibliyografya (Eski Sefer:104) (1244–1245 Turkish–Russian War and the Edirne Pact).

Ahmet Muhtar (Topçu Erkân-ı Harbiye Kaymakam-ı); *Çapı Büyük Seri Ateşli Toplar.* İstanbul, Mekteb-i Harbiye Matbaası, 1309 (1893), 198 Sayfa, 27x20, Önsöz, Giriş, 38 Şekil 4 Fotoğraf 26 Çizelge, Bibliyografya (Türk Silahlı Kuvvetleri:305) (Large caliber automatic artillery).

Ahmet Muhtar (Miralay); *A'yâd-ı Mefahir-i Milliye-i Osmaniye'den: Osmanlılığın Avrupa'da Tarz-ı Teessüsü Yahut Feth-i Celile-i Konstantiniye* (H-857/M.1453), Tab ve Neşri "Malumat" ve "servet" Gazeteleri İmtiyaz Sahibi Es-seyid Mehmet Tahir, Maarip Nezaret-i Celilesi-nin ruhsatıyla İstanbul'Tahir Bey Matbassı'nda Bastırılmıştir, 1316 (1900), 311 Şayfa, 18, 5x26, 5, Fihrist, Giriş, 26 Resim, 1 Harita, 4 Kroki (Tarih:812) (The sources of Ottoman pride, or the conquest of Istanbul).

Ahmet Muhtar (Miralay); *Osmanlı Topçiuları.* İstanbul, Mekteb-i Fünun-u Harbiye Matbaasi, 1315 (1899), 406 Sayfa, 28x20, Önsöz, Giriş. 2-Resim, 1 Harita, Çizelge, Bibliyografya (Tarih:348) (The Ottoman artilleryman).

Ahmet Muhtar (Erkân-ı Harp Ferik); *Esfar-ı Osmaniye Hatıraları: 1073-1075 Seferi'nin Vakayi-i Esasiyesi Sengotar'da Osmanlı Ordusu,* Kitabhane-i İslam ve Askeri Tüccarzade Ibrahim Hilmi, İstanbul, 1326 (1910) 80 Sayfa, 15, 5x23, Giriş, 7 Resim, 2 Kroki, Bibliyografya (Eski Sefer:72) (The memoirs of the old Ottoman campaigns).

Ahmet Muhtar Paşa; *Muharebat-ı Meşhure Muhakeme ve Mubahesatı,* İstanbul, Mekteb-i Harbiye Matbassı, 1306 (1890), 222 Sayfa, 16x26, 65 Kroki (Tarih:856) (Review of famous battles).

Ahmet Nihad (Kaymakam); *1897 Osmanlı-Yunan Seferi'nde Teselya Harekâtı,* Harbiye Mektebi Matbaası, 1926, 45 Sayfa, 15x20, Önsöz (Türk-Yunan:5) (Operations in Thessaly during the 1897 Ottoman–Greek War).

A. R.; *11 Nisan İnkılâbı,* İstanbul Kütüphane-i İslam ve Askeri, 1325 (1909), 95 Sayfa, 17x12, Giriş, 15 Adet Resim (Büyük Harp:19) (The revolution of 11 April 1909).

Ahmet Rasim; *Türkiye Adalar Denizi Kılavuzu, İmroz'dan Marmaris Burnuna Kadar,* İstanbul, Matbaayı Bahriye, 1926, 215 Sayfa, 23x16, Önsöz, Fihrist, 43 Şekil (Deniz:67) (The Aegean Sea guide from Imroz to the Cape of Marmaris).

Ahmet Refik; *Meşhur Osmanlı Kumandanları,* İbrahim Hilmi, İstanbul, Kütüphane-i İslam ve Askerî 1318 (1912), 388 Sayfa, 11x17, 5 (Tarib:95) (Famous commanders of the Ottoman Empire).

Ahmet Refik; *Tarihte Osmanlı Neferi,* Süleymaniye (İstanbul), Matbaası Askeriye 1331 (1915) 26 Sayfa, 13x18, 5 (Genel Eser:74) (The history of the Ottoman soldier).

Ahmet Refik; *Yirmibeş Sene Siper Kavgası,* İstanbul, Orhaniye Matbaası, 1333 (1917), 217 Sayfa, 12x17 (Genel Eser:124) (Twenty-five years long trench warfare).

Ahmet Saip; *1877 Osmanlı Rus Seferi,* Kahire, Hindiye Matbaası, 1327 (1911), 381 Sayfa, 13x19, Giriş (93 Seferi:26) (1877 Ottoman–Russian War).

Ahmet Sedat (Erkân-ı Harbiye Kolağası); *Karadağlılarda Sevkülceyş ve Tabiye,* İstanbul, Mekteb-i Harbiye Matbaası, 1327 (1911), 57 Sayfa, 13x20, Fihrist, 7 Kroki (Kaybol-muştur). (Harp tarihi Yardımcı Eserler:55) (The tactics and strategy of the Montenegran Army).

Ahmet Sedat (Erkân-ı Harp Binbaşı); *Yunan Ordusu Ahval ve Tensikat-ı Askeriyesinden Bir Mebze,* İstanbul Mekteb-i Fünun-u Harbiye-i Şahane Matbaası, 1320 (1904), 26 Sayfa, 23x15 (İstiklâl:78) (A brief review of the military reorganization of the Greek Army).

Ahmet Suat (Piyade Yüzbaşı); *Balkan Darülharbine Dair Tetkikat-ı Coğrafya ve Mütalaat-ı Sevkülceyşiye,* ı nci Kitap, İstanbul Mühendishane-i Berri-i Hümayun Matbaası, 1330 (1914), 62 Sayfa, 15x23 (Harp Tarihi Yardımcı Eserler:66) (The geographical study of the Balkan War and strategic opinions).

Akgün; *İzmir'in Kurtarılışı,* Jandarma Matbaası, 1341 (1925), 24 Sayfa, 23x16, Giriş, 1 Resim (İstiklâl:343) (The liberation of Smyrna).

Alaaddin (Miralay); *Balkan Harbi'nde 4 ncü Fırka'nın Harekâtı,* Erkân-ı Harbiye-i Umumiye (Genelkurmay Başkanlığı) Yayınlarından 61 No. lu Askeri Mecmua'ya Ek olarak Neşredilmiştir. İstanbul, 1926, 86 Sayfa, 23x15, 5, Fihrist, 2 Kroki, 2 Çizelge (Balkan:20) (The operations of the 4th Division during the Balkan War).

Alaşehir Kongresi Mukarrerati (16/25 Ağustos 1919), 13 Sayfa, 21x14 (İstiklâl:166) (The results of the Alaşehir Congress [16–25 August 1919]).

Ali Fethi (OKYAR); *Bolayır Muharebesi'nde Adem-i Muvaffakiyetin Esbabı,* Tabı ve Neşri İbrahim Hilmi, İstanbul, Kütüphane-i İslam ve Askeri, 1330 (1914), 26 Sayfa, 11, 5x17, 5 Giriş (Balkan:63) (The reasons for failure in the Bolayir War).

Ali Fuat (Erkân-ı Harp. Miralayı); *Süleyman Paşa Ordusu'nun Balkandaki Harekâtı,* İstanbul Matbaayı Askeriye 1340 (1924), 107 Sayfa, 17x25, Fihrist, Giriş, 26 Kroki (93 Seferi:11) (The operations of Süleyman Pasha's Army in the Balkans).

Ali Haydar (Kolağası); *Kosova Meydan Muharebesi,* Konstantiniye (İstanbul), Matbaayı Ebuzziya, 1328 (1912), 59 Sayfa, 12x18, Önsöz, Giriş, Dört Adet Resim (Eski Sefer:62) (The battle of Kosova).

Ali Haydar Emir; *İmroz Baskını,* Yıldız, Askeri Akademiler Kumandanlığ ı Matbaası, 1927, 20 Sayfa, 23x16 (Deniz:153) (The Imroz raid).

Ali Haydar Emir; *Türkiye–İtalya Harbi 1327–1328 (1911–1912),* İstanbul, 1339 (1923), 297 Sayfa, 23x17 (Deniz:171) (The Turkish–Italian War [1911–1912]).

Ali Rıza (Erkân-ı Harbiye Kaymakamı); *1897 Türk-Yunan Seferi,* İstanbul, Erkân-ı Harbiye, 1927, 231 Sayfa, 13x20, Çizelge, Bibliyografya, Harita (Türk-Yunan:9) (The 1897 Turco–Greek campaign).

Ali Rıza (Piyade Binbaşı); *Harb-i Umumi' de Yunan Ordusu,* Karargâh-ı Umumi İstihbarat Şubesi, İstanbul, 1916, 39 Sayfa, 17x12, 5, Fihrist, 13 Adet Cetvel (Büyük Harp:17) (The Greek Army during the First World War).

Ali Rıza Seyfi; *Barboros Hayreddin,* İstanbul, Bahriye Matbaası, 1330 (1914) 55 Sayfa, 24x16, 2 Resim (Deniz:89) (The great Admiral Barboros Hayrettin).

Ali Saib; *Kilikya Facialar ve Urfa'nın KurtuluşMücadeleleri,* Ankara, 1340 (1924), 262 Sayfa, 20x13, Önsöz, 1 Resim (İstiklâl:94) (The tragedy of Kilikya and the fighting for independence of Urfa).

Arifî (Piyade Miralay); *Askeri İstatistik,* İstanbul, Şirket-i Mürettebiye Matbaası, 1334 (1918), Önsöz, Fihrist, 111 Sayfa, 19x12 (Genel Eser:81) (Military statistics).

Esfar-ı Osmaniye tetkikatından 1293–1294 (Osmanlı-Rus) Seferinde Kafkas Cephesi; 54 Sayfa, 16x23, 2 Kroki (93 Seferi:13) (The Caucasian front during the 1877–1878 Ottoman–Russian War [from a study on the campaigns of the Ottoman Empire]).

Bağdat'a Doğru; Times Gazetesi'nin Tarih'i Harbi'nden Çev: Hüsameddin, İstanbul, Matbaayı Amire, 1333 (1917), 43 Sayfa, 15, 5x23, Fihrist (Büyük Harp Irak:10) (Toward Bagdad).

Bahri (Yüzbaşı); *Balkan Harbi'nde Sırp Ordusu,* İstanbul, Tanin Matbaası, 1913 (1329) 77 Sayfa, 12x19, Giriş, İçindekiler (Balkan:38) (The Serbian Army during the Balkan wars).

Bahriye Salnamesi 1878 (1293 H.); Bahriye Nezareti 1 nci Daire 3 ncü Şubesi, İstanbul, Bahriye Matbaası, 1330 (1914), 309 Sayfa, 23x15, Fihrist (Müracaat:164) (The Naval almanac—1878).

Behçet (Mütekait Miralay); *Büyük Harpte Mısır Seferi,* İstanbul, Askeri Matbaa, 1930, 34 Sayfa, 25x18, Giriş, 1 Harita (Birinci Dünya Harbi:45) (The Egyptian campaign during the First World War).

1910 Tarihli Bulgar Hizmet-i Seferiye Nizamnamesi'nin Muharebe Kısmı; İstanbul Matbaayı Askeriye, 1330 (1914) 61 Sayfa, 13x20, Çizelge (Balkan:77) (Combat section of the Bulgarian Army service regulations dated 1910).

1877–1878 Osmanlı-Rus Seferi'nde Osmanlı Kumandanları; Çev: Halil Rüş tü Matbaa-ı Ebüzziya, İstanbul, 1329 (1913), 68 Sayfa, 11x16, Önsöz, Giriş (93 Seferi:27) (The Ottoman commanders of the 1877–1878 Ottoman–Russian War).

1335–1336 Seneleri Kafkasya'da İslamlara Karşı İcra Olunduğu Tebeyyün Eden Ermeni Mezalimi, Türkiye Büyük Millet Meclisi Hükümeti Saek Cephesi Kumandanlığı, Kars 1.1.1337 (1921), 32 Sayfa 18x14, 6 Belge (İstiklâl:165) (The Armenian atrocities on Islams in 1919–1920 at Caucasia).

1328 Balkan Harbi'nde Şark Ordusu Kumandanı Abdullah Paşa'nın Hatıratı; İstanbul, Erkân-ı Harbiye Mektebi Matbaası, 1336 (1920), 332 Sayfa, 22x15, Fihrist, Onsöz, Giriş, Metin Haricinde Cetvel ve Haritalar Fihristi (Balkan:26) (The Eastern Corps Commander Abdullah Pasha's diary of the 1912 Balkan War).

Bulgaristan ile Mütterfikîn Arasında Aktedilip 15 Kânunusani (Ocak) 1920'de İrade-i Kraliye İktiran Eyleyen Nöyyi Muahedesi'nin Mevadd-ı Askeriyesi; Erkân-ı Harbiye-i Umumiye Riyaseti 2 nci şube, İstanbul, 1337 (1921), 24 Sayfa, 26x15, 5 Çizelge (İstiklâl:270) (The military paragraphs of the Noyon Pact).

Burhanettin Bey (Erkân-ı Harbiye Miralayı); *Türk Cepheleri: Çanakkale Muharebesi Notları,* İstanbul, Harp Akademileri Komutanlığı Matbaası, 1929, 80 Sayfa, 15x22, 1 Adet Kroki (Çanakkale:60) (Notes on the War of the Dardanelles).

Bursalı Mehmed Tahir; *Menakib-i Harb,* Dersaadet (İstanbul), Ahmet İhsan Matbaası, 1333 (1917), 23 Sayfa, 12x20, 5 (Eski Sefer:46) (Real-life war stories).

Büyük Harp-Türk Cepheleri, Çanakkale Cephesi; Kısım:2, İstanbul, Yıldız Askeri Akademiler Kumandanlığı Matbaası, 1927, 112 Sayfa 16x23 (Çanakkale:23) (The Turkish fronts during the First World War: The Dardanelles front).

Büyük Harp-Türk Cepheleri. Filistin Cephesi; Kısım:3, İstanbul, Yıldız Askeri Akademiler Kumandanlığı Matbaası, 1927, 955 Sayfa, 16x24 (Filistin:30) (The Turkish fronts during the First World War: The Palestinian front).

Cavid (Mütekait Mirliva); *Irak Seferi ve İttihat Hükümetinin Hayalat ve Cehalat-ı Siyasiyesi,* İstanbul, Müdafaa Matbaası, 1334 (1918), 49 Sayfa, 14x20, Önsöz (Büyük Harp Irak:16) (The Iraq campaign and the ignorant policy and illusions of the Committee of Union and Progress Government).

Cenevre Mukavelenâmesi ve Mevadd-ı Müteferriası; İstanbul, Matbaa-i Askeriye, 1327 (1911), 36 Sayfa, 15, 5x22, 5 (Tarih:547) (The paragraphs of the Geneva Pact in detail).

Ceride-i Askeriye; Sayı 14 Erkân-ı Harbıye i Umumiye Talim ve Terbiye Şubesi, İstanbul, 30 Eylül 1338 (1922), 9 Sayfa, 30x20, Önsöz, Bir Adet Kroki (Harp Tarihi Yardımcı Eser:1) (The military journal [No. 14]).

Cevdet Kerim (Erkân-ı Harbiye Binbaşısı); *Türk İstiklâl Harbi (Garp Cephesi),* Erkân-ı Harbiye-i Umumiye Talim ve Terbiye Dairesi, İstanbul, Matbaayı Ebuziya 1341 (1925), 222 Sayfa, Fihrist, Önsöz, 30 Kroki, 25x19 (İstiklâl:26) (The Turkish War of Independence [Western Front]).

Cevdet Kerim (Erkân-ı Harp Binbaşısı); *Halk Konferanslari; Türk İstiklâl Mücadelesi Konferansları,* Maarif Vekâleti Milli Talim ve Terbiye Dairesi Halk Terbiyesi Şubesi, İstanbul, 1927, 227 Sayfa, 20x14, Önsöz, 2 Harita, 1 Kroki (İstiklâl:92) (Lectures on the Turkish struggle for independence).

Cihan Harbi'nde Osmanlı Harekâtı Tarihçesi—Çanakkale Muharebatı; Dersaadet (İstanbul), Matbaayı Askeriye 1338 (1922), Cüzü:1 (Cilt:1), 75 Sayfa, 16x24, Fihrist, Önsöz (Çanakkale:21) (The history of the operations of the Ottoman Empire during the First World War: The battles of the Dardanelles).

Çanakkale Raporu; Çev.: Hüsamettin, İstanbul, Matbaa-ı Amire, 1333 (1917), 82 Sayfa, 23,5x16,1 Kroki (Çanakkale:84) (The Dardanelles report).

Çanakkale'de Torpillere Karşı Korunma; Karargâh-ı Umumi 12. Mevaki-i Müstahkem Şubesi, 1332 (1916), 11 Sayfa, 19x13 (Çanakkale:74) (Defense against torpedo attack at the Dardanelles).

Çobanoğlu A. Z.; *Balkan Harbi Şark Ordusu'nun Hezimeti* (1 nci Nizamiye Kolordusu Hatıratından), Birinci Kısım, İbrahim Hilmi, İstanbul, 1332 (1916), 105 Sayfa, 12x18, Giriş (Türkçesi vardır) (Balkan:36) (The failure of the Eastern Army Corps during the Balkan War).

Devlet-i Âliyye ile Sulh Muahedesi; Öğüt Matbaası, Konya 1336 (1920), 176 Sayfa, 23x15 (İstiklâl:148) (The peace agreements reached with the Ottoman State).

Devlet-i Âliyye ile Sulh Şerâiti; İstanbul, Matbaayı Amire, 1336 (1920), 111 Sayfa, 29x20 (İstiklâl:143) (The conditions of the Peace Agreements).

Dördüncü Kolordu Manevrası; Erkân-ı Harbiye-i Umumiye Talim ve Terbiye Dairesi, İstanbul, 1927, 230 Sayfa, 23x15, Fihrist, 20 Kroki, 2 Harita, 4 Kurulu (Türk Silahlı Kuvvetleri:108) (The maneuvers of the 4th Army Corps).

Dukakinzade Feridun (Mütekait Yüzbaşı); *(1736–1739) Türk-Avusturya-Rus Seferi,* Erkân-ı Harbiye-i Umumiye Onuncu Şubesi, İstanbul, 1928, 24 Sayfa, 23x16, Fihrist, Dipnot, 1 Adet Kroki (Eski Sefer:110) (1736–1739 Turkish–Austrian–Russian Campaign).

Dukakinzade Feridun (Erkân-ı Harp Yüzbaşı); *Büyük Harp-Türk Cepheleri, Filistin Cephesi,* Harp Akademisi 1926–1927 Tedrisat , Yıldız-Harp Akademileri Komutanlığı Matbaası, 1927, 91 Sayfa, 23x15 (Filistin:30) (The Turkish fronts during the First World War: The Palestinian Front [by Captain Dukakinzade Feridun]).

Dumlupınar-Başkumandan Meydan Muharebesi Devr-i Senevisi Merasimi; Matbuat Müdüriyet-i Umumiyesi, Ankara, 1340 (1924), 23 Sayfa, 18x24 (İstiklâl:237) (Anniversary of the battle of Dumlupinar victory ceremony).

Düvel-i Mutelife Tarafından Verilen Muahede Projesine Askeri Cevaplar; Dersaadet (İstanbul), Matbaa-ı Askeri, 1337 (1921), 62 Sayfa, 16, 5x25 (İstiklâl:269) (The military response of the Ottoman Empire to the pact proposed by the Allied Powers).

Edirne, Yanya Kaleleriyle Rumeli Garp ve Çatalca Orduları Taltifat Defteri; İstanbul, Matbaa-ı Askeriye, 1329 (1913), 133 Sayfa, 20x13, Doğru-Yalnış Cetveli (Balkan:73) (The honor book of Western Rumelian and Çatalcan armies).

Emin (Mirliva); *Yanya Müdafaası* I, II. Cilt), Erkân-ı Harbiye-i Umumiye Talim ve Terbiye Dairesi, İstanbul, 1927, 117 Sayfa, 26x19, Yanlış-Doğru Cetveli, Önsöz, Giriş, 38 Adet Kroki, 4 Levha, 3 Nizam-ı Harb, 23 Adet Harita, 6 Kuvve Cetveli (Balkan:12) (Defense of Yanya).

Erkân-ı Harbiye Mekteb-i Külliyatı; Adet 10, İstanbul, 10 Eylül 1336 (1920), 40 Sayfa, 13, 5x21, Fihrist (Büyük Harp Filistin:15) (The bibliography of the General Staff School).

Ermeni Komitelerinin Âmâl ve Harekât-ı İhtilaliyesi; Erkân-ı Harbiye-i Umumiye Riyaseti, İstanbul 1332 (1916), 323 Sayfa, 18x32, Giriş, 66 Resim. Harp Tarihi Yardımcı Eserler:24 (The desires of the Armenian Committee and their attempts at rebellion).

Fahreddin (Ferik); *Kudüs Muharebesi 26 ncı Fırka'nın Harekâtı,* Konya, Vilayet Matbaası, 1341 (1925) 23 Sayfa, 14x23, Önsöz, Krokiler kaybolmuştur (Filistin:25) (The operations of the 26th Division during the Jerusalem War).

Fahreddin (Ferik); *Türkiye İstiklâl Muharebatında Süvari Kolordusunun Harekâtı,* Konya Vilayet Matbaası, 1925 (1341), 52 Sayfa, 21x15, İçindekiler, Giriş (İstiklâl:56) (The operations of the Cavalry Army Corps during the Turkish War of Independence).

Fatma Aliye; *Kosova Zaferi-Ankara Hezimeti,* Dersaadet (İstanbul), Kanaat Matbaası, 1331 (1915), 143 Sayfa, 12, 5x17, 5, Önsöz, Giriş (Eski Sefer:58) (Kosova victory—Ankara defeat).

Fevzi (Yüzbaşı); *Cihan Harbi'nde Deniz Muharebeleri ve İskajerak,* Ahmet Kemal Matbaası, 1928, 114 Sayfa, 21x15, İçindekiler, Giriş, Kroki ve Tablo (Deniz:164) (Naval campaigns during the First World War).

Fevzi; *Deniz Muharebeleri (1793–1905),* Bahriye Matbaası, 1927, 296 Sayfa, 23x16, Fihrist, Önsöz, 43 Resim, 30 Kroki (Deniz:90) (Naval wars [1793–1905]).

Fevzi (Çakmak-Müşir); *Garb-i Rumeli'nin Suret-i Ziya-ı Balkan Harbi'nde Garp Cephesi,* İstanbul, Erkân-ı Harbiye Mektebi Matbaası, 480 Sayfa, 26x19, Doğru-Yanlış Cetveli, Fihrist, Giriş (Balkan:10) (The western front during the Balkan War).

Fransızlara Nazaran Suriye ve Kilikya Muharebatı; Çev.: Kurmay Albay Kadri, Erkân-ı Harbiye-i Umumiye, İstihbarat Dairesi, İstanbul, 1341 (1925), 130 Sayfa, 24x18, Fihrist, Giriş, 5 Kroki (İstiklâl:254) (Syrian and Kilikyan battles according to the French).

Ganaim-i Bahriye Kanunu Sureti; Matbaa-ı Bahriye, İstanbul, 1328 (1912), 13 Sayfa, 26x18 (Deniz:24) (A copy of the Naval War Code).

Gece Harekât ve Muharebeleri; Erkân-ı Harbiye-i Umumiye Talim ve Terbiye Dairesi, İstanbul 1927, 120 Sayfa, 23x15, Fihrist (Türk Silahl Kuvvetleri:219) (Night operations and battles).

General Boa; *1914–1918 Harbi Esnasında Alman Ordusu,* Çev.: İstihkâm Albay Ali Galip, İstanbul Matbaayı Askeriye 1339 (1923), 39 Sayfa, 23x15, Fihrist, Önsöz, Kroki (Büyük Harp:41) (The German Army during World War I [1914–1918]).

Goltz (Müşir); *Osmanlı Yunan Seferi 1897 (1313),* İstanbul Mekteb-i Fünun-u Harbiye-i Osmani Matbaası, 1326 (1910), 297 Sayfa, 15x22, Önsöz, Giriş (Türk-Yunan:4) (The Ottoman–Greek Campaign, 1897).

H. Cemal; *Yeni Harp, Başımıza Tekrar Gelenler, Edirne Harbi Muhasarası, Esaret ve Esbab-ı Felaket,* İstanbul, Şemsi Matbaası, 1917, 601 Sayfa, 17, 5x11, 5, Önsöz, Giriş (Balkan:28) (The new war, recurrences, the siege of Edirne [Adrianople]).

H. Sami (Yüzbaşı); *Tabiye-i Bahriye,* İstanbul, Matbaayı Bahriye, 1338 (1922), 58 Sayfa, 23x15, Giriş, 14 Kroki (Deniz:181) (Naval War Tactics).

Harb-i Bahri Esasları; İstanbul, Bahriye Matbaası, 1329 (1913), 223 Sayfa, 16x11 (Deniz:195) (The bases of naval warfare).

Harb-i Umumi'de Çanakkale Muharebat-ı Bahriyesi; İstanbul, Erkân-ı Harbiye Mektebi Matbaası, 1336 (1920), 26 Sayfa, 23x15 (Deniz:120) (The Dardanelles naval battles during World War I).

Harb-î Umumi'de Osmanlı Cepheleri Vakayi'i; 80 Sayfa, 15x23, Giriş, 8 Krokisi Olan Kitabın 2 Krokisi Kaybolmuştur (Büyük Harp Kafkas:19) (The battles on the Ottoman fronts during World War I).

Harb-î Umumi'de Osmanlı Tarih'i Harbi-Çanakkale Muharebatı, 1330–1331; Harbiye Nezareti, 111 Sayfa, 24x31, 3 Kroki, 1 Çizelge (Çanakkale:1) (The Ottoman history during World War I and the Dardanelles battles).

Hasan Sırrı; *Hukuk-u Düvel Noktay-ı Nazarından Osmanlı-İtalya Muharebesi,* Konstantiniye (İstanbul), Matbaa-i Ebuzziya, 1330 (1914), 40 Sayfa, 9x19 (Türk-İtalyan:4) (The Ottoman–Italian War from the viewpoint of international law).

Haydarizâde İbrahim; *Irak Ordusu'na Hitab,* İstanbul, Matbaayı Amire, 1335 (1919), 16 Sayfa, 19x12, 5 (Harp Tarihi Yardımcı Eserler:214) (Irak:17) (The address to the Iraqi Army).

Hayri Bey (Kaymakam); *Harb-i Umumi'de Çanakkale Muharebat-ı Berriyesi, Anafartalar Grubu Muharebatı,* İstanbul, Erkân-ı Harbiye Mektebi Matbaası, 1336 (1920), 61 Sayfa, 16x23, Önsöz (Çanakkaale:73) (During World War I the Dardanelles battles and Anafartalar battles).

Hayreddin (Binbaşı); *Harb-i Bahri San'atı,* İstanbul, Bahriye Matbaası, 1926, 119 Sayfa, 24x16, Önsöz, 11 şekil, 13 Çizelge (Türk Silahlı Kuvvetleri:330) (The art of naval warfare).

Hindistan Ordusu ve Mısır'daki Kıtaat-ı İşgaliye, İstanbul, Matbaa-ı Askeriye, 1331 (1915), 11 Sayfa, 24x33, 1 Harita, 9 Kuruluş, 7 Cetvel (Yabancı Cephe:26) (The Indian Army and the occupation troops in Egypt).

Hükümet-i Osmaniye Kuvve-i Bahriyesi; Matbaa-ı Bahriye, 10 Haziran 1328 (1912), 7 Sayfa, 32x24 (Deniz:134) (The naval power of the Ottoman state).

Hüseyin Fuat (Mütekait Miralay); *Kuva-yi Umumiye Bahriye,* Matbaayı Bahriye, 1329 (1913), 218 Sayfa, 28x19, Önsöz (Deniz:8) (The Ottoman naval force).

Hüseyin Hüsnü; *Erkân-ı Harbiye Meslek Vezaîf ve Teşkilât Tarihi ve İlmi Tetkikat,* İstanbul, Erkân-ı Harbiye Mektebi Matbaası, 1340 (1924), 184 Sayfa, 16x24, Fihrist, 3 Kroki (Harp Tarihi Yardımcı Eserler:122) (General staff professional duties and organizational history and scientific investigation).

Irak'i Dair Harp Notları; Çev.: Hüsameddin, Erkân-ı Harbiye-i Umumiye İstihbarat Şubesi, Dersaadet (İstanbul), 1333 (1917), 88 Sayfa, 16, 5x24 (Irak:28) (Büyük Harp Irak:8) (The war memorandums on Iraq).

İhsan (Erkân-ı Harp Binbaşısı); *Askeri Tarih,* III Cüz, İstanbul, Mektebi Harbiye Matbaası, 1341 (1925), 515 Sayfa, 20x13, 3 Resim, 10 Harita (Tarih:83) (Military history).

İhsan (Erkân-ı Harp Binbaşısı); *Meşhur Osmanlı Seferlerinden Birinci Kosova-Niğbolu-Varna-Feth-i Konstantiniye-Çaldıran Meydan Muharebeleri,* II. Cuz, İstanbul Mekteb-i Harbiye Matbaası, 1341 (1925), 156 Sayfa, 13x20, 11 Krokisinin Olduğu Yazılmış Olmakla Beraber Kaybolmuştur (Eski Sefer:68) (The first conquest of Kosova–Niğbolu–Varna–Constantinople–Çaldiran pitched battles of the great Ottoman campaigns).

İ. Münir (Kaymakam); *Mayın Tarayıcılığı,* TC Büyük Erkân-ı Harbiye Reisliği 12 nci Deniz Şubesi, İstanbul, Deniz Matbaası, 1929, 74 Sayfa, 23x16, Fihrist (Deniz:65) (Mine sweeping).

İngiliz Bahr-i Sefid Kuvve-i Seferiyesi Başkumandanı Sir Ian Hamilton'un Çanakkale Muharebeleri'ne Dair İngiltere Harbiye Nezareti'ne Sun-

duğu Rapor; 21 Eylül 1915 tarihli *Times* Gazetesi'nden, Çev.: Dz.Yzb. Rahmi, İstanbul, Matbaayı Amire, 1331 (1915), 83 Sayfa, 23x15 (Çanakkale:58) (The report presented to the English War Office by Sir Ian Hamilton, the Commander in Chief of the English campaign in the Mediterranean, concerning the Dardanellas battles).

İran Ordusu Tarihçesi; Matbaayı Askeriye, 1326 (1910), 19 Sayfa, 20, 5x15 (Harp Tarihi Yardımcı Eserler:174) (The short history of the Iranian Army).

İran'a Dair Askeri Raporlar; 2 Cilt, Karargâh-ı Umumi, İstihbarat Şubesi, İstanbul, 1332 (1917), 125 Sayfa, 23x15, 5, 3 Çizelge (Harp Tarihi Yardımcı Eserler:36) (The military reports about Iran).

İran ve Ordusu; Erkân-ı Harbiyeyi Umumiye İstihbarat Dairesi, İstanbul, 1927, 172 Sayfa, 23x16, Fihrist, 39 Resim, 2 Kroki (Harp Tarihi Yardımcı Eserler:173) (Iran and its army).

İsmail Hakkı (Erkân-ı Harp Binbaşısı); *Şanlı Asker Ali Çavuş,* 1327 (1911) Tanin Matbaası, 118 Sayfa, 23x15 (İstiklâl:292) (The famous soldier, Sergeant Ali).

İstiklâl Harbi Sıhhiye Raporu; 30 Sayfa, 23x16, 3 Grafik, 3 Harita, 4 Kroki (İstiklâl:267) (The medical report on the Turkish War of Independence).

İzmir, Ayvalık, Aydın ve Havalisinin Yunan Tarafından İşgali; İstanbul, Matbaayı Amire 1335 (1919), 40 Sayfa, 23, 5x16, 5 (İstiklâl:35) (The occupation by the Greeks of Izmir, Ayvalik, Aydin, and their environs).

İzmir'in Yunanlılar Tarafından İşgaline Müteallik Olarak Makamat-ı Askeriyeden Mevrud Raporlar; İstanbul, Matbaayı Askeriye 1335 (1919), 20 Sayfa, 24x17 (İstiklâl:35) (The reports which came from the military authorities concerning the occupation by the Greeks of Izmir).

İzzet; *Asker-i İslamiyeye Mahsus Dini ve Vatani Cihaddan Bahis Mevizedir,* İstanbul, Matbaa-ı Askeriye, 1331 (1915), 77 Sayfa, 13x19, Önsöz (Genel Eser:593) (The subject matters from the religions and patriotic war to the Islamic military).

İzzet (Ferik); *Osmanlı-Yunan Seferi,* Kitaphane-i Askeri İbrahim Hilmi, 1325 (1909), 35 Sayfa, 19x12, 3 Harita (Türk-Yunan:8) (The Ottoman–Greek campaign).

İzzettin Bey (Kaymakam); *Çanakkale Arıburnu (Şimal Grubu) Muharebatı,* Erkân-ı Harbiye Mektebi, İstanbul, 1336 (1920), 34 Sayfa, 16x24 (Çanakkale:18) (The Dardanellas, Ariburnu [Northern Group] battles).

Jorj Remon; *Mağlublarla Beraber Edirne Sahralarında,* Çev.: H. Cevdet, İstanbul, Kanaat Matbaası, 1916, 243 Sayfa, 17, 5x12, Giriş (Balkan:56) (In the Edirne open plains with the defeated).

Kafkas Cephesi'nde Üçüncü Ordu; Mecmuayı Askeriye, 1 Kasım 1920-1 Şubat 1921, No:20–24, 11 Sayfa, 16x23, 2 Harita, 5 Kroki, 7 Çizelge, 2 Kuruluş (Kafkas:23) (The 3rd Army on the Caucasian front).

Karadağ Ordusu Hakkında Muhtasar Risale; Karargâh-ı Umumi İstihbarat Şubesi, İstanbul, 1915, 14 Sayfa, 16, 5x12, Fihrist, 4 Adet Cetvel, 1 Adet Harita (Büyük Harp:53) (The brief brochure on the Montenegran Army).

Karadağ Ordusu Ahval ve Tensikat-ı Askeriyesi; Umum Erkân-ı Harbiye Dairesi İkinci Şubesi, Hicri 1328 Rumi 1325 (1921), 26 Sayfa, 14x21 (Eski Sefer:44) (Haarp Tarihi Yardımcı Eserler:165) (The affairs and military ordinances and reorganization of the Montenegran Army).
Keçecizade İzzet Fuat (Ferik); *Kaçırılan Fırsatlar,* İstanbul, Matbaa-ı Ahmet İhsan, 1320 (1904), 326 Sayfa, 17x24, Giriş, 1 Fotoğraf, 10 Kroki (93 Seferi:14) (The lost opportunities).
Ksenofon İstratikos; *Sakarya Muharebatı,* Çeviren ve Yayına Haz.: Erkân-ı Harbiye-i Umumiye İstihbarat Şubesi, İstanbul, 1329 (1913), 29 Sayfa, 21x29, 2 Kroki (İstiklâl:328) (The Sakarya battles).
Lohanizade Mustafa Nureddin; *"Hubb-u İstiklâl" in Abıdesi Gaziantep Müdafaası,* İstanbul, Matbaa-ı Milli, 1342 (1926), 398 Sayfa, 19x13, Giriş. 99 Resim ve 1 Kroki (İstiklâl:88) (The Independence Memorial, the defense of Gaziantep).
M. Abadi; *Dağda Harb Hareketleri Hakkında Bir Tetkik,* İstanbul Askeri Matbaa, 1926, 271 Sayfa, 22x15, Fihrist, 5 Kroki, 15 Lahika (Türk Silahlı Kuvvetleri:136) (An investigation into war operations on the mountain).
Mahmut Beliğ (Mütekait Miralay); *Balkan Harbi'nde Mürettep 1 nci Kolordu'nun Harekâtı* (74 Numaralı Askeri Mecmuanın Tarih Kısmı Olarak Yayınlanmıştır), İstanbul, Askeri Matbaa, 1929, 234 Sayfa, 19x26, Giriş, Harita, Kroki, Çizelge (Balkan:41) (The operations of the Allatted 1st Corps during the Balkan War).
Mahmut Beliğ (Mütekait Miralay); *Balkan Harbi'nde Mürettep 4 ncü Kolordu'nun Harekâtı* (Mart 1928, 68 No.lu Askeri Mecmuaya Mülhak Olarak Neşr Olunmuştur. Sayı 19), İstanbul Askeri Matbaası, 1928, 536 Sayfa, 16x23, 5, Fihrist, Metin Dahilinde 18, Metin Haricinde 14 Adet Harita Kroki ve Nizam-ı Harb Cetveli, Bir Adet Resim (Balkan:16) (The operations of the Allatted 4th Corps during the Balkan War).
Mahmut Celalettin (Yüzbaşı); *Kumkale Muharebatı,* Erkân-ı Harbiye-i Umumiye Riyaseti, İstanbul, 15 Ağustos 1336 (1920), 51 Sayfa, 21x13, Giriş, Metin Dısında 1 Kroki (Çanakkale:37) (The Kumkale battles).
Mahmut Muhtar (Paşa); *1328 Balkan Harbi'nde Şark Ordusu Kumandanı Abdullah Paşa'nin Hatıratına 2 nci Şark Ordusu Kumandanı Mahmut Muhtar Paşa'nın Cevabı,* Kahire, Emirriye Matbassı, 1932, 51 Sayfa, 13x19, 1 Çizelge, 1 Kroki (Balkan:23) (The 2nd Eastern Army Commander Mahmut Muhtar Pasha's reply to the Eastern Army Commander Abdullah Pasha's Memoirs, during the Balkan War in 1912 [1328]).
Mahmut Muhtar (Paşa); *Üçüncü Kolordu'nun, İkinci Şark Ordusu'nun Muharebatı,* İstanbul, Kanaat Matbaası, 1915, 393 Sayfa, 18x12, Yanlış-Doğru Cetveli (Balkan:25) (The 3rd Army Corps, the 2nd Eastern Army's battles).
Mahmut Şevket (Paşa); *Osmanlı Teşkilât ve Kıyafet-i Askeriyesi* (Osmanlı Ordusunun Bidayet-i Tesisinden Zamanımıza Kadar), İstanbul, Mekteb-i Harbiye Matbaası, 1325 (1909), 53 Sayfa, 25x18, Önsöz, Resim (Müracaat:89) (The Ottoman organization and military costumes [dress]).

Mahmut Talat (Mütekait Miralay) "Plevne Müdafaası," *Mecmua-i Askeri,* Sayı 66, Tarih Kısmı, İstanbul Askeri Matbaa, 1927, 231 Sayfa, 16x23, Fihrist, Giriş, 10 Harita, 4 Pafta, 8 Nizam-ı Harp (93 Seferi:15) (The military review, defense of Plevne).

Mecmua-i Askeriye, İstanbul, Matbaa-ı Askeriye, 12 Nisan 1336 (1920), 48 Sayfa 23x15, Fihrist, 6 Kroki (Çanakkale:13) (The military review, April 1920).

Mecmua-i Askeriye; Erkân-ı Harbiye-i Umumiye Riyaseti, Alıncı, İstanbul, 1336 (1920), 898 Sayfa, 23x14, 15 Kroki (Büyük Harp Çanakkale:13) (The military review, 1920).

Mehmet Ali Nüzhet (Mirliva); 1912, *Balkan Harbi'nde Süvarinin Harekâtı,* Cemiyet Kütüphanesi, 1331 (1915), 88 Sayfa, 12x17, 5, Önsöz (Balkan:31) (The cavalry operations during the Balkan War of 1912).

M. Neşet (Miralay); *Büyük Harpte Romanya Cephesi'nde 6 ncı Türk Kolordusu* (78 Numarlı Askeri Mecmuanın Tarih Kısmı Olarak Yayımıanmıştır), İstanbul, Askeri Matbaa, 1930, 169 Sayfa, 19x26, Fihrist, Giriş, Harita, Kroki, Çizelge (Büyük Harp Yabancı Cephe:9) (The 6th Turkish Army Corps on the Rumanian front during World War I).

Mehmet Atıf (Kaymakam); *1293 Sensinde Kars'ın Sukûtu Sebepleri Hakkında Rapor,* Askeri Mecmua'nın Tarih Kısmı, Kânunevvel 1926 Tarihinde 63 Numaralı Askeri Mecmu'ya Ek Olarak Neşrolunmuştur: Sayı 4, İstanbul, Askeri Matbaa, 17 Sayfa, 15x23, 1 Kroki (93 Seferi:19) (The report on the forfeiture of Kars).

Mehmet Atıf; *Nazarı Şeriatte Kuvve-i Berriye ve Bahriyenin Ehemmiyet ve Vücubu,* Donanmayı Osmani Muaveneti Milliye Cemiyeti Beyoğlu Merkezi, İstanbul, 1326 (1910), 39 Sayfa, 16x12 (Deniz:197) (The land forces in theoretical law code and the importance and the necessity of the Navy).

Mehmet Emin (Erkân-ı Harbiye Kolağası); *Muharebat-ı Kılâ,* İstanbul, Matbaa-ı Askeriye, 1327 (1911), 43 Sayfa, 23, 5x16, 3 Adet Cetvel (Balkan:58) (Eski Sefer:85) (The Kilâ battles).

Mehmet Emin; (Erkân-ı Harp Binbaşsı); *Selmanpak Meydan Muharebesi,* Erkân-ı Harbiye-i Umumiye Tarih-i Harp Neşiyatı, İstanbul 1337 (1921), 147 Sayfa, 16x24, Önsöz, Fihrist, Nizam-ı Harp Cetveli (Büyük Harp Irak:6) (The Selmanpak pitched battle).

Mehmet Emin (Erkân-ı Harp Binbasısı); *Harb-i Umumi'de Osmanlı Cepheleri Vakayii,* İstanbul, Erkân-ı Harbiye-i Umumiye Matbaası, 1 Ekim 1922, 164 Sayfa, 24x16, Fihrist (Birinci Dünya Harbi:27) (The battles on the Ottoman fronts during World War I).

Mehmet Hulusi (Yüzbaşı); *1326 Senesi Osmanlı Ordusunun Sonbahar Manevraları Hakkında Müşahedat ve Mütalaatın,* Kitabhane-i İslâm ve Askeri, İstanbul, 1326 (1910), 199 Sayfa, 15x24, 2 Harita, 3 Çizelge, 5 Şema (Balkan:47) (Observations and opinions concerning the Ottoman Army's autumn maneuvers in 1910).

Mehmet Nihat (Erkân-ı Harp Kaymakamı; *Balkan Harbi, 1328–1329 Trakya Seferi,* I. Cilt, İstanbul Matbaa-i Askeri 1340 (1924), 206 Sayfa, 15, 5x33, Fihrist, Önsöz, Giriş Metin Haricinde 1-30 Numaralı 40 Parça Zeyl (Ek), Bibliyografya (Balkan:14) (The Thracian campaign during the Balkan War of 1912–1913 [1328–1329]).

Mehmet Nihat (Erkân-ı Harp Kaymakamı); *Balkan Harbi'nde Çatalca Muharebesi* (Konferans), IV. Cilt Erkân-ı Harbiye-i Umumiye Riyaseti, İstanbul, Matbaayı Askeri, 1341 (1925), 70 Sayfa, 23, 5x16, Fihrist, Metin Harici 2 Kroki, Bibliyografya (Balkan:40) (The battle of Çatalca during the Balkan War).

Mehmet Nihat (Erkân-ı Harp Kaymakam); *1870–1871 Seferi,* Erkân-ı Harbiye Mektebi Külliyatı, Sayı 18, İstanbul, 1341 (1925), 217 Sayfa, 15x22, Fihrist, Giriş, 6 Kroki Kaybolmuştur (Eski Sefer:89) (The campaign of 1870–1871).

Mehmet Nihat (Öğretmen Binbaşı); *Irak Cephesi Muharebatından,* 998 Sayfa, 15, 5x22, 5 Giriş, 9 Kroki, 1 Çizelge (Irak:19) (The battles on the Iraq front).

Mehmet Niyazi; *Şark Ordusu'nda Aziz Paşa Fırkası,* Cemiyet Kütüphanesi, İstanbul, 1915, 95 Sayfa, 18x12, Önsöz, 1 Adet Harita, 1 Kuruluş Cetveli, 5 Adet Kroki (Balkan:34) (Aziz Pasha's division in the Eastern Army).

Mehmet Suphi (Erkân-ı Harbiye Kolağası); *Karadağve Ordusu,* İstanbul, Feridiye Matbaası, 1901, 95 Sayfa, 19x14, Fihrist, 1 Adet Cetvel, 5 Adet Resim (Eski Sefer:53) (Montenegro and its army).

Mehmet Süreyya; *Sicill-i Osmani Yahut Tezkere-i Meşahir-i Osmaniye,* II. Cilt, İstanbul, Matbaa-ı Amire, 1311 (1895), 442 Sayfa, 15x24 (Tarih:847) (Famous Ottoman memorandums).

Mehmet Şükrü (Yüzbaşı); *Esfar-ı Bahriye-i Osmaniye,* İstanbul Karabet Matbaası, 1306 (1890), 501 Sayfa, 20x13, 5 Resim (Deniz:189) (Ottoman naval campaigns).

Mehmet Tevfik (Erkân-ı Harp Kaymakamı); *Tarih-i Osmani,* İstanbul, Mekteb-i Fünun-u Harbiye-i Şahane Matbaası, 1308 (1892), İkinci Baskı, 308 Sayfa, 16x24, Önsöz, Fihrist (Tarih:136) (Ottoman history).

Mevzi-i Harbde Müdafaa (Def ve Tard); İstanbul, Askeri Matbaa, 1337 (1921), 182 Sayfa, 12x17 (Türk Silahlı Kuvvetleri:332) (Defense in local war).

Mısır Seferi; Çev.: Erkân-ı Harp Kıdemli Yüzbaşısı Rahmı, Times'ın Tarih-i Harbi'nden, İstanbul, Matbaa-ı Amire, 1332 (1916), 45 Sayfa, 16, 5x24, 5, Fihrist (Filistin:7) (The Egyptian campaign).

Mısır'ın Müdafaası, Çev.: Erkân-ı Harp Kıdemli Yüzbaşısı Rahmi, İstanbul, 1332 (1916), 14 Sayfa, 16, 5x23, 5 (Büyük Harp Filistin:10) (The defense of Egypt).

Mustafa Necip Efendi; *Sultan Selim-i Salis Asrı,* İstanbul, Matbaa-ı Amire, 1280 (1864), 118 Sayfa, 12x18, Önsöz (Tarih:290) (The reign of Sultan Selim III).

Mustafa Nuri Paşa; *Netayic'ül-Vukuât,* I. Cilt, İstanbul, Matbaa-ı Amire, 1294 (1879), 133 Sayfa, 16x24, Fihrist, Önsöz (Tarih:138) (The results of the events).

Muzaffer (Erkân-ı Harp Miralayı;) *Kuva-yı Havaiye Renberi,* Erkân-ı Harbiye-i Umumiye Talim ve Terbiye Dairesi, İstanbul, 1342 (1926), 60 Sayfa, 23x16, Fihrist, Önsöz, Grafik, Şekil (Genel Eser:155) (The guidebook to the Air Force).

Molman; *Çanakkale Muharebesi,* Çev.: Halil Kemal, Erkân-ı Harbiye Umumiye Talim ve Terbiye Dairesi, İstanbul, 1927, 127 Sayfa, 23, 5x16, Fihrist, Giriş, 61 Resim (Çanakkale:84) (The Dardanelles battles).

Moraja Dohson; *Moğol Tarihi,* Çev.: Mustafa Rahmi, Telif ve Tercüme Encümeni'nce Kabul Edilmiştir. İstanbul, Matbaaı Amire, 1340–1342, 315 Sayfa, 13x19, Fihrist, Önsöz (Tarih:273) (Mongolian history).

Naci (Yüzbaşı); *Balkan Harbi'nde Edirne Muhasarasma Ait Harp Ceridesi,* Erkân-ı Harbiye-i Umumiye, İstanbul, 1926, 88 Sayfa, 23x15, 5, Fihrist, Metin içinde 4 Kroki, 4 Nizam-ı Harp, Metin Haricinde 8 Parça Nizam-ı Harp, Kroki ve Grafik (Balkan:21) (War diary of the siege of Edirne).

Namık Kemal; *Kanije Muhasarası,* İkinci Baskı , İstanbul, Matbaa-ı Amire, 1335 (1919), 235 Sayfa, 12x19, Önsöz, Istılahat ve Tabirata (Terimlere) Dair Bir İndeks ve Tiryaki Hasan Paşa'ya Ait Bir Resim (Tarih:295) (The siege of Kanije).

Necd Kıt'ası Meselesi; İstanbul, Matbaa-ı Amire, 1334 (1918), 15 Sayfa, 15x23 (Harp Tarihi Yardımcı Eserler:37) (The question of the Necd detachment).

Necib Asım; Mehmet Arif; *Osmanlı Tarihi,* I. Cilt, Tarih-i Osmani Encümeni, İstanbul, 1335 (1919), 638 Sayfa, 16x24, Fihrist, Önsöz, Giriş, Bibliyografya (Tarih:30) (Ottoman history).

Nihat (Öğretemen Binbaşı); *Harb-i Umumi-de Sedd'ül-bahir "Cenup Grubu" Muharebatı,* İstanbul, Matbaa-ı Askeriye, 15 Haziran 1336 (1920), 61 Sayfa, 16x23 (Çanakkale:35) (The Sedd'Ul-bahir "Southern Group" battles during World War I).

Nişancı Mehmet (Paşa); *Tarih-i Nişancı,* İstanbul, Matbaa-ı Amire, 1290 H. (1873), 316 Sayfa, 12x17, Fihrist (Tarih:826) (The marksman in history).

Nuri (Erkân-ı Harp Binbaşısı); *1805 Seferi,* İstanbul, Mektebi Harbiye-i Şahane Matbaası, 1320 (1904), 200 Sayfa, 24x17, Fiyatı 30 Kuruştur (Eski Sefer:95) (The 1805 campaign).

14 ncü Kolordu Kumandanlığının 19.8.1335 Tarihli Tezkiresine Merbuten Vürud Eden Yunan Fecayiine Muğlak Liste; İstanbul, Matbaa-ı Askeriye, 1335 (1919), 31 Sayfa, 24x16 (İstiklâl:234) (The records of the Greek atrocities noted in the reports of the 14th Corps, August 19, 1919).

Orduda Terfiat; İstanbul, Matbaa-ı Askeriye, 1334 (1918), 46 Sayfa, 19x14 (Müracaat:392) (Promotions in the army).

Ordu-yu Osmaniye'nin Terhis Projesi; Harbiye Nezareti, Ordu Dairesi, Dersaadet (İstanbul), Matbaa-ı Askeriye 1334 (1918), 51 Sayfa, 27x19, Fihrist, 3 Resim (Büyük Harp:35) (Discharging the Ottoman Army).

Orta Anadolu'da Yunan Mezalimi; 3 Cilt, Orhaniye Matbaası Teşrinil evvel (Ekim) 1337 (1921), 245 Sayfa, 19x14, Önsöz, 50 Adet Resim. Kitapta 3 Harita Bulunduğu Belirtildiği Halde 1 Adet Harita Vardır (İstiklâl:103) (The Greek atrocities in Central Anatolia).

Osman Nuri (Kıdemli Yüzbaşı); *Büyük Harp'de İtalya Bahriyesi 1915–1918,* TC Büyük Erkân-ı Harbiye Reisliği 12 nci Deniz Şubesi, İstanbul, 1929, 77 Sayfa, 16x23, Fihrist Resim, Çizelge (Deniz:69) (The Italian Navy, 1915–1918 in World Wart I).

Osman Senai (Erkân-ı Harp Kolağası; *Osmanlı-Yunan Seferi:Dömeke Meydan Muharebesi,* 3 Cilt (bir arada), Kitabhane-i Askeri, İstanbul, 1314 (1898), 671 Sayfa, 20x13, 5, Fihrist, 5 Kroki (Türk-Yunan:6) (The Ottoman–Greek Campaign: The Dömeke pitched battle).

MILITARY HISTORY PUBLICATIONS (1930–1960)

ABD Dışişleri Bakanlığı; *Amerikan Askeri Yardumı,* Çev.: Asteğmen Aydın Sinanoğlu, Ankara, Genelkurmay Başkanlığı Yayınları, 1949, 35 Sayfa, 14x18, 5, İçindekiler, 7 Çizelge, Ekler (Türk Silahlı Kuvvetleri:88) (U.S. military aid).

Ahmet Faik; *Askerliğin Psikolojisi,* İstanbul Burhaneddin Matbaası , 1933, 224 Sayfa, 21x15, Önsöz, Fihrist, Resim (Genel Eserler:414) (Military psychology).

Ahmet Rasim (Deniz Kaymakam); *Denize Ait Tarihi Makalât,* İstanbul, Deniz Matbaası, 1931, 67 Sayfa, 24x15 (Deniz:110) (Historical articles pertaining to the navy).

Aker, Şefik (Em. Alb.); *Çanakkale, Arıburnu Savaşları ve 27 nci Alay,* 99 sayıh Askeri Mecmua'nın Tarih Kısmı, İstanbul, Askeri Matbaa, 1935, 98 Sayfa, 27x19, İçindekiler, Giriş, 4 Kroki, 5 Fotoğraf (Çanakkale:3) (Dardanelles: Battles of Ariburnu and the 27th Regiment).

Alaftaroğlu, Ziya İbrahim (Miralay); *Imha Muharebesi,* 3 Cilt, Büyük Erkân-ı Harbiye Riyaseti X. Şube Yayını, İstanbul, 1931, 118 Sayfa, 26, 5x19, 5, Fihrist, Giriş, 14 Harita, 6 Kroki (Eski Seferler:91) (Internecine war [War of Extermination]).

Ali Cevat; *Ikiuci Meşrutiyet'in Ilân,* Yayına Harırlayan: Faik Reşit Unat, Ankara 16x24, Fihrist, Önsöz, Giriş, İndeks (Declaration of 2nd constitutional period and the event of 31 March).

Ali Haydar Emir; *Balkan Harbi'nde Türk Filosu,* Dz. Hrp. Akademisi Neşriyatından, Sayı: 11, Istanbul, Deniz Matbaası, 1932, 475 Sayfa, 16x24, Fihrist, 18 Harita, 14 Resim (Balkan:17) (The Turkish Squadron [nav.] during the Balkan War).

Alkoç, Celâl (Kur. Bnb.); *Tanklar ve Muharebeleri,* 123 sayılı Askeri Mecmuaya ek olarak çıkarılmıştır. İstanbul, Askeri Matbaa, 1941, 107 Sayfa, 26, 5x19, Fihrist, 14 Kroki (Türk Silahlı Kuvvetleri:58) (Tanks and tank combat).

Alkan, Etem (Kur. Öyzb.); *Gizleme (Kamuflaj),* Genelkurmay Başkanlığı X. Şube Yayını, İstanbul, Askeri Basımevi, 1947, 104 Sayfa, 16x22, 5, İçindekiler, Önsöz, 1 Kroki, 19 Fotoğraf, 38 Şekil, 4 Cetvel (Türk Silahlı Kuvvetleri:235) (Camouflage).

Alkan, Etem-Ulubay, Necdet; *Topyekûn Savunma,* İstanbul, 1955, 154 Sayfa, 15x20, 5, Fihrist, 17 Kroki (İkinci Dünya Harbi:44) (Total defense).

Alpkartal, Nurettin (Yzb.); *Büyük Harpte Makedonya Cephesi,* Genelkurmay Başkanlığı X. Şubesi'nce yayımlanmıştır Ankara, 1938, 153 Safya, 26x18, İçindekiler, Giriş, Kaynak Eserler, 14 Kroki (Yabancı Cep) (The Macedonian front during the First World War).

Apak, Rahmi; *İstiklâl Savaşı'nda Garp Cephesi Nasıl Kuruldu,* İstanbul, Güven Basımevi, 1942, 108 Sayfa, 23x15, 5, Önsöz, Fihrist, 41 Resim (İstiklâl:253) (How the west front was organized during the Turkish War of Independence).

Aras, Kâzım (Bnb.); *İstiklâl Savaşı 'nda Kocaeli Bölgesindeki Harekât,* İstanbul, Askeri Matbaa, 1936, 176 Sayfa, 25, 5x18, Fihrist, Önsöz, 9 Kroki (İstiklâl:16) (Operations in Kocaeli Region during the Turkish War of Independence).

Ataç, Nazmi (Kur. Alb.); *Türk Harp Tarihi SevkülceyşMoseleleri,* İstanbul, Harp Akademisi Matbaası, 1941, 81 Sayfa, 24x16, Fihrist, 16 Kroki (Türk Silahlı Kuvvetleri:19) (Strategical cases in the history of the Turkish military).

Ataç, N. B. (Kur. Yb.); *Türk Harp Tarihi Meseleleri,* İstanbul, Harp Akademisi Basımevi, 1936, 101 Sayfa, 15x23, 20 Kroki (Türk Silahl Kuvvetleri:18) (The subjects of Turkish military history).

Atasü, A. Remzi (Kur. Bnb.); *Büyük Harpte Demiryollarının Askeri Rolleri ve Yarına Hazırlanışları,* İstanbul, Askeri Matbaa, 1939, 103 Sayfa, 16x24, Fihrist, Doğru-Yanlış Cetveli Kaynakça, 15 Kroki (Birinci Dünya Harbi:86) (The military roles of railways during the First World War and their preparation for the future).

Aykut, Fahri (Kur. Öyzb.); *İstiklâl Savaşı'nda Dördüncü Kolordu,* İstanbul, Askeri Matbaa, 1935, 276 Sayfa, 26, 5x18, 5, Fihrist, Önsöz, 50 Kroki, Doğru-Yanlış Cetveli (İstiklâl:21) (The 4th Army Corps during the Turkish War of Independence).

Aykut, Fahri (Kur. Alb.); *İstiklâl Savaşı'nda Kütahya ve Eskişehir Muharebeleri,* İstanbul, Askeri Matbaa, 1936, 166 Sayfa, 26x18, Fihrist, Önsöz, 9 Kroki, 1 Kuruluş Cetveli (İstiklâl:29) (Battles of Kütahya and Eskişehir during the Turkish War of Independence).

Aysan, Emin (Kur. Yb.); *Büyük Harpte İran Cephesi,* III. Cilt, İstanbul, Askeri, Matbaa, 1938, 54 Sayfa, 18x24, Fihrist, 18 Kroki (Kafkas:15) (Iranian front during the First World War).

Bahattin (Em. Kaymakam); *Ordu ve Donanmanın Müşterek Harekâtı,* İstanbul, Deniz Matbaası, 1935, 46 Sayfa, 24x15 (Deniz:94) (Joint operations of the army and the navy).

Baki (Em. Miralay); *Büyük Harpte Kafkas Cephesi,* Cilt I–II, İstanbul, Askeri Matbaa, 1933, 180 Sayfa, 18x26, Fihrist, Önsöz, 3 Harita, 37 Kroki, 8 Cetvel, 5 Kuruluş (Kafkas:1) (Caucasian front during the First World War).

Balkan, Recep (Sv. Alb.); *Büyük Harpte Şark Cephesinde Sağ Kanat Harekâtı* (Murat, Van Gölü havzasında Türk-Rus süvarilerinin operatif hedefleri) (1914 Ekim: 20 Ağustos 1915), İstanbul, Gnkur, Bşk. lığı Askeri Basımevi, 1946, 249 Sayfa, 18x26, 18 Kroki, Fihrist, Önsöz, 1 Harita, 2 Kuruluş (Kafkas:12) (The right wing operations on the eastern front during the First World War).

Barbara, Nicola; *Konstantiniye Muhasarası Ruznamesi 1453,* Cev.: Ş. T. Diler, İstanbul, Fethi Derneği, 1953, 77 Sayfa, 17x24, Giriş, Bibliyografya, Esere Enrico Cornet tarafından notlar ve vesikalar ilave edilmiştir (Tarih:175) (The war diary of the Constantinople siege, 1453).

Bayur, Hikmet; *Mustafa Kemal'in Falkenhayn İle Çatışmasıyla İlgili Henüz Yayınlanmamış Bir Raporu,* Ankara, TTK Basımevi, 1956, 34 Sayfa, 18x23 (Atatürk:59) (An unreleased report about the controversy between Mustafa Kemal and Falkenhayn).

Bekman, Münir Müeyyet-Tülbentçi, Feridun Fazıl; *Ikinci Cihan Harbi Kronolojisi,* 6 Cilt, İstanbul, Başvekâlet Basın ve Yayın Umum Müdürlüğü Yayını, 1943–1948, 110+171+128+239+176+116 Sayfa, 16x22, 5, İndeks (İkinci Dünya Harbi:30) (The Second World War chronology).

Belen, Fahri (Ög. Kur. Alb.); *Çanakkale Savaşı*, İstanbul, Harp Akademisi Matbaası, 1935, 158 Sayfa, 23x16, İçindekiler, Önsöz, Bibliyografya, Sonuç (Çanakkale:8) (The battle for the Dardanelles).

Benlioğlu, Mehmed; *Türklerin Harp San'atına Hizmetleri, Altıyüz Yıl Evvelki Türk Tabiyesi,* Genelkurmay X. Şube, İstanbul, 1936, 24 Sayfa, 26x18, Fihrist, Önsöz (Harp Tarihi Yardimcı Eserler:12) (The Turks' contributions to the art of war and their tactics 600 years ago).

Berkman, Tahsin (Kur. Alb.); *Harp Tarihi,* Ankara, Harp Okulu Basımevi, 1949, 299 Sayfa, 24x17, 124 Kroki, 1 Garfik, 2 Tablo (Tarih:533) (Military history).

1912–1913 Balkan Harbi'nde Türk-Bulgar Harbi, Çev.: Murat Tunca, 3 Cilt, İstanbul, Askeri Matbaa, 1943, 385+519+553 Sayfa, 18x26, Fihrist, Önsöz, 4 Kroki, 18 Harita, 2 Kuruluş, 1 İsaret Levhası (Balkan:1) (The Turkish–Hungarian battle during the Balkan War [1912–1913]).

Cebesoy, Ali Fuat (Konya Saylavı, Em. Gen.); *Birüssebi-Gazze Meydan Muharebesi ve 20 nci Kolordu,* İstanbul, Askeri Matbaa, 1938, 80 Sayfa, 18x26, Fihrist, Önsöz, 19 Kroki (Filistin:5) (The Birüssebi-Gaza battle and the 20th Army Corps).

Celâloğu, Mustafa; *(Tabakatülmemalik ve Derecâtülmesalik) Osmanlı Imparatorluğu'nun Yükselme Devrinde Türk Ordusunun Savaşları ve Devletin Durumu, iç ve Dış Siyasası,* Türkçeleştiren: Sadettin Tokdemir (Em. Bnb.), 107 sayılı Askeri Mecmua'nın ekidir, İstanbul, Askeri Matbaa, 1937, 257 Sayfa, 26, 5x19, 5, Fihrist, Önsöz, Giriş (Harp Tarihi Yardımcı Eserler:6) (The Wars of the Turkish Army and the governmental situation during the rise of the Ottoman Empire).

Çakmak, Fevzi; *Büyük Harpte Şark Cephesi Hareketleri, Şark Vilayetlerimizde, Kafkasya'da ve İran'da,* Ankara, Gnkur. Matbaası, 1936, 363 Sayfa, 18x26, Fihrist, 72 Kroki, 3 Cetvel, 27 Harita (Kafkas:4) (Operations on the Eastern Front, Caucasia, Iran, and Eastern Provinces during the First World War).

Çesme Deniz Muharebesi Faciası ve Akdenizde İlk Rus Donanması; Çev. Ali Rıza Seyfi, İstanbul, Deniz Matbaası, 1943, 107 Sayfa, 24x16, 2 Muharebe Planı (Deniz:59) (The tragedy of the Çeşme Naval War and the First Russian Fleet in the Mediterranean).

Deniz Harp Tarihi Notları (Ecnebi Seferleri); Çev.: Bnb. Tekirdağlı H. Sami, İstanbul, Deniz Matbaası, 1932, 223 Sayfa, 24x16, 31 Adet Şekil (Deniz:108) (Naval military history notes [foreign campaigns]).

Deniz Mecmuası Makale Bibliyografyası; Toplayan: Dz. Bnb. Sadettin Kursan, İstanbul Matbaası, 1943, 118 Sayfa, 24x16 (Deniz:113) (Bibliography of the Maritime Magazine notes).

Dukakinzade, Feridun (Em. Yzb.); *Memleketin Harbe Hazırlanması,* Büyük Erkân-ı Harbiye Riyaseti X. Şube, İstanbul, 1932, 66 Sayfa, Doğru Cetveli (Türk Silahlı Kuvvetleri:140). (Preparation of the nation for war).

Hün, İhsan (Em. Kur. Alb.); *Osmanlı Ordusunda Genelkurmayın Ne Suretle Teşekkül Ettiği ve Geçirdiği Safhalar,* Genelkurmay Başkanlığı Yayınları, İstanbul Basımevi, 1952, 123 Sayfa, 23x16, Fihrist, Önsöz (Türk Silahlı Kuvvetleri:128) (The establishment and progress of the General Staff in the Ottoman Army).

Karabekir, Kâzım; *Cihan Harbi'ne Neden Girdik, Nasıl Girdik, Nasıl İdare Ettik?* Cilt: I, II, İstanbul, Tecelli Basımevi, 1937, 747 Sayfa, 12x18, Fihrist, Önsöz, 9 Resim (Birinci Dünya Harbi:16) (Why and how we participated in the First World War, how we conducted [managed] it).

Kore Harbi'nde Türk SilahlıKuvvetleri Muharebeleri (1950–1953), Ankara, Erkân-ı Harbiye-i Umumiye Riyaseti Harp Tarihi Dairesi Yayını, 1959, 88 Sayfa, 21x28, İçindekiler, Önsöz, 1 Harita, 1 Kuruluş, 17 Kroki (Kore:46) (Battles of the Turkish armed forces during the Korean War).

Kurtbek, Seyfi (Kur. Alb.); *Harp ve Ekonomi,* İstanbul, İnsel Kitabevi, 1942, 190 Sayfa, 21x15, Önsöz, Fihrist (Genel Esaslar:250) (War and economies).

Sancar, Necdet; *Tarihte Türk-İtalyan Savaşları,* İstanbul, Arkadaş Basımevi, 1942, 115 Sayfa, 20x26, Fihrist, Önsöz, 1 Harita, Bibliyografya (Türk-İtalyan:1) (Turkish–Italian wars in history).

Şakir, Ziya; *1914–18 Cihan Harbini Nasil Idare Ettik,* İstanbul, Muallim Fuat Gücüyener Matbaası, 1944, 328 Sayfa, 12x18 (Büyük Harp:15) (How we conducted the First World War 1914–1918).

Tümerdem, İ. Hakkı (Em. Kur. Yb.); *Türk Harp Tarihi, Osmanlı Imparatorluğu Devrinde Büyük Meydan Muharebeleri,* İstanbul, Cumhuriyet Matbaası, 1939, 164 Sayfa, 23x14, Önsöz, İçindekiler (Çanakkale) (History of the Turkish military, important battles during the Ottoman Empire).

Uzunçarşılı, İsmail Hakkı (Ord. Prof.); *Osmanlı Devleti Teşkilâtından Kapıkulu Ocakları,* 2 Cilt, Ankara, TTK Basımevi, 1943–1944, 1061 Sayfa, 16x24, İçindekiler, Önsöz, Bibliyografya, İndeks, 44 Levha (Türk Tarih Kurumu:41) (The Janissary organization of the Ottoman Empire).

Uzunçarşılı, İsmail Hakkı (Ord. Prof.); *OsmanlıDevletinin Merhez ve Bahriye Teşkilâtı,* Ankara, TTK Basımevi, 1948, 632 Sayfa, 15x23, İçindekiler, Bibliyografya, İndeks, 95 Levha (Türk Tarih Kurumu:43) (The administrative and naval organizations of the Ottoman Empire).

MILITARY HISTORY PUBLICATIONS (SINCE 1960)

1897 Osmanli–Yunan Harbi; Selim Sun. Ankara, Genelkurmay Basimevi, 1965. 335 s. hrt., kroki, 24 cm. (1897 Ottoman–Greek War).

Türk Silahh Kuvvetleri Tarihi, Osmanli Devri, *Osmanah-Italyan Harbi (1911–1912);* Hamdi Ertuna. Ankara, Genelkurmay Basumevi, 1981. 544 s. res., hrt., kroki, 24 cm. (The Ottoman–Italian War [1911–1912]).

Türk Silahh Kuvvetleri Tarihi, Osmanli Devri, *Osmanli–Rus Kirim Harbi, Kafkas Cephesi Harekâtu (1853–1856);* Hikmet Süer. Ankara, Genelkurmay Basumevi, 1986. 200 s. res., hrt., kroki, 24 cm. (The Ottoman–Russian, Crimean War, The Caucasian front operations [1853–1856]).

1853–1856 Osmanli–Rus ve Kirim Savasi, Deniz Harekâtu; Saim Besbelli. Ankara, Genelkurmay Basumevi, 1977. 136 s. res., hrt., kroki, 25 cm. (Ottoman–Russian and Crimean War, the naval operations 1853–1856).

Türk Silahh Kuvvetleri Tarihi, Osmanli *Devri, 1877–1878 Osmanli–Rus Harbi Kafkas Cephesi Harekâtu;* Sadi Sükan, II. Cilt. Ankara, Genelkurmay Basumevi, 1985. 230 s. hrt., kroki, 24 cm. (The Ottoman period, 1877–1878 Ottoman–Russian War, the Caucasian front operations).

Türk Silahh Kuvvetleri Tarihi, *Malazgirt Meydan Muharebesi (26 A ustos 1071);* Selahattin Karatanau, II. Cilt Eki. Ankara Genelkurmay Basumevi, 1970. 190 s. res., hrt., 24 cm. (The Malazgirt [Manzikert] pitched battle [26 August 1071]).

Türk Silahh Kuvvetleri Tarihi, Osmanli Devri, *1877–1878 Osmanli–Rus Harbi, Deniz Harekâtu;* Saim Besbelli, III. Cilt. Ankara, Genelkurmay Basumevi, 1980. 95 s. res., hrt. kroki, 24 cm. (The Ottoman period, 1877–1878 Ottoman–Russian War, the naval operations).

Türk Silahh Kuvvetleri Tarihi, *Osmanli Tarihi, 1911–1912 Osmanli–Italyan Harbi, Deniz Harekâtu;* Saim Besbelli [ve] Mustafa Ülman, III. Cilt. Ankara, Genelkurmay Basumevi, 1980. 166 s. res., hrt., kroki, 24 cm. (The Turkish–Italian War of 1911–1912).

Türk Silahh Kuvvetleri Tarihi (1299–1453); Rahmi Egemen [ve] Hayri Aytepe, III. Cilt, 1. Kisum, ETÜT. Ankara, Genelkurmay Basumevi, 1964. 352 s. kroki, 24 cm. (The Turkish armed forces history [1299–1453]).

Türk Silahh Kuvvetleri Tarihi, Deniz Kismi (1299–1452); Sirri Altiparmak, Abdullah Yetisen [ve] Yuluğ Tekin Kurat, III. Cilt, 1. Kism'a Ek, ETÜT. Istanbul, Kara Kuvvetleri Komutanhği Askeri Basumevi, 1964. 67 s. kroki, 24 cm.(The Turkish armed forces history, the naval section [1299–1452]).

Türk Silahh Kuvvetleri Tarihi (1451–1566); Rahmi Egemen, Lütfü Güvenç [ve] Riza Bozkurt, III. Cilt, 2. Kism. Ankara, Genelkurmay Basumevi, 1977. 800 s. res., kroki, 24 cm. (The Turkish armed forces history [1451–1566]).

Türk Silahh Kuvvetleri Tarihi, Osmanli–Iran Savasi, Çaldiran Meydan Muharebesi 1514; Emin Aysan [ve] Nafiz Orhon, III. Cilt, 2. Kisim Eki. Ankara, Genelkurmay Basumevi, 1979. 173 s. kroki, 24 cm. (The Turkish armed forces history, Ottoman–Iran War, Çaldiran pitched battle 1514).

Türk Silahh Kuvvetleri Tarihi, Osmanli Devri, Othukbeli Meydan Muharebesi (11 Ağustos 1473); Hazim Isgüven, III. Cilt, II. Kisim Eki. Ankara, Genelkurmay Basumevi, 1986. 158 s. kroki, 24 cm. (The Otlukbeli pitched battle [11 August 1473]).

Türk Silahh Kuvvetleri Tarihi, Osmanli Dönemi, Rodos'un Fethi 1512; Rebi Önal, III. Cilt, 2. Kisum Eki. Ankara, Genelkurmay Basumevi, 1979. 78 s. hrt., kroki, 24 cm. (The Turkish armed forces history, the Ottoman period, the conquest of Rhodes [1512]).

Türk Silahh Kuvvetleri Tarihi, *Osmanli Devri, Kanuni nin Ölümünden Ikinei Viyana Kuşatmasi'na Kadar Olan Devre 1566–1683;* Hayri Aytepe [ve] Lütfü Güvenç, III. Cilt, 3. Kisum. Ankara, Genelkurmay Basumevi, 1981. 541 s. res., kroki, 24 cm. (The Ottoman period, from the death of Sultan Süleyman to the 2nd Siege of Vienna [1566–1683]).

Türk Silahah Kuvvetler Tarihi, *Fas Seferi (1551–1578);* Burhanettin Hünoğ lu, III. Cilt, III. Kisum Eki, Ankara, Genelkurmay Basumevi, 1978. 85 s. hrt., kroki, 24 cm. (The Morocco campaign [1551–1578]).

Türk Silahh Kuvvetleri Tarihi, *Girit Seferi (1645–1669);* Kemal Yükep, III. Cilt, 3. Kisum Eki. Ankara, Genelkurmay Basumevi, 1977. 116 s. res., kroki, 24 cm. (The Crete campaign [1645–1669]).

Türk Silahh Kuvvetleri Tarihi, *Istanbul'un Fethi (1453);* Rahmi Egemen [ve] Naci Çakin, III. Cilt, 3. Kisum Eki, ETÜT. Ankara, Genelkurmay Basumevi, 1979. 191 s. res., kroki, 24 cm. (The conquest of Istanbul [1453]).

Türk Silahh Kuvvetleri Tarihi, *Kibris Seferi (1570–1571);* Emin Aysan, III. Cilt, 3. Kisum Eki. Ankara, Genelkurmay Basumevi, 1971. 186 s. hrt., kroki, 24 cm. (The Cyprus campaign [1570–1571]).

Türk Silahh Kuvvetleri Tarihi, *Osmanli Devni, Osmanli–Avusturya Harbi 1593–1606;* Lütfü Güvernç, III. Cilt, III. Kisum Eki. Ankara, Genelkurmay Basumevi, 1985. 180 s. hrt., kroki, 24 cm. (The Ottoman–Austrian War [1593–1606]).

Türk Silahh Kuvvetleri Tarihi, *Sentagor Muharebesi 1664;* Kemal Yükep, III. Cilt, 3. Kisum Eki, ETÜT. Ankara, Genelkurmay Basumevi, 1978. 61 s. hrt., kroki, 24 cm. (The Sentagor battle 1664).

Türk Silahh Kuvvetleri Tarihi, *Tunus'un Fethi (1574);* Ahmet Riza Açan. III. Cilt, 3. Kisum Eki. Ankara, Genelkurmay Basumevi 1978. 83 s. hrt., kroki, 24 cm. (The conquest of Tunis [1574]).

Türk Silahh Kuvvetleri Tarihi Osmanli Devri, *Ikinei Viyana Kuşatmasi'ndan Nizam-1 Cedid'in Teşkiline Kadar Olan Devre (1683–1793);* Aşir Erkayin [ve] A. Riza Bozkurt, III. Cilt, 4. Kisum. Ankara, Genelkurmay Basumevi, 1982. 336 s. res., kroki. 24 cm. (The period from the 2nd siege of Vienna to the formation of the new regular troops [1683–1793]).

Türk Silahh Kuvvetleri Tarihi, Osmanli Devri, *Ikinci Viyana Kuşatmasi 1683;* Aşir Erkayin, III. Cilt, IV. Kisum Eki. Ankara, Genelkurmay Basumevi, 1983. 122 s. hrt., kroki, 24 cm. (The 2nd siege of Vienna 1683).

Türk Silahh Kuvvetleri Tarihi Osmanli Devri, *Prut Seferi (1711);* Hazim Işgüven, III. Cilt, 4. Kisum Eki. Ankara, Genelkurmay Basumevi, 1981, 217 s. hrt., kroki, 24 cm. (The Prut campaign [1711]).

Türk Silahh Kuvvetleri Tarihi (1793–1908); Naci Çakim [ve] Nafiz Orhon, III. Cilt, 5. Kisum. Ankara, Genelkurmay Basumevi, 1978. 753 s. hrt., kroki, 24 cm. (The Turkish armed forces history [1793–1908]).

Türk Silahh Kuvvetleri Tarihi, Osmanli–Rus Harbi (1828–1829); Naci Çakin, III. Cilt, 5. Kisum Eki, ETÜT. Ankara, Genelkurmay Basumevi, 1978. 247 s. hrt., kroki, 24 cm. (The Ottoman–Russian War [1828–1829]).

Türk Silahh Kuvvetleri Tarihi (1908–1920); Selahattin Karatamu, III. Cilt, 6. Kisum. Ankara, Genelkurmay Basumevi, 1971. 510 s. res., hrt., kroki, 24 cm. (The Turkish armed forces history [1908–1920]).

Türk Silahh Kuvvetleri Tarihi, Türkiye Büyük Millet Meclisi Ifükümet Dönemi (23 Nisan 1920–29 Ekim 1923); Şükrü Erkal, IV. Cilt, 1. Kisum. Ankara, Genelkurmay Basumevi, 1984. 598 s. res., kroki, 24 cm. (The Turkish Grand National Assembly Government period [23 April 1920–29 October 1923]).

Balkan Harbi Serisi (The Balkan War Series)

Balkan Harbi (1912–1913); Harbin Sebepleri, Askeri Hazirliklar ve Osmanli Devleti'nin Harbe Girişi Reşat Hall, I. Cilt. Ankara, Genelkurmay Basumevi, 1970. 286 s. hrt., kroki, 24 cm. (The Balkan War [1912–1913]; the reason for the war, the military preparations, and the entrance of the Ottoman State into the war).

Türk Silahh Kuvvetleri Tarihi, *Balkan Harbi Şark Ordusu, Birinci Çatalca Muharebesi;* M. Kadri Alasya, II. Cilt, I. Kitap. Ankara, Genelkurmay Basumevi, 1983. 321 s. hrt., kroki, 24 cm. (The Balkan War, the Eastern Army, the 1st Çatalca battle).

Türk Silahah Kuvvetleri Tarihai, *Osmanli Devri Balkan Harbi, Sark Ordusu Ikinci Caatalca Muharebesi ve Sarköv Cikartmasi;* Hikmet Süer, II. Cilt, 2. Kisum, 2. Kitap. Ankara, Genelkurmay Basumevi, 1981. 554 s. res., kroki, 24 cm. (The Ottoman period, the Balkan War, the Eastern Army, the 2nd Çatalca Battle, and the arköy landing).

Türk Silahh Kuvvetleri Tarihi, *Osmanli Devri Balkan Harbi (1912–1913), Edirne Kalesi Etrafundaki Muharebeler;* Şadi Sükan, II. Cilt, 3. Kisum. Ankara, Genelkurmay Basumevi, 1980. 484 s. res., hrt., kroki, 24 cm. (The Ottoman Period, the Balkan War [1912–1913], the battles around the fort at Edirne).

Türk Silahh Kuvvetleri Tarihi, *Balkan Harbi (1912–1913), Garp Ordusu, Vardar Ordusu ve Ustruma Kolordusu;* Reşat Halli, III. Cilt, 7. Kisum. Ankara, Genelkurmay Basumevi, 1979. 536 s. res., hrt., kroki, 24 cm. (Balkan War [1912–1913], the Western Army, the Vardar Army, and Ustruma Corps).

Türk Silahh Kuvvetleri Tarihi, Osmanli Devri, *Balkan Harbi (1912–1913), Garp Ordusu Yunan Cephesi Harekâtu;* Raif Yaşar [ve] Hüseyin Kabasakal, III. Cilt, 2. Kisum. Ankara, Genelkurmay Basumevi, 1981. 813 s. res., hrt., kroki, 24 cm. (The Balkan War [1912–1913], the Western Army, the Greek front operation).

Türk Silahh Kuvvetleri Tarihi, *Balkan Harbi, Garp Ordusu Karadağ Cephesi;* Fehmi Özatalay. Ankara, Genelkurmay Basumevi, 1984. 232 s. res., kroki, 24 cm. (The Balkan War, the Western Army, the Montenegro front).

Balkan Harbi Tarihi, Osmanli Deniz Harekâtu 1912–1913; Afif Büyüktuğ rul, VII. Cilt. Istanbul, Kara Kuvvetleri Komutanliği Askeri Basumevi, 1965. 244 s. kroki, 24 cm. (The Balkan War history, the Ottoman naval operations [1912–1913]).

Birinei Dünya Harbi Serisi (World War I Series)

Birinei Dünya Harbi'nde, Türk Harbi, *Osmanli Imparatorluğu'nun Siyasi ve Askeri Hazirhklari ve Harbe Girisi;* Cemal Akbay, I. Cilt. Ankara, Genelkurmay Basumevi, 1970. 292 s. res., kroki, 24 cm. (In World War I, the political and military preparations of the Ottoman Empire and its entrance into the war).

Birinci Dünya Harbi'nde Türk Harbi, *Kafkas Cephesi, 2 nci Ordu Harekâtu 1916–1918;* Fikri Güleç, II. Cilt. 2. Kisum. Ankara, Genelkurmay

Basumevi, 1978. 352 s. kroki, 24 cm. (In World War I, the Caucasian front, the 2nd Army operations 1916–1918).

Birinci Dünya Harbi'nde Türk Harbi, *Irak–Iran Cephesi 1914–1918;* Nezihi Firat, III. Cilt, 1. Kisum. Ankara, Genelkurmay Basumevi, 1979. 840 s. res., hrt., krok, 24 cm. (In World War I, the Iraq–Iran front 1914–1918).

Birinci Dünya Harbi'nde Türk Harbi, *Sina-Filistin Cephesi, Harbin Başlangicmdan lkinci Gazze Muharebeleri Sonuna Kadar;* Yahya Okçu, IV. Cilt, 1. Kisum. Ankara, Genelkurmay Basumevi, 1979. 825 s. res., hrt., kroki, 24 cm. (In World War I, the Sinai–Palestine front from the beginning of the war to the end of the Gaza battles).

Birinci Dünya Harbi'nde Türk Harbi, *Sina–Filistin Cephesi, Ikinci Gazze Muharebesi Sonundan Mondros Mütarekesi'ne Kadar Yapilan Harekât (21 Nisan 1917–30 Ekim 1918);* Kâmil Önalp, Hilmi Üstünsoy [ve] Kâmuran Dengiz, IV. Cilt, 2. Kisum. Ankara, Genelkurmay Basumevi, 1986. 823 s. res., hrt., kroki, 24 cm. (In World War I, the Sinai–Palestine front, the operations from the end of the Gaza battle to the Mudros armistice).

Birinci Dünya Harbi'nde Türk Harbi, Çanakkale Cephesi, Amfibi Harekât; Remzi Yiğitgüden, Muhterem Saral [ve] Reşat Halli, V. Cilt, 2. Kitap. Ankara, Genelkurmay Basumevi, 1978. 507 s. res., hrt., kroki, 24 cm. (In World War I, the Dardanelles front, the amphibious operations).

Türk Silahh Kuvvetleri Tarihi, Osmanli Devri, *Birinci Dünya Harbi'nde Türk Harabi, Çanakkale Cephesi Harekâti (Haziran 1915–Ocak 1916);* Irfan Tekşüt [ve] Necati Ökse, V. Cilt, 3. Kitap. Ankara, Genelkurmay Basumevi, 1980. 626 s. hrt., kroki, 24 cm. (In World War I, the Dardanelles front operations [June 1915–January 1916]).

Birinci Dünya Harbi'nde Türk Harbi, *Hicaz, Asir, Yemen Cepheleri ve Libya Harekâtu 1914–1918;* Şükrü Erkal, VI. Cilt. Ankara, Genelkurmay Basumevi, 1978. 944 s. res., hrt., kroki, 24 cm. (In World War, the Hejaz, Asir, Yemen fronts and Libyan operations 1914–1918).

Birinci Dünya Harbi, Avrupa Cepheleri, *Galiçya Cephesi;* Cihat Akçakayahoğlu, VII. Cilt, 1. Kisum. Ankara, Genelkurmay Basumevi, 1967. 116 s. res., kroki, 24 cm. (In World War I, the Galicia front).

Birinci Dünya Harbi Avrupa Cepheleri, *Romanya Cephesi;* Fikri Güleç. VII. Cilt, 2. Kisum. Ankara, Genelkurmay Basumevi, 1967. 166 s. res., kroki, 24 cm. (In World War I, the European fronts, the Rumanian front).

Birinci Dünya Harbi Avrupa Cepheleri, *Makedonya Cephesi;* Fazil Karhdağ [ve] Kâni Ciner, VII. Cilt, 2. Kisum. Ankara, Genelkurmay Basumevi, 1964. 85 s. res., hrt., kroki, 24 cm. (In World War I, the European fronts, the Macedonian front).

Birinci Dünya Harbi'nde Türk Harbi, *Deniz Harekâtu;* Saim Besbelli, VIII. Cilt. Ankara, Genelkurmay Basumevi, 1976. 664 s. res., kroki, 24 cm. (In World War I, the naval operations).

Birinci Dünya Harbi, Türk Hava Harekâti; Ihsan Göymen, IX. Cilt. Ankara, Genelkurmay Basumevi, 1969. 258 s. kroki, 24 cm. (In World War I, the Turkish air operations).

Türk Silahh Kuvvetleri Tarihi, Osmanli Devri, *Birinci Dünya Harbi, Idari Faaliyetler ve Lojistik;* X ncu Cilt. Ankara, Genelkurmay Basumevi, 1985. 792 s. hrt., kroki, 24 cm. (In World War I, the administrative activities and logistics).

Türk Istiklal Harbi Serisi (The Turkish War of Independence Series)

Türk Istiklâl Harbi, Mondros Mütarekesi ve Tatbikatu; Tevfik Biyikhoğlu, I. Cilt. Ankara, Genelkurmay Basumevi, 1962. 233 s. hrt. kroki, 24 cm. (The Turkish War of independence, the Mudros truce, and its application).

Türk Istiklâl Harbi, Bati Cephesi, Yunanhlarm Bati Anadolu'da Istila Hareketlerine Başlamalari, Izmir'in Işgali, Mustafa Kemal Paşa'nin Samsun'a Çikmasi, Milli Mukavemetin Kurulmasi (15 Mayis–4 Eylül 1919); Hakku Güvendik, II. Cilt, 1. Kisum. Ankara, Genelkurmay Basumevi, 1963. 229 s. hrt., kroki, 24 cm. (The Turkish War of Independence, the Western front, the start of the Greek invasion of Anatolia. The occupation of Izmir, the landing on Samsun by Mustafa Kemal Pasha, the Foundation of the national resistance [15 May–4 September 1919]).

Türk Istiklâl Harbi, Bati Cephesi, Sivas Kongresi ve Heyeti Temsiliye Devri, Istanbul'un Itilâf Devletleri Tarafindan Resmen Işgali, Türkiye Büyük Millet Meclisi Hükümetinin Kurulmasi, Bati Anadolu ve Trakya Cephelerinde Yunan Ileri Harekati (4 Eylül 1919–9 Kasim 1920); Rahmi Apak, Reşat Halli [ve] Kadri Coşkuner, II. Cilt, 2. Kisum. Ankara, Genelkurmay Basumevi, 1965. 407 s. kroki, 24 cm. (The Turkish War of Independence, the western front, the Sivas congress and the period of representative delegation, the action of occupation of Istanbul by the Allied powers, the establishment of the Turkish Grand National Assembly, the Greek forward operations on the Western Anatolian and Thracian fronts [4 September 1919–9 November 1920]).

Türk Istiklâl Harbi Batu Cephesi, Birinci–Ikinci Inönü, Ashhanlilar, Dumlupnar Muharaebeleri (9 Kasum 1920–15 Nisan 1921); Kâmil Önalp, II. Cilt. 3. Kisum. Ankara, Genelkurmay Basumevi, 1966. 608 s. kroki, 24 cm. (The Turkish War of Independence, the western front, 1st–2nd Inönü, Aslihanlilar, and Dumlupinar battles [9 November 1920–15 April 1921]).

Türk Istiklâl Harbi, Batu Cephesi, Kütahya-Eskişehir Muharebeleri (15 Mayis 1921–25 Temmuz 1921); Kâmil Önalp, Şadi Sükan [ve] I. Hakki Alpay, II. Cilt, 4. Kisum. Ankara, Genelkurmay Basumevi, 1974. 606. s. kroki, 24 cm. (The Turkish War of Independence, the western front, Kütahya-Eskişehir battles [15 May 1921–25 July 1921]).

Türk Istiklâl Harbi, Batu Cephesi, Sakarya Meydan Muharebesinden Önceki Olaylar ve Mevzi Ilerisindeki Harekât (25 Temmuz–22 Ağustos 1921); Kâmil Önalp, II. Cilt, 5. Kisum, 1. Kitap. Ankara, Genelkurmay Basumevi, 1972. 314 s. kroki, 24 cm. (The Turkish

War of Independence, the western front, the events prior to the Sakarya pitched battle and the operations in the forward position [25 July–22 August 1921]).

Türk Istiklâl Harbi, Batu Cephesi, Sakarya Meydan Muharebesi (23 Ağustos–13 Eylül 1921) ve Sonraki Harekât (14 Eylü'–10 Ekim 1921); II. Cilt, 5. Kisum, 2. Kitap. Ankara, Genelkurmay Basumevi, 1973. 504 s. kroki, 24 cm. (The Turkish War of Independence, the western front, the Sakarya pitched battle [23 August–13 September 1921], and the subsequent operations [14 September–10 October 1921]).

Türk Istiklâl Harbi, Batu Cephesi, Büyük Taarruza Hazirlik ve Büyük Taarruz (10 Ekim 1921–31 Temmuz 1922); Şükrü Erkal, II. Cilt, 6. Kisum, 1. Kitap. Ankara, Genelkurmay Basumevi, 1967. 386 s. kroki, 24 cm. (The Turkish War of Independence, the western front, the preparations for the great offensive operation, and the great offensive [10 October 1921–31 July 1922]).

Türk Istiklâl Harbi, Batu Cephesi, Büyük Taarruz (1–31 Ağustos 1922); Kemal Niş, II. Cilt, 6. Kisum, 2. Kitap. Ankara, Genelkurmay Basumevi, 1968. 335 s. kroki, 24 cm. (The Turkish War of Independence, the western front, the great offensive [1–31 August 1922]).

Türk Istiklâl Harbi, Batu Cephesi, Büyük Taarruzda Takip Harekâti (31 Ağustos–18 Eylül 1922); Kemal Niş [ve] Reşat Söker, II. Cilt, 6. Kisum, 3. Kitap. Ankara, Genelkurmay Basumevi, 1969. 265 s. kroki, 24 cm. (The Turkish War of Independence, the western front, the follow-up operations during the great offensive [31 August–18 September 1922]).

Türk Istiklâl Harbi, Bati Cephesi, Istiklâl Harbinin Son Safhasu (18 Eylül 1922–1 Kasum 1923), Boğazlara Karşi Harekât, Mudanya Mütarekesi, Mütarekeyi Izleyen Olaylar ve Harekât, Lozan Antlaş, masi, Türk Silah Kuvveltlerinin Barişa Dönüşü; Abidin Tüzel, 2. Cilt, 6. Kisum, 4. Kitap. Ankara, Genelkurmay Basumevi, 1969. 280 s. kroki, 24 cm. (The Turkish War of Independence, the western front, the final phase of this war [18 September 1922–1 November 1923], the operations conducted against the Straits, the Mudanya truce, the follow-up events operations, the Lausanne agreement, and the return to peace by the Turkish armed forces).

Türk Istiklâl Harbi, Doğu Cephesi (1919–1921); Hüsamettin Tugaç, III. Cilt. Ankara, Genelkurmay Basumevi, 1965. 326 s. hrt., kroki, 24 cm. (The Turkish War of Independence, the eastern front [1919–1921]).

Türk Istiklâl Harbi, Güney Cephesi, Ingiliz ve Fransizlarm Güney-Doğu Anadolu'yu Işgal Etmeleri Milli Mücadele Hareketleri, Bu Bölgede Yapilan Muharebeler ve Revandiz Harekâtu (15 Mayis 1919–20 Ekim 1921); Ahmet Hulki Saral, IV. Cilt. Ankara, Genelkurmay Basumevi, 1966. 294 s. kroki, 24 cm. (The Turkish War of Independence, the southern front, the occupation of southeastern Anatolia by Britain and France, the national struggle movements, the battles, and the Revandiz operations [15 May 1919–20 October 1921] in this region).

Türk Istiklâl Harbi, Deniz Cephesi ve Hava Harekâti; Saim Besbelli [ve] Ihsan Göymen, V. Cilt. Ankara, Genelkurmay Basumevi, 1964. 255

s. res., kroki, 24 cm. (The Turkish War of Independence, the naval front and the air operations).

Türk Istiklâl Harbi, Iç Ayaklanmalar (1919–1921); Rahmi Apak, VI. Cilt. Ankara, Genelkurmay Basumevi, 1964. 172 s. kroki, 24 cm. (The Turkish War of Independence, the internal rebellions [1919–1921]).

Türk Istiklâl Harbi, Istiklâl Harbinde Ayaklanmalar (1919–1921); Hamdi Ertuna, VI. Cilt. Ankara, Genelkurmay Basumevi, 1974. 360 s. kroki, 24 cm. (The Turkish War of Independence, the rebellions during the war [1919–1921]).

Türk Istiklâl Harbi, Idari Faaliyetler (15 Mayis 1919–Kasum 1923), VII. Cilt. Ankara, Genelkurmay Basumevi, 1975. 663 s. hrt., kroki, 24 cm. (The Turkish War of Independence, administrative activities [15 May 1919–November 1923]).

Türk Istiklâl Harbine Katulan Tümen ve Daha Üst Kademelerdeki Komutanlarin Biyografileri. Ankara, Genelkurmay Basumevi, 1972. 245 s. res., 24 cm. (The biographies of the commanders of divisions and higher echelons that participated in the Turkish War of Independence).

Şehir ve Kasabalarin Harp Bölgeleri, Bombardman, Işgal ve Kurtuluş Tarihleri 1911–1922. Ankara, Genelkurmay Basumevi, 1977. 158 s. 24 cm. (The war regions of the cities and towns, the bombardment, the occupation, and the salvation dates [1911–1922]).

23

The United Kingdom

Official Histories of the Royal Air Force

Group Captain Ian Madelin, Director,
Air Historical Branch, Ministry of Defence

The history of British air power in World War I was published in the six-volume *The War in the Air,* Raleigh and Jones, Oxford University Press (1922–1936). There were no official histories of the RAF to appear in the interwar years, with the single exception of *A Short History of the RAF,* brought out by the Air Ministry in 1929 as *Air Publication (AP) 125,* for training use within the service (but see also under Air Historical Branch Narratives).

For World War II, the term "Official History" properly describes the volumes brought out under the auspices of the Cabinet Office Historical Section in the major series *History of the Second World War.* For the most part these volumes cover the role of the RAF in context within the various campaign and theater studies, and only two are more particularly concerned with air matters. The first is Basil Collier's *The Defence of the United Kingdom* (in which about half the chapters concern air operations). The second is the outstanding four-volume set *The Strategic Air Offensive Against Germany.* Written by Sir Charles Webster, a highly regarded diplomatic historian, and Dr. Noble Frankland Ph.D. (Oxon), an ex–Bomber Command navigator, it appeared in 1961 and despite much that has been written since on this still-controversial subject it has not been surpassed.

This series of official histories is published by Her Majesty's Stationery Office, as was the three-volume history *The Royal Air Force 1939–1945* by Denis Richards and Hilary St. George Saunders. This is a more popular treatment but is nevertheless a respectable historical study, sound in its use of sources, and it still serves a very useful purpose by being the only work among the official histories where the whole story of the RAF in World War II is covered.

By far the most important and comprehensive treatment of the role of the RAF in World War II appears in the extended series of studies and narratives produced by the Air Historical Branch, comprising nearly ninety volumes. When they first appeared these were all classified, and allowed for official access only. Virtually all have now been downgraded, with copies lodged in the Public Record Office, and a few have been published commercially. In their particular fields most of them remain the standard reference sources. A list appears at the end of this essay.

Note, however, that in this category of works (albeit not all produced by AHB) there are a few which deal with developments in the interwar years. These include, for example, AP 3233 *Aircrew Training 1934–42* (two volumes plus synopsis); *The Expansion of the RAF 1934–39,* J. M. Spaight; and *Growth and Progress of (Fighter) Operations Rooms 1929–37.* Furthermore, the majority of the others, although nominally about World War II themes, nevertheless pick up their stories in the interwar years. This applies to the studies on functional themes like *Works* (AP 3236), *Maintenance* (AP 3397), and *Operational Research in the RAF* (AP 3369); to the specialist themes like *Women's Auxiliary Air Force* (AP 3234); and to most of the operational narratives, except those dedicated to specific theater campaigns. For example, Volume I of the series *The RAF in the Bombing Offensive Against Germany* is titled *Pre-War Evolution of Bomber Command 1917–1939.*

The production of official histories (i.e., those emanating from the Cabinet Office Historical Section) continues into the postwar years, but the series is required to cover all aspects of government activity and only one book has dealt with a military campaign—namely, Korea—a campaign, however, in which the RAF played only a very small part (*The British Role in the Korean War*, Farrar-Hockley, HMSO, Vol. I, 1990, Vol. II, published in 1995). But one must also mention here a most important set in this series which, although still on a World War II theme, came out only recently. This is the five-volume *British Intelligence in the Second World War,* by F. H. Hinsley and others, published between 1979 and 1990 (Volume III is in two parts).

The Air Historical Branch also continues the production of its studies into the postwar period, but on a much reduced scale and the coverage is not continuous. A few of these studies are similar in style to the formal narratives of World War II. Like their predecessors, they all appeared in the first instance under a security grading, for internal circulation only. But at the expiry of the thirty-year point they are released to the Public Record Office and a few are published for commercial release. Other AHB studies, notably the trilogy by Sir David Lee dealing with RAF postwar operations in the Middle East, Far East, and Mediterranean, respectively, went straight into commercial publication.

Among the latest titles currently with HMSO and due to come out in 1995 are *A History of RAF Transport Command,* Wynn, and *Defence Policy and the Royal Air Force 1956–1963,* James.

ROYAL AIR FORCE BIBLIOGRAPHY

First World War

War in the Air	
Vol. I	Raleigh: Pub. OUP 1922
Vol. II	Jones: Pub. OUP 1928
Vol. III	Jones: Pub. OUP 1931
Vol. IV	Jones: Pub. OUP 1934
Vol. V	Jones: Pub. OUP 1935
Vol. VI	Jones: Pub. OUP 1937
Appendices	Jones: Pub. OUP 1937

Interwar Years

Balloon Defences (1914–45)	PRO Air 41 items 1–2
Photographic Reconnaissance Vol. 1, 1914–April 1941	PRO Air 41 item 6
The Expansion of the RAF 1934–1939	PRO Air 41 item 8
The RAF in the Bombing Offensive Against Germany	
Vol. 1, The Pre-War Evolution of Bomber Command 1917–1939	PRO Air 41 item 39
The Air Defence of Great Britain Vol. 1, The Growth of Fighter Command 1936–June 1940	PRO Air 41 item 14
The RAF in Maritime War	
Vol. 1, Atlantic and Home Waters—The Prelude 1918–1939	PRO Air 41 item 45
Growth and Progress of (Fighter) Operations Rooms 1929–1937	PRO Air 16 item 195

Second World War

Airborne Forces (AP 3231)	PRO Air 41 item 80
Air/Sea Rescue (AP 3232)	PRO Air 10 item 5553
Anglo-American Collaboration in the Air War Over North-West Europe 1940–42.	PRO Air 41 item 62
Armament	
Vol. 1, Bombs and Bombing Equipment (SD 719)	PRO Air 41 item 81
Vol. 2, Guns, Gunsights, Turrets, Ammunition and Pyrotechnics (SD 737)	PRO Air 41 item 82
Deception and Decoy	PRO Air 41 item 3 To be published by HMSO
The Defence of the United Kingdom	Official History Series: Collier: Pub. HMSO 1957
Escape from Germany	Crawley: Pub. HMSO 1985
Flying Training	
Aircrew Training (Synoptic Volume) 1934–1942	PRO Air 41 item 4
Vol. 1, Policy and Planning (AP 3233)	PRO Air 10 item 5551
Vol. 2, Organisation	PRO Air 41 items 69–71
International Law of the Air 1939–45	PRO Air 41 item 5
Maintenance (AP 3397)	PRO Air 10 item 5552
Manning Plans and Policy	PRO Air 41 item 65
Meteorology (CD 1134)	PRO Air 10 item 5550
Photographic Reconnaissance	
Vol. 1, (see Interwar Years)	
Vol. 2, May 1941–August 1945	PRO Air 41 item 7
Photographic Reconnaissance	
Vol. I, *The Fight at Odds: The Royal Air Force, 1939–1945*	Richards & Saunders: Pub. HMSO 1953
Vol. II, *The Fight Avails*	Richards & Saunders: Pub. HMSO 1954
Vol. III, *The Fight Is Won*	Richards & Saunders: Pub. HMSO 1954
Propaganda and Publicity	PRO Air 41 item 9
Rise and Fall of the German Air Force	Marsh: Published by Arms and Armour Press, 1983
Royal Observer Corps	PRO Air 41 item 11

Signals	
Vol. 1, Signals Branch Policy and Organisation (AP 3237)	PRO Air 10 item 5554
Vol. 2, Telecommunications (AP 3237)	PRO Air 10 item 5554
Vol. 3, Aircraft Radio (AP 1136)	PRO Air 10 item 5557
Vol. 4, Radar in Raid Reporting (CD 1063)	PRO Air 41 item 12
Vol. 5, Fighter Control and Interception (AP 1116)	PRO Air 10 item 5556
Vol. 6, Radio in Maritime War (AP 736)	PRO Air 10 item 5555
Vol. 7, Radio Countermeasures (AP 3407)	PRO Air 41 item 13
Air Support (AP 3235)	PRO Air 10 item 5547
Women's Auxiliary Air Force (AP 3234)	PRO Air 10 item 5546
Works (AP 3236)	PRO Air 10 item 5559 To be published by HMSO 1995
Operational Research in the RAF	Hartcup: Published by HMSO 1963
The Strategic Air Offensive Against Germany	Official History Series:
Vol. 1, *Preparation*	Webster & Frankland: Pub. HMSO 1961
Vol. 2, *Endeavour*	Webster & Frankland: Pub. HMSO 1961
Vol. 3, *Victor*	Webster & Frankland: Pub. HMSO 1961
Annexes and Appendices	Webster & Frankland: Pub. HMSO 1961
The RAF in the Bombing Offensive Against Germany	
Vol. 1, (see Interwar Years)	
Vol. 2, Restricted Bombing Sept. 1939–1941	PRO Air 41 item 40
Vol. 3, Area Bombing and and the Makeshift Force June 1941–Feb. 1943	PRO Air 41 item 41
Vol. 4, Experiment and Development Feb. 1942–Feb. 1943	PRO Air 41 item 42

Vol. 5, The Full Offensive March 1943–Feb. 1944	PRO Air 41 item 43
Vol. 6, The Final Phase March 1944–May 1945	PRO Air 41 item 56
Vol. 7, Planning of the Strategic Bombing Offensive and Its Contribution to German Collapse	PRO Air 41 item 57

The Air Defence of Great Britain

Vol. 1, (see Interwar Years)	
Vol. 2, The Battle of Britain July–Oct. 1940	PRO Air 41 items 15–16
Vol. 3, Night Air Defence June 1940–Dec. 1941	PRO Air 41 item 17
Vol. 4, The Beginning of the Fighter Offensive Nov. 1940–Dec. 1941	PRO Air 41 item 18
Vol. 5, Struggle of Air Supremacy 1942–1944	PRO Air 41 item 49
Vol. 6, The Flying Bomb and Rocket Campaigns 1944–1945	PRO Air 41 items 55 and 72

The RAF in Maritime War

Vol. 1 (see Interwar Years)	
Vol. 2, Atlantic and Home Waters—The Defensive Phase Sept. 1939–June 1941	PRO Air 41 item 73
Vol. 3, Atlantic and Home Waters—The Preparative Phase July 1941–Feb. 1943	PRO Air 41 item 47
Vol. 4, Atlantic and Home Waters—The Offensive Phase Feb. 1943–May 1944	PRO Air 41 item 48
Vol. 5, Atlantic and Home Waters—The Victorious Phase May 1944–May 1945	PRO Air 41 item 74
Vol. 6, The Mediterranean and Red Sea Sept. 1939–May 1943	PRO Air 41 item 19
Vol. 7, Parts I–II Mediterranean May 1943–May 1945	PRO Air 41 items 54, 75–76

Vol. 7, Part III, Nov. 1943–Aug. 1945	PRO Air 41 item 77
Vol. 8, Statistics	PRO Air 41 item 79
The Campaign in Norway April–June 1940	PRO Air 41 item 20
The Campaign in France and the Low Countries Sept. 1939–June 1940	PRO Air 41 items 21–22
The Liberation of North-West Europe	
Vol. 1, The Planning and Preparation of the Allied Expeditionary Air Force for the Invasion of North-West France	PRO Air 41 item 66
Vol. 2, The Administrative Preparations	PRO Air 41 item 23
Vol. 3, The Landings in Normandy	PRO Air 41 item 24
Vol. 4, The Breakout and Advance to the Lower Rhine 12 June–30 Sept. 1944	PRO Air 41 item 67
Vol. 5, From the Rhine to the Baltic Oct. 1944–May 1945	PRO Air 41 item 68
Special Duties Operations in Europe	PRO Air 41 item 84
The Middle East Campaigns	
Vol. 1, Operations in Libya and the Western Desert Sept. 1939–June 1941	PRO Air 41 item 44
Vol. 2, Operations in Libya and the Western Desert June 1941–Jan. 1942	PRO Air 41 item 25
Vol. 3, Operations in Libya and the Western Desert Jan. 1942–June 1942	PRO Air 41 item 26
Vol. 4, Operations in Libya and the Western Desert July 1942–May 1943	PRO Air 41 item 50
Vol. 5, The Campaign in East Africa 1940–1941	PRO Air 41 item 27
Vol. 6, The Campaign in Greece 1940–1941	PRO Air 41 item 28

Vol. 7, The Campaign in Crete May 1941	PRO Air 41 item 29
Vol. 8, Operations in Iraq May 1941	PRO Air 41 item 30
Vol. 9, The Campaign in Syria June 1941	PRO Air 41 item 31
Vol. 10, The West African Air Reinforcement Route	PRO Air 41 item 32
The North African Campaign Nov. 1942–May 1943	PRO Air 41 item 33
The Sicilian Campaign (Including Pantellaria and Lampedusa) June–Aug. 1943	PRO Air 41 items 52 and 59
The Italian Campaign 1943–1945	
Vol. 1, Planning and Invasion to the Fall of Rome	PRO Air 41 item 34
Vol. 2, Operations June 1944–May 1945	PRO Air 41 item 58
Operations in the Dodecanese Islands	PRO Air 41 items 53 and 61
The Campaign in Southern France	PRO Air 41 item 60
The Campaigns in the Far East	
Vol. 1, Far East Defence Policy and Preparations for War	PRO Air 41 item 35
Vol. 2, Malaya, Netherlands, East Indies and Burma	PRO Air 41 item 63
Vol. 3, India Command Sept. 1939–Nov. 1943	PRO Air 41 item 36
Vol. 4, SEAC Nov. 1943–Aug. 1945	PRO Air 41 item 64
Vol. 5, Air Supply Operations in Burma 1942–1945	PRO Air 41 item 37
Vol. 6, Air Transport in South West Pacific Area Feb. 1945–Feb. 1946	PRO Air 41 item 38

Postwar Years

The RAF in Maritime War	
Vol. 7, Part IV Post War Operations Aug. 1945–Nov. 1946	PRO Air 41 item 78

Operation Firedog—Air Support in the Malayan Emergency 1948–1960	Postgate: Due for publication HMSO 1992. Also, PRO Air 41 item 83
Flight from the Middle East—A History of the Royal Air Force in the Arabian Peninsula and Adjacent Territories 1945–1972	Lee: Published by HMSO 1980
Eastward—A History of the Royal Air Force in the Far East 1945–1972	Lee: Published by HMSO 1984
Wings in the Sun—A History of the Royal Air Force in the Mediterranean 1945–1986	Lee: Published by HMSO 1989
Watching the Skies—A History of Ground Radar in the Air Defence of the United Kingdom	Gough: Due for publication HMSO 1992
The History of Royal Air Force Cranwell	Haslam: Published by HMSO 1982
High Commanders of the Royal Air Force	Probert: Published by HMSO 1991
RAF Helicopters. The First Twenty Years Part I 1950–60 Part II 1960–70	Dowling: Due for publication HMSO 1992
The RAF Strategic Nuclear Deterrent Forces: Their Origins, Roles and Deployment 1946–1969. A Documentary History.	Wynn: Published by HMSO 1994
A History of RAF Transport Command	Wynn: To be published by HMSO 1995
Defence Policy and the Royal Air Force 1956–1963	James: To be published by HMSO 1995

The United Kingdom

Robin Higham, Kansas State University

The history of the Second World War was completed with the publication in 1988 of the last of the military campaign volumes, *The Mediterranean and Middle East*, Volume 6, Part 3; by General Sir William Jackson and, in 1990, the last two volumes of the series on British intelligence during the war (Volume 4, *Security and Counter-Intelligence,* by Professor Sir Harry Hinsley and C.A.G. Simkins, and Volume 5, *Strategic Deception,* by Professor Sir Michael Howard).

Of the peacetime history series announced by Prime Minister Harold Wilson in 1966, *The Nationalization of British Industry 1945–51* by Professor Sir Norman Chester was published in 1975, four volumes on environmental planning by J. B. Cullingworth and G. E. Cherry appeared between 1975 and 1981, and *Colonial Development* by D. J. Morgan was published in five volumes in 1980.

Volume 1 of *External Economic Policy since the War* by Professor L. S. Pressnell was published in 1987, and Volume 1 of *The History of the Health Services since the War* by Dr. Charles Webster in 1988; Volume 2 of both histories are in course of preparation. Volume 1 of *The History of the British Part in the Korean War* by General Sir Anthony Farrar-Hockley was published in 1990, Volume 2 is to be published early in 1995.

A history of defense organization since 1945 is being prepared by Professor D. Cameron Watt, and Professor Alan Milward started work in 1993 on a two-volume history of the United Kingdom's accession to the European Community.

Further topics for inclusion in the programme of official histories are under interdepartmental consideration, and are brought forward as earlier histories are completed.

BIBLIOGRAPHY

World War II

F. H. Hinsley, et al. *British Intelligence in the Second World War.*

I. Hinsley, F. H. with E. E. Thomas. *Its Influence on Strategy and Operations.* C.F.G. Ransom and R. C. Knight. 1979.

II. Hinsley, F. H. with E. E. Thomas. *Its Influence on Strategy and Operations.* C.F.G. Ransom and R. C. Knight. 1981.

III. Hinsley, F. H. with E. E. Thomas. Part I. *Its Influence on Strategy and Operations.* C.F.G. Ransom and R. C. Knight. 1988.

Thomas, E. E., C.F.G. Ranson, and C.A.G. Simkins. Part II. *Its Influence on Strategy and Operations.* 1988.

IV. Hinsley, F. H. and C.A.G. Simkins. *Security and Counter-Intelligence.* 1990.

V. Howard, Sir Michael. *Strategic Deception.* 1990.

Hinsley, F. H. *British Intelligence in the Second World War.* Abridged. 1993.

Jackson, General Sir William. *The Mediterranean.*

VI. Jackson, General Sir William with T. P. Gleave. Part III. *November 1944 to May 1945.*

Peacetime Series

Chester, Sir Norman. *The Nationalization of British Industry, 1945–1951.* 1975.

Cullingworth, J. B. and G. E. Cherry, *Environmental Planning, 1939–1969.*

I. Cullingworth, J. B. *Reconstruction and Land Use Planning, 1939–1947.* 1975.

II. Cherry, G. D. *National Parks and Recreation in the Countryside.* 1975.

III. Cullingworth, J. B. *New Towns Policy.* 1979.

IV. Cullingworth, J. B. *Land Values, Compensation and Betterment.* 1980.

Morgan, D. J. *Colonial Development.*

I. *The Origins of British Aid Policy, 1924–1945.* 1980.

II. *Developing British Colonial Resources, 1945–1951.* 1980.

III. *A Reassessment of British Aid Policy, 1951–1965.* 1980.

IV. *Changes in British Aid Policy, 1951–1970.* 1980.

V. *Guidance Towards Self-Government in British Colonies, 1941–1971.* 1980.

Pressnell, Professor L. S. *External Economic Policy Since the War.*

I. *The Post-War Financial Settlement.* 1986.

(others to come)

Webster, Dr. Charles. *The Health Services Since the War.*

I. *Problems of Health Care: The National Health Service before 1957.* 1988.

Farrar-Hockley, General Sir Anthony. *The British Part in the Korean War.*

I. *A Distant Obligation.* 1990.

II. *An Honourable Discharge.* 1995.

Watt, Professor D. Cameron. *A History of British Defence Organization.* (In preparation).

Milward, Professor Alan. *The United Kingdom's Accession to the European Community.* (2 vols., in preparation).

24

The USSR and Russia

The Institute of Military History of the USSR (Historical Information)

I. U. Shevedov, Senior Scientific Worker for General Dimitri A. Volkoganov, Chief of the Institute of Military History of the USSR, Translated by John C. K. Daly

EDITOR'S NOTE

Like the essay on the DDR historical service written in 1990, the following piece is from the same transitional period.

The Institute of Military History of the Ministry of Defense of the USSR appears as the fundamental scientific establishment engaged in the study and working out of military-historical problems.

The institute was founded on 5 November 1956 with the aims of subsequently broadening and heightening the theoretical level of scientific research in the area of military history for improvement in the work of military-patriotic training of the workers.

In organizational relations the institute is under the direction of the Ministry of Defense of the USSR. Scientific-methodological guidance is accomplished through the Academy of Sciences of the USSR; the institute is connected to the Historical Section of the Academy of Sciences of the USSR.

The Institute of Military History of the Ministry of Defense of the USSR is charged with the fulfillment of the following duties:

- The working out of questions of military-historical methodology.
- Research concerning the scientific-historical problems of the Great Patriotic War of the Soviet people and the Second World War.

- The generalization of military-historical experience of war and the national liberation movements of peoples.
- The working out of fundamental problems of the history of the armed forces of the USSR and the history of military art.
- The participation in patriotic and internationalist training of peoples of different nations.
- The coordination of scientific research works in the field of military history.
- Research on the actual problems of foreign military historiography.
- The analysis of foreign military historiography.

Attached to the institute is a scientific council, founded to coordinate research in the area of military history, its mission being to accomplish the coordination of research in the country independently from established and organizational departmental subordination.

The first head of the institute was the corresponding member of the Academy of Sciences of the USSR, holder of the Order of Lenin, General-Lieutenant Pavel Andreevich Zhilin. Since 1988 the institute collective has been headed by Doctor of Philosophical Science Professor General-Colonel Dmitrii Antonovich Volkoganov, a name which is widely known, not only in our country, but also abroad.

In a relatively short time the Institute of Military History of the USSR has become acknowledged as the scientific center in the area of military history. Within its walls have worked and continue to labor many well-known specialists in the realm of military history and doctors of history, philosophy and military science: N. N. Azovtsev, D. A. Volkoganov, P. A. Zhilin, Iu. Ia. Kurshin, M. M. Kir'ian, R. A. Savushkin, A. G. Khor'kov, S. A. Tiushkevich, and others.

At present, a large consideration of the institute is the preparation of young scholars. The institute acts as a postgraduate facility in which are raised the future generation of Soviet military historians.

Members of the institute researched and published more than 400 scientific works of various volumes with more than 15 million published pages, covering a wide range of questions of military history, of which one-third are devoted to interpreting the events of the Great Patriotic and Second World War. Sixty works have been translated into foreign languages and have been published in foreign countries.

Among the works undertaken by the institute a special place is taken by the multivolume fundamental works: *The History of the Second World War, 1939–1945* (12 volumes) and *The Soviet Military Encyclopedia* (8 volumes). Both publications received deservedly high recognition from the Soviet and foreign scientific communities. The works had subscribers in thirty-nine countries of the world. Side by side with the fundamental historical works, a large consideration has always been the preparation of works intended for the general public. Among these one is able to note a series of brochures appearing at the twenty-fifth and thirtieth anniversaries of the victory of the Soviet people in the Great Patriotic War, among them *The Battle for the Caucausus, The Battle for the Kursk Bulge, Operation Bagration, The Liberation of Belorussia, The Liberation of Ukraine, The Liberation Mission of the Soviet Armed Forces in the Second World War,* and others. The authors of these works, grounded in rich and various factual materials, succeeded in giving the reader all the stresses of most bloody fighting and battle on the battleground. Many members of the institute during the war defended with rifles in hand the freedom and independence of our Motherland. The geography of their military service was varied. It stretched from the Barents Sea to the Black Sea, from the walls of Moscow and the shores of the Volga to the borders of the Soviet Union.

Many of them participated in the liberation mission of the Soviet Army in Central and Southeastern Europe. All of them for courage, heroism, and military mastery were awarded orders and medals, but three of them, A. E. Borovykh, S. F. Likhovidov, and G. F. Samoilovich, were awarded the highest decoration Hero of the Soviet Union, with A. E. Borovykh receiving the decoration twice. After the war N. V. Usenko was awarded the Hero of the Soviet Union.

The institute collective is engaged in a great deal of scientific-methodological and consultative work on the creation of monumental memorials, museums, and expositions in Moscow, Leningrad, Volgograd, Kursk, and other towns devoted to the victory of the Soviet people and the Soviet Armed Forces in the Great Patriotic War. Among them are the following:

- The architectural-sculptural ensemble-memorial "Victory of the Soviet people in the Great Patriotic War 1941–1945," erected in Moscow.
- The State Museum of the Defense of Moscow.
- In Volgograd, the Museum of the Battle of Stalingrad; in Kiev, the Museum of the Great Patriotic War.
- The memorial complex "The Line of Glory" of Moscow and other cities.
- The monument to the Battle of Kursk.

Systematic scientific consultations are held for film and telefilm projects, among them multiseries presentations such as "The Great Patriotic War" (twenty episodes), and "The Strategy of Victory" (fifteen episodes), prepared for the commemoration of the thirtieth and fortieth anniversaries of the end of the Great Patriotic War.

The scientific work of the members of the institute has been assessed and recognized by the Soviet government. On 6 May 1983, by proclamation of the Presidium of the Supreme Soviet of the USSR, the Institute of Military History of the Ministry of Defense of the USSR was awarded the Order of the Red Star for service in the field of military-historical science.

At the present time the primary focus of the scientific efforts undertaken by the institute collective (independently or jointly) with other scientific units is in the area of scientific-historical problems.

Among important works currently being undertaken by the institute is the preparation for publication of a ten-volume work, *The Great Patriotic War of the Soviet People.* In this work other institutes of the Academy of Sciences are also taking part. The ten-volume history will survey and assess political, economic, diplomatic, ideological and military activities of Fascist Germany and the USSR, analyzing military, economic, political, ideological, and other factors determining the beginning and outcome of the Great Patriotic War. It is planned, in light of new political thinking, to determine, based on the documents and analysis, the onset of the war and its opening phases, especially studying the questions of strategic deployment, military preparedness, and mobilization of both sides; the management of troops, subjected to the unexpected blows of the enemy; the conducting of a strategic defense, the restoration of a strategic front, the interception of initiative, and its retention in sectors of the operational lines; and the creation of the anti-Hitler coalition and the contribution of the Allied governments in the achievement of victory over Fascism and its allies.

One of the central problems of the Institute of Military History is the preparation for publication of the second edition of *The Soviet Military Encyclopedia* in eight volumes. Questions of military-historical problems are a major aspect of the work—more than 3,500 articles. The problems of military-historical research developing at the present time involve the following directions:

- A methodological basis for the research of the history of war in light of new political thinking, the study of the theoretical legacy of V. I. Lenin, and its creativity in the fulfillment of the condition of *perestroika.*
- The uncovering and summarizing of the history of the Soviet armed forces.
- Research on the problems of military mastery and the development of the military art in civilian operations and the Great Patriotic War (*The Revolutionary Military Council of the Republic 1918–1924, Documents of the High Command 1918–1941, Methods of Work of Commanders and*

Staffs for Preparation and Introduction of Military Activities in Light of Experience in the Great Patriotic War, and other works).

- Research on complex theoretical and practical questions connected with the education of troops and youth about the experience of military history (*Military History and Actual Problems of Contemporary Military Practice, Bearers of Three Orders of Glory, A Short Biographical Dictionary*, and other works).
- Research on the military experience of socialist nations and joint preparation of military-historical works.
- Research on the military structure and military art of foreign governments in the years of the Second World War and in the postwar period (*Armed Forces of the USA: History and Present, Military Art in Local Conflicts*, and other works).
- Research on foreign historiography on problems of Soviet military history.
- The summarizing of experiences in the coordination of activity in the field of military history.

In appearing as the coordinating organ of scientific-research work in the field of military history, the Institute of Military History of the USSR maintains contacts with 465 scientific establishments and organizations.

The combined coordinated plan of scientific research in the area of military history developed with military and foreign establishments and higher educational institutions of the country in 1986–1990 covers 274 different military-historical subjects. The scientific council on coordination of research in the area of military history compiled an outstanding subject list of military-historical research and recommendations for work for the period 1986–1990 and up to the year 2000. These themes contain 234 complex military-historical subjects.

The Institute of Military History creatively and fruitfully collaborates with the military-historical establishments of socialist countries, but also maintains scientific relations with military historians of other foreign countries and with international military-historical organizations. This work significantly increased after the appointment in May 1988 of Professor General-Colonel D. A. Volkoganov, Ph.D., as head of the institute.

The staff of the institute participate together with members of the Institutes of the Academy of Sciences in international meetings, and in organizing the National Committee of Historians of the USSR, in which they are representatives of the military historians section.

The head of the Institute of Military History was chosen as vice-president of the International Commission on Military History and as a member of the Bureau of the International Committee of the History of the Second World War.

Cooperation between the members of the institute and their foreign colleagues takes many forms. Examples of scientific cooperation with socialist countries include the following:

- Work on joint commissions of historians of socialist countries (USSR–Bulgaria, USSR–Hungary, etc.).
- The writing of joint scientific works (in all, twelve works have been put together, including *The Belgrade Operation, NATO and Military Conflicts, Brotherhood in Arms*, etc.).
- The exchange of scientific information.
- The providing of access for colleagues to archives.
- The participation in preparation and work of scientific conferences, with the presentation of papers.
- Annual meetings of heads of military-historical establishments.

Examples of scientific relations with other foreign countries include the following:

- Participation in joint military-historical conferences and symposiums.
- The exchange of delegations of military historians.
- Lectures on military-historical problems.
- The exchange of newly published military-historical literature.

Examples of participation in the work of international military-historical organizations include the following:

- Participation of delegations of Soviet students in international congresses of historical science, in international congresses and colloquiums in military history, and by contacts with the International Commission on the History of the Second World War and the International Commission of Military History.
- By participation in the meetings of the International Commission on Military History and the International Commission on the History of the Second World War.
- The periodic publication of Soviet edition of the *International Military-Historical Journal* (No. 44 in 1979, No. 59 in 1985).

Cooperation of the institute with scientific organizations continues to broaden. In 1989 alone, about fifty meetings were held with foreign scholars. For the first time in its history the institute was visited by a distinguished delegation from the United States of

America, headed by the director of Military-Historical Section of the American Army, General W. Stofft.

The staff of the institute took part in an International Colloquium in Paris on the 200th anniversary of the French Revolution and the fourth Far Eastern meeting of representatives of Soviet and Japanese communities in the town of Sapporo. General-Colonel D. A. Volkoganov has presented papers in England, the Federal Republic of Germany, Finland, and France. A series of other activities is also being undertaken.

Fundamental Works of the Institute of Military History of the USSR

V. Iudina, Fellow of the Institute of Military History of the USSR Ministry of Defense, Translated by John C. K. Daly

ВОЕННАЯ ИСТОРИЯ
(MILITARY HISTORY)

Военно–теоретическое наследие классиков марксизма–ленинизма
(The Military-Theoretical Legacy of the Classics of Marxism–Leninism)

Классики марсизма–ленинизма и военная истории/ Жилин, П. А.; Бабин, А. И.; Бешенцев, А. В. и др. М.: Воениздат, 1983. 344 с.

(Classics of Marxism–Leninism and Military History. Zhilin, P. A.; Babin, A. I.; Beshentsev, A. V.; and others; Moscow: Voenizdat, 1983. 344 pages.)

Карл Маркс и военная историа/ Редкол.: М. Х. Калашник, П. А. Жилин, Ю. И. Кораблев и др. М.: Воениздат, 1969. 240 с.

(Karl Marx and Military History. Editorial Board: M. Kh. Kalishnik, P. A. Zhilin, Iu. I. Korablev, and others. Moscow: Voenizdat, 1969. 240 pages.)

Фридрих Энгелс и военная история/ Редкол. П. А. Жилин, В. Т. Логин, Е. И. Рыбкин и др. М.: Воениздат, 1972. 336 с.

(Friedrich Engels and Military History. Editorial Board: P. A. Zhilin, V. T. Login, E. I. Rybkin, and others. Moscow: Voenizdat, 1972. 366 pages.

Бабин, А. И. Формирование и развитие военно–теоретических взглядов Ф. Энгельса. М.: Наука, 1975. 275 с.

(Babin A. I. The Formation and Development of the Military-Theoretical Views of F. Engels. Moscow: Nauka, 1975. 275 pages.)

Бабин, А. И. Энгелс – выдающийся военный теоретик рабочего класса. М.: Воениздат, 1970. 320 с.

(Babin, A. I. Engels—A Distinguished Military Theoretician of the Working Class. Moscow; Voenizdat, 1970. 320 pages.)

В. И. Ленин и военная история/ Редкол.: М. В. Захаров, М. Х. Калашник, П. А. Жилин и др. М.: Воениздат, 1970 . 323 с.

(V. I. Lenin and Military History. Editorial Board: M. V. Zakharov, M. Kh. Kalachnik, P. A. Zhilin, and others. Moscow: Voenizdat, 1970. 323 pages.)

Азовцев, Н.Н. В. И. Ленин и советская военная наука. 2–е изд. М.: Наука, 1981. 350 с.

(Azovtsev, N. N. V. I. Lenin and Soviet Military Science. 2nd ed. Moscow: Nauka, 1981. 350 pages.)

Азовцев, Н. Н. Военные вопросы в трудах В. И. Ленина: Аннот. указ. произведений и высказыванний В.И. Ленина по важнейшим воп. войны, армии и воен. науки. 2–е изд., доп. и перераб. М.: Воениздат, 1972. 454 с.

(Azovtsev, N. N. Military Questions in the Works of V. I. Lenin: Annotated Decrees, Produced by and Expressed by V. I. Lenin on Important Questions of War, the Army and Military Science. 2nd ed., supplemented and revised. Moscow: Voenizdat, 1972. 454 pages.)

Зверев, Б. И. В. И. Ленин и флот (1918–1920). М.: Воениздат, 1978. 296 с.

(Zverev, B. I. V. I. Lenin and the Fleet [1918–1920]. Moscow: Voenizdat, 1978. 296 pages.)

Кораблев, Ю. И. В. И. Ленин н создание Красной Армии. М.: Наука, 1970. 462 с.

(Korablev, Iu. I. V. I. Lenin and the Creation of the Red Army. Moscow: Nauka, 1970. 462 pages.)

Селяничев, А. К. В. И. Ленин и становление Советского Военно–Морского флота. М.: Наука, 1979. 230 с.

(Selianichev, A. K. V. I. Lenin and the Formation of the Soviet Navy. Moscow: Nauka, 1979. 230 pages.)

Строков, А. А. В. И. Ленин о войне и военном искусстве. М.: Наука, 1971. 184 с.

(Strokov, A. A. V. I. Lenin on War and the Military Art. Moscow: Nauka, 1971. 184 pages.)

Проблемы методологии
(Problems of Methodology)

XXУ сьезд КПСС и военно–историческая наука: Науч. сб./ Редкол.: Кирьян, М. М.; Логин, В. Т.; Тюшкевич, С. А. М.: Воениздат, 1977. 215 с.

(25th Congress of the CPUSSR and Military-Historical Science: Scientific Collection. S. A. Moscow: Voenizdat, 1977. 215 pages.)

Марксистско–ленинская методология военной истории/ П. А. Жилин, П. Ф. Исаков. В. Т. Логин и др. 2–е изд. М.: Наука. 1976. 375 с.

(The Marxist–Leninist Methodology of Military History. P. A. Zhilin, P. F. Isakov, V. T. Login and others. 2nd edition. Moscow: Nauka, 1976. 375 pages.)

Война, история, идеология/ Бешенцев, А. В.; Громова, В. В.; Коротков, Г. И. и др. М.: Политиздат, 1974. 383 с.

(War, History, Ideology. Beshentsev, A. V.; Gromova, V. V.; Korotkov, G. I.; and others. Moscow: Politizdat, 1974. 383 pages.)

Жилин, П. А. Проблемы военной истории. М.: Воениздат, 1975. 399 с.

(Zhilin, P. A. Problems of Military History. Moscow: Voenizdat, 1975. 399 pages.)

Киршин, Ю. Я.; Попов, В. М.; Савушкин, Р. А. Политическое содержание современных войн. М.: Наука, 1987. 335 с.

(Kirshin, Iu. Ia.; Popov, V. M.; Savushkin, P. A. The Political Content of Contemporary War. Moscow: Nauka, 1987. 335 pages.)

Логин, В. Т. Диалектика военно–исторического исследования. М.: Наука, 1979. 221 с.

(Login V. T. The Dialectic of Military-Historical Research. Moscow: Nauka, 1979. 221 pages.)

Опыт войн в зашиту социалистического Отечества: Ист.–теоркт. исслед./ В. Т. Логин, С. Д. Гусаревич, В. И. Карпушенко и др. М.: Наука, 1985. 256 с.

(The Exerience of Wars in Defense of the Socialist Fatherland: Historical-Theoretical Research. V. T. Login, S. D. Gusarevich, V. I. Karpushenko, and others. Moscow: Nauka, 1985. 256 pages.)

Рыбкин, Е. И. Критика буржуазных учений о причинах и роли войн в истории: филос.–ист. очерк. М.: Наука, 1979. 240 с.

(Rybkin, E. I. A Critique of Bourgeois Doctorine about the Causes and Role of War in History: A Philosophical-Historical Essay. Moscow: Nauka, 1979. 240 pages.)

Тюшкевич, С. А. Философия и военная теория. М.: Наука. 1975, 312 с.

(Tiushkevich, S. A. Philosophy and Military Theory. Moscow: Nauka, 1975. 312 pages.)

Философия и военная история/ Рыбкин, Е. И.; Логин, В. Т.; Бабин, А. И. и др. М.: Наука, 1979. 327 с.

(Philosophy and Military History. Rybkin, E. I.; Login, V. T.; Babin, A. A. I.; and others. Moscow: Nauka, 1979. 327 pages.)

Шабардин, П. А. Армия в современной политической борьбе. М.: Наука, 1988. 221 с.

(Shabardin, P. A..The Army in the Contemporary Political Struggle. Moscow: Nauka, 1988. 221 pages.)

Общие проблемы
(General Problems)

Вестник военной истории: Науч. зап. М.: Воениздат, 1970–71. Вып. 1–2.

(The Herald of Military History: Scientific Notes. Moscow: Voenizdat, 1970–1971. Issues 1–2.)

Военный энциклопедический словарь/ Гл. ред. комис.: С. Ф. Ахромеев, П. А. Жилин, М. М. Кирьян и др. 2-е изд. М.: Воениздат, 1986. 863 с.

(Military Encyclopedic Dictionary. Main Editorial Commission: S. F. Akhromeev, P. A. Zhilin, M. M. Kir'ian, and others. 2nd edition. Moscow: Voenizdat, 1986. 863 pages.)

Волкогонов, Д. А. Триумф и трагедия: в 2 кн. Полит. портрет И. В. Сталина. М.: Изд-во Агенства печати "Новости", 1989. Кн. 1-2.

(Volkkogonov, D. A. Triumph and Tragedy: In 2 books. A Political Portrait of I. V. Stalin. Moscow: Publisher Agency Publication "Novosti," 1989. Books 1–2.)

Жилин, П. А. О войне и военной истории. М.: Наука, 1984. 544 с.

(Zhilin, P. A. Of War and Military History. Moscow: Nauka, 1984. 544 pages.)

Зарождение и разитие советской военной историографии, 1917-1941 / И. И. Ростунов, П. А. Жилин, М. М. Кирьян и др. М.: Наука, 1985. 183 с.

(The Origin and Development of Soviet Military Historiography, 1917–1941. I. I. Rostunov, P. A. Zhilin, M. M. Kir'ian, and others. Moscow: Nauka, 1985. 183 pages.)

История военного искуства: Учебник/ М. М. Кирьян, А. И. Бабин, Ю. Г. Перечнев и др.; Под. ред. П. А. Жилина. М.: Воениздат, 1986. 446 с.

(History of the Military Art: A Manual. M. M. Kir'ian, A. I. Babin, Iu. Perechnev, and others; Edited by P. A. Zhilin. Moscow: Voenizdat, 1986. 466 pages.)

История отечественной военно-энциклопедической литературы / А. И. Бабин, Д. И. Винокуров, М. М. Кирьян, И. И. Ростунов. М.: Наука, 1980. 174 с.

(History of the Fatherland's Military-Encyclopedic Literature. A. I. Babin, D. I. Vinokurov, M. M. Kir'ian, I. I. Rostunov. Moscow: Nauka, 1980. 174 pages.)

Кирьян, М. М. Проблемы военной теории в советских научно-справочных изданиях. М.: Наука, 1985. 161 с.

(Kir'ian, M. M. Problems of Military Theory in Soviet Scientific-Reference Books. Moscow: Nauka, 1985. 161 pages.)

Коротков, И. А. История советской военной мысли: Крат.очерк, 1917-июнь 1941. М.: Наука, 1980. 272 с.

(Korotkov, I. A. History of Soviet Military Thought: A Brief Note, 1917–June 1941. Moscow: Nauka, 1980. 272 pages.)

Очерки советской военной историографии / Бабин, А. И.; Быстров, В. Е.; Жилин, П. А. и др. М.: Воениздат, 1974. 415 с.

(Notes on Soviet Military History. Babin, A. I.; Bystrov, V. E.; Zhilin, P. A.; and others. Moscow: Voenizdat, 1974. 415 pages.)

Советская военная энциклопедия: в 8 т. / Гл. ред. комис-: А. А. Гречко, Н. В. Огарков, П. А. Жилин и др. М.: Воениздат, 1976-80. Т. 1-8. (Готовится 2-е изд.).

(The Soviet Military Encyclopedia: In 8 Vols.. Main Editorial Commission: A. A. Grechko, N. V. Ogarkov, P. A. Zhilin, and others. Moscow: Voenizdat, 1976–1980. Vols. 1–8. [Second edition in preparation.])

Тюшкевич, С. А. Война и современность. М.: Наука, 1986. 213 с.

(Tiushkevich, S. A. War and the Present. Moscow: Nauka, 1986. 213 pages.)

Б. М. Шапошников и его военно-теоретическое наследие: (К 100-летию со дня рождения). М.: Воениздат, 1983. 216 с.

(B. M. Shaposhnikov and His Military-Theoretical Legacy: [On the 100th Aniversary of his Birthday] Moscow: Voenizdat, 1983. 216 pages.)

Военная история дореволюционной России (Military History of Pre-Revolutionary Russia)

Отечественная артиллерия: 600 лет / Г. Т. Хорошилов, Р. Б. Брагинский, А. И. Матвеев и др. М.: Воениздат, 1986. 362 с.

(Artillery of the Fatherland: 600 Years. G. T. Khoroshilov, R. B. Braginskii, A. I. Matveev, and others. Moscow: Voenizdat, 1986. 362 pages.)

Русские землепроходы и мореходы: Из истории открытия и освоения Сибири и Дал. Востока / В. А. Авдеев, А. А. Измайлов, М. Н. Осипова, Ю. Ф. Соколов. М.: Воениздат, 1982. 80 с.

(Russian Passages and Voyages: From the History of the Opening and Assimalation of Siberia and the Far East. V. A. Avdeev, A. A. Izmailov, M. N. Osipova, Iu. F. Sokolov. Moscow: Voenizdat, 1982. 80 pages.)

Мещеряков, Г. П. Русская военная мысль в XIX в. М. : Наука, 1973. 315 с.

(Meshcheriakov, G. P. Russian Military Thought in the 19th Century. Moscow: Nauka, 1973. 315 pages.)

История Северной войны, 1700,1721 гг./ И. И. Ростунов, В. А. Авдеев, М. Н. Н. Осипова, Ю. Ф. Соколов. М.: Наука, 1987. 212 с.

(History of the Northern War, 1700–1721. I. I. Rostunov, V. A. Avdeev, M. N. Osipova, Iu. F. Sokolov. Moscow: Nauka, 1987. 212 pages.)

Ростунов, И. И. Александр Васильевич Суворов: Жизнь и полководческская деятельность. М.: Воениздат, 1989. 495 с.

(Rostunov, I. I. Aleksandr Vasil'evich Suvorov: Life and Command Activities. Moscow: Voenizdat, 1989. 495 pages.)

Жилин, П. А. Гибель наполеоновской армии в России. 2-е изд., испр. и доп. М.: Наука, 1974. 451 с.

(Zhilin, P. A. The Destruction of the Napoleonic Army in Russia. 2nd edition, revised and supplemented. Moscow: Nauka, 1974. 451 pages.)

Жилин, П. А. Михаил Илларионович Кутузов: Жизинь и полководческская деятельность. 2-е изд. М.: Воениздат, 1983. 368 с.

(Zhilin, P. A. Mikhail Illarionovich Kutuzov: Life and Command Activities. 2nd edition. Moscow: Voenizdat, 1983. 368 pages.)

Жилин, П. А. Отечественная война 1812 года. 3-е изд., испр. и доп. М.: Наука, 1988. 495 с.

(Zhilin, P. A. The Fatherland War of 1812. 3rd edition, revised and supplemented. Moscow: Nauka, 1988. 495 pages.)

Ростунов, И. И. Отечественная война 1812 года. М.: Знание, 1987. 64 с.

(Rostunov, I. I. The Fatherland War of 1812. Moscow: Znanie, 1987. 64 pages.)

Русская военная мысль: конец XIX – начало XX вв./ В. А. Авдеев, П. А. Жилин, М. М. Кирьян и др. М. : Наука, 1973. 252 с.

(Russian Military Thought: End of the XIXth—Beginning of the XXth Century. V. A. Avdeev, P. A. Zhilin, M. M. Kir'ian, and others. Moscow: Nauka, 1973. 252 pages.)

Русско–турецая война, 1877–1878 гг. В. И. Ачкасов, А.П. Тарвасов, И. И. Ростунов и др. М.: Воениздат, 1977. 260 с.

(The Russo–Turkish War, 1877–1878. V. I. Achkasov, A. P. Tarvasov, I. I. Rostunov, and others. Moscow: Voenizdat, 1977. 260 pages.)

Сенчакова, Л. Т. Революционное движение в русское армии и флоте в конце XIX – начале XX в. (1879–1904 гг.). М.: Наука, 1972. 216 с.

(Senchakova, L. T. The Revolutionary Movement in the Russian Army and Navy at the End of the XIX—Beginning of the XXth Century [1879–1904]. Moscow: Nauka, 1972. 216 pages.)

Военные организации российского пролетариата и опыт его вооруженной борьбы, 1903–1917 гг. / В. Н. Багров, Л. М. Гаврилов, Л. М. Гаркавенко и др. М.: Наука, 1974. 418 с.

(The Military Organization of the Russian Proletariat and Its Experience of Armed Conflict, 1903–1917. V. N. Bagrov, L. M. Gavrilov, L. M. Garkavenko, and others. Moscow: Nauka, 1974. 418 pages.)

История русско–японской войны, 1904–1905 гг. / И. И. Ростунов, Л. А. Зайцев, Ю. Ф. Соколов и др. М.: Наука, 1977. 381 с.

(History of the Russo–Japanese War, 1904–1905. I. I. Rostunov, L. A. Zaitsev, Iu. F. Sokolov and others. Moscow: Nauka, 1977. 381 pages.)

История первой мировой войны, 1914–1918 гг. / И. И. Ростунов, А. М. Агеев, Ю. Ф. Соколов и др. М.: Наука, 1975. Т. 1–2.

(History of the First World War, 1914–1918. I. I. Rostunov, A. M. Ageev, Iu. F. Sokolov, and others. Moscow: Nauka, 1975. Vols. 1–2.)

Ростунов, И. И. Русслий фронт первой мировой войны, 1914–1918 гг. / М.: Навка. 1975. Т. 1–2.

(Rostunov, I. I. The Russian Front in the First World War, 1914–1918. Moscow: Nauka, 1975. Vols. 1–2.)

нная история СССР
(Military History of the USSR)

Великая Октябрьская социадистическая революция и гражданская война в СССР
(The Great October Socialist Revolution and Civil War in the USSR)

Вокнно–революционные комитеты действующей армии, 25 окт. 1917 г. – март 1918 г. / Сост. Е. П. Воронин, Л. М. Гаврилов, Е. А. Елпатьевская и др. М.: Наука, 1977. 658 с.

(The Military-Revolutionary Committee of the Standing Army, 25 October 1917–March 1918. Compiled by E. P. Voronin, L. M. Gavrilov, E. A. Elpat'evskaia, and others. Moscow: Nauka, 1977. 658 pages.)

Вооруженные силы Великого Октября / В. Г. Колычев, Л. М. Гаврилов, С. М. Гончаров и др. М.: Наука, 1977. 288 с.

(The Armed Forces of the Great October. V. G. Kolychev, L. M. Gavrilov, S. M. Goncharov, and others. Moscow: Nauka, 1977. 288 pages.)

Венгерские интернационалисты в Октябрьской революции и граждансой войне в СССР: Сб. документов в 2 т. / Сост. О. С. Рябухина, Л. М. Чижова, А. Йожа и др. М.: Политиздат, 1968. Т. 1–2.

(Hungarian Internationalists in the October Revolution and Civil War in the USSR: A Collection of Documents in 2 vols. Compiled by O. S.

Riabukin, L. M. Chizhov, A. Iozh, and others. Moscow: Politzdat, 1968. Vols. 1–2.)

Октябрьская революция и армия, 25 окт. 1917 г. – март 1918 г.: Сб. документов / Сост. Е. П. Бородин, Л. М. Гаврилов, Т. Ф. Кузьмина и др. М.: Наука, 1973. 455 с.

(The October Revolution and the Army, 25 October 1917–March 1918.: A Collection of Documents. Compiled by E. P. Borodin, L. M. Gavrilov, T. F. Kuzmina, and others. Moscow: Nauka, 1973. 455 pages.)

Конев, А. М. Красная гвардия на защите Октября. 2–е изд., доп. М.: Наука, 1989. 333 с.

(Konev, A. M. The Red Guard in the Defense of October, 2nd edition supplemented. Moscow: Nauka, 1989. 333 pages.)

Гражданская война в СССР: В 2 т./ Азовцев, Н. Н.; Гусаревич, С. Д.; Тинин, А, Л. и др. М.: Воениздат, 1980–86. Т. 1–2.

(Civil War in the USSR: In 2 vols. Azovtsev, N. N.; Gusarevich, S. D.; Tinin, A. L.; and others. Moscow: Voenizdat, 1980–86. Vols. 1–2.)

Гражданская война и военная интервенция в СССР: Энциклопедия / Редкол.: С. С. Хромов, Н. Н. Азовцев, С. Д. Гусарев и др. М.: Сов. энцикл., 1983. 698 с.

(Civil War and Military Intervention in the USSR; An Encyclopedia. Editorial Board: S. S. Khromov, N. N. Azovtsev, S. D. Gusarev, and others. Moscow: Sov. Entsikl., 1983. 698 pages.)

Директивы Главного Командования Красной Армии (1917–1920 гг.): сб. документов / Сост. Н. М. Вьюнова, Н. И. Деева, Т. Ф. Каряева. М.: Воениздат, 1969. 883 с.

(Directives of the Main Command of the Red Army [1917–1920]: Collection of Documents. Compiled by N. M. V'iunov, N. I. Deev, T. F. Kariaev. Moscow: Voenizdat, 1969. 883 pages.)

Директивы командования фронтов Красной Армии (1917–1922 гг.): сб. документов: В 4 т. /Сост. Т. Ф. Каряева, Н. М. Вьюнова, З. Ф. Павлова и др. М.: Воениздат, 1971–78. Т. 1–4.

(Directives of the Command of the Red Army Fronts [1917–1922]: Collection of Documents: In 4 vols.. Compiled by T. F. Kariaev, N. M. V'iunov, Z. F. Pavlov, and others. Moscow: Voenizdat, 1971–78. Vols. 1–4.)

Из истории гражданской войны и интервенции, 1917–1922 гг. Сб. статей / Редкол.: И. И. Минц, Н. Н. Азовцев, П. Н. Дмитриев и др. М.: Наука, 1974. 480 с.

(From the History of the Civil War and Intervention, 1917–1922. Collection of Documents. Editorial Board: I. I. Mints, N. N. Azovtsev, P. N. Dmitriev, and others. Moscow: Nauka, 1974. 480 pages.)

Крах первого нашествия империалистов на страну Советов / Н. Н. Азовцев, А. М. Конев и др. М.: Воениздат, 1973. 439 с.

(The Failure of the First Invasion of the Imperialists in the Country of the Soviets. N. N. Azovtsev, A. M. Konev and others. Moscow: Voenizdat, 1973. 439 pages.)

2–я армия в боях за освобождение Прикамья и Приуралья, 1918–1919: Документы. Устинов: Удмуртия, 1987. 316 с.

(The 2nd Army in the Battle for the Liberation of Prikam'ia and Priural'ia, 1918–1919: Documents. Ustinov: Udmurtiia, 1987. 316 pages.)

...И на Тихом океане, 1920–1922: Нар. рев. армия ДВР в освобождении Приамурья и Приморья: Сб. документов / Сост. В. О. Дайнес и др. Иркутск: Вост.–Сиб. кн. изд., 1988. 358 с.

(. . . And on the Pacific Ocean, 1920–1922: The Peoples' Revolutionary Army of th DVR and the Liberation of Priamur'ia and Primor'ia: A Collection of Documents. Compiled by V. O. Daines and others. Irkutsk: Vost.-Sib. Kn. izd., 1988. 358 pages.)

Якушевский, А. С. Пропагандистская работа большевиков среди войск интервентов в 1918–1920 гг. М.: Наука, 1974. 187 с.

(Iakushevskii, A. S. Bolshevik Propaganda Work among the Interventionist Troops in 1918–1920. Moscow: Nauke, 1974. 187 pages.)

Интернациональная помощь XI армии в борьбе за победу советсой власти в Азербайджане: Документы и материалы, 1920–1921 гг. / Сост. Дайнес, В.О. и др. Баку: Азернешр, 1989. 194 с.

(The International Aid of the XIth Army in the Battle for the Victory of Soviet Power in Azerbaidzhan: Documents and Materials, 1920–1921. Compiled by V. O. Dains and others. Baku: Azerneshr, 1989. 194 pages.)

М. Фрунзе на Восточном фронте: Сб. документов. Куйбышев: Кн. изд–во, 1985. 272 с.

(M. Frunze and the Eastern Front: Collection of Documents. Kuibyshev: Kn. izd-vo, 1985. 272 pages.)

Шли дивизи вперед: Нар. рев. армия (Дальневост. респ.) в освобождении Забайкалья, 1920–1921: Сб. документов / Сост. В.О. Дайнес, В.Г. Краснов. Иркутск: Вост.–Сиб. кн. изд., 1987. 484 с.

(The Division Went Forward: The Peoples' Revolutionary Army [Far-Eastern Republic] in the Liberation of TransBiakal, 1920–1921: Collection of Documents. Compiled by V. O. Daines, V. G. Krasnov. Irkutsk: Vost.-Sib. kn. izd., 1987. 484 pages.)

Межвоенный период
(Interwar Period)

Конфликт на КВЖД: Из истории Сов. Вооруж. Сил / В. Н. Вартанов, И. М. Калинина, Е. В. Маркелов и др.; ред. В. П. Зимонин. Хабаровск: Кн. изд–во, 1989. 176 с.

(Conflict in the KVZhD: From the History of the Soviet Armed Forces. V. N. Vartanov, I. M. Kalinina, E. V. Markelov, and others; Editor V. P. Zimonin. Khabarovsk: Kn. izd-vo, 1989. 176 pages.)

Победа на реке Халхин–Гол: (Материалы науч. конф.) П. А. Жилин, А. И. Бабин, Д. Цэдэв и др. М.: Наука, 1981. 144 с.

(Vistory on the Khalkhin-Gol River: [Materials for a Study of the Conflict]. P. A. Zhilin, A. I. Babin, D. Tsedev, and others. Moscow: Nauka, 1981. 144 pages.)

Великая Отечественная война Советского Союза 1941–1945 гг.
(The Great Patriotic War of the Soviet Union, 1941–1945)

Великая Отечественная война: Крат. науч.–попул. очерк / В. Е. Быстров, П. А. Жилин, Г. А. Колтунов и др. 2–е изд. М.: Политиздат, 1973. 542 с.

(The Great Patriotic War: Short Scientific-Popular Notes. V. E. Bystrov, P. A. Zhilin, G. A. Koltunov, and others. 2nd edition. Moscow: Politzdat, 1973. 542 pages.)

Великая Отечественная народная, 1941–1945: Крат. ист. очерк / П. А. Жилин, А. И. Бабин, М. М. Кирьян и др. М.: Мысль, 1985. 368 с.

(The Great Patriotic People's 1941–1945: Short Historical Note. P. A. Zhilin, A. I. Babin, M. M. Kir'ian, and others. Moscow: Mysl', 1985. 368 pages.)

Великая Отечественная война, 1941–1945: Словарь–справочник. М.: Политиздат, 1988. 559 с.

(The Great Patriotic War, 1941–1945: Dictionary–Reference Book. Moscow: Politzdat, 1988. 559 pages.)

Великая Отечественная война, 1941–1945: Энциклопедия / Редкол.: Ю. Я. Барабаш, П. А. Жилин, Г. П. Михайловский и др. М.: Сов. энцикл., 1985. 832с.

(The Great Patriotic War, 1941–1945: Encyclopedia, Editorial Board.: Iu. Ia. Barabash, P. A. Zhilin, G. P. Mikhailovskii, and others. Moscow: Sov. entsikl., 1985. 832 pages.)

Историография Великой Отечественной войны: Сб. статей / Редкол.: М. П. Ким, А. И. Бабин, Ю. В. Плотников и др. М.: Наука, 1980. 288 с.

(Historigraphy of the Great Patriotic War: Collection of Articles. Editorial Board: M. P. Kim, A. I. Babin, Iu. V. Plotnikov, and others. M.: Nauka, 1980. 288 pages.)

Всемирно–историческая победа советского народа, 1941–1945 гг. : Материалы науч. конф., посвящ. 25–летию победы над фашист. Германией / Редкол.: М. В. Захаров, П. Н. Федосеев, П. А. Жилин и др. М.: Наука, 1971. 648 с.

(The Global Historical Victory of the Soviet People, 1941–1945: Materials of a Scientific Conference, Devoted to the 25th Anniversary of the Victory Over Fascist Germany. Editorial Board: M. V. Zakharov, P. H. Fedoceev, P.A. Zhilin, and others. Moscow: Nauka, 1971. 648 pages.)

Великая победа советского народа, 1941–1945: Материалы науч. конф., посвящ. 30–летию победы сов. народа в Великой Отеч. войне 1941–1945 гг. Редкол.: А. А. Гречко, А. А. Епишев, П. А. Жилин и др. М.: Наука, 1976. 648 с.

(The Great Victory of the Soviet People, 1941–1945: Materials of a Scientific Conference, Devoted to the 30th Anniversary of the Victory of the Soviet People in the Great Patriotic War 1941–1945. Editorial Board: A. A. Grechko, A. A. Epishev, P. A. Zhilin, and others. Moscow: Nauka, 1976. 648 pages.)

Подвиг народа / П. А. Жилин, А. А. Бабаков, М. М. Кирьян и др. М.: Наука, 1981. 224 с.

(The Victory of the People. P. A. Zhlin, A. A. Babkov, M. M. Kir'ian, and others. Moaxow: Nauka, 1981. 224 pages.)

40 лет Великой Победы. М.: Наука, 1987. 408 с.

(40 Years of the Great Victory. M.: Nauka, 1987. 408 pages.)

Ленинский комсомол в Великой Отечественной войне / Редкол.: Ганичев, В. Н.; Исаков, П. Ф.; Куманев, Г. А. и др. М.: Мол. гвардия, 1975. 335 с.

(The Leninist Konsomol in the Great Patriotic War. Editorial Board.: Ganichev, V. N.; Isakov, P. F.; Kumanev, G. A., and others. Moscow: Mol. Gvardiia, 1975. 335 pages.)

Величие подвига советского народа: Зарубеж. отклики и высказывания 1941–1945 гг. о Великой Отеч. войне /Сост. А. И. Бабин, М. М. Кирьян, Г. И. Коротков, А. С. Якушевский. М.: Международные отношения, 1985. 384 с.

(The Grandeur of the Heroic Deed of the Soviet People: Foreign Comments and Statements 1941–1945 about the Great Patriotic War. Compiled by A. I. Babin, M. M. Kir'ian, G. I. Korotkov, A. S. Iakushevshii. Moscow: Mezhdunarodnie Otnosheniia, 1985. 384 pages.)

Азясский, Н. Ф.; Князьков, А. С. Парптизанская операция "Рельсовая война". М.: Знание, 1985. 63 с. (Новое в жизни, науке, технике. Сер. "Защита Отечества"; II).

(Aziasskii, N. F.; Kniaz'kov, A. S. The Partisan Operation "Railway War." Moscow: Znanie, 1985. 63 pages [The Modern in Life, Science, Technology. Series "Zashchita Otechestva"; II]).

Антосяк, А. В. В боях за свободу Руминии. М.: Воениздат, 1974. 288 с.

(A. V. Antosiak, A. B. In the Battle for the Liberation of Rumania. M.: Voenizdat, 1974. 288 pages.)

Баженов, А, Н.; Шевчук, В. П. В боях под Смоленском. М.: Моск. рабочий, 1984. 61 с.

(Bazhenov, A. N.; Shevchuk, V. P. In the Battle for Smolensk. M.: Mosk. rabochii, 1984. 61 pages.)

Басов, А. В. Флот в Великой Отечественной войне 1941–1945 гг. М.: 1980. 301 с.

(Basov, A. V. The Navy in the Great Patriotic War 1941–1945. Moscow: 1980. 301 pages.)

Батов, П. И. Форсирование рек, 1942–1945 гг.: (Из опыта 65–й армии). М.: Воениздат, 1986. 160 с.

(Batov, P. I. The Forcing of Rivers 1942–1945: [from the Experience of the 65th Army]. M.: Voenizdat, 1986. 160 pages.)

Беспримерный подвиг: Материали науч. конф., посвящ. 25–летию нем.–фашист. войск под Москвой / Редкол.: П. А. Жилин, К. И. Буков, А. Н. Грылев и др. М.: Наука, 1968. 462 с.

(An Unsurpassed Accomplishment: Material from a Scientific Conference Devoted to the 25th Anniversary of the German-Fascist Troops before Moscow. Editorial Board: Zhilin, P. A.: Bukov, K. I.: Grulev, A. N., and others. Moscow: Nauka, 1968. 462 pages.)

Битва на Курской дуге / Редкол.: Н.И. Шеховцов, Г.А. Колтунов, Ю.В. Плотников и др. М.: Наука, 1975. 192 с.

(The Battle at the Kursk Bulge. Editorial Board: N. I. Shekhotsov, G. A. Koltunov, Iu. V. Plotnikov, and others. M.: Nauka, 1975. 192 pages.)

Битва под Москвой / Н.Г. Андроников, П.П. Ионов, Р.В. Мазуркевич, В.П. Смирнов. М.: Воениздат, 1989. 320 с.

(The Battle for Moscow. N. G. Andronikov, P. P. Ionov, P. V. Mazurkrvich, V. P. Smirnov. Moscow: Voenizdat, 1989. 320 pages.)

Борисов, Н. В. Они повторили подвиг Сусанина. 2–е изд. М.: Просвещуние, 1979. 143 с.

(Borisov, N. V. They Repeated the Accomplishment of Susanin. 2nd ed. Moscow: Prosveshchenie, 1979. 143 pages.)

Великий освободительный поход / Сост. М. Н. Горбунов. М: Политиздат, 1970. 312 с.

(The Great Liberation March. Compiled by M. N. Gorbunov. Moscow: Politizdat, 1970. 312 pages.)

Внезапность в наступательных операциях Великой Отечественной войны / Отв. ред. М.М. Кирьян. М.: Наука, 1986. 208 с.

(Surprise in Offensive Operation in the Great Patriotic War. Editor in Chief M. M. Kir'ian. Moscow: Nauka, 1986. 208 pages.)

Воробьев, Ф. Д.; Паротькин, И. В.; Шиманский, А. Н. Последний штурм: Берлин операция 1945 г. 2-е изд., испр. и доп. М.: Воениздат, 1975. 455 с.

(Vorob'ev, F. D. Parot'kin, I. V.; Shimanskii, A. N. The Last Storm: The Berlin Operation 1945. 2nd ed., revised and supplemented. Moscow: Voenizdat, 1975. 455 pages.)

Восемнадцатая в сраженях за Родину: боевой путь 18-й армии / М. И. Повалий, Ю. В. Плотников, И. М. Ананьев и др. М.: Воениздат, 1982. 528 с.

(The Eighteenth in the Battle for the Motherland; the Militaty Path of the 18th Army. M. I. Povalii, Iu. V. Plotnikov, I. M. Anan'ev, and others. Moscow: Voenizdat, 1982. 528 pages.)

Герои огненных лет: Очерки о москвичах – Героях Сов. Союза / Редкол.: П. А. Жилин, А. И. Бабин, А. М. Синицин и др. М.: Моск. рабочий, 1975–85. Кн. 1–8.

(Heroes of the Fiery Years: Notes about the Muscovites—Heroes of the Soviet Union. Editorial Board: P. A. Ahilin, A. I. Babin, A. M. Sinitsin, and others. Moscow: Mosk. rabochii, 1975–85. books 1–8.)

Герои Советского Союза: Ист.–стат. очерк / Д. Н. Артамонов, А. А. Бабаков, Н. В. Борисов и др. М.: Воениздат, 1984. 288 с.

(Heroes of the Soviet Union: A Historical-Statistical Note. D. N. Artamonov, A. A. Babokov, N. V. Borison, and others. Moscow: Voenizdat, 1984. 288 pages.)

Герои Советского Союза: Крат.биогр. словар: В 2 т. / А. А. Бабаков, Ф. Н. Абрамов, А. М. Агеев и др. М.: Воениздат, 1987–88. Т. 1–2.

(Heroes of the Soviet Union: A Short Biographical Dictionary: In 2 vols. A. A. Babakov, F. M. Abramov, A. M. Ageev, and others. Moscow: Voenizdat, 1987–88. Vols. 1–2.)

Елисеев, Е. П. На Белостокском направлении. М.: Наука, 1971. 230 с.

(Eliseev, E. P. In the Direction of Belostok. Moscow: Nauka, 1971. 230 pages.)

Ибрагимбейли, Х. М. Битва за Кавказ. М.: Знание, 1983. 62 с. (Новое в жизни, науке, технике. Сер. "Защита Отечества"; 10).

(Ibragimbeili, Kh. M. The Battle for the Caucasus. Moscow: Znanie, 1983. 62 pages. [Modernity in Life, Science, Technology. Series "Defense of the Fatherland"; 101.)

Исаев, С. И.; Левченко, В. Н. Герои–освободители Харьковщины. Харьков: Прапор, 1988. 316 с.

(Isaev, S. I.; Levchenko, V. N. Hero-Liberators of Khar'kov. Khar'kov: Prapor, 1988. 316 pages.)

Исторический подвиг Сталинграда / Подгот.: Ю. В. Плотников, В. А. Дорофеев, А. С. Князьков и др. М.: Мысль, 1985. 416 с.

(The Historic Accomplishment of Stalingrad. Prepared by Iu. V. Plotnikov, V. A. Dorofeev, A. S. Knias'kov, and others. Moscow: Misl', 1985. 416 pages.)

Карельский фронт в Великой Отечественной войне 1941–1945 гг.: Военн.–ист. очерк / Бабин, А. И.; Ананьев, И. М.; Желтов, А. С. и др. М.: Наука, 1984. 359 с.

(The Karelian Front in the Great Patriotic War 1941–1945: A Military-Historical Note. Babin, A. I.; Anan'ev, I. M.; Zheltov, A. S., and others. Moscow: Nauka, 1984. 359 pages.)

Кожевников, М. Н. Командование и штаб ВВС Советской Армии в Великой Отечественной войне 1941–1945 гг.: 2–е изд., испр. и доп. М.: Наука, 1985.

(Kozhevnikov, M. N. Command and the Staff of the VVS of the Soviet Army in the Patriotic War 1941–1945: 2nd ed., revised and supplemented. Moscow: Nauka, 1985. 288 pages.)

Колтунов, Г.А.; Соловьев, Б. Г. Курская битва. М.: Воениздат, 1983. 128 с.

(Koltunov, G. A.; Solov'ev, B. G. The Battle of Kursk. Moscow: Voenizdat, 1983. 128 pages.)

Колтунов, Г. А.; Соловьев, Б. Г. Огненная дуга. М.: Воениздат, 1973. 176 с.

(Koltunov, G. A.; Solov'ev, B. G. The Fiery Bulge. Moscow: Voenizdat, 1973. 176 pages.)

Краснознаменный Балтийский флот в ьитве за Ленинград, 1941–1944 гг. / Редкол.: А. В. Басов, Ю. Г. Перечнев и др. М.: Наука, 1973. 446 с.

(The Red Banner Baltic Fleet in the Battle for Leningrad, 1941–1944. Editorial Board: A. V. Basov, Iu. G. Perechnev, and others. Moscow: Nayka, 1973. 446 pages.)

Краснознаменный Балтийский флот в завершающий период Великой Отечественной войне 1944–1945 гг./ Редкол.: А. В. Басов, Д. Д. Кодола, Ю. Г. Перечнев. М.: Наука, 1975. 488 с.

(The Red Banner Baltic Fleet in the Concluding Period of the Great Patriotic War, 1944–1945. Editorial Board: A. V. Basov, D. D. Kadola, Iu. G. Perechnev. Moscow: Nauka, 1975. 488 pages.)

Крах блицкрига: Урок милитаристам и агрессорам / Подгот. М. М. Кирьян, В. Ф. Бутурлинов, В. П. Зимонин и др. М.: Воениздат, 1987. 208 с.

(The Failure of Blitzkrieg; A Lesson of Militarism and Aggression. Prepared by M. M. Kir'ian, V. F. Buturlinov, V. P. Zimonin, and others. Moscow: Voenizdat, 1987. 208 pages.)

Курская битва. / Редкол.: Б. И. Баромыкин, Г. А. Колтунов, Е. П. Михайлова и др. М.: Наука, 1970. 543 с.

(The Battle of Kursk. Editorial Board: B. I. Baromykin, G. A. Koltunov, E. P. Mikhailova, and others. Moscow: Nauka, 1970. 543 pages.)

Мазуркевич, Р. В. В трудную пору: О нач. периоде Великой Отеч. войны. Минск: Беларусь, 1985. 48 с.

(Mazurekevich, P. V. In a Difficult Time: About the Opening Period of the Great Patriotic War. Minsk: Belarus', 1985. 48 pages.)

Мазуркевич, Р. В. Сплав мужества и стали: Танкисты в Курской битве. Воронеж: Центр.–Чернозем. кн. изд–во, 1986. 238 с.

(Mazurekevich, P. V. The Fusion of Courage and Steel: Armor in the Kursk Battle. Voronezh: Tsentr.-Chernozem. kn. izd-vo, 1986. 238 pages.)

На Волховском фронте, 1941–1944 гг. / Отв. ред. А. И. Бабин. М.: Наука, 1982. 298 с.

(On the Volkhov Front, 1941–1944. Editor in Chief A. I. Babin. Moscow: Nauka, 1982. 298 pages.)

На северо–Западном фронте, 1941–1943 гг. / Сост. Ф. Н. Утенков. М.: Наука, 1969. 447 с.

(On the North-West Front, 1941–1943. Compiled by F. N. Utenkov. Moscow: Nauka, 1969. 447 pages.)

Освободительная миссия Советских Вооруженных Сил во второй мировой войне / Подгот.: И. В. Пароткин, Н. Г. Андроников, А. В. Антосяк и др. 2–е изд. М.: Политиздат, 1974. 502 с.

(The Liberation Mission of the Soviet Armed Forces in the Second World War. Prepared by: I. V. Parotkin, N. G. Andronikov, A. V. Antosiak and others. 2nd ed., Moscow: Politizdat, 1974. 502 pages.)

Освободительная миссия Советских Вооруженных Сил в Европе во второй мировой войне: Документы и материалы / Редкол.: П. А. Жилин, А. И. Бабин, В. В. Семин и др. М.: Воениздат, 1985. 640 с.

(The Liberation Mission of the Soviet Armed Forces in Europe in the Second World War: Documents and Materials. Editorial Board: P. A. Zhilin, A. I. Babin, V. V. Semin, and others. M.: Voenizdat, 1985. 640 pages.)

Освободительная миссия Советских Вооруженных Сил на Балканах / А. В. Антосяк, Н. В. Васильева, П. А. Кочегура и др. М.: Наука, 1989. 264 с.

(The Liberation Mission of the Soviet Armed Forces in Europe in the Balkans. A. V. Antosiak, H. V. Vasil'eva, P. A. Kochegura and others. Moscow: Nauka, 1989. 264 pages.)

Освобождение городов: Справочник по освобождению городов в период Великой Отеч. войны, 1941–1945 / М. Л. Дударенко, Ю. Г. Перечнев, С. П. Абрамов и др. М.: Воениздат, 1985. 598 с.

(The Liberation of Towns: A Reference Book on the Liberation of Towns during the Great Patriotic War, 1941–1945. M. L. Dudarenko, Iu. G. Perechnev, S. P. Abramov, and others. Moscow: Voenizdat, 1985. 598 pages.)

Ю. Г. Перечнев, Уроки "блицкрига". М.: Моск. рабочий, 1985. 88 с.

(Iu. G. Perechnev, Lessons of "Blitzkrieg." Moscow: Mosk. rabochii, 1985. 88 pages.)

Победа под Москвой: По материалам воен.–науч. конф. / Подгот.: М. М. Кирьян, Ю. Г. Перечнев, А. М. Соколов, Г. Т. Хорошилов. М.: Воениздат, 1982. 157 с.

(Victory Before Moscow: Materials of a Military-Scientific Conference. Prepared by: M. M. Kir'ian, Iu. G. Perechnev, A. M. Sokolov, G. T. Khoroshilov. Moscow: Voenizdat, 1982. 157 pages.)

Победа на востоке: к 40–летию разгрома милитарист. Японии / О. Б. Борисов, В. Ф. Бутурлинов, А. М. Носков, Ю. М. Шевенков. М.: Воениздат, 1985. 127 с.

(Victory in the East: the 40th Anniversary of the Destruction of Militarist Japan. O. V. Borisov, V. F. Buturlianov, A. M. Noskov, Iu. M. Shchevenkov. Moscow: Voenizdat, 1985. 127 pages.)

Победа СССР в воине с милитаристской Японией и послевоенное развитие Восточной и Юго–Восточной Азии: Материалы конф. / Редкол.: А. Д. Педосов, В. А. Власов, А. И. Картунова и др. М.: Наука, 1977. 254 с.

(The Victory of the USSR in the War with Militarist Japan and the Postwar Development of East and South-Eastern Asia: Conference materials. Editorial Board: A. D. Pedosov, V. A. Vlasov, A. I. Kartunova, and others. Moscow: Nauka, 1977. 254 pages.)

Приказы Верховного Главнокомандующего в Великой Отечественной войны: С 25 янв. 1943 г. по 3 сент. 1945 г. / И. М. Ананьев, Н. И. Шеховцов, П. Ф. Шкорувский и др. М.: Воениздат, 1976. 648 с.

(Directives of the Supreme Command in the Great Patriotic War: From 25 January 1943 to 3 September 1945. I. M. Anan'ev, N. I. Shekhovtsov, P. F. Shkoruvshii, and others. Moscow: Voenizdat, 1976. 648 pages.)

Разгром милитаристской Япониии и освободительная ииссия СССР в Азии: Сб. документов / Сост. В. Ф. Бутурлинов и др. М.: Изд–во Агенства печати "Новости". 1985. 119 с.

(The Destruction of Militarist Japan and the Liberation Mission of the USSR in Asia: Collection of Documents. Compiled by V. F. Buturlinov and others. Moscow: Izd-vo Agenstva pechati “Novosti,” 1985. 119 pages.)

Светлишин, Н. А. Войска ПВО страны в Великой Отечественной войне: Вопр. оператив.–стратег. применения. М.: Наука, 1979. 295 с.

(Svetlishin, N. A. Troops of the PVO Countries in the Great Patriotic War: Questions of Operational-Strategic Application. Moscow: Nauka, 1979. 295 pages.)

Соловьев, Б. Г. Верхмат на пути к гибели: Крушение планов нем.–фашист. командования летом и осенью 1943 г. М.: Наука, 1973. 312 с.

(Solov'ev, B. G. The Wehrmacht on the Road to Destruction: The Wreck of the Plans of the German-Fascist Command in the Summer and Autumn of 1943. Moscow: Nauka, 1973. 312 pages.)

Тыл Советских Вооруженных Сил в Великой Отечественной войне 1941–1945 гг. / И. М. Голушко, Ю. В. Плотников, Н. А. Антипенко и др. М.: Воениздат, 1977. 559 с.

(The Rear of Soviet Armed forces in the Great Patriotic War 1941–1945. I. M. Golushko Iu. V. Plotnikov, N. A. Antipenko, and others. Moscow: Voenizdat, 1977. 559 pages.)

Федоров, А. Ф. Авиация в битве под Москвой. 2–е изд., доп. и испр. М.: Наука, 1975. 344 с.

(Fedorov, A. F. Aviation in the Battle for Moscow. 2nd ed., supplemented and revised. Moscow: Nauka, 1975. 344 pages.)

Фронты наступали: По опыту Великой Отеч. войны: Крат. ист.–теорет. очерк / В. Б. Сеоев, В. П. Андреев, М. Ф. Бегунов и др. М.: Наука, 1987. 254 с.

(The Front Was Attacked: In the Experience of the Great Patriotic War: A Short Historical-Theoretical Note. V. B. Seoev, V. P. Andreev, M. F. Begunov, and others. Moscow: Nauka, 1987. 254 pages.)

Шумихин, В. С.; Борисов, Н. В. Немеркнущий подвиг: Героизм сов. воинов в годы Великой Отеч. войны. М.: Наука, 1985. 271 с.

(Shumikhin, V. S.; Borisov, N. V. The Unfading Accomplishment: The Heroism of Soviet Soldiers in the Years of the Great Patriotic War. Moscow: 1985. 271 pages.)

Шумихин, В. С. Подвиг Героев Советского Союза. М.: Знание, 1987. 64 с.

(Shumikhin, V. The Accomplishment of the Heroes of the Soviet Union. Moscow: Znanie, 1987. 64 pages.)

Всеобщая история
(General History)

Вторая мировая война 1939–1945 гг. Послевоенный период
(The Second World War 1939–1945. The Postwar Period)

История Вторая мировая война, 1939–1945 гг.: В 12 т. / Гл. ред. комис.: А. А. Гречко, Д. Ф. Устинов, П. А. Жилин, и др. М.: Воениздат, 1973–82. Т. 1–12.

(History of the Second World War 1939–1945: In 12 vols. Main Editorial Commission.: A. A. Grechko, D. F. Ustinov, P. A. Zhilin, and others. Moscow: Voenizdat, 1973–82. Vols. 1–12.)

Вторая мировая война: Итоги и уроки / Гл. ред. комис.: С. Л. Соколов, С. Ф. Ахромеев, П. А. Жилин, и др. М.: Воениздат, 1985. 447 с.

(The Second World War: Results and Lessons. The Main Editorial Commission.: S. L. Sokolov, S. F. Akhromeev, P. A. Zhilin, and others. Moscow: Voenizdat, 1985. 447 pages.)

Вторая мировая война: Крат. история / Д. Айххольц, А. И. Бабин, П. А. Жилин, и др. М.: Наука, 1984. 591 с.

(The Second World War: A Short History. D. Aikhkhol'ts, A. I. Babin, P. A. Zhilin, and others. Moscow: Nauka, 1984. 591 pages.)

Вторая мировая война и современность: Сб. статей / Редкол.: П. А. Жилин, П. М. Деревянко, Г. Д. Комлев и др. М.: Наука, 1972. 355 с.

(The Second World War and the Present: A Collection of Articles. Editorial Board: P. A. Zhilin, P. M. Derevianko, G. D. Komlev, and others. Moscow: Nauka, 1972. 355 pages.)

Вторая мировая война 1939–1945: фотоальбом / Сост. и авт. текста Т. Бушуева, А. Другов, А. Савин. М.: Планета, 1989. 415 с.

(The Second World War 1939–1945: Photoalbum. Compiled and authored text, T. Bushueva, A. Drugov, A. Savin. Moscow: Planeta, 1989. 415 pages.)

Жилин, П. А., Якушевский, А. С., Кульков, Е. Н. Критика основных концепций буржуазной историографии второй мировой войны. М.: Наука, 1983. 384 с.

(Zhilin, P. A.; Iakushevskii, A. S.; Kul'kov, E. N. A Criticism of the Fundamental Conceptions of Bourgeois Historiography of the Second World War. Moscow: Nauka, 1983. 384 pages.)

Коренной перелом во второй мировой войне: По материалам воен.–науч. конф. / Подгот.: М. М. Кирьян, Ю. Г. Перечнев, В. Т. Елисеев и др. М.: Воениздат, 1985. 216 с.

(The Fundamental Turning Point of the Second World War: Materials of a Military-Scientific Conference. Prepared by M. M. Kir'ian, Iu. G. Perechnev, V. T. Eliseev, and others. Moscow: Voenizdat, 1985. 216 pages.)

Лютов, И. С.; Носков, А. М. Коалиционное взаимодействие союзиков: По опыту первой и второй мировых войн. М.: Наука, 1988. 245 с.

(Liutov, I. S.; Noskov, A. M. Coalition Cooperation of the Allies: The Experience of the First and Second World Wars. Moscow: Nauka, 1988. 245 pages.)

Носков, А. М. Норвегия во второй мировой войне, 1940–1945. М.: Наука, 1973. 276 с.

(Noskov, A. M. Norway in the Second World War, 1940–1945. Moscow: Nauka, 1973. 276 pages.)

Носков, А. М. Скандинавский плацдарм во второй мировой войне. М.: Наука. 1977. 248 с.

(Noskov, A. M. Scandinavian Brigehead in the Second World War. Moscow: Nauka, 1977. 248 pages.)

Орлов, А. С.; Новоселов, Б. Н. Факты против мифов: Подлин. и мнимая история второй мировой войны. М.: Мол. гвардая, 1986. 239 с.

(Orlov, A. S.; Novoselov, B. N. Facts against Myths: The Authentic and Imaginary History of the Second World War. Moscow: Mol. gvardiia, 1986. 239 pages.)

Правда истории: (Против буржуаз. фальсификации истории второй мировой войны) / Сост. И. Поморов. М.: Знание, 1971. 80 с.

(The Truth of History: [Against the Bourgeois Falsificators of History of the Second World War]. Compiled by M. Promorov. Moscow: Znanie, 1977. 80 pages.)

Преступные цели гитлеровской Германии в войне против Советского Союза: Документы, материали / Авт.–сост. А. С. Орлов, В. П. Зимонин, Г. М Иваницскии и др. М.: Воениздат, 1987. 301 с.

(The Criminal Goals of Hitler's Germany in the War against the Soviet Union; Documents, Materials. Author-Compilers A. S. Orlov, V. P. Zimonin, G. M. Ivanitsskii, and others. Moscow: Voenizdat, 1987. 301 pages.)

Против общего врага: Сов. люди во франц. движении Сопротивления / Сост. и авт. введ. Н. Г. Цырульников. М.: Наука, 1972. 395 с.

(Against the Common Enemy: Soviet Citizens in the French Resistance. Compiler and Introductory Author H. G. Tsul'nikov. Moscow: Nauka, 1972. 395 pages.)

Разгром японского милитаризма во второй мировой войне / Подгот. к изд. М. М. Кирьян, В. Ф. Бутурлинов, В. Н. Вартанов и др. М.: Воениздат, 1986. 381 с.

(The Destruction of Japanese Militarism in the Second World War. Prepared for publication by M. M. Kir'ian, V. F. Buturlinov, V. N. Vartanov, and others. Moscow: Voenizdat, 1986. 381 pages.)

Ржешевский, О. А. Война и история: Буржуаз. историография США о второй мировой войне. М.: Мысль, 1976. 292 с.

(Rzhexhevskii, O. A. War and History: Bourgeois History of the USA about the Second World War. Moscow: Misl', 1976. 292 pages.)

Савин, А. С. Японский милитаризм в период второй мировой войны, 1939–1945 гг. М.: Наука, 1979. 239 с.

(Savin, A. S. Japanese Militarism in the Period of the Second World War, 1939–1945. Moscow: Nauka, 1979. 239 pages.)

Семиряга, М. И. Немецо–фашистская политика национального порабощения в оккупированных странах Западной и северной Европы. М.: Наука, 1980. 240 с.

(Semiriaga, M. I. The German-Fascist Policy of National Enslavement in the Occupation of the Countries of Western and Northern Europe. Moscow: Nauka, 1980. 240 pages.)

Семиряга, М. И. Советские люди в европейском Сопротивлении. М.: Наука, 1970. 351 с.

(Semiriaga, M. I. Soviet Citizens in the European Resistance. Moscow: Nauka, 1970. 351 pages.)

Советские люди в освободительной борьбе югославского народа, 1941–1945 гг. (Воспоминания, документы и материалы) / Т. А. Бушуева. М.: Наука, 1973. 207 с.

(Soviet Citizens in the Liberation Struggle of the Yugoslavian People, 1941–1945 [Reminiscences, Documents and Material]. T. A. Bushueva. Moscow.: Nauka, 1973. 207 pages.)

Страны Централюной и Юго–Восточной Европы во второй мировой войне: Воен.– –ист. справочник / Подгот.: Семиряга, М. И.; Васильева, Н. В.; Шинкарев, И. И. и др. М.: Воениздат, 1972. 302 с.

(The countries of Central and South-Eastern Europe in the Second World War: A Military-Historical Reference Work. Prepared by: Semiriaga, M. I.; Vasil'eva, N. V.; Shikarev, I. I., and others. Moscow: Voenizdat, 1972. 302 pages.)

Вооруженная борьба народов Азии за свободу и независимость, 1945–1980 / Л. Л. Круглов, В. Ф. Бутурлинов, А. Ф. Дмитриев и др. М.: Наука, 1984. 341 с.

(The Armed Struggle of the Peoples of Asia for Freedom and Independence, 1945–1980. I. L. Kruglov, V. F. Buturlinov, A. F. Dmitriev, and others. Moscow: Nauka, 1984. 341 pages.)

Вооруженная борьба народов Африки за свободу и независимость / Л. Л. Круг–лов, А. С. Аветян, В. А. Высоцкий и др. М.: Наука, 1974. 444 с.

(The Armed Struggle of the Peoples of Africa for Freedom and Independence. L. L. Kruglov, A. S. Avetian, V. A. Vysotskii, and others. Moscow: Nauka, 1974. 444 pages.)

За антифашистскую демократическую Германию, Сб. Дк., 1945–1949 гг. / Редкол.: Жилин, П. А.; Белов, Г. А.; Дёрнберг, С. и др. М.: Политиздат, 703 с.

(Behind the Antifascist Democratic Germany: A Collection of Documents, 1945–1949. Editorial Board.: Zhilin, P. A.; Belov, G. A.; Dernberg, S.; and others. Moscow: Politizdat, 1969. 703 pages.)

ВООРУЖЕННЫЕ СИЛЫ (ARMED FORCES)

Вооруженные Силы СССР (Armed Forces of the USSR)

КПСС и военное строительство / Махалов, В. С.; Бабаков, А. А.; Артамов, Д Н. и др. М.: Воениздат, 1982 311 с.

(The CPSS and Military Construction. Makhalov, V. S.; Babakov, A. A.; Artamov, D. N.; and others. Moscow: Voenizdat, 1982. 311 pages.)

Бабаков, А. А. Вооруженные Силы СССР после войны (1945–1986 гг.) История строительства. М.: Воениздат, 1987. 288 с.

(Babakov, A. A. The Armed Forces of the USSR after the War [1945–1986]. A History of Construction. Moscow: Voenizdat, 1987. 288 pages.)

Дружба и братство народов СССР – источник могущества Советских Вооруженных Сил: Материалы конф., посвящ. 60–летию образования СССР / Редкол.: Н. Д. Козлов, А. С. Гудков, В. Ф. Молчанов, Л. А. Бублик. Москва, 1983. 115 с.

(The Friendship and Brotherhood of the Peoples of the USSR—A Source of Power of the Soviet Armed Forces: Materials from a Conference Dedicated to the 60th Anniversary of the Formation of the USSR. Editorial Board: N. D. Kozlov, A. S. Gudkov, V. F. Molchanov, L. A. Bubnik. Moscow: 1983. 115 pages.)

Советские Вооруженные Силы: История строительства / Тюшкевич, С. А.; Зверев, Б. И.; Кораблев, Ю. И. и др. М.: Воениздат, 1978. 515 с.

(The Soviet Armed Forces: History of their Formation. Tiushkevich, S. A.; Zverev, B. I.; Korablev, Iu. I., and others. Moscow: Voenizdat, 1978. 515 pages.)

Советские Вооруженные Силы в условиях развитого социализма / Ю. Я. Киршин, В. С. Ещенко, П. Ф. Исаков и др. М.: Наука, 1985. 296 с.

(The Soviet Armed Forces in the Conditions of the Development of Socialism. Iu. Ia. Kirshin, V. S. Eshchenko, P. F. Isakov, and others. Moscow: Nauka, 1985. 296 pages.)

Советские Вооруженные Силы на стража мира и социализма / Ю. Я. Киршин, Н. Н. Грачев, И. А. Даунис и др. М.: Наука, 1988. 350 с.

(The Soviet Armed Forces on Guard for Peace and Socialism. Iu. Ia. N. N. Kirshin, N. N. Grachev, I. A. Daunis, and others. Moscow: Nauka, 1988. 350 pages.)

Военно–технический прогресс и Вооруженные Силы СССР: (Анализ развития вооружения, организации и способов действий) М. М. Кирьян, А. А. Бабаков, А. Н. Баженов и др. М.: Воениздат, 1982. 355 с.

(Military-Technical Progress and the Armed Forces of the USSR: [An Analysis of the Development of the Armament, Organization, and Means of Action]. M. M. Kir'ian, A. A. Babakov, A. N. Bazhenov, and others. Moscow: Voenizdat, 1982. 355 pages.)

Идеологическая работа в Вооруженных Силах СССР: Ист.–теорет. очерк / Исаков, П. Ф.; Ильин, С. К.; Артамошин, Ю. Н. и др. М.: Воениздат, 1983. 334 с.

(Ideological Work in the Armed Forces of the USSR: A Historical-Theoretical Note. Isakov, P. F.; Il'in, S. K.; Artamoshin, Iu. N.; and others. Moscow: Voenizdat, 1983. 334 pages.)

Всеармейские совещания политработников, 1918–1940 гг.: (Резолюции) / Сост. Т. Ф. Караева, Н. Е. Елисеева, В. Ф. Клочков и др. М.: Наука, 1984. 335 с.

(The All-Army Conference of Political Workers, 1918–1940: [Resolutions]. Compiled by T. F. Karaeva, N. E. Eliseeva, V. F. Klochkov, and others. Moscow: Nauka, 1984. 335 pages.)

Парийно–политическая работа в Красной Армии: Документы, 1921–1929 гг. / Сост. Т. Ф. Караева, В. Г. Колычев, В. Ф. Клочков и др. М.: Воениздат, 1981. 576 с.

(Party-Political Work in the Red Army: Documents, 1921–1929. Compiled by T. F. Karaeva, V. G. Kolychev, V. F. Klochkov, and others. Moscow: Voenizdat, 1981. 576 pages.)

Парийно–политическая работа в Крамной Артии: Документы, июль 1929 г.–май 1941 г. / Сост. Т. Ф. Караева, В. Ф. Клочков, Е. С. Степанов, В. П. Шевчук. М.: Воениздат, 1985. 535 с.

(Party-Political Work in the Red Army: Documents, July 1929–May 1941. Compiled by T. F. Karaeva, V. F. Klochkov, E. S. Stepanov, V. P. Shevchuk. Moscow: Voenizdat, 1985. 535 pages.)

Парийно–политическая работа в Вооруженных Силах СССР, 1918–1973 гг.: Ист. очерк / Исаков, П. Ф.; Колычев, В. Г.; Волков, А. М. и др. М: Воениздат, 1974. 366 с.

(Party-Political Work in the Armed Forces of the USSR, 1918–1973: An Historical Note. Isakov, P. F.; Kolychev, V. G.; Volkov, A. M.; and others. M.: Voenizdat, 1974. 366 pages.)

Политорганы Советских Вооруженных Сил: Ист–.теорет. очерк / П. Ф. Исаков, А. М. Волков, Г. В. Средин и др. М.: Воениздат, 1984. 400 с.

(Political Organs of the Soviet Armed Forces: An Historical-Theoretical Note. P. F. Isakov, A. M. Volkov, G. V. Sredin, and others. Moscow: Voenizdat, 1984. 400 pages.)

Колычев, В. Г. Партийно–политическая работа в Красной Армии в годы гражданской войны, 1918–1920. М.: Наука, 1979. 407 с.

(Kolychev, V. G. Party-Political Work in the Red Army in the Years of the Civil War, 1918–1920. Moscow: Nauka, 1979. 407 pages.)

Клочков, В. Ф. Красная Армия – школа коммунистическкого воспитания воинов, 1918–1941. М.: Наука, 1984. 229 с.

(Klochkov, V. F. The Red Army—A School of Communist Education of Troops, 1918–1941. Moscow: Nauka, 1984. 229 pages.)

Сувениров, О. Ф. Коммунистическая партия – организатор политического воспитания Красной Армии и флота, 1921–1928. М.: Наука, 1976. 291 с.

(Suvenirov, O. F. The Communist Party—The Organisor of Political Education of the Red Army and Fleet, 1921–1928. Moscow: Nauka, 1976. 291 pages.)

Инженерные войска Советской Армии, 1918–1945 / Е. П. Егоров, В. П. Андреев, С. Ф. Бегунов и др. М.: Воениздат, 1985. 488 с.

(Engineer Troops of the Soviet Army 1918–1945. E. P. Egorov, V. P. Andreev, S. F. Begunov, and others. Moscow: Voenizdat, 1985. 488 pages.)

Перечнев, Ю. Г. Советская береговая артиллерия: (История развития и боевого применения, 1921–1945 гг.) М.: Наука, 1976. 335 с.

(Perechnev, Iu. G. Soviet Shore Artillery: [The Historiy of Development and Military Application, 1921–1945]. Moscow: Nauka, 1976. 335 pages.)

Шумихин, В. С. Советская военная авиация, 1917–1941. М.: Наука, 1986. 284 с.

(Shumikhin, V. S. Soviet Military Aviation, 1917–1941. Moscow: Nauka, 1986. 284 pages.)

Боевое содружество Вооруженных Сил СССР и вооруженных сил других стран
(The Military Cooperation of the Armed Forces of the USSR and Armed Forces of Other Countries)

Боевое содружество = ДайчинОнхОрлОл: О сов.–монг. содружестве / А. И. Бабин, Д. Цэдэв, А. В. Антосяк и др. М.: Воениздат, 1983. 334 с.

(Military Cooperation=Daichinonkhorlol: About Soviet-Mongolian Cooperation. A. I. Babin, D. Tsedev, A. V. Antosiak, and others. Moscow: Voenizdat, 1983. 334 pages.)

Боевое содружество братских народов и армий / Штемемко, С. М.; Антосяк, А. В., Фомин, В. И. и др. М.: Воениздат, 1975. 295 с.

(Military Cooperation of Fraternal Peoples and Armies. Shtemeko, S. M.; Antosiak, A. V.; Fomin, V. I., and others. Moscow: Voenizdat, 1975. 295 pages.)

Боевое содружество, рожденное Великим Октябрем: О сов.–венг. содружестве / А. И. Бабин, П. А. Жилин, К. Деркеи и др. М.: Воениздат, 1987. 351 с.

(Military Cooperation, Born of the Great October: Of Soviet-Hungarian Friendship. A. I. Babin, P. A. Zhilin, K. Deren, and others. Moscow: Voenizdat, 1987. 351 pages.)

Боевое содружество советского и польского народа / Редкол.: П. А. Жилин, А. В. Антосяк, И. М. Игнатенко и др. М.: Мысль, 1973. 277 с.

(Military Cooperation of the Soviet and Polish People. Editorial Board: P. A. Zhilin, A. V. Antosiak, I. M. Ignatenko, and others. Moscow: Misl', 1973. 277 pages.)

Братсво по оружию = Braterstwo broni / А. В. Антосяк, С. Гаць, Ю. В. Плотников и др. М.: Воениздат, 1975. 383 с.

(Brotherhood in Arms—Braterstwo broni. A. V. Antosiak, S. Gats', Iu. V. Plotnikov, and others. Moscow: Voenizdat, 1975. 383 pages.)

Варшавский Договор – союз во имя мира и социализма / Антосяк, А. В.; Кочегура П. А.; Фомин, В. И. и др. М.: Воениздат, 1980. 295 с.

(The Warsaw Pact—A Union in the Name of Peace and Socialism. Antosiak, A. V.; Kochegura, P. A.; Fomin, V. I.; and others. Moscow: Voenizdat, 1980. 295 pages.)

Вековая дружба, боевое братство = Вековна дружба, боино братство / А. В. Антосяк, Н. Н. Азовцев, А. И. Бабин и др. М.: Воениздат, 1980. 336 с.

(An Age-Old Friendship, Military Brotherhood—Vekovna druzhba, boino bratstvo. A. V. Antosiak, N. N. Azovtsev, A. I. Babin, and others. Moscow: Voenizdat, 1980. 336 pages.)

Военно–политическое сотрудничество социалистических стран / А. В. Антосяк, В. В. Сёмин, Н. В. Васильева и др. М.: Наука, 1988. 320 с.

(The Military-Political Cooperation of Socialist Countries. A. V. Antosiak, V. V. Semin, N. V. Vasi'eva, and others. Moscow: Nauka, 1988. 320 pages.)

Зарождение народных армий стран – участниц Варшавского Договора, 1941–1949 гг. / А. В. Антосяк, Н. П. Афанасьев, Л. П. Макаров и др. М.: Наука, 1975. 392 с.

(The Growth of Peoples' Armies of Countries—Participants of the Warsaw Pact, 1941–1949. A. V. Antosiak, N. P. Afanas'ev, L. P. Makarov, and others. Moscow; Nauka, 1975. 392 pages.)

Мужество и братство = Valentia i fraternidad / И. Д. Стаценко, Э. Буснего Родригес, А. Д. Бекаревич и др. М.: Воениздат, 1982. 240 с.

(Courage and Brotherhood—Valentia i fraternidad. I. D. Statsenko, E. E. Busnego Rodriges, A. D. Bekarevich, and others. Moscow: Voenizdat, 1982. 240 pages.)

На вечные времена = na vecne casy / А. И. Бабин, Я. Липтак, Г. Д. Мишустин и др. 2–е изд., испр. и доп. М. Воениздат, 1985. 359 с.

(For Ever=Na vecne casy. A. I. Babin, Ia. Liptak, G. D. Mishustin, and others. 2nd ed., revised and supplemented. Moscow: Voenizdat, 1985. 359 pages.)

Под знаменем боевой дружбы: (По материалам конф. сов. и польских историков, состоявшейся в Москве 23–27 окт. 1972 г.) / Редкол.: В. Г. Гаврилов, И. И. Костюшко, П. А. Кочегура и др. М.: Знание, 1977. 198 с.

(Under the Banner of Military Friendship: [Materials of a Conference of Soviet and Polish Historians, Meeting in Moscow 23–27 Oct. 1972]. Editorial Board: V. G. Gavrilov, I. I. Kostiushko, P. A. Kochegura, and others. Moscow: Znanie, 1977. 198 pages.)

Строительство армий европейских стран социалистического содружества, 1949–1949–1980 / А. В. Антосяк, Н. П. Афанасьев, П. А. Кочегура и др. М.: Наука, 1984. 310 с.

(The Construction of Armies of European Countries of Socialist Amity, 1949–1980. A. V. Antosiak, N. P. Afanas'ev, P. A. Kochegura, and others. Moscow: Nauka, 1984. 310 pages.)

Вооруженные силы капиталистических стран
(The Armed Forces of Capitalist Countries)

Внезапность в операциях вооруженных сил США / Ржешевский, О. А.; Кирьян, М. М.; Кульков, Е.Н. и др. М.: Воениздат, 1982. 328 с.

(Surprise in the Operation of the Armed Forces of the USA. Rzheshevskii, O. A.; Kir'ian, M. M.; Kul'kov, E. N.; and others. Moscow: Voenizdat, 1982. 328 pages.)

Военно–блоковая политика империализма: История и современность / О. А. Ржешевский, Н. Н. Азовцев, А. В. Антосяк и др. М.: Воениздат, 1980. 454 с.

(Military-Bloc Politicc of Imperialism: History and the Present. O. A. Rzheshevskii, N. N. Azovtsev, A. V. Antosiak, and others. Moscow: Voenizdat, 1980. 454 pages.)

Вооруженные силы Японии: История и современность: (К 40–летию разгрома милитарист. Японии во второй мировой войне) / А. С. Савин, А. М. Носков, В. П. Зиммонин и др. М.: Наука, 1985. 326 с.

(The Armed Forces of Japan: History and the Present: [The 40th Anniversary of the Destruction of Militarist Japan in the Second World War]. A. S. Savin, A. M. Noskov, V. P. Zimonin, and others. Moscow: Nauka, 1985. 326 pages.)

География милитаризма / Антосяк, А. В.; Арзуманов, Г. А.; Волович, В. Г. и др. М.: Мысль, 1984. 268 с.

(The Geography of Militarism. Antosiak, A. V.; Arzumanovc, G. A.; Volovich, V. G.; and others. Moscow: Misl', 1984. 268 pages.)

Государства НАТО и военные конфликты: Воен.–ист. очерк / М. М. Кирьян, Б. Хайман, А.С. Якушевский и др. М.: Наука, 1987. 311 с.

(The Governments of NATO and Military Conflict: A Military-Historical Note. M. M. Kir'ian, B. Khaiman, A. S. Iakushevskii and others. Moscow: Nauka, 1987. 311 pages.)

Иваницкий, Г. М.; Орлов, А.С.; Якушевский, А. С. Фашистские преступники на свободе. М.: Воениздат, 1987. 96 с.

(Ivanitskii, G. M.; Orlov, A. S.; Iakushevshii, A. S. The Fascist Criminals at Liberty. Moscow: Voenizdat, 1987. 96 pages.)

Кто кому угрожает: Вымыслы врагов социализма и действительность / Ю. И. Садчиков, Е. И. Гвоздев, А. И. Евсеев и др. М.: Воениздат, 1981. 87 с.

(Who Threatens Whom: Fabrication of the Enemies of Socialism and Reality. Iu. I. Sadchikov, E. I. Gvozdev, A. I. Evseev, and others. Moscow: Voenizdat, 1981. 87 pages.)

Милитаризм – угроза миру и цивилизации / Ю. Я. Кирщин, В. С. Ещенко, Н. Ф. Ковалевский и др. М.: Наука, 1987. 127 с.

(Militarism—A Threat to Peace and Civilisation. Iu. Ia. Kirshin, V. S. Eshchenko, N. F. Kovalevskii, and others. Moscow: Nauka, 1987. 127 pages.)

Носков, А. М. Северная Европа в военных планах империализма: Ист. очерк. М.: Наука, 1987. 127 с.

(Noskov, A. M. Northern Europe in the Military Plans of Imperialsm: A Historical Note. Moscow: Nauka, 1987. 127 pages.)

Орлов, А. С. В поисках "абсолютного" оружия. М.: Мол. гвардия, 1989. 286 с.

(Orlov, A. S. In Search of the "Ultimate" Weapon. M.: Mol. gvardiia, 1989. 268 pages.)

Сухопутные войка капиталистических государств / Макиев, Д. Ф.; Глазунов, Н. К.; Жуков, П. А.; Масленников, П. Е. М.: Воениздат, 1974. 560 с.

(Ground Forces of the Capitalist Governments. Makiev, D. F.; Glazunov, N. K.; Zhukov, P. A.; Maslennikov, P. E. Moscow: Voenizdat, 1974. 560 pages.)

Японский милитаризм: (Воен.–ист. исслед.) / Е. М. Жуков, Б. Г. Сапожников, А. С. Савин и др. М.: Наука, 1972. 376 с.

(Japanese Militarism: [Military-Historical Research]. E. M. Zhukov, B. G. Sapozhnikov, A. S. Savin, and others. M.: Nauka, 1972. 376 pages.)

Залетный А.Ф. Милитаризация ФРГ. М.: Наука, 1969. 478 с.

(Zaletnyi A. F. Militarisation of the Federal Republic of Germany: Moscow, Nauka, 1969. 478 pages.)

25

Zimbabwe

Zimbabwe (Formerly The Rhodesias)

Lewis H. Gann, Hoover Institution

Between 1953 and 1963 Northern Rhodesia (then a British protectorate) and Southern Rhodesia (a British self-governing colony) were linked with Nyasaland (later Malawi) in the Federation of Rhodesia and Nyasaland, which took over defense as a federal function. No official history was issued, but the federal government published an official *Handbook to the Federation of Rhodesia and Nyasaland*, edited by W. V. Brelsford (Government Printer, Salisbury, 1960) which contains a chapter titled "The Armed Forces" (pp. 666–677).

The federation broke up in 1963, and in 1964 Northern Rhodesia—now named Zambia—achieved independence. Southern Rhodesia then assumed the name of Rhodesia and regained control over its defense forces. From 1967 to 1980 Rhodesia was involved in a lengthy guerrilla war which pitted the white-controlled government forces against two African opposition movements, the Zimbabwe African National Union (ZANU) and the Zimbabwe African People's Union (ZAPU). In 1980 the contenders, under British mediation, concluded a compromise peace, and Rhodesia achieved internationally recognized independence as Zimbabwe.

Neither the former Rhodesian government nor its African successor government issued an official history.

BIBLIOGRAPHY

Brelsford, William Vernon, ed. *Handbook to the Federation of Rhodesia and Nyasaland*. Salisbury: Government Printer, 1986.

Brelsford, W. V. *The Story of the Northern Rhodesia Regiment.* Lusaka (Northern Rhodesia): Government Printer, 1954. viii, 134 pp., plates (part col.), ports, maps, 25cm.

Evans, M. *Fighting against Chimurenga: An Analysis of Counter-Insurgency in Rhodesia.* Salisbury: Historical Association of Rhodesia, 1981.

Index

ABOUT THE EDITOR

Robin Higham taught military history at Kansas State University from 1963 to 1998. He is the author of more than 140 articles, 14 monographs, and the editor of many bibliographical volumes. He was the editor of *Military Affairs* from 1968 to 1988 and *Aerospace Historian* from 1970 to 1988, and has been editor of *The Journal of the West* since 1976.

ISBN 0-313-28684-1
90000>
EAN
9 780313 286841
HARDCOVER BAR CODE